STRATEGIC ASIA 2006–07

STRATEGIC ASIA 2006–07

TRADE, INTERDEPENDENCE, AND SECURITY

Edited by

Ashley J. Tellis and Michael Wills

With contributions from

Michael R. Chambers, Stephen D. Cohen, Kavita Iyengar, David C. Kang, Devesh Kapur, Ann Marie Kimball, Michael Mastanduno, Minxin Pei, David P. Rapkin, Peter Rutland, Dina R. Spechler, Martin C. Spechler, William R. Thompson, and Donald E. Weatherbee

THE NATIONAL BUREAU *of* ASIAN RESEARCH
Seattle and Washington, D.C.

THE NATIONAL BUREAU *of* ASIAN RESEARCH

Published in the United States of America by
The National Bureau of Asian Research, Seattle, WA and Washington, DC
www.nbr.org

This material is based upon work supported by the Department of Energy (National Nuclear Security Administration) under Award Number DE-FG52-03SF22724.

This report was prepared as an account of work sponsored by an agency of the United States Government. Neither the United States Government nor any agency thereof, nor any of their employees, makes any warranty, express or implied, or assumes any legal liability or responsibility for the accuracy, completeness, or usefulness of any information, apparatus, product, or process disclosed, or represents that its use would not infringe privately owned rights. Reference herein to any specific commercial product, process, or service by trade name, trademark, manufacturer, or otherwise does not constitute or imply its endorsement, recommendation, or favoring by the United States Government or any agency thereof. The views and opinions of authors expressed herein do not necessarily state or reflect those of the United States Government or any agency thereof.

NBR makes no warranties or representations regarding the accuracy of any map in this volume. Depicted boundaries are meant as guidelines only and do not represent the views of NBR or NBR's funders.

Publisher's Cataloging-In-Publication Data
(Prepared by The Donohue Group, Inc.)

Strategic Asia 2006-07 : trade, interdependence, and security / edited by Ashley J. Tellis and Michael Wills ; with contributions from Michael R. Chambers ... [et al.]
    p. : ill., maps ; cm.
    Based upon work supported by the Department of Energy (National Nuclear Security Administration) under Award Number DE-FG52-03SF22724.
    Includes bibliographical references and index.
    ISBN: 0-9713938-7-7

    1. Asia--Commerce. 2. Asia--Economic conditions. 3. Asia--Economic integration. 4. Asia--Commercial policy. 5. Asia--Defenses. 6. Asia--Strategic aspects. 7. Asia--Foreign economic relations--United States. 8. United States--Foreign economic relations--Asia. 9. National security--Asia. I. Tellis, Ashley J. II. Wills, Michael, 1970- III. Chambers, Michael R. IV. National Bureau of Asian Research (U.S.)

HF3752.3 .S77 2006
382.095

Design and publishing services by The National Bureau of Asian Research

Cover design by Stefanie Choi

Printed in Canada

The paper used in this publication meets the minimum requirement of the American National Standard for Information Sciences—Permanence of Paper for Printed Library Materials, ANSI Z39.48-1992.

Contents

> An exploration of how growing levels of trade and interdependence
> fit into the grand strategies of Asian states and how changing
> economic relationships could affect regional stability.

Strategic Asia: Country Studies

> An examination of why the ongoing refusal of the United States to
> live within its economic means poses challenges to U.S. domestic
> prosperity, dilutes U.S. credibility as a global superpower, and
> elevates U.S.-East Asian economic interdependence to uncharted
> levels of complexity.

> An analysis of the growth of China's trade and economic
> interdependence with both its Asian neighbors and the United
> States and assessment of the impact these developments will have
> on China's security and the security of the Asia-Pacific region.

Strategic Asia: Regional Studies

Strategic Asia: Special Studies

Strategic Asia: Indicators

Preface

Richard J. Ellings

Strategic Asia 2006–07: Trade, Interdependence, and Security is the sixth in the series of annual reports produced by the Strategic Asia Program at NBR. This year's volume investigates the growing economic interdependence among Asian states and assesses the implications of these burgeoning economic ties for security in the region. Although some scholars postulate that economic interdependence sublimates conflict among nations, the historical record proves inconclusive. The first great era of globalization ended in the breakdown of the British-enforced international free trade system and the tragedy of World War I. The regional fault lines in Asia, well documented in previous volumes of Strategic Asia, necessitate a hard look at how trade can ameliorate or exacerbate existing tensions.

The changing strategic landscape is fraught with an uncertain mix of opportunity and challenge. Amid tensions over the meaning and impact of China's and India's rise and Japan's increasing assertiveness in global affairs, barriers to trade and economic interaction are falling. The degree to which states in the region are integrated into the global economy varies immensely from advanced states like Japan to WTO-hopefuls Vietnam and Russia to the pariah states of Myanmar (Burma) and North Korea. In many countries, most notably the great powers of the Asia-Pacific (China, Japan, Russia, India, and the United States), economic ties are both strengthening and complicating states' relations with profound implications for policy decisions. In many Asian states, policymakers wary of China face opposition to their national security strategies by powerful business and economic interest groups opposed to any policy which might destabilize relations with China. Nowhere can this be seen more clearly than in Sino-Japanese relations, where a hot economic relationship belies frosty political interaction. It is within the realm of this regional and great power interaction and competition for influence that the effects of intense economic interaction need close examination.

Because it merits an entire volume itself, the effects of globalization on governmental change—especially on democratization, for example—is not tackled in the pages that follow. This will be the topic of a future NBR study, as the expectation of this effect lies at the core of long-term U.S. strategy toward China and many other non-democratic states.

The National Bureau of Asian Research developed the Strategic Asia Program to fulfill three objectives: (1) to provide the best possible understanding of the current strategic environment in Asia;[1] (2) to look forward five years, and in some cases beyond, to contemplate the region's future; and (3) to establish a record of data and assessment for those interested in understanding changes taking place in the Asian strategic landscape.

Keeping within the scope of the annual volumes, *Strategic Asia 2006–07: Trade, Interdependence, and Security* is designed to be an integrated set of original studies that aims to provide the most authoritative information and analysis possible. Through a series of country, regional, and special studies, this volume discusses the depths and varieties of trade, degrees of economic interdependency, and future expectations of trade, all within broader analyses of states' strategic objectives. The implications for the United States are assessed in the hope that identifying the potential consequences of these economic developments and state strategies in the region will assist U.S. decisionmakers in their efforts to craft effective policy toward Asia. A companion website provides free access to the comprehensive Strategic Asia database, which contains a wealth of indicators for Asian demographic, trade, communication, and financial trends; measures of states' economic and military capabilities; and information on political and energy dynamics. Drawing together data from disparate sources, the database allows users to compare these statistics across a range of years, countries, and indicators, providing an invaluable resource to illustrate and assess the momentous changes underway in Asia.

---

[1] The Strategic Asia Program considers as "Asia" the entire eastern half of the Eurasian landmass and the arc of offshore islands in the western Pacific. This vast expanse can be pictured as an area centered on China and consisting of four distinct sub-regions arrayed clockwise around it: Northeast Asia (including the Russian Far East, the Korean Peninsula, and Japan), Southeast Asia (including both its mainland and maritime components), South Asia (including India and Pakistan, and bordered to the west by Afghanistan), and Central Asia (Kazakhstan, Kyrgyzstan, Tajikistan, Turkmenistan, Uzbekistan, and southern Russia). The Strategic Asia Program also tracks significant developments across the Asia-Pacific to the United States and Canada.

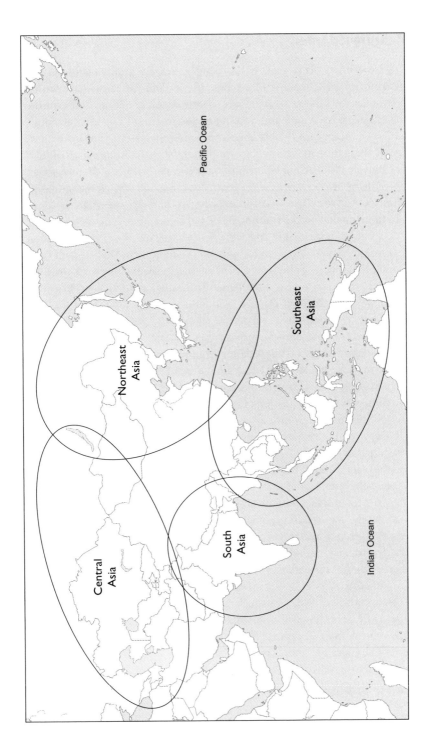

Acknowledgments

Now in its sixth year, it has been extremely gratifying to see this dynamic program mature. More than fifty leading specialists have written for the series, adding their unique talents to each volume and ensuring that Strategic Asia maintains a fresh perspective on the region. Many of the authors have appeared before concerned committees of Congress, which is a testament to the sophisticated, forward-looking analysis that is the hallmark of Strategic Asia. A public seminar and private briefings for government regularly accompany the release of each book. Beyond the policy community, Strategic Asia finds use by corporate planners and in university classrooms as a fundamental part of training the next generation of Asia specialists.

Strategic Asia's growth and achievement have relied on the sage wisdom and insightfulness of two senior advisors: General John Shalikashvili (ret.), former Chairman of the Joint Chiefs of Staff, and the program's founding research director Aaron Friedberg, Professor of Politics at Princeton University and former Deputy National Security Advisor to the Vice President. Without John's and Aaron's thoughtful guidance, Strategic Asia might have become simply another edited volume—or less—and for that, I owe them my profound appreciation. It is in this spirit, in fact, that NBR is endowing the Shalikashvili Chair for National Security Studies, dedicated to policy-relevant scholarship in the field of national security studies, and building upon the foundation of the Strategic Asia program.

Ashley Tellis has once again done a superb job as Research Director. He designed the research agenda, co-led the spring planning meeting in Washington, D.C., and, together with Program Director Michael Wills, ably led the team through the research, writing, and editing processes. Early this year, Ashley took a brief leave of absence to serve on assignment at the State Department as senior advisor to Undersecretary of State Nicholas Burns and was closely involved in negotiating the civil nuclear agreement with India. Ashley's grasp of the major policy issues facing Asia and the United States is extraordinary, and we were deeply appreciative to have him back with us again with the conclusion of his latest government service.

Equal gratitude is due to the numerous contributions of Program Director Michael Wills. Michael has balanced more roles than ever this year as we have launched a new Center for Asian Security Studies (housing the Strategic Asia Program, "Shali Chair," and other initiatives), expanded existing programs, and asked him to lead the coordination of research efforts across NBR—all a testament to his exceptional organizational and management skills. His and Ashley's deft leadership has made the program a continuing success.

Likewise, I want to acknowledge the tremendous role that NBR staff and program associates have played behind the scenes. Ashley and Michael were adroitly assisted by Jessica Keough, who as Program Manager, handled much of daily running of the program, including managing relations with the authors, organizing meetings and presentations, and assisting with the volume's production. The quality of this volume owes much to the talents and numerous proficiencies of Andrew Marble, NBR's Editor, who directed the reviews, editing, and production of the volume. Sandra Ward provided valuable assistance in these regards and Jannette Whippy did a wonderful job laying out the entire volume. Debbie Cooper provided fantastic logistical support to many of the meetings in Washington, D.C. Senior Programmer Erick Thompson and Programmer Ben Andrews provided essential IT support and maintained the Strategic Asia database.

Special thanks are due to the hard work of this year's program associates and Next Generation Program fellow. Much of the work undertaken in the Strategic Asia Program has relied on their outstanding talents and dedication. Program Associates Peter Mattis and Evan Morrisey provided superb research assistance to the authors, previewed drafts, compiled the appendix, and supported the program throughout the year. Next Generation fellow Tim Cook did a marvelous job drafting much of the companion Executive Summary, contributing to the appendix, previewing drafts, and assisting in the proofreading and indexing of the volume. Michael Jones provided helpful support to the Publications team. John Graham, Teresa Reimers, Tim Cook, and Jessica Keough were responsible for proofreading the volume.

Many people at NBR contribute throughout the year to the Strategic Asia Program, from the timely wisdom and experience of George Russell, NBR's Chairman, and counsel of other members of our Board of Directors, to the guidance and fundraising help of Brigitte Allen and Karolos Karnikis, Vice Presidents for Institutional Development and for Programs and Administration, respectively. In 2005 NBR opened an office in Washington, DC and special thanks go to Daniel Wright, Roy Kamphausen, and Raelyn Campbell for their outreach efforts to raise the profile of Strategic Asia–related and NBR work inside the Beltway.

The most important work fell to the authors, of course, who embraced the difficult puzzle of the relationship between economic integration and security to produce a policy-relevant and superbly researched volume. I would like to acknowledge their hard work, dedication, and flexibility in meeting NBR's tight deadlines and requirements—a difficult feat for which they deserve much credit. The anonymous reviewers, both scholarly specialists and government analysts, deserve thanks as well for their important task of reviewing the draft chapters. Their insightful comments and critiques contributed to high quality of this year's book.

Last but certainly not least, I would like to extend my deep appreciation to the sponsors of Strategic Asia—the Lynde and Harry Bradley Foundation, National Nuclear Security Administration at the Department of Energy, and GE Foundation. Their generous support and commitment to the Strategic Asia Program has allowed us to transform it from an idea into a reality, and for that I am grateful beyond measure.

Richard J. Ellings
President
The National Bureau of Asian Research
August 2006

STRATEGIC ASIA 2006–07

OVERVIEW

EXECUTIVE SUMMARY

This overview explores how growing levels of trade and interdependence fit into the grand strategies of Asian states and how changing economic relationships could affect regional stability.

MAIN ARGUMENT:

This volume suggests that trade is a critical instrument in Asia's economic growth. China's explosive growth during the last three decades, in particular, has created a web of interdependence conducive to rapid growth, linking both friends and rivals. Even India and Russia, which previously had not emphasized foreign trade, now have focused on increasing links with the global economy.

POLICY IMPLICATIONS:

- The complex and variegated growing trade dependence in Asia offers no assurance that interdependence will make violent conflict between states irrelevant.

- Asian states appear to view trading relations as vehicles to increase national wealth rather than as a means for procurement of collective security. These states have yet, however, to exhibit acute fears about their partners' relative gains from such relationships.

- This nonchalance may derive from three judgments relevant to the future of Asia: (1) The primacy of the United States is robust enough to ensure that differentials in relative gains are strategically insignificant; (2) Asian states expect regional peace to continue, thereby strengthening positive expectations for future trade; and (3) even if gains are diverted to military purposes in some states (such as China), these states do not yet pose consequential military threats and could potentially be contained without forgoing profitable trading relationships.

- Since Asian leaders appear content to straddle the divide on interdependence versus security, Asian countries will continue to enjoy gains from international commerce so long as these two goals are not perceived to be in absolute conflict.

Overview

Trade, Interdependence, and Security in Asia

Ashley J. Tellis

The production of order remains the central problem of international politics. Since the beginning of recorded reflection on the interstate system, political philosophers and theorists have sought to understand the causes of discord among nations and how these might be ameliorated. The realist tradition, the oldest and most venerable perspective on international politics, assesses the roots of conflict to lie in the security-seeking or power-maximizing behavior of contending political entities and suggests that peace—understood as the moderation of conflict but not the absence of competition—derives principally from the balance of power where the ambitions of one are contained by the countervailing strength of another. The liberal tradition, even when it accepts the realist phenomenology of the origins of conflict, offers a more hopeful perspective. This tradition suggests that the Hobbesian "war of all against all" can be moderated either by normative variables—such as the presence of democracy, which represents an incarnation of moral claims in politics—or by calculations of self-interest—as, for example, through economic interdependence, which provides opportunities even for egoistical agents to realize joint gains and thereby minimize the prospects of violent conflict.[1]

Ashley J. Tellis is Senior Associate at the Carnegie Endowment for International Peace and Research Director of the Strategic Asia Program at NBR. He is the author of *India's Emerging Nuclear Posture* (2001) and co-author of *Interpreting China's Grand Strategy: Past, Present, and Future* (2000). He can be reached at <atellis@carnegieendowment.org>.

[1] A good survey of the contrasting perspectives can be found in Michael W. Doyle, *Ways of War and Peace: Realism, Liberalism, and Socialism* (New York: W.W. Norton, 1997).

Interdependence and the "Hobbesian Problem"

Whether economic interdependence offers a solution to the traditional "Hobbesian problem of order"[2] in the international system is of more than academic interest. Rather, it represents an important policy concern insofar as trade and interdependence could provide a foundation for durable stability in the international system, "after hegemony."[3] Whether holding a realist or a liberal view of international politics, one can easily acknowledge that systemic stability today is owed greatly to the hegemony of the United States—whether attributing to overwhelming concentration of U.S. capabilities or to the U.S. role as a standard bearer of liberal values worldwide. The liberal international economic order that Washington has promoted since the end of the Second World War has on the one hand had the desirable effect of ushering in prosperity on a huge scale in Europe and Asia. This same order could on the other hand also create the very conditions by which U.S. primacy might be decisively undermined if the resulting diffusion of economic growth produces new geopolitical competitors to the United States. The prospect of such an evolution—represented in the American mind most obviously by the rise of China—then raises the following question: will future international politics witness once again the violent struggles associated with a hegemonic transition (as many realists expect), or will the most recent bout of economic interdependence in fact mitigate the otherwise relentless momentum toward a conflict that might lead to major war (as many liberals hope)?[4]

Even apart from this question of the effects of interdependence on the quality of a potential systemic power transition, the issue of whether trade mitigates security competition is for many reasons an important one, especially in Asia. To begin with, the Asian continent is poised to become the largest single concentration of power in global politics, contributing close to half of the international product by 2025. Further, Asia hosts several major centers of economic power (Japan, China, South Korea, India, Australia, Russia, and Southeast Asia)—each of which is in different ways consequential for regional and global politics—as well as four major claimants for power-political recognition on a global scale (Russia, China, Japan, and India). Finally, the key Asian powers each possess significant

---

[2] Talcott Parsons first formulated this phrase in his classic work, *The Structure of Social Action* (New York: Free Press, 1937).

[3] The affirmative claim is asserted and defended in Robert O. Keohane, *After Hegemony: Cooperation and Discord in the World Political Economy* (Princeton, N.J.: Princeton University Press, 1984).

[4] The classic statement on the relationship between differential economic growth and hegemonic war can be found in Robert Gilpin, *War and Change in World Politics* (New York: Cambridge University Press, 1981).

military capabilities and, interestingly, are increasingly bound to one or another by deepening economic linkages while continuing to remain enmeshed in various forms of manifest or latent geopolitical rivalry.[5]

The question whether growing economic interdependence can lead to political pacification of various Asian dyadic rivalries takes on added interest in light of Asia's circumstances. If the liberal tradition is correct, the existence of uneven growth in an otherwise rising Asia would matter less so long as the major powers were tied to one another in dense bonds of economic dependency: such bonds would be costly to break, thus providing insurance against the predations of conflict and thereby becoming instruments through which order is produced in an otherwise anarchic system.[6] If the realist tradition is correct, the existence of dense interdependence between various key Asian states (including the United States as an Asian power) not only will fail to provide any antidote to the prospect of conflict but may in fact simply exacerbate the situation: since economic interdependence inevitably brings strategic vulnerability—in that states become dependent on others for vital goods or markets for their survival or prosperity—states become compelled "to control what they depend on or to lessen the extent of their dependency,"[7] thereby creating a situation where interdependence leads "probably...to greater security competition."[8]

This volume, *Strategic Asia 2006–07: Trade, Interdependence, and Security*, is conceived against the backdrop of this critical debate. The chapters herein are anchored in the proposition that, irrespective of whether one holds a realist or a liberal view, the question whether economic interdependence among states conduces to war or peace cannot be examined without first establishing the realities of trade and investment in various Asian economies and across important dyads. If significant current or prospective economic interdependence does not characterize the relations between key Asian countries, the issue of whether trade and investment has inflaming or pacifying effects becomes irrelevant. Accordingly, the first task intellectually is simply to establish the facts as they pertain to trade and

---

[5] For more on this issue, see Ashley J. Tellis, "Overview: Military Modernization in Asia," in *Strategic Asia 2005–06: Military Modernization in an Era of Uncertainty*, ed. Ashley J. Tellis and Michael Wills (Seattle: National Bureau of Asian Research, 2005), 3–37.

[6] Susan McMillan, "Interdependence and Conflict," *Mershon International Studies Review* 41 (1997): 33–58; and Richard Rosecrance, *The Rise of the Trading State: Commerce and Conquest in the Modern World* (New York: Basic Books, 1986). See also Richard Rosecrance, "War, Trade and Interdependence," in *Interdependence and Conflict in World Politics*, ed. James N. Rosenau and Hylke Tromp (Aldershot, U.K.: Avebury, 1989), 48–57.

[7] Kenneth Waltz, *Theory of International Politics* (New York: Random House, 1979), 106.

[8] John J. Mearsheimer, "Disorder Restored," in *Rethinking America's Security*, ed. Graham Allison and Gregory F. Treverton (New York: W.W. Norton, 1992), 223.

economic interdependence in Asia in a systematic way. Such an approach would allow for focused scrutiny of any individual state and, by implication, for synoptic comparisons across countries.

Given the explosive deepening of globalization over the last two decades—understood as the growing share of global economic activity between people who live in different countries—this volume seeks to examine the role of trade and interdependence in the grand strategies of various Asian states. The focus is on understanding a number of issues in this context:

- how key Asian states view trade as advancing their national economic, political, and strategic objectives;

- how these states conceive of their trading relations with other regional powers as well as with the larger world;

- how the trade links that tie various Asian countries to one another as well as to the global economic order might affect national security and regional stability, and by implication the larger question whether and how trade and interdependence might conduce to war or peace.

An examination of this kind is undoubtedly challenging because it requires addressing issues of economics, political economy, and international relations simultaneously. Yet, undertaking at least an initial cut at such an examination is worthwhile for at least three reasons.

First, there is a large literature in political science, mainly associated with liberal international relations theory, that holds growing international trade—and specifically strong economic interdependence—to be positively correlated with international peace.[9] This argument, which draws from the classical liberal tradition going back to Adam Smith and Immanuel Kant, has spawned a modern research program that uses quantitative statistical analysis to conclude that economic interdependence does indeed promote peace among states. The general causal argument underlying these statistical inferences is relatively simple: trade between states increases specialization across national boundaries; increased specialization increases the gains from trade on one hand, while deepening mutual dependency on the other hand; and growing mutual dependency makes war more costly and thereby

---

[9] The literature on this issue is huge. Useful surveys can be found in Edward D. Mansfield and Brian M. Pollins, eds., *Economic Interdependence and International Conflict: New Perspectives on an Enduring Debate* (Ann Arbor: University of Michigan Press, 2003); Gerald Schneider, Katherine Barbieri, and Nils Peter Gleditsch, eds., *Globalization and Armed Conflict* (Lanham: Rowman and Littlefield, 2003); and Bruce Russett and John R. Oneal, *Triangulating Peace: Democracy, Interdependence, and International Organizations* (New York: Norton, 2001). An excellent critique of the interdepedence and peace thesis can be found in Katherine Barbieri, *The Liberal Illusion: Does Trade Promote Peace?* (Ann Arbor: University of Michigan Press, 2002).

constrains states from seeking recourse to military force. This basic argument recently has been modified in two innovative ways. One argument made, for example, is that deepening interdependence leads to peace only when high levels of trade are expected to survive indefinitely into the future.[10] Another argument maintains that increased trade enhances the prospects for peace mainly when a state's military power is based overwhelmingly on the domestically abundant resources in its factor endowment mix.[11] Predictably, all these arguments are open to challenge both by realist theorists of international relations as well as by other scholars on both methodological and substantive grounds. This volume is not intended to resolve these debates but, against the backdrop of these discussions, it is intended to explore whether and how the economic interdependence that characterizes any given Asian state might conduce to peace or conflict in the specific circumstances facing it.

Second, even as trade and interdependence are rising in Asia and beyond, the geopolitical structure of the Asian (and global) system is changing in ways that potentially could have serious consequences for structural stability over the long run. Increasingly obvious today is that China and, to a lesser degree, India have begun a successful ascent to great-power status that, if continued uninterruptedly, would alter both the composition and the ranking of the world's major powers. The historical evidence thus far suggests that rising powers have invariably generated disruptive forces in the international order, usually leading to systemic wars that result in the replacement of one hegemonic state by another.[12] Even if systemic war is not at issue, the question whether the rise of China and eventually India could precipitate regional conflicts—or even serious crises short of war in their local environments—remains an important one. If China and India are moderated in their political ambitions precisely because they owe their national growth to dense international trade and interdependence linkages with countries that might otherwise be their political competitors, then the future of the current international system could be unlike that of the past: the rise of previous powers involved no such moderating effects, and the growth of the rising powers of the eighteenth and nineteenth centuries, unlike that of these two states, was primarily as a result of accelerated internal accumulation (or, when external accumulation was at issue, did not

---

[10] Dale C. Copeland, "Economic Interdependence and War: A Theory of Trade Expectations," *International Security* 20, no. 4 (Spring 1996): 5–41.

[11] David M. Rowe, "The Tragedy of Liberalism—How Globalization Caused the First World War," *Security Studies* 14, no. 3 (July–September 2005): 407–47.

[12] George Modelski, *Long Cycles in World Politics* (Seattle: University of Washington Press, 1987).

involve tight interdependence with their principal rivals).[13] "Mapping" the nature and the extent of the dependence of each of Asia's major states on foreign trade, as well as identifying the webs of interdependence that arise as a result of various trading patterns, would thus provide the raw material to make some judgments about the hopeful view of Asia's future for which liberal international relations theorists might argue. The result of these judgments, in turn, would also condition arguments as to how the United States ought to respond to the current growth of Asian economic power.

Third, if the pacifying effects of trade are affected not only by the perceived durability of interdependence relationships over time but also by the composition of trade itself, then it is important to document not only the volume and direction of trade of key Asian states but also the dependence of these states on trade for certain key ingredients that contribute to national power. Accordingly, helpful in providing a textured picture of how in any given case trade may conduce to (or detract from) national growth and international security would be an examination of the following: how a country's trade performance is divided by merchandise versus invisibles, raw materials versus finished goods, high value added versus low valued added products, direct versus portfolio investments, and products versus people as well as and whether that trade emphasizes certain key elements such as the acquisition of science and technology and weapons and defense goods. Additionally, of importance would be an understanding of how a country's trade and interdependence affect the domestic political environment in a number of issue areas: how trade and economic interdependences cohere with a country's grand strategy; whether (and how) trade creates constituencies at the mass or elite level that shape the country's national choices; and, finally, whether (and how) the patterns and direction of trade condition the political relations enjoyed by a country with key economic partners in Asia and beyond. An examination of these factors would provide a more nuanced understanding of the benefits and the limits of growing interdependence for regional and global security.

A comprehensive study of trade and interdependence in Asia along all these dimensions would constitute an entire research program that could not be reduced to a single volume. Accordingly, the chapters in this survey ought to be viewed primarily as a first step toward addressing these questions. They incorporate many, but not all, of the variables highlighted above to some degree or another. Rather, they seek primarily to elucidate the importance of trade in the grand strategies of key Asian states and to

[13] For details, see George Modelski and William R. Thompson, *Leading Sectors and World Powers: The Coevolution of Global Politics and Economics* (Columbia, S.C.: University of South Carolina Press, 1996).

describe the pattern of their trading relationships so as to establish a baseline that would allow future editions of *Strategic Asia* to interrogate more deeply the larger question of whether the ongoing processes of globalization in Asia would contribute to a peaceful evolution of regional politics (and of the international system more generally) or whether they are likely to be even more disruptive than usual in that they accelerate the differences in national growth and thereby exacerbate the potential disequilibrium in the regional and global balances of power.

Because this volume has more modest aims, it does not investigate, for example, the intriguing question of whether globalization as experienced in Asia is transforming the domestic political systems in key Asian states in a way that helpfully influences critical political decisions pertaining to war and peace. The volume also does not assess at any length how trade, interdependence, and globalization may be creating new interest groups in domestic politics and how these groups affect the distribution of state power and preferences in regard to questions of high politics. The unified state as rational actor is, therefore, retained largely as the unit of analysis primarily for reasons of convenience since the main objective of the research work reported here is to provide, first, the relevant information pertaining to trade and interdependence in regard to the principal states in Asia and, second, a set of analytical judgments about how such interdependence affects specific issues of peace and security associated with each country of interest in this volume. As such, *Strategic Asia 2006–07* provides a survey of how trade and interdependence affect security in complex ways in various Asian states and in the continent as a whole.

Interdependence and Security in Asia

The chapters in this volume of *Strategic Asia* suggest a complex picture of growing trade dependence on the part of almost all Asian states (see **Table 1**), yet no assurance that such interdependence promises to make violent power-political conflict irrelevant. The lack of such assurance derives from a variety of factors, ranging from a relatively weak trade intensity to a continuing primacy of power-political goals. The former, for example, is the case with the most important state in the international system, the United States, and the latter with the China-Taiwan-United States triangle. Consequently, the growing economic interdependence that defines all Asian states ought to be viewed, at least for the moment, as providing a vehicle for increasing national wealth rather than as a device that confidently assures the attenuation of power-political rivalry. More interestingly and to the point, however, is that most of the key Asian nations seem to focus on trade principally as a device for maximizing "power and plenty," that is, as an instrumental mechanism for assuring the fastest increases in gross national product, which can then be used by the governing regime to secure whatever goals—domestic or external—that may be of interest to the state.[14] The significance of trade for most Asian powers thus derives from fundamentally realist impulses—expanding the national product to secure specific political aims—rather than from liberal instincts centered on achieving "peace on earth" through "free trade among men."[15] Even in those cases where trade is specifically directed toward mitigating conflicts—as for example in Chinese efforts at attracting Taiwanese and Japanese business investments to the mainland, Southeast Asian efforts at developing tight economic relations with China, or Sino-Indian efforts at deepening bilateral trade relations—the calculus in each instance appears to center on how trade and interdependence might be used "strategically" to advance certain geopolitical and geo-economic goals rather than because of the conviction, as Richard Cobden held, that free trade "unites" states, "making each equally anxious for the prosperity and happiness of both."[16]

Stephen D. Cohen's chapter on the United States provides a fascinating analysis of how the world's most powerful country views—and exploits— foreign trade in a unique way born of the exceptional position of the United States in the international system. Cohen underscores that although the United States remains the world's most powerful economy as well as its premier military power, "exports and imports both represent a smaller percentage of U.S. gross domestic product (GDP) than is the case in every other major economy and most minor ones." As a result, the United States is not unduly dependent on the global economy for the country's continued wealth and power. Such dependence is manifested mainly through the extraordinary American indebtedness, which because of unparalleled U.S. power and the reserve currency role of the dollar has permitted the United States to accumulate "so much external debt for so long" that the country is "at—if not already beyond—the boundaries of prudent economic behavior." Cohen's analysis leads inevitably to the conclusion that the United States enjoys great, although not untrammeled, freedom of action in international politics not only because it possesses enormous military and economic power but also because the country takes advantage of a peculiar benefit of interdependence arising from the fact that U.S. creditors have no choice but

---

[14] The classic statement of this strategy is Jacob Viner, "Power and Plenty as Objectives of Foreign Policy in the Seventeenth and Eighteenth Centuries," *World Politics* 1, no. 1 (October 1948).

[15] These phrases are borrowed from Daniel T. Griswold, "Peace on Earth? Try Free Trade among Men," CATO Institute, December 28, 2005.

[16] Richard Cobden, *The Political Writings of Richard Cobden* (London: T. Fischer Unwin, 1903), 225.

to offer what are in effect dollar tributes—whereby these creditors exchange real resources for paper currency—so long as they remain reluctant to rely on domestic demand as the main engine for generating economic growth in their own countries.

This reluctance, in the case of China for example, is rooted in an economic strategy centered on the logic of export-led growth. In the final analysis, however, this hesitancy may be driven as much by the political imperatives of eschewing the creation of real consumers who might inevitably demand full political rights. The reasons that other Asian states, such as Japan, subsidize continued U.S. overconsumption differ from those of China at a political level. At an economic level, however, the reasons remain the same: these states, reluctant or unable to create genuine effective demand at home, are compelled to mortgage their economic growth to continued U.S. consumption of their exported products. Given this strategy, these states simply have no choice but to finance the continuing U.S. trade deficits if they are to stand some chance of maintaining their growth rates in the absence of significant internal consumption. In such circumstances, the U.S. dependence on trade, which is relatively modest to begin with, could have even less of a political restraining effect than might otherwise be case, which is arguably good news for the pursuit of U.S. strategic objectives in Asia, especially when these embody some risk of conflict with a country such as China.

Michael Chambers' chapter on China provides a superb case study of a country that is disproportionately dependent on trade with the international system for its growth in national power yet seeks to exploit that interdependence in order to "create a buffer zone to help Beijing resist any hostile pressure," especially from the United States. In Chambers' reading, the PRC's export-led economic strategy, conceived and directed consciously by a purposeful state, is centered fundamentally on creating the wherewithal to support China's rise as a traditional great power with the full panoply of political, economic, and military capabilities. Export-led growth then becomes the instrumentality that enables Beijing to keep the United States invested in strong economic links with China, thereby hopefully dissuading Washington from constraining China's rise. At the same time, however, such growth creates webs of interdependence that tightly tie the prosperity of China's regional neighbors to their relations with Beijing. The high trade intensity that characterizes the Chinese economy is thus oriented toward realizing economic and strategic objectives simultaneously: trade is clearly viewed as providing the fastest means of enlarging the national product, which in turn provides the state with the resources required both to maintain the social contract that preserves the state's power and to secure those capabilities deemed necessary to protect national interests. Simultaneously, however, trade is seen as providing a strategic instrument that could tie the hands of China's most important adversaries, such as the United States and Japan, through exactly the mechanism highlighted by liberal interdependence theory—namely the high costs of conflict among specialized trading partners—while concurrently limiting the freedom of action of China's regional neighbors, who presumably would be unwilling to bandwagon with countries that might imperil the source of their current prosperity.

This same strategy is now conceived by Beijing as helping to wean the Taiwanese from any temptations to independence. In an anomaly from the perspective of liberal interdependence theory, however, Beijing appears to be willing to put all economic achievements of the last three decades at risk if necessary to prevent Taiwanese secessionism—by refusing to rule out war with China's principal trading partner, the United States. This response appears to derive from complex considerations involving the unity of China as a state, the legitimacy and survival of China's ruling Communist party, and the fear of further strengthening China's foreign competitors. Therefore the pacifying benefits usually attributed to deep economic interdependence by liberal thought appear to be at conspicuous risk at least as far as this contingency is concerned. And while arguing that China's zeal for great power capabilities via economic growth provides reasonable assurance that Beijing's geopolitical behavior will be moderated for the next decade or so, Chambers also notes that "as China's economic power, military capabilities, and political influence expand, the PRC may develop new interests at odds with the current international system." If the current patterns of Chinese economic growth continue to hold, this moment would undoubtedly embody a critical test of whether economic interdependence does in fact conduce to peace.

There is perhaps no better example in the postwar era of how trade can contribute to rapid economic growth and the accumulation of great power capabilities than Japan. A country with poor natural resources and a political order destroyed by war, Japan rose from the ashes of defeat to become the second largest economy in the world through the exploitation of an asymmetrically open international economy, especially the U.S. market, while relying on the security offered by its U.S. protector. As **Table 1** indicates, Japan still exhibits a remarkably low degree of openness to foreign trade, second only to Central Asia among the key economic centers surveyed in this volume. Michael Mastanduno's chapter describes this dynamic in some detail and explores how Japan, the trading state par excellence, is struggling to become a "normal" country able to sustain high

TABLE 1   Trade intensity in Asia, 2004

Country or region	% of trade with Asia	% of trade with the United States	% of trade with rest of the world	Trade as % of GDP
Central Asia	39.2	3.4	57.3	19.9
China	53.9	15.1	31.0	65.3
India	28.2	10.7	61.1	41.6
Japan	48.0	18.8	33.1	22.1
Russia	19.8	4.9	75.3	57.3
South Korea	51.7	15.1	33.2	83.8
Southeast Asia	61.1	13.3	25.6	47.8
United States	33.5	–	66.5	23.7

SOURCE: International Monetary Fund, *Direction of Trade Statistics Yearbook*, 2005.

NOTE: No data for Southeast Asia was available for Brunei or Burma. No data for Central Asia was available for Turkmenistan.

levels of economic performance even while pursuing new power-political goals. After a disastrous recessionary decade, ironically rooted in the supernormal success of Japanese mercantilism up to the 1980s, the Japanese economy appears to be slowly returning to the path of renewed economic growth. Although Tokyo recognizes that creating effective domestic demand is critical to the country's economic resurgence, the structure of the Japanese economy—including conspicuously unfavorable demographic trends—ensures that Japan will continue to remain dependent on overseas markets for sustained growth over the long term.

Whether Japan can become a true great power in such circumstances— where the country continues to remain noticeably dependent on external sources for almost all its raw material inputs as well as for markets for the bulk of finished goods—remains an interesting question. What is even more intriguing about the Japanese case is that Tokyo's deepened integration with the East Asian economic system—which promises to rapidly eclipse trading relations with Japan's most important traditional partner, the United States—involves reliance on partners that are either suspicious of Japan because of the burdens of history (for example, China, South Korea, and Southeast Asia) or likely to be deeply competitive with Japan for reasons associated with conventional balance-of-power politics. Japan thus far appears to have avoided the worst consequences of this tension: key Asian trading partners, each for their own reasons, have welcomed tightening economic interdependence with Japan, even as they continue with considerable wariness to watch the country's transition into a "normal" power. As Mastanduno emphasizes, the oddity is that Tokyo's political and security relations with key neighbors have worsened despite Japan's greater economic integration with East Asia. This leads him to speculatively conclude that economic interdependence may not conduce to peaceable relations, at least in this region.

This conclusion, however, has profound consequences. The absence of peace could over time erode the webs of interdependence now developing in the region, thus undermining especially those powers, such as Japan, that depend most on regional trade for continued growth. In such circumstances, Tokyo would have little choice. With a predominantly domestic driven economic expansion unlikely at least in the immediate future, Japan's desire to sustain its current strategy of maintaining high economic growth while becoming a normal state may leave it with no other real option than to rely asymmetrically on the U.S. market (and those of other non-East Asian states) even more intensively than before. Whether this option of deepened economic dependence on the United States and other non-East Asian markets can be sustained, however, will depend greatly on the state of Sino-U.S. relations, Japan's relations with emerging states outside East Asia proper, and China's own behavior as a rising power. Yet as Mastanduno points out, "Japan could play an important regional role as an alternative to China…" for smaller states that "prefer having options rather than being excessively dependent on one powerful neighboring economy."

In the case of South Korea, the intersection of trade, interdependence, and high politics, forms a similar picture but with notable differences. Like Japan, South Korea has traditionally been a poster child for the success of trade-driven growth in the postwar era. The protection offered by the United States, coupled with asymmetric access to the American market, enabled Seoul to rapidly garner the benefits of development while warding off the North Korean (DPRK) threat without undue dissipation of South Korea's dramatic economic gains. As David Kang describes, emboldened by its success, South Korea today seeks to exploit the beneficial potential of trade-driven interdependence to advance simultaneously both strategic and economic goals. One element involves a dramatic new effort by South Korea to integrate longstanding adversary North Korea into a new peninsular rapprochement that Seoul hopes will simultaneously attenuate the military threats posed by a still powerful, though clearly weakening, Pyongyang; minimize the prospect of DPRK collapse (with a view to eliminating all instabilities associated with that outcome); and eventually pave the way for a gradual and peaceful unification of the peninsula. The other element involves efforts by South Korea to deepen economic and political ties with China, both because Beijing shares Seoul's priorities with respect to North Korea—in contrast to the United States which, mindful of global consequences, emphasizes the elimination of Pyongyang's nuclear weapons—and because the rapidly growing Chinese economy now offers more and increasingly profitable opportunities for South Korean trade and investment.

In relative terms, therefore, the United States comes out the loser as a result of these trends. Although Kang emphasizes that Seoul "firmly desires to continue its close relationship with the United States," the structural factors he describes clearly forecast a tightening of economic and political ties between Seoul and Beijing that is likely to complicate U.S. strategic goals in Northeast Asia. The political benefits of economic interdependence between the two Koreas may not just yet be fully realized in the manner hoped for by liberal theorists—in part because genuine interdependence between the two sides of the Korean peninsula is still far away but also because the DPRK regime is still sufficiently eccentric in regard to the use of force. Yet the growing ties between Seoul and Pyongyang and between Seoul and Beijing, when contrasted both with the persisting alienation in relations between Seoul and Tokyo and with the growing uncertainty in future ties between Washington and Seoul, might turn out to be just the combination necessary to compromise South Korea's autonomy in Northeast Asia. Kang's analysis suggests that although neither foreordained nor desirable, such an outcome may be inevitable if the emerging patterns of economic interdependence come to strongly dominate national security decisionmaking in Beijing and Seoul.

The strength of the growing Chinese economy as a magnet for trade and by implication political influence, a strength that is so strongly evident in the case of relations between Seoul and Beijing, is also manifest in the interactions between Southeast Asia and China—but with an interesting twist. As Donald Weatherbee convincingly documents in his chapter, a rising China no doubt exercises a powerful gravitational pull on Southeast Asia, but the region's states—in sharp contrast with Seoul—have consciously attempted to avoid being sucked into Beijing's vortex. The patterns of economic interdependence witnessed in the region only empower the Association of Southeast Asian Nations (ASEAN) in one regard: although regional trade with China has risen (not surprisingly, given Beijing's impressive trade-driven growth in recent decades) the United States remains Southeast Asia's largest partner when all economic transactions—trade, investment, and development assistance—are taken into account. The Bush administration's new "Enterprise for ASEAN Initiative" (EAI), which provides a roadmap for steadily moving from bilateral trade and investment framework agreements (TIFA) to region-wide free trade agreements, will further consolidate the U.S. presence in Southeast Asia over the long term and provide powerful countervailing assistance to ASEAN, which appears determined to steer clear of becoming locked into tributary relations with China.

The intersection of economics and politics in Southeast Asia thus appears to satisfy realist expectations of interstate behavior. At one level, most of the region's small states have sought to pursue different kinds of free trade agreements with one another in order both to increase national economic growth in the fastest way possible and to mitigate any potentially adverse intra-regional rivalry. The pursuit of these two objectives, however, is shaped by the recognition that the ASEAN states are essentially minnows in a sea of whales. Hence, the efforts by these states at internal balancing and regional coalition building are consciously supplemented by the forging of strong economic ties with Japan, the European Union, and the United States, even as the security relations enjoyed by key local actors with Washington continue to be viewed as the ultimate guarantor of the region's autonomy. Deeply desirous of minimizing the threat posed by China, the Southeast Asian states have sought to integrate Beijing into their lattice of multilayered economic relations, while continuing to reach out to other major regional balancers such as Japan and India. As Weatherbee emphasizes, this does not imply that the Southeast Asian states are being assimilated into a web with China at its hub. Rather, ASEAN seeks to remain the hub of its own global network, with spokes of different sizes running to the United States, the European Union, Japan, China, and India. Thus the dense set of bilateral trade and investment relations pursued by the individual ASEAN states with all these outside actors would come to create "a peaceful and politically stable Southeast Asia open to all." Peace and order in the ASEAN strategy, then, do not derive merely from the fact of dense economic interdependence, but rather from the assurance that any attempt either by intra-regional or extra-regional actors to disrupt that interdependence by force would challenge the interests of other major powers, who would then respond in the manner necessary to restore the lost equilibrium.

The patterns of trade, interdependence, and security that dominate the Southeast Asian region are as far removed as can be imagined from South Asia for many reasons. Unlike Southeast Asia, which is populated by states and economies of comparable size (with the exception of Indonesia, which is large but physically separated from the other regional states), the South Asian region is dominated—physically, politically, economically, and strategically—by India. India is the geographically unifying entity because the country happens to share borders with every other state in the region, none of whom share a common border. One way that this central geographical fact defines regional politics is by making India the convenient object of all regional resentments, no matter what individual disagreements India's neighbors may have with one another. India's asymmetrically larger size, dramatically greater power-political standing, and conspicuously larger economy relative to neighboring countries only accentuate this dynamic further. Given that India's traditional economic strategy centered on self-reliance, New Delhi's trading relations with its neighbors historically have been essentially marginal: India did not need its neighbors for anything essential to its prosperity. In their detailed survey of South Asia in this volume, Kavita Iyengar and Devesh Kapur illustrate how a number of factors combine to produce remarkably low levels of economic integration: chronic political tensions within the region, poor physical connectivity, the lack of trade complementarity and similarities in comparative advantage, high tariff and non-tariff barriers (NTBs), and burdensome "behind the border" constraints.

New efforts such as the South Asian Free Trade Agreement are now underway to increase intra-regional trade. Similarly, attempts are also being made to boost extra-regional trade, with India in particular pushing to conclude various bilateral and regional economic cooperation agreements for both economic and political reasons; yet the pace of change is maddeningly slow. Intra-regional trade continues to be stymied by fear that smaller neighbors have of being overwhelmed by India's larger and more sophisticated economy. The slow growth of extra-regional trade, on the other hand, is attributable to other reasons. India's large size, history of emphasizing self-reliance, and relative self-sufficiency in terms of most natural resources (with the conspicuous exception of energy) invariably puts a premium on internal rather than trade-driven growth—just like the United States. True, the ideological rationales that traditionally reinforced this strategy are changing, as New Delhi gradually liberalizes India's economy. The democratic political system, however, restrains the government from rapidly and comprehensively integrating the economy with the liberal international trading order because the resulting gains and losses would deleteriously affect the fortunes of many key domestic constituencies.

The beneficial effects of interdependence on regional peace and security, for example between India and Pakistan, are therefore modest at best. As Iyengar and Kapur correctly conclude, "not only is the level of trade [within South Asia] too small, but even if it were to grow substantially, bilateral trade [within the region] will remain a modest fraction of overall trade—too small to matter, especially given the high degree of substitutability of products available in highly competitive global trade markets. Trade disruption will not impose onerous costs on any of these countries and hence will not be a factor" that compels them to change their strategic attitudes. Even in the case of Sino-Indian relations, where dramatic increases in trade have been realized in recent years, this growth in "interdependence" is driven entirely by the realist goal of maximizing national power in both countries. Consequently, this growth is complemented by efforts that involve "quietly developing security assets to counter each other," even as China appears poised "to emerge as India's largest trading partner by the end of this decade." On balance, therefore, increased interdependence in the Sino-Indian relationship will certainly complicate the political and strategic calculus in both countries but does not as yet assure a lasting peace, with significant consequences for the future of the balance of power in Asia.

Dina and Martin Spechler's chapter on Central Asia graphically depicts a region—now populated by five "increasingly disparate states with different growth strategies, results, and political orientations"—that has lost the economic and political unity that characterized it during the Soviet era. The Spechlers note that while the energy, mineral, and human resources have enabled at least three states—Kazakhstan, Turkmenistan, and Uzbekistan—to pursue autonomous foreign policies, the presence of oil and natural gas has drawn several major outside powers (Russia, China, India, and the United States) to develop significant interests in the region. Two questions concerning trade, interdependence, and security are relevant to the region. First, are the intra-regional trade patterns and the use of natural resources likely to increase the probability of conflict among the Central Asian states or with outsiders? Second, does the role of outside powers in developing Central Asia's energy resources increase the probability of violent conflict or to reduce power-political tensions?

The data adduced by the Spechlers suggests that intra-regional trade remains relatively modest, although informal trade is likely to be more substantial than official statistics suggest. The reality of relatively low intra-regional trade densities implies that regional economic relations are likely to have a marginal impact on questions of war and peace. These questions are likely to be affected more by local precipitants such as Islamist extremism, the trans-border drug trade, and border disputes than by local economic intercourse. The authors conclude that major conflict between the Central Asian states is in any event unlikely, but that contestation over water could precipitate localized tensions. Where strife between the major powers over regional resources is concerned, the authors again draw sanguine conclusions, arguing that secure energy supplies to Russia, China, India, or other Eurasian powers will reduce the probability of violent conflict. This inference is obviously reassuring, although much will depend on the strategies adopted by large local consumers of energy such as China, Japan, and India; so long as these actors view markets as the principal mechanism for mediating oil and natural gas demands, the potential for armed conflict ought to be mitigated. Not to be overlooked, however, are circumstances in which the mercantilist approaches toward securing energy supplies might come to dominate the national strategies of these states, an issue that, at least in the case of China and to a lesser degree India, is not yet settled completely and in the case of Japan could change in the future. In such cases, the risk of conflict would increase to the degree that these nations came to view natural resources in foreign lands as assets to be "captured" for one's exclusive use, a challenge that even the "export globalism" currently pursued by the Central Asian states may be unable to prevent.

Rounding up the country studies in this volume, Peter Rutland's chapter on Russia focuses on a major global power that is currently enjoying an economic renaissance almost entirely because of upward price movements in the global energy markets. This fact underscores, among other things, the remarkable nature of Russia's economic evolution from an autarkic, inward-looking, economic machine during the Soviet Union to the trading state that the country has become during the current era. Russia's growing dependence on trade ought to augur well both for integration with the Western political community (an objective Moscow has assiduously pursued since the demise of the Soviet Union) and for regional peace and stability (if the liberal vision of interdependence is correct). Rutland's analysis, however, highlights several variables that cast shadows on what is otherwise a welcome development.

To begin with, Russia's integration with the global economy centers primarily on the country's exports of energy and critical raw materials—a situation well understood by economists to have the potential to reinforce the "resource curse."[17] Contemporary developments seem to corroborate this expectation: the Russian state, flush with cash from rising energy prices, has moved swiftly to retard the country's movement toward democratization. Favored instead is a state-supported corporatism that has targeted liberal political elements within the country and, as a result, precipitated great unease within the West. Furthermore, given that the infrastructure associated with Russia's energy estate appears to be rapidly aging, whether Russia will be able to sustain the country's currently lucrative energy production and export strategy over the long term is unclear. Finally, there is a significant risk that Russia's current strategy of selling advanced

---

[17] Jeffrey D. Sachs and Andrew M. Warner, "Natural Resource Abundance and Economic Growth," National Bureau of Economic Research, NBER Working Paper, no. 5398, December 1995; Ragnar Torvik, "Natural Resources, Rent Seeking and Welfare," *Journal of Development Economics* 67, no. 2 (April 15, 2002): 455–70; and Sweder van Wijnbergen, "The 'Dutch Disease': A Disease After All?" *Economic Journal*, 94 (March 1984): 41–55.

weaponry to China could backfire, insofar as such sales could strengthen what is clearly a rising power and a potential Russian adversary. Not at all certain at this time is whether the Russian defense industry will be able to maintain the technological superiority that will help blunt future Chinese challenges, whether the Chinese economic penetration of the vulnerable Russian Far East—the locus of many critical Russian resources—will diminish, and whether the strength and capabilities of Russia's conventional defense forces will remain adequate given the enormous security challenges that continue to confront the country.

All told the Russian economy appears well-placed to benefit from the growing energy demands in Asia and elsewhere; there remain, however, considerable uncertainties as to whether these advantages can be sustained over the long-term and to the advantage of Russian democracy. Gnawing doubts also persist about whether the growing interdependence that now characterizes the Russian economy will actually contribute toward mitigating the security threats that are likely to confront Moscow in the future.

In addition to the country and regional chapters on trade and interdependence—this volume, continuing a tradition begun with the very first edition of Strategic Asia in 2001—includes three special studies that in interesting ways relate to the theme of this year's research.

The first study by Minxin Pei addresses what is probably the central question surrounding the rise of China as a great power and one that is intimately linked to the emerging patterns of trade and interdependence now witnessed in Asia: can Beijing sustain its meteoric economic growth over the secular period without political reforms? If the answer to this question is affirmative, not only will China have succeeded in blazing a new path not witnessed historically but from both a realist and a liberal perspective China's economic growth would also likely give way to serious political apprehensions. Pei answers this critical question in the negative, however, noting that "China will not likely continue this course of rapid growth without undertaking the necessary political reforms to make the Chinese political system more responsive and respectful of property and individual rights." Noting that a period of strong economic growth may obscure the need for fundamental political and structural reforms, Pei urges U.S. policymakers in particular not to take China's future economic success for granted. Instead, he argues that the West ought to focus on encouraging domestic political change within China as a means of helping the country both to sustain economic growth and to become a responsible global power. Such a policy, however, could increase tensions in Sino-U.S. relations in the near term; whether current and future U.S. administrations ought to take these risks in light of the presumed benefits Pei highlights in his chapter, therefore, ought to become an important element of the U.S. debate on China in the years to come.

As the special study by William Thompson and David Rapkin on the emergence of China and India reminds us, there are two power transitions occurring in Asia today, with two large powers growing in strength and pressing claims for recognition on the global stage. Unlike most previous work, which has focused predominantly on the political facets of Sino-Indian rivalry, Thompson and Rapkin attempt to depict this "dual transition" in terms of the structural elements: the modes and relations of production in the global economy. Since the birth of new great powers has historically engendered considerable violence, the question whether the concurrent rise of China and India to great power status would prove the exception to this historical norm in the current age of interdependence remains a matter of great theoretical and policy interest. Thompson and Rapkin soberly conclude that although interdependence may accelerate the growth of national capabilities in both these countries, it cannot assuredly pacify conspicuous rivalries. Rather, the economic friction that interdependence autonomously generates can "offset or overwhelm its conflict-suppressing effects," depending on various factors. What is important in the Sino-Indian cases, however, is that their impact on the global system is still open because, the authors argue, "the explication of historical patterns" ought to be viewed "as opportunities for social, or more aptly strategic, learning that can lessen the probability that the deadly dynamics of great power interactions characteristic of prior centuries will be repeated." If the realists are correct in their assessments of international politics, however, no amount of learning may be sufficient for China and India to avoid the adjustment traumas associated with the rise of new great powers because other states, fearful of the worst outcomes for their security, are condemned to engage in individually beneficial but systemically sub-optimal behaviors that have the effect of exacerbating strategic rivalry. Whether this outcome can yet be escaped in the case of China and India remains to be seen, but the record that Thompson and Rapkin have themselves adduced and analyzed leaves little room for unalloyed optimism.

In addition to great-power rivalry, perhaps no other issue can do more to undermine the optimism concerning Asia's continuing growth in economic and political power than the spread of pandemic disease—again, ironically encouraged by that increased movement of goods, services, and people that defines interdependence. Ann Marie Kimball's special study on infectious diseases and their impact on interdependence highlights the transformative role of epidemics and their potential to retard growth in

East and Southeast Asia—the reason that is most likely to emerge as the source of such a scourge despite their being among the most productive quadrants of the Asian continent. Despite the improvements in international cooperation that have occurred since the SARS epidemic, Kimball warns that the region still lacks the capabilities to cope with a truly virulent outbreak of infectious disease. If unmanaged, such a contingency could deeply undermine the "Asian miracle" through its corrosive impact on labor availability, irremediable alterations in family size and structure, pressure on savings and investment, and even increased suspicions between states (both those who are victims and those who are bystanders in an epidemic). Given the importance of this issue to the Asian countries themselves as well as to the United States, Kimball notes the importance of Washington investing in collaborative efforts to detect, treat, and manage the outbreak of infectious disease in a way that goes beyond simply being obsessed with "thwarting potential bioterror attacks against the American people."

Taking Stock

When viewed synoptically, the country and regional studies in this volume of Strategic Asia leave no doubt that trade has become a critical instrument in the drive to sustain national economic growth. The smaller countries of East Asia had settled on trade-driven growth strategies in the early postwar period; their success was sufficiently obvious by the late 1970s to entice China to follow suit. This decision had dramatic consequences in that it propelled China's explosive economic growth during the last three decades and, as a result, has created a web of interdependence that links many East and Southeast Asian states—both friends and rivals—into a network that has been very conducive to rapid growth. Even large continental-sized states such as India and Russia, which for different reasons had not emphasized foreign trade previously, have now focused on increasing their links with the global economy. The emerging trend in Strategic Asia's area of focus thus seems clear: growing trade and interdependence will increasingly be the norm between both friends and competitors, with all countries coming to realize the value of accelerated economic growth for achieving their national purposes.

This "rush to trade" as a strategy for increasing growth, and as manifested in Asia over the last few decades, has intriguing characteristics. Although all trade expansion at an economic level is invariably accompanied by the need to manage the character and consequences of that expansion domestically, the major trading states in Asia do not as yet appear to exhibit any acute fears about the problem of relative gains.[18] That is, these states remain at least thus far noticeably unconcerned about how much their partners may be profiting from any given trading relationship, so long as they are all seen to come out ahead in absolute terms relative to not trading at all. To the degree that concerns about relative gains are manifest, these states seem to be driven more by sub-national issues involving domestic political groups (who may be winners or losers in specific trading interactions) than by issues at the state level, where national security decisionmakers fret about the economic performance of their country relative to some competitors. In this sense, the behavior of these states seems to comport with liberal theories of international politics and may derive from three specific judgments that are relevant to the future of Asia:

- That the hegemonic status of the United States and its security commitments in Asia are right now so robust as to ensure that any differentials in relative gains have insignificant strategic meaning.

- That peace among the Asian states will continue for some time to come, thereby strengthening positive expectations for future trade among national decisionmakers in these countries and inducing them to expand their interdependence in order to realize its growth and welfare gains, without being unduly fearful about the consequences for long-term strategic competition.

- That even if in some states, such as China, the gains from trade are generating resources that are being diverted to military purposes, these states are still not able to pose consequential military threats. Such threats can in any event be contained by other political instruments that do not require their partners to forgo any profitable trading relationships in the interim.[19]

That the Asian states can continue to expand their trading links on these premises is particularly interesting because most of the regional states appear to view trade as a device for maximizing national power.

---

[18] This issue is discussed systematically in Joseph M. Grieco, "Anarchy and the Limits of Cooperation: A Realist Critique of the Newest Liberal Institutionalism," *International Organization* 42, no. 3 (Summer 1988): 485–529.

[19] Whether this judgment is accurate is another matter altogether. The historical record is littered with examples of countries that failed to make accurate assessments of the pre-conflict balance of military capabilities, only to discover—too late sometimes—that the balance of power had indeed changed unexpectedly despite careful watching. For sobering judgments about the art of military assessment, see Aaron Friedberg, "The Assessment of Military Power: A Review Essay," *International Security* 12, no. 3 (Winter 1987/88): 190–202, and Eliot Cohen, "Guessing Game: A Reappraisal of Systems Analysis," in *The Strategic Imperative*, ed. Samuel Huntington (Cambridge, MA: Ballinger, 1982), 163–92.

The chapters in this volume illustrate clearly that the trading states in Asia perceive the deepening in regional interdependence less in terms of collective security and more in terms of latching on to the most efficient device capable of increasing national growth rates in comparison to some alternative economic strategy. Although domestic political considerations are ever present in this context, the state-level drivers nonetheless revolve primarily around a number of considerations:

- increasing national strength;

- providing the state with resources to advance power-political goals;

- minimizing the prospects of balancing on the part of one's competitors;

- creating networks of dependency that limit a rival's choices;

- expanding access and influence in strategic areas;

- generating conditions that would limit the freedom of action on the part of important extra-continental powers such as the United States.

Given such objectives, the fact that the Asian states currently neglect relative gains issues in their trading relationships may appear surprising at first sight. Yet on reconsideration, these attitudes are understandable because, as Albert Hirschman appreciated as early as 1945, decisions to trade generally involve efforts to maximize both economic and political utility.[20] So long as these two objectives are not perceived to be in absolute conflict, political rivals might continue to engage in productive trading relations because of their judgment that economic or political benefits are to be derived from trade with one's competitors. In fact, concerns about differential growth rates may themselves compel states to engage more vigorously in trading relationships than usual—despite all the risks arising from interdependence—if these interactions are seen to provide more effective mechanisms of increasing national economic capacity relative to all other alternatives.[21] This calculus probably accounts for why even great powers pursued relationships involving economic interdependence at various points in history, including when security competition between them was particularly intense, as was the case between 1880 and 1914. Because most of the Asian states today find themselves encompassed

---

[20] Albert O. Hirschman, *National Power and the Structure of Foreign Trade* (Berkeley, CA: University of California Press, 1945).

[21] For a good discussion of why states may trade despite concerns for relative gains see especially the essays by Duncan Snidal, Robert Powell, and Robert Keohane, in *Neorealism and Neoliberalism: The Contemporary Debate*, ed. David A. Baldwin (New York: Columbia University Press, 1993).

by exactly the same logic (while simultaneously remaining—despite the growth in intra-Asian trade—critically dependent on important markets outside Asia), their dependence on foreign trade as an engine for ensuring economic growth will likely continue for some time to come.

The behavior of the Asian states, therefore, suggests that their leaders have understood both the lessons of economics and the lessons of international politics all too well. They appreciate that robust economic growth alone enables them to protect their states in the manner they deem desirable, that trade enables these states to expand their national power faster in comparison to alternative national strategies, and that the growth in power, which derives from both trade and internal resource mobilization, enables them to ward off threats and manage risks while strengthening their ability to secure whatever strategic goals they may happen to pursue. In so doing, Asian states appear to straddle the realist-liberal divide on trade, interdependence, and security: they recognize that the demands of power and the demands of plenty may be opposed in the limiting case; until that point is reached, however, they want to enjoy the gains deriving from international commerce precisely in order to be better able to manage the tensions that all utility- and security-maximizing states must confront in an "anarchic" global environment. To the degree that such behaviors are likely to persist in a regional strategic environment that is "between the times," the liberal hypothesis regarding interdependence and peace cannot yet be conclusively tested in Asia. And, if the realist reading of international politics is correct, such a test may continue to elude the continent, if not necessarily every dyad within it, for some time to come.

STRATEGIC ASIA 2006–07

COUNTRY STUDIES

EXECUTIVE SUMMARY

This chapter examines why the ongoing refusal of the United States to live within its economic means poses challenges to U.S. domestic prosperity, dilutes U.S. credibility as a global superpower, and elevates U.S.-East Asian economic interdependence to uncharted levels of complexity.

MAIN ARGUMENT:
- Having accumulated so much external debt for so long, the United States is at—if not already beyond—the boundaries of prudent economic behavior. A paradox of American "exceptionalism" is that this situation reflects both U.S. weakness and strength.

- Several Asian countries have become super-creditors due to over-reliance on exports to the U.S. market and under-reliance on internal growth. The compulsion of these countries to export and the U.S. craving for imports are complementary excesses. Imprudent dependence on a ballooning global balance of payments disequilibrium has created a precarious interdependence between the super-debtor and its Asian super-creditors.

- Though the likelihood of an economic crisis caused by a rapid depreciation of the dollar is neither inevitable nor imminent, the danger is credible enough that governments should be taking the situation more seriously.

POLICY IMPLICATIONS:
- The ability of the United States to endure the financial burdens of being the world's sole superpower depends on "good" macroeconomic policy, a system that encourages innovation and the entrepreneurial spirit, a capacity for self-reinvention, and efficient capital markets.

- By relying excessively on debt, the U.S. government has effectively abdicated short- to medium-term control over the dollar's value to the mostly Asian super-creditors and profit-seeking speculators everywhere.

- Washington has not yet allowed U.S. gratitude for the roles that Asian super-creditors play in stabilizing the dollar's exchange rate to influence U.S. security policy relating to Asia. Less U.S. dependence on external borrowing would preserve the firewall separating economic and security issues.

The Superpower as Super-Debtor: Implications of Economic Disequilibria for U.S.-Asian Relations

Stephen D. Cohen

The United States has taken no meaningful action to contain ten years of steadily worsening, record-breaking trade deficits. The policy of inaction that by default has encouraged these deficits has been praised as a brilliant, wealth-maximizing strategy but also has been condemned as a dangerously irresponsible indifference to increasingly untenable international economic imbalances. Passionate believers in reliance on free market forces as the optimal strategy are unconcerned, remaining confident that the invisible hand of the marketplace will devise a more efficient solution than anything that politicians and civil servants can concoct. Believing that market imperfections inevitably make matters worse, skeptics are concerned that inaction by the U.S. government risks severe economic upheaval that, among other things, will harm Washington's role in world affairs in general and in Asia in particular. This chapter argues that, on balance, the de facto U.S. pursuit of a familiar but risky short-cut to prosperity—massive borrowing and postponed sacrifices—poses a *potential* danger to U.S. economic and foreign policy interests as well as to the global economy.

A cloud of uncertainty hovers over the "exceptionalism" label commonly affixed to U.S. economic prosperity and to the role that the United States plays in the world. The uncertainty is about mounting debt. An imminent threat to U.S. economic growth, global leadership, or military power can be inferred but not categorically demonstrated. The dependence of other

Stephen D. Cohen is Professor, School of International Service, American University, Washington, D.C. and Director of the International Economic Relations Field. His new book, tentatively titled *Foreign Direct Investment and Multinational Corporations: Avoiding Simplicity, Embracing Complexity*, will be published later this year. He can be reached at <scohen@american.edu>.

countries, especially in Asia, on exports to the U.S. market has never been greater. When approaching or having already passed the line of excessive borrowing, however, a superpower courts both economic instability and complications in its relations with foreign countries. The world's sole superpower and biggest national economy is addicted to borrowing and consuming at the same time that foreign economies, mainly in East Asia, are addicted to lending and exporting. The result is an international economic order that has slipped into the uncharted waters of record balance-of-payments disequilibria. The inherently intricate linkage between the domestic economy, the international balance of payments position, and the foreign relations of the United States has never been more complicated and precarious. Countries having a large trade surplus face their own version of complexity and precariousness. This situation is well summarized by the old axiom, attributed to J. Paul Getty, that "If you owe the bank $100, that's your problem. If you owe the bank $100 million, that's the bank's problem."

In the continued absence of greater sensitivity to the new vulnerabilities, Washington will continue to base U.S. economic policy strategy mainly on inertia mixed with denial. No one can say for sure how well or how poorly the United States can continue to reconcile its role of superpower with the potentially debilitating baggage associated with the role of super-borrower/debtor. On the one hand, the United States' international power and prestige have not been enhanced by the domestic economy's increased dependence on the kindness of strangers with cash to lend. On the other hand, the Asian super-creditors have gained little practical leverage over their biggest borrower. These countries too have an increased economic dependence. Shunning an emphasis on stimulating economic growth through increased internal demand, the big surplus countries hold fast to a calculated decision to rely inordinately on increased U.S. consumption for their growth. Furthermore, the super-creditors have amassed such large dollar holdings that their exchange-rate policy options are limited: super-creditors have a strong vested interest in preventing a sizable fall in the dollar's value. The analysis that follows examines the major elements that collectively have created an epic contest between two forces. The first is preservation of American exceptionalism—the dynamism of the U.S. economy, the ability and will to actively pursue national interests on a global basis, the ability to run prolonged balance of payments deficits, and so on. The second is a vulnerability and potential weakness born of dependence on overseas lenders.

The first section of this chapter examines the source of rising U.S. external indebtedness: the extraordinary size, duration, impact, and foreign support of U.S. balance of payments deficits. The second section lays out the arguments as to why the unique U.S. ability to finance an excess of foreign expenditures over earnings could be close to a breaking point. The critical role of large-trade-surplus-countries in East Asia in determining how long U.S. deficits and debt build-up can endure is the subject of the third section. The chapter then reviews the reasons why a United States living within its means should have the economic size, strength, and vigor to finance the obligations associated with global superpower status. A case study of U.S.-Chinese economic relations then illustrates many of the points raised in previous sections. The concluding section suggests future economic scenarios and reviews the policy implications of massive U.S. foreign borrowing and massive Asian lending.

American Exceptionalism: Enabler of Extraordinary U.S. External Deficits

After more than 55 years in which their country's international expenditures exceeded international earnings on a virtually uninterrupted basis, few Americans consider external deficits to be abnormal. As discussed below, this way of thinking is aided and abetted by the fact that the U.S. economy is more insulated from international stresses and strains than are economies of other countries. Not even the nearly unbroken chain of record-breaking annual trade deficits since the mid-1990s has been sufficient to cause the American public to become anxious about the deteriorating—but little understood—balance of payments. This is not an irrational reaction. The U.S. economy to date has suffered no visible injury from these deficits, thanks mainly to accommodating Asian creditors. The body politic has given no thought to pressuring its elected leaders to launch a growth-retarding, pre-emptive strike against current consumption and government expenditures as a move to deter a potential international economic crisis that might not occur in their lifetimes.

The administration and Congress have heard this silence and reacted accordingly. More than 60 years of giving priority to foreign policy concerns and domestic consumption over export expansion or import reduction has imbued senior U.S. economic policymakers with a uniquely high tolerance for net dollar outflows. This trait is the direct opposite of the export-maximization imperative that dominates the trade policies of every other country. Only the U.S. government does not view foreign trade first and foremost as an adjunct of promoting the economic health and size of the domestic industrial sector. The rest of the world reveres exports and at best tolerates imports of goods competing with those produced domestically. Washington arguably is the capital city least convinced of the need to proactively pursue the core tenet of mercantilism: a country's wealth, power, and influence all increase in proportion to the size of that country's surplus of exports over imports. The United States is the country least committed to genuinely making export maximization its top trade priority.

Several factors unique to the United States explain why U.S. trade policy has been so distinctive as to be in a class by itself since the late 1940s. The common denominator among these factors is that the costs of maintaining a distinctive trade policy have been uniquely low, while benefits to foreign policy have been substantial. The initial explanatory factor was a dramatic turnaround in attitudes after the United States abandoned an isolationist foreign policy and embraced global leadership following World War II. Trade policy was soon co-opted by postwar national security priorities. This move followed a quick consensus regarding the value of assisting the postwar economic recovery of Cold War allies in Western Europe and Asia by, among other things, keeping the super-strong U.S. market open to exports from these regions while tolerating their discriminatory import barriers against U.S. goods. The domestic drawbacks to this approach were not felt until many years later, after the war-torn economies of Western Europe and Japan recovered and once again became strong competitors in the international marketplace.

While the period of unequivocal U.S. economic hegemony ended in the early 1960s, one important economic indicator is still valid: exports and imports both represent a smaller percentage of U.S. gross domestic product (GDP) than is the case in every other major economy and most minor ones. The value of U.S. exports of goods in 2005 equated to 7% of (nominal) GDP, while imports were equal to 13% of total economic output. Germany's exports and imports of goods in the same year were 35% and 28% of GDP, respectively.[1] Exports as a percent of GDP in East and Southeast Asia are also high. The figures in 2005 were: China, 34%; Taiwan, 55%; and Korea, 36%. Inflated by re-exports of processed goods, the percentage for Singapore was 167%; Hong Kong, 163%; and Malaysia, 108%.[2]

Relatively small inward and outward foreign trade flows minimize the macro impact (as distinct from a few major sectoral, or micro, effects) on total U.S. production, jobs, and corporate profits. Increased exports offer relatively small benefits to, and increased imports impose relatively small

---

[1] Data for the United States derived from the U.S. Department of Commerce; for Germany, the International Monetary Fund and the World Trade Organization. The inclusion of trade in services marginally raises the GDP percentages for both countries.

[2] Andy Xie, "A Stormy Summer Ahead," Morgan Stanley Global Economic Forum, July 18, 2006, http://www.morganstanley.com/GEFdata/digests/latest-digest.html.

costs on, the American economy as a whole.³ An economic rule of thumb holds that a country's overall economic growth and job creation are mainly determined by domestic trends. This rule is more applicable to the United States than elsewhere because domestic economic trends and performance so heavily dominate determination of GDP growth and employment. For example, employment in the manufacturing sector, where workers are most vulnerable to import competition, now accounts for a mere 11% of the total workforce.⁴ This calculus also largely explains why the U.S. government has long been way out in front in its willingness to restrict export sales in the interest of furthering national security, foreign policy, or humanitarian goals. The rest of the world largely retains a mercantilist view that exports lost to sanctions are unacceptably costly, especially since trade sanctions have seldom forced targeted governments to abandon their offending behavior.

A second critically important contributing factor to the exceptional nature of U.S. trade beliefs and practices since the end of World War II was the emergence of the dollar as the world's main transactions and reserve currency. The dollar's exalted status has given the United States the unique ability to simply use a small fraction of its own money supply to pay for all the imports the country needs. Compared to other countries, the United States is therefore under far less pressure to export in order to earn hard currency to pay for imports.

Third, U.S. attitudes toward foreign trade are further skewed from the international norm by the fact that, with only sporadic interruptions, the rest of the world has welcomed a net outflow of dollars from a spendthrift United States. Relatively weak economies are forced to curtail imports of needed goods (especially high-tech goods that they cannot produce domestically) and are always seeking additional dollars to pay for more imports. The most practical way for these countries to obtain additional hard currency is through rising U.S. imports that increase the net outflow of dollars from the United States. If the private and public sectors in other countries have an infinite and perpetual desire (or at least willingness) to hold onto accumulated dollars, the United States can in theory run a large current account deficit indefinitely. Some have viewed this unique ability as an unfair arrangement that should not be perpetuated. Charles de Gaulle

---

³ This conclusion is not invalidated by the fact that exports and imports today represent a larger share of the U.S. economy than in the mid- and late-twentieth century. Trade is still statistically a marginal factor in the total economic picture.

⁴ U.S. Labor Department: Bureau of Labor Statistics, "The Employment Situation, June 2006," Press Release, July 7, 2006, http://www.bls.gov/bls/newsrels.htm. The politics of trade are such that no matter how small a percentage of the total workforce they may constitute, workers at risk of losing their jobs to imports can and do exercise their right to demand that their leaders offer protection.

in the 1960s acerbically described this U.S. practice as an "exorbitant privilege."

Uniquely negative attitudes toward industrial policy are a fourth reason that the attitude of the United States toward foreign trade bears so little resemblance to those of its trading partners. Other countries deem it desirable to use government resources to promote the growth of targeted industries and to use foreign trade to promote domestic industries. These countries believe, therefore, that providing subsidies to export industries and imposing import barriers serve legitimate purposes. Most Americans are skeptical that government interference in the marketplace is cost-effective and accept the corollary that market-driven trade flows are more beneficial than government-mandated trade barriers or export subsidies. Washington generally approaches domestic economic policy and trade policy as distinct entities; foreign trade strategy is not an adjunct for (non-existent) economic planning. By taking a strong leadership role in negotiating reductions in trade barriers, the U.S. government has come closer than any of its counterparts to acting in accordance with free trade theory. The core argument of this theory is that the ultimate rationale for a country to engage in international trade is to reap the benefits of acquiring goods that are made more efficiently and cheaply in other countries.[5] A final factor creating a distinctive U.S. trade policy is that U.S. manufacturing companies as a group are well ahead of their foreign competition in the extent of their reliance upon foreign direct investment, rather than upon traditional exporting, as the main vehicle for generating sales to customers in other countries.

Prior to the early 1970s, the United States spent more money overseas than it was earning, but did so in a very unusual and positive manner. Unlike the typical country with a balance of payments deficit, the United States enjoyed a highly competitive economy that was generating large trade surpluses. These surpluses were, however, dwarfed by larger net capital outflows, most of which were completely consistent with what a political and economic hegemon should have been doing. Responding to the onset of the Cold War, the U.S. government began spending money overseas for foreign aid and military bases. The private sector began exporting capital in record amounts in order to acquire attractive overseas assets. Much of this trend took the form of the first sustained surge in foreign direct investment by U.S. manufacturing companies. In addition, U.S. banks sharply increased

---

[5] The theory further suggests that outflows of real wealth (commonly referred to as exports) are beneficial mainly for generating the capital to pay for imports; given that domestic policies are more effective in increasing aggregate demand within a country, exporting is seen as the means to import real wealth, not an end in itself.

loans to overseas borrowers. Repatriated profits and interest payments were sufficiently large that, over the long-term, American companies brought back more capital from abroad than was originally sent out.

In light of non-stop U.S. merchandise trade deficits since 1976, attention has turned to the country's deteriorating current account position, the most watched component of a country's balance of payments. The major component of the current account is exports and imports of goods and services.[6] The account also measures international income and payments (mostly dividends and interest) and unilateral transfer payments and receipts (mostly local worker remittances to other countries). Although the numbers clearly show steadily increasing, record-shattering U.S. current account deficits, assessments of the implications of this trend are sharply divided.

The optimistic school of thought emphasizes positive economic trends as the main underlying cause of the current account deficits. This school asserts that the relatively strong, sustained increase in U.S. imports can be traced largely to the fact that the U.S. economy has been growing faster than its major trading partners for several years. The average annual growth rate in real U.S. GDP was 2.7% in the 2001–2005 period; this rate compares favorably to the average growth rates of 1.5% and 1.2% for the European Union countries and Japan, respectively.[7] A second favorable factor offered by the optimists is that the trade deficit is the *result*, not the cause, of large net capital inflows. Given the nature of the accounting principles governing the compilation of balance of payments statistics, a country with a financial account surplus normally has a roughly corresponding current account deficit, and vice versa.[8] The relative attractiveness of the U.S. economic and political environment accounts for much of the large volume of capital the United States draws from foreign investors. A relative shortage of attractive investment opportunities in less dynamic economies suggests a higher return can be had by acquiring such U.S.-based assets as corporations (direct investment), stocks, corporate bonds, and real estate. In arguing that a U.S. current account deficit is a logical and sustainable economic phenomenon, Richard Cooper has written that the deficit is "a natural consequence of excess saving in the rest of the world," noting that the comparative advantage of the United States in producing financial assets has

---

[6] This chapter follows the common practice of using the terms "current account" and "balance of payments" interchangeably.

[7] Joint Economic Committee of the U.S. Congress, *U.S. Economy Outperformed the Canadian, European, and Japanese Economies since 2001*, December 2005, http://www.house.gov/jec/publications/109/rr109-25.pdf.

[8] In accounting, assets and liabilities always offset one another (i.e., they net out to zero); this is why the balance of payments always balances.

been highly attractive to foreign investors.[9] In any event, it is not possible to scientifically demonstrate whether a current account imbalance is the cause of an offsetting financial account imbalance or vice versa; in most cases, it is probably some combination of the two—i.e., a two-way cause and effect. Remarkably, foreign governments have not made public demands that the United States quickly adopt adjustment measures to reduce the U.S. trade deficit. This silence reflects the beliefs of these foreign governments that their interests have been served by a decade of rising U.S. deficits and that it is in their interest to prevent their trade surpluses from declining or disappearing. The beneficiaries of robust U.S. demand for imports are not well situated to lose what for several countries has been their single greatest source of economic growth. Reflecting the relatively soft economies of the other large industrial countries, the combined dollar value of U.S. GDP growth and increased U.S. imports accounted for an estimated 63% of the cumulative increase in the dollar value of world GDP during the seven year period ending in 2001.[10] Countries enamored with export-led growth do not want to bite the hand that has been crucial to satisfying their preoccupation with export maximization. In the U.S. equivalent of economic deference, Washington does not want to bite the hands of big foreign lenders to the United States.

Exceptionalism at Risk: The U.S. Current Account Deficit

Since the closing years of the last century, a relatively prosperous international economy has coexisted with unprecedented divergences between balance of payments surpluses and deficits. This is not necessarily a dangerous or untenable situation. Adherents of the sustainability school of thought correctly observe that all alternatives to more-of-the-same policies are deemed by both surplus and deficit countries to be prohibitively costly in economic and in political terms. No U.S. president wants to raise taxes in order to narrow the budget deficit. No foreign government wants to be blamed for the slower growth, lost jobs, and lower business profits that would follow policy initiatives that shrank exports without providing offsetting increases in aggregate domestic demand.

For several reasons, however, the rosy scenario appears too optimistic for current circumstances. Facts, trends, and economic theory favor the less

[9] Richard N. Cooper, "Living with Global Imbalances: A Contrarian View," Institute for International Economics, November 2005, 6, http://www.iie.com.

[10] Stephen Roach, "An Historic Moment?" Morgan Stanley Global Economic Forum, June 23, 2003, http://www.morganstanley.com/GEFdata/digests/20030623-mon.html. (A 63% contribution to world growth would be approximately twice the U.S. share of world GDP.)

optimistic assessment of the large and growing U.S. current account deficit. The forces necessary for a correction in the massive U.S. current account deficit have not begun to coalesce. Time may be running out for the status quo. The longer this disequilibrium continues, the more American economic well-being will be vulnerable to a sharp correction in the foreign exchange market. This correction could come in the form of speculators massively selling dollars, foreign governments refusing to accumulate additional dollars, or both.

An explanation of contemporary U.S. current account deficits can be summarized in one word: excess. Excess derives from two interconnected economic strategies of questionable wisdom and durability: excessive spending by the United States and excessive dependence by the East Asian super-creditors on American consumers for increased economic growth and jobs. A bleak scenario is even more likely to occur because of the absence of any consequential adjustment measures taken by either the country with the biggest current account deficit or the countries with the largest trade surpluses. No changes appear to be in the offing. The two sides remain content to hope that the international economic status quo, believed by many to be unsustainable, does not suddenly and violently unravel.

The current era of net dollar outflows in many ways is a godsend to the world economy just as it was in the years after World War II. Despite the parallels, important differences do exist in the economic and foreign policy implications of these two episodes of American economic exceptionalism. Contemporary U.S. balance of payments deficits are bigger in size and lower in quality. As Richard Cooper concedes, the deficit cannot continue increasing indefinitely as a percentage of GDP without negative repercussions. A deteriorating U.S. external position is also suggested by the declining credibility of the argument that the growing current account deficit results from a torrent of private foreign investment flows lured by the relatively dynamic American economy. This assertion could be backed by statistics in the late 1990s, but not today. The belief that foreign private investors still cause the trade deficit suffers from a serious flaw: failure to differentiate between two distinct kinds of capital inflows, each of which carries a very different implication.

A simple indicator of foreign confidence both in the U.S. economy and in dollar assets is the respective shares of capital inflows accounted for by the overseas private sector and by foreign governments. Most inflows from "official" sources consist of foreign central banks investing dollars bought through interventions in the foreign exchange market, the result of efforts to prop up a weak dollar. Such inflows reflect perceived weakness, and should not be construed as a case of a strong economy attracting massive amounts of private capital. Since it is statistically necessary for a financial account surplus to approximately offset a current account deficit, official flows are the reciprocal of private flows. The larger the latter, the less is the need for official intervention to absorb unwanted dollars. In 2000, amidst a booming U.S. economy, net capital inflows of slightly more than $1.05 trillion were divided between incoming private flows of $1 trillion (much of which in effect financed efficiency-enhancing U.S. corporate investments in information technology) and official flows of $43 billion, a mere 4% of the total.[11]

Times and attitudes have changed. Private foreign investors have become less enamored with continued accumulations of dollar assets in the United States. Motivated by the desire to protect their exports to the United States rather than a passion for investing there, foreign central banks have needed to expand their role in financing the U.S. deficit. The greater the share of foreign central bank dollar purchases relative to private foreign investors, the more the case for a U.S. financial account surplus generating a current account deficit is undermined. In 2004, recorded net official inflows of $388 billion accounted for 27% of total net U.S. inflows of $1.45 trillion. This figure reflects increased intervention, mostly by a number of central banks in Asia, designed to prevent their respective currencies from significantly appreciating in value against the dollar.

Being a big borrower—whether an individual, company, or country—is not necessarily a dangerous or undesirable position to be in, especially if the borrowed capital is used mainly for productive purposes rather than for one-time consumer gratification. The more that borrowing is used to increase the debtor's capacity to generate long-term income, the easier the repayment process should be. Since 2001, however, the growing U.S. current account deficit and increased foreign borrowing have reflected increased purchases of consumer goods far more than they have reflected investment in capital goods to modernize and expand productive capacity. This trend can be deduced by continued increases in U.S. capital inflows and consumption concurrent with a relative slowdown in new investment.

Government decisionmakers in Asia and the United States have not overtly voiced the concerns expressed by many private sector economists regarding the sustainability of the growing global economic disequilibrium in general and the sustainability of U.S. current account deficits and financial account surpluses in particular. Complacency has raised the official tolerance for risk on both sides of the Pacific and has increased willingness by the big creditor countries as well as the super-borrower to

---

[11] "Balance of Payments (International Transactions)," U.S. Department of Commerce, Bureau of Economic Affairs, http://www.bea.gov/bea/di/home/bop.htm.

stick with what is seen as a good way to achieve economic priorities. All of these countries have good reason to seek to preserve the economic status quo. Consumption in the United States, exports from Asia, and the general economic growth of both regions have been rising. It is a nearly inviolable law of political economy that politicians do not implement unpopular measures to choke off economic growth when things are going well and it is uncertain that the turmoil predicted by pessimists will ever materialize. Meanwhile, the political leadership of the super-creditors in Asia continues to exhibit little confidence in the efficacy of greater reliance on internally-generated demand to spur economic growth.

Americans have not sated their desire for additional consumption nor have they rekindled their desire to save. No interest groups have voiced willingness to pay higher taxes or to accept reductions in federal social safety net programs like Social Security and Medicare in order to reduce federal budget deficits. Politicians in the United States see no reason to make the voters angry by inflicting austerity on the public at a time when the cost to the country of living well beyond its means has been minimal and might stay that way for a long while. The U.S. economy to date has been none the worse for wear despite continued record-breaking borrowing and record-breaking trade deficits. Economic output, employment, and disposable income (at least in the upper income brackets) have steadily increased since the mid-1990s.[12] The risky combination of prolonged increases in deficits and debt has thus far allowed the United States to evade the traditional dilemma of having to choose between guns and butter. Better yet, Americans have been able to spend far more on consumption and investment than what they produced on their own. Income tax rates have been reduced even as federal spending keeps growing. Should the day of reckoning be many years away, governmental inaction will prove to be the functional equivalent of a rational choice to not pay its own way domestically or internationally. If a punitive judgment day in fact is near, however, apathetic U.S. economic policy will be judged as disastrously inept. Only the passage of time will indicate which of these scenarios will play out and provide a definitive judgment as to the wisdom or the folly of allowing a prolonged upward spiral of debt in the United States.

Prevention of a destabilizing plunge in the value of the dollar should not be assumed, no matter how much reassurance is offered by the optimistic school of thought. Such a plunge occurred in the past, most notably

---

[12] Relatively high U.S. growth rates and relatively low rates of unemployment despite a growing trade deficit are consistent with the argument made by most economic analysts that domestic trends are by far the most important determinants of aggregate U.S. economic activity and that the level of imports is only a marginally important macro-economic indicator.

in 1971, 1973, and 1978. The traumatic collapse of the Bretton Woods system of fixed exchange rates in 1973 was caused by a combination of an arguably irresponsible U.S. refusal to adopt effective measures to address its deteriorating current account position and the arguably irresponsible refusal by several European countries to adopt measures to reduce their chronic current account surpluses. History is largely repeating itself in 2006. The two major causes of the current global balance of payments disequilibrium have been the lack of U.S. resolve to live within its economic means and an aggressive commitment by several Asian governments (who have assumed the role previously played by Europeans) to maintain their arguably overvalued currencies and preserve their trade surpluses. The biggest difference is that record-breaking U.S. current account deficits are vastly larger than those of the early 1970s. Another key difference is that recent deficits can be largely attributed to undesirable factors—mainly inadequate saving, consumers' love affair with foreign goods and services, large government budget deficits, and apparent lack of competitiveness in parts of the U.S. industrial sector.

The U.S. current account deficit in 2006 also can be legitimately labeled "perilous" because economic indicators suggest it will remain at or near current levels if not continue increasing for the foreseeable future. The relatively limited dollar depreciation (as of mid-2006), the outlook for relatively high rates of growth both in the U.S. economy and in aggregate demand, Washington's continued embrace of tax cuts, rising oil prices, and so on are exactly the opposite of what is needed to induce meaningful correction.

The exceptional U.S. dependence on borrowing—viewed in abstract terms as a decline in U.S. economic discipline regarding the need to "pay its way" in the global marketplace—can be demonstrated in hard numbers. Though the largest creditor country in the world at the beginning of the 1980s, the United States had become the world's largest debtor by the end of 2005; the international liabilities of the United States exceeded international assets by $2.7 trillion, an attention-getting 22% of U.S. GDP. [13]

The federal budget deficit averaged $370 billion in fiscal years 2003 through 2005, the highest in recorded history. [14] Outstanding federal debt

---

[13] U.S. Department of Commerce, Bureau of Economic Analysis, http://www.bea.gov/bea/ newsrelarchive/2006/intinv05_fax.pdf. The negative U.S. international investment position should exceed $3 trillion at the end of 2006.

[14] Council of Economic Advisors, *Economic Indicators*, Joint Economic Committee, March 2006, http://www.gpoaccess.gov/indicators/index.html. The reduction in the budget deficit projected for fiscal 2006 is generally assumed to be temporary. Furthermore, skeptics have argued that the projected deficit reduction is hardly grounds for rejoicing given that the deficit would still be relatively large for a period of strong economic growth.

climbed to $8.2 trillion at year-end 2005 and is likely to pass the $8.5 trillion mark by the end of 2006.[15]

U.S. external deficits have progressively set world records on an annual basis in virtually every year from the early 1990s through 2005. The U.S. merchandise trade deficit in 2005 rose to a world record $767 billion, an amount four and one-half times its size in 1995. The value of U.S. merchandise imports increased by $1 trillion between 1994 and 2005 (looked at from the opposite direction, foreign countries' exports to the United States increased by approximately the same amount).[16] At $1.7 trillion dollars in 2005, U.S. merchandise imports were nearly twice as large as exports of $900 billion. The size of this gap suggests the difficulty of attaining a large, sustained reduction in the U.S. trade deficit. The steady trajectory of this deficit is depicted in **Figure 1**.

In 2005 the United States incurred the largest current account deficit ever recorded: $792 billion. The number one cause by far was the steady increase in the merchandise trade deficit. At the same time, the U.S. surplus in trade in services remained below its ten-year average, and the surplus in international income shrank due to rising interest payments to foreign lenders. Increasing outflows of worker remittances enlarged the deficit in unilateral transfers. A perverse form of economic exceptionalism is also seen in cumulative U.S. current account deficits of about $6 trillion from 1982 through 2006. Equally exceptional is the need and ability of the United States to attract net capital inflows of an approximately equal amount in order to finance or offset these deficits.[17] Concern about the growing size of the U.S. trade and current account deficits no longer can be dispelled by the argument that relative size is a more important indicator than absolute size. Arguably, nothing is necessarily amiss when the world's largest economy exhibits the world's biggest current account deficit. Economists believe that the size of the external deficit in relation to GDP is a more relevant

---

[15] Despite conventional wisdom, a budget deficit is seldom by itself the direct cause of an external deficit, nor does a budget deficit necessarily prolong an existing trade deficit. A government's budget deficit or surplus is only one of several variables in a larger equation. This chapter avoids any reference to the frequently used term "twin deficits" because the term connotes the oversimplified and frequently incorrect notion that there is a permanent one-to-one relationship between a budget deficit and a current account deficit. The two are not related in any fixed manner. The overall determinant—the savings-investment relationship—varies according to other variables as well, the most important being private sector saving, investment outlays, and a country's relative industrial competitiveness.

[16] U.S. Department of Commerce, *FT-990* report, December 1994 and December 2005, http://www.census.gov/foreign-trade/www.

[17] Being an "extreme" net taker of real economic resources and capital from the rest of the world means that the current U.S. balance of payments position is more appropriate for developing countries; developing countries are the ones that should be both net takers of real economic resources (i.e., have current account deficits caused by relatively large imports of growth-promoting goods) and net importers of capital from wealthier countries.

FIGURE 1   Growth of the U.S. deficit in goods and services trade, 1980–2005

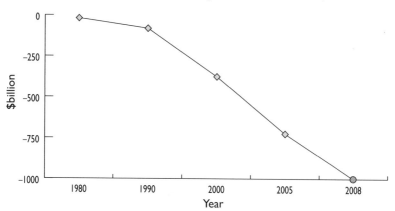

SOURCE: U.S. Commerce Department, various publications.

NOTE: 2008 number projected by the author.

statistic. The problem is that the U.S. current account deficit has been steadily growing faster than GDP; the former grew seven-fold between 1995 and 2005 while the latter grew by only 70%. The inevitable arithmetic result is that the current account deficit represents a growing percentage of total economic activity. The deficit in the fourth quarter of 2005 rose to an annualized rate above 7% of GDP.[18] This is an alarming number.

Studies of past currency crises have found that after a country's current account deficit rises above 5% of its GDP, there is a growing statistical probability that a crisis in confidence will trigger massive selling of the country's currency by speculators and investors (for purchase of currencies perceived to have stronger fundamentals).[19] As the threat grows that its monetary reserves will be depleted, the affected country must implement painful balance of payments corrective measures, mainly more restrictive macroeconomic policies that will reduce imports through slower growth and increased unemployment. It must be noted that the economies that suffered currency crises over the past twenty years were neither as developed nor as resilient as the U.S. economy. Moreover, the "emerging

---

[18] Council of Economic Advisors, *Economic Indicators*. The U.S. current account deficit as a percentage of GDP declined fractionally in the first quarter of 2006.

[19] The most frequently cited of these studies is Caroline L. Freund, "Current Account Adjustment in Industrialized Countries," International Finance Discussion Paper, no. 692, December 2000, http://www.federalreserve.gov/pubs/ifdp. Also see Lawrence Summers, "The United States and the Global Adjustment Process," speech at the Third Annual Stavros S. Niarchos Lecture, Institute for International Economics, Washington, D.C., March 23, 2004, http://www.iie.com/publications/pubs.cfm (Speeches, Testimonies, Papers).

market" countries hit by these crises did not have the benefit of foreign central banks regularly intervening to support their currencies in order to prevent exchange rate realignments that would jeopardize their exports to a large, critically important market.

Enablers of the Disequilibrium: America's Asian Cash Cows

Geographically, Asia accounts both for a major portion of the U.S. merchandise trade deficit and a major source of its offsetting capital inflows. A complete and precise assessment requires that the data be disaggregated on a sub-regional basis because U.S. bilateral trade is heavily concentrated in East and Southeast Asia (see **Table 1**). Bilateral deficits with China and Japan accounted for 37% of the total U.S. multilateral deficit in 2005 according to U.S. trade statistics; adding in Korea and Taiwan raises this figure to 41%. Meanwhile, total exports to and imports from the countries of South Asia were only $10 billion and $27 billion, respectively, in 2005. Except for India, South Asian countries are of minimal statistical significance to overall U.S. trade (and foreign direct investment). Trade with the five Central Asian countries is even less statistically significant to aggregate U.S. trade.[20]

U.S. imports of goods from what the Commerce Department designates as Pacific Rim countries jumped from $289 billion in 1995 to $552 billion in 2005, an increase of $263 billion.[21] Nevertheless, their share of the faster-growing overall U.S. trade deficit dropped from 68% to 43% in this time period as bilateral trade deficits with the other countries of North America and Europe grew at a faster rate.[22] "Asia" as a cause of U.S. trade woes declines significantly from a second statistical disaggregation that takes into account the spectacular increases both in imports from China and in the bilateral deficit with that country. According to U.S. data, imports from China totaled $3.86 billion in 1985, a mere $6 million greater than U.S. exports to that country. Goods imported from China skyrocketed to $244 billion in 2005, raising the bilateral imbalance to $202 billion and creating the largest bilateral trade deficit in history.[23] China alone accounted

---

[20] The five countries are Kazakhstan, Kyrgyzstan, Tajikistan, Turkmenistan, and Uzbekistan.

[21] Pacific Rim countries include Australia, Brunei, China, Hong Kong, Indonesia, Japan, Korea, Macao, Malaysia, New Zealand, Papua New Guinea, Philippines, Singapore, and Taiwan.

[22] U.S. Department of Commerce, *FT-990* report, December 1995 and December 2005, http://www.census.gov/foreign-trade/www.

[23] Data from the U.S. Department of Commerce, "Foreign Trade Statistics," U.S. Census Bureau, http://www.census.gov/foreign-trade/balance/c5700.html.

TABLE 1   U.S. trade with major Asian trading partners, 2005 ($billion)

Country	Imports	Rank	Exports	Rank	U.S. deficit	Rank
China	243.5	2	41.8	4	201.6	1
Japan	138.1	4	55.4	3	82.7	2
Korea	43.8	7	27.7	7	16.1	12
Taiwan	34.8	8	22.1	10	12.8	13
Malaysia	33.7	11	10.5	18	23.3	7
Thailand	19.9	17	7.2	23	12.7	14
India	18.8	18	8	2	10.8	18
Singapore	15.1	21	20.6	11	+ 5.5	–
Indonesia	12	26	3	39	9	22
Philippines	9.2	28	6.9	25	2.4	38
Hong Kong	8.9	30	16.3	13	+ 7	–
Australia	7.3	35	15.8	14	+ 8.4	–
Vietnam	6.6	38	1.2	58	5.4	27
Pakistan	3.3	51	1.2	57	2	41
New Zealand	3.2	52	2.6	41	0.5	65
Bangladesh	2.7	56	0.3	90	2.4	35

SOURCE: U.S. Commerce Department, *FT-990* report, http://www.census.gov/foreign-trade/ Press-Release/2005pr/12/exh14.pdf.

NOTE: Rank is measured by bilateral trade flows and deficits according to U.S. statistics.

for nearly $200 billion of the abovementioned $263 billion increase in U.S. imports from Pacific Rim countries between 1995 and 2005.[24]

Trade diversion is another factor behind the reduction in Asia's share (excluding China) of the U.S. multilateral trade deficit. Countless billions of dollars of labor-intensive imports—such as textiles and apparel, shoes, consumer electronics, and toys—that earlier came from now relatively affluent Asian countries, are being produced and shipped from low-cost China. For this reason, U.S. imports from the original "Newly Industrialized Countries" (Hong Kong, Korea, Singapore, and Taiwan) increased only moderately between 1985 and 2005.

As has been implicitly suggested, big foreign lenders were necessary to enable the United States to become the world's biggest international debtor by spending (consuming and investing) well in excess of the value

[24] U.S. Department of Commerce, *FT-990* report, December 1995 and December 2005.

of domestic production.[25] A few East and Southeast Asian countries— and, more recently, major oil exporting countries—are the super-lenders and super-exporters that have provided trillions of dollars in goods and services that augment U.S. production. In doing so, these countries have boosted consumption and raised the standard of living in the United States. Producing much more than consuming and investing, these countries have generously ignored the indifference of the U.S. government to rising, occasionally record-setting budget deficits. The surplus Asian countries are not overtly upset with a falling U.S. net personal saving rate that tumbled, incredibly, to a negative rate in 2005.[26] Furthermore, the super-creditors have turned a blind eye to the regularity with which the United States has achieved world record current account and trade deficits. Whatever concerns they may privately harbor about continuing to add to their dollar holdings are overshadowed by the priority of increasing exports to the United States. This objective requires super-creditor indulgence.

The super-borrower and the super-creditors have informally joined hands to create what effectively is an economics-based "coalition of the willing." The ties that bind this partnership of convenience cannot be characterized as a clearly sustainable commonality of interests based on equal rewards. A structural economic disequilibrium of any kind tends to be inherently unstable. The far more important glue binding this coalition is the opposite but complementary addictions to excess, the result of which, in the minds of (mainly American) economists, is a perverse division of labor. The United States eagerly consumes, imports, and borrows. Other countries, mainly in Asia, eagerly produce, save, export, and lend. The Asian countries with large trade surpluses have remained resolute in their debatable desire to send a significant portion of the output of their labors to feed the voracious consumption habit of the United States.

Private foreign investors accumulate assets in the United States on a pro-active, market-driven basis in search of profits. Governments usually acquire dollars on a defensive, reactive basis, born of the perceived need to minimize depreciation in the currency of their most prized export market. A steep fall in the dollar's exchange rate would likely cause higher interest rates, reduced U.S. economic growth, and a fall in U.S. demand for Asian

---

[25] In a closed world economy where international capital flows are prohibited by national controls, a country could not import the supplemental capital that would allow it to invest more than it saved (i.e., that which is left over after consumption). Similarly, in a closed world economy where imports are severely restricted, a country could not import the supplemental resources that would allow it to spend at levels well above what it produces.

[26] The Department of Commerce estimated that in the year 2005 personal savings in the United States amounted to *negative* $42 billion. See U.S. Department of Commerce, Bureau of Economic Analysis, http://www.bea.gov/bea/dn/nipaweb/SelectTable.asp?Selected=Y.

exports. The governments of surplus countries have not been willing to risk dollar depreciation and write-downs in the (local currency) value of their remaining dollar holdings by engaging in large-scale purchases of other reserve currencies such as euros or Japanese yen.[27] In seeking to avoid this potentially costly strategy, the Asian surplus countries have had no choice but to accumulate and retain massive amounts of dollars. These holdings in turn leave them no choice but to mostly invest in and make loans to the United States.[28] Buying assets in a third country would require sales of dollars and purchases of that country's currency.[29]

The super-creditors' choice of which kinds of dollar assets to purchase is also limited. Investing in relatively volatile stocks and commodities is considered too risky and imprudent by the traditionally conservative finance ministries that manage state-owned funds. Consequently, creditor governments turn mainly to the safe and highly liquid (easy to sell quickly and in large amounts without affecting price) debt instruments of the U.S. government, mainly IOUs issued by the Treasury Department. The result is that foreigners have become major players in financing the U.S. federal budget deficit. The creditor countries quite literally help Americans to live beyond their means. In return, Americans help their creditors to increase exports.

For trade surplus countries, an open question is what are the ultimate net economic benefits that accrue from large purchases of U.S. Treasury bonds in lieu of increased domestic consumption. When the standard of living and average per capita income of the deficit country living beyond its means continue to exceed those of the net exporters, the verdict of most economists is that the debtor is getting a very good deal in real economic terms from its export-enamored foreign benefactors. The Asian super-creditors are paying a price for rigidities in their domestic economies and for short-sighted policy management. Whereas the United States has had little-to-no difficulty over time in generating economic growth through increased domestic demand, many other countries—most notably in East Asia—have felt compelled to rely heavily on export-led growth. This is a distinctly second-best choice in economic theory terms because exports

---

[27] A write-down is an accounting reduction in the book value of an asset that reflects a drop in market price.

[28] Current account surplus countries not wanting to buy dollar assets have one theoretical alternative to investing in the United States—they could convert their dollar earnings into cash and bury banknotes in the ground. This practice remains theoretical because it is neither cost-effective nor practical.

[29] Foreign holdings of dollars in the aggregate can only be reduced by foreigners increasing their imports of U.S. goods or by increased foreign investment in the United States. Dollars sold by one foreign-based owner to another merely change ownership.

of real economic resources (i.e., goods and services) above current and anticipated import needs represent a transfer of real wealth from domestic consumers to foreigners. Net exports are foregone domestic consumption. This is an undesirable situation in general, but especially so for residents of trade surplus countries living at or below the poverty level. A country with a current account deficit expands its consumption beyond domestic production by means of net transfers abroad of money, which is a means of exchange and a unit of account rather than a real economic resource.

The United States is ideally situated to be a massive net importer of real wealth and thereby to play the role of international consumer of first and last resort. All U.S. imports are paid for simply by diverting a small fraction of the U.S. domestic money supply that does not have to be earned by exporting real wealth. Financing trade and budget deficits is easy when your currency is the world transactions currency and is universally accepted as payment by foreign exporters. [30]

The reserves of the United States' principal Asian creditor countries have grown by nearly $2 trillion dollars since the mid-1990s. The absence to date of sustained or loud demands that the United States actively take steps to shrink its trade deficit suggests that these countries are prepared to continue acquiring dollars in large amounts if their currencies begin to appreciate in value. Large accumulations of dollars signify successful pursuit by surplus countries of the strategy of relying primarily on exports to generate economic growth and increase employment. The super-creditors have no credible need at this point to further add to their reserves in preparation for the proverbial rainy day. These countries are not formally committed to underwriting continuous increases in the American standard of living or in financing U.S. budget deficits. Furthermore, they do not harbor illusions that U.S. Treasury bills and bonds provide a higher yield and greater opportunity for appreciation than other assets. The bottom line is that a strong export sector has offset the weak domestic demand that has burdened Asian economies for several years. The Asian super-creditors' seemingly insatiable appetite for dollar accumulation does not indicate an "irrational affinity" for the United States. "Asia would export anywhere if it could and happily finance any resulting imbalances." [31] However, no other market is as big and open. The European Union currently cannot absorb

---

[30] Maintaining these deficits for years on end is facilitated by the rule of thumb discussed previously that foreign countries with large current account surpluses must return a major portion of their net dollar earnings to the United States as loans and investments.

[31] Michael Dooley, David Folkerts-Landau, and Peter Garber, "An Essay on the Revived Bretton Woods System," National Bureau of Economic Research, Paper no. 9971, September 2003, 9, http://www.nber.org.

a comparable flood of imports from Asia due to structural economic problems and the burden of absorbing Eastern Europe.[32]

Some of the super-creditor countries are still suffering negative fall-out from the so-called Asian economic contagion crisis that began in 1997 when the deteriorating economic situation in Thailand lead to a run on its currency, the baht. What followed was an unprecedented geographical spread of severe speculative attacks on the currencies of Korea, Indonesia, Malaysia, and the Philippines. Massive outflows of capital in turn caused exchange rates and stock market prices to plummet, interest rates to soar, and recessions to wreak havoc in these countries. The International Monetary Fund (IMF) imposed unusually intensive and invasive conditions for extending loans to rescue Thailand, Korea, and Indonesia—conditions that exacerbated an already bad situation and led to deep resentment of the Fund. It is safe to assume that East Asian countries want to have sufficiently large holdings of foreign exchange reserves to minimize the chance of future currency crises and minimize any future need to seek loans from the IMF. These desires partially explain why some East Asian governments have been content to indefinitely accumulate reserves accruing from prolonged current account surpluses. These governments seem to "prefer relying more on exports to supply the demand for domestic production. Heightened risk aversion renders them happy to accumulate a large cushion of international reserves."[33] Yet another residual of the 1990s turmoil relevant to contemporary U.S.-East Asian economic relations is weakness in Asia's domestic demand that enhances the perceived importance of export growth. The rate of corporate investment in new plant and capital equipment declined throughout Asia (excluding China) in the late 1990s and has yet to fully recover, presumably because of still weakened corporate balance sheets and excess capacity stemming from the recession induced by the economic crisis.

An additional source of soft domestic demand is the relatively strong preference for saving over consumption exhibited by Asian workers (including those in China). High savings rates and low investment expenditures are the parents of current account surpluses. Together they explain most of the jump in the aggregate surpluses of developing Asia from

---

[32] Dooley, Folkerts-Landau, and Garber, "An Essay on the Revived Bretton Woods System."

[33] Barry Eichengreen, "The Blind Men and the Elephant," (unpublished manuscript, University of California, Berkeley, November 2005), 13, http://emlab.berkeley.edu/users/eichengr/policy/KyotoPaper.pdf.

$85 billion in 2000 to an estimated $241 billion in 2005.[34] Asia was on the mind of then Federal Reserve Governor Ben Bernanke when he introduced the term "global saving glut" as a new explanation for the rapid rise and persistence of U.S. current account deficits since the mid-1990s.[35] Whereas consumption in China as a share of GDP appears to have fallen to a record low of less than 50% in 2005, consumption as a percentage of GDP in the United States has been holding at a record high of about 71% since 2002. China's total gross saving in 2005 represented 45% of GDP, an amount three times greater than the percentage of gross saving in the United States.[36]

Certain Asian central banks have made major contributions to financing the increase in U.S. debt and consumption through their willingness to accumulate large increments in dollar reserves. As noted above, this willingness stems from their intention to prevent significant dollar depreciation that would put upward pressures on U.S. interest rates and put downward pressures on U.S. GDP growth rates. These contributions can be tracked by the growth in their publicly announced foreign exchange reserves, most of which are held in U.S. dollars. Again, "unprecedented" and "record breaking" are the appropriate modifiers for recent statistical trends. In the three-year period beginning 2003, Asian central banks added upwards of $1 trillion to their reserves, roughly one-half the cumulative U.S. current account during that time. Published statistics shown in **Table 2** indicate a surge equivalent to $1.6 trillion in the total monetary reserves of seven major Asian surplus countries between 2000 and 2005.[37]

Foreign central banks, again mainly in Asia, have been especially active in investing in the safe refuge of the U.S. Treasury market since 2000. It was then that inflows of private capital into the United States began failing to keep pace with the acceleration in the current account deficit. Increased dollar purchases by foreign central banks became necessary to assure that

[34] Note that the term "developing Asia" excludes Japan and the four original "NICs" (Hong Kong, Korea, Singapore, and Taiwan). This data was calculated from data in *World Economic Outlook*. See International Monetary Fund Research Department, *World Economic Outlook April 2006*, (Washington, D.C.: International Monetary Fund, 2006): Appendix Table 25, http://www.imf.org.

[35] Ben Bernanke, "The Global Saving Glut and the U.S. Current Account Deficit" (remarks at the Sandridge Lecture, Virginia Association of Economics, Richmond, VA, March 10, 2005), http://www.federalreserve.gov/boarddocs/speeches/2005/20050414/default.htm.

[36] Stephen Roach, "Passing Ships in the Night," Morgan Stanley Global Economic Forum, February 3, 2006, http://www.morganstanley.com/GEFdata/digests/20060203-fri.html. Gross saving is a more inclusive measure than the net personal saving figure mentioned earlier; the former includes corporate savings, government savings, and depreciation write-offs (consumption of fixed capital), as well as personal savings.

[37] Although this increase was mostly comprised of dollars, "monetary reserves" also includes other foreign currencies and a country's guaranteed access to borrowing at the International Monetary Fund. Some of the increases in reserves shown in **Table 2** may be higher for some countries; large accumulators of dollars sometimes are tempted to keep a portion of their new holdings "off the books" to dampen accusations of exchange rate manipulation.

TABLE 2   Major Asian holdings of monetary reserves, excluding gold
($billion at year-end)

Country	2000	2005
China	168	822
Japan	355	834
Korea	96	210
Taiwan	107	253
India	38	132
Singapore	80	116
Malaysia	30	71
Total	874	2,438
Change	–	+1,564

SOURCES: International Monetary Fund, *International Financial Statistics*, March 2006; and Central Bank of China for Taiwan, http://www.cbc.gov.tw/EngHome/Eeconomic/Statistics/FS/history/ERESERVE-H.pdf.

NOTE: China's announced reserve holdings of $941 billion at the end of June 2006, a one-third increase over the same period one year earlier, made China the world's largest holder of dollar reserves.

supply and demand for dollars in the foreign exchange market remained in approximate equilibrium lest Asian currencies substantially appreciate against the dollar. Some $4.2 trillion of the $8.2 trillion in outstanding U.S. Treasury securities at the end of 2005 was owned by U.S. government agencies (mainly the Federal Reserve System). Of the remaining $4 trillion of these debt instruments, approximately one-half had been purchased by domestic institutions and individuals while the other half was owned by foreign governments and private foreign investors.[38] The roughly 50% of non-U.S. government holdings of Treasury debt owned by foreigners at year-end 2005 was exactly double the percentage they owned at the end of 1995.

Furthermore, whereas the total amount of U.S. Treasury bills and bonds held by non-U.S. government agencies increased by $1.1 trillion between year-end 2000 and year-end 2005, the amount held by foreigners increased by $1 trillion in the same period.[39] In other words, foreigners accounted for almost 100% of the increase in outstanding Treasury debt that was not bought by U.S. government agencies during the first five years

[38] U.S. Department of the Treasury, *U.S. Treasury Bulletin*, various issues, http://www.fms.treas.gov/bulletin. A small fraction of purchases by foreign sources is made by international organizations.

[39] Ibid., June, 2006.

of the George W. Bush administration. More specifically, just six Asian economies—Japan, China, Taiwan, Korea, Hong Kong, and Singapore—accounted for approximately 53% of the $2 trillion in total foreign holdings of U.S. Treasury securities at the end of 2005. These six super-creditors more than doubled their Treasury holdings from $508 billion to $1.15 trillion between year-end 2000 and year-end 2005, an increase of $643 billion.[40] Purchases of U.S. government debt of this magnitude certify these creditors as major financiers of the $1.3 trillion in aggregate U.S. budget deficits that accumulated from the time of their return in fiscal 2002 through fiscal 2005. The question of whether this symbiotic creditor/debtor interdependence will hold at a steady state, continue growing, or unravel is as unclear as it is important.[41]

Pessimists claim that the law of supply and demand will have to be revised if the United States is to be able to continue hemorrhaging dollars overseas at current levels without precipitating a costly and disruptive currency crisis. They warn that a steep, disorderly fall in the dollar would likely lead to an unfortunate chain of events including rising U.S. interest rates, declining investor and consumer confidence, a decline in U.S. economic growth, and economic weakness in other countries as their exports and stock markets felt the shockwaves and trended downward.[42] Political factors might force a costly confrontation. A non-partisan Wall Street economist expressed concern about a rising overseas backlash against the Bush administration's aggressive foreign policy, noting that "nearly 70% of global currency reserves are now in the hands of the developing nations, arming them, as a bloc, with a potential geopolitical weapon pointed straight at the United States."[43]

Optimists claim that a decade of erroneous forecasts by doomsayers of a meltdown of the dollar followed by global recession is indicative of

---

[40] U.S. Department of the Treasury, *Treasury International Capital System*, May 2006, http://www.treas.gov/tic.

[41] Rumors that Asian countries desire to diversify their reserves or are reluctant to continue making large additions to their dollar holdings are virtually always based on pure guesswork. Although the total value of monetary reserves is published, most governments keep secret the composition on a currency-by-currency basis. It is absolutely in the interest of governments with large dollar holdings to withhold any information about sales that might trigger a large, sustained depreciation of the dollar.

[42] A typical expression of these warnings can be found in the Organization for Economic Cooperation and Development's May, 2006 *Economic Outlook*: A "brutal unfolding" of today's unsustainable current account imbalances "would hurt the world economy…" It is uncertain, however, "whether the needed changes in domestic policies required to avert worst-case scenarios [will] come into place in the foreseeable future." See *OECD Economic Outlook*, no. 79, May 23, 2006 at http://www.oecd.org/publications.

[43] Joseph Quinlan, "Memo to Wall Street: 'America Is at War'" Bank of America Investment Strategies Group, electronic mailing, May 16, 2006.

an underlying stability in the global balance of payments situation. The counterargument is that this stability can suddenly and unexpectedly end at any time. The optimistic school of thought also notes, however, that nothing in economic theory dictates that a borrower-lender partnership of convenience cannot continue indefinitely. The dynamism of the U.S. economy may well hold a permanent attraction for foreign investors seeking higher rates of return than are available in their more sluggish, more regulated home economies. The counterargument to this is that the U.S. economy is not likely to be the most dynamic and attractive national economy on a permanent, uninterrupted basis. Optimists also claim that the major surplus/creditor countries will stubbornly cling both to their reliance on export-led growth and to their determination to buy and hold U.S. currency in whatever amounts are necessary to keep their currencies' exchange rates relatively stable against the dollar. The counterargument here is that the ability of governments to control exchange rates has been, and will likely continue to be, periodically undermined by massive selling and buying by speculators. The collapse of the fixed exchange rate standard is testament to the limited power of governments to maintain the exchange rates they prefer.

The same counterargument applies to the related positivist argument that the super-creditors have painted themselves into a corner by virtue of their already enormous dollar holdings. Each creditor has a compelling vested interest in keeping its currency's exchange rate relatively stable vis-à-vis the dollar. In addition to wanting to prevent exports from being priced out of the lucrative U.S. market, the major East Asian dollar holders would want to avoid the painful internal accounting loss that would result in the event of major dollar depreciation. The value of their dollar holdings in such a case would have to be restated downward in local currency terms (which is how a foreign central bank values reserves in its books). By way of example, if the dollar were to appreciate by 10% against the Chinese yuan, the accounting loss in local currency terms for China's central bank, assuming total dollar holdings of $1 trillion, would be the yuan equivalent of $100 billion, about 5% of that country's GDP in 2005.[44]

Former U.S. treasury secretary Lawrence Summers inferred that a built-in set of stabilizers exists in the new U.S.-Asian interdependence because of what he called a "kind of balance of financial terror."[45] This is an

---

[44] None of these downside risks precludes the possibility of limited and discreet reserve diversification by countries enjoying large trade surpluses. The impact of such sales on the dollar's exchange rate would depend on the skill of a central bank in timing relatively small-scale currency sales to coincide with temporary dollar strength in the foreign exchange market and conducting these sales without detection by market watchers.

[45] Summers, "The United States and the Global Adjustment Process."

appropriate but slightly oversimplified assessment. No guarantees exist that the super-creditors in Asia or the major Middle Eastern oil exporters can ensure a relatively stable exchange rate for the dollar. Non-state actors could determine, as they have done in the past, whether the dollar remains stable or dramatically depreciates. A chain reaction could unexpectedly erupt at any time; all that is needed is for the number of individual speculators and multinational corporations to reach critical mass in thinking that the dollar is headed for a fall and big profits can be had by being ahead of the tidal wave of dollars being sold for other currencies. When enough speculators rush to the exit at the same time, a self-fulfilling prophesy invariably materializes (as happened to the United States in the 1970s and to several Asian countries in 1997). Frenzied dollar selling could be so massive and unrelenting as to overwhelm even China's and Japan's ample appetites for dollars. Super-creditors and the super-debtor could pay dearly in such a negative-sum game.

Will Rising External Debt Be the Undoing of the U. S. as Superpower?

Two big questions arise from the worsening international debtor status of the United States. One is whether Washington will still be able to afford the economic burdens associated with its expansive definition of how to play the role of lone global superpower. The second is whether the major creditors will drop their current accommodating stance and seek to diminish America's global power and prestige. Thus far, U.S. economic limitations—real or perceived—have not stood in the way of foreign policy ambitions. No cracks indicating "imperial overstretch" were visible to the naked eye as of mid-2006.[46] For better or worse, neither U.S. foreign policy efforts nor military spending had been diminished or diluted to compensate for the debt burden arising from the record-breaking U.S. budget and current account deficits. Potentially disruptive structural deficits in the U.S. balance of payments have not caused a scaling back of the U.S. fight against terrorism, military intervention in Iraq and Afghanistan, or the effort to prevent "axis of evil" countries from developing nuclear weapons.

This absence of linkage between U.S. foreign policy and international economics parallels the first round of U.S. balance of payments crises

---

[46] This is an important caveat in view of the thesis advanced here that excessive American indebtedness and growing current account deficits are potentially serious problems that could quickly become critical. The prospect for accumulating much more debt precludes any guarantee that escalating U.S. economic problems will not suddenly and forcefully undermine Washington's influence, credibility, and prestige among foreign friends and "strategic competitors" alike.

in the 1960s and 1970s. Neither the intensified demands by European surplus countries for a reduction in U.S. balance of payments deficits nor subsequent threats to dollar stability ever caused a reduction of U.S. troops in Western Europe, a move that would have been a natural way to reduce U.S. overseas expenditures. Two traumatic dollar devaluations followed by periodic declines in a floating dollar did nothing to cause a scaling back of the U.S. effort to win the cold war. Balance of payments deficits and an occasionally shaky dollar did not prevent the U.S. government from hastening the collapse of communism and the Soviet Empire, in part by aggressively outspending Moscow in the arms race.

In his classic study of the rise and fall of great powers, Paul Kennedy posed two critical questions regarding the ability of the United States to better endure the costs associated with being a global superpower than did previous great powers, nearly all of which eventually went broke from the burdens of empire. The first question was whether the United States could remain in a "class of its own" by being able to preserve a reasonable balance between the cost of its perceived defense requirements and the economic means available to fulfill those commitments. The second question was whether the United States could "preserve the technological and economic basis of its power from relative erosion in the face of the ever-shifting patterns of global production."[47] The correct answer to both questions is "yes"— subject, however, to two caveats. The first deals with military logistics in that a finite number of U.S. combat troops limits the number of countries where the U.S. government can intervene militarily. Absent resumption of a draft to populate a dramatic increase in the size of its armed forces, not even the United States can project military power to every hot spot.

The second caveat is economic in nature. An overextended economy operating for many years on deficit spending and inadequate savings is vulnerable to prolonged weakness that could eventually interfere with international goals. The remedy is quite simple: return to sound fundamentals. A U.S. economy operating in a more fiscally prudent manner and demonstrating something resembling the international average for personal saving should have no problem supporting the burdens of superpower status for the foreseeable future. Nominal U.S. GDP passed the $13 trillion mark in the first quarter of 2006. More importantly, the U.S. economy's flexible structure and relatively high efficiency and innovation levels, together with the effects of a growing population, suggest an economy

---

[47] Paul Kennedy, *The Rise and Fall of the Great Powers* (New York: Random House, 1987), 514–15.

capable of sustained real growth of 3% or more annually; this figure is currently the equivalent of $400–500 billion expressed in current dollars.[48]

Not even the costs of a military budget that accounted for approximately one-half of the world's military outlays in 2005 are beyond the financial capabilities of an economy with these quantitative and qualitative credentials.[49] Total U.S. military and arms production expenditures now exceed $500 billion dollars annually.[50] Though large in absolute terms, these outlays represent less than 4% of total U.S. economic output and in future years would typically be about equal in absolute size to future annual net *increments* in nominal GDP. Whether the United States becomes an overextended super-power is mainly a function of whether sound economic policies and more moderate personal consumption will prevail over prolonged self-indulgence.

Budget and trade deficits of unprecedented magnitudes, which are the main sources of the current U.S. economic vulnerability, begin with a nation-wide fondness for comfort and instant gratification. These deficits are more directly the result of implicit preferences expressed by the public and inaction by their elected leaders, not structural weaknesses and inadequacies in the U.S. economy. If Americans were willing to pay a modest amount of additional taxes and save more, the budget and current account deficits, all other things held constant, would recede gradually. The issue is about commitment, not capability. By following such an economic strategy, the United States could afford the tremendous expenses of projecting an extraordinary (but not unlimited) combination of power, presence, and influence throughout the world without needing significant financial assistance from other countries. U.S. economic resources and potential are not inadequate to the task of supporting superpower status.

No hard evidence exists that the United States has suffered diminished hard or soft power in East and Southeast Asia as a result of dependence on capital inflows from the region to finance its current account and budget deficits. Although clearly not immune to a rapid and forceful turnaround, this situation can be depicted as sustainable in the medium term. One

---

[48] Because of compounding, a 3% GDP increase in future years will continue growing in absolute terms beyond the current range cited.

[49] Data source: Stockholm International Peace Research Institute, *SIPRI Yearbook 2006*, chapter 8, http://yearbook2006.sipri.org/chap8/. Increased military spending by the United States in Iraq could result in the U.S. defense budget accounting for more than half of world military expenditures in 2006 and beyond.

[50] To put this total in context, the annual U.S. military budget and supplemental appropriations would be the equivalent in size to the GDP of the seventeenth largest national economy in the world.

reason is the previously discussed dependence by much of East Asia on exporting to a relatively open and healthy U.S. market.

Another argument in support of the thesis that the U.S. role and influence in this region has not diminished is political in nature: the steady if not rising dependence by much of Asia on U.S. military power. Ironically, the growing view that a strong U.S. presence is necessary is largely attributable to Washington's nemesis, Pyongyang. North Korea's missile-rattling and quest for nuclear weapons does nothing to encourage Japan and South Korea to use their rising dollar holdings as leverage to demand that the United States remove troops from their territory or lower its overall profile in Asia more to their liking. India and Vietnam also are not in the "attack mode." They are pursuing closer political and economic relations with the United States, presumably to boost exports and to address concerns about China's rising power and influence. The Asian country that would be most happy to exploit U.S. vulnerability is the PRC. Whatever ambitions Beijing has in this direction, however, are hampered by China's own vulnerabilities.

U.S.-Chinese Relations: A Case Study in Extreme Economics

The relationship with China has become the United States' most important in Asia, if not in the world. Economic relations between these two powers offer an excellent case study in the complexities and uncertainties emanating from the mutual dependence that has arisen between big debtor and big creditor. Bilateral economic relations also vividly illustrate Washington's increasingly complicated balancing act between economic policy and foreign policy priorities. How to deal with China in economic and political terms presents special challenges. Should the United States consider China a useful friend and lucrative export market, a dangerous threat to U.S. national security and economic interests, a scheming but occasionally cooperative strategic competitor, or all three?

U.S. policies toward China also are illustrative of how "compartmentalization" continues to keep foreign policy and international economic policy separate and distinct. It is difficult to make the case that U.S. foreign policy has become more genteel toward China as a result of the PRC's status as the world's largest holder of dollars as foreign reserves and consequently as a major creditor financing the U.S. budget and current account deficits. The Chinese government has not been the recipient of any measurable decrease in criticism from Washington regarding Beijing's dealings with the Iranian government, exports of military equipment, human rights abuses, and so on. On the other hand, the fact that the United States' largest bilateral trade deficit is with China has not resulted in Beijing being the recipient of any measurable increase in U.S. foreign policy antagonism.

Only between sectors of U.S. international economic policy is there a clear-cut example of the debtor-creditor relationship suggesting an accommodation of Beijing. The U.S. Treasury Department is grateful that capital inflows from China have contributed to keeping U.S. interest rates down, thereby holding down the U.S. government's cost of borrowing to finance its deficit. Presumably, this situation explains the Bush administration's remarkable, perhaps excessive, exhibition of patience in maintaining a non-confrontational posture toward what is widely regarded as China's exchange rate manipulation to prevent appreciation. The wish to avoid goading China into becoming a less avid accumulator of dollars, along with desire to recruit its help in moderating North Korean behavior, has kept the administration from threatening retaliation if Beijing refuses to ease its aggressive intervention in the foreign exchange market to buy dollars. The Bush administration has drawn growing criticism on Capitol Hill by refusing to officially designate China as a currency manipulator under U.S. law.[51] If intervention in the foreign exchange market by Beijing was curtailed, China's massive trade surplus and inflows of foreign direct investment would almost certainly cause significant yuan appreciation relative to the dollar. A more expensive yuan could (to an unknown extent) dampen exports to the United States while making U.S. exports more price competitive in China, trends not to the liking of a country that has grown more accustomed to and dependent on export-led growth than on domestic demand-driven growth.

The extent to which the miraculous growth of China's GDP and export sector poses a political or economic threat to the United States cannot be stated with precision or certainty. Too many complexities and ambiguities are involved to allow for anything more than perceptions and educated guesses; the result is two sharply divergent viewpoints. On one hand, the speed and magnitude that characterize the recent escalation of the U.S. bilateral deficit with China is a concern to many Americans. So too is the fact that U.S. statistics show U.S. imports from China jumping from $1.9

---

[51] Section 3004 of the Omnibus Trade and Competitiveness Act of 1988 directs the Treasury Department to submit semi-annual reports to Congress analyzing the exchange rate policies of other countries while seeking specifically to identify any countries that are manipulating the value of their currencies vis-à-vis the dollar to seek unfair competitive advantage in international trade. If any country meets the specified manipulation criteria, the congressionally written provision directs the treasury secretary to initiate bilateral negotiations for the purpose of ensuring that the offending government(s) agree to allow appropriate exchange rate adjustments (i.e., permit their currency's exchange rate to appreciate).

billion in 1981 to $244 billion in 2005, an incredible increase of more than 10,000%. *Business Week* asserted in 2004 that the three "scariest" words to U.S. industry are "the China price." In general, this is a price "30% to 50% less than what you can possibly make something for in the U.S. In the worst cases, it means below your cost of materials."[52] Whereas broad cost differentials were once limited to low-skilled, labor-intensive sectors, China is becoming price competitive in a growing number of high-tech, capital-intensive products. Rising salaries in China mean that hourly workers are now available for less in other Asian countries (e.g., Vietnam and Cambodia). China's expanding trade surplus exemplifies the truism, however, that wages are only one factor among many in determining total production costs. China remains very competitive in other variables in the cost of doing business, such as the extent and nature of government regulations, quality of physical infrastructure, labor force skills and discipline, taxes, corruption, and the cost and reliability of electrical power.

On the other hand, China's economy displays significant vulnerabilities despite its extraordinary past successes and tremendous future potential. It may rely too heavily on exporting. The extent of China's dependence on the American market can be seen by the fact that according to U.S. trade statistics, the United States accounted for 30–38% of Chinese exports from 2000 to 2005.[53] Converting China's GDP into dollars on an exchange rate basis, the value of the PRC's exports to the United States in 2004 was equivalent to 12% of China's total domestic output (i.e., GDP). More significantly, the $100 billion increase in U.S. imports (again using U.S. trade statistics) from the PRC between 2000 and 2004 accounted for approximately 18% of the increase in China's GDP ($568 billion) during the same time period.

The United States has been by far the most important destination for China's rapidly growing exports, which in turn have been a critically important source of the country's rapid GDP growth. Surging exports clearly have been of incalculable help in easing the pain of China's transition from a purely command economy to a mixed economy. The strong Chinese export sector provides a ready-made source of new employment for the millions of workers that have been and are being dismissed from inefficient, grossly overstaffed state-owned enterprises. Yet to call the country "dependent"

---

[52] "The China Price," *BusinesWeek*, December 6, 2004, 102.

[53] The data may overstate the case for China's trade dependence on the United States. U.S. trade numbers record much higher import numbers than do PRC statistics for Chinese exports to the United States. This difference is mainly a result of different methodologies for estimating the value of transshipments through Hong Kong. Since Chinese data seems to understate the value of bilateral trade flows, the most accurate measure of two-way trade would seem to lie somewhere between the two governments' published data.

on the U.S. market would be subjective labeling at best. The level of future dependence on exports to the United States is a function of the ability of Chinese economic planners to stimulate internal demand and expand export markets elsewhere.

Any important source of economic growth and job creation is especially important to the leadership in Beijing. In political terms, the seemingly limitless U.S. appetite for cheap Chinese goods has indirectly enhanced the domestic legitimacy of the Chinese Communist Party (CCP). Soaring exports to the American market have played an integral part in sustaining the informal social contract that the Party has entered into with the masses: in return for their accepting the CCP's monopoly on political power, the leadership promises sustained delivery of high economic growth rates, a rising standard of living, and reduced poverty. The legitimacy of the CCP is based on its success in bringing unprecedented prosperity to a large portion of the Chinese people. As one China watcher noted, "Communist ideology, by contrast, plays very little role in maintaining popular support for the CCP-led government or in providing the cement that holds the Party itself together."[54]

The past and present success of the Chinese economy is absolutely no guarantee of sustained strength over the medium and long term. Its limited reliance on market forces to guide production, prices, and capital allocation decisions is a potentially serious flaw. The euphoria attending the growth trajectory of the Chinese economy may be as mistaken as the overly optimistic extrapolations in the late 1980s of Japan's future economic growth.[55] China's economy suffers from distortions similar to those that caused the economies of the other fast-growth Asian economies to veer off course. At the top of the list are inefficient allocations of capital encouraged by extensive government intervention in the economy and a dysfunctional banking system caused by poor lending practices based on the personal connections of the borrower rather than sound balance sheet analysis. In many respects the Chinese economy in 2006 is a bubble waiting to burst. Like Japan in the 1980s, China has overheated real estate and stock markets as well as the makings of excessive industrial capacity. Chinese policymakers have the additional burden of trying to facilitate economic growth amidst a political environment that limits civil liberties and the free flow of ideas.

---

[54] Dwight Perkins, "China's Economic Growth: Implications for the Defense Budget," in *Strategic Asia 2005–06: Military Modernization in an Era of Uncertainty*, ed. Ashley J. Tellis and Michael Wills (Seattle: National Bureau of Asian Research, 2005), 63.

[55] For an example of this overly optimistic view, see Stephen D. Cohen, *Cowboys and Samurai: Why the United States Is Losing the Industrial Battle and Why It Matters* (New York: HarperBusiness, 1991).

The conflicting conclusions as to whether the rise of Chinese economic power will marginalize the U.S. position in Asia reflect a classic example of what usually emerges from the fine art of selectively using data that supports a preconceived conclusion. China's successful efforts to increase its influence over neighboring countries has led to a rash of warnings—of unknown validity—that a new Asian order is on the horizon, one in which Washington will play an insignificant role. In the first place, this is not a zero-sum game in which Chinese gains must come at U.S. expense. Bilateral trade flows between China and most other Asian countries have been rising faster than the flows between the United States and these other Asian countries; but this difference is due in part to the initial, one-time boost in trade from the recent implementation of the free trade agreement between China and the Association of Southeast Asian Nations (ASEAN).[56] In any event, China's growing presence and clout are based on more than economic growth; the PRC's increased military spending has not gone unnoticed by nearby countries.

China's claim to the "commanding heights" of the Asian economy is weakened by a number of limitations. China's trade statistics with Asia are inflated by the country's large (but unquantifiable) role in assembling parts made elsewhere in Asia into finished products that are then re-exported, most often to North America. Because only the value-added is truly a Chinese product, trade flow numbers exaggerate China's importance as a buyer of goods manufactured in other Asian countries. Given that East and Southeast Asia are more dependent on the American market than on China for exporting, most of these countries have been highly receptive to the U.S. government's overtures to conclude bilateral free trade agreements (FTAs). Such agreements are in force in Asia with Singapore and Australia and are being negotiated with Korea, Malaysia, and Thailand. Additional U.S. FTAs are likely in Asia given that other countries, including Indonesia and the Philippines, have expressed interest. In addition, U.S. trade policymakers favor such agreements (the "WTO-plus" approach) because they offer closer political relations with key countries, are able to go beyond the scope of multilateral trade liberalization agreements, and offer U.S. companies a solid commercial foothold in the markets of free trade partners.

Trade is only half of contemporary international commerce. Foreign direct investment (FDI) at times is the larger, more important half. The positive effects of incoming FDI have become so evident—most notably in Singapore, China, and Malaysia—that countries throughout Asia (and elsewhere) are actively seeking the establishment of foreign subsidiaries.

---

[56] See Donald Weatherbee's chapter in this volume.

Incoming FDI has come extensively from U.S. companies and very little from China. In the 2000–2004 period, recorded FDI from U.S. multinationals totaled $19 billion, about one-fifth of total incoming direct investment in ASEAN countries. With net FDI of $348 billion during these five years, Chinese companies accounted for less than 0.05% of total direct investment flows to ASEAN.[57]

Conclusions, Outlook, and Policy Implications

Current international economic conditions are far too complicated and sui generis to identify which of the many variables in the public and private sectors will dominate the others and determine how the debtor-creditor disequilibrium will play out. The dangers of a serious, growth-choking economic crisis are potential, not inevitable. Still, the risks are credible enough that they should be taken more seriously by governments. Borrowing so heavily against the future is a high-stakes bet that continued debtor status will not eventually diminish American prosperity and weaken U.S. global influence and prestige. Policymakers would be well advised to take more seriously the economic excesses that are both exposing the dollar to the risk of a large, disorderly depreciation and exposing the global economy to the repercussions of its main currency in free fall. The unique ability of the United States to incur large, non-stop balance of payments deficits is in question because this "exorbitant privilege" does not extend to generating massive international IOUs forever.

A plummeting dollar could lead to economic malaise (higher interest rates, slower growth, and more unemployment) in the United States so severe that a more isolationist, lower-cost foreign policy becomes attractive to a majority of the voting public. The firewall separating U.S. economic and foreign policies is not indestructible. Although there is at present a lack of evidence to predict that the powerful American foreign policy eagle will be grounded, it is neither alarmist nor extremist to suggest it might have to alter course to avoid being buffeted by the tailwinds of a precipitous drop in confidence in the dollar. Since a substantial improvement in the U.S. international economic position is not likely in the short term, the major East Asian creditor countries and currency speculators world-wide will be the main actors determining whether a sword of Damocles continues dangling precariously over the global economy or drops on it. A superpower should want greater control over its economic and foreign affairs destiny.

---

[57] ASEAN, "Foreign Direct Investment Statistics," http://www.aseansec.org/18144.htm.

In calculating the odds on scenarios that might materialize over the next two years, the most likely outcome is muddling through, perhaps facilitated by changing economic conditions beginning with faster economic growth in Europe and Japan and slower growth in the United States. Such changes in relative aggregate demand would probably lead to increased demand for imports by other countries. This would at least reduce the rate of growth of the U.S. trade/current account deficit and possibly lead to a modest reduction in its absolute size that in either case would be sufficient to prevent a full-blown currency crisis. The status quo would also be bolstered to the extent that the super-creditors continue seeing no viable alternative to continuous dollar accumulations, lest their vast holdings depreciate in value.

A second scenario is one in which the dollar depreciates on a steady but moderate and orderly basis. This outcome would likely be triggered by a slight increase in dollar sales by speculators, possibly combined with at least one of the super-creditors, most likely China, initiating a modest program of diversifying its reserve holdings by small, but regular, dollar sales. Americans would suffer increases in import prices, but many U.S. goods potentially would become more price competitive in the global marketplace. Assuming that Americans would reduce their demand for higher cost imports, the result would be a slow but welcomed reduction in the U.S. trade deficit. The added variable of relatively faster GDP growth in the major U.S. trading partners would accelerate and enlarge this correction.

A third plausible scenario is a severe international economic crisis and downturn fomented by a frenzied and sustained dumping of dollars by speculators anxious to take refuge in other currencies and gold. This would be a likely result if the growth of the U.S. trade and current account deficits continues unabated or if the performance of the U.S. economy deteriorated relative to others. In any event, the main wild card between relatively positive and negative scenarios is the extent to which inflows of capital from private foreign investors will remain steady, diminish, or increase, whether for economic reasons or due to unforeseen international political events.

Perhaps the least likely scenario is an improved U.S. current account position resulting from adoption of fundamental changes in U.S. domestic economic policy, e.g. tax increases to narrow the budget deficit, as well as structural initiatives by domestic companies that make U.S. exports more appealing.

An essential course of action for the United States is to follow what most economists would identify as first-best policies. One is a genuine coming to terms with the perils of living so long and so far beyond its means. Pay-as-you-go government expenditures should gradually replace deficit financing, and fiscal measures that provide more incentives to save and more disincentives to consume would be useful. Equally essential is preservation and enhancement of the U.S. economy's many internal strengths that helped attract more than $1 trillion from private foreign investors in 2005 for foreign direct investment, purchases of stocks and bonds, bank deposits, and so on. A plunge in these inflows could have catastrophic consequences for the dollar's value and international monetary stability. The United States would do well to preserve that which makes its economy relatively efficient and attractive, beginning with its business and entrepreneurial-friendly environment, excellence in technological innovation, limited government regulation, and lack of rigidity in labor markets. The more that the federal and state governments educate and train Americans for the jobs of the future rather than try to perpetuate the jobs of the past, the better off the U.S. economy will be.

If doing nothing and hoping the status quo holds is second-best policy, then the imposition of new import barriers would be a third-best policy. The long-standing emphasis on reducing the U.S. trade deficit through export expansion rather than through import reduction remains the only sensible strategy. This approach justifies aggressive efforts by U.S. officials to remove or reduce foreign trade barriers in force in Asia and elsewhere. Furthermore, Washington would both advance free trade and solidify the U.S. presence in East Asia by seeking to revive the moribund negotiations in the APEC forum to create an Asia-Pacific free trade area.

The super-debtor and its major foreign creditors need to better understand and more effectively discuss their unique mutual dependency stemming from opposite but complementary economic strategies. They also need to talk about their mutual susceptibility to the possibility that the current global balance of payments disequilibrium could escalate into a serious, costly, and avoidable international economic crisis. No quick fixes exist, but policymakers of the relevant governments would do well to initiate extended talks to discuss contingency planning and mutual policy adjustments. Both U.S. foreign policy and economic objectives would benefit from making such consultations a part of wider U.S. government efforts to understand the needs and desires of Asian countries.

No matter what directions the domestic economy or the current account deficit take, U.S. foreign policy toward Asia ought to be more proactive. American exceptionalism is not so powerful and entrenched that it can thrive on autopilot.

EXECUTIVE SUMMARY

This chapter analyzes the growth of China's trade and economic interdependence with both its Asian neighbors and the United States and assesses the impact these developments will have on China's security and the security of the Asia-Pacific region.

MAIN ARGUMENT:

China currently is engaged in a process of strategic economic development that will enhance the People's Republic of China's (PRC) comprehensive national power. The purpose of this development is to enhance national wealth, creating a reasonably prosperous China by 2020 and providing the economic basis for China's emergence as a regional and global great power. Toward these ends, China has sought to develop webs of economic interdependence with its regional neighbors. These connections are both supporting the PRC's economic development and linking these neighbors to China in friendly and cooperative relations. China is also exhibiting restraint and greater cooperation with its neighbors—behavior explained by economic interdependence as well as Beijing's own foreign policy strategy.

POLICY IMPLICATIONS:

- The webs of interdependence, coupled with Beijing's desire for regional peace and stability, likely will constrain militaristic adventurism by the Chinese around their periphery over the next five to ten years.

- Given the growth of economic interdependence between China and its Asia-Pacific neighbors, several of these countries would be reluctant to jeopardize the benefits of trade with the PRC in the event of Sino-U.S. conflict over Taiwan. This reluctance will complicate U.S. military operations in the event of such conflict.

- The U.S. and the international community should continue to encourage China's active participation in the global economy and multilateral international institutions. Once China's rise to great power status is achieved, China's interests may change from basic acceptance of the international status quo to more revisionist goals. Engagement and socialization today are the best hedge against a future revisionist China.

Rising China:
The Search for Power and Plenty

Michael R. Chambers

This chapter seeks to outline the current and future impact of China's growing trade and economic interdependence on the security both of China and of the Asia-Pacific region. The chapter will seek to answer two basic questions. First, how do growing trade and interdependence relate to and impact China's grand strategy as it is rising to great power status? Second, will China's increasing involvement with and integration into global trade help to constrain China from military adventurism?

The People's Republic of China (PRC) is currently engaged in strategic economic growth with the goal of becoming a moderately well-off society by the year 2020 and providing the economic basis for China's drive to become a great power. Beijing sees not a mutually exclusive choice between wealth and power but a close interrelationship between economic development and security, with each dependent on the other. The key themes and arguments of this chapter are threefold: First, China's goal to become a great power is based on the development of "comprehensive national power" that is rooted in a strong and prosperous economy. Beijing is using foreign trade and investment as key drivers for the development of its economy.

Second, China seeks to develop webs of interdependence with its regional neighbors in order to link them to the PRC as well as to create a buffer zone to help Beijing resist any hostile pressure from the United States. China's efforts to build interdependence also are intended to dampen Asian

Michael R. Chambers, Associate Professor of Political Science at Indiana State Univesity, is an editor of *Asian Security*. He can be reached at <mchambers3@indstate.edu>.

The author wishes to thank Brandy Jolliff, Shyam Kulkarni, Peter Mattis, and Evan Morrisey for research assistance.

anxieties about the "China threat" as the PRC rises. These efforts appear to be generally successful.

Finally, economic interdependence appears to be constraining China in cooperative relations with its neighbors. Also at work, however, is Chinese self-restraint—based on Beijing's strategic desire for a peaceful and stable regional security environment in which to pursue economic development.

Based on the analysis presented below, three main policy implications both for the United States and for the international community become evident. First, the webs of interdependence, coupled with Beijing's desire for regional peace and stability, will likely constrain militaristic adventurism by the Chinese around their periphery over the next five to ten years.

Second, given the growth of economic interdependence between China and its Asia-Pacific neighbors, several of these countries would be reluctant to jeopardize the benefits of trade with the PRC in the event of Sino-U.S. conflict over Taiwan. This reluctance will complicate U.S. military operations in the event of such conflict.

Finally, the United States and the international community should continue to encourage China's active participation in the global economy and multilateral international institutions. Once China's rise to great power status is achieved, the PRC's interests may change from basic acceptance of the international status quo to more revisionist goals. Engagement and socialization today are the best hedge against a future revisionist China.

The chapter is organized as follows. The first section reviews the grand strategy guiding China's rise and examines the importance of international trade and foreign investment for China's economic development. The section that follows examines the extent of economic interdependence in China's relations with its Asian neighbors and major trade partners. A third section considers security implications of this interdependence, and a conclusion offers policy implications.

Grand Strategy, Trade, and Economic Interdependence

Ever since Chairman Mao Zedong's announcement on October 1, 1949 that the Chinese people had finally "stood up," the Chinese leadership has sought to return China to its position of traditional international and regional status. During the Maoist era (1949–76), China made some progress toward this goal (e.g., the development of nuclear weapons). Nevertheless, many of the radical political and economic policies of Mao thwarted Beijing's efforts. Not until the late 1970s, with the rise of pragmatic reformers under the leadership of Deng Xiaoping, did the PRC finally set the country on the path to sustained economic modernization and development. Averaging

9% annual economic growth since the reforms of 1978, China has set the stage for its rise to great power status. Deng and the pragmatic reformers understood that economic modernization and development would need to be the basis for growth of China's comprehensive national power and that the PRC would need to open up to the international economy—including international trade and foreign investment—in order to help spur continued economic development.

Grand Strategy with "Chinese Characteristics"

China's long-term strategic goal—to become a great power in the Asia-Pacific region and beyond—is guiding China's overall foreign policy.[1] To achieve this goal, the PRC needs to develop its "comprehensive national power" or "overall national strength," which includes economic, political, and military components. This is a long-term plan that will require a few decades to achieve, based as it is on the modernization and development of China's economy. Beijing is also adopting a gradual approach so as not to unduly antagonize other great powers, especially the United States; the Chinese recognize the current international structure of U.S. unipolarity and do not want to provoke counterbalancing actions to China's, rise either by the United States or by any Asian neighbors.[2]

Emphasizing China's goal of rising to great power status is not to deny the importance of the more basic priorities of maintaining regime security and preserving the territorial integrity of the PRC. These remain critical for the Chinese Communist Party (CCP) leadership, and Beijing perceives that the longer-term goal of great powerdom cannot be achieved without

---

[1] There is some debate among analysts of Chinese foreign relations as to the existence of a Chinese grand strategy. Thomas Christensen has argued that China lacks a unified grand strategic plan to bind together the PRC's economic, security, and foreign policy objectives, while Avery Goldstein, Michael Swaine, and Ashley Tellis admit the lack of an explicit strategy but see a de facto grand strategy both accepted by the Chinese leadership and guiding their policies. There is also some debate over the relative weighting of the Communist Party leadership's emphasis on maintaining regime security, domestic stability, and national unity versus the CCP's drive for influence and great power status at the regional and global levels. See Thomas J. Christensen, "China," in *Strategic Asia 2001–2002: Power and Purpose*, ed. Richard J. Ellings and Aaron L. Friedberg (Seattle: National Bureau of Asian Research, 2001), 27–69; Avery Goldstein, *Rising to the Challenge: China's Grand Strategy and International Security* (Stanford: Stanford University Press, 2005); and Michael D. Swaine and Ashley J. Tellis, *Interpreting China's Grand Strategy: Past, Present, and Future* (Santa Monica: Project Air Force and RAND, 2000).

[2] For a discussion of this Chinese wariness, see Goldstein, *Rising to the Challenge*, especially pages 130–35, and chapter 7; and Wang Jisi, "China's Changing Role in Asia" (occasional paper of the Atlantic Council of the U.S., January 2004).

ensuring these prior two security goals.[3] Allowing organized resistance and opposition to the party's leadership or allowing the loss of national territory—whether it be Tibet or Taiwan—would prove the leadership to be weak both domestically and internationally and would undermine China's comprehensive national power.

The best way for China to achieve all three of these strategic priorities is through continued strong economic growth. By bringing increasing prosperity to the Chinese people, economic growth will strengthen popular support for (or at least reduce their dissatisfaction with) the leadership, thereby enhancing the legitimacy of continued CCP rule. Economic growth, funneled through increased tax revenues and other resources, will allow the PRC to increase funding to poorer regions and minority areas where there might otherwise be disturbances against the government.[4] The increase in government revenues resulting from economic growth will also allow continued double-digit growth in the official military budget, which is gradually strengthening the PLA's military capabilities to address threats to China's security and territorial integrity—particularly vis-à-vis Taiwan. Economic growth also will increase the PRC's international influence: Beijing will have additional resources to use as leverage in relations with other countries (e.g., via foreign aid or investment) as well as in international organizations. Likewise, continued growth in the size of the Chinese economy will bring the PRC international influence, as the size of the Chinese market grows in relation to the international economy.

For the Chinese economy to continue the trend of high growth that China has enjoyed for the last twenty-five years, the PRC must have a relatively peaceful international security environment, especially in the East Asian region. China also needs strong trade relations with other countries. By developing these economic linkages with neighboring countries, China will gain important inputs for the Chinese economy (such as natural resources, investments, and technology) as well as provide markets in which to sell Chinese exports. By importing neighbors' goods, investing in neighbors' economies, and even increasing aid to poorer neighbors, the PRC will demonstrate that China is a good neighbor—and thereby

---

[3] For examples of statements by the Chinese leadership that link together regime security, territorial integrity, and the drive for regional and global influence, see Jiang Zemin, "Build a Well-Off Society in an All-Round Way and Create a New Situation in Building Socialism with Chinese Characteristics" (report to the 16th National Congress of the Chinese Communist Party, November 8, 2002), available at http://english.people.com.cn/200211/18/eng20021118_106983.shtml; Information Office of the State Council, *China's Peaceful Development Road*, December 12, 2005, available at http://www.china.org.cn/english/2005/Dec/152669.htm; and Information Office of the State Council, *China's National Defense in 2004*, available at http://www.china.org.cn/e-white/20041227/index.htm.

[4] Thomas J. Christensen, "China," 32–33.

likely dampen fears the region may have of a rising China. Through these linkages of economic interdependence, Beijing hopes not only to influence these neighbors but also to surround China with a buffer zone of friends that will help the PRC resist hostile pressure from the United States. Given that Beijing views the United States as the principal long-term challenge to China's rise to great power status, the PRC worries that such pressure will indeed occur.

China's Economic Development Strategy

Opening China to the international economy has been an important emphasis of Beijing's economic strategy since the start of the reform era in 1978. For most of the Maoist period, China followed a largely autarkic economic policy, limiting its economic interactions with foreigners. With the launching of the Four Modernizations and the Open Door Policy in late 1978, however, the post-Mao leadership sought to link economic modernization with opening of the economy to foreign investment and foreign trade. Seeking to emulate the economic successes of Japan and the East Asian "tigers" (South Korea, Taiwan, Hong Kong, and Singapore), Beijing implemented over the course of the 1980s the PRC's version of the East Asian development model.[5] Though implementation of this model was less than smooth, China gradually became committed to using foreign investment to make up for domestic capital shortages and backward technologies, emphasizing exports to drive economic growth and liberalizing trade to allow global market forces to bring greater efficiency to Chinese production. The culmination of this process was China's 2001 accession to the World Trade Organization (WTO), which required the PRC to agree both to some of the toughest market-opening measures of any member of the group and to accept safeguard measures for other WTO members against spikes in Chinese exports to their countries.[6]

Because of the importance of continued economic growth for China's strategic goals, the Chinese government has generally supported the export-led growth strategy. Several scholars caution, however, against jumping to the conclusion that China's development strategy closely mimics the state-guided growth of Japan and the East Asian tigers. In particular, these

---

[5] For discussion of the reforms and economic development policies, see Harry Harding, *China's Second Revolution: Reform after Mao* (Washington, D.C.: Brookings Institution Press, 1987); Barry Naughton, *Growing Out of the Plan: Chinese Economic Reform, 1978–1993* (Cambridge: Cambridge University Press, 1995); and Susan L. Shirk, *The Political Logic of Economic Reform in China* (Berkeley: University of California Press, 1993).

[6] Nicholas R. Lardy, *Integrating China into the Global Economy* (Washington, D.C.: Brookings Institution Press, 2002), chapters 1 and 3.

scholars point to China's lack of policy coherence in guiding the reforms, lack of an agency analogous to Japan's Ministry of International Trade and Industry (MITI), and decentralized decisionmaking process in the export regime.[7]

The CCP leadership currently argues that China is in a twenty-year period of "strategic opportunity" during which the chances for a world war are low and the international environment around China should be favorable for the country's continued economic development. The PRC is attempting to seize this opportunity to develop a "well-off society" so that China can become a "strong, prosperous, democratic, and culturally advanced socialist country" by the middle of the twenty-first century.[8] The party leadership wants to quadruple China's 2000 gross domestic product (GDP) by 2020, an accomplishment that would not only help to bring prosperity to the Chinese people but also increase "China's overall national strength and international competitiveness." As part of this effort, former party leader Jiang Zemin called on his colleagues both to increase China's participation in international trade—expanding exports and optimizing the import mix to focus on imported advanced technology and key equipment—and to increase the PRC's utilization of foreign direct investment.

Growth of Trade

The emphasis on trade as a key driver of China's strategic economic development has achieved impressive results (see **Table 1**). In 2004 China surpassed Japan as the third largest trading power in the world and in 2005 surpassed France as the fourth largest economy.[9] In addition to this emergence as one of the world's major trade powers, the PRC's integration into the global economy also is evident from China's increasing reliance on trade: total trade as a percentage of GDP has grown from only 12% in 1980 to 64% in 2005 (see **Figure 1**).[10] As is evident in Table 1 and Figure 1, accession to the WTO appears to have accelerated China's total trade

---

[7] For analysis that suggests China is not closely following a protectionist, "developmental state" model, see Thomas G. Moore, "China as a Latecomer: Toward a Global Logic of the Open Policy," *Journal of Contemporary China* 5, no. 12 (July 1996); Nicholas Lardy, *Integrating China into the Global Economy* (Washington, D.C.: Brookings Institution Press, 2002); and Scott Kennedy, "China's Porous Protectionism: The Changing Political Economy of Trade Policy," *Political Science Quarterly* 120, no. 3 (October 2005).

[8] Jiang, "Build a Well-Off Society."

[9] Keith Bradsher, "China Reports Another Year of Strong (or Even Better) Growth," *New York Times*, January 26, 2006, C5.

[10] These percentages were calculated based on the total trade figures presented in Table 1 and China's GDP figures available in the International Monetary Fund (IMF) World Economic Outlook Database (WEO), April 2006 available at http://www.imf.org/external/pubs/ft/weo/2006/01/data/index.htm.

TABLE 1   China's trade, 1980–2005 ($billion)

	Imports	Exports	Total	Balance
1980	19.5	18.1	37.6	−1.4
1985	42.5	27.3	69.8	−15.2
1990	53.9	62.9	116.8	9.0
1995	132.2	148.8	281.0	16.6
1996	138.9	151.2	290.1	12.3
1997	142.2	182.9	325.1	40.7
1998	140.4	183.7	324.1	43.3
1999	165.7	194.9	360.6	29.2
2000	225.1	249.2	474.3	24.1
2001	243.6	266.7	510.3	23.1
2002	295.4	325.7	621.1	30.3
2003	412.8	438.2	851.0	25.4
2004	561.4	593.2	1154.6	31.8
2005	660.1	762.0	1422.1	101.9

SOURCES: IMF *Direction of Trade Statistics (DOTS) Yearbook*, 1987, 1995, 2000, 2001, and 2005; and IMF *DOTS Quarterly*, June 2006.

growth and reliance on trade. Moreover, both the growth in China's exports and the country's overall trade surplus have enabled the PRC to build the largest foreign exchange reserves in the world: PRC holdings surpassed Japan's reserves of $850 billion in February 2006, and by the end of March 2006 China had amassed $875 billion.[11]

In the process of integrating China into the world economy, the PRC has capitalized on China's relatively cheap labor force to become the "workshop of the world"—or at least the assembly location of the world. China imports raw materials and components (as well as the necessary machinery) for manufacturing consumer goods and then exports the finished products. As a result, the broad composition of China's trade has shifted since the start of the reform period. In 1980 China's imports were comprised of 34% primary goods and 65% manufactured goods yet by 2004 the balance stood at 21% and 79%, respectively. The shift is even more dramatic in China's exports, where the balance changed from approximately 7% to 93% in favor of manufactured goods.[12] The composition of the manufactured

[11] Andrew Browne, "China Move Is Unlikely to Boost Yuan," *Wall Street Journal*, April 15, 2006, A4.

[12] Data on composition of trade is from *Zhongguo Tongji Nianjian*, 2005 [*China Statistical Yearbook*, 2005], tables 18-4 and 18-5.

FIGURE 1   Trade as a percentage of GDP

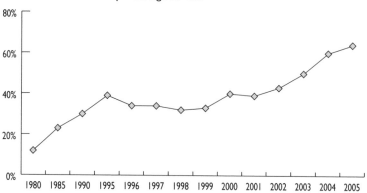

SOURCES: IMF *DOTS Yearbook,* 1987, 1995, 2000, and 2001; IMF *DOTS Quarterly* (June 2006); and IMF World Economic Outlook Database, April 2006.

goods that China imports and exports also has undergone a transformation as the Chinese have moved up the technology ladder. In 1995 clothing and apparel represented 14% of Chinese exports compared to 12.8% for electrical machinery and electronics, but in 2005 electrical machinery and electronics represented 22% of exports (the top category, valued at $172.4 billion) while clothing and apparel had slipped to less than 9%. Electrical machinery and electronics (especially components for these goods) also constituted China's top import category in 2005 at $174.9 billion (26.5% of all Chinese imports), followed by imported components for office machines and various industrial machinery.[13]

To feed its rapidly growing economy, the PRC has become a major importer of several commodities, including mineral fuel and oil, plastics, chemicals, iron and steel, various ores, and copper. For some of these items, China's increasing imports have raised the possibility that Chinese demand could begin to shape world prices for the commodity. For example, in 2002 China's net imports of crude oil represented 5% of world trade in that commodity; copper, 15%; and soybeans, 20%.[14]

The most important of these resource imports is energy, particularly oil. The rapid rise of China's economy has led to increasing demand for energy.

[13] *Global Trade Atlas* http://www.gtis.com/gta. According to the data in *Global Trade Atlas,* China supplanted the United States in 2005 as the top global trader in the electrical machinery and electronics category (HS-85), with $347.3 billion in total trade compared to $336.9 billion for the United States.

[14] Thomas Lum and Dick K. Nanto, "China's Trade with the United States and the World," *CRS Report for Congress* no. RL31403 (Washington, D.C.: Congressional Research Service, updated March 14, 2006), 9.

Although China relies heavily on domestically produced coal for energy, oil has become an increasingly important part of the energy equation. Chinese demand for oil doubled from 1.7 million barrels per day (MMBD) in 1984 to 3.4 MMBD in 1995 and doubled again to 6.8 MMBD by 2005. China, which by 2003 had surpassed Japan to become the world's second largest consumer of oil behind the United States, is now the third largest importer of oil behind these two countries. China currently imports more than 40% of its oil needs, a figure that could jump to 80% by 2030.[15] Given this growing dependence on imported oil, Beijing has become increasingly concerned about China's energy security. Disruptions to this supply of oil could lead to stagnation in the Chinese economy, which could in turn undermine one of the CCP's two primary bases of legitimacy. Substantial price increases could have a similar effect. Moreover, approximately 80% of China's imported oil comes through the Strait of Malacca from the Persian Gulf and Africa, a vulnerability—known as the "Malacca Dilemma"—that gives Chinese leaders cause for concern. To address such concerns, the Chinese have considered building pipelines to avoid the Strait, attempted to diversify China's sources of oil, and sought equity control of oil sources rather than rely on market forces (the last of which is an approach that is leading to tensions with the United States).[16]

The Role of Foreign Investment

Just as the growth of foreign trade has helped to drive China's economic development, foreign direct investment (FDI) into China has brought factories and businesses to supply the local market with goods and services, created firms directed toward the export market (with all the trade-related benefits those entail), provided new jobs (often with higher pay than offered by domestic firms), and provided sources of new technologies and capital. From 1979 to 2004 China contracted $1,096.6 billion in FDI, with $562.1 billion utilized.[17] In 2002 through 2004 the PRC was the leading recipient of FDI in the world, replacing the previous front runner, the United States. The flow of FDI into China was $72.4 billion in 2005, up 19% from 2004

---

[15] Mikkal E. Herberg, "China's Search for Energy Security and Implications for Southeast Asia," in *Contending Perspectives: Southeast Asian and American Views of a Rising China*, ed. Evelyn Goh, Sheldon Simon, and Michael Wills (New York: Routledge, *forthcoming*).

[16] See Kenneth Lieberthal and Mikkal Herberg, "China's Search for Energy Security: Implications for U.S. Policy," *NBR Analysis* 17, no. 1 (April 2006), available at http://www.nbr.org. See also David Zweig and Bi Jianhai, "China's Global Hunt for Energy," *Foreign Affairs* 84, no. 5 (September/October 2005).

[17] *Zhongguo Tongji Nianjian,* 2005 [China Statistical Yearbook, 2005], "Utilization of Foreign Capital," table 18–13.

($60.6 billion).[18] Much of this investment has gone into the manufacturing sector as production and assembly factories have moved from other Asian countries into China: the investment into manufacturing was $25.8 billion in 2000 (63% of utilized FDI) and $43.0 billion in 2004 (71% of utilized FDI).[19] FDI from other Asian countries represented 61% of the total utilized in 2004.[20] Additionally, several of China's East Asian neighbors regularly place as top investors in the PRC (see **Table 2**). The importance of these foreign-funded enterprises is indicated by their prominence in Chinese export production (58% of Chinese exports in 2005).[21]

Although much of the focus is on FDI flows into China, the PRC also is increasing China's overseas investments as a way to integrate with the world economy. China's stock of outward FDI had reached US$27.8 billion by 2000 and $38.8 billion by 2004.[22] The PRC invested a further $6.9 billion overseas in 2005. Chinese overseas investment has primarily targeted the mining, transport, manufacturing, and wholesale and retail trade sectors.[23] Over the years, Asia has been the recipient of the bulk of China's outward investment (receiving 75% according to the PRC's white paper, "China's Peaceful Development Road"), but in 2004 Latin America and the Caribbean (especially the Cayman Islands) together were the largest recipient of this Chinese investment.[24]

China's Participation in International Economic Institutions

Beijing views participation in international economic institutions as an important component of China's peaceful development. Such participation will bring China greater international influence and prestige by enabling

---

[18] Geoff Dyer and Andrew Yeh, "Beijing Revises Inflow Figures up to Dollars 72.4bn Foreign Investment," *Financial Times*, June 9, 2006, 9.

[19] *Zhongguo Tongji Nianjian*, 2005.

[20] Ibid. This total includes South Asian and East Asian neighbors.

[21] Wayne M. Morrison, "China's Economic Conditions," *CRS Issue Brief for Congress* no. IB98014 (Washington, D.C.: Congressional Research Service, updated March 17, 2006), 9. See also David Barboza, "Some Assembly Needed: China as Asia's Factory," *New York Times*, February 9, 2006.

[22] UN Conference on Trade and Development (UNCTAD), *World Investment Report 2005* (New York and Geneva, 2005), annex table B.2.

[23] *Zhongguo Tongji Nianjian*, 2005. The 2005 overseas investment figure is from Ministry of Commerce, People's Republic of China, "Main Indicators of Foreign Trade and Economy in Total (2005/1–12)," March 16, 2006, available at http://english.mofcom.gov.cn.

[24] See http://www.china.org.cn (Foreign Economic Relations/China Facts and Figures). This is the authorized government Internet portal run under the auspices of the Information Office of the PRC State Council. The fact that the Cayman Islands serves as both a major recipient of and a major source for FDI suggests that much of the Chinese investment into the Caymans is finding its way back into the PRC via tax breaks and other incentives accorded foreign investment by Beijing.

TABLE 2   China's utilized FDI inflows, top foreign investors, selected years ($billion)

Rank	1985		1990		1995		2000		2004	
1	Hong Kong	0.95	Hong Kong and Macao	1.91	Hong Kong	20.2	Hong Kong	15.5	Hong Kong	19.0
2	United States	0.36	Japan	0.50	Japan	3.2	United States	4.4	Virgin Islands	6.7
3	Japan	0.31	United States	0.46	Taiwan	3.2	Virgin Islands	3.8	South Korea	6.2
4	UK	0.07	F.R. Germany	0.06	United States	3.1	Japan	2.9	Japan	5.4
5	France	0.03	Singapore	0.05	Singapore	1.9	Taiwan	2.3	United States	3.9
6	F.R. Germany	0.02	Australia	0.02	South Korea	1.0	Singapore	2.2	Taiwan	3.1
7	Italy	0.02	Kuwait	0.02	UK	0.96	South Korea	1.5	Cayman Is.	2.0
8	Australia	0.01	France	0.02	Macao	0.44	UK	1.2	Singapore	2.0
9	Singapore	0.01	Netherlands	0.01	Germany	0.39	Germany	1.0	Samoa	1.1
10	Canada	0.01	UK	0.01	Virgin Islands	0.30	France	0.8	Germany	1.1
Total FDI		1.95		3.50		37.8		40.6		60.6

SOURCE: *Zhongguo Tongji Nianjian*, 2005 [China Statistical Yearbook, 2005].

NOTE: The Virgin Islands, Cayman Islands, and Western Samoa are used by many foreign firms for tax purposes. Total number of countries that contributed FDI to China in 1985: 24, 1990: 29, 1995: 58, 2000: 118, and 2004: 149.

Beijing to help shape the rules of the international economic order. Participation will also bolster the PRC's image as a cooperative partner, thereby alleviating concerns that China may be a threat to others. China is an active member in the major global multilateral economic institutions, including the World Bank, the International Monetary Fund (IMF), and the WTO. China also is a full participant in regional economic institutions such as the Asian Development Bank (ADB), the APEC Forum, and the "ASEAN+3" dialogue process.[25] Similarly, the PRC participates in such subregional economic cooperation as the Greater Mekong Subregion Economic Cooperation Program as well as in such cross-regional groupings as the Asia-Europe Meeting (ASEM). Chinese leaders regularly attend less formal international economic dialogues such as the annual World Economic Forum in Davos, Switzerland. Additionally, though not a member of the G-8, the PRC on occasion has been invited to attend as a guest of the host country.

Increasing Interdependence in China's Foreign Relations

While integrating into the world economy, China has significantly increased trade and economic interdependence with major trade partners and Asian neighbors (see **Table 3** and **Table 4**). This development fits well with the PRC's strategic goal of becoming a great power. These intensified economic linkages are providing material inputs, export markets, foreign investment, and new technologies to help drive China's economic growth. Such linkages also are creating avenues for cooperation between China and its neighbors that could reduce regional anxieties about the PRC's rise while simultaneously creating mechanisms for Beijing to increase its influence with these regional neighbors and other trade partners. This section examines China's economic relations with these partners in order to shed light on Chinese efforts to create these webs of interdependence. Quite evident are China's growing trade imbalances with certain types of countries: China has trade deficits with several Asian neighbors that supply the raw materials and intermediate products to China's factories but has large trade surpluses with the developed Western countries (and Hong Kong, which serves as an export corridor) that are the major markets for China's manufacturing exports.

---

[25] ASEAN+3 consists of the ten Southeast Asian countries (Brunei, Cambodia, Indonesia, Laos, Malaysia, Myanmar [Burma], Philippines, Singapore, Thailand, and Vietnam) plus China, Japan, and South Korea.

TABLE 3   China's top ten trade partners, 1995 and 2005 ($billion)

	Rank	Partner	China's imports	China's exports	Total trade	Balance
1995	1	Hong Kong	57.9	69.7	127.6	11.8
	2	United States	11.7	48.5	60.2	36.8
	3	Japan	21.9	35.9	57.8	14.0
	4	Germany	6.1	12.4	18.5	6.3
	5	Taiwan*	14.8	3.1	17.9	-11.7
	6	South Korea	9.2	7.4	16.6	-1.8
	7	France	3.4	6.6	10.0	3.2
	8	Italy	2.5	4.4	6.9	1.9
	9	Singapore	2.8	4.0	6.8	1.2
	10	UK	1.5	4.1	5.6	2.6
2005	1	United States	41.8	259.8	301.6	218
	2	Hong Kong	130.3	135.1	265.4	4.8
	3	Japan	80.0	108.4	188.4	28.4
	4	South Korea	69.9	38.6	108.5	-31.3
	5	Taiwan*	74.7	16.5	91.2	-58.2
	6	Germany	26.4	49.4	75.8	23
	7	Singapore	19.7	20.5	40.2	0.8
	8	Netherlands	3.2	32.1	35.3	28.9
	9	Malaysia	18.3	11.7	30.0	-6.6
	10	UK	5.1	23.9	29.0	18.8

SOURCES: IMF *DOTS Yearbook*, 1998; (1995 data); IMF *DOTS Quarterly*, June 2006 (2005 data); and 2005 data for Taiwan from Ministry of Commerce of the People's Republic of China, http://english.mofcom.gov.cn.

NOTE: Based on partner-reported data.

* Data as reported by China. Significant variation exists between data as reported by China and Taiwan. In 2005, Taiwan reported direct exports to China of $40.9 billion and direct imports from China of $19.9 billion, for a total of $60.8 billion and a surplus of $21.0 billion. Interestingly, for trade with mainland China and Hong Kong combined, Taiwan reported exports of $71.6 billion and imports of $21.8 billion, for total trade of $93.4 billion and a surplus of $49.8 billion, which is much closer to the PRC-reported data.

Trade with East Asian and Pacific Neighbors

As mentioned above, China's trade patterns with East Asian and Pacific neighbors suggest that the PRC is largely importing both the necessary raw materials for China's growing economy and the necessary intermediate

TABLE 4 China's trade with regional partners ($billion)

	1995				2005			
	China's imp.	China's exp.	Total	Balance	China's imp.	China's exp.	Total	Balance
Japan	21.9	35.9	57.8	14.0	80.0	108.4	188.4	28.4
North Korea[a]	0.06	0.48	0.54	0.42	0.5	1.1	1.6	0.6
South Korea	9.2	7.4	16.6	−1.8	69.9	38.6	108.5	−31.3
Taiwan[a, b]	14.8	3.1	17.9	−11.7	74.7	16.5	91.2	−58.2
ASEAN[c]	8.6	10.2	18.8	1.6	67.7	65.2	132.9	−2.5
Brunei	0.00	0.04	0.04	0.04	0.19	0.06	0.25	−0.13
Cambodia	0.01	0.06	0.07	0.05	0.02	0.59	0.61	0.57
Indonesia	1.8	1.6	3.4	−0.2	7.7	9.2	16.9	1.5
Laos[d]	0.01	0.02	0.03	0.01	0.01	0.11	0.12	0.1
Malaysia	1.9	1.7	3.6	−0.2	18.3	11.7	30.0	−6.6
Myanmar	0.1	0.7	0.8	0.6	0.2	1.0	1.2	0.8
Philippines	0.2	0.7	0.9	0.5	10.2	4.6	14.8	−5.6
Singapore	2.8	4.0	6.8	1.2	19.7	20.5	40.2	0.8
Thailand	1.6	2.1	3.7	0.5	9.1	11.2	20.3	2.1
Vietnam	0.3	0.02	0.32	−0.28	2.3	6.2	8.5	3.9
Australia	2.3	2.9	5.2	0.6	12.1	16.3	28.4	4.2
New Zealand	0.35	0.48	0.83	0.13	1.2	1.5	2.7	0.3
Russia	3.4	0.9	4.3	−2.5	13.0	7.2	20.2	−5.8
Kazakhstan	0.3	0.03	0.33	−0.27	2.6	4.3	6.9	1.7
Kyrgyzstan	0.00	0.03	0.03	0.03	0.1	1.0	1.1	0.9
Tajikistan	0.01	0.00	0.01	−0.01	0.01	0.16	0.17	0.15
Turkmenistan	0.01	0.01	0.02	0.0	0.02	0.1	0.12	0.08
Uzbekistan	0.06	0.05	0.11	−0.01	0.41	0.25	0.66	−0.16
Afghanistan[d]	0.02	0.03	0.05	0.01	0.00	0.06	0.06	0.06
Mongolia[d]	0.09	0.07	0.16	−0.02	0.4	0.2	0.6	−0.2
Bangladesh	0.05	0.62	0.67	0.57	0.05	1.87	1.92	1.82
India	0.3	0.8	1.1	0.5	8.9	9.8	18.7	0.9
Nepal[d]	0.00	0.06	0.06	0.06	0.01	0.18	0.19	0.17
Pakistan	0.1	0.5	0.6	0.4	0.8	3.8	4.6	3.0
Sri Lanka	0.00	0.16	0.16	0.16	0.03	1.04	1.07	1.01

SOURCES: IMF *DOTS Yearbook*, 1998 (1995 data) and 2005 (2004 data); IMF *DOTS Quarterly*, June 2006 (2005 data); and *Global Trade Atlas* (2005 data).

NOTE: Based on partner–reported data; a = data as reported by China in IMF *DOTS* (significant variation exists between data as reported by China and Taiwan); b = 2005 data is from the *Global Trade Atlas*, as reported by China (significant variation exists between data as reported by China and Taiwan); c = in 1995, ASEAN consisted of only Brunei, Indonesia, Malaysia, the Philippines, Singapore, Thailand, and Vietnam; by 2005, Cambodia, Laos, and Myanmar were also members; and d = includes 2004 partner-reported data since 2005 data is missing.

parts for assembling export goods. China's significant 2005 trade deficits with South Korea and Taiwan (and more modest deficits with Malaysia and the Philippines) were based largely on the importation of both optical instruments and intermediate components for electrical machinery, electronics, and office machines. Even countries with which the PRC had a modest trade surplus for 2005 (such as Vietnam, Myanmar [Burma], Laos, Australia, and New Zealand) provided China with important raw materials such as wood, rubber, ores, and mineral fuels.[26] With so many countries in the region contributing to China's economic development through trade and investment—and becoming connected through this process—the PRC is achieving its goal of building interdependence with its Asian neighbors. Additionally, by importing so heavily, China also is helping to share the benefits of its economic rise, creating the promised "win-win" situation. This economic cooperation should help to dampen concerns that China's rise might pose a threat to its neighbors. Yet there is a problem with this scenario. Chinese trade data suggests that the PRC has more and larger deficits with its Asian neighbors than does the data from these partners. China reported deficits with Australia (US$5.1 billion), Indonesia ($0.1 billion), Japan ($16.4 billion), and Thailand ($6.2 billion), but each of these partners reported that they had the deficit with China. While China's trade statistics show its neighbors benefiting through trade from China's rise, the picture looks different through the eyes of these neighbors.

The Chinese also have been promoting further integration with these regional neighbors, both by agreeing to create a free trade area (FTA) with ASEAN and by supporting an eventual linkage of this FTA into a broader East Asian FTA under the ASEAN+3 process, possibly culminating in an East Asian Community. In addition, Beijing is negotiating FTAs with Australia and New Zealand. Though most of China's regional relationships are yielding positive political results from interdependence, this is not true in all cases—with Japan perhaps being the most significant exception.

Japan. Given that Japan is the second most powerful country in East Asia, the relationship with Japan is extremely important for China. Over the past decade Japan has continued to be one of China's primary trade partners, although Japan has slipped from first to third position in 2005 (Japan's share of China's total trade declined from just over 20% in 1995 to 13% in 2005 as Chinese trade diversified). The PRC has maintained its position as the second largest trade partner for Japan through 2004. Japan

---

[26] Data in this section on 2005 trade balances and major components of trades draws on the IMF, *Direction of Trade Statistics (DOTS) Quarterly,* June 2006; and *Global Trade Atlas,* available at http://www.gtis.con/gta. Data for earlier trade draws on *DOTS Yearbook,* 2005 and selected other years, available at http://www.imf.org/external/data.htm.

also has been a major source of FDI into China (in 2005 Japanese FDI into the PRC surged nearly 20%, reaching $6.5 billion) as well as a source of aid through its official development assistance (ODA) program (Tokyo provided $25.6 billion in loans between 1979 and May 2005).[27] With China's rising wealth, growing military power, and several points of friction between the two countries, however, Tokyo has stated that ODA to China would not continue past the 2008 Olympics in Beijing.

Despite the increasingly close economic relationship between China and Japan, political relations became quite strained during 2005 and early 2006. These tensions relate not only to the legacies of Japanese aggression during the 1930s to 1940s (the source of Chinese anger at Prime Minister Junichiro Koizumi's continued visits to the Yasukuni Shrine) but also to the Sino-Japanese rivalry for influence in the region and beyond. These tensions boiled over in April 2005 when demonstrations that broke out in several Chinese cities caused damage to many Japanese businesses.[28] As a result of these political tensions, in March 2006 Tokyo acted to temporarily freeze Japan's yen loan ODA to China but resumed the loans in June.[29] Periodic tensions also have erupted over trade, such as the heated dispute in 2001 over Japan's efforts to limit imports of Chinese tatami mats, scallions, and shiitake mushrooms.[30] Moreover, the two countries are in competition for energy resources in the region, as evidenced by the squabble over natural gas deposits in the East China Sea as well as by the jockeying over whether a new Russian oil pipeline (the East Siberian-Pacific Ocean pipeline) would run to China or to the Pacific coast to meet tankers bound for Japan. Though increased Sino-Japanese economic interaction has helped China's economy to grow, the enhanced interdependence apparently has not led to increased Chinese influence in Tokyo.

The Korean Peninsula. Similarly, China's economic interactions with North Korea (DPRK) have not led to increased political influence over Pyongyang. The PRC has developed a relationship of asymmetrical interdependence with North Korea: the DPRK is heavily dependent on the PRC (Pyongyang's top trade partner), but North Korea matters only slightly to the Chinese economy. As the only remaining ally of North Korea, China is this stricken neighbor's major source of fuel and food (providing perhaps

---

[27] Associated Press, "Japan Invested Record $6.53 Billion in China in 2005," *Washington Post*, April 4, 2006, D5.

[28] These violent demonstrations seem to have had little effect, however, on Japanese business decisions, since both bilateral trade and Japanese FDI reached record levels in 2005.

[29] Kana Inagaki, "Japan to Freeze Loans to China over Worsening Relations," Associated Press, March 23, 2006. Announcement of the resumed loans is available on the Japanese Ministry of Foreign Affairs website, http://www.mofa.go.jp/policy/oda.

[30] "Japan, China Ministers Cut Deal on Import Trade Battle," *Nikkei Weekly*, December 25, 2001.

as much as 75% of Pyongyang's imports of each).[31] Moreover, China is a major source of foreign investment. President Hu Jintao, when visiting North Korea in October 2005, reportedly pledged to invest $2 billion over the next few years.[32] North Korean dependence on China should give the PRC leverage with the DPRK, which Beijing has tried to use to encourage economic reforms that would bring to the Korean peninsula the peace and stability needed by the PRC for China's own strategic economic development. The Chinese could also use this leverage to halt Pyongyang's nuclear brinksmanship. Beijing's top concern—avoiding regional instability that could affect China's own economic growth—unfortunately keeps China from putting heavy pressure on Pyongyang out of fear that doing so could result in a collapse of the North Korean regime and massive refugee flows into the PRC. China thus is content with exerting milder pressure on North Korea to maintain periodic discussions in the Six-Party Talks aimed at achieving a political solution to the North Korean crisis. Yet as made evident by the DPRK's July 5, 2006 missile tests, Pyongyang appears willing to ignore Chinese admonitions to behave in a cooperative manner.

In contrast, growing trade and economic interaction between China and South Korea (ROK) seem to have built the friendly linkages with Seoul hoped for by Beijing. Bilateral trade has shown strong growth since the normalization of Sino-South Korean relations in 1992. Just as South Korea became a more important trade partner for China, Beijing today is Seoul's top trading partner (up from third in 1995). Of particular note is that Chinese imports from South Korea increased 600% (a surge that led to a $31.3 billion Chinese trade deficit with the ROK in 2005); these imports have helped both to fuel the South Korean economy and to create a South Korean stake in China's economic health. The ROK also has been one of the major foreign investors in the PRC for the last decade and was the third largest supplier of FDI into China in 2004 ($6.2 billion utilized). In 2001 China supplanted the United States as the primary target of South Korean FDI.[33]

As the PRC has supplanted the United States as the ROK's major trade and investment partner, Sino-South Korean economic closeness has been coupled with a growing sense of popular affinity for the PRC among many South Koreans, especially the younger generations. Many analysts have

[31] Andrew Scobell, "China and North Korea: From Comrades-in-Arms to Allies at Arm's Length," Strategic Studies Institute, U.S. Army War College, March 2004, 6–7.

[32] Scott Snyder, "China-Korea Relations: Hu Visits the Two Koreas," *Comparative Connections* 7, no. 4 January 12, 2006.

[33] Thomas G. Moore, "China's International Relations: The Economic Dimension," in *The International Relations of Northeast Asia*, ed. Samuel S. Kim (Lanham: Rowman and Littlefield, 2004), 110.

also noted that South Korea's position regarding the current North Korean nuclear crisis—using carrots more than sticks to encourage a political resolution—is often closer to Beijing's than to Washington's, suggesting that China's economic influence on the ROK is leading to greater political influence as well. Moreover, increasing interdependence is pushing the leadership in Seoul to reconsider how the ROK should respond to a U.S. request for assistance in the event that the United States and China go to war (particularly in the area around Taiwan). This potential neutralization of South Korea as a U.S. ally in the most likely scenario for U.S. military action in East Asia aligns well with Beijing's strategic goals.

Despite close economic ties, South Korea and China have over the years had some trade troubles, such as the "garlic war" of 2000 and the "kimchee war" of 2005. Seoul also has increasing worries about the closing technological gap between Chinese and South Korean producers as well as the possibility that South Koreans will be squeezed out of certain industries should this issue not be managed well. Contributing to such concerns were reports in late 2005 both that Hyundai Motors was being forced to provide technology "offsets" in order to expand the company's production lines and facilities in China and that a Chinese partner had revealed confidential data to local competitors.[34] Nevertheless, the overall thrust of Sino-South Korean relations over the past decade has been toward greater friendship and cooperation based on closer economic interdependence.

Taiwan. Arguably the neighbor with whom Beijing's strategy of encouraging economic interdependence has had the most success is Taiwan. China-Taiwan economic linkages have been intended not only to help drive Chinese economic growth but also to bind the economic health of Taiwanese industry to the PRC's economy and to decrease support for Taiwan independence among the Taiwanese people. Beijing's efforts have realized success. Despite the continuing official restrictions on direct trade between Taiwan and the PRC, trade has risen sharply over the last decade, particularly over the last five years. Since Taipei initiated the three "mini-links" in 2001 total trade has nearly tripled from $32.3 billion to almost $100 billion, particularly on the strength of Chinese imports from the island (which have tripled since 2000).[35] Taiwan is one of the PRC's top five trade partners—and the PRC's largest trade deficit is with its political rival.

---

[34] See Scott Snyder, "Hu Visits the Two Koreas"; and Scott Snyder, "China-Korea Relations: Kim Jong-il Pays Tribute to Beijing—In His Own Way," *Comparative Connections* 8, no. 1, April 12, 2006.

[35] The three "mini-links" is a term that refers to direct transport, commerce, and postal exchange between the mainland and Taiwan's two coastal islands of Jinmen (Quemoy) and Mazu (Matsu). Beijing has long called on Taipei to allow direct links between the mainland and Taiwan proper, a step which has yet to occur.

(There is significant variation in the trade data as reported by the PRC and Taiwan. See **Table 3** for a comparison of the two.)

Taiwan is also one of the PRC's major investors, with much of the island's manufacturing base having shifted across the strait to China. Although Taiwanese FDI into the PRC was $3.1 billion in 2004, Thomas Moore has noted that Taiwanese businesses are understood to be significant contributors to the large increase in FDI into China from the Virgin Islands and other tax havens (such as the Caymans and Samoa). Many analysts suggest that actual Taiwanese FDI into the PRC is double the official figures.[36]

The economic relationship remains limited primarily by the Chen Shui-bian administration's wariness of becoming economically over-dependent on the mainland. Such dependence, however, is precisely what Beijing wishes to encourage: if the Taiwanese economy becomes highly integrated with the PRC economy, the likelihood that Taiwan would declare independence—and risk severing economic ties—would be minimized. Although the first direct air linkages (charter flights to ferry businessmen during the Lunar New Year festival) between Taiwan and the PRC occurred in 2005 and were repeated in 2006, Chen has refrained from lifting the limits on the amount of capital that Taiwanese firms can invest in the PRC. In early 2006 Chen announced that the government would more effectively "manage" economic interactions across the Strait, including more closely watching for unauthorized investments in the PRC.[37] The PRC is likely to continue its wooing of Taiwanese opposition leaders (such as Lien Chan and Ma Ying-jeou of the Nationalist Party) who are in favor of loosening such restrictions and establishing direct airline and mail connections—and who might defeat whomever the DPP chooses to run in the 2008 presidential elections.

ASEAN. Another area where China has seen positive results from its efforts to promote enhanced interdependence is Southeast Asia, a region where trade with China has grown rapidly over the past decade (see **Table 4**). Collectively, China's Southeast Asian neighbors are one of China's major trade partners (fourth largest in 2005), and individually many of these countries are major trading partners of China as well. In 2005, while the original ASEAN 5 plus Vietnam all were in China's top thirty trade partners, both Singapore and Malaysia were among China's top ten trading partners. Except for Brunei (ninth), China was in the second, third, or fourth position as a trade partner for the Southeast Asian countries.

---

[36] Thomas Moore, "China's International Relations: The Economic Dimension," 111.

[37] See David G. Brown, "China-Taiwan Relations: Missed Opportunities," *Comparative Connections* 8, no. 1, April 12, 2006.

Trade data for 2005 show that Chinese pledges to share the benefits of its economic rise with Southeast Asia met with limited success. China had a small trade deficit with ASEAN ($2.5 billion) rather than the modest surplus of the previous few years, and ran trade deficits with three ASEAN countries. What is particularly interesting is that Chinese data show a much larger deficit ($19.6 billion), with China having deficits with five (rather than three) of its Southeast Asian neighbors, including all the industrialized countries in Southeast Asia except Singapore.[38] Due to the shift of manufacturing production to the PRC from around the region, Chinese imports from ASEAN consist mainly of either components for electrical machinery, electronics, and office machines (from Singapore, Thailand, and Malaysia) or natural resources and raw materials (fuels and oil from Brunei, Indonesia, and Vietnam; wood from Laos and Myanmar). Electrical machinery, electronics, and office machines comprise a large portion of China's exports to the region. The growth of China as a manufacturing hub has also spurred an increase of Southeast Asian FDI into the PRC: in 2004 all ten of the ASEAN member countries sent FDI (totaling $3.0 billion) into the PRC.[39] China in turn has invested in these neighbors, sending a total of $631.4 million in FDI to ASEAN between 1995 and 2003.[40]

Beijing has worked hard to assuage Southeast Asian fears that China's economic rise will lead to Chinese dominance. The shift of FDI away from Southeast Asia toward China has hurt the Southeast Asians, and the emerging position of China in the manufacture and assembly of consumer electronics as well as clothing presents an economic challenge to both low-tech and higher-tech industries in the region. To alleviate such fears, China has since 1997 engaged in "good neighbor" diplomacy with promises that Southeast Asians will mutually benefit from the PRC's economic development in a "win-win" situation. Toward this end, the PRC has strengthened political cooperation with ASEAN (e.g., by acceding to the Treaty of Amity and Cooperation and through active participation in ASEAN+3) and has tried to share the economic benefits of its rise through its agreement to the China-ASEAN FTA (as well as the "early harvests" program for trade in agricultural produce). Beijing also has pledged to increase Chinese investment in Southeast Asia, has provided economic aid to poorer members of ASEAN (e.g., Cambodia and Laos), and has provided China's largest-ever humanitarian assistance to countries stricken by the Boxing Day tsunami of 2004. The PRC has also increased the number

---

[38] See IMF, *DOTS Quarterly*, June 2006.

[39] *Zhongguo Tongji Nianjian*, 2005.

[40] ASEAN Secretariat, *Statistics of Foreign Direct Investment in ASEAN*, 7th ed. (Jakarta: ASEAN Secretariat, 2005), tables 2.1.2 and 2.1.3, http://www.aseasnsec.org/18177.htm.

of Chinese tourists to the Southeast Asian region as a way to spread the wealth—from 795,000 in 1995 to 3,163,000 in 2004, by which time China was the fourth largest source of foreign visitors to the ASEAN countries.[41] These Chinese efforts have paid off. The Southeast Asian countries in turn have largely tried to accommodate China's rise and have acceded to Chinese wishes on a few issues, including tolerating Beijing's desires to isolate the Dalai Lama and Falun Gong, adhering to Beijing's line on Taiwan, and even extending "market economy" status to the PRC at the WTO (a designation that will help Beijing move toward undoing one of the restrictions China accepted during WTO accession). By all appearances, increasing China's economic interdependence with Southeast Asia has helped the PRC achieve the Chinese goals of economic development and enhancing China's regional influence.

Australia. China's trade with Australia has grown sharply since 1995, with total trade rising from $5.2 billion in 1995 to $28.4 billion in 2005. In 2005 Australia was China's eleventh largest trade partner, accounting for 1.9% of Chinese trade, while China was Australia's second largest trade partner.[42] Australia serves as a source of primary goods to the Chinese economy, providing various ores (especially iron and copper) as well as wool and coal. Making Australia worthy of note here, though, is the country's recent emergence as a major supplier of Chinese energy needs. In addition to coal exports, Australia in April 2006 signed a major deal to supply uranium ore for the PRC's nuclear power plants. These plants will assist Beijing greatly in meeting China's energy needs. Additionally, the first shipments of liquid natural gas from a Sino-Australian deal were delivered by Australia in late May 2006. The two countries are looking to further enhance their bilateral trade relationship, with Beijing and Canberra having started to negotiate an FTA in April 2005. The benefits that the PRC receives from this tightening of the Sino-Australian economic relationship also extend beyond the powering of the Chinese economy: Prime Minister John Howard has let it be known that in the event of a Sino-American conflict over Taiwan the Australians might be reluctant to sacrifice their economic ties to China in order to assist the U.S. armed forces.

---

[41] "ASEAN Tourism Arrivals Statistics," http://www.aseansec.org/4952.htm (ASEAN Tourist Statistics).

[42] See "Bilateral Trade and Investment Fact Sheet" on Australian-Chinese relations, available at http://www.dfat.gov.au/geo/china/index.html.

Trade with Russia and Central Asia

China's trade with its northern and western neighbors has grown over the past decade as the Chinese economy has developed and has needed raw materials to fuel its development. For the most part, however, trade levels remain fairly low. Much of China's imports from and investment in this region focus on natural resources—primarily oil but also metal ores and cotton. In addition to the bilateral economic relations, China not only helped to create the Shanghai Cooperation Organization (SCO) in 2001 as a way to enhance political-security cooperation between China, Russia, and the Central Asian republics but also has been urging the SCO to move toward facilitating economic cooperation among its members. Nevertheless, the level of integration between China and these neighbors (except for Russia) remains far below that with the countries of Eastern Asia.

Russia. The Sino-Russian trade relationship is an interesting one, with China reliant on Russia for energy (Russia supplied 10% of China's crude oil imports in 2005)[43] as well as for modern military weaponry. Having long been one of China's top trade partners, Russia ranked ninth largest in 2005 based on Beijing's trade figures, but missed the top ten based on partner-provided data. (The PRC ranked fourth among Russia's trade partners in 2004, up from eighth in 1995.) The total value of this trade has increased nearly 400% since 1995, with strong increases occurring in both Chinese imports (oil and natural resources) and exports (clothing and electronics). Recently, Moscow has become concerned about the structure of trade between Russia and China given that Chinese imports of Russian-made machinery and electronic products have fallen drastically since 2001 while PRC imports of Russian oil, lumber, and other raw materials continue to climb.[44]

Despite this surge in the oil trade, closer energy relations between the PRC and Russia are hindered by the lack of oil pipelines connecting the two neighbors (Russian oil exports must travel by rail) and by Russia's desires to use oil (and gas) pipelines as strategic "cards" to be played between China and Japan as well as between Asia and Europe.[45] Chinese oil companies are very interested in helping to build such pipelines; the China National Petroleum Corporation (CNPC) has promised a "gift" of $400 million to Transneft (Russia's monopoly oil pipeline operator) to finance the extension

[43] David E. Sanger, "China's Oil Needs Are High on U.S. Agenda," *New York Times*, April 19, 2006, A1.

[44] See Yu Bin, "China-Russia Relations: China's Year of Russia and the Gathering Nuclear Storm," *Comparative Connections* 8, no. 1, April 12, 2006; and *Global Trade Atlas*, http://gtis.com.

[45] Yu, "China's Year of Russia and the Gathering Nuclear Storm."

of the East Siberian-Pacific Ocean (ESPO) oil pipeline to China.[46] During Russian president Vladimir Putin's March 2006 visit to Beijing, deals were signed on a feasibility study of the ESPO branch pipeline to China, on pipelines to deliver Russian gas to the PRC, and on the creation of Sino-Russian joint ventures for the exploration, production, and retailing of oil.

In addition to oil, Russia is a major source of armaments for the PRC. Since the 1990s China has purchased several hundred Su-27 and Su-30 fighters, twelve *Kilo*-class submarines, four *Sovremenny*-class destroyers, and several air defense missile systems, as well as associated weaponry for these arms. Though valued at an estimated $1.2 billion per year for the 1990s, these sales are believed to have doubled in average value since 1999.[47]

China's reliance on Russia both for oil and for much of China's modern armaments points toward some asymmetry in the relationship that could favor Russia. Yet Russia needs the arms sales to China nearly as much as the PRC needs the weaponry: without these sales, the Russian military industries would be bordering on financial trouble. Additionally, because of Moscow's games with the pipelines China is less dependent on Russia than otherwise might be the case. Moreover, the PRC's efforts to strike energy deals in Central Asia, Africa, Latin America, and elsewhere should reduce Beijing's dependence on Russian oil. The implications of this uneven interdependence are discussed below.

Central Asia. Except for trade with Kazakhstan, China's trade with the countries of Central Asia is not very significant. In 2005 China's trade with Kazakhstan, Kyrgyzstan, Tajikistan, Turkmenistan, and Uzbekistan totaled only 0.6% of China's global trade. The opportunity for future trade is growing because the Chinese have been investing in Central Asia over the last decade as Beijing has sought to access Central Asia's natural resources, particularly oil and gas. For example, China has helped build an oil pipeline from Kazakhstan to the PRC, and in October 2005 the CNPC bought PetroKazakhstan for $4.2 billion. In April 2006 China and Turkmenistan struck deals for the sale of Turkmen natural gas to the PRC starting in 2009 and for construction of a pipeline to carry the gas to China.[48] As has been noted by many analysts, these Chinese energy deals and investments in Central Asia suggest a willingness by the PRC to compete with Russia both

---

[46] "CNPC to Issue $400Mln Grant to Build ESPO Pipeline Branch to China," *Interfax*, March 22, 2006.

[47] U.S. Secretary of Defense, "Annual Report on the Military Power of the People's Republic of China, 2004," 30.

[48] For analysis of this deal, see Stephen Blank, "Turkmenistan Completes China's Triple Play in Energy," *China Brief* VI, issue 10, May 10, 2006, 6–8.

for control over the resources of the region (in order to fuel the growing Chinese economy) and for influence with these countries.[49]

Trade with South Asia

South Asia is a region comprised of Chinese friends and a former adversary, and the PRC is clearly attempting to promote interdependence as a means to enhance relations with the latter while maintaining its friendships. While China's economic interactions with the region in general have grown, Sino-Indian trade has blossomed following the PRC's 2001 accession into the WTO (and following the return to policies of engagement after the Indian and Pakistani nuclear tests of 1998). In 2005 China reported that India was the PRC's fifteenth largest trade partner, representing 1.3% of China's global trade, while in 2004 the PRC ranked third as a trading partner for both Bangladesh and India and fourth for Pakistan. During Premier Wen Jiabao's April 2005 trip to the region, China agreed to a number of steps to increase its economic ties to India, including the Five-Year Sino-Indian Economic Cooperation Program (which should boost bilateral trade to $25 billion by 2010) as well as agreements both to study the feasibility of a Regional Trading Arrangement (which could lead to the FTA that China hopes to create) and to promote cooperation in a number of issue areas (such as health care and science and technology). In Bangalore, Wen promoted high-tech integration between the two countries and called on Chinese and Indian firms to cooperate based on India's strengths in computer software and on China's assets in hardware.[50] While previously there has not been a great flow of FDI between China and India, the situation appears to be changing, particularly in the information technology (IT) sector: India's Infosys Technologies announced a planned investment of $65 million in fall 2005, and these plans are being mirrored by other Indian IT firms.[51] Chinese IT firms are also starting to head in the other direction: in 2005 Huawei Technologies announced plans to invest $60 million in a manufacturing plant in Bangalore, and TCL Corporation announced tentative plans to set up a manufacturing hub to produce televisions and other consumer goods with a $22 million investment.[52]

---

[49] For example, see Blank, "Turkmenistan Completes China's Triple Play in Energy."

[50] See Xiao Qiang, "Premier Wen's South Asian Tour Produces Abundant Results," *Renmin Ribao*, April 13, 2005; and "Construct a Bridge Leading to the Future," *People's Daily Online*, April 13, 2005.

[51] Howard W. French, "India and China Take on the World and Each Other," *New York Times*, November 8, 2005, C9.

[52] "China's Huawei to Set Up Manufacturing Plant in India," *Asia Pulse*, October 25, 2005; and "China's TCL to Put Up a Manufacturing Unit in India," *Asia Pulse*, October 25, 2005.

Sino-Indian cooperation has also moved into the energy sector: in January 2006 China and India took a step toward energy cooperation with the signing of a memorandum of understanding both to end "unrestricted" competition between their energy companies for energy sources in third countries and to cooperate in other aspects of the oil industry. The purpose of this agreement—which followed successful cooperation between India's Oil and Natural Gas Corporation (ONGC) and China's CNPC in December 2005 to buy a stake in a Syrian oilfield—was to bring greater stability to the Asian energy market (and prevent the bidding up of asset purchases).[53] The effectiveness of this MOU remains in question, however: in July, even as the Indians were requesting talks to work out the details of the cooperative agreement, a Sino-Angolan consortium led by Sinopec more than doubled ONGC's bid in order to secure a stake in Angola's Block 18.[54]

Sino-Pakistani trade relations, which remain far behind those with India (despite the PRC and Pakistan being informal security allies), are nevertheless beginning to show signs of improvement. During his April 2005 visit, Wen agreed to begin negotiations on a Sino-Pakistani FTA and to implement an "early harvests program" beginning January 1, 2006 that would help to address China's trade surplus with Pakistan. The PRC has also established many joint ventures in Pakistan, especially in the mining, telecommunications, and energy sectors. The most significant Chinese investment in Pakistan, however, is in infrastructure.[55] In 2001 Beijing agreed to help Pakistan develop the deep-harbor port at Gwadar, promising to contribute $400 million for the first stage of the project.[56] During Wen's visit in April 2005 the Chinese offered nearly $200 million in financing for the second phase of the Gwadar project, including deepening of the harbor. The Chinese also agreed to provide $350 million in financing for the Chasma-II nuclear power project and to construct 1,200 low-cost housing units at a total cost of $85 million.[57] During President Pervez Musharraf's February 2006 visit to Beijing, the two sides reached additional agreements

---

[53] Carola Hoyos, Jo Johnson, and Richard McGregor, "China and India Forge Alliance on Oil with Aim of Ending 'Mindless Rivalry,'" *Financial Times*, January 13, 2006, 1.

[54] "India's ONGC Loses Bid for Angola Block,: *Asia Pulse*, July 17, 2006.

[55] "China's Trade with Pakistan and South Asian Nations Soars," *Asia Pulse*, January 12, 2005.

[56] For analysis of the importance of this project in Sino-Pakistani relations, see John W. Garver, "The Future of the Sino-Pakistani *Entente Cordiale*," in *South Asia in 2020: Future Strategic Balances and Alliances*, ed., Michael R. Chambers (Carlisle: Strategic Studies Institute, U.S. Army War College, November 2002), 414–18.

[57] Nadeem Malik, "China to Invest in Gwadar-II Project," *The News* (Islamabad), April 5, 2005; and Mariana Baabar, "Prime Minister Wen Accorded Warm Welcome," *The News* (Islamabad), April 6, 2005.

on joint ventures worth $500 million.[58] Such deals demonstrate China's commitment to the economic health and security of Pakistan, helping Pakistan maintain a sense of balance against India and thus preserving peace and stability in this region of importance to Beijing.

Trade with the Developed West

The United States and the European Union (EU) continue to serve both as the primary export markets for China and as important sources of FDI and technology to support economic development in the PRC. The strong growth in trade has been dominated by the increase in Chinese manufactured exports to these partners (although Chinese imports have also risen), leading to ever-increasing trade surpluses for Beijing. As a result, although interdependence is increasing, so are trade frictions. Taken collectively, the EU has been the top trading partner of China since 2004 (according to Chinese trade data), and several EU member states are among the top fifteen trade partners of China; China was the EU's second largest trade partner in 2005 after the United States. Due to China's role as a global manufacturing and assembly hub, the EU—like the United States—had a significant trade imbalance with the PRC in 2005: $70.1 billion based on Chinese data, but $132 billion based on European figures.[59] European FDI flows into China have been significant over the years ($4.6 billion in 2004),[60] and Chinese firms are now starting to invest in Europe as well (e.g., Chinese electronics firm TCL bought the television and DVD player business of France's Thomson Electronics in 2004). Given that Sino-EU trade and economic interdependence is not a major factor in Asia-Pacific security, these relations will not be considered in depth in this chapter.

United States. China has used its exports to and FDI from the United States as important drivers of economic growth. Moreover, as a result of the PRC's overall economic and trade success the United States and China each rank among the other's most important economic partners. As can be seen in Table 3, Sino-American trade increased 400% between 1995 and 2005, with Chinese exports growing more strongly. As a result, China's trade surplus with the United States has increased from $8.6 billion in 1995 to $114.4 billion in 2005 according to Chinese data—or from $36.8 billion

[58] "Pakistani, Chinese Private Firms Sign US$500 MLN in Accords," *Asia Pulse*, February 23, 2006; and "Pakistan and China to Set Up Joint Investment Company," *Business Recorder*, February 26, 2006.

[59] The EU trade figure is from Morrison, "China's Economic Conditions," 9.

[60] *Zhongguo Tongji Nianjian*, 2005.

to $218.0 billion using U.S. trade data.[61] Either way, the 2005 imbalance was a record. The United States was the PRC's top trade partner in 2005, representing just under 15% of China's global trade. China moved from fifth largest trade partner for the United States in 1995 to third largest in 2005.

The United States has been one of the leading sources of FDI into China and had been the second largest source of cumulative FDI after Hong Kong until 2005, when Japan bumped the United States to the third position. In 2005 U.S. FDI into China was fifth largest at $3.1 billion, down slightly from $3.9 billion in 2004.[62] Chinese FDI into the United States, though not as significant, has received attention over the past two years. In 2004 Lenovo purchased IBM's personal computer division, and 2005 saw the failed bid by China National Offshore Oil Corporation (CNOOC) to purchase Unocal for $18.5 billion. In 1999 Haier invested $40 million in an industrial park to manufacture refrigerators and other appliances in South Carolina, and the company announced plans in April 2006 to invest a further $150 million to expand the facility.[63] Such cross-investment is enhancing the economic interdependence between the two countries.

Driven largely by the huge imbalance in trade, tensions have arisen in U.S.-China economic relations over a number of issues, including the undervaluing of the Chinese *renminbi*, piracy of intellectual property, and U.S. job losses. These issues have been a regular focus of high-level political exchanges over the past couple of years (and, in the case of intellectual piracy, for over a decade). The currency issue has received significant attention over the past year or so, in large part because it underlies the Sino-American trade imbalance. Under pressure from the United States and other countries, in July 2005 Beijing unpegged the renminbi from the U.S. dollar and revalued it by 2.1% as a first step in adjusting the renminbi's value to be more in line with what many consider to be the currency's market value. Through May 15, 2006 Beijing had allowed the currency to move a further 1.4%, crossing the 8 renminbi to the dollar mark for the first time.[64] Beijing's actions remained a far cry from what many in Washington wanted to see, leading to calls for the Bush administration to declare Beijing a currency manipulator. Based on Beijing's statement of intent to allow a gradual increase in the value of the renminbi, Treasury Secretary John

---

[61] Compare the China-reported to the partner-reported data in IMF, *DOTS Yearbook*, 1998 and *DOTS Quarterly*, June 2006.

[62] Morrison, "China's Economic Conditions," 5.

[63] "Haier to Create 1,000 Jobs in Kershaw County," *The State.Com*, http://www.thestate.com, April 11, 2006.

[64] Keith Bradsher, "China Lets Currency Rise Past Key Level," *New York Times*, May 16, 2006, C1.

Snow opted in April 2006 not to cite the Chinese government for currency manipulation, thereby avoiding a showdown over the issue.[65]

Washington's decision not to confront Beijing over the currency rate provides a prime example of the economic interdependence of the two countries. On the strength of China's trade surplus, the PRC has become the leading holder of foreign exchange reserves: in February 2006 China had accumulated $854 billion in reserves (much of it in U.S. dollars), surpassing Japan's reported stockpile of $850 billion.[66] The PRC is also the second largest holder of U.S. Treasury securities (after Japan), with an estimated $257 billion.[67] Whereas China is dependent to a large degree on U.S. imports of its goods, the United States is dependent on China's holdings of U.S. dollars and Treasury notes, holdings that have helped to keep interest rates low and fund the U.S. national budget deficit. As a result of this economic interdependence, as well as of Washington's need for Beijing's assistance in dealing with a number of international issues, unnamed U.S. officials have acknowledged that they could not be as tough on Beijing with regards to the currency issue as they might otherwise be.[68] China clearly not only has benefited economically from increasing interdependence (through the strong growth of the Chinese economy) but also has complicated decisionmaking in Washington, thereby benefiting politically as well.

Implications of Increased Chinese Interdependence for Peace and Security

China has greatly increased its integration with the international economy since the start of the economic reforms in 1978 and has strengthened its interdependence with economic partners over the past decade. Much of this interdependence is based on China's increasing involvement in global trade and in the amount of FDI that has been invested in the PRC. Outward flows of FDI from China to other countries have not achieved the same levels as the inward flows. Over the past five years, however, Beijing has been encouraging Chinese firms to invest abroad as part of China's "go out" strategy. Chinese overseas investment is increasing, and such investment will tighten China's integration with the international economy. As a result of these efforts, China has been achieving its strategic

---

[65] See Steven R. Weisman, "U.S. Won't Press China Over Yuan," *New York Times*, May 11, 2006.

[66] David Cohen, "China's Huge Currency Reserves Pique U.S. Interest," Business Week Online, March 28, 2006, http://www.businessweek.com.

[67] Morrison, "China's Economic Conditions," 14.

[68] Weisman, "U.S. Won't Press China Over Yuan."

goal of economic development, which in turn is strengthening the country's comprehensive national power and thereby fostering the PRC's drive to achieve regional and global status as a great power.

Becoming globalized and more economically interdependent with the world is very much a conscious strategy of the Chinese leadership, as laid out both in Jiang Zemin's November 2002 report to the 16th Party Congress and in the more recent white paper on "China's Peaceful Development Road." These closer economic interactions are seen as ways to improve the quality of Chinese products and to enhance the technological level of Chinese firms. Such outcomes are particularly important to Beijing as China seeks to develop more technology- and capital-intensive products (e.g., consumer electronics and even automobiles)—while at the same time trying to maintain the Chinese position in labor-intensive, low-cost goods. The PRC also sees developing webs of interdependence with neighboring countries as a way to link these countries to China not only economically but also politically, as is discussed below.

What implications does China's increasing economic interdependence with its neighbors and the United States have for peace and security in the Asia-Pacific region? Will this deepened interdependence constrain China from military adventurism? Scholars in the liberal camp of international relations theory argue that the likelihood of war will be reduced as countries become integrated into the global economy. Given the increased costs of war and the decreased benefits from war that have occurred over the last one hundred years or so, these scholars argue that a country can more cheaply gain necessary resources through trade, rather than through attempted conquest. Trading for goods and services based on an international division of labor is a mutually beneficial interaction. Moreover, by going to war against an economic partner a country would be harming its own economic interests via the destruction to its foreign market—and possibly even factories, mines, or other assets owned by that country's own corporations in the other country.[69] Recent scholarship has sought to modify and add nuance to these arguments. Dale Copeland has argued that such choices are influenced not only by the level of interdependence but also by a country's expectations that trade will continue into the future: namely that expectations of continued trade and interdependence will lead a state's policy toward peace, whereas expectations that trade will cease and that

---

[69] For arguments along these lines, see Normal Angell, *The Great Illusion*, 2nd ed. (New York: G.P. Putnam's Sons, 1933); and Richard Rosecrance, *The Rise of the Trading State* (New York: Basic Books, 1986). For a cogent summary of these arguments, see Dale C. Copeland, "Economic Interdependence and War: A Theory of Trade Expectations," *International Security* 20, no. 4 (Spring 1996): 5–41.

the country's vulnerability for resources will be exploited will lead toward conflict.[70]

The data presented above clearly shows that China has become increasingly economically interdependent: a trade-to-GDP ratio of 64%, heavy reliance on FDI inflows, and strengthening Chinese FDI outflows all point in this direction. Also clear is that China expects to continue a high volume of international trade over the next five to ten years: not only is China's economic strategy dependent upon continuing international trade, but the number of FTAs that China is negotiating and implementing (FTAs with ASEAN, Australia, Chile, and Pakistan as well as hopes for FTAs with India and even with Japan and South Korea) likewise points to expectations for continued high levels of trade. This expectation for continued high levels of trade will likely obtain even if China's trade-to-GDP ratio falls over the next five to ten years. The Chinese are sensitive to the political implications of the PRC's record trade surplus in 2005 and of the mammoth surpluses with the United States, Japan, and the EU in particular. Beijing also intends to begin shifting its development strategy away from export-led growth to growth based on increasing domestic demand and consumption.[71] For both reasons, the future should bring a diminution of the trade-to-GDP ratio but continuing high levels of international trade.

At a general level then, the predictions of liberal arguments on the pacifying effects of interdependence are likely to be borne out over the next five to ten years. The problem, however, is that China's grand strategy requires similar levels of Chinese political and security cooperation over the next five to ten years in order to maintain a peaceful and stable international environment. Thus if China's grand strategy—rather than the forces of interdependence—is what is restraining the PRC from military adventurism, this might become apparent only after China's rise is complete and Beijing shifts strategy. On the other hand, if both factors are at work then Chinese restraint over this period should be doubly assured. Consideration of China's bilateral relations may shed some light on this situation.

East Asia and the Pacific

China's efforts to use interdependence to foster improved political relations have met with much success in East Asia and the Pacific. This is particularly true with respect to South Korea, ASEAN, and Australia. As

---

[70] Copeland, "Economic Interdependence and War."

[71] See "China's Peaceful Development Road," especially Part III. See also the interview with Commerce Minister Bo Xilai in "Drive Growth by Opening Up, Seek Win-Win via Cooperation," *People's Daily*, December 28, 2005.

discussed above, these countries have largely accommodated China's rise, have developed strong political relations with the PRC, and have indicated their reluctance to jeopardize their strong economic ties to China in the event of Sino-American conflict. That the PRC would aggressively use armed force against these neighbors to resolve disputes is increasingly unlikely, as relations with these countries seem to be creating the ring of friendly countries that the Chinese grand strategy desires. The willingness of these countries to interact commercially with China also militates against economic bases for potential Chinese aggression.

This is not to say that China has "stolen" South Korea and Australia from the United States; both countries remain U.S. friends and allies, and neither country sees a zero-sum situation where friendship with China requires a loss of friendship with the United States. Nor has Southeast Asia been made into a sphere of Chinese influence, as some analysts fear. First, the increased economic integration has not led to a situation of asymmetrical interdependence in which the PRC would have strong political influence over these neighbors. In fact, as noted above, China is not the top trade partner with any of the members of ASEAN and is typically only the third or fourth largest trade partner with these countries. Second, although perceptions of China vary to some extent among the Southeast Asian countries, most still harbor lingering suspicions about China's rising power and intentions. While accommodating—and seeking to benefit economically from—the PRC's rise, Southeast Asians are following a hedge strategy of maintaining good relations with other major powers as well, particularly with the United States, Japan, and even India. ASEAN is also reluctant to cede regional leadership to China, as was demonstrated at the 2005 East Asian Summit. Rather, ASEAN plans to maintain as much control over the regional agenda as possible. Nevertheless, as a result of the enhanced interdependence with the PRC, Southeast Asian countries desire to avoid having to choose between China and the United States—particularly in the event of armed conflict over Taiwan. Given this reluctance on the part of these countries to choose sides, should U.S. and Chinese forces find themselves at war over the next five to ten years, the United States might be without access to the facilities in Singapore and other parts of Southeast Asia that the U.S. military is coming to depend on in this era of "places, not bases." This neutralization would likely extend to the U.S. alliances with Thailand and the Philippines, further hampering U.S. military operations in such a war.

Enhanced economic interdependence between China and ASEAN is spilling over into cooperation in two maritime areas as well. The first involves the Spratly Islands area of the South China Sea, where China has overlapping claims with several Southeast Asian countries. For much of the 1990s this was an area of potential conflict between the PRC and its neighbors, epitomized by China's 1995 seizure of and subsequent fortification of Mischief Reef. Competition for fish stocks, potential submarine energy sources, and geostrategic location contributed to the tensions. With aggressive implementation of the Chinese "good neighbor" since diplomacy in 1997 and the conclusion of the Declaration on Conduct of Parties in the South China Sea in 2002, however, Chinese and Philippine oil companies agreed in September 2004 to a joint exploration project in an area over which they have been in dispute; the Vietnamese joined the project in March 2005.[72] The second area of cooperation involves Chinese offers to enhance military cooperation with Indonesia, Malaysia, and Singapore to better secure the sea-lines of communication through the Strait of Malacca. Chinese dependence on this strait for the bulk of China's imported energy and for so much of China's trade leaves the PRC vulnerable should this sea-line be closed. Beijing's offers of financial and other assistance to enhance security of the strait represent another avenue of potential security consequences resulting from China's economic interdependence with Southeast Asia.

China's strategy of using economic interdependence for political and security goals is most evident with Taiwan: Beijing is attempting to tie the two economies so closely together that Taiwanese leaders cannot declare formal independence from China without destroying the island's economy.[73] The flip side, however, also becomes true: Taiwan's importance to the Chinese economy constrains Beijing's ability to use force against this political rival. (The possibility of international sanctions and the likelihood that other countries would perceive China as an aggressor may also constrain Chinese aggression against Taiwan.) Yet even Richard Rosecrance has acknowledged that for some countries (especially those in the Third World) nationalism and territoriality may trump economic interdependence.[74] Emergent Chinese nationalism—including heavy emphasis on territorial integrity— could lead the PRC to override concerns about the economic costs of armed conflict with Taiwan. For the PRC, using military force to resolve the Taiwan issue may defy economic sense but could make immense political sense, which is why such a possibility cannot be ruled out. Still, Chinese behavior

---

[72] T. J. Burgonio, "Accord on Spratlys Launches GMA's China Visit," *Philippine Daily Inquirer*, September 2, 2004; and "Philippines, China, Vietnam to Conduct Joint Marine Seismic Research in South China Sea," Xinhua News Agency, March 14, 2005.

[73] See Suisheng Zhao, "Economic Interdependence and Political Divergence: The Emerging Pattern of Relations Across the Taiwan Strait," *Journal of Contemporary China* 6, issue 15 (July 1997), 177–97.

[74] Richard Rosecrance, *The Rise of the Trading State*, 43 and 204–07.

and statements over the past half-decade suggest that China can live with the status quo and will not aggress against the island unless provoked.

The two countries in the region where the implications of China's enhanced interdependence are less positive are North Korea and Japan. In the case of North Korea, the PRC has developed asymmetrical interdependence with this ally based on the DPRK's heavy economic dependence on China. Nevertheless, the prickliness of the regime in Pyongyang, combined with Beijing's reluctance to press North Korea too hard, limits Chinese influence. Though unlikely that China would aggress against this neighbor, should there be war between the United States and the DPRK, Chinese troops might cross the border to secure Chinese interests in North Korea.

Despite the very strong economic ties that have developed between China and Japan, the growing tensions in Sino-Japanese political and security relations pose a challenge to arguments that economic interdependence will lead to cooperation and away from conflict. These tensions are generated by the legacies of World War II and by territorial disputes (including energy resources) in the East China Sea. Emerging nationalisms in both China and Japan also perceive the other country as a major long-term security threat: the Chinese fear the return of militarism as Japanese leaders seek to turn Japan into a "normal" country (with a military that can act together with those of Japan's allies for the common benefit), whereas Japanese fear China's military rise and desire for predominance in East Asia. Chinese efforts to expand their influence in the region, particularly in Southeast Asia, have forced Japan to try to play catch up by following the Chinese lead in signing ASEAN's Treaty of Amity and Cooperation or moving (haltingly) toward an FTA with ASEAN. These Sino-Japanese tensions suggest that the forces of economic interdependence can be trumped by nationalistic sentiments, competition for important resources (e.g., energy deposits in the East China Sea), and rivalry for political influence. The prospects for mutual economic benefits may, however, have helped to dampen somewhat the potential for conflict. For example, the April 2005 anti-Japanese demonstrations lasted only three weekends and, despite resulting damage to Japanese business and government properties, Japanese trade with and investment in China surged in 2005. Similarly, in mid-2005 tensions were rising over the disputed Chunxiao natural gas field in the East China Sea, but talks were commenced in an attempt to resolve the issue before the dispute got out of hand. Additionally, the Chinese—both the public and the government—appear to understand the logic of interdependence: as Peter Gries has noted, many of the Chinese demonstrators in April 2005 called for a boycott of Japanese goods in an attempt to leverage Japan's vulnerability in this interdependent relationship.[75] The Chinese leadership sought to maintain dialogue and economic interaction with Tokyo as a way to maintain the economic interdependence with Japan, thereby hoping to constrain Japanese reactions. Given that Beijing clearly sees the prospect for high levels of trade and interdependence with Japan over the next five to ten years, the arguments on interdependence might hold. Yet, Sino-Japanese rivalry and competing nationalisms bear watching as these factors could alter expectations of interdependence and thus modify the pacifying efficacy of interdependence.

Neighbors North and West

China's interdependence with Russia, Central Asia, and South Asia is growing and should continue to grow over the next five to ten years based on the continuing development of the Chinese economy as well as on increasing cross-border investments and FTA negotiations. Current levels of interdependence, however, are not terribly high, except with India and Russia. Although the traditional arguments on interdependence should lead us to worry about China's intentions toward these countries, the emergence over the last decade of peaceful and cooperative relations supports the modified argument that expectations about continued trade and interdependence are on the mark. The PRC's grand strategy also leads China toward these cooperative relations. In Central Asia, Beijing has promoted political and security cooperation both bilaterally as well as through the SCO. The PRC has pursued continued friendly relations with the countries of South Asia and has developed good relations with India. The past five years have seen an increased number of exchanges among senior Chinese and Indian political and military officials, joint military exercises, and progress on the border issue. As Beijing and New Delhi have become more comfortable with each other in the realm of geopolitics and security, the economic relationship has taken off. The PRC's desire for peace and stability on its border (so as to further China's strategic economic development) has prompted this growing interdependence with India, which should reinforce the more peaceful and secure nature of the Sino-Indian relationship. If the two countries can negotiate an FTA over the next few years, further momentum will be gained in this direction.

This general improvement in Sino-Indian relations, as well as Beijing's desire for a peaceful regional environment, prompted the Chinese leadership

---

[75] See Peter Gries, "Nationalism, Indignation and China's Japan Policy," *SAIS Review* xxv, no. 2 (Summer/Fall 2005): 105–14.

to urge restraint on the part of Islamabad during the 1999 Kargil crisis and the 2001–02 India-Pakistan border crisis (following the December 12, 2001 terrorist attack on the Indian Parliament). As China and India become increasingly interdependent, Beijing's desire for stability in South Asia may lead China to further press restraint on Pakistan in the event of any crises over the next five to ten years. This does not mean, however, that China is forsaking its ally: China's huge investments in the Gwadar project—which indirectly support Pakistan's ability to resist possible Indian military pressures through creation of a second major port away from the Indian-Pakistani border—are evidence that China continues to see its security as dependent on the existence and security of Pakistan. A strong and secure Pakistan will be able to provide a stable balance to a strong and prosperous India.

Trade and interdependence also should continue to grow between China and Russia over the next five to ten years, suggesting that relative peace and stability will obtain in the relationship between the two. This interdependence might, however, be a little fragile. Rising tensions between these two major powers is possible, based on some combination of: (a) a reduction in Chinese reliance on Russian energy as Beijing diversifies its supplies, (b) intensified Russian unease if the composition of trade continues to skew such that Moscow is essentially a supplier of raw materials for China while the PRC exports higher cost manufactured goods, and (c) diminished Chinese reliance on Russian arms if the PLA is able to resolve some of its quality problems with indigenous weapons production. Tensions between China and Russia might also increase as the PRC increasingly becomes a major economic partner of several Central Asian countries (particularly Kazakhstan, Kyrgyzstan, and Uzbekistan). Russian efforts to use monopolies on energy pipelines out of the Central Asian region for political influence in these former Soviet republics will be undermined as Chinese energy companies move in. With China rapidly becoming a key player in the new "great game" in Central Asia, Sino-Russian rivalry could develop. The existence of the SCO and Beijing's desire to maintain peace and stability around China's periphery could lead to a Sino-Russian condominium rather than rivalry in the region—much like China and India have recently agreed to avoid such competition in their energy deals.

Implications for the United States

The depth of the Sino-American economic interdependence described above and the expectations that these high levels of trade will continue suggest the improbability that either side will instigate conflict with the other anytime during the next five to ten years; the economic costs of such a conflict will force national leaders to think long and hard before such an engagement. China has embraced globalization and interdependence as its path to strategic economic development, which will provide Beijing the means to maintain domestic stability, increase national wealth, and achieve regional and global great power status. China benefits from the international economic order constructed and maintained by the United States; despite suggesting the need to "democratize international relations" in order to reduce U.S. dominance and to give more countries a say in international decisionmaking, China has given no indication that the PRC desires to overturn and radically reshape this system.[76] Moreover, Beijing recognizes the current economic and military gaps that exist between the United States and China and understands the need to work within the current unipolar system.

Nevertheless, the possibility of conflict cannot be ruled out. One area of possible conflict is the Korean peninsula. If the North Korean nuclear crisis goes horribly wrong and the United States invades the North, the PLA quite possibly might also intervene to protect Chinese interests. A second potential location of Sino-American conflict is the East China Sea. In this scenario, Sino-Japanese jostling over disputed territory or maritime areas and competition for scarce energy supplies, paired with the strong nationalism in both countries, could lead to conflict. Were this to occur, the United States could be pulled into the conflict on the side of its ally. The third and perhaps most likely scenario involves Taiwan. Should the PRC attack Taiwan—and should Washington decide that the attack was unprovoked—the United States would likely honor its commitment to help defend the island. Economic interdependence will not prevent these conflicts from occurring, since the security issues leading to Sino-American conflict in each of these scenarios would likely trump the economic considerations.[77] Economic interdependence would, however, affect each of these conflicts. The reasons are twofold. The first is that because of the interdependence that has emerged between China and its neighbors in the Asia-Pacific and the desires of these countries not to be forced to choose between China and the United States in the even of conflict, Beijing may have neutralized the U.S. ability to draw on facilities and support from South Korea, ASEAN, and even Australia in the prosecution of such armed

---

[76] Moore, "Chinese Foreign Policy in the Age of Globalization."

[77] For China, these interests would include border security, national identity, territorial sovereignty, and perhaps the drive for scarce resources; for the United States, these interests would include halting nuclear proliferation, defense of an ally or major trade partner, and resisting aggression by a rising great power.

conflicts. Second, although not able to stop the conflict from occurring, the costs associated with economic interdependence may cause the second mover in the conflict to pause long enough to allow the first mover time to gain a greater military advantage; realization of this possibility could affect how both sides prosecute the conflict.

Conclusion and Policy Implications

Economic interdependence is a key element of China's grand strategy, and Beijing's pursuit of economic development through trade is intended to bring China both power and plenty. Developing the Chinese economy will increase both the wealth of the nation and the personal wealth of the Chinese people, providing the Communist Party leadership with the resources necessary to maintain the legitimacy of their rule and the stability of the country. Economic development will also serve as the base for China's growth into a great power both regionally and globally, as economic power will be convertible into political influence and military capabilities.

Beijing is also using interdependence to link other countries to the PRC in friendly relations that will promote not only economic cooperation but also political and security cooperation. Whether China is becoming similarly restrained from military adventurism due to interdependence is not quite clear. While there is some evidence to support such a view, the real causal factor may be Chinese self-restraint based on its grand strategy. That both factors appear to point toward Chinese restraint over the next five to ten years is good news both for the United States and for China's neighbors.

What about the longer term? The rise of Japan and West Germany to international prominence after World War II by emphasizing trade and economics and eschewing military power (under the U.S. security umbrella) led to the notion of the "trading state."[78] China's rise suggests that this paradigm for emerging great powers may have to be left behind with the Cold War era. While the PRC is certainly engaging in international trade as the path to economic development and great power status, Beijing is also following the more traditional route of developing military power to match China's economic power. As enunciated both in Jiang Zemin's report to the 16th Party Congress in 2002 and in China's defense white papers of 2002 and 2004, China seeks to develop comprehensive national power, which marries economic and military capabilities for overall political influence. The growth of Chinese military capabilities, however, is not occurring at a break-neck pace: military modernization is to take place in line with

---

[78] Rosecrance, *The Rise of the Trading State.*

China's "national conditions," so that the PRC does not follow the fate of the Soviet Union, which built a military apparatus that the economy could not sustain.[79] When this process is completed, the United States may face a superpower peer with more staying power than the Soviet Union had.

Yet even as China is following the more traditional path for the rise of a new great power, the PRC is rising both in an international system that is more institutionalized and in an international economy that is more marketized than was the case for previous rising great powers. The institutionalization of the international system means that states agree to abide by the norms and rules of the institutions of which they are members. Available evidence suggests that China has been participating well in and abiding by the norms and rules of the institutions that Beijing has joined.[80] Moreover, China has supported the creation of new regional institutions in East Asia. In the more marketized international economy, states are pushed away from mercantilist trading practices toward more liberal, free market trading behavior. Though still in transition toward a true market economy at home, China does not appear to be engaging in a mercantilist search for "colonies" as markets or for resources. Rather, the PRC appears to be living up to the rules of the liberal international economic system and largely appears to be living up to its WTO accession commitments. Moreover, Beijing is actively negotiating FTAs with regional neighbors and other countries (e.g., Chile) and has proposed the creation of even more such agreements. Adherence to the rules of both international society and the international economy may dampen fears of China's rise as a more traditional great power.

Over the next five to ten years, while Beijing focuses on developing its economy during this "period of strategic opportunity," China's current behavior is likely to continue. The United States and the international community should encourage China along this path, as such behavior is in conformity with Washington's desire to engage Beijing as a "stakeholder" in the international system. Beyond this period, as China's economic power, military capabilities, and political influence expand, the PRC may develop new interests at odds with the current international system and more actively seek to change the current norms and rules. The more China is engaged and has a stake in today's system and its accompanying norms and

---

[79] "China's National Defense in 2004," Section II.

[80] Margaret M. Pearson, "The Major Multilateral Economic Institutions Engage China," and Alastair Iain Johnston and Paul Evans, "China's Engagement with Multilateral Security Institutions," both in *Engaging China: The Management of an Emerging Power*, ed. Alastair Iain Johnston and Robert S. Ross (London and New York: Routledge, 1999).

rules, the less likely the scenario of a revisionist China emerging in ten to fifteen years becomes.

The one possible exception to this characterization of Chinese behavior is Beijing's more mercantilist drive for energy security. The Chinese leadership is very concerned about the PRC's access to stable and secure sources of energy to power China's economic growth. To cope with these insecurities, Chinese oil companies are working with the assistance of PRC diplomats to gain long-term supply contracts and equity stakes in oil and gas fields—and have targeted Central Asia, Africa, and Latin America in an effort to diversify their sources. Moreover, the Chinese are making these deals in some instances with countries that Washington deems to be unsavory (such as Sudan, Myanmar, Iran, and even Venezuela). Washington's fear is that by striking these equity deals and long-term supply contracts (and doing so on occasion with anti-U.S. regimes), China is seeking to "lock up" energy supplies in ways that will further drive up the price of energy. As Kenneth Lieberthal and Mikkal Herberg have recently argued, however, "Chinese national oil companies have equity oil production overseas equal to only 15% of Chinese oil imports—a far cry from the perception. In fact, China must rely on the market for the vast majority of its oil imports." Moreover, Lieberthal and Herberg's analysis of energy policymaking in Beijing reveals that "although the Chinese leadership has a mercantilist bent in their approach to energy, the Chinese national oil companies themselves are often driven by commercial interests as much as they are by state interests."[81] To the extent that the Chinese continue to pursue this mercantilist approach to energy resources, there is the potential that China's behavior could lead to conflict with the United States—or Japan or Russia. If the Chinese national oil companies can be somehow integrated into the global economy, however, then China's more commercial interests may prevail.

---

[81] Lieberthal and Herberg, "China's Search for Energy Security," 13–19.

EXECUTIVE SUMMARY

This chapter examines the three significant challenges facing Japan: to restore sustained economic growth, to maintain the positive momentum that has developed in relations with the U.S., and to deepen economic interdependence while improving security relations in its region.

MAIN ARGUMENT:

- Japan finally appears poised to return to sustained economic growth. Growth depends on an end to deflationary expectations, the stimulation of domestic demand, and continued progress in economic reform.

- Though Japan has drawn closer to the U.S. in the past five years, even deeper relations with the U.S. may raise expectations unreasonably and may complicate Japan's regional relationships.

- Over the past decade Japan has become more integrated economically into East Asia; at the same time, however, Japan's political and security relations with key neighbors have worsened.

- Regional economic interdependence is, on balance, a positive factor in regional security but cannot be counted on to resolve regional conflicts or to forestall rivalry between Japan and China.

POLICY IMPLICATIONS:

- As Japanese economic growth is in the national security interest of the U.S., Washington would benefit from encouraging continued economic reform.

- The maintenance of a healthy and stable U.S. economy has a significant positive impact on regional stability in East Asia.

- The U.S. is a pivotal player in the China-Japan rivalry. A U.S.-Japanese alliance that is too aggressive alarms China, whereas one that is too weak raises abandonment anxieties in Japan.

- Given the high economic and security stakes, remaining deeply engaged in East Asia is critical for the U.S., notwithstanding the formidable challenges the country faces elsewhere in the world.

Back to Normal? The Promise and Pitfalls of Japan's Economic Integration

Michael Mastanduno

Japanese government officials might understandably look back on the Cold War with at least some degree of nostalgia. During this time of serious international tension, Japan nonetheless did enjoy remarkable economic success and prosperity, a high degree of security, and clarity in terms of its international identity. Japan, like West Germany, was forced by historical circumstance to accept the limited diplomatic and military role of a "civilian power." Japan made a virtue of necessity by maximizing its wealth and competitive position in the world economy.

The post-Cold War era has posed a different set of challenges for Japan. Since 1990 the Japanese economy has moved from success to stagnation, and international observers have shifted from admiring what went right to puzzling over what went wrong. In the area of security, the stable and predictable tensions of the Cold War have been replaced by greater uncertainty and fluidity. Japan's East Asian neighborhood is a troubled one, characterized by an insecure rising power, a provocative and desperate smaller power, unresolved Cold War conflicts, and a political atmosphere of suspicion and resentment that continues to linger some sixty years after World War II. Tokyo retains a close security relationship with Washington, but the United States is now a unipolar power, unconstrained by any peer competitor and fashioning more unilaterally a provocative strategy for meeting threats and transforming world politics.

Michael Mastanduno (PhD, Princeton University) is Nelson A. Rockefeller Professor of Government and Associate Dean for the Social Sciences at Dartmouth College. He can be reached at <michael. mastanduno@dartmouth.edu>.

The author would like to thank Maia Fedyszyn for research assistance and the external referees for their comments on earlier drafts.

Japan faces three important and related challenges, the resolution of which will shape its future. The first concerns the domestic economy: will Japan finally return to steady economic growth? Signs of the long-awaited transition have begun to appear in the last two years. Sustained growth requires Tokyo both to stimulate domestic demand and to continue reforms as Japan struggles to shed the consequences of the so-called bubble economy of the late 1980s. Steady economic growth not only matters for Japan's prosperity but also has profound implications for Japan's role in regional and global security.

The second challenge involves relations with the United States. In the wake of the Cold War, Japan has staked its security on the continuity of a close relationship with the United States. As Washington's demands have increased, Tokyo has done more in order to be an effective and reliable security partner. This dynamic has been especially true over the past five years, during which Japan, under the leadership of Prime Minister Junichiro Koizumi, seems to be working to become the "Great Britain" of the Pacific—a loyal and privileged ally that works side by side with the United States bilaterally, regionally, and even globally.[1] Although particular economic frictions continue to arise, the overall relationship (both economic and security) is now characterized more by cooperation than by conflict. Though beneficial to Japan, the ever-closer relationship with the United States carries risks for Japan as well. On the one hand, Japan must be careful not to raise bilateral expectations that the Japanese are unable to fulfill, whether for political or constitutional reasons. Such a situation might incur U.S. resentment or lead to mutual disappointment in what both sides are touting as a transformed partnership. On the other hand, Tokyo must assure that closer relations with the United States do not worsen relations with Japan's own neighbors, in particular China.

The third challenge concerns regional politics and Japan's role within East Asia. In the early 1990s Aaron Friedberg made the prominent observation that East Asia, in contrast to Europe, might be "ripe for rivalry" after the Cold War.[2] In the subsequent decade, Japan's regional relationships, particularly with China and South Korea, have deteriorated. Relations with North Korea have worsened even more significantly. At the same time, Japan's regional economic ties have strengthened. Can the increase in economic interdependence help to resolve regional security tensions? The

---

[1] The Japan-Britain comparison has been raised in various contexts, including in the report by the influential Armitage Commission, *The United States and Japan: Advancing Toward a Mature Partnership*, INSS Special Report (Washington, D.C.: Institute for National Strategic Studies, National Defense University, October 11, 2000).

[2] Aaron Friedberg, "Ripe for Rivalry: Prospects for Peace in a Multipolar Asia," *International Security* 18, no. 3 (Winter 1993–94): 5–33.

challenge for Japan is to use positive economic relationships to improve security outcomes—and to prevent security tensions from spilling over and threatening deepening regional economic ties.

This chapter explores each of these three areas of challenge and the related implications for stability in East Asia. Japan is a critical player in the region. A return to economic growth for Japan would bring economic benefits to other actors as well as help to mitigate regional tensions. Japan's strengthening relationship with the United States can similarly be a source of stability—as long as the stronger bilateral alliance is not directed provocatively at China. In the short term, North Korea poses a clear threat to Japanese and regional security; over the longer term, the deteriorating relationship and emerging competition between Japan and China likely will be the most pressing problem for regional stability. Although regional economic interdependence is growing and is a positive force for stability, this alone will not be sufficient to resolve the underlying tensions in relations between Japan and Japan's neighbors. A concluding section considers implications for the United States and the role the United States might play in helping to promote positive outcomes for Japan and the region.

Japan's Economy: Are Happy Days Here Again?

A statistical snapshot of contemporary Japan depicts a prosperous, stable and sophisticated economy with significant links to the global economy. Japan's population in 2003 was 128 million, a bit less than half of the United States' population and one-tenth of China's.[3] Japan ranks near the top of the developed world in quality-of-life indicators such as life expectancy (82 years) and adult literacy (99%). With a GDP of roughly $4 trillion—40% of the United States' GDP and three times China's—Japan is the world's second largest economy.[4] As of 2003, Japan was the world's fourth largest exporter, with a 6% share of world exports, and possessed the world's largest current account balance at $112 billion. Japan exports industrial and technology-intensive goods, with machinery (electrical and non-electrical) and transportation equipment accounting for almost 75% of exports. Japan's principal imports include mineral fuels, chemicals, food, and raw materials; machinery and equipment imports have increased as well as Japanese firms have developed global production networks. In 2003

---

[3] Figures in this paragraph are taken from *The Economist Pocket World in Figures*, 2005 ed. (London: Profile Books, 2005); and *Statistical Handbook of Japan*, ed. Statistical Research and Training Institute (Statistics Bureau, 2005), 125–26.

[4] In terms of purchasing power parity (PPP), the Chinese economy is second largest and the Japanese economy is third. *Pocket World in Figures*, 2005 ed., 26.

the United States was Japan's main export destination, accounting for 30% of Japan's overseas sales, while China, South Korea, Taiwan, and Hong Kong accounted for an additional 30%. Japan's two largest sources of imports were China (18%) and the United States (17%).

This snapshot only hints at the key changes taking place over time both in the Japanese economy and its relation to the world economy. Over the past two decades Japan has become less dependent on trade with the United States and more meaningfully integrated into the burgeoning regional economy of East Asia. Japan has deepened interdependence with China even as China has begun to surpass Japan as the economic powerhouse of the region. (These economic developments and their security implications are discussed in section three below.) Equally important developments have occurred in the Japanese domestic economy. The key turning point came in the early 1990s as Japan made an unfortunate transition from steady growth to an economic stagnation that has lasted some fifteen years.

Japan's economic performance between 1950 and 1990 is indeed a "miracle." Japanese GDP grew at roughly 9% annually between 1950 and 1970, about double the average annual growth rate for the industrialized West. During the inflation-ridden 1970s, Japan managed to average nearly 5% growth while its economic peers struggled to maintain 3%. Japan continued to outpace OECD countries during the 1980s and by the end of that decade already possessed the world's second largest economy—a remarkable achievement for a resource-poor island economy that had been thoroughly destroyed during World War II.

Enjoying not only growth but the economic diversification that accompanies development, Japan appeared to have mastered a new model of capitalism—developmental capitalism—that other Asian developing countries saw fit to emulate.[5] Industrial success bred financial success; at the beginning of the 1990s Japan was the world's leading foreign aid donor and second-largest contributor to the International Monetary Fund (IMF).[6]

The postwar economic miracle rested on three foundations—domestic, international, and strategic. First, Japan's domestic political and social system was organized to maximize the interests of producers. The Liberal Democratic Party (LDP) provided a stable, pro-business environment for some 35 years upon taking power in 1955. Politicians left economic management in the capable hands of Japan's permanent bureaucracy, in particular the powerful Ministry of International Trade and Industry

---

[5] The World Bank, *The East Asian Miracle: Economic Growth and Public Policy* (New York: Oxford University Press, 1993); and Chalmers Johnson, *MITI and the Japanese Miracle: The Growth of Japanese Industrial Policy, 1920-1975* (Stanford: Stanford University Press, 1982).

[6] *Statistical Handbook of Japan*, 2005, 136.

(MITI) and Ministry of Finance (MOF). Large corporations along with their suppliers and affiliated firms were integrated vertically into *keiretsu*, or industrial groupings, whose members held each other's stock and together coordinated the group's overall business strategies. The largest corporations and banks worked closely with and accepted "administrative guidance" from government officials and provided lifetime employment benefits to their own workforces. The remarkably high savings rate of the Japanese public facilitated capital accumulation and business investment.[7]

Second, Japan was a great beneficiary of the open world economy promoted by the United States after World War II. In the interest of Japanese economic recovery, Washington provided preferential access to Japanese exports in the U.S. market and worked to facilitate Japanese entry into markets in Western Europe and Southeast Asia as well.[8] With the U.S. nuclear and security umbrella, Japanese defense spending could remain relatively modest relative to GDP, leaving Japan free to focus on the pursuit of economic competitiveness.

The third foundation of the economic miracle was the successful long-term strategy of export-led growth. Japan was able to act as a mercantilist state in a liberalizing world economy. The state served as a gatekeeper, regulating relations between the Japanese and world economy with a consistent focus on maximizing export competitiveness. Monetary authorities maintained an undervalued yen until the 1980s, and MITI practiced the industrial policy of "picking winners"—subsidizing and promoting leading sectors of economic activity such as automobiles in the 1960s and computers and electronics in the 1970s and 1980s.[9]

What Went Wrong?

The irony is that just as the United States and Western Europe came to fully appreciate—and fear—the economic power of Japan, that power began to wane. In retrospect, the evidence is clear that by 1990 Japan had entered an economic crisis, one that would last some fifteen years and shatter the image of Japan as the global economic frontrunner.

Trouble began as Japan accumulated massive wealth by the mid-1980s. As the yen began to rise, Japan's imports became cheaper while Japanese

[7] See Karel Van Wolferen, *The Enigma of Japanese Power* (New York: Knopf, 1989); and Clyde V. Prestowitz, Jr., *Trading Places: How We Are Giving Our Future to Japan and How to Reclaim It*, 2nd ed. (New York: Basic Books, 1990).

[8] Michael Schaller, *Altered States: The United States and Japan Since the Occupation* (New York: Oxford University Press, 1997).

[9] Maria Anchordoguy, *Computers, Inc.: Japan's Challenge to IBM* (Cambridge: Harvard University Press, 1989).

exports, though now more expensive, continued to surge on global markets before foreign customers made the expected adjustments to higher prices. Japan's central bank, fearing the eventual growth-retarding effects of currency appreciation, eased the money supply. With so much capital available, Japanese firms over-invested while land and stock prices rose precipitously, creating Japan's infamous bubble economy.

The bubble burst in the early 1990s. Monetary authorities overcorrected and tightened the money supply just as economic recession in the West and foreign adjustments to the stronger yen sapped Japanese export performance. Economic growth halted abruptly, leading to a classic economic hangover. Land and stock prices crashed, businesses faced overcapacity, and banks were saddled with bad loans

If the bubble economy precipitated the crisis, Japan's response exacerbated and prolonged it. Recovery required flexibility, but the Japanese economy proved inflexible. Corporations and industrial groupings were slow to shed unneeded labor, and government officials were reluctant to allow overexposed banks to fail. Japan's envied industrial policy seemed to work well when Japan was catching up to existing market leaders but was less effective once the country found itself at the technological frontier.[10] Japan's standard response to slowdowns in prior decades—i.e., increased exports— no longer worked due to the strong yen and the political intolerance that had developed in the West after years of Japanese current account surpluses. Recovery required new thinking, but Japanese politicians tended to be caretakers rather than visionaries, and Japan's permanent bureaucracy was better suited to implement an existing strategy than to devise a new one.

The government responded throughout the 1990s with monetary and fiscal policy, but these efforts were largely frustrated. Government spending as a percentage of GDP almost doubled between 1996 and 2001. This effort had some stimulating effect but seemed more to serve vested interests— construction firms, workers and companies in regulated industries, and local communities with political clout—than to create a cycle of self-sustaining growth.[11] In order to encourage spending, monetary authorities cut interest rates essentially to zero; Japanese consumers, long conditioned to save, seemed unwilling now to reverse course and spend, particularly in an atmosphere of economic uncertainty. Japan's household savings rate increased by 6% between 1997 and 2002, and the annual inflation rate was a

---

[10] Scott Callon, *Divided Sun: MITI and the Breakdown of Japanese High Tech Industrial Policy* (Stanford: Stanford University Press, 1995).

[11] William K. Black, "The Dango Tango: Why Corruption Blocks Real Reform in Japan," *Business Ethics Quarterly* 14, no. 4 (2004): 603–23.

negative 0.6%, even though the average annual increase in the money supply (M1) was a *positive* 11.2%.[12]

Revival at Last?

Since 2002, the economic picture has brightened. Real GDP growth picked up from an average of 0.9% between 1992 and 2002 to 1.4% in 2003, 2.6% in 2004, and an estimated 2.4% in 2005.[13] Until 2004 this recovery appeared fragile, being based largely on a boom in Japan's exports to China, primarily in the form of industrial machinery to equip China's rapidly growing production and export activity. Japanese exports to China as a percentage of total exports increased sharply from 9.6% in 2002 to 13.1% in 2004.[14] Although the emphasis may have shifted in terms of destination, the pattern was familiar—Japan relying on the export sector to generate recovery. To break the deflationary cycle, however, requires an increase in domestic demand.

Strong signs of domestic-led growth began to show by 2004, suggesting that this time self-sustaining recovery may be for real. The key indicator is found in Japan's labor markets. During the long recession, and in keeping with Japan's social consensus, many large companies were reluctant to hire permanent workers but also chose not to shed labor, asking existing workers to accept pay cuts instead.[15] Japanese firms did, however, hire part-time and temporary workers in significant numbers and at much lower cost than regular full-time workers.[16] Workers, whether full- or part-time, were forced to accept lower wages, which made it difficult for the consumer sector to generate domestic demand. Lower labor costs, however, combined with the surge in exports to China and eventually helped to increase Japanese corporate profits. As corporations have rebounded, they have begun once again to hire workers on a full-time basis and to pay higher wages. 2005 marked the first year since 1997 during which Japan experienced an overall

---

[12] *Pocket Book in Figures*, 2005 ed., 168.

[13] "Country Report: Japan," The Economist Intelligence Unit, December 2005, 5.

[14] "Country Report: Japan, The Economist Intelligence Unit; and *Pocket Book in Figures*, 2005 ed., 169.

[15] Bill Emmott, "The Sun Also Rises," *The Economist*, October 8, 2005. It is revealing that Japan's average annual unemployment rate between 1995 and 2002 was 4.2%; the United States, with a GDP that grew more than three times more rapidly, had an average unemployment rate of 4.9%.

[16] Ibid. In 1990 part-time workers accounted for 19% of the Japanese workforce; by 2005, they accounted for almost 30%—20 million out of 65 million total workers. To cite one specific example, in 2005 Canon employed 70% of its Japanese workforce as non-permanent. Ten years earlier, the figure was 10%.

growth in real wages.[17] Wage growth is the key to self-sustaining recovery; as wages rise, people spend more and companies produce more. As profits rise, corporations demand more labor and pay higher wages, reinforcing the virtuous cycle. With economic growth reaching an annualized 5% during the fourth quarter of 2005, this cycle appears underway in Japan.

Other indicators similarly point away from deflation and toward self-sustaining growth. By late 2005, Japanese businesses reported that excess capacity—a drag on investment and growth for over a decade—had largely disappeared. Capital spending in 2005 grew at 7.7%; consumer spending, 2.1%.[18] The portion of non-performing loans in Japanese bank portfolios reached over 40% in 2001; by 2004, this portion was under 20%.[19] In October 2005 the Bank of Japan reported that with core prices expected to continue to rise through 2007, the bank would have the opportunity to decrease the money supply as the prospect of deflation recedes.[20]

If Japan has finally turned the corner, what might be the explanation? Japan's economy never endured a decisive "shock therapy" similar to Thatcher's Britain during the 1980s or Yeltsin's Russia in the early 1990s. Nor did Japan's economy respond to recession with the flexibility of the United States' more unregulated and less socially forgiving style of capitalism. Rather, Japan appears to have adjusted slowly and incrementally over fifteen years. The long "lost decade" of the 1990s was actually one of gradual but steady progress in regulatory reform. Adjustments to employment law enabled firms to hire temporary workers. Gradually acknowledging the mountain of bad debt, banks slowly worked the debt off. The "big bang" financial reform of 1998 strengthened government supervision of financial institutions and their accounting practices. Corporate takeovers—a standard way to rationalize excess capacity but one long considered taboo in Japanese political economy—slowly became an accepted activity, even to the point of allowing foreign firms to participate. The new trend was captured by French auto maker Renault's 1999 purchase of a controlling stake in Nissan, which included the installation of a cost-cutting foreigner, Carlos Ghosn, as chief operating officer.[21] In 1992, 40% of the equity in Japanese companies was in the form of cross shareholdings belonging to other, affiliated Japanese

---

[17] Sebastian Moffett, "In Japan, Wages are Fueling Growth," *Wall Street Journal*, February 16, 2006, A6; and Emmott, "The Sun Also Rises."

[18] "Japan's June Consumer Sentiment Falls on Stocks Drop," *Bloomberg News*, July 11, 2005, http://www.bloomberg.com.

[19] Emmott, "The Sun Also Rises," 5.

[20] Economist Intelligence Unit, "Country Report: Japan," 9. For the first time in six years, the Bank of Japan raised interest rates in July 2006.

[21] Ibid., 32.

companies, and only 6% was held by foreign investors. By 2004, cross shareholdings represented only 24%, and the foreign portion had increased to 22%. Relative to that of the United States, the Japanese economy is still regulated and insulated, but the perceptible if incremental trend over time has been to reduce the role of the state, allowing market forces to operate in the interest of greater efficiency.

The most dramatic political indicator of the commitment to reform is Koizumi's postal initiative. Japan's postal system, which in the postwar era has collected and allocated massive amounts of private capital (usually with as much political as economic logic), is symbolic of Japan's traditional, state-led growth strategy.[22] Koizumi staked his political future on the effort to privatize the system. His postal reform legislation barely passed the lower house of the Diet in July 2005 and was defeated in the upper house in August 2005. Koizumi called for an election in September 2005 to serve, in effect, as a referendum on the government's continued commitment to reform. His gamble paid off as the LDP earned a decisive victory, capturing 296 of 480 seats in the Diet—a gain of 84 since the prior election in 2003.[23] With small gains made by New Komeito, the LDP's coalition partner, the LDP now enjoys a sufficient majority in the legislature to override vetoes and essentially govern with minimal resistance from the main opposition party, the Democratic Party of Japan (DPJ), which for now is in political disarray.

The prospects for continued economic reform, and thus for sustained growth, appear promising over the next several years. Although Koizumi is scheduled in accordance with party rules to step down in September 2006, he has established economic reform as the priority agenda of the once again dominant LDP. The postal reform victory should also carry political momentum into the next phase of reform, including the restructuring and privatization of eight state-owned financial institutions.

Japan's path may be fairly clear, yet is not without significant obstacles. In the short term, sustained growth will require effective management of monetary and fiscal policy. After years of providing massive amounts of liquidity, the Bank of Japan is eager for the chance to move interest rates higher and slow the growth of the money supply. After years of government spending in an effort to revive the economy, Japanese fiscal authorities face sizable fiscal deficits and seek opportunities to raise taxes and lower public sector consumption. The risk is that either monetary or fiscal policy, or

---

[22] See Johnson, *MITI and the Japanese Miracle*; and Emmott, "The Sun Also Rises," 10, whose estimates indicate that the postal system takes in about 30% of Japanese personal deposits and 40% of life insurance payments.

[23] Economic Intelligence Unit, "Country Report: Japan," 13.

both, will be tightened prematurely or too severely, choking off the fragile shoots of economic growth that have recently appeared. High oil prices are an additional complicating factor that could discourage investment and production in energy-sensitive sectors such as steel, automobiles, and chemicals.

The longer-term and more fundamental challenge to Japanese economic growth is demographic. The Ministry of Health, Labor, and Welfare anticipates that the Japanese workforce will decline by 0.7% each year, and total population could fall from 128 million to 100 million by the middle of the century.[24] A shrinking workforce implies a more pressing national need for women to take employment; having more working women, however, is likely to exacerbate the demographic challenge by resulting in less children per family. Instead of extricating the country from fiscal distress, the Japanese state might end up having to increase outlays to provide more child care for working families just as more health and retirement care provisions are required for the aging Japanese population. One obvious remedy to the labor challenge is immigration. Japan, however, is not the United States; Japan's commitment to national homogeneity has brought with it a resistance to immigration on a meaningful scale. Barring changes to this pattern, economic reform takes on even greater significance. The less workers there are the more critical is the need to increase the productivity or output per worker, a shift that will only come as the economy continues to move in the direction of greater flexibility in response to market signals.

Japan and the United States: An Ever-Closer Partnership?

Mike Mansfield, U.S. Ambassador to Japan during the Cold War, famously repeated the mantra that the U.S.-Japan relationship was "the most important bilateral relationship in the world, bar none." Japan was the cornerstone of U.S. strategy in Asia—a stable, democratic ally whose geographic location was crucial both for the containment of the Soviet Union in the North Pacific and the projection of U.S. power in the wider East Asian region.[25] Mansfield's statement was all the more true for Japan. The relationship with the United States provided security protection when Japan was constrained from fully providing its own, provided markets and

---

[24] Emmott, "The Sun Also Rises," 16.

[25] Paul Giarra, "U.S. Bases in Japan: Historical Background and Innovative Approaches to Maintaining Strategic Presence," in *The US-Japan Alliance: Past, Present, and Future*, ed. Michael J. Green and Patrick M. Cronin (New York: Council on Foreign Relations, 1999), 114–38.

access to supply needed for economic recovery, and helped to promote Japan's new national identity as a civilian power within a community of democratic nations. Although Japanese government officials may have preferred terms like "comprehensive security" and "omnidirectional foreign policy" to characterize their postwar geopolitical orientation, the obvious center of gravity in Japanese grand strategy was the relationship with the United States.

That postwar relationship was mutually beneficial yet asymmetrical. The asymmetry existed in the formal sense that the bilateral treaty signed in 1951 obliged the United States to come to the defense of Japan, but not vice versa. Also operative in the political sense was that the United States tacitly reserved the right to set the bilateral agenda, to act unilaterally, and to modify the terms of the bilateral deal as Washington saw fit. Alliance theory suggests that the more dependent partner in an asymmetrical relationship will be forced to manage the twin fears of abandonment and entrapment.[26] The dependent power may also face the problem of resentment or the sense in the stronger power that the weaker is free riding, shirking its fair share of the cost of alliance obligations.

For Japan, the entrapment problem has surfaced periodically, such as near the end of the Vietnam War, when Japanese officials worried that the United States might press Japan to join the fight, or more recently, when Japan feared being dragged into a supporting role in a military conflict in the Taiwan Strait or on the Korean Peninsula.[27] The far more pressing problems for Japan have been dealing with the fear of abandonment prompted by periodic changes in U.S geopolitical strategy and managing the resentment generated by the pressures of U.S. domestic politics. Not surprisingly, the twists and turns in U.S. domestic politics and foreign policy have typically left Japanese officials frustrated and in turn resentful of the United States.[28] Over time, however, Japan's response to these alliance dilemmas has been not to seek out serious alternatives to dependence on the United States but to draw even closer both diplomatically and strategically.[29]

---

[26] See Glenn Snyder, *Alliance Politics* (Ithaca: Cornell University Press, 1997). With special reference to East Asia, see Victor Cha, *Alignment Despite Antagonism: The U.S.-Korea-Japan Security Triangle* (Stanford: Stanford University Press, 1999); and "Abandonment, Entrapment, and Neoclassical Realism in Asia," *International Studies Quarterly* 44 (2000): 261–87.

[27] Walter LaFeber, *The Clash* (New York: W. W. Norton, 1997), 348–49.

[28] Michael Mastanduno, "U.S. Foreign Policy and the Pragmatic Use of International Institutions," *Australian Journal of International Affairs* 59, no. 3 (September 2005): 317–33.

[29] Cha suggests this is a predictable response from a weaker ally. See Cha, "Abandonment, Entrapment, and Neoclassical Realism in Asia," 265.

After the Cold War

The problems of resentment and fear of abandonment have persisted for Japan since 1990 and have been magnified by the collapse of global bipolarity. The absence of the unifying Soviet threat naturally has raised questions about the purpose and future of an alliance that essentially developed to contain that threat. As a unipolar power, the United States has become less constrained and enjoys greater discretion in its global and regional foreign policy.

Japan's overall response to this alliance uncertainty has been to remain a steadfast ally in support of the United States. Tokyo's diplomatic efforts, however, have not always had the desired effect. During the 1990-91 Persian Gulf War, Japan interpreted its constitution as preventing the rear area logistical support requested by the United States.[30] Japan compensated by raising taxes to finance a very sizable contribution, some $13 billion, to the U.S. war effort. This well-intentioned approach inspired more criticism than praise from the U.S. Congress and media who saw Japan, even more dependent on Middle Eastern oil, practicing "checkbook diplomacy" out of harm's way. U.S. resentment, of course, was framed in the context of an economic competition that Japan still appeared to be winning. The Clinton administration initiated the U.S.-Japan Framework Talks to force Japan to make concessions on an array of outstanding trade disputes. Japan proved it could sometimes say "no" and resisted, and in February 1994 both sides walked away without even a cosmetic agreement. The United States threatened sanctions; Japan countered by threatening to drag its alliance partner through the new dispute settlement procedures of the WTO.

A respite came in 1996. The Joint Declaration between President Clinton and Prime Minister Ryutaro Hashimoto signaled that bilateral economic conflicts would take a back seat to a renewed emphasis on security cooperation. Regional tensions—the North Korean nuclear crisis of 1994 and the Chinese military exercises and missile tests near Taiwan in 1995-96—motivated Japan to revise defense cooperation guidelines with the United States. These developments convinced Washington that the end of the Cold War did not afford the United States the luxury of pulling back from a role as stabilizer of regional conflicts. The Defense Department plan known as the Nye Initiative halted any contemplated U.S. force reductions and called for the maintenance of U.S. troop levels at 100,000 in East Asia for the indefinite future. The plan called for a strategy of "deep engagement" centered both on this forward military presence and on a revitalization of

---

[30] See Mike M. Mochizuki, "Japan: Between Alliance and Autonomy," in *Strategic Asia 2004-05: Confronting Terrorism in the Pursuit of Power*, ed. Ashley J. Tellis and Michael Wills (Seattle: National Bureau of Asian Research, 2004).

the bilateral alliance with Japan.[31] The realization in Washington by 1995 that Japan's stagnant economy no longer constituted a serious threat also helped to reinforce the new bilateral focus on security cooperation. For Tokyo the respite was brief, with renewed fears of abandonment surfacing by the late 1990s. U.S. attention turned to China, and the Clinton team sought to develop a strategic partnership with China as a means to integrate and make compatible China's growing power and ambitions with a U.S.-centered global and regional order. From the perspective of Japan, the frustration of U.S. "Japan-bashing" was now replaced by the anxiety of "Japan-passing." Clinton's ten-day visit to China in 1999, without even a stop in Japan, captured literally the "passing" concern.[32]

Koizumi and Bush: A New Dawn and New Challenges

The Armitage Commission Report of 2000 reflected concern (shared by alliance watchers on both sides of the Pacific) that the U.S.-Japan alliance was in dire need of redefinition and renewal.[33] That effort has been strikingly successful, so much so that the past five years might be characterized as a golden age in the bilateral relationship.[34] The two sides have deepened their cooperation bilaterally, regionally, and globally. By the end of 2005 the Security Consultative Committee, made up of the foreign affairs and defense heads for Japan and the United States, ratified an interim agreement on the realignment of U.S. security forces in Japan that is generally acknowledged as a precondition for a transformed alliance. Secretary of State Condoleeza Rice remarked that "a relationship that was once about the defense of Japan or perhaps about the stability of the region, has truly become a global alliance." Japanese Defense Agency Director General Ohno Yoshinori agreed and spoke of an opening of a new era, calling the consultations and

---

[31] *United States Security Strategy for the East Asia-Pacific Region*, Office of International Security Affairs, U.S. Department of Defense (Washington, D.C.: U.S. Government Printing Office, 1995); and Joseph S. Nye, Jr., "The Case for Deep Engagement," *Foreign Affairs* 74 (1995): 90–102.

[32] For discussion see Neil E. Silver, *The United States, Japan, and China: Setting the Course* (occasional paper, New York, Council on Foreign Relations, 2000); and Michael Mastanduno, "The U.S.-Japan Alliance and Models of Regional Security Order," in *Reinventing the Alliance: U.S.-Japan Security Partnership in an Era of Change*, ed. G. John Ikenberry and Takashi Inoguchi (New York: Palgrave MacMillan, 2003).

[33] See Armitage Commission, *The United States and Japan: Advancing Toward a More Mature Partnership*; and Ikenberry and Inoguchi, *Reinventing the Alliance*.

[34] In a 2006 interview with the on-line newsletter *The Oriental Economist*, Richard Armitage observed that the two sides had clearly exceeded the goals and expectations put forth in the 2000 report. See "Armitage on Asia," *PacNet* 12 (March 23, 2006), available on-line at http://www.csis.org/media/csis/pubs/pac0612.pdf.

agreement "a truly historical process for a transformation of the U.S.-Japan alliance.[35]

What Has Gone Right?

There are at least four main reasons for this "new era." First, the regional crises of the 1990s appear to have convinced Japanese officials that there was no alternative to a U.S.-centered security strategy, and these officials have responded with accelerated willingness to meet U.S. concerns and engage in deeper security collaboration.[36] Since 1997, Japanese government officials have agreed to revise the bilateral defense cooperation guidelines (which had been in effect some twenty years) in order to allow Japan to provide rear support for U.S. military operations in areas surrounding Japan. The Japanese have worked to lessen the political burden of the U.S. military presence in Okinawa—even agreeing after some diplomatic posturing to pay more that half of the estimated $10 billion cost of relocating U.S. Marines from Okinawa to Guam.[37] Prompted by the 1998 North Korean missile launch, the Japanese have joined with the United States in a missile defense initiative; in March 2006 the two sides successfully conducted a joint missile interceptor test. In a reversal of the debacle following the 1990–91 Gulf War, Japan has provided tangible (if circumscribed) support to the United States in the global war on terrorism, including unprecedented deployments of Japanese forces in Iraq and the Indian Ocean.

These foreign policy moves have required a concomitant effort in domestic politics, including the passage of new legislation and creation of new crisis management instruments. Since 1990, Japanese officials have undertaken two revisions of National Defense Program Guidelines in support of military modernization and alliance cooperation.[38] The Japanese government and public have taken up a serious reappraisal of Article Nine, the constitutional provision that guides the country's participation in international security affairs.[39] The cumulative impact of these and other initiatives has been to raise the question of whether Japan is "back in

---

[35] Quotes are found in Brad Glosserman, "U.S.-Japan Relations: The Alliance Transformed?" *Comparative Connections* 7, no. 4 (January 12, 2006).

[36] Brad Glosserman, "Changing Asia Needs the U.S.-Japan Alliance," *PacNet* 47 (October 21, 2004), http://www.csis.org/media/csis/pubs/pac0447.pdf.

[37] "U.S., Japan Agree on Troop Realignment," *Los Angeles Times*, April 24, 2006.

[38] Christopher W. Hughes, "Japanese Military Modernization: In Search of a More Normal Security Role," in *Strategic Asia 2005–06: Military Modernization in an Era of Uncertainty*, ed. Ashley J. Tellis and Michael Wills (Seattle: National Bureau of Asian Research, 2005).

[39] J. Patrick Boyd and Richard J. Samuels, *Nine Lives? The Politics of Constitutional Reform in Japan* (Washington, D.C.: East-West Center, 2005).

world politics," preparing to take on a military and diplomatic role more commensurate with the country's economic and technological power. From the perspective of the United States, these developments are welcome. The traditional alliance behavior pattern—in which the United States makes demands and Japan resists or cooperates grudgingly only at the last moment—appears at least to some extent to have been replaced by a greater Japanese responsiveness to U.S. alliance concerns—even if that means sidestepping domestic or constitutional constraints.

Second, Japan's new assertiveness dovetails with an increasing U.S. reliance on Japan. Given that so much of U.S. diplomatic attention and resources have been diverted to the Middle East, Japan's role as the cornerstone of U.S. security strategy in East Asia has taken on greater significance. With continued rise of China, the Bush administration has pursued a mixed strategy of maintaining economic engagement and laying at least the groundwork for military containment. As the most powerful economic and military player in China's region, Japan obviously is crucial to the latter effort. Also relevant is that U.S. relations with South Korea have deteriorated due to differences over how to handle North Korea, the emergence of a new democratic assertiveness in South Korea, and Washington's decision to relocate U.S. forces from the central front in South Korea in order to serve more effectively U.S. efforts in the war on terrorism. The United States has a strong relationship with Australia and (not surprisingly) has been cultivating one with India. Yet for Washington these relationships are supplements to—rather than substitutes for—the indispensable role U.S. officials expect of Japan. Tokyo has been eager to demonstrate its willingness not only to take on that role regionally but also to take the next step of cooperating more fully with U.S. foreign policy initiatives globally.

Third, the most common source of alliance friction—economic conflict and competition—has receded. There remain, to be sure, nagging bilateral economic issues such as Japan's ban on beef exports due to fears of "mad cow" disease and U.S. complaints that anti-competitive practices persist in the Japanese corporate sector. Yet these types of issues no longer are the priority focus of the bilateral agenda. For the United States, China has replaced Japan as the rising economic giant of concern and as the leading practitioner of unfair trade practices. China is now the first to incur the public wrath of the U.S. Congress and import-sensitive business community. On the positive side, Japan is quietly providing a crucial financial service to the United States. The Japanese central bank has been accumulating and holding in reserve massive amounts of U.S. dollars, allowing the Bush administration to finance external debts without having to raise taxes or scale back the administration's ambitious and costly global foreign policy. As of September 2005, Japan held some 33% of U.S. federal debt, with mainland China a distant second at about 12%.[40]

Fourth, not to be underestimated is the power of personal relationships among leaders. Bush and Koizumi have developed a rapport over the past five years that rivals the positive chemistry between President Reagan and Prime Minister Nakasone during the 1980s. This special relationship insures that Japan receives the benefit of the doubt within internal U.S. policy debates over trade and other issues.[41] Bush's high regard for personal loyalties has helped assure that Koizumi remains immune from U.S. criticism (Koizumi's provocative visits to the Yasukuni Shrine nothwithstanding) and has encouraged the Prime Minister to continue to push a U.S.-friendly agenda in Japan.

Two Challenges

This recent consolidation of Japan's relationship with the United States is a major diplomatic success for Japan, helping both to re-anchor Japanese security in the uncertain environment of the post-Cold War world and to provide political space for Tokyo to transform and expand Japan's regional and global role. Nonetheless, important to recognize is that diplomatic success is a mixed blessing, raising two important challenges that Japan must manage in the years ahead.

The first concerns the bilateral relationship itself. Proclamations of a new partnership or transformed alliance naturally raise expectations. Higher expectations, if not met, result in even greater disappointment and possible resentment. The United States, for example, might plausibly be expected to count on the active support of Japan in dealing with a likely crisis in the Middle East—the prospect of a nuclear-armed Iran. The potential for alliance conflict is clear. The United States wants to isolate Iran whereas Japan, interested both in secure access to Iranian petroleum reserves and in contracts to rebuild the energy infrastructure, has a strong preference to engage the regime. As of early 2006, Japan was facing diplomatic pressure to back the hard line of the United States. John Bolton, U.S. Ambassador to the UN, stated publicly that "we can understand Japan's energy problem,

[40] Justin Murray and Marc Labonte, *Foreign Holdings of Federal Debt, CRS Report for Congress* (Washington, D.C.: Congressional Research Service, November 23, 2005).

[41] See, for example, the comments of Richard Armitage in "Armitage on Asia."

but...it is far more important for Japan to work together to prevent Iran from possessing nuclear weapons."[42]

Similarly, the all-important base redeployment deal, announced with great fanfare in October 2005, has a long way to go before being implemented effectively. The burden-sharing problem over cost was resolved in April 2006, but the more difficult hurdle involves local politics. One Japanese community after another has expressed "not in my backyard" reservations about hosting the U.S. forces that will remain in Japan. In March 2006, 58% of voters in Yamaguchi Prefecture turned out for a referendum on whether to accept Tokyo's plan for the redeployment from Atsugi to Iwakuni of some 60 aircraft from the nuclear-powered carrier, the USS Kitty Hawk; 80% voted against the move.[43] While not impossible, overriding these domestic political concerns is likely to be politically difficult for Koizumi or his successor. Failure to deliver will earn Japan the wrath of the U.S. defense community, which continually reminds Japan that the United States— having waited patiently since the late 1990s for Japan's force relocation solution—will not wait forever.

Long experience suggests that the Japanese government must be mindful not only of the current U.S. administration but also of the role and sentiment of the U.S. Congress. Members of Congress have applauded the transformed bilateral relationship yet also made clear in 2005 their interest in reasserting an oversight role in relations with Japan.[44] Congress expressed concern over the deterioration in Japan's relations with its neighbors, the impact of the weak yen on U.S. competitiveness, and impediments in the Japanese market to U.S. exports of beef and advanced technology products. China may be the current focus of congressional criticism but Japan is not immune; ironically, Japan may be more exposed to criticism precisely because so much is now expected of Japan's renewed connection to the United States. Members of Congress await the tangible benefits that the transformed partnership will bring to their constituents in the U.S. business community.

The risk of dashed expectations is likely to be reciprocal. Tokyo has counted on Washington's support for the Japanese bid for a permanent seat on the UN Security Council, and the United States has pledged that support. For the Bush administration, however, this is not a sufficiently high priority

---

[42] Brad Glosserman, "U.S.-Japan Relations: Unfinished Business," *Comparative Connection* 8, no. 1 (April 12, 2006).

[43] Glosserman, "U.S.-Japan Relations: Unfinished Business."

[44] See for example, House Committee on International Relations, Subcommittee on Asia and the Pacific, *Focus on a Changing Japan*, hearing, 109th Cong., 1st sess., April 4, 2005; and Senate Committee on Foreign Relations, *A Review of U.S.-Japan Relations*, hearing, 109th Cong., 1st sess., September 29, 2005.

to expend the political capital necessary to give Japan's bid a chance for success—a reality that is increasingly clear to Japanese officials. Japan teamed up with Brazil, Germany, and India in a collective bid for seats; the U.S. position as of 2006 was that the United States supported Japan's—and only Japan's—bid, thereby undermining the diplomatic strategy chosen by Japan and disappointing the Koizumi government. The broader point is that in becoming more of a normal ally, Japan will expect not only U.S. diplomatic support but also a greater say in alliance decisionmaking. This expectation runs counter to the longstanding alliance pattern in which the United States initiates, often unilaterally, and Japan follows, often reluctantly.

Complicating the problem further for Tokyo is the need to manage simultaneously the heightened expectations of the United States and the domestic politics of Japan's emerging security transformation. Japanese politics clearly have come a long way from the diffusion of authority and balance of opinion during the Cold War period that made revision of Article Nine and a more robust security posture politically impractical. In the 1990s the political ground began to shift in favor of constitutional and security policy revisionism.[45] Leftist parties, the institutional manifestation of Japanese pacifism, weakened considerably during the 1990s: the Japan Socialist Party held over 130 seats in the lower house in 1990 but only 6 seats by 2003. Within the dominant LDP the power of factional leaders—who are often divided on the issue of constitutional revision—has weakened, and the power of the prime minister and cabinet has strengthened. Interpretation of Article Nine previously rested in the hands of cautious bureaucrats within the Cabinet Legislation Bureau and now resides with the prime minister and his foreign policy team. This institutional development is all the more critical since the current and popular prime minister is a constitutional and security policy revisionist. Public opinion has shifted as well. By 2005 both major political parties proposed revisions to the constitution, and opinion polls suggested a majority of the public was supportive as well.

These internal developments and Japan's recent behavior might tempt U.S. officials to think that a transformed Japanese foreign policy is now a foregone conclusion. Such a finding would be premature. Although meaningful adjustment in Japanese security policy is already taking place, how far and how fast such change will go remains to be seen. The Japanese public is tolerant but not necessarily enthusiastic about expanding Japan's security role, and some politicians remain wary of being dragged into

---

[45] A useful discussion of the domestic transformation can be found in Samuels and Boyd, *Nine Lives?* 7–8, 29–30, and 36–37.

conflicts by a globally activist United States.[46] As the previous discussion of economic reform suggested, Japan prefers to make policy changes incrementally and with deliberation. The door to security policy change is now partially open, but if Japanese revisionists or U.S. government officials try to push too hard, the result might be a domestic political backlash against a Japan that is more assertive in global security affairs.

Japan's second challenge involves the potential conflict between Japan's relations both with the United States and with the country's East Asian neighbors. In moving closer to Washington, Tokyo has become more isolated in the East Asian region. This is more than a mere coincidence. While placing more of its eggs in the U.S. basket, Japan has perceived less of an incentive to expend the diplomatic effort needed to reassure and improve relations with neighboring countries. The most obvious problems are with South Korea and China. Japan's relationship with South Korea has deteriorated over the issue of Koizumi's visits to Yasukuni as well as due to Japan's edging closer to the U.S. position on North Korea. Chinese leaders are alarmed by deeper levels of U.S.-Japan security cooperation. For China, the U.S. alliance with Japan may serve either as the "cork in the bottle," restraining Japanese militarization, or as the "protective eggshell," nurturing and promoting that threatening outcome. The Japanese regional challenge is to continue improving relations with the United States along with, rather than at the expense of, Japan's relations in a troubled neighborhood.

Can Economic Interdependence Mitigate Security Tensions in the Region?

Since the end of the Cold War, the extent to which economic and security trends in East Asia have moved in opposite directions is striking. The security environment is one of increasing tension; the regional economic environment is one of increasing cooperation. The Chinese economy is central to the latter development. Japan—with a sizable population, technological sophistication, and established links to other states—is a key player as well. As Sino-Japanese security relations have deteriorated, bilateral economic relations have progressed positively.

Can economic interdependence mitigate security tensions in East Asia? This is a natural question in light of the divergent trends and an important one given the stakes involved. International relations theory provides mixed guidance: liberals are optimistic that interdependence promotes or

---

[46] See, for example, Thomas Berger's statement in the April 4, 2005 House Committee on International Relations, Subcommittee on Asia and the Pacific hearing, *Focus on a Changing Japan*.

reinforces peace, whereas realists tend to be more skeptical. The context in East Asia lends some support to both positions. Economic relations—in particular those involving Japan—have the potential to play a constructive supporting role in the security environment yet are no panacea. Sound economic relations cannot be counted on to solve the long-term security problem of China-Japan rivalry, even though such relationships can help to soften some aspects of that rivalry.

Security Asia: Tensions Rising

Richard Ellings and Aaron Friedberg opened an earlier volume of *Strategic Asia* by noting that "the most serious threats to U.S. security are likely to come from Asia, where an increasing proportion of the world's economic and military power has come to reside, and where domestic instability and international conflict are virtually certain."[47] That assessment was certainly plausible looking backward to the 1990s. Unlike Europe after the Cold War, Asia offered an array of regime types rather than an abundance of democracies, rapidly growing and unstable economies rather than mature capitalist ones, weak regional institutions instead of strong ones, and festering border disputes rather than resolved ones. In Asia the burdens of history weigh more heavily as well, and among Asian states there is a heightened rather than diminished sense of nationalism.[48] A series of crises—involving North Korean nuclear capabilities in 1994, conflict between China and Taiwan in 1996, the Asian financial meltdown in 1997–98, the North Korean missile launch in 1998, and fear of war between India and Pakistan in 1998 and 2000—reinforced the more pessimistic view of Asia's prospects. Since 2000, the pessimistic assessment continues to be credible. The prospect of a conflict across the Taiwan Strait that might draw in the United States and even Japan cannot be counted out. The crisis over North Korea's nuclear ambitions recurred in 2004, sparking both military threats from the United States and a concerted diplomatic effort from major states in the region. North Korea's test launch of multiple rockets on July 4, 2006 escalated tensions and created a renewed sense of regional insecurity. Dealing with China-Taiwan tensions and a provocative North Korean regime represent the region's more immediate challenges; over time, the more ominous security problem involves China and Japan.

---

[47] Richard J. Ellings and Aaron L. Friedberg, *Strategic Asia 2001–02: Power and Purpose* (Seattle: National Bureau of Asian Research, 2001), i.

[48] In the early 1990s, Stephen Van Evera made the case that Europe was "primed for peace," in contrast to Aaron Friedberg's concern that Asia might be "ripe for rivalry." See Van Evera, "Primed for Peace: Europe after the Cold War," *International Security* 15, no. 3 (Winter 1990–91): 7–57; and Friedberg, "Ripe for Rivalry."

Relations between the two Asian giants have become increasingly troubled. Japan and China did not hold a summit between 2001 and 2006. According to diplomats from each country, as of 2006 channels of communication were restricted and relations damaged "at every level."[49] Japan now officially regards China as an economic and military threat. China is furious that Japan has meddled in its internal affairs by, in tandem with the United States, declaring Taiwan a security concern. Late in 2004, the Japanese navy chased a Chinese submarine out of Japan's territorial waters near Okinawa. The two energy-dependent countries have disagreements over oil and gas reserves in the East China Sea, and China has escalated the problem by beginning to extract some of the gas. Koizumi's regular visits to the Yasukuni Shrine are a continuing source of friction with China. The same is true for what China perceives as Japan's unwillingness to come to terms with how Japan has portrayed its history in textbooks. "Spontaneous" and occasionally violent demonstrations against Japanese consulates and businesses in China broke out in 2005 over the textbook revision issue, prompting Japan to demand that China rein in violent protestors and make amends. The Japanese public has an increasingly unfavorable view of China; many in the Chinese public, especially younger Chinese, find Japan equally distasteful.[50]

It is not surprising that each country finds the other at fault for the troubled relationship. China is upset by the deepening of the U.S.-Japan alliance and by the accompanying normalization of Japan's military role that seems to be proceeding at a rapid pace. Japan is cooperating on a missile defense system with the United States that is a direct response to North Korea, but also, at least indirectly, to China. Japan's explicit public tilt towards the U.S. position on Taiwan adds fuel to the fire. Additionally, in China's eyes Koizumi's five visits to Yasukuni in five years (despite regional protests) demonstrate at best a remarkable lack of sensitivity and at worst a desire to glorify Japan's militarist past. Japan, for its part, perceives China as the region's source of instability. China's regime is undemocratic. Though China's military currently may be technologically unsophisticated, defense spending in the People's Republic of China (PRC) is rising steadily as China

---

[49] "Japan and its Neighbors: A Giant Stirs, a Region Bridles," *The Economist*, May 13, 2006, 25–27. See also Kent Calder, "China and Japan's Simmering Rivalry," *Foreign Affairs* 85, no. 2 (March/ April 2006): 129–39.

[50] Calder reports that in October 2001, 48% of Japanese polled had a favorable view of China. By October 2005 the number dropped to 32%. In China, 44 million people reportedly signed an electronic petition opposing a permanent UN Security Council seat for Japan. See Calder, "China and Japan's Simmering Rivalry," 133.

modernizes the country's armed forces.[51] The missiles pointed at Taiwan could also reach Japan. In Japan's eyes, China's permanent UN Security Council seat is an accident of history, and China is now exploiting this privileged position to deny the Japanese their rightful international role. Koizumi's repeated visits to the controversial shrine in part reflect the new assertiveness and accompanying unwillingness of Japan to back down and apologize whenever China complains.

There is, however, a deep, longer-term structural problem, one that is captured by the law of uneven development.[52] China is a rising power while Japan is a mature one. In the past, when China was strong Japan tended to be weak, and when Japan was strong China was weak. Both are strong for the first time in modern history, and each aspires to be a dominant regional power. The power transition is troubling to Japan, which sees China's political and economic influence increasing regionally (e.g., in Southeast Asia) and globally (e.g., in relations with the United States) at the expense of Japan. The transition is troubling to a China that aspires to prestige and influence, including a Japanese acknowledgement of China that is commensurate with the growth of the PRC's material power. Domestic politics in each country are exacerbating the tensions. Apparent to Japan is that China bolsters the legitimacy of the country's undemocratic regime by stirring up nationalist sentiment and positioning the regime as the protector of China in the face of an aggressive Japan.[53] Apparent to China is that the traditionally pacifist left in Japan is no longer a serious political force, that both major parties support constitutional revision, and that a majority of the Japanese public appears supportive also. Regional transformations are heightening the rivalry as well. The prospect of a united Korea, for example, raises threats and opportunities for both Japan and China that neither was forced to contemplate during the long Cold War.

Japanese relations with South Korea have similarly moved in a more negative direction. Bilateral ties had improved during the 1990s due to prodding by the United States, Japan's assistance to South Korea after the 1997–98 financial crisis, and most importantly South Korean President Kim Dae Jung's historic visit to Japan in October 1998.[54] In the past several

---

[51] A multi-country poll carried out in 2005 found Japan to be among the countries most concerned by China's growing military power. Of Japanese polled 78% viewed China's military power negatively, and only 3% positively. Interestingly, only 23% of Japanese polled viewed China's economic power negatively, and 35% positively. See "22-Nation Poll Showed China Viewed Positively by Most Countries," Program on International Policy Attitudes (PIPA), March 6, 2005.

[52] Robert Gilpin, *War and Change in World Politics* (New York: Cambridge University Press, 1981).

[53] Thomas Christensen, "China, the U.S.-Japan Alliance, and the Security Dilemma in East Asia," *International Security* 23, no. 4 (Spring 1999): 49–80.

[54] Mochizuki, "Japan: Between Alliance and Autonomy," 118.

years, however, relations have soured somewhat. Both Koizumi's Yasukuni diplomacy and the politics of Japanese textbooks have inflamed sentiment in Korea the same way and with roughly the same intensity as in China. Since 2005, neither Koizumi nor South Korean President Roh Moo-hyun has been prepared to take the steps necessary to restore summit meetings and relax tensions. Each instead has pointed to the other's lack of understanding of the history issue.[55] A conflict erupted in early 2006 over the disputed islets known as Dodko by South Korea and Takeshima by Japan.[56] South Korea controls the islets, but Japan announced the dispatch of unarmed ships to map the seabed in the area. South Korea considered this action provocative and sent armed patrol boats to the site. A compromise was reached, but the conflict itself and the importance each side attributes to this seemingly innocuous prize (note that the Japanese even celebrate a "Takeshima Day" in February) demonstrate the current level of fragility and irritability in the bilateral relationship.

Initial responses to the North Korean missile tests of 2006 reinforced the antagonism between Japan and South Korea. Japan responded with alarm and took the initiative in calling for UN sanctions. Japanese officials, including chief cabinet secretary Shinzo Abe (a possible successor to Koizumi) and the head of the Japanese defense agency questioned publicly whether Japan's constitution would permit pre-emptive attacks against North Korean missile sites in self-defense. South Korean officials reacted as much to Japan's reaction as to North Korea's action. The South Korean president's office issued a statement accusing Japan of heightening regional tensions by creating a big fuss over the missile tests. Japan called South Korea's statement "regrettable," and the United States was left to wonder how a unified response to North Korea might be forged in light of the growing divide between its two important East Asian allies.[57]

Unsurprisingly, Japan's relations with North Korea have declined even more precipitously. The North Korean missile launch over Japan in 1998 raised anxieties and prompted Japan to work more closely on missile defense with the United States, to launch Japan's own spy satellites, and to improve Japan's submarine-detection technology. Bilateral relations took an even more decisive turn for the worse in 2002 when, in the context of a visit to North Korea by Koizumi that was designed to improve relations, North

---

[55] David Kang and Ji-young Lee, "Japan-Korea Relations: Seirei Ketsuzetsu [Cold Politics, Warm Economics], *Comparative Connections* 7, no. 4 (January 12, 2006).

[56] *The Economist*, "Japan and Its Neighbors," 27.

[57] Norimitsu Onishi, "Missile Tests Divide Seoul from Tokyo," *New York Times*, July 11, 2006, A6; and Martin Fackler, "Japan Finds Still Harsher Words for North Korea's Missile Tests," *New York Times*, July 11, 2006, A6.

Korea revealed (with apology) that North Korean agents had abducted Japanese citizens during the 1970s and 1980s. The acknowledgment that some had died only increased the indignation among the Japanese government and public. The abduction issue has poisoned bilateral ties and created reciprocity of historical grievance—North Korea insists Japan make amends for its colonial past, and Japan demands amends from North Korea for crimes against Japanese citizens. The conflict has also edged Japan closer to the United States on the North Korean nuclear issue. Japan initially sought to distance itself from the U.S. hard line on North Korea in the Six-Party Talks. By early 2006, Japan's position was to "squeeze but negotiate"— continue talking to North Korea but at the same time remain open to imposing economic or diplomatic pressure on the recalcitrant regime. In early 2006 Japan reassured the United States that normalization of ties with North Korea would not take place unless the abduction, nuclear, missile, and other issues were comprehensively resolved. Japan and North Korea did resume bilateral talks in February 2006, but the dialogue of the deaf led to no agreements given that Japan focused on the abduction and nuclear issues while North Korea demanded compensation for Japan's imperial past.[58] The July 2006 missile tests and Japan's call for international sanctions all but guarantee a continuation of bilateral hostility and suspicion.

The above discussions should not be taken to imply that Japan is isolated in the region. Japan's positive relations with Australia, for example, have been deepened by the decision in March 2006 to initiate historic trilateral talks at the ministerial level among Japan, Australia, and the United States. The joint statement found common ground on the bid of North Korea, Iran, and Japan for a UN Security Council Seat.[59] Russian President Vladimir Putin visited Japan in November 2005. The two leaders continued to disagree over the disputed Northern Territories but signed twelve bilateral agreements aimed at improving Japanese access to Russian energy supplies and expressing Japanese support for Russia's bid to join the WTO.[60] These positive steps, however, have been overshadowed by the regional anxiety created by the deterioration in Japan's relations—especially relations with China and also with the two Koreas.

---

[58] Kang and Lee, "Japan-Korea Relations."

[59] Glosserman, "U.S.-Japan Relations: Unfinished Business."

[60] Economist Intelligence Unit, "Country Report: Japan," 16.

Economic Asia: Deepening Regional Interdependence

Economic indicators tell a different story, pointing to a region coming together more than drifting apart.[61] The share of intra-regional trade as a proportion of total trade for East Asian countries increased significantly from 35% in 1980 to 57% in 2001. The comparative figure for the deeply integrated European Union in 2001 was 62%, while the North American free trade area came in at 48%.[62] Financial cooperation is also advancing. In the wake of the Asian financial crisis, ASEAN members created the ASEAN Surveillance Process to monitor and provide early detection of problems that could lead to financial distress. The Chiang Mai Initiative of ASEAN+3 members developed a liquidity support mechanism which complements IMF resources by expanding credit lines and swap arrangements among East Asian central banks.[63] Deepening economic integration is both state- and market-driven. Alongside the existing APEC forum, ASEAN members decided in 1992 to set up an ASEAN Free Trade Area (AFTA) to be achieved by 2008. East Asian states are also increasing their involvement with each other in bilateral free trade or economic partnership agreements: two agreements are in effect, six are under negotiation, and several more are under consideration. These arrangements typically are not limited to tariff agreements but aspire to deeper integration—including the liberalization of services, the harmonization of government standards and procedures, and the elimination of other non-tariff barriers. Firms in the region are moving from simple assembly relationships between countries to denser, region-wide production and distribution networks.[64]

China and Japan are the key players advancing regional interdependence and their roles have shifted over time. As of the mid-1980s Japan was the clear leader in regional integration and other states sought not only to follow Japan but to emulate Japan's domestic practices, leading analysts to employ the familiar metaphor of a flying-geese formation to describe East Asian regionalism. As Japan's economy stalled by the mid-1990s, this leadership role faltered. Japanese banks were forced to halt the expansion of their lending to other East Asian economies, and Japanese corporations, fearful of exporting jobs in the face of domestic stagnation, cut back

[61] T.J. Pempel, ed., *Remapping East Asia: The Construction of a Region* (Ithaca: Cornell University Press, 2005); and Edward Lincoln, *East Asian Regionalism* (Washington, D.C.: Brookings Institution Press, 2004).

[62] Mario B. Lamberte, "An Overview of Economic Cooperation and Integration in Asia," in *Asian Economic Cooperation and Integration: Progress, Prospects, and Challenges* (Asian Development Bank, 2005), 9. The fifteen East Asian economic regions include the ten members of ASEAN along with the People's Republic of China, Japan, South Korea, Hong Kong, and Taiwan.

[63] Lamberte, "An Overview of Economic Cooperation and Integration in Asia," 23–25.

[64] Ibid., 14, 17.

on foreign direct investment.[65] Although lacking the deep financial and technological resources of Japan, China in some ways has taken up the slack. Since the decision to liberalize its economy in 1978, China's growth rate has approached 8–10% annually and exports have grown by close to 15% annually. China has become the region's—and to some extent the world's—production center and export platform, particularly for labor-intensive goods. China is the largest recipient of FDI among developing countries and is the leading export market in Asia for South Korea, Taiwan, and Singapore. China is both attracting investments from some East Asian states and to some extent taking investments away from others, particularly middle income countries in ASEAN that share China's development stage and export profile.

Even though no longer the undisputed leader, Japan has both a regional role that remains significant and regional ties that have deepened over the past five years. Japan's overall trade has increased steadily over the past decade, with exports jumping from ¥41.5 trillion in 1995 to ¥51 trillion in 2000 and ¥61.2 trillion in 2004. Imports moved from ¥31.5 trillion in 1995 to ¥40.9 trillion in 2000 to ¥49.2 trillion in 2004.[66] The geographic shift has been more striking. Exports to Asia increased from ¥21.2 trillion to ¥29.9 trillion between 2000 and 2004, while imports from Asia went from ¥17 trillion in 2000 to ¥22.2 trillion in 2004. During that same period, trade with the United States actually *decreased*, with exports dropping from ¥15.4 trillion to ¥13.7 trillion, and imports declining from ¥7.8 trillion to ¥6.8 trillion.[67] A slightly longer time frame suggests a similar pattern: as a portion of Japan's total exports, exports to Asia increased from 27% in 1991 to 38% in 2001, while imports increased from 28% to 37%. Exports to the United States dropped from 34% to 29%, and imports from 22% to 21%.[68] Trade within the region is growing faster than, and displacing trade with, Japan's traditional postwar partner, the United States.

In the initial postwar decades, Japan imported raw materials and exported manufactured items, primarily to the United States and secondarily to Europe and Asia. Japanese foreign direct investment was minimal. The United States and Europe complained that Japan exported machinery and manufactured goods without importing the same in return and thus

---

[65] Andrew MacIntyre and Barry Naughton, "The Decline of a Japan-Led Model of the East Asian Economy," in *Remapping East Asia*, ed. T.J. Pempel (Ithaca: Cornell University Press, 2005), 85–86.

[66] See *Statistical Handbook of Japan*, 2005 ed., 124, 129.

[67] Ibid., 124, 129.

[68] Tim Callen and Warwick McKibbon, "The Impact of Japanese Economic Policies on the Asia Region," in *Japan's Lost Decade*, ed. Tim Callen and Jonathan D. Ostry (Washington, D.C.: International Monetary Fund, 2003), 253.

devastated trading partners in certain sectors (e.g., automobiles and semiconductors).[69] The rise of the yen beginning in 1985 made it harder for Japan to export manufactured goods and thus spurred Japanese companies to invest in facilities abroad. Japan became the largest foreign investor in ASEAN, particularly in middle income destinations such as Thailand and Indonesia. As more Japanese facilities have been established in Asia and elsewhere, Japan's intra-firm trade (international trade among affiliates of the same company) has increased significantly. Intra-firm trade by Japanese companies now accounts for some 60% of their total trade within Asia. [70] The composition of Japanese trade is less "unequal" than twenty years ago: Japan now imports roughly the same percentage of manufactured goods that the country exports and both sells and buys significant amounts of machinery and equipment from Asia.[71]

Trade in semiconductors, the essential building blocks for computers and peripheral equipment, further highlights Japan's regional integration. Almost two-thirds of Japanese semiconductor exports are destined for East Asia—33% to China, 10% to Taiwan, 12% to South Korea, and 8% to Singapore. Additionally 22% of Japan's semiconductor imports are from Taiwan and 17% from South Korea.[72]

The recent growth of Japan's trade with China has been striking. Bilateral trade roughly quadrupled between 1995 and 2004, with Japan's exports increasing from ¥2 trillion to ¥8 trillion, and imports climbing from ¥3 trillion to ¥10 trillion.[73] Since 2002 Japan has imported more from China than has the United States, and—if recent trends continue—in several years Japan's exports to China will also outpace those to the United States.

Institutional developments within East Asia reflect both Japan's interest in deepening interdependence and the changing positions of Japan and China. Japan's regional dominance coincided with the rise of APEC as a consensual, informal, and non-binding forum that gave East Asian governments an opportunity to build trust and explore policy coordination without having to make costly commitments. APEC declined in the face of the more demanding economic environment brought on by the Asian financial crisis. In the wake of that crisis Japan sought to assert leadership by proposing an Asian Monetary Fund both to help stabilize currency

---

[69] Lincoln, *Japan's Unequal Trade.*

[70] Lamberte, "An Overview of Economic Cooperation and Integration in Asia," 9–10.

[71] Japanese imports of machinery and transport equipment jumped from 5% of total imports in 1985 to 35% by 2000. See Callen and McKibbon, "The Impact of Japanese Economic Policies on the Asian Region," 252.

[72] *Statistical Handbook of Japan,* 126.

[73] Ibid., 129–30.

fluctuations and to ward off future crises. This initiative was rebuffed by the United States out of concern that such a move might diminish the role of the IMF. Since both the value of the yen and lending by Japanese banks were dropping significantly at the time, how prominent a leadership role Japan would have been able to assume is unclear in any event.[74] By 2001 China seized the regional initiative by proposing, to the exclusion of Japan, a China-ASEAN free trade agreement to come into effect within ten years. Initially caught by surprise, the Japanese eventually responded with Tokyo's own sub-regional initiatives. Japan has concluded a bilateral free trade agreement with Singapore and currently is negotiating for similar deals with South Korea, Thailand, the Philippines, and Malaysia. Free trade agreements with ASEAN and Indonesia, as well as a trilateral one with China and South Korea, are also under consideration.

Interdependence and Security

The scholarly literature is mixed on the question of whether economic interdependence promotes peace.[75] Liberal thinkers emphasize the constraining effects of interdependence on governments calculating costly foreign policy conflicts. Realists tend to believe that non-economic factors are more important drivers of security cooperation and conflict. The impact of economic interdependence is likely to be modest, although in some instances the vulnerabilities created by interdependence might actually increase the probabilities of security conflict.

The debate is unlikely to be resolved, and current dynamics in East Asia lend some support to each position. Economic interdependence is no panacea; counting on this factor to resolve outstanding security problems—in particular the emerging China-Japan rivalry—would be foolish. Economic interdependence can, however, help to ease tensions and mitigate conflict in other, less obvious ways.

The Limited Role of Economic Interdependence

China and Japan are great powers, and their foreign policy stakes are too high for economic interdependence to drive foreign policy outcomes. In other contexts, great powers have demonstrated a willingness to forego

---

[74] MacIntyre and Naughton, "The Decline of a Japan-Led Model," 94–95.

[75] The literature is immense. Good recent treatments include Edward D. Mansfield and Brian M. Pollins, eds., *Economic Interdependence and International Conflict: New Perspectives on an Enduring Debate* (Ann Arbor: University of Michigan Press, 2003); and Jean-Marc Blanchard, Edward D. Mansfield, and Norrin M. Ripsman, eds., *Power and the Purse: Economic Statecraft, Interdependence, and National Security* (London: Frank Cass, 2000).

economic benefits in order to preserve foreign policy autonomy. High levels of interdependence did not prevent Britain and Germany from engaging in what became World War I.[76] The United States employed economic weapons against the Soviet Union and Soviet allies throughout the Cold War, even at the United States' own expense economically.[77] Additionally, although the China-Japan relationship may not be on the verge of war or even an enduring cold war, a striking dynamic is that as bilateral economic interdependence has deepened over the past decade, the bilateral security relationship has become increasingly problematic.

The rupturing of current bilateral economic ties would be costly for each side, yet hardly insurmountable. China is an important destination for Japanese manufacturing plants, equipment, and semiconductors, but there are other states in the region, at stages of development similar to China's, who would be happy to expand their roles as manufacturing export platforms. Japan currently draws some 80% of total clothing imports from China; other sources exist, though perhaps at slightly higher prices. Japan's energy comes from the Middle East, and Japan's financial connections with the United States are deep but minimal with China. China, for its part, would be able to look to the United States, Western Europe, and even the region itself for ready alternatives both to Japanese industrial exports and to the Japanese market for consumer goods.

The global interdependence of Japan and China could lead to conflict between the two in at least one sector. Both countries are energy dependent and, notwithstanding the fact that oil and gas are commodities readily available on the global market, each seems to believe that more security lies in greater political or territorial control over sources of supply. Japan and China could come into conflict over the competition to secure the most favorable arrangements from energy producers in the Middle East, Central Asia, or Russia. The two countries have already demonstrated a willingness to contest each other for the possible energy resources of the East China Sea.

China-Japan security tensions could also be exacerbated by emerging rivalry of the two over economic leadership in East Asian regionalism. China's recent diplomacy suggests eagerness to take a leadership position even at the expense of Japan, and China's economic potential and emerging production networks make such a challenge viable. As MacIntyre and

[76] Paul Papayounou goes further, arguing that economic interdependence helped to cause the conflict by diluting both the signal and reality of Britain's willingness to deter a rising Germany. See Paul Papayoanou, *Power Ties: Economic Interdependence, Balancing, and War* (Ann Arbor: University of Michigan Press, 1999).

[77] Michael Mastanduno, *Economic Containment: CoCom and the Politics of East-West Trade* (Ithaca: Cornell University Press, 1992).

Naughton note, "it is inevitable that there will be a rivalry between China and Japan without a clear outcome…the concerns of other East Asian nations will be subordinated to the interests of the new great powers as they struggle to define their economic interests and their relations with each other."[78]

How Economic Interdependence Might Help

Although not likely to discourage the Japan-China rivalry, economic interdependence can contribute to regional security in several ways. First, the fact that Chinese economic development is taking place *within* an integrated regional and global economy makes it more difficult for China to pose a revisionist challenge to the existing international order. China's future power depends on economic growth, and growth in turn depends on maintaining good relations with the major players in the world economy, including the United States, Japan, and the European Union. Those powers have a reasonable degree of influence over the pace of Chinese growth and the foreign policy that goes along with such growth.[79] Interwar Germany and the postwar Soviet Union mobilized their challenger strategies more as "outsiders"—they enjoyed an economic position of strength relative to smaller countries in their region but had economic ties to other great powers that were more modest.

Second, Japan can play an important regional role as an alternative to China. Smaller countries prefer having options rather than being excessively dependent on one powerful neighboring economy. As Albert Hirschman showed long ago, dependence on a single supplier or market leads to political vulnerability.[80] China is emerging with the potential to play that type of dominant regional role, particularly with respect to countries in Southeast Asia. The maintenance and expansion of Japan's ties in the region provide a second option and thereby help to deflect some of the potential vulnerability of the region's smaller states.[81] In the past, the smaller states had good reason to fear Japan's regional economic clout; today these states can welcome a forward Japanese presence—and a growing Japanese domestic

---

[78] MacIntrye and Naughton, "The Decline of a Japan-Led Model," 100.

[79] Leaders in Beijing may have sought to contain recent anti-Japanese outbursts in China in a move to ensure these incidents did not seriously jeopardize bilateral economic ties.

[80] Albert O. Hirschman, *National Power and the Structure of Foreign Trade* (Berkeley: University of California Press, 1980).

[81] The Unites States, of course, provides a third option, although China's growing appeal has begun to threaten the United States' traditionally dominant position. See, for example, Jane Perlez, "Chinese Move to Eclipse U.S. Appeal in South Asia," *New York Times*, November 18, 2004.

market—as an alternative to, and balancer of, the possibly dominant role of China.

At a global level, the world economy needs Japan to restore growth. A mere 2% increase in the Japanese growth rate would generate some US$100 billion in income—the entire GDP of a smaller Asian economy such as the Philippines or Singapore.[82] The Japanese economy is sufficiently large to be a global engine of growth, particularly if that growth can be generated through increases in domestic demand. That role was anticipated for Japan during the 1970s and 1980s; the Carter administration, for example, held out the prospect of collective leadership, with Japan serving along with the United States and West Germany as one of three "locomotives" pulling the world economy towards greater growth.[83] During the 1990s, the European engine turned inward while the Japanese engine stalled, leaving the United States as the primary source of global growth. This dependence on the U.S. economy places the world economy in a precarious position because the United States, saddled by large deficits and extensive foreign borrowing, could itself stall in the foreseeable future.[84] A healthy Japanese economy would make a positive contribution to global economic stability.

The same point holds for the Asian regional economy. Following the Japanese example, the countries of East Asia typically generate growth through the export sector, being highly dependent on markets in North America and Europe. The possibility that higher energy prices, higher interest rates, and the bursting of the housing bubble in the United States could cause a slowdown in these developed markets raises the question of the extent to which Asia can sustain its own growth regionally. Given that China's developing economy competes with low cost producers and exporters elsewhere in Asia to a far greater extent than does the Japanese economy, the expansion of domestic demand in Japan would be a key source of regional growth.[85]

In short, sustained economic interdependence can promote regional stability indirectly by creating the conditions for growth and prosperity within individual states and the region as a whole. Economic interdependence—even if it cannot be counted on to solve the region's most knotty security problems—has an important role to play. This is all the

[82] See Andrew Batson, "Can Asia Fuel its own Growth in 2006?" *Wall Street Journal*, December 6, 2005.

[83] Robert Putnam and Nicholas Bayne, *Hanging Together: Cooperation and Conflict in the Seven Power Summits* (New York: Sage Publications, 1987).

[84] As argued in Stephen Cohen's chapter in this volume.

[85] Tim Callen and Warwick McKibbon have run a series of simulations that demonstrate the significance of projected Japanese economic growth on the smaller economies of the region. See Callen and McKibbon, "The Impact of Japanese Economic Policies on the Asian Region," 251–72.

more reason to manage the region's security problems effectively in order to assure that they do not undermine the continued growth of regional economic interdependence.

Policy Implications for the United States

This chapter has suggested that Japan faces three significant challenges: to restore sustained economic growth, to maintain the positive momentum that has developed in relations with the United States, and to deepen economic interdependence while improving security relations in its region. Japan's ability to attain these outcomes over the next five years is uncertain. Much will depend on the evolution of Japanese politics and policy in a post-Koizumi era.

LDP candidates vying to replace Koizumi express support for continuing economic reform. This support is not surprising in light of Koizumi's electoral success. Though reform momentum may be sustained, particularly in the absence of a strong leader, the possibility remains that factional politics and public works spending in the service of vested interests will regain importance in the LDP. Koizumi forced the LDP to embrace his personal agenda; whether and to what extent the party takes on that agenda as its own after his departure remains to be seen.

It is similarly premature to assume that U.S.-Japan relations are now on a glide path to success. It will be difficult for any new prime minister, and new U.S. president, to replicate the special relationship of Koizumi and Bush. Subsequent U.S. leaders might expect too much too quickly of Japan, and Japanese leaders might overestimate the extent to which the United States is prepared to share decisionmaking initiative even in a transformed partnership. A more "normal" Japan will be a more autonomous Japan, both seeking to pursue interests that do not always line up with the preferences of the United States and seeking greater voice in collective alliance endeavors.

Regional economic interdependence is likely to deepen in the years ahead, particularly if Japan can sustain growth and China can avoid crisis. Economic interdependence can, however, contribute only modestly to resolving the region's seemingly intractable security problems on the Korean peninsula, in the Taiwan Strait, and in the emerging rivalry between Japan and China. LDP politicians likely to replace Koizumi appear poised to continue his more assertive foreign policy that on balance has exacerbated more than ameliorated regional tensions.

In light of these factors, several policy implications are relevant for the United States. First, important to recognize is that Japanese economic growth is in the national security interest of the United States. Such growth brings benefits to the regional and global economy, to regional security, and to U.S.-Japanese relations. Economic stagnation exacerbates the law of uneven development in Japan's relations with China and constrains Japan's ability to play a constructive regional role. Economic growth depends significantly on economic reform; the maintenance of reform ultimately depends on political will in Japan. The United States can help by encouraging the reformist coalition and gently pressing post-Koizumi Japan to continue moving in that direction.

Second, the maintenance of the U.S. domestic economy has important implications for regional security. The U.S. economy remains sufficiently large and powerful to serve as an engine of growth—or as a transmitter of economic stasis. Moreover, U.S. growth must be accompanied by economic stability. Large external deficits have in the past proven to be a source of instability, bringing the risks of economic slowdown, dollar crisis, and protectionist pressure. That pressure was directed at Japan during the 1980s and is increasingly aimed at China today. Such pressure could also be turned against Japan, however, particularly if Japan proves less willing to finance U.S. deficits—an outcome that will become more likely if Japan manages to rely on domestic demand more so than the export sector to generate sustained growth.

Third, the United States is a pivotal player in managing the Japan-China rivalry. The U.S.-Japanese alliance can reassure Japan about China but can also reassure China about Japan. An alliance that is "too strong" alarms China, while one that is "too weak" raises abandonment anxieties in Japan. The balance is a delicate one—yet crucial to get right. If the problem in the last half of the 1990s was Japanese fear of being "passed," the problem today is the opposite—i.e., that that alliance is moving too rapidly in directions that alarm China. The U.S. interest lies both in communicating that Washington desires strong relations with the two rivals and in encouraging them to have more positive ties with each other. In short, the United States requires not just a bilateral strategy with Japan and one with China, but a more comprehensive regional strategy.

Finally, rising regional tensions remind us that there is still a need for the United States to play a stabilizing role in East Asia. The United States was "deeply engaged" during the 1990s and offered constructive help in managing regional crises, tempering Chinese-Japanese competition, and serving as a export market of last resort. U.S. officials continue to express good intentions but since September 11, 2001 have been preoccupied and to some extent distracted by the war on terrorism and the war in Iraq. The realities of East Asian security and economics suggest that the United States must find a way to remain an engaged player, notwithstanding the formidable challenges the country may face elsewhere in the world.

EXECUTIVE SUMMARY

This chapter analyzes the current and future impact of South Korea's growing trade and economic interdependence for ROK security and relations in Northeast Asia. The chapter will seek to answer two basic questions: (1) Why has South Korea pursued a strategy of engagement toward North Korea? and (2) What is the impact of South Korea's changing foreign policy on the U.S.-ROK alliance?

MAIN ARGUMENT:

- South Korea's commitment over the past decade to a strategy of interdependence and engagement with North Korea constitutes a fundamental shift in South Korea's foreign policy strategy.

- South Korea's economic development has depended upon significant engagement with the regional and global economies—an engagement that has increased during the past decade.

- South Korea's priorities are regional, and the ROK is primarily concerned with national reconciliation with the DPRK. This preoccupation stands in contrast to the global concerns of the U.S., which sets policy in East Asia as an extension of U.S. national security policies.

POLICY IMPLICATIONS:

- The younger generation in South Korea is increasingly influential in policymaking circles. Washington will benefit from recognizing and preparing to work with—rather than against—this emerging elite.

- U.S. and ROK goals and policies toward the DPRK are likely to continue to diverge. China's clear preference for engagement with North Korea means that Washington faces a difficult choice: either continue following a restrained containment policy that risks achieving no progress on the peninsula or change directions to engage the North—a course that also appears unlikely.

- South Korea's support for the U.S. operation in Iraq, cooperation on trade and other regional issues, and common values such as democracy and capitalism form the basis of the U.S.-ROK alliance. Perhaps most importantly, the successful creation of a U.S.-ROK Free Trade Agreement could both strengthen the alliance and the U.S. presence in Northeast Asia.

South Korea's Embrace of Interdependence in Pursuit of Security

David C. Kang

This chapter analyzes the current and future impact of South Korea's growing trade and economic interdependence for the country's security and relations in Northeast Asia. The chapter will seek to answer two basic questions: (1) Why has the Republic of Korea (ROK) pursued a strategy of engagement toward North Korea? and (2) What is the impact of South Korea's changing foreign policy on the U.S.-ROK alliance?

South Korea's international position is comprised of a complex mix of pressures. Focused overwhelmingly upon the last vestige of the Cold War—the unresolved division of the Korean peninsula into northern and southern portions—the ROK must also manage an alliance with the United States, devise a modus vivendi with a massive and dynamic China, and resolve the ROK relationship with Japan. Toward that end, a fairly clear South Korean grand strategy has emerged over the past decade, one that emphasizes economic over military issues, accommodation rather than confrontation with China, and a slowly evolving alliance with the United States. The centerpiece of this grand strategy has been a willingness to engage North Korea economically while downplaying the nuclear issue.

Why has the ROK continued to pursue both an engagement strategy toward North Korea and an interdependence grand strategy in general? What is the impact of South Korea's changing foreign policy on the U.S.-ROK alliance?

This chapter will make three main arguments. First, in terms of overall national security strategy, South Korea has committed itself to a strategy of

David C. Kang (PhD, UC Berkeley) is Associate Professor of Government and Adjunct Associate Professor and Research Director at the Center for International Business at the Tuck School of Business at Dartmouth College. He can be reached at <dave.kang@dartmouth.edu>.

interdependence and engagement with the Democratic Peoples Republic of Korea (DPRK). This seemingly deep-rooted commitment, which stems from a number of factors, constitutes a fundamental shift over the past decade in South Korea's foreign policy strategy. South Korea's emergence over the past half century has been predicated upon an economic development model that catapulted the ROK into the ranks of the developed nations; thus the fact that this strategy is being continued in South Korea's broader foreign economic policy is not surprising. Furthermore, the economic weakness of North Korea, South Korea's democratization, the end of the Cold War, and a change in South Korea's national identity have all contributed to the current belief within South Korea that military issues are secondary to economic issues. As a result, South Korea's engagement strategy will continue to carry consequences for regional policy toward North Korea, the U.S. role in the region, and the influence of China.

Second, this chapter argues that in terms of foreign economic policy, South Korea's development has depended upon extensive engagement with the regional and global economies, an orientation that has actually increased in the wake of the Asian financial crisis of a decade ago. South Korea continues to reform its domestic economy, move toward creating a number of bilateral and multilateral free trade agreements, and support and participate in other regional and global economic fora. As with many East Asian states, however, South Korea has increasingly begun to look within the region for economic partners (especially to China) and away from the United States. To use T.J. Pempel's terminology, this increased regional focus is comprised of both *regionalism* (top-down, government-led institutional creation) and *regionalization* (bottom-up, societally driven interactions).[1]

Third, South Korea firmly desires to continue its close relationship with the United States. Whenever possible, South Korea cooperates with the United States. For Seoul, North Korean nuclear weapons are not an issue of primary importance. South Korea is first and foremost concerned with national reconciliation—i.e., how best to integrate North Korea back into the world's most dynamic region, regardless of nuclear status—and what the foreign policy of a unified Korea should be. In contrast to South Korea's regional issues, U.S. concerns are global in outlook. For the foreseeable future, the United States will be concerned mainly with counterterrorism, the proliferation of weapons of mass destruction, and homeland defense; thus Washington views U.S. policy in East Asia as an extension of these national security priorities. Beyond such concerns, the United States is not particularly focused on economic integration in the region, promotion

---

[1] T.J. Pempel, ed., *Remapping East Asia: The Construction of a Region* (Ithaca, N.Y.: Cornell University Press, 2005).

of regional stability, or attempts to shape the pace and manner of Korean unification.

There are three main implications that arise from this analysis. First, U.S.-ROK relations will continue to diverge over the North Korea question. This difference means that the United States will have a difficult time pursuing a more coercive stance toward the DPRK, and the most likely medium-term result will be continued stalemate over North Korea's nuclear programs. Second, as economic integration with its massive neighbor continues, South Korea will continue to increase political, cultural, and diplomatic interactions with China. This increasing orientation toward China will have implications for the strained U.S.-ROK alliance. Although both Seoul and Washington desire to maintain a strong alliance, these two trends will continue to put pressure on U.S.-ROK relations and, without careful management by both sides, could lead to a suboptimal outcome. Finally, South Korea's pursuit of regional economic ties will lead to increased interactions with the region. Whether these interactions will result in a fundamental reorientation of Seoul's foreign policy remains to be seen, but the trend is markedly different from that of the past half century, during which time South Korea was focused mainly on its alliance with the United States.

This chapter is divided into three main sections. The first provides an overview of South Korea's economic policy during the past half century. The second section surveys current ROK foreign policy priorities, covering South Korea's engagement policy toward the DPRK as well as ROK relations with China and Japan. A third section explores the implications of South Korea's foreign policy for U.S. interests in the region.

ROK Foreign Economic Policy Before the 1997 Financial Crisis

From the beginning of the Cold War until perhaps a decade ago, East Asia was stable if not peaceful: Korea and Japan were staunch anti-communist allies of the United States, both focused on deterring the Soviet Union and North Korea from military adventurism in the region. China, though large, was politically isolated and economically unimportant. When the U.S.-ROK alliance was signed in 1953, South Korea was devastated by the Korean War. Building domestic political and economic institutions following decades of harsh Japanese colonial rule, South Korea was almost entirely dependent upon the United States for its continued survival. This first half century of South Korean foreign policy was marked by two enduring strands. One strand was a security policy focused almost exclusively on deterring North Korea by embedding the ROK within an anti-communist U.S. alliance.[2] The other strand was an economic development strategy based on export-orientation, close private-public cooperation, and interaction with the regional and global economies that became known as the "developmental state."[3]

These two foreign policy pillars had spectacular results. South Korean economic growth averaged over 9% per year from 1961 to 1992, the highest in the world.[4] South Korean companies rapidly moved up the industrial ladder, and South Korean exports flooded Western and U.S. markets. By 1995 per capita income in South Korea had reached $10,000, up from $82 per capita in 1961. In the wake of economic development, South Korea managed a peaceful transition to democratic rule in 1987 when the military government allowed free and fair elections. In 1996 South Korea joined the OECD, and today South Korea is both the tenth largest economy in the world and a vibrant and stable democracy. In terms of national security, a strong anti-communist stance emphasized close U.S. ties, deterrence of and competition with North Korea, and deep integration into the U.S. Cold War alliance structure. Fears of a second North Korean attack remained high throughout the Cold War.

These twin foreign policy pillars began to weaken rapidly in the late 1990s. Democratization in 1987 allowed different domestic interest groups to emerge and weakened, but did not eliminate, the power held by traditional actors and institutions such as the central government, large industrial groups (*chaebol*), and the entrenched bureaucratic and political elites that had ruled South Korea for decades.[5] The end of the Cold War also reduced South Korean security concerns vis-à-vis North Korea. Not only had South Korea's economy far surpassed that of the DPRK, but North Korea also suffered mightily during the 1990s as both its traditional allies (China and the Soviet Union) rapidly normalized relations with South

---

[2] Victor Cha, *Alignment Despite Antagonism* (Stanford, CA.: Stanford University Press, 1999).

[3] Stephan Haggard, *Pathways from the Periphery* (Ithaca, N.Y.: Cornell University Press, 1991); and Jung-en Woo, *Race to the Swift* (New York: Columbia University Press, 1990).

[4] Robert Wade, "East Asia's Economic Success: Conflicting Perspectives, Partial Insights, Shaky Evidence," *World Politics* 44, no. 2 (January 1992): 270–320.

[5] David Kang, *Crony Capitalism: Corruption and Development in South Korea and the Philippines* (Cambridge: Cambridge University Press, 2002), chapters 4 and 5; and Stephan Haggard and Robert Kaufman, "The Political Economy of Democratic Transitions," *Comparative Politics* 29, no. 3 (April 1997): 263–83.

Korea and reduced economic, diplomatic, and military support for North Korea.[6]

Amid these broad changes, two critical events stand out as major turning points for South Korean foreign policy: the 1997 Asian financial crisis and the 2000 summit between South Korean president Kim Dae-jung and North Korean leader Kim Jong-il.

The 1997 Asian financial crisis changed South Korean perceptions of the United States, ROK relations with the world, and the relative power of South Korean domestic coalitions.[7] In November 1997 South Korea's currency halved in value in less than a week, dropping from 900 to 1900 won to the dollar. Six of the thirty largest chaebol went bankrupt. December 4, 1997—the day the South Korean government appealed to the International Monetary Fund (IMF) for help—has come to be known as the "day of national humiliation," and South Koreans began to reassess the policies that had first brought them economic success and then crisis. For a country that was in the midst of performing so well economically, such a crisis proved humbling. Ultimately, South Korea agreed to a $58 billion bailout package from the IMF in exchange for undertaking extensive domestic economic reform measures. South Korea agreed to pursue market-oriented reform in the financial, corporate, and labor markets as well as open the ROK economy to much greater foreign investment and trade.

The second major event that has helped reshape South Korea's foreign policy was the June 2000 summit meeting between Kim Jong-il and president Kim Dae-jung. The summit marked the culmination of a change in South Korean attitudes toward North Korea. Four decades of rapid economic development has created a generation of young South Koreans who have nothing more than book knowledge about the Korean War, poverty, or a genuine North Korean threat. By contrast, Kim Dae-jung's "sunshine policy" has reaped an important political and psychological benefit—the first sustained exposure to the DPRK and the regime's reclusive leader Kim Jong-il. In the midst of President Clinton's generally benign foreign policy toward the DPRK, South Korea thus began to pursue economic and cultural engagement with North Korea and turned away from its previous policy of competition and hostility. Ever since the 2000 summit, South Korean trade

---

[6] For example, Chinese coal exports to North Korea fell from 1.64 million tons in 1989 to 0.05 million tons by 1997. Similar decreases were seen in oil exports. Figures from Stephan Haggard and Marcus Noland, *Famine in North Korea: Aid, Markets and Reform* (New York: Columbia University Press, forthcoming).

[7] T.J. Pempel, ed., *The Asian Financial Crisis* (Ithaca, NY: Cornell University Press, 1999); Robert Wade, "The Asian Debt-and-development crisis of 1997–? Causes and Consequences," *World Development* 26, no. 8 (August 1998): 1535–53; and Paul Krugman, "What Happened to Asia?" (manuscript, M.I.T., 1998), http://web.mit.edu/krugman/www/DISINTER.html.

and investment into North Korea has expanded rapidly, averaging increases of over 50% per year. With the election of U.S. President George W. Bush, a second nuclear crisis in 2002, and a U.S. administration that was generally more suspicious of North Korea, U.S. and ROK foreign policy attitudes have openly diverged.

South Korea's Current Foreign Economic Policy

Trade comprises over 50% of South Korea's GDP, and as a result South Korean foreign policy is unsurprisingly oriented to maintaining and strengthening the regional and world trading order. Furthermore, South Korea's success at economic development based on exports has tightly tied South Korea into the world and regional economic orders. In this sense, South Korea's overall foreign policy is as focused on economics as it is on security.

Furthermore, the past decade has seen a major change in the geopolitical situation in Northeast Asia. China is emerging as the most vibrant and powerful economy in the region, the Soviet Union has disappeared (to be replaced by a Russia concerned more with business than with military expansion), Japan is exploring ways to exert its influence through a more assertive foreign policy, and interaction between North and South Korea has increased to the point that paved roads and railroads now traverse the Demilitarized Zone (DMZ). Despite being a genuine competitor with South Korea during the Cold War, by the 1990s North Korea had fallen far behind South Korea in terms of economic growth and military strength.

Given that South Korea's democratization of 1987 allowed previously silenced domestic interests to voice their opinions regarding national politics, domestic politics have played a major part in this transformation. Furthermore, South Korea has undergone a major shift in the past decade, from viewing North Korea as a threat to viewing it as a "poor cousin." While external security threats to Seoul appear to have diminished over the past decade, economic motivations—a consistently important aspect of South Korea's foreign and domestic policy since World War II—have increased. At many levels of South Korean society there is concern over decreasing international economic competitiveness and growing inequality at home. These worries are driving domestic market-oriented reforms, support for regional institution building, trade and foreign direct investment (FDI) with China, and the engagement strategy with North Korea. Though strategic motivations are important, economic motivations for engagement have become more crucial, especially since the 2000 summit.

This changed regional and domestic context has caused South Korea's long-term strategic concerns to shift from Seoul's previous Cold War focus. Instead of the Cold War policy that emphasized deterrence of the North, South Korea's priority has now adjusted; although deterrence remains important, the South is increasingly focused on reconciliation with the North. This change in South Korean foreign policy focus, however, should not be overstated: South Koreans still overwhelmingly view the United States in a positive light, and despite the strain on the alliance brought about by the events of the 1990s and 2000s, South Koreans generally desire both the security alliance and close economic relations with the United States to continue.

South Korea's Relations with China

Much like every other country in the region, South Korea increasingly sees its economic fate tied to the future of the Chinese economy. The potential benefits are large, especially given the two countries' geographic proximity and shared cultural similarities. Though there are clearly worries in South Korea over the rapid rise of Chinese manufacturing and technological prowess, this concern has not stopped the headlong rush of South Korean firms into China. Nor does the South Korean government resist regional moves—mostly initiated by China—to further both economic integration and open borders.

In terms of economic cooperation, China's attraction to South Korea was exemplified in 2003 when the PRC surpassed the United States as the largest export market for South Korean products—a position the United States had held since 1965.[8] **Figure 1** shows total trade (imports and exports) between South Korea and the countries of China, Japan, and the United States. Most notable is not only that China has become the largest trading partner of South Korea but also how quickly that transition took place.[9] In 2003 South Korea invested more in China than did the United States ($4.7 billion to $4.2 billion). In 2003 ROK exports to China increased 35% to $47.5 billion, far surpassing South Korean exports to the United States, which increased 7% to $36.7 billion. Over 25,000 South Korean companies now have production facilities in China.[10] South Korea's Woori Bank has a 150-member research group focused on China, and by 2004 all the major South Korean banks had opened branch offices in China.[11]

---

[8] Korea International Trade Association, *Bridging the Pacific* no. XXXIV (January 2004).

[9] Scott Snyder, "The Beginning of the End of the U.S.-ROK Alliance?" PacNET 36, August 26, 2004.

[10] Moon Ihlwan, "Korea's China Play," *BusinessWeek*, March 29, 2004, 32.

[11] Kim Chang-gyu, "Korean banks race into China market," *Joongang Ilbo*, July 1, 2004.

The number of Chinese language schools in South Korea increased 44% in the two-year period from 2003 to 2005.[12] Over 1.6 million South Koreans visit China each year, a number that continues to grow.[13] In 2003, 35,000 South Koreans were studying at Chinese universities (comprising 46% of all foreign students in China), while over 180,000 South Koreans had become long-term residents in China.[14]

FIGURE 1 South Korea's major trade partners, 1990–2005

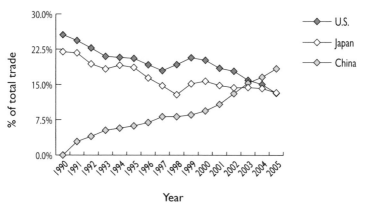

SOURCE: International Monetary Fund, *Direction of Trade Statistics*, 2005.

China's increased importance to South Koreans is due to more than economic interactions. In a survey of ROK National Assembly members in 2004, the newspaper *Donga Ilbo* found that 55% of newly elected members regarded China as the most important target of South Korea's future diplomacy, compared to the only 42% of "old-timers" who held the same view.[15] Jae-ho Chung notes that "despite the formidable threat that China may pose for Korea, no trace of concern for South Korea's security is evident in Seoul."[16] South Korea's 2004 National Security Strategy labels the ROK-China relationship a "comprehensive cooperative partnership" and calls for

---

[12] Park Sung-ha and Han Ae-ran, "Nihao mom? A Mandarin Approach to Child-Rearing Schools for Overseas Chinese See More Korean Students than Ever," *Joongang Ilbo*, March 14, 2006.

[13] James Brooke, "China 'Looming Large' in South Korea as Biggest Player, Replacing the U.S.," *New York Times*, January 3, 2003.

[14] Jae-ho Chung, "The 'Rise' of China and Its Impact on South Korea's Strategic Soul-Searching," in James Lister, ed., *The Newly Emerging Asian Order and the Korean Peninsula* (Washington, D.C.: Korea Economic Institute, 2005), 1–12.

[15] *Donga Ilbo*, April 19, 2004.

[16] Chung, "The 'Rise' of China and Its Impact on South Korea's Strategic Soul-Searching," 4.

greater military exchanges between the two countries.[17] In 2006 a senior South Korean government official stated that "China has no intention of threatening the Korean peninsula. China wants stability on its borders, and it has very good relations with us. We are also deeply intertwined on economic issues as well as cooperating on security issues."[18]

A U.S. Department of State poll conducted in late 2005 was particularly revealing.[19] When asked which country would be the future power center of Asia in five to ten years, 74% of South Koreans chose China, while only 9% chose the United States. When asked to predict who the closest economic partner would be in five to ten years, 11% of South Korean respondents indicated the United States, versus 68% who indicated China. Yet when polled about their attitudes, 53% of South Koreans held favorable opinions of both China and the United States. When asked about bilateral relationships, 78% of respondents felt that South Korea's bilateral relations with China were good, while 58% felt that bilateral relations with the United States were good. In sum, though South Korean public opinion views China as increasingly powerful in the region, the general view of China is positive.

ROK-China relations have not been completely smooth, however. In recent years the two countries have clashed verbally over the nature of the ancient kingdom of Koguryo (37 BC–668 AD), with both sides claiming that Koguryo was an historical antedecent to their modern nation. This dispute does not, however, appear likely to have any substantive effect on relations between the two countries, in part because the dispute is not a function of official Chinese government policy but rather is limited to unofficial claims made by Chinese academics.[20] China and North Korea formally delineated their border in 1962, with China ceding 60% of the disputed territory. In contrast to South Korea's territorial dispute with Japan (discussed below), the dispute over Koguryo is restricted to claims about history, and at no

[17] National Security Council, *Peace, Prosperity, and National Security: National Security Strategy of the Republic of Korea* (Seoul: National Security Council, 2004), http://www.korea.net/kois/pds/pdf/policy/security_en.pdf.

[18] Author interview with South Korean government official, March 17, 2006.

[19] U.S. State Department, Bureau of Intelligence and Research, "INF Poll: Asian Views of China," Foreign Broadcast Information Service, November 16, 2005. Poll results are from face-to-face interview surveys conducted in the summer and fall of 2005 with representative samples of adults in seven East Asian countries. Samples were chosen by multi-stage probability selection techniques.

[20] David Scofield, "China Puts Korean Spat on the Map," *Asia Times*, August 19, 2004, http://www.atimes.com/atimes/Korea/FH19Dg01.html.

time has the Chinese government made any attempt to abrogate the 1962 treaty or to re-negotiate the actual border.[21]

Of more relevance is the nascent competition between South Korea and China for influence in North Korea as well as the rapidity with which China is catching up to South Korea's technological lead in manufacturing. As will be discussed later in this section, both China and South Korea are firmly engaged with North Korea. This engagement could lead China to have more influence than South Korea on the future of North Korea. As one experienced member of an NGO that has deep ties with North Korea noted recently, "China is essentially pushing aid and economic relations over the border to the North. They have far more access to the North than does South Korea, and this is worrying the South Koreans as they look to the coming years."[22] Some South Koreans are concerned that overall Chinese economic and political importance to the peninsula will provide Beijing too great an influence over both Koreas, to the detriment of South Korea's own interests.

Furthermore, South Korean manufacturing firms are increasingly finding themselves in direct competition with Chinese firms. Korea's technological lead over Chinese firms has shrunk more rapidly than might have been anticipated even a few years ago. South Korean firms currently have an estimated three-to-five-year lead on Chinese firms, down from the ten-year lead of just a few years ago.[23]

In sum, despite some tensions in the ROK-China relationship, on the whole China has rapidly become an extremely important economic and diplomatic partner for South Korea. South Korea has warm and increasingly close relations with China along a range of security, economic, and diplomatic issues and does not want to be forced to choose between Beijing or Washington. Although there is little sentiment in Seoul to replace the United States with China as South Korea's closest ally—and despite Seoul regarding Beijing's influence in Pyongyang as worrisome—continued improvement in Seoul's relations with Beijing means that South Korea's foreign policy orientation is gradually shifting. Though still important, the United States is no longer the only powerful country to which South Korea must pay attention.

---

[21] For a detailed study of China's territorial dispute resolution, see Taylor Fravel, "Regime Insecurity and International Cooperation: Explaining China's Compromises in Territorial Disputes," *International Security* 30, no. 2 (Fall 2005): 46–83.

[22] Author's interview with a member of an NGO, April 22, 2006.

[23] Author's personal communication from a senior official of South Korea's Ministry of Finance and the Economy, June 12, 2006.

South Korea-Japan Relations

In recent years, friction between Japan and South Korea has erupted over Japanese junior high school textbooks, visits by the Japanese prime minister to the Yasukuni shrine, and the issue of "comfort women."[24] In the past few years tension has particularly arisen over rival Japanese and South Korean claims to ownership of a set of islands in the East Sea. Though South Korea currently exercises de facto control over the islands, the two countries have never officially delineated ownership in a formal treaty.

Given that South Korea and Japan are both advanced capitalist democracies that maintain deep alliances with the United States, South Korea's recent troubles with Japan are somewhat surprising. Furthermore, both countries are linked by deep economic ties.

Relations between South Korea and Japan have worsened in part because of domestic politics: leaders of both sides have been pandering to their domestic constituents, with making an issue over a meaningless set of rocks being easier than focusing on divisive and difficult issues such as North Korean nuclear proliferation, free trade agreements, and how to deal with the United States and China. Both sides suffer partly from a lack of leadership: whereas Koizumi and Roh should be taking the lead in moving the Japan-ROK relationship forward, both are content to dwell on historical matters. Finally, such issues are a convenient substitute for other frustrations the two sides have with each other: South Korea is concerned over Tokyo's moves to change Japan's military stance, while Japan is frustrated that South Korea continues to engage rather than contain North Korea. All these issues combine to make an explosive mix of sentiment and anger.

Gilbert Rozman notes that accusations between the two countries have been cultural rather than strategic or economic.[25] For example, on the occasion marking the 87th anniversary of the March 1st Independence Movement in South Korea, Roh advised Koizumi that an act of a nation's leader should be judged by the standard of whether such an act is proper in light of universal conscience and historical experience. Roh's remarks that Japan's status as an "ordinary country" should not necessarily entail a military build-up (referring to Japan's efforts to revise its pacifist constitution) were followed by Koizumi's advice to Roh to take a close look at both Japan's record during the 60-year postwar period and Tokyo's efforts

---

[24] "Comfort women" were East Asians (mostly South Koreans and Filipinos) who the Japanese forced into sexual slavery during World War II.

[25] Gilbert Rozman, *Northeast Asia's Stunted Regionalism: Bilateral Distrust in the Shadow of Globalization* (Cambridge: Cambridge University Press, 2004).

toward a friendly relationship with Seoul.[26] While the leaders of both nations were busy giving each other advice, the problems threatened to spiral out of control.[27]

Yet it is important to keep these diplomatic disputes in context: very few of these disputes have had actual consequences for policies or relations between Japan and South Korea. The long-discussed free trade agreement (FTA) between the two countries is dormant not because of clashes over history but rather due to much more mundane domestic politics and an unwillingness by either side to give ground on agricultural issues. Though ROK policy toward North Korea was stalled in 2006, this lack of movement was because the Six-Party Talks themselves have not seen progress. In fact, absolute trade and investment flows between the two countries continue to increase, despite the fact that the relative share of Japan's total trade with South Korea has declined. Indeed, total trade between Japan and South Korea increased almost $30 billion between 2001 and 2005.[28] Japan and South Korea have also continued to work together on a number of other issues. For example, in 2005 the two countries agreed to a bilateral currency swap. The agreement, worth $3 billion, will help stabilize South Korean and Japanese financial markets and allow for the lending of short-term capital to either side when foreign currency reserves run short. Nobuhiro Hiwatari notes that "there has been little complaint from Japanese multinational corporations that their businesses have been hurt in Korea."[29] Thus, although diplomatic relations between Seoul and Tokyo are hardly warm, such disputes have remained the province of rhetoric and domestic showmanship and have not affected actual interactions between the two states to a significant degree.

U.S.-ROK Relations

As ROK-China relations continue to become closer and ROK-Japan relations remain stalled, the U.S.-ROK alliance is under greater strain than ever before. True, South Korea has clearly not abandoned the United States for the embrace of China and cooperation and interaction is still deeper

---

[26] Quoted in David Kang and Jiyoung Lee, "Japan-Korea Relations: *seirei keinetsu (cold politics, warm economics)*," *Comparative Connections* (April 1, 2006): 5.

[27] In spring of 2006, the Japanese announced plans to send a survey vessel into what South Korea considers its territorial waters. The ROK government responded by announcing plans to send four naval vessels to meet the Japanese ship and if necessary board the ship.

[28] Figures quoted in Wonhyuk Lim, "KORUS FTA: A Strategic and Pragmatic View," Policy Forum Online 06-46A (Nautilus Institute, June 13, 2006), 6.

[29] Nobuhiro Hiwatari, "Japan in 2005: Koizumi's Finest Hour," *Asian Survey* 46, no. 1 (January/February 2006): 22–36.

with the United States than with China; Seoul has, however, moved in the direction of warmer ties with Beijing and less dependence on the United States—a transition that, while slow, has accelerated in the past few years. Indeed, it is becoming increasingly possible that the U.S.-ROK alliance will undergo a fundamental change. Though in part this is a natural evolution, this process also reflects starkly different perspectives between the two countries on major international issues. As Scott Snyder notes, "the alliance appears demonstrably less important to both Americans and South Koreans than it was during the Cold War."[30]

The U.S.-ROK alliance has succeeded beyond expectations, however, in maintaining peace at the strategic crossroads of Northeast Asia, promoting South Korean economic development, and helping to enable the emergence of one of East Asia's most vibrant and successful democracies. The United States, of course, pursued mutual U.S.-ROK security interests in maintaining regional peace, which was the prerequisite for South Korean development. Economically, South Korea is now the tenth largest economy in the world and the seventh largest trading partner of the United States. The United States is the largest foreign investor in South Korea and total trade between the two countries amounted to $70 billion in 2005.

South Koreans overwhelmingly value the U.S.-ROK alliance and welcome a U.S. military presence in South Korea. Press reports in the United States have often overstated the level of anti-Americanism in South Korea. Contrary to public perception, both sides value the alliance and the long-standing U.S.-ROK relationship. In hopes of strengthening the alliance, the ROK has particularly sought to cooperate with the United States in many diverse areas. For example, South Korea is providing the largest contingent of troops to Iraq after the United States and United Kingdom. The relocation of U.S. military bases outside of Seoul proceeded with minimal protest, and U.S. and South Korean negotiators are beginning discussions over a FTA between the two countries. Indeed, there remains deep appreciation and warmth for the United States in South Korea. Erik Larson notes that there continues to be "substantial support for the alliance and a continued U.S. military presence in South Korea."[31]

In sum, South Korea desires to maintain a close alliance with the United States and continues to see the United States as an important economic and political partner. There are deep cultural ties between the two countries as well. Yet South Korea's foreign policy has begun to shift, perhaps inevitably,

---

[30] Scott Snyder, "The Beginning of the End of the U.S.-ROK Alliance?" PacNET 36, August 26, 2004.

[31] Erik Larson, "An Analysis of The September 2003 *Joongang Ilbo*-CSIS Polls of South Korean Attitudes Toward the U.S.," paper prepared for the CSIS Study group on South Korean Attitudes toward the United States, December 13, 2003, 1.

toward East Asia and China. This shift includes a major emphasis on multilateral and bilateral trade and investment arrangements with both regional and global actors.

South Korea's Increasing Regional Orientation

The trend away from a U.S. focus and toward East Asia was given further impetus by the 1997 Asian financial crisis. This major shock to economies throughout the region revealed both the increasingly interconnected nature of regional economies and a number of deep problems with the way many of the economies were organized. In the wake of the crisis, South Korea engaged in comprehensive economic reforms and by 2006 has become far more open to investors and corporate governance reform and transparency than during the country's era of high growth. South Korea has also begun to put more energy and resources into ROK economic relations in the region. Despite these changes, however, South Korea remains far from being a decentralized economy in which the government merely performs regulatory functions.

In some areas South Korea has dealt forthrightly with the structural problems in its economy. For example, South Korea has vigorously pursued reform of the financial sector and openness to foreign investment. The banking crisis also appears to have largely ended—though non-performing loans comprised over 16% of total loans in 1998, the percentage of non-performing loans by 2001 was only 2.4%.[32] In terms of foreign direct investment, FDI flows increased rapidly following both the 1997 crisis and Kim Dae-jung's liberalization of the Korean market (see **Figure 2**).[33] Since 1997 U.S. FDI commitments have surpassed $20 billion.

In other areas, however, reform has been more difficult. Chaebol reform in particular has proven to be partial at best. Some groups were dismantled: the Hyundai Group, for example, was split into three separate companies. The excessively high debt ratios of the major chaebols have also been significantly reduced—publicly listed firms had an average debt-equity ratio of 96.7% in 2004, down from 396% in 1997.[34]

---

[32] Peter Chow, "Financial Restructuring and Corporate Governance in Korea and Taiwan after 1997: Toward Sustainable Development in East Asia," in James Lister, ed., *The Newly Emerging Asian Order and the Korean Peninsula* (Washington, D.C.: Korea Economic Institute, 2006), 77–102.

[33] Mark Manyin, "South Korea-U.S. Economic Relations: Cooperation, Friction, and Prospects for a Free Trade Agreement (FTA)," CRS Report for Congress (Washington, D.C.: Congressional Research Service, February 9, 2006), 3.

[34] Peter Chow, "Financial Restructuring and Corporate Governance in Korea and Taiwan after 1997: Toward Sustainable Development in East Asia," in James Lister, ed., *The Newly Emerging Asian Order and the Korean Peninsula* (Washington, D.C.: Korea Economic Institute, 2006), 88.

FIGURE 2   Foreign direct investment in South Korea, 1996–2005

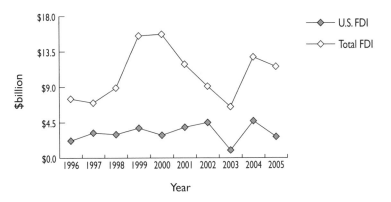

SOURCE: Republic of Korea Ministry of Commerce, Industry, and Energy, 2005.

Progress in reforming corporate governance and increasing transparency, however, has been more partial. Vestiges of the developmental state, with its interference into the economy, and a nationalist mindset all remain in South Korea. These attitudes and institutions have proven fairly difficult to change. Although inward FDI has been liberalized, South Korean nationalism continues to pose problems for foreign investors. Chaebol owners themselves resist foreign ownership or even board membership by foreigners. Perhaps the most notable example was Sovereign's ultimately failed bid to put outside members on the board of SK corporation, despite both Sovereign being the largest shareholder in the company and the SK chairman having been convicted of accounting fraud.[35]

In addition to domestic economic reforms, the ROK also began to pursue economic and institutional ties more actively throughout the region; these ties are both formal, such as the ASEAN+3, and informal, such as increased outward FDI by individual South Korean companies. Although the causes and consequences of the 1997 financial crisis have been hotly debated, worth noting is that Western and Asian perceptions of these causes and consequences tend to be at odds with each other. Western analyses have tended to emphasize the poor business practices of Asian firms (e.g., leveling allegations of "crony capitalism"), while Asian analyses tend to emphasize the indifferent attitude of the IMF and, in particular, the U.S. government.[36]

---

[35] Moon Ilhwan, "Staging a Revolt at the SK Chaebol," *BusinessWeek* March 14, 2005, http://www.businessweek.com/magazine/content/05_11/b3924076.htm.

[36] Michael Vatikiotis, "Pacific Divide: Southeast Asians are Smouldering over What They See as America's Cool Response to Their Economic Woes," *Far Eastern Economic Review*, November 6, 1997, 14.

Donald Emmerson notes that "…from within ASEAN…Washington was reproached for hostility, or indifference, or both—for torching the region's economies and then letting them burn."[37] More important than the reality of what caused the crisis is noting that these different perceptions exist and have shaped the way in which some countries (such as South Korea) have viewed their foreign economic policies and relations. As Marcus Noland has noted, "the crisis served to make Asian countries more aware of their Asian identity."[38]

Despite spanning the globe, South Korea's current trade, investment, and production networks are increasingly focused on East Asia. In 2005 South Korea hosted the APEC summit meeting. South Korea has also joined numerous regional and international organizations such as ASEAN+3, the ASEAN Regional Forum, and the Chiang Mai initiative, the last of which is a currency swap arrangement among Asian states designed to help prevent the currency crisis that led to the financial crisis. South Korea's shift to a regional emphasis is perhaps best exemplified by its outward foreign direct

TABLE 1   South Korean outward FDI by region ($million)

	2000	2001	2002	2003	2004
North America	1,401	1,462	564	1,040	1,376
Asia	1,532	1,332	1,677	2,242	3,190
Europe	289	2,129	957	211	683
Other	1,774	152	368	305	465
Total	4,996	5,075	3,566	3,797	5,715

SOURCE: Economist Intelligence Unit, *South Korea: Country Profile 2005* (London: Economist Intelligence Unit, 2005).

investment. Although the United States was as recently as 2000 the largest recipient of outward FDI, by 2004 well over twice as much South Korean investment went to Asia than to North America (see **Table 1**).

South Korea has also begun to pursue a number of FTAs with various countries.[39] Since ratifying its first FTA with Chile in 2004, South Korea

---

[37] Donald K. Emmerson, "What Do the Blind-Sided See? Reapproaching Regionalism in Southeast Asia," *The Pacific Review* 18, no. 1 (March 2005): 1–21.

[38] Marcus Noland, quoted on Marketplace, May 5, 2006, http://marketplace.org.

[39] T.J. Pempel and Shujiro Urata, "Japan: A New Move toward Bilateral Trade Agreements," in Vinod K. Aggarwal and Shujiro Urata, eds., *Bilateral Trade Arrangements in the Asia-Pacific: Origins, Evolution, and Implications* (London: Routledge, 2005); and Chung-in Moon, "In the Shadow of Broken Cheers: The Dynamics of Globalization in South Korea," in Aseem Prakash and Jeffrey Hart, eds., *Responding to Globalization* (London: Routledge, 2000).

has concluded such agreements with Singapore and the European Union and begun feasibility studies or actual negotiations with Canada, Mexico, MERCOSUR, ASEAN, and India. In the meantime, FTA talks between South Korea and ASEAN have made substantial progress, with last-minute negotiations at the 2005 APEC summit aimed at finalizing the deal. For South Korea, the most important potential FTAs are those with China, Japan, and the United States, agreements which are all currently under negotiation.

Despite the fact that South Korea has gone through six rounds of negotiations with Japan over an FTA, there has to date been little progress. This lack of progress is in large part due to domestic opposition from agricultural interests in both countries. Japan and South Korea found themselves in a similar negotiating stance over agricultural trade during the 2005 Doha Round of WTO talks that were held in Hong Kong. Both South Korea and Japan have been under strong and diametrically opposed pressure from inside and outside of the country. Domestic agricultural interests in both countries linked the cultural tradition of viewing "rice as 'the life of our nation'" as a justification for continued governmental support for, and defense of, agriculture; criticism from rice producing countries over the Japanese and South Korean protective approach increased during the Hong Kong talks. In order to placate such criticism, in November 2005 following negotiations with the United States, China, Thailand, and six other rice producers—South Korea's National Assembly passed legislation allowing increased imports of rice. The South Korean government will double its current 4% limit on rice imports by 2014 and eventually open the rice market fully, all while increasing subsides to rice farmers.

Within the business community, however, there is widespread support for a China-Japan-South Korea FTA. The Trilateral Joint Research Team conducted a survey of business enterprises in these three countries and found that 85% of Chinese businesses, 79% of Japanese businesses, and 71% of South Korean businesses support the idea.[40] Estimates hold that a Korea-China FTA would increase South Korea's GDP somewhere between 0.14% and 2.47%. Because Japan and South Korea's economies are similar— and thus competitive—the effects of a Japan-South Korea FTA on South Korea's GDP is estimated to be less beneficial.[41] Given this, South Korea's

---

[40] Quoted in Inkyo Cheong, "East Asian Economic Integration: Implications for a U.S.-Korea FTA," (manuscript, Inha University, 2004), 9.

[41] See, for example, Inkyo Cheong, *Hanil FTA kyungjaejeork hyokawa sisajeon* [Economic Effects of Korea-Japan FTA and Policy implications for Korea], KIEP Policy Analysis 01-04 (Seoul: KIEP, 2001); and Bank of Korea, *Hanjoongil Kukjaemooyeokeui bikyobunseokwa jeonmang* [Comparative Analysis and Prospects for International Trade between China, Korea, and Japan], (Seoul: Bank of Korea, 2001).

manufacturing sector is more cautious than Japan's about moving forward too quickly.

One of the most important of the potential FTAs currently under negotiation is that between South Korea and the United States. In May 2006 the United States and South Korea began negotiations over a U.S.-ROK FTA. Scheduled to be completed by March 2007 due to the expiration of the U.S. president's "trade promotion authority" in July of the same year, the negotiations are on a tight timeline. Because domestic interests—in particular, agriculture—in both the United States and ROK have virtual veto power over an agreement, however, actual ratification and implementation is likely to be a long and difficult process.

A successful FTA could have a potentially positive economic and political impact on U.S.-ROK relations. By removing tariff and non-tariff barriers to trade, the FTA would bring even further significant gains to both countries. Many studies of the economic impact of a U.S.-ROK FTA conclude that because industrial structures in South Korea and the United States are complementary rather than competitive, South Korea's GDP would increase between 0.36% and 1.73%.[42] The South Korean government estimates that an FTA with the United States could increase the ROK GDP by 2%, ROK exports to the United States by 15%, and South Korean manufacturing employment by 6.5%. A similar study by the Korea Institute for International Economic Policy predicted U.S. exports to South Korea would rise $12.2 billion and South Korea's exports to the U.S. would increase $7.1 billion.[43]

Much of the opposition to the FTA is coming from powerful and well-organized interest groups in South Korea, notably the agricultural sector. There is widespread skepticism in South Korea that an FTA would actually prove beneficial, and the FTA could fall prey to domestic politics given that a presidential election is coming up in December 2007.[44]

---

[42] Seungjoo Lee, "The Political Economy of FTAs in Northeast Asia: A South Korean Perspective," (paper presented at the conference Northeast Asia's Economic and Security Regionalism: Old Constraints and New Prospects, Center for International Studies, University of Southern California, Los Angeles, March 3–4, 2006).

[43] Lee Tae-sik, "U.S.-South Korea Trade Ties," *Washington Times*, February 19, 2006, http://www.washtimes.com/commentary/20060218-100154-6636r.htm; and U.S. Department of State, "U.S.-Republic of Korea Free Trade Agreement," February 7, 2006, www.scoop.co.nz/stories/WO0602/S00078.htm.

[44] Wonhyuk Lim, "KORUS FTA: A Strategic and Pragmatic View," Policy Forum Online 06-46A (Nautilus Institute, June 13, 2006).

South-North Economic Relations

Within the larger context of a foreign policy that emphasizes interdependence and a focus on economic issues, the issue that most visibly reveals the changing nature of South Korea's overall foreign policy approach is Seoul's strategy for solving the North Korea problem. U.S. and South Korean policies were relatively in accord during the entire Cold War period and well into the first North Korean nuclear crisis of 1993–94. As recently as the mid-1990s, South Korea viewed North Korea primarily as an imminent military threat.[45] Yet the past decade has seen a major change in how South Korea views itself, North Korea, and the ROK's own preferred method for resolving the issue of a divided Korean Peninsula. The 2002 crisis over North Korea's nuclear programs showed how far the two countries had drifted apart in their foreign policies and perceptions and how far South Korean fears had progressed that the United States would initiate a conflict on the peninsula that could devastate the ROK.[46]

The United States continues to view North Korea primarily in military terms and is worried about North Korean military strength, in particular Pyongyang's nuclear weapons program. The United States is concerned over the potential sale of either nuclear material or missiles to terrorist groups such as Al Qaeda, which would in turn use such weapons against the United States. Furthermore, although from 1999 to 2006, Pyongyang placed a voluntary moratorium on tests of its ICBMs, its unsuccessful test of a Taepodong-2 missile in July 2006 heightened fears throughout the region about its weapons program.[47] In response, the United States has generally attempted to isolate North Korea and is pursuing a complex mix of negotiation and coercion in an attempt to convince North Korea to halt its nuclear programs.[48]

By contrast, South Korea has come to view the North Korea problem primarily in economic and political terms and is now more concerned over the weak nature of the North Korean state, which could likely lead the government to collapse or descend into chaos. South Koreans believe that North Korea can be deterred and are instead worried about the economic and political consequences of a collapsed regime. To put the matter in

---

[45] Victor Cha notes that historically it was South Korea's fear that the U.S. would not take this threat perception seriously that drove the U.S.-Korea relationship. See Cha, *Alignment Despite Antagonism* (Stanford, CA: 1999).

[46] Much of this section draws on Victor Cha and David Kang, *Nuclear North Korea: A Debate on Engagement Strategies* (New York: Columbia University Press, 2003).

[47] P. Parameswaran, "North Korea Flexes Missile Muscle to Grab US Attention," Agence France-Presse, June 13, 2006, http://www.defencetalk.com/news/publish/printer/printer_6415.php.

[48] For overviews of the 2002 crisis and its aftermath, see Victor Cha and David Kang, "Can North Korea Be Engaged?" *Survival* 46 (2) (Summer 2004): 89–108.

perspective, should North Korea collapse, the number of refugees could potentially exceed the entire global refugee population of 2004.[49] Even assuming a best-case scenario in which such a collapse did not turn violent, the regional economic and political effects would be severe.[50]

In preparation for such an outcome, South Korea has embarked on a path of economic interdependence and political reconciliation with North Korea. Having begun a decade ago, this new policy will most likely continue to be South Korea's primary foreign policy direction. The goal is to slowly change North Korea through increased economic and cultural ties and to promote reform in the DPRK through aid and investment. South Korea appears to be solidly on course to pursue interdependence relative to North Korea, and this policy appears to fit comfortably with China's approach to the region.

This change in South Korea's foreign policy toward North Korea appears to be quite deeply rooted. South Korea's much deeper long-term question has proven more complex: how best to manage and ultimately solve the North Korean issue—even if nuclear weapons are no longer a factor—and simultaneously arrive at a sustainable long-term economic, political, and military relationship with an increasingly powerful China. As a result, managing the nuclear issue has been a necessary step to reintegration, and South Korea's foreign policy over the past decade has reflected this more fundamental goal of unifying the peninsula.

South Korean engagement of North Korea actually began under the Kim Young-sam government, when South Korean non-governmental organizations, most of which were Christian-based, ignored governmental prohibitions against sending aid to North Korea during its famine.[51] With the Kim Dae-jung administration (1998–2003) and continuing with the Roh Moo-hyun administration (2003–08), South Korean official policy changed as well. Kim had long criticized the conservative military governments for both excessively politicizing the North Korean threat and impeding inter-Korea reconciliation efforts. As president, Kim called for a "sunshine policy" that would engage North Korea and begin the reconciliation process.

Currently, official ROK policy toward North Korea is explicitly based upon the idea both that trade and interdependence can promote peace and stability on the peninsula and that encouraging North Korea to continue

---

[49] *World Refugee Survey 2004*, U.S. Committee for Refugees and Immigrants, http://www.refugees.org/data/wrs/04/pdf/key_statistics.pdf and www.refugees.org/article.aspx?id=1156.

[50] See, for example, Richard Ellings and Nicholas Eberstadt, eds., *Korea's Future and the Great Powers* (Seattle, WA.: University of Washington Press, 2001).

[51] L. Gordon Flake and Scott A. Snyder, eds., *Paved with Good Intentions: The NGO Experience in North Korea* (Westport, CT: Praeger, 2003).

economic reforms and opening to the international community is the best path toward achieving stability and peace on the peninsula. Regarding the increasing economic and cultural ties between North and South Korea, for instance, the South Korean Ministry of Unification stated that "with the peaceful use of the demilitarized zone, the eased military tension, and confidence building measures, the foundation for peaceful unification will be prepared."[52]

Thus, for almost a decade, South Korea has consistently pursued a policy of economic engagement toward North Korea that has been designed to encourage North Korean economic reforms. Following the shift to the sunshine policy, South Korea rapidly increased its relations with North Korea: North-South merchandise trade has rapidly increased over the past five years, with merchandise trade between the two sides increasing 50% from 2004 to 2005, exceeding $1 billion for the first time (see **Figure 3**).[53] Commercial trade amounted to 65% of total North-South trade in 2005, while non-commercial (government) trade accounted for less than 35%.

FIGURE 3   Total trade between North and South Korea, 1989–2005

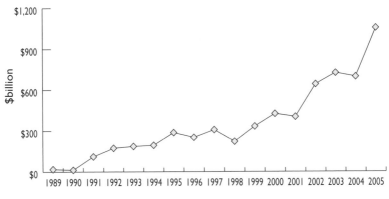

SOURCE: Ministry of Unification, "Statistics on Inter-Korean Trade," http://www.unikorea.go.kr.

Thus, while the government is supporting the economic integration of the

---

[52] Ministry of Unification, "Peace and Prosperity: White Paper on Korean Unification 2005," (Seoul: Ministry of Unification, 2005), 106–108. See also MOU, "Kaesong Kongdan geonseol silmu jobchuk bodo chamgojaryo," (Seoul: Ministry of Unification, December 8, 2002).

[53] "Inter-Korean Trade Beats $1 Billion in 2005," *JoongAng Ilbo*, January 23, 2006; and Economist Intelligence Unit, *North Korea: Country Report 2003* (London: The Economist Intelligence Unit, 2003), 19.

two Koreas, private firms are also heavily involved. Trade with South Korea accounted for 20% of North Korea's total trade in 2004, while South Korea's $256 million worth of economic assistance comprised 61% of total external assistance to the North.

With the official approval of both South and North Korean governments, South Korean conglomerates rapidly expanded their activities in the DPRK. Thirty-nine South Korean firms were granted permission in 2002 to establish cooperation partnership arrangements with North Korea.[54] Perhaps the most notable success has been the Kaesong Industrial Park, a special economic zone or industrial park just north of the DMZ in the ancient capital city of Kaesong. Designed to use South Korean capital and North Korean labor, the zone will consist of a railroad and roads that connect the two sides by crossing the DMZ.[55] The first products from Kaesong, North Korean-made iron kitchen pots, became available in Seoul in December 2004 and sold out in one day.[56] Currently shoes, clothes, electronic products, machinery, and some semiconductors and communication equipment are being produced at Kaesong.[57]

Kaesong in some ways represents the most visible success of South Korea's policy of engagement with North Korea. The actual economic benefit of Kaesong at this initial stage is minimal: North Korean earnings are estimated to be less than $20 million annually in rent and taxes, and of the less than twenty South Korean companies currently operating in Kaesong, few are profitable. The South Korean government currently has plans to license another twenty firms to operate in Kaesong by the end of 2006, however, and South Korea explicitly excluded Kaesong when reducing aid to North Korea following the DPRK missile tests of July 2006.[58]

South-North negotiations have covered a wide range of issues, such as reconnecting the railroads across and repaving a road through the DMZ, creation of joint sports teams, family reunions, economic assistance, and—most significantly—military discussions.[59] In 2004 the two sides agreed to the establishment of a hotline between North and South Korea, held the

---

[54] *Joongang Ilbo*, April 16, 2000, http://www.joins.com/top.html.

[55] *Donga Ilbo*, "Road Connecting the Two Koreas Opens," December 1, 2004.

[56] *Yonhap News*, "First Products from Inter-Korean Project Due on Sale in South This Week," December 13, 2004.

[57] Sang-young Rhyu, "North Korea's Economy and East Asia's Regionalism: Opportunities and Challenges" (paper presented at the conference Northeast Asia's Economic and Security Regionalism: Old Constraints and New Prospects, Center for International Studies, University of Southern California, Los Angeles, March 3–4, 2006).

[58] Author's personal communication from a senior U.S. official, August 1, 2006.

[59] David Kang, "North Korea's Economy," in Robert Worden, ed., *North Korea: A Country Study* (Washington, D.C.: Federal Research Bureau, 2005).

first high-level meeting between North and South Korean military generals since the Korean War, and halted the decades-long propaganda efforts along the DMZ.[60] In 2005 North and South Korea established three hundred direct telephone lines linking South Korea with the Kaesong industrial zone for the first time since the Soviet troops severed telephone lines in 1945.

Growing contacts with North Korea reinforced the perception in South Korea that their neighbor to the north was more to be pitied than feared. For example, the Hyundai group established a tour of Mt. Kumgang on the east coast of North Korea, a destination that more than 275,000 South Koreans visited in 2005 and over 1.1 million total have visited since 2000. In 2005 alone, the two governments allowed 660 family members who had been separated by the division to hold reunions.[61] Meetings between divided families have occurred on an intermittent basis, and both countries agreed to march together in the Olympics under the "unification flag."[62]

To be sure, there is much skepticism both about Kim Jong-il's intentions and about the extent of North Korea's market-socialism reform policies. Observers in the United States and South Korea remain divided over the extent and likely success of the reforms.[63] Peter Hayes notes that "the regime is investing in minerals development, niche markets for exporting cheap labor or embodied labor, a boot-strapping sector, and real estate development on the DMZ that combined represent a long-term and slowly growing economic foundation for a nuclear-armed DPRK."[64] Alternatively, Marcus Noland has an "essentially pessimistic" view of the North Korean reforms, noting that "it is fair to say that the reforms have been a mixed bag, not delivering as expected and contributing to increasing social differentiation and inequality."[65] Regardless of North Korean intentions,

---

[60] James Brooke, "2 Koreas Sidestep U.S. to Forge Pragmatic Links," *New York Times*, June 26, 2004.

[61] Christine Ahn, "Reunification Is on the March," *International Herald Tribune*, February 9, 2006.

[62] Ruediger Frank, "Economic Reforms in North Korea (1998–2003): Systemic Restrictions, Quantitative Analysis, Ideological Background," *Journal of the Asia Pacific Economy* 10, no. 3 (2005): 278–311.

[63] See, for example, Stephan Haggard and Marcus Noland, *Famine in North Korea: Aid, Markets and Reform* (New York: Columbia University Press, 2006); Bradley Babson, "Visualizing a North Korean "Bold Switchover": International Financial Institutions and Economic Development in the DPRK," *Asia Policy* 2 (July 2006); and Marcus Noland, "Transition from the Bottom-Up: Institutional Change in North Korea," (paper presented at the Institute for International Economics, Washington, D.C., March 20, 2006).

[64] Peter Hayes, "US Misses Mines for Nukes Opportunity," Nautilus Institute Special Report 06-34A, May 2, 2006.

[65] Marcus Noland, "How North Korea Funds Its Regime," testimony before the Senate Subcommittee on Federal Financial Management, Government Information, and International Security, Committee on Homeland Security and Governmental Affairs, Washington, D.C., April 26, 2006. See also Marcus Noland, "Transition from the Bottom-Up: Institutional Change in North Korea," (paper presented at the Institute for International Economics, Washington, D.C., March 20, 2006).

however, South Korea (along with China) has continued to follow a comprehensive engagement strategy toward the North. South Korea's policy has had the effect of increasing strains in the U.S.-ROK alliance, and the difference in the two countries' approaches to North Korea became clear soon after the election of George W. Bush in 2000. When a second North Korean nuclear program spurred a crisis in October 2002, U.S. and South Korean positions openly diverged. The South Korean populace and leadership urged restraint, whereas the Bush administration took a harder line. The South Koreans were concerned that, as a result of the Bush administration's open embrace of preemptive war as an instrument of national policy, North Korea would become a potential target of such a preemptive strike, with South Korea—particularly Seoul— being the victim and bearing the brunt of the ensuing devastation.

South Korean Identity

The 2002 South Korean presidential election revealed the degree of distance between the United States and South Korea on how to deal with North Korea. In large part, the election came down to a referendum on South Korea's stance toward North Korea and the United States. By a ratio of 49.8% to 48.1%, voters chose Roh Moo-hyun, who favored continued engagement with North Korea, over the more conservative Lee Hoi-chang, whose stance toward North Korea—suspending assistance until the DPRK cooperates on issues like arms control—more closely reflected that of the United States. In electing Roh Moo-hyun by the largest share in modern Korean political history, voters voiced their displeasure with the Bush administration's inflexible stance.[66] In January 2003, newly elected Roh Moo-hyun stated that "South Korea ranks as the twelfth to thirteenth largest economy in the world and I want to preside over our strong nation as its strong president. All I am asking is an equal partnership with the United States."[67]

The divergence between the United States and South Korea continued. With Bush's reelection in 2004, the United States continued attempts to isolate North Korea, refusing to engage in negotiations until Pyongyang had dismantled any nuclear weapons programs.[68] Conversely, South Korea

---

[66] In 1987, Roh Tae-woo received 36.5% of the popular vote; in 1992, Kim Young-sam received 41.4%, and in 1997 Kim Dae-jung received 40.3%.

[67] *Chosun Ilbo, No Dangsunja bukhaekdeung kwallyun chŏt tv toron* [President-elect Roh Speaks about North Korea's Nuclear Program in His First TV Forum], January 18, 2003, http://www. chosun.com/w21data/html/news/200301/200301180131.html.

[68] See Victor Cha and David Kang, "Can North Korea Be Engaged?" *Survival* 46, no. 2 (Summer 2004): 89–108.

continued an engagement strategy, leading to open friction between the two military allies. The South Korean 2004 defense white paper downgraded North Korea from "main enemy" to a "direct and substantial threat to our military." Despite a vocal, hard-line minority opinion in South Korea, in the past few years opinion polls regularly have shown over 70% of the population continuing to favor engagement.

Numerous skeptics question the wisdom of South Korea's policy toward North Korea. Indeed, South Korea's adamant refusal to take a harder line toward North Korea has both led some analysts to call South Korea's foreign policy "appeasement" and increased friction with the United States. Nicholas Eberstadt has called South Korea "a runaway ally," arguing that the United States ought to "work around" the Roh administration.[69] Ted Galen Carpenter and Doug Bandow have called for an "amicable divorce" between South Korea and the United States, suggesting that the U.S.-ROK alliance should be dissolved.[70]

While differences between South Korea and the United States over how to deal with North Korea are nothing new, in the past such differences often were tactical and so were resolved in large part because of the common perception that North Korea represented a serious security threat. In recent years, however, Seoul has viewed the Bush administration's apparent interest in fostering Pyongyang's collapse or in using military force as unacceptable, since either option would threaten the progress made over the past decade. Magnified by other tensions in the relationship—such as South Korea's increasing self-confidence and pride, anti-Americanism, and concerns about U.S. unilateralism—the Bush approach to North Korea has become the prism through which many South Koreans view the U.S.-ROK security relationship.

Disagreement over how best to deal with North Korea has both led to open friction between the United States and South Korea and put a severe strain on the alliance. In a series of speeches during his tenure, Roh Moo-hyun has reiterated the rationale behind engagement of North Korea. In a speech to the World Affairs Council of Los Angeles on November 12, 2004, Roh said he hoped that the United States would not use "hard-line measures" against the North and that "North Korea will not develop nuclear arms."[71] The South Korean Embassy in Washington, D.C. argued in a press

[69] Nicholas Eberstadt, "Tear Down This Tyranny," *The Weekly Standard*, November 29, 2004, http://www.weeklystandard.com/Content/Public/Articles/000/000/004/951szxxd.asp.

[70] Ted Galen Carpenter and Douglas Bandow, *The Korean Conundrum: America's Troubled Relations with North and South Korea* (London: Palgrave MacMillan, 2004).

[71] Roh Moo-hyun, quoted in *Yonhap*, "Roh Urges U.S. Not to Take Hard-Line Policy on N. Korea," November 13, 2004.

release that "a more confrontational U.S. policy approach is not likely to bear fruit. North Korea has never succumbed to external pressure over the past fifty years, despite the wishes of foreign ideologues."[72] The South Korean liberal newspaper *Hankyoreh Sinmun* editorialized that "the Koreans should resolve their own problems, including the nuclear issue."[73] Over one hundred respected figures in Korean society, including Catholic Cardinal Stephen Kim, sent the U.S. Embassy in Seoul an open letter urging the U.S. ambassador to reject military options.[74]

At one point in 2005, President Roh Moo-hyun's comments regarding U.S. policies toward North Korea were unusually direct. The United States had begun to publicly pressure South Korea to take a more active stance against North Korea's illegal financial activities, such as counterfeiting U.S. money. Roh said that:

> I don't agree (with) some opinions inside the U.S. that appear to be wanting to take issue with North Korea's regime, apply pressure, and sometimes wishing for its collapse. If the U.S. government tries to resolve the problem that way, there will be friction and disagreement between South Korea and the United States.[75]

When the United States released a press statement through the U.S. Embassy in Seoul "urging" South Korea to take action against North Korean financial transactions, the South Korean Foreign Ministry released a response calling the U.S. press release "inappropriate."[76]

South Korean popular support for an engagement policy appears to be deeply rooted and reflects the changing nature of South Korea's national identity. Over the past decade Seoul has begun to formulate a positive image and role for the ROK by rethinking South Korea's relationship to North Korea. After decades of demonizing North Korea and defining itself as North Korea's opposite, South Korea has begun to redefine itself as a "distant relative." Now feeling in a position of strength, South Korea is prodding North Korea to change. In a way, it is not surprising that South Korean national identity with respect to North Korea has begun to change. Not only do the two share a common history and culture, but by any measure—economic, political, cultural, or diplomatic—South Korea won

---

[72] Soo-dong O, "Defusing North Korea," press release by the Embassy of the Republic of Korea, Washington, D.C., December 1, 2004.

[73] Editorial, *Hankyoreh Sinmun*, November 7, 2004.

[74] *Donga Ilbo*, January 12, 2005.

[75] *The News*, "South Korean President Warns U.S. against Seeking Collapse of the North," January 26, 2006, http://www.ipcs.org/Jan_06_japan.pdf.

[76] Andrew Salmon, "Roh Opposes U.S. on Regime Change Plans for North, Warns of 'Difference of Opinion,'" *Washington Times*, January 26, 2006.

the competition with North Korea. Thus, it is relatively easy for Seoul to be magnanimous with Pyongyang.

Although some argue that only the younger generation of South Koreans supports the engagement policy toward North Korea, this is not the case. Indeed, discussion about a generational rift in South Korea is somewhat overstated.[77] In reality, among the South Korean populace there is widespread agreement that engagement is the proper strategy to follow. For example, a March 2005 opinion poll published in the South Korean newspaper *Donga Ilbo* showed 77% of Koreans supporting the use of diplomatic means and talks with North Korea in response to Pyongyang's nuclear weapons development and kidnapping of foreign civilians. Significantly, even those from the "older generations" were solidly in favor of engagement. Of those in their 60s or older, 63.6% supported diplomatic means.[78] In 2005, a Korean Institute for National Unification poll found that 85% of the general public and 95% of opinion leaders approved of North-South economic cooperation.[79]

In fact, a leftist (or "progressive") strand of South Korean politics is not new. Though masked during the Cold War, a long-running leftist element has existed in South Korean politics since the 1940s. Kim Kyung-won, a former ambassador to the United Nations and the United States under Chun Doo-hwan, made the following statement:

> South Korea has always had a deeply-held leftist strand of politics. Back in the 1940s it was probably stronger than the conservative forces, and only the U.S. military government allowed the right to win power. We thought [this strand] had disappeared under the military governments, but it did not. And now, it is back, reasserting itself.[80]

This leftist strand of politics was so strong that Park Chung-hee was forced to declare martial law from 1972 to 1979, during which time he temporarily closed the universities because of extensive student protests. After a coup d'etat in 1980, the entire city of Kwangju rose up in protest, and the demonstrations were only put down by the direct use of South Korean military units that were pulled off the DMZ.[81]

---

[77] Derek Mitchell, ed., *Strategy and Sentiment: South Korean Views of the United States and the U.S.-ROK Alliance* (Washington, D.C.: Center for Strategic and International Studies, 2004).

[78] *Donga Ilbo*, "Opinion Poll on South Korean Attitudes Toward Japan and Other Nations," March 4–31, 2005, http://www.donga.com/fbin/output?f=aps&n=20050460247&main=1.

[79] Ahn, "Reunification Is on the March."

[80] Author's interview with Kim Kyung-won, August 31, 2003.

[81] John Adams Wickham, *Korea on the Brink: From the "12/12 Incident" to the Kwangju Uprising, 1979–1980* (Washington, D.C.: National Defense University Press, 1999); and Linda Lewis, ed., *Laying Claim to the Memory of May: A Look Back at the 1980 Kwangju Uprising* (Honolulu: University of Hawai`i Press: Center for Korean Studies, University of Hawai`i, 2002).

Given widespread South Korean popular support for engagement, both the opposition and ruling parties are motivated by electoral purposes to back engagement toward North Korea. In 2005, for example, the opposition Grand National Party—often considered more hard line toward North Korea than the ruling Uri Party—submitted a proposal to establish a special economic zone along the entire border with North Korea to foster inter-Korean economic cooperation. The proposed zone, which would extend the current Kaesong industrial zone to Paju in South Korea's Kyeonggi province, includes plans to expand the economic boundary from Haeju in North Korea to Incheon in South Korea as a joint inter-Korean project similar to the Kaesong zone.[82]

South Korea's engagement and interdependence policies toward North Korea are echoed by China's approach. Arguing that North Korea was on the path to reform, Chinese officials have made public pronouncements urging a conciliatory line toward North Korea. In January 2005, Chinese ambassador to South Korea, Li Bin, argued that "to think that North Korea will collapse is far-fetched speculation. The fundamental problem is the North's ailing economy. If the economic situation improves, I think we can resolve the defector problem. The support of the South Korean government will greatly help North Korea in this respect."[83] In fact, Chinese trade and investment into North Korea far outstrips that of even South Korea; over half of total North Korean trade in 2005 was with China—almost double inter-Korean trade.[84] Without Chinese cooperation, the United States will find attempting to isolate North Korea to be difficult, if not impossible. Indeed, Kim Jong-il's nine-day visit to Chinese industrial zones in January 2006 was evidence not only that China continues to have warm relations with North Korea but also intends to continue a policy of engagement while showing no signs of a more coercive stance toward North Korea.

Three factors—China's role as mediator in the North Korean nuclear issue, South Korea's focus on long-term reintegration of North Korea rather than on nuclear weapons, and a U.S. concern with weapons of mass destruction—have combined to create a situation in which the United States and South Korea have come into increasing conflict over their respective goals and strategies toward North Korea.

In sum, South Korea's foreign policy orientation appears to be firmly focused on interdependence with North Korea as the keystone of its overall

[82] Annie I. Bang, "Bill on Inter-Korean Special Zone Proposed, Move Aims to Build Economic Community," *Korea Herald*, February 14, 2006.

[83] Li Bin, quoted in the *JoongAng Ilbo*, January 14, 2005.

[84] Robert Marquand, "North Korea's Border Trade Getting Busier," *Christian Science Monitor*, April 14, 2005, http://www.csmonitor.com/2005/0414/p01s04-woap.html.

foreign policy. The widespread popular support that exists for this policy shows few signs of abating. Indeed, until national reconciliation or some type of unification is achieved, North Korea will overwhelmingly be the first priority of South Korean foreign policy. Within that context, China's rapid economic development and similar perspective on the best policy to adopt toward North Korea have combined to cause South Korea to shift its foreign policy attention away from the United States. The strains in the U.S.-ROK alliance are real and reflect genuine policy differences over how to deal with North Korea.

Implications for U.S. Policy in the Region

South Korea's enduring geopolitical problem is its location at the intersection of a number of great powers. The Cold War, which allowed South Korea to concentrate primarily on bilateral relations with the United States, was an exception to this fundamental regional dynamic. Confronted with three major concerns—China's emergence, Japan's moves toward a "normal" foreign policy, and continued U.S. concern over North Korean nuclear weapons—Seoul faces the unenviable task of formulating a strategy that allows South Korea to retain some control over its own fate and pursue the primary goal of reconciliation with North Korea while at the same time juggling competing interests from a number of great powers.[85]

South Korea has no obvious choices about how best to craft its long-term foreign policy, and the actions of other states—especially those of the United States—will go a long way toward determining the constraints within which South Korea operates. Important to note, however, is this fundamental Korean dynamic: neither emotionalism nor anti-Americanism has been the cause of strife in the U.S.–ROK alliance.

South Korean Foreign Policy in the Next Five Years

Looking ahead five years, one can draw a number of tentative conclusions about the impact that Seoul's policies will have on both South Korea and the region. First, South Korea remains focused on reforming its domestic economy and realizing stable economic growth. Although South Korea's economy continues to expand—with growth from 1999 to 2004 averaging 6.4% per year—the era of double-digit economic growth is over. Thus, as South Korea's economy enters a mature phase, a main driver for foreign policy is Seoul's search for relationships and institutions that can

---

[85] Christopher Hughes, "Japan's Re-Emergence as a 'Normal' Military Power," International Institute for Strategic Studies, London, Adelphi Papers 368–9, 2005.

provide South Korea the means by which to realize stable and continued economic growth. Included in this endeavor will be regional efforts to build multilateral economic institutions, forge FTAs, and increase investment and other relationships around the region as well as efforts to strengthen the global trade and investment climate for South Korean growth, which is highly predicated on an open international economy.

Second, China-ROK economic relations will continue to grow both in size and in depth. The two economies are increasingly intertwined in both the range of relations and the size of those relations. South Korea appears to find much more in common with the foreign policy of China than with that of Japan or even the United States. From policy toward North Korea to skepticism about Japan's increasingly muscular foreign policy, China and South Korea appear to have similar foreign policy orientations.

Third, in terms of North-South economic relations the trend of economic integration is clearly increasing. Intra-Korean trade, although continuing to be a miniscule portion of South Korea's overall trade, is both a much larger portion of North Korea's trade and politically far more significant for South Korea than its volume would suggest. Although the nuclear issue will not likely be resolved anytime soon, within five years North-South economic relations will likely be even deeper than they are today. This has implications both for the nuclear issue and for North-South relations. Coercive U.S. measures against the North (such as sanctions) are unlikely to be successful if South Korea and China do not participate. Yet capitalism and economic trade may very well bring unintended consequences to the North; that is, greater information about the outside world may begin to change North Korean citizens' perceptions about themselves, their leader, and their place in the world. With the government having severed its direct link to the people by scaling back the public distribution system, citizens are increasingly forced to plan for their own economic security in ways that did not exist in the past.[86] Though the limited economic reforms will not likely destabilize the regime, such reforms could significantly weaken the regime.

Two potential events could affect these overall trends. First, following the 2007 presidential election in South Korea a new president may decide to adopt a different foreign policy toward North Korea. A president from the opposition Hannaradang could very well slow down or reverse the trend toward engagement. For example, Seoul's mayor Lee Myung-back has promised to "stem the red tide…of nascent socialism" if he were elected.[87] Yet worth noting is that, given the deep support for engagement of North

---

[86] Ser Myo-ja, "Marx meets Madison Avenue in North Korea," *Joongang Ilbo*, June 12, 2006.

[87] "Seoul Mayor Vows to Stem Red Tide," *Chosun Ilbo*, March 14, 2006, http://english.chosun.com/ w21data/html/news/200603/200603140023.html.

Korea—and the willingness of the South Korean populace to loudly and quickly voice their displeasure with governmental actions—such a reversal seems unlikely. Fully abandoning an engagement strategy would be difficult for Seoul given the widespread popular support in South Korea and the extensive institutional and infrastructural ties already in place over the past decade.

The second potential event that could affect current trends in South Korean policy is an unexpected crisis with Pyongyang: a North Korean nuclear weapons test or rapid regime collapse could lead South Korea's popular support for engagement to change quite quickly. Although support for engagement appears to be deeply rooted, the depth of public commitment to such a policy—should it become prohibitively costly or appear to be having negative results—is difficult to gauge.

The Future of U.S.-ROK Relations

That the U.S.-ROK alliance itself may change is to be expected and not feared. Furthermore, the relationship between the United States and South Korea—far deeper than just an alliance—comprises economic and cultural flows, immigration, and enduring values such as a firm commitment to capitalism and democracy. This relationship will continue to deepen no matter what form the military alliance between these two countries takes. To promote both U.S. and South Korean national interests and to further the goal of peace and stability in the region, however, both sides will need to avoid petty emotional squabbles and focus on the real issues confronting the alliance.

Three main implications for the United States arise from South Korea's foreign economic policy. First, the influence of South Korea's younger generation in policymaking circles is increasing and will only continue to increase over time. To retain influence on the peninsula the United States must recognize and prepare to work with, rather than against, this emerging South Korean policymaking elite.

Second, U.S. and ROK goals and policies toward North Korea are likely to continue to diverge. This trend may change with South Korea facing a presidential election in 2007, although a major foreign policy turn toward confrontation with North Korea is somewhat unlikely. Given China's clear preference for a stance of engaging North Korea, the United States will face a dilemma regarding peninsular policy: continue to follow a restrained containment policy at the risk of making no progress on the peninsula, or change direction toward an engagement strategy—an equally unlikely course.

Third, the United States and South Korea continue to work and cooperate quite closely on a number of other issues. South Korean support for the global war on terrorism has continued despite domestic skepticism regarding the deployment of South Korean troops to Iraq. Certain measures, such as a U.S. visa-waiver program, would help to strengthen ties between the two countries. Also important is timely completion of the U.S.-ROK FTA. U.S.-ROK relations can continue to improve through progress toward a free trade agreement. A successful FTA could be a positive force in the region, fostering competitive moves by other countries to conclude their own FTAs both with each other and with the United States. The FTA is not, however, a panacea that will solve the larger issues between the United States and South Korea; an agreement would be only one element of a diverse and deep relationship between the two countries.

The assessment presented here, although seemingly rather bleak, is not necessarily so pessimistic. Disagreements that arise because of strategic and substantive interests are more easily resolved than are disagreements over core values and attitudes. There exists a natural foundation upon which to further strengthen U.S.-ROK ties—strong economic and military ties bind the U.S. and ROK, and South Korean values are deeply rooted in capitalism and democracy. As South Korea becomes a mature and important regional and global economic power, the relationship with the United States is bound to change. If both the United States and South Korea recognize this and make adjustments, their relationship can continue to be a cornerstone of peace and prosperity in Northeast Asia.

EXECUTIVE SUMMARY

This chapter examines Russia's role in Asia, including to what extent Russia is turning eastward from Europe in its foreign economic and political strategies and what forces are driving Russia's actions.

MAIN ARGUMENT:

- Europe is Russia's principal trade partner. Looking ahead, however, Moscow desires to develop deeper economic ties with Asia, in part because of political differences with its European partners.

- Key to Russia's new Asia strategy is the building of an export pipeline for Siberian oil. With a growing global energy shortage, Russia's Siberian energy resources have a ready market in China, Japan, and South Korea. Further development of Russia's economic integration with Asia will, however, be a long and costly process.

POLICY IMPLICATIONS:

- With Sakhalin and Siberian oil and gas coming on-stream, Russia's economic presence in Asia will substantially increase. This development should lower U.S. anxiety over energy security in China and Japan.

- Moscow seems uninclined to link economic interests tightly with strategic goals. Japanese hopes that increased trade will lead to resolution of the Northern Territories question, therefore, may be misplaced.

- Though chances of sharing in the fruits of this Siberian oil boom are high, U.S. oil companies will need patience, a long-term perspective, and a willingness to play by Russia's rules of the game.

- With high oil prices and strong economic growth, Moscow will not be taking risks nor embarking on radical policy changes. The U.S. should not take too seriously scare scenarios such as the specter of a close Russian-Chinese alliance. The U.S. is a key partner for both Russia and China, and neither country wants to damage its relations with Washington.

Russia's Economic Role in Asia: Toward Deeper Integration

Peter Rutland

Russia is unique in being a country with a presence both in Asia and Europe. Less than eight million Russians, a mere 5% of the population, live in the Russian Far East (RFE)—yet Russia occupies one-fifth of the Asian landmass and holds immense mineral wealth. The country's energy resources are the key to Russia's economic and strategic role in Asia.

Russia sees both threats and opportunities in Asia. Similarly, Western commentary tends to emphasize two extremes. On one side is the vision of a bonanza of Russian resources flooding into energy-starved East Asian markets. On the other side are alarming scenarios—such as the thinly populated RFE being swamped by migrants from China to the south or a Russo-Chinese alliance challenging the United States for global hegemony.

None of these extreme scenarios are likely to come to pass—certainly not within the next five years. The Russian leadership, under no pressure to take any drastic and risky decisions, is most likely to follow a policy of cautious continuity in Russia's relations with Asia in the immediate future.

Rising world oil prices have helped fuel a seven-year economic boom in Russia, during which GDP has grown by more than 50%. As the world's leading natural gas supplier and second largest oil exporter, Moscow is confident that Russia's favorable economic situation will persist into the foreseeable future. As noted by the respected analyst Dmitri Trenin, "The Russian leadership is certain that Russia's energy resources make Russia

Peter Rutland is Professor of Government at Wesleyan University. He can be reached at <prutland@wesleyan.edu>.

The author would like to thank Derrin Culp, Vladimir Kontorovich, and Shinichiro Tabata for assistance with this paper.

truly 'irreplaceable' in the global economy, and consequently in world politics."[1] This situation gives President Vladimir Putin the luxury of carefully weighing all foreign policy options.

In contrast, Russia in 2006 is definitely feeling embattled politically. The Russian leadership saw the wave of "color revolutions" that swept through Georgia, Ukraine, and Kyrgyzstan between 2003 and 2005 as part of a deliberate U.S. strategy to loosen Moscow's influence over the "near abroad." This impression was reinforced when the United States set up military bases in Kyrgyzstan and Uzbekistan to pursue the war in Afghanistan.[2] At the same time Russia has been berated by the United States and European Union (EU) for the Kremlin's retreat from democracy and "extortion" of higher gas prices from Ukraine (by cutting deliveries on January 2, 2006). Russia is told by U.S. think-tanks that the country is headed in the "wrong direction"—and even that the Russian military can no longer defend the country from U.S. nuclear attack.[3]

In response to these challenges, Russia has shed some of its illusions about closer integration with the West and has started to look more seriously for Asian partners to balance U.S. pressure. Dmitri Trenin bluntly states that "Russia's leaders have given up on becoming part of the West and have started creating their own Moscow-centered system. Russia has a choice between accepting subservience and reasserting its status as a great power, thereby claiming its rightful place in the world alongside the United States and China."[4] Germany's leading Russia expert, Alexander Rahr, argues that Europe is experiencing a "cold peace" and that "Russia feels rejected by the West and pushed off to Asia."[5] Andrew Kuchins even argues that 2005 saw the most serious strategic shift in Russian foreign policy since the collapse of the Soviet Union in the form of a reorientation of Russian policy toward the East.[6]

Speaking in Tomsk after talks with German Chancellor Angela Merkel on April 26, 2006, Putin said "We hear statements about a threat of

---

[1] Dmitri Trenin, "The Post-Imperial Project," *Nezavisimaya gazeta-dipkurier*, no. 2 (January 2006).

[2] The United States quit the Uzbekistan base by November 2005.

[3] "Russia's Wrong Direction. What the U.S. Can and Should Do," Council on Foreign Relations, March 2006; and Keir Lieber and Daryl Press, "The Rise of U.S. Nuclear Primacy," *Foreign Affairs* 85, no. 2 (March/April 2006). Similar warnings can be found in the report from the London-based Foreign Policy Center, "Russia and the G8: A Summit Scorecard" (June 2006), available on-line at http://fpc.org.uk/fsblob/796.pdf. For a reply, see Vitalii Ivanov and Konstantin Simonov, "Russia's Right Path," *Nezavisimaya gazeta*, May 2, 2006.

[4] Dmitri Trenin, "Russia leaves the West," *Foreign Affairs* 85, no. 4 (July/August 2006).

[5] "Europe Experiences a 'Cold Peace,'" *Die Welt*, December 20, 2005.

[6] Andrew Kuchins, "New Directions in Russian Foreign Policy: Is the East Wind Prevailing Over the West in Moscow?" (paper presented at the Wilton Park conference, November 29, 2005), reprinted in Johnson's Russian List, no. 9314, December 6, 2005, http://www.cdi.org/russia/johnson.

dependence on Russia, about the need to restrict Russian companies' access to European markets. What can we do, when we hear the same thing every day? We are beginning to look for other markets."[7]

At the same time, Russian policy is deeply conflicted. Many Russians are concerned by the growing power of China. They do not want to jump from the frying pan into the fire and aid the rise of a new rival to the East by providing Beijing with energy resources and advanced military hardware.[8] Dmitri Trenin argues that "Russia lacks an overall political strategy in Asia—something that would outline Russia's multilateral relations with East Asia and bilateral relations with Asian states."[9]

This reorientation away from the West is increasingly connected to energy policy. These changes come at a pivotal time in the evolution of Russia's energy policy. Though having profited from the recent boom in oil prices, Russia is confronting an urgent need for massive investment to develop new fields now that existing oil and gas fields have passed their peak. At the same time, Russia's hydrocarbon export infrastructure is operating at full capacity, and new pipelines are needed to shift the oil and gas currently being used domestically into the more lucrative export market.

The first section of this chapter reviews the general state of the Russian economy and the role of international economic integration in Moscow's development strategy. The next section outlines the existing structure of Russian trade with Asia and examines the two main elements in Russia's Asian trade: energy and arms. The third section examines Russia's role in regional associations, particularly the effort to turn the Shanghai Cooperation Organization into an effective regional body for security cooperation in Central Asia—and one that tries to limit the U.S. role in the region. The chapter continues with a review of Russia's relations with individual Asian countries and concludes with a discussion of the policy debates over Russia's role in Asia.

The Role of Foreign Economic Relations in Russia's National Strategy

Since 1991 Russia has been going through a period of wrenching political and economic transformation. The outcome of this transformation

---

[7] Saed Shah, "Putin Rails Against Western 'Double Standards,'" *The Independent*, April 28, 2006.

[8] Max Verbitz, "Russian-Chinese Military Cooperation: Can a Bear Trust a Dragon?" *Perspective* 26, no. 3 (May 2006). The author is a Russian using a pseudonym.

[9] Interview with Dmitri Trenin in Rustem Falyakhov "Continuing the Old Dispute Deprives Both Sides of Potential Benefits," *Gazeta*, November 18, 2005.

is still uncertain, though the contours have become clearer since the consolidation of state power under Putin. Russian foreign policy is still heavily influenced by domestic concerns: the need to maintain political and economic stability and the state's struggle both to assert control over warring factions and to implement a coherent policy. These domestic considerations are hindering efforts to deepen Russian engagement with Asia.

Under both Putin and his predecessor, Boris Yeltsin, Russia has been trying to reform its economic structure and adopt market institutions. This strategy has emphasized increased participation in the international economy through trade and investment. Energy is Russia's trump card. Russia produced 459 million tons of crude oil in 2005, 11.9% of global output and second only to Saudi Arabia with 13.1%. Russia was the world leader in natural gas, with 215 billion cubic meters of exports accounting for 27% of the world market, well ahead of Canada (13%) and Norway (9%).[10] Between 1998 and 2004, booming oil exports from Russia satisfied half of global demand growth.[11]

In the Yeltsin period, Russia's integration into the global economy proceeded at a rapid but uneven pace, with individual corporate leaders (the oligarchs) often playing the leading role. Putin has taken decisive steps to reassert state control over domestic and foreign economic development. Yet companies such as the pipeline operator Transneft and the energy giants Gazprom and Rosneft are still to a degree independent players, despite the fact that the state owns a controlling block of company shares and when necessary forces company leadership to follow the Kremlin line. This situation underscores the need for caution in making generalizations about Russia's "grand strategy," since these debates assume a greater coherence in Russian policy than may in fact be the case.

Development of the energy sector has been the main driver of Russia's economic recovery since the August 1998 financial crisis. The Russian economy has experienced steady growth, 6% a year on average since 1999.[12] (See **Table 1.**) Much of the growth has been led by the surge in exports, which rose from $72 billion in 1998 to $183 billion in 2004—and $245 billion in 2005, when oil and gas accounted for 61% of earnings.[13] (See

---

[10] International Monetary Fund World Economic Outlook Database, http://www.imf.org/external/data.htm (World Economic Outlook Databases).

[11] William Tomson and Rudiger Ahrend, "Realizing the Oil Supply Potential of the CIS," Organization for Economic Cooperation and Development, May 18, 2006, http://www.oecd.org.

[12] Organization for Economic Cooperation and Development, *Economic Survey Russian Federation 2004* (Paris: OECD, 2004); World Bank, *From Transition to Development*, April 2004; and World Bank, *Russian Economic Report*, no. 12 (April 2006), http://www.worldbank.org.ru.

[13] "Russian Economic Report #8," World Bank, June 2004. In 2005 imports dropped 25% to $125 billion, leaving a trade surplus of $118 billion.

Table 2.) Trade now accounts for 48% of Russia's GDP. The proportion of the population living in poverty has halved from 1999 to 2005, while state revenues have doubled—thanks to more effective taxation of the soaring oil and gas rents. The federal budget ran a surplus equal to 7.5% of GDP in 2005. High oil prices also led to a large trade surplus, the accumulation of capital reserves of $180 billion, and the paying down of some international debts ahead of schedule ($15 billion in 2005 alone).

Putin has not rolled back the market reforms laid down by Yeltsin in the 1990s. On the contrary, the Russian leader has pushed ahead with some institutional reforms, especially in regard to codifying Russian law and reducing bureaucratic obstacles to business, though much work remains to be done. For example, liberalization of domestic gas and electricity prices is still blocked by the Kremlin out of fear that such a policy would provoke popular protests.[14] Putin has stripped the oligarchs of their political power by taking over their media empires and by putting the State Duma under the control of a single, pro-presidential party, United Russia. Putin has constructed a system of state corporatism in Russia, displacing the model of independent, private corporations controlled by swashbuckling oligarchs that was the pattern of the 1990s. Though the prime target for this strategy was the energy sector (in the form of the private Yukos oil company) the past year has seen the model extended to the defense industry as well as to aircraft, engineering, and even auto manufacturing. Opinions differ as to whether this state corporatism is compatible with a market economy and whether such corporatism will be able to produce sustainable economic growth in Russia. Within Russia the optimists outnumber the skeptics, while among Western observers the balance of opinion is reversed.

The Kremlin believes that a more market-driven approach would not work given Russia's geographic isolation and resource endowment. The Russian leadership points to the chaotic experiences of the 1990s, which culminated in the financial crash of August 1998, to prove the point that radical market liberalization was ill-suited to Russia's unique circumstances. The state wants to prevent Russia from slipping into dependency on energy exports; the strategy then is to capture the rents from the energy trade and channel them back into investment in high-tech research and manufacturing in order to rebuild Russia's now-outdated industrial base. The rent-capture is taking place both through taxation and through the formation of vertically-integrated state corporations, whose boards are headed by loyal Kremlin appointees.

---

[14] Gas still retails at $30 per 1000 cubic meter (cm) for industrial consumers, compared to the $230 paid by European customers.

TABLE 1   Macroeconomic indicators

	1996	1997	1998	1999	2000	2001	2002	2003	2004	2005
Industrial production (%)	–4.5	2.0	–5.2	11.0	11.9	2.9	3.1	8.9	7.3	4.0
Fixed investments (%)	–18.0	–5.0	–12.0	5.3	17.4	10.0	2.8	12.5	11.7	10.7
Unemployment (%)[†]	9.3	9.0	13.2	12.4	9.9	8.7	9.0	8.7	7.6	7.7
Exports of goods ($billion)	89.7	86.9	74.4	75.6	105.0	101.9	107.3	135.9	183.5	245.3
Imports of goods ($billion)	68.1	72.0	58.0	39.5	44.9	53.8	61.0	76.1	96.3	125.1
Current account ($billion)	10.8	–0.1	0.2	24.6	46.8	33.9	29.1	35.4	58.6	84.2
GDP (%)	–3.6	1.4	–5.3	6.4	10.0	5.1	4.7	7.3	7.2	6.4

SOURCE: Rosstat and Central Bank, as reported in Bank of Finland, *Russia Review*, no. 4 (April 12, 2006), http://www.bof.fi/bofit/eng/4ruec/index.stm.

NOTE: In 1995, 76% of Russia's trade was with CIS members; this fell slightly to 72% by 2004.

† End of the period.

Uncertainty exists, however, over whether Russia will be able to generate the energy exports that the strategy requires. Most of Russia's network of 49,000 km of oil pipelines and 150,000 km of gas lines was laid down more than 30 years ago. A massive program of investment is needed to upgrade this infrastructure and add new capacity. At the same time, existing oil and gas fields are past their peak and little exploration and development has taken place over the past twenty years. The Organization for Economic Cooperation and Development (OECD) predicts that Russian oil and gas production will plateau for the next fifteen to twenty years.[15]

Over the long term, considerable uncertainty remains regarding the cost-effectiveness of investments in Russian energy.[16] If oil stays above $40 per barrel for ten years, exploiting the oil and gas basins of central Siberia may be not only technically feasible but also cost-effective. Building a 3,000 km pipeline to export these resources to China and Japan might even be

---

[15] Tomson and Ahrend, "Realizing the Oil Supply Potential of the CIS." The authors cite data from the Institute for Energy Policy and the U.S. Geological Survey: Russia has 72 billion barrels of proven reserves (6.1% of world total); in 2004 Russia produced 9.3 million barrels/day (8.7% of world output) of which 5.1 million were exported.

[16] Leslie Dienes, "Observations on the Problematic Potential of Russian Oil and the Complexities of Siberia," *Eurasian Geography and Economics* 45, no. 4 (July 2004).

TABLE 2   Russia's major trading partners ($million)

	Exports			Imports		
	1998	2001	2004	1998	2001	2004
Germany	5,697	8,178	13,295	5,404	5,716	10,571
Ukraine	5,531	4,931	10,633	3,219	3,777	6,097
Netherlands	3,930	3,870	15,207	905	840	1,373
PRC	3,144	4,021	10,020	1,146	1,611	4,733
Italy	3,203	6,844	10,271	1,787	1,341	3,197
U.S.	5,995	5,944	8,354	4,052	3,199	3,205
Switzerland	3,216	1,522	7,798	426	394	650
Turkey	1,923	2,980	7,200	512	509	1,225
Finland	2,063	3,032	5,764	1,432	1,275	2,331
Poland	2,173	3,952	5,682	1,032	950	2,302
UK	2,927	3,182	5,645	1,205	980	2,064
Japan	2,171	2,438	3,471	810	813	3,937
Cyprus	375	1,398	5,310	27	28	22
EU total	32,280	46,798	88,325	18,828	17,544	33,967
Total trade	74,884	101,884	183,452	63,817	59,140	105,938

SOURCE: IMF *Direction of Trade Statistics*, 2005 (Washington, D.C.: International Monetary Fund, 2006).

profitable. There are, however, many variables in the mix. With oil at that price, oil shale and tar sands may become competitive rival sources, or a world recession could at any time cause oil prices to plummet.

Western companies understand that they are now facing new rules of the game. Though still welcome as partners, especially for the technology and managerial expertise that they bring, Western companies will be limited to a minority stake in Russian-led companies and joint ventures. Western companies interested in investing in Russia are expected as a quid pro quo to form joint ventures in other countries to help Russian corporations such as Gazprom, Rosneft, and Lukoil gain access to more lucrative downstream markets in Western countries through ownership of refineries and distribution networks.

Russian integration into international economic institutions has lagged behind the increased role for foreign trade in Russia's economy. Although Russia is a member of the Group of Eight (G8), the world's leading industrial countries, that membership is mainly of symbolic value. Russia yielded to EU entreaties and agreed to join the Kyoto Protocol in March

2005—in return for the EU's backing for Russian entry to the World Trade Organization (WTO) despite EU objections to Russia's low domestic energy prices. Russia is the only major economy that is not a WTO member, and though Russia began negotiating WTO entry in 1993, hopes for joining in 2006 have not materialized. Putin was unable to realize his goal of securing U.S. support of Russia entering the WTO in time for the G8 summit in St. Petersburg in July 2006. The main obstacles now are U.S. objections to weak intellectual property protections and limited access to banking and insurance markets inside Russia.

The economic and political challenges of forging a new development strategy are slowing down an eastward shift in Russia's foreign economic policy. Strategic considerations—a desire both to protect Russia from U.S. encirclement and EU exclusion and to assert Russia's pride as an independent power—are pushing Moscow to speed up the collaboration with new partners in Asia. For the time being, westward integration seems to have reached its natural limits; on the other hand, Asia has vast and growing economies whose demand for resources, arms, and capital machinery suit the Russian economy's strengths. Asia offers an additional advantage of having political structures more compatible with Russia's "managed democracy"—and the Asian countries do not have the Western habit of making political criteria a condition for trade.

Russia's Economic Integration with Asia

Trade

Though still heavily dependent on trade with Europe, Russia has good prospects for a rapid increase in trade with Asia in the next few years. The bulk of Russia's trade (upwards of 75%) still flows west to Europe. (See **Table 3**.) Russia's largest trading partners are Germany and Ukraine, with the EU-25 taking 51% of Russian exports and providing 33% of Russia's imports in 2004.[17] Out of a total trade turnover of $289 billion, only $36 billion was with Asia and another $14 billion with Central Asia.

This pattern is in no way surprising. Not only does most of the Russian population live in European Russia but the railway and port infrastructure was built for trade with Europe. Oil and gas pipelines, built between the 1960s and 1980s, connected Russia to her socialist bloc partners in East Europe, Germany, and beyond. Russia has a common border with the EU members of Finland, Estonia, Latvia, and Lithuania, and Russia's

---

[17] Prior to the ten new members joining the EU in 2004, the EU-15 accounted for only 33% of Russian trade.

TABLE 3   Russian trade with Asia ($million)

	Exports			Imports		
	1998	2001	2004	1998	2001	2004
PRC	3,144	4,021	10,020	1,146	1,611	4,733
Japan	2,171	2,438	3,471	810	813	3,937
S. Korea	516	842	1,963	1,004	782	2,025
India	580	695	2,461	660	541	643
Taiwan	142	263	1,999	74	163	342
Vietnam	275	164	706	56	79	100
Thailand	32	69	372	61	105	355
Malaysia	117	261	114	120	157	423
Mongolia	133	211	363	50	35	21
Indonesia	13	30	145	88	95	221
Singapore	56	719	186	104	106	162
Hong Kong	144	126	318	8	15	10
Philippines	33	45	217	9	22	50
Pakistan	21	57	227	14	26	25
N. Korea	54	58	205	8	16	5
Afghanistan	14	8	76	7	3	4
Bangladesh	49	24	60	11	4	11
Asia total	7,479	10,060	22,958	4,297	4,640	13,230

SOURCE: IMF *Direction of Trade Statistics*, 2005.

Kaliningrad province is an exclave physically located between Poland and Lithuania. By plane Moscow is three hours from Brussels but seven hours from Beijing. St. Petersburg is a one-hour flight from Helsinki.

Over the past decade Asia has become the powerhouse of the global economy—one whose weight will only increase in future decades. Russia must step up economic cooperation with Asia in order to adapt to this new reality. Energy clearly is the key: Russia has the resources; China, South Korea, and Japan, the demand (and the capital); and Japan, the technology.

Not at all clear is whether Russia fully shares this vision of deeper integration. Some of the Russian political elite still see Asia as a greater source of threat than opportunity. Moscow is aware not only of the huge potential for growth in the export of resources to Asian markets but also of the costs and political implications of such projects as well as the need to strike a good deal.

Energy: The Pipeline Puzzle

Key to Russia's new Asia strategy is the building of an export pipeline for Siberian oil. Substantial new oil and gas reserves found in Siberia amount to an estimated 17% of global oil reserves. Russia's plan is to build a pipeline—known as the East Siberia-Pacific Ocean pipeline (VSTO in Russian)—to carry 600,000 barrels of oil per day (80 million tons per year) across the continent to customers in East Asia. This pipeline, together with the projects on the island of Sakhalin, would increase the proportion of Russia's oil exports to Asia from the current 3% to 30% by 2020.

For China and Japan, securing new energy sources that do not depend on the flow of supplies from the Persian Gulf is a major strategic priority.[18] China is keen to develop secure overland supply routes from Russia and Kazakhstan because the sea routes that bring Persian Gulf oil to East Asia through the Strait of Malacca could easily be blockaded should there be a future confrontation with the United States.

China and Russia have mulled over an oil export pipeline since 1993. The past few years have seen a remarkable back-and-forth between two alternative routes for the pipeline. The original plan was for a 2,500 km line from Angarsk in Siberia directly across Mongolia to Daqing in northeast China. Mikhail Khodorkovsky, the ambitious head of Russia's largest oil company, Yukos, won China's agreement to finance the building of the line; the agreement was signed by President Hu Jintao in the presence of Putin during a state visit to Moscow in May 2003. This line would have been the first privately owned oil export pipeline in Russia. The other Russian pipelines are owned and operated by the state-owned Transneft corporation. The exact track still had not been decided: the Russian government preferred a longer route that would follow around the Russian border rather than cross Mongolia.

In July 2003, however, Putin authorized the arrest of five Yukos executives on charges of fraud and tax evasion; Khodorkovsky himself was arrested in October 2003. The Yukos head was seen as a threat to the Kremlin on several fronts. Khodorkovsky was believed to be preparing to sell Yukos to a foreign oil major (going against the Kremlin policy of keeping natural resources in Russian hands), investing heavily in political representation in the State Duma, and possibly preparing a run for the presidency in 2008. With Khodorkovsky out of the way (in 2005 he began an eight-year jail term), an energetic struggle began for control of Yukos assets. In December 2004 the majority state-owned company Rosneft bought the main Yukos production subsidiary for $9.5 billion (helped by a $6 billion loan from

---

[18] Stephen Blank, "China's Energy Crossroads," *Perspective* 26, no. 3 (May 2006): 2–7.

the Chinese National Petroleum Corporation [CNPC]). Gazprom's plan to absorb Rosneft and form one giant energy conglomerate was blocked after months of backroom maneuvering.[19] In November 2005 Gazprom went on to buy the private oil company Sibneft (owned by oligarch Roman Abramovich) for $13 billion, bringing 60% of hydrocarbon production back into state hands. This new model of state corporatism poses a distinct challenge to foreign investors. For example, BP-TNK is now under pressure to share its giant Kovykta natural gas field in Siberia with Gazprom. BP-TNK has been lobbying for permission to build an export pipeline to China, but Gazprom has stated a preference for waiting until Sakhalin comes on stream. China got a taste of the new Russian approach in December 2002 when the Chinese were shut out of the bidding for a Russian oil company, Slavneft. A new subsoil resources bill introduced into Russia's parliament in 2006 will bar foreign companies from more than 50% ownership of any field deemed "strategic."

Meanwhile, debate continued over the route of the export pipeline. Much to China's chagrin, in the summer of 2003 Russia backed out of the Angarsk-Daqing deal and started entertaining a Japanese proposal for a 4,000 km pipeline extending down to the port of Nakhodka. Though more costly, this pipeline would enable tankers to ship the oil to Japan or other customers, thus keeping Russia from dependence on a single buyer—China. Both Japan and China offered to lend billions of dollars to finance the project. The start point of the pipeline in Siberia was switched from Angarsk, site of a Yukos oilfield, to Taishet, the location of a Rosneft refinery. The official Russian position as of July 2006 is to favor *both* routes. The first segment of the VSTO will run from Taishet to Skovorodino and will cost an estimated $6.5 billion. A second phase Skovorodino to Perevoznaya bay (now favored over Nakhodka) will cost another $5 billion. China is willing to pay for the Skovorodino-Daqing branch. It is not clear if the double line will be commercially viable, or even if there is enough oil to justify the project.

Irkutsk governor Aleksandr Tishanin and other provincial leaders want to have more money spent on developing the infrastructure in Siberia (such as connecting outlying cities to the natural gas grid) rather than to have the region's resources shipped out to China in return for money sent back to Moscow.[20] A strong lobby favors investing in the development of the Baikal-Amur railway, a Brezhnev-era extension of the Trans-Siberian railway

[19] Both companies are run by close allies of Putin. Dmitri Medvedev, promoted to first deputy prime minister in November 2005, simultaneously serves as chairman of the Gazprom board, while the deputy head of the Presidential Administration, Igor Sechin, is in charge at Rosneft.

[20] V.I. Suslov and A.G. Korzhubaev, "Energy-Transport Routes in Siberia and the Far East," *EKO*, no. 8 (2005): 47–67; and Marina Zabolotskaya, "How to Tame the Asian Tigers," *Rossiiskaya gazeta*, no. 287 (December 2005).

running north of Lake Baikal that can be used as an interim solution for oil exports by rail. President Mikhail Nikolaev, head of the diamond-rich but isolated northern republic of Sakha (Yakutiya) is among those arguing for more investment in Siberian development rather than in resource exports.

For two years Putin has been unable or unwilling to come down with a clear decision on the project, much to the frustration of his Chinese and Japanese interlocutors. In April 2005 Moscow issued an order for the pipeline to be constructed from Taishet to the halfway point at Skovorodino near the Russo-Chinese border. In July 2005 remarks Putin suggested that the first extension of the pipeline will be the branch to China, remarks that he repeated in September 2005. Yet during a visit to Beijing in March 2006 Putin—still unable to give a firm commitment to the Chinese—stated that a final decision must await the result of feasibility studies dealing with environmental and financial issues.[21] Ground finally was broken on the Taishet-Skovorodino section of the pipeline on April 28, 2006.[22]

Why was Moscow being so indecisive about the final destination of the pipeline? Part of the problem is price. The Chinese, notorious hard-bargainers, reportedly were offering low-ball prices: $25 a barrel for oil and $40 per cubic meter for gas.[23] These prices are one third and one fifth of what Russia's European customers are currently paying for oil and gas respectively. According to one report, "the breakthrough came [in September 2004] when the Chinese comrades were persuaded to link the price of Russian gas to petroleum product prices in China, which correspond to world prices rather than to the price of coal."[24]

Russia's leaders occasionally have raised the specter of energy sales to Asia in order to scare European customers into agreeing to Russian

---

[21] Zhang Guobao, vice minister of the National Development and Reform Commission, complained "One moment Russia is saying they have made a decision, the next saying that no decision has been made. To date, there has been no correct information. This is regrettable." Quoted in Carl Motished, "Russia Holds the Solution to its Neighbour's Shortage," *Times*, March 21, 2006, http://timesonline.co.uk/global/. During Putin's March 2006 visit to Beijing Gazprom did sign a protocol with CNPC expressing intention to build two pipelines to export 80 billion cubic meters of gas to China by 2011 (of which 10% would come from Sakhalin). See Irina Reznik, "The Great Pipeline of China," *Vedomosti*, March 22, 2006.

[22] Speaking at a meeting of Siberian regional leaders in the Siberian city of Tomsk on April 26, Putin ordered that the pipeline be routed 40 kilometers north of Lake Baikal in order to avoid possible pollution. See Sergei Blagov, "Putin Pleases Environmentalists," *Eurasia Daily Monitor*, April 27, 2006. In a subsequent meeting with Putin on May 26, however, Transneft head Semyon Vainshtok said that because of impassable mountains the new pipeline route would in fact have to run 400 km north of Lake Baikal, adding considerably to the cost. Transcript of speech from meeting in Sochi, May 26, 2006, available at http://www.kremlin.ru/eng/ (Speeches). Vainstok had earlier estimated that the detour would cost $900 million: see Ekho Moskvy, April 20, 2006.

[23] Vladimir Milov, "How Sustainable is Russia's Future as an Energy Superpower?" Carnegie Endowment, Washington, D.C., March 16, 2006, http://www.carnegieendowment.org.

[24] Aleksander Chudodeev, "Going East," *Itogi*, no.13 (March 27, 2006).

demands—for example, for ownership of downstream assets. In April 2006 Gazprom's Aleksei Miller told the EU ambassadors in Moscow that "it would be a mistake to forget that we are actively expanding into new markets like North America and China. What if we reroute to the East? Supply will decrease. At first, we plan to reroute 30 million tons of oil there, and that means that Europe will not receive this amount. Prices in Europe will rise."[25] That same month Putin told journalists that "[Russia] should look for sellers' markets" and "prioritize the Asia-Pacific region."[26]

While the struggle continues around the VSTO, the development of the oil and gas fields on the island of Sakhalin is proceeding apace.[27] The $10 billion being invested in oil and gas extraction on Sakhalin represents the largest single foreign investment in Russia ever (and the final total invested may rise to $50 billion). Exxon's Sakhalin 1 holds about 300 million tons of oil reserves, and Sakhalin 2 about 150 million tons.[28] Each project has some 500 billion cubic meters of gas. Sakhalin 1 began pumping oil on a modest scale in 2005. Royal Dutch Shell is managing the challenging offshore development Sakhalin 2, which is 60% complete.[29] Ecological concerns, geological difficulties, and some renegotiation of licenses have delayed the projects by several years. Once extracted, the oil and gas will be piped 800 km to ice-free ports at the island's southern tip, where a liquefied natural gas (LNG) facility is being built with a capacity of 10 billion cubic meters per year (8% of current world demand). In January 2004, the Russian government cancelled the license for the development of the Sakhalin 3 field that had been won by ExxonMobil back in 1993. Now Rosneft holds a 75% stake in Sakhalin 3. Shell is under pressure to bring Gazprom into its Sakhalin 2 project. Given the political and ecological uncertainties surrounding both ocean-floor pipeline construction to Japan and land-lines across North Korea, LNG will likely be the main vehicle for natural gas exports from Sakhalin.

---

[25] Nataliya Grib, "Europe's Raised Eyebrows," *Kommersant*, April 25, 2006.

[26] "Putin Blasts West, Siberian Economy at Meeting with Governors," *RIA-Novosti*, April 26, 2006.

[27] Michael Bradshaw, "Sakhalin Projects Show Why Russia Still Needs Foreign Investors," *Pacific Russia Oil and Gas Report* (Winter 2005).

[28] Exxon is the lead operator with a 30% stake; Exxon's partners include India's ONC (20%), Japan's Sodeco (30%), and Rosneft (20%). http://www.sakhalin1.com/.

[29] Shell has a 55% stake in Sakhalin 2, along with Mitsui (25%) and Mitsubishi (20%). See http://www.sakhalin-2.com/. See also "Make or Break for Shell in Russia," *Sunday Times*, March 12, 2006.

Arms Trade

The arms trade remains a significant source of revenue for Russia, with China and India as the leading partners. Russian arms sales, which had been lagging, increased from $2.9 billion in 1998 to $5.6 billion in 2004. In the 2001 to 2005 period 43% of Russia's deliveries went to China and 25% to India.[30] In 2005 Russia sold $6.13 billion worth of arms, of which 70% went to China and India, and had some $23 billion in booked orders.[31] It is important to remember that throughout the 1990s arms sales accounted for a mere 5% of Russia's total exports, with the proportion further shrinking as oil prices boomed. This revenue has, however, been vitally important in keeping Russia's once-proud defense industry afloat, as for most of the 1990s the cash-starved Russian armed forces were not buying new weapons. "The exports of arms to China in the 1990s ensured the survival not just of individual plants, but whole regions."[32] Russian defense procurement has doubled since 2000, reaching $6.5 billion in 2005 and $8 billion in 2006, but in spring 2006 Russia's defense plants were operating at only 40% of capacity.[33] Hence the sector still needs foreign sales to survive—and to fund the development of next-generation weapons.[34]

Following a 30-year hiatus, in 1992 China again began buying arms from Russia. China since has received 12 kilo-class submarines, 4 Sovremennyi class destroyers equipped with SS-N-22 Sunburn anti-ship missiles, 12 S-300 and 27 Tor M-1 air-defense complexes, 200 fourth-generation fighters (SU-27 and SU-30) as well as a license to produce 450 more domestically.[35] Two of the subs will be built at Komsomol'sk-na-Amur, in Russia's Far East, providing a vital source of revenue for the Amur shipyard.[36] Wen Jiabao, Chair of China's State Council, announced a year ago that the practice of buying finished arms supplies from Russia had exhausted itself and called

---

[30] Bjorn Hagelin et al., "International Arms Transfers," in *SIPRI Yearbook 2006: Armaments, Disarmament and International Security* (Stockholm International Peace Research Institute, 2006), chapter 10.

[31] *Nezavisimaya gazeta*, February 10, 2006; and Konstantin Lantratov, "One Billion in Four Days," *Kommersant*, February 20, 2006.

[32] Aleksandr Golts, "Trade Partner, Military Ally. The Evolution of Military-Technical Cooperation Between Russia and China," *Pro et Contra* 9, no. 3 (2005).

[33] Viktor Baranets, "Why Would Russia Equip Foreign Armies?" *Komsomol'skaya pravda*, March 9–16 2006; and Viktor Myasnikov, "Military Industry Slides into Bankruptcy," *Nezavisimoe voennoe obozrenie*, no. 14 (April 28, 2006).

[34] To date, Russia has been selling mainly 1980s-era technology.

[35] Golts, "Trade Partner, Military Ally." See also Stockholm International Peace Research Institute, *Arms Trade Register* (Boston: MIT Press, 1975).

[36] Since 1992 the Amur shipyard has not completed a single submarine for the Russian navy, lacking funds to finish the three boats under construction. See "Komsomol'sk-na-Amur," GlobalSecurity, http://www.globalsecurity.org.

TABLE 4   Russian arms exports ($million)

	2000	2001	2002	2003	2004	2005
PRC	1,457	2,600	1,943	1,511	1,771	1,350
India	431	463	1148	1,948	1,377	485
Yemen	53	14	521	–	329	239
Algeria	226	365	84	143	246	103
Greece	245	117	39	20	22	257
Vietnam	–	6	121	12	259	212
Sudan	–	134	55	90	270	–
Iran	84	114	74	162	–	87
Kazakhstan	144	31	83	62	27	68
Eritrea	–	60	–	–	202	276
Ethiopia	72	–	–	193	192	–
Syria	420	–	–	–	–	–
Burma	–	125	185	–	–	–
Total	3,250	4,680	4,545	4,546	4,963	3,581

SOURCE: SIPRI Arms Transfers Database, Stockholm International Peace Research Institute, http://www.sipri.org/contents/armstrad/at_data.html.

NOTE: This total is for all 48 countries reported receiving Russian arms from 2000 to 2005.

for more licensing agreements.[37] In the past, aircraft accounted for more than 60% of exports, but in 2005 naval sales accounted for 45% of total Russian arms exports—due in part to $450 million earned from the delivery to China of two Kilo-class submarines. Future deals with China include the sale of 34 Il-76MD military transport planes and 4 Il-78 refueling tankers worth $1.2 billion.[38]

Russia has $7 billion worth of orders booked with India. The largest deals include a contract to sell 3 frigates (worth $1.56 billion), 30 MIG-29Ks for the carrier Vikramaditya ($1.5 billion), 6 Amur-1650 submarines ($2 billion), and joint development of a transport plane ($1.5 billion).[39] In

[37] Interview with Aleksander Denisov, Senior Deputy Director of the Federal Military Technology Cooperation Service in Aleksei Khazbiev, "Arms Reconfiguration," *Ekspert*, no. 46 (December 5, 2005).

[38] Konstantin Lantratov, "One Billion in Four Days."

[39] Konstatin Lantratov, "Russia will Flood India with Military Hardware," *Kommersant*, February 3, 2006.

2004 Russia began delivery of parts for 140 SU-30MKI fighters that will be assembled in India and will earn Russia $3.5 billion.[40]

Russia is striving to find new customers beyond China and India. In 2003 Putin signed a $900 million contract with Malaysia for 18 SU-30MKM fighters.[41] In 2005 Russia sold 10 Ka-32 helicopters to South Korea and 2 S-300PMU1 air defense systems to Vietnam for a combined price of $250 million. Russian arms sales dipped in 2005 due to a variety of factors, such as financial problems in Indonesia and Thailand following the tsunami.[42] Still, Indonesia plans to buy 6 Kilo-class submarines (worth $1.9 billion) by 2010. In April 2006 Russia hosted a delegation from Myanmar after a three-year hiatus in sales to that country: Russia is interested in selling arms in return for oil and gas concessions.[43]

In 1995 Russia made a secret agreement with the United States not to sign any new contracts for arms sales to Iran (the "Gore-Chernomyrdin pact"). The Russians withdrew from the arrangement in 2000 but sold only $300–400 million in arms to Iran over the next five years. In December 2005 Russia signed a contract with Iran for the delivery of 29 Tor-M1 and Pechora-A2 air defense systems (which are less sophisticated than the S-300) worth $700 million.[44]

The Russians have been wary of selling top-of-the-line technologies (such as airborne radar aircraft or AWACs) to China and India for fear of disturbing the strategic balance in ways that might threaten Russian interests. Academic Viktor Baranets asked "Where are the guarantees that [the Chinese military], enhanced with Russia's help, will never be turned against Russia itself?"[45] As a case in point, in November 2005 Igor Reshetin, director of the TsNIIMASH-Export company, was arrested along with two of his deputies for illegally selling space technology to China. When asked about the wisdom of selling advanced weapons to foreigners, Rosoboronexport Director Sergei Chemezov bluntly replied: "Let's face it: if we do not do it, somebody else will."[46] In April 2006 Defense Minister Sergei Ivanov stated:

---

[40] Konstantin Lantratov, "Let Down by the Wings," *Kommersant*, December 1, 2005.

[41] Dmitri Litovkin, "Russia Dilutes the Military Aircraft Market with Civilian Planes," *Izvestiya*, December 7, 2005.

[42] Aleksei Khazbiev, "Arms Reconfiguration."

[43] Konstantin Lantratov, "Air-to-Minerals Missiles," *Kommersant*, April 4, 2006.

[44] Aleksei Nikolskii, "Revenue from a Rogue," *Vedomosti*, December 2, 2005. Russia is happy to sell weapons to countries on the Pentagon's blacklist, such as Sudan or Venezuela. See Igor Dmitriev, "Hello to Arms," *Versiya*, no. 19 (May 22–28, 2006).

[45] Viktor Baranets, "Why Would Russia Equip Foreign Armies?," *Komsomol'skaya pravda*, March 9–16, 2006.

[46] Andrei Vandenko, "An Armed Man," *Itogi*, no. 44 (October 2005): 22–4.

I don't rule out that we might discuss selling the SU-34 [bomber] to China in the future. There are no such negotiations yet. The same is applicable to the fifth-generation fighters. To begin negotiations we need to settle a very important judicial issue, that is to sign an agreement on protection of intellectual property.[47]

In the view of most analysts, Russia's arms trade is driven primarily by the need to generate revenue for the Russian industry rather than by a grand strategy that seeks to build a multipolar alliance with China and India. Separating the strategic from the economic logic behind the arms trade is not easy.

Relations with Countries of the Region

After taking office in 2000 Putin gave repeated signals that he saw Russia as primarily a European power, a view reflecting the realities of geography, history, and culture. Russian foreign policy priorities generally ran in a west-to-east direction: the top priority was Europe, followed by the western former Soviet countries (Ukraine, Belarus, Caucasus), then by Central Asia, then Northeast Asia, and finally South/Southeast Asia. This pattern of priorities has begun to shift over the past two years, however, as Moscow has focused more attention on Central Asia and East Asia. Russia has ambitious plans to boost trade with China and in the past two years has for the first time ever held military exercises with China and India.

China

Russia and China have much in common. China, like Russia, has nuclear weapons, a seat on the UN Security Council, and an authoritarian regime that is the target of frequent Western criticism. The two countries reached agreement in 2004 on the last remaining unresolved issue in their relations—the drawing of their 4,000 km mutual border.[48]

Russia is acutely aware of China's growing role in the world economy and of the business opportunities that are opening up as a result. China's share in world trade rose from 0.8% in 1978 to 7.7% in 2005, while that of Russia fell from 3.4% in 1990 to 1.8% in 2005.[49] Russia also is somewhat wary of making China stronger and of becoming more economically dependent on this giant Asian neighbor. Moscow sees China as an economic rival in

---

[47] Dmitri Litovkin, "The Shanghai Cooperation Organization is Not NATO," *Izvestiya*, May 3, 2006.

[48] Though delimitation of three islands in the Ussuri river remains to be completed.

[49] Giorgio Navaretti, "Patterns of Trade and Protection," World Bank, May 2004; and World Trade Organization, "World Trade 2005," April 11, 2006.

developing Central Asian energy but also recognizes Beijing as a strategic partner whose interests include preserving stability in Central Asia and limiting the U.S. presence in the region.

During Hu Jintao's visit to Moscow in July 2005 the two countries' leaders issued a grandiose joint declaration on world order in the 21st century.[50] The document stressed the role of multipolarity and the importance of non-interference in internal affairs and mutual respect for other nations' sovereignty.

The rhetoric may, however, be running ahead of reality. The distinct gulf that exists between professions of strategic partnership by the nations' leaders and the anemic economic relations between the two countries has been characterized as a "gap between 'hot' contacts at the top and 'cold' contacts further down."[51] Russian-Chinese trade was $29.1 billion in 2005, up 37% from the previous year and well up from the $11 billion logged in 2001.[52] Though the trend is encouraging, this level still pales in comparison to China's annual trade of $210 billion with the United States or of $185 billion with Japan. Russia accounts for less than 2% of China's trade, and China provides about 8% of Russia's trade.[53]

Not all is smooth sailing. In November 2005 Prime Minister Mikhail Fradkov visited Beijing to try to clear up what he diplomatically called "current difficulties" in the trade relationship.[54] Yevgeny Verlin noted: "Russia's caution in military-technical cooperation or in permitting expansion of Chinese capital into Russian innovation zones and the construction market, all of that irritates Beijing immensely."[55] In 2003 China, a member of the WTO since 2001, launched four anti-dumping suits against Russia concerning $500–600 million of steel imports. Russia-China talks regarding Russian entry to the WTO were suspended from January through September of 2003 but concluded in 2004, at which time China agreed to terms for Russian entry.[56]

On the Russian side, the main concern is to diversify exports away from their current dependence on fuel and raw materials. During his March 2006 visit to Beijing, Putin complained that deliveries of machinery and

---

[50] Text is available in Russian at: http://www.kremlin.ru/interdocs/2005/07/01.

[51] Aleksander Lomanov, "Oil and Gas Mediation," *Vremya novostei*, March 23, 2006.

[52] In the first three months of 2006 Russia-China trade hit $12 billion, or up 53% year-on-year. RIA-Novosti, June 15, 2006.

[53] At their 2004 meeting Putin and Hu Jintao set the goal of quadrupling trade turnover somewhere between $60 and 80 billion by 2010.

[54] Mikhail Vorobiev, "Political Necessity," *Vremya novostei*, November 7, 2005.

[55] Yevgeny Verlin, "What Kind of China We Need," *Profil*, no. 10 (March 2006).

[56] *Delovoi Kitai* 4 (2004).

equipment to China almost halved in 2005.[57] Russia's imports from China
are led by electrical equipment (30.4%), consumer durables (23.3%), and
shoes (4.9%), while Russian exports consist of oil (33.7%), ships (9.9%),
timber (9.5%), weapons (5.5%), fertilizer (5.5%), and ferrous metals
(5.2%).[58] In 2005 Russia delivered 5.18 million tons of oil to China by rail
and hopes by 2010 to boost that to 15 million tons (10% of China's import
demand).[59]

Chinese businesses have invested about $2 billion in Russia, and Russian
firms have invested some $500 million in China—although most of these
are reportedly run by Chinese returning from Russia. These sums amount
to only 1.8% of Chinese investment abroad, 0.8% of all FDI in Russia, 6.3%
of Russian investment abroad, and 0.09% of all FDI in China.[60]

Energy and arms remain the two principal elements in Russian exports.
Apart from plans to build oil and gas pipelines, Russia is currently building
the two reactors at the Tianwan nuclear power station; a tender for two new
reactors will be held in 2007. China intends to build 30 new reactors by
2020, and Russia is keen to share in that market. Each year Russia sells to
China 500 to 900 million kilowatt/hours of electricity—and ambitious plans
are in the works to raise the amount to 18 billion kilowatt/hours per year by
2010.

China's economic rise is causing some anxiety in Moscow. There is
a growing realization that "China is well ahead of Russia and India as to
the degree of its engagement in the global economy."[61] From 1978 to 2004,
China attracted foreign direct investment amounting to $562 billion,
including $61 billion in 2004, while Russia attracted just $9.4 billion towards
a cumulative total of about $30 billion. Given China's aggressive policy of
deep integration with the global economy, Moscow may no longer have an
advantage in R&D from its days as the Soviet superpower. Russia's current

[57] Dmitri Zhantiyev, "A Bridge to the Celestial Kingdom," *Rossiiskie vesti*, March 23, 2006.

[58] "Rossiiskaya federatsiya i strana mir. Kitai [Russian Federation and the Countries of the World. China] 2005 October–December," retrieved via ISI Emerging Markets database. The data, presumably from the State Customs Service, is for the fourth quarter 2005. The proportions were roughly the same in previous quarters, though ferrous metals dropped from 17% in the first half of the year to 8% in the second.

[59] The main companies handling Russian exports as of the fourth quarter 2005 were Rosneft (31.4%), Tomskneft (8.6%), and Rosoboroneksport (8.0%). In the first quarter 2005 the three leaders were Lukoil (7.4%), Yukos 7.4%, and the steelmaker Magnitogorsk MK (8.5%). The city of Moscow books 34.0% of the exports, followed by Arkhangelsk (30.3%), the Siberian provinces of Tomsk (5.8%), and Irkutsk (4.2%). See Tselyanin, "Regional Cooperation of China and Russia," *EKO*, no. 10 (2005): 126–33.

[60] Li Tseyan'min', "China as Investor," *EKO*, no. 9 (2005): 105–11.

[61] Vladimir Portyakov, "Russia, China and India in the World Economy," *Russia in Global Affairs*, no. 2, April 2006; Kseniya Yudaeva, "How Can We Diversify Our Exports?" *Pro et Contra* 9, no. 3 (2005).

share on the global innovations market stands at 0.5% versus China's share of 6%.[62] In the World Economic Forum Competitiveness index, Russia ranks 75 out of 117 countries, lagging behind China (49) and India (50).[63]

Given Russia's low birth rate and high male mortality, World Bank projections are that Russia's population will fall from the current 144 million to 119 million by 2050. This population decline likely will lead Russia to rely increasingly on immigrant workers, with China as a likely source. Public opinion is not reconciled to this idea. In a recent poll of the Russian public, negative opinion was greatest toward immigrants from the Caucasus (50% of respondents), with those from China in the second place of opprobrium (46%), followed by Vietnam (42%) and Central Asia (31%).[64] Although many Russians see China as Russia's strategic partner (34%) and even ally (22%), most favor restrictions on Chinese imports (61%), businesses (66%), and immigrant labor (69%).[65] Only 8% said that trade between the two countries was more advantageous for Russia, whereas more than 50% said China benefited most.

Since the Soviet collapse, there has been a revival of informal cross-border trade with China, with exports of commodities such as fish and timber matched by imports of consumer goods from clothing to cars. This border trade accounts for an estimated $10–12 billion a year, much of which goes unreported and untaxed.[66] The transportation infrastructure between the two countries is being expanded, and Chinese entrepreneurs are leasing Russian forests, farmland, and factories. Not clear is how willing Russian officials at the national or local level are to accelerate this process. Cross-border relations were damaged by the December 2005 benzene spill from a Chinese factory into the Sungari river that threatened the water supply of Khabarovsk and triggered anti-Chinese protests.[67]

A startling reminder of the illegal dimensions of the cross-border trade came with the May 2006 dismissal of a dozen senior officials from the State Customs Service and their alleged high-level "protectors" in the procuracy, Interior Ministry, and Federal Security Service. The scandal also forced the resignation of four members of the Federation Council (the upper house of the national parliament), including Igor Ivanov from Primore. The affair

---

[62] Yudaeva, "How Can We Diversify Our Exports?"

[63] Augusto Lopez-Claros, "Russia: Competitiveness, Economic Growth and the Next Stage of Development," World Economic Forum, Global Competitiveness Report 2005, September 28, 2005, chapter 2.6, http://www.weforum.org/.

[64] Vasily Zubkov, "Immigration to Russia, a Boon or a Curse?" RIAN, November 16, 2005.

[65] Interfax, August 15, 2005. According to a VTsIOM poll.

[66] Delovoi Kitai 4 (2004).

[67] Igor Verba, "Campaign Chemotherapy," Nezavisimaya gazeta, November 30, 2005.

was the result of a sting operation involving boxcars of unregistered Chinese goods.[68]

Japan

Russo-Japanese relations remain stymied by Japan's refusal to accept the Russian occupation of the four southern Kurile islands (what the Japanese call the "Northern Territories") seized by Stalin in 1945. In the absence of an agreement, no peace treaty yet exists between the two countries. The Japanese assumption is that Russia eventually will be obliged to return all four islands.

Russia at various points has hinted at possible openness to a compromise. For example, a November 2004 statement by Foreign Minister Sergei Lavrov affirmed Moscow's recognition of the Soviet-Japanese Joint Declaration of 1956, in which the Soviet Union expressed willingness to negotiate with Japan the handing over of the two southern islands of Shikotan and Habomai. Due, however, to a 2002 political scandal over a possible backdoor compromise deal with Russia, Japan has reverted to insistence on the eventual return of all four islands. Given Russia's increasing political and economic strength, it seems unlikely that Russia will return any of the islands. During a 2005 visit to the Kuriles, Defense Minister Sergei Ivanov stressed that the Russians "do not intend to make any territorial concessions; we do not intend to leave."[69] Putin is keen to resolve the issue and move on.[70]

Moscow is puzzled by Japan's obstinance over the Kuriles. Japan's view apparently is that economic involvement with Russia—such as Japanese investments in Sakhalin and the VSTO pipeline—will bind Moscow closer to Tokyo and increase the likelihood of Putin compromising. Russia, however, regards these as mutually beneficial projects that do not require a political quid pro quo.

Despite a Japanese-Russian Action Plan signed in 2003, the relationship has been marked by a distinct lack of progress. During a November 2005 visit to Japan Putin signed a package of agreements that included LNG purchases from Sakhalin and confirmation of the Taishet-Perevoznaya oil pipeline. Koizumi also achieved his objective: a public assurance from Putin that the search for a solution to the territorial dispute will continue.[71]

---

[68] Maksim Agarkov, "Resignations," *Profil*, no. 19 (May 2006).

[69] *Taipei Times*, July 31, 2005.

[70] Marat Khairullin, "Purely Business, Nothing Personal. Japan Gives Russia Some Lessons in Diplomacy," *Gazeta*, February 8, 2006.

[71] Aleksander Sadchikov, "Gas Today, Islands Tomorrow," *Izvestiya*, November 23, 2005.

Meanwhile, Japan's trade with Russia rose from $3.2 billion in 2001 to $7.4 billion in 2005. Japanese investment in Russia also increased sharply, from $117 million in 2000 to around $1 billion in 2003. Contributing to this increased investment, for example, is Toyota's planned opening of a $150 million assembly plant in Petersburg.

Moscow was not thrilled by the April 2006 conclusion of a U.S.-Japanese agreement to relocate U.S. military bases in Japan and increase military cooperation. As Andrei Fesyun has written: "The United States is drawing Japan into its policy of global dominance in all regions of the world—with the intention of using Japan as a shield to absorb a first strike."[72] In contrast, however, to the Russian public's ambiguity regarding China the public does not see Japan as a threat. According to a VTsIOM survey, 61% of respondents had a positive view of Japan (as a friend or partner) while only 12% saw Japan as a rival and 6% as an enemy. Nevertheless, 73% felt the time had come for Russia to stop discussing the territorial problem.[73]

India

The Soviet Union enjoyed good but somewhat distant relations with India. Both countries were wary of the United States and China, and India was a regular purchaser of Soviet weapons. India has purchased more than $7 billion worth of weapons from Russia in the last five years; in the Indian armed forces, up to 70% of the military hardware was made in Russia or the former Soviet Union.[74] Between 1992 and 2004 Russia sold India 60 fighters (MIG-29s, SU-30MKIs, and SU-30Ks) and upgraded 125 previously delivered MIG-21s. Components for the assembly of 140 SU-30MKI aircraft are being delivered. India also bought six IL-78MKI flying tankers and three A-50 AWACS-type planes and is in discussion with Russia for the joint development of a transport aircraft.[75] The visit of President George W. Bush to India in March 2006 sparked Russian fears that the United States might take over as a primary military supplier (for example of F-16 fighters). The India-United States accord on nuclear cooperation that was signed during that visit puts into question future Russian nuclear sales. Russia is currently building two reactors at a nuclear power plant in Kudankulam.

---

[72] Andrei Fesyun, "Will Japan and the U.S. Go to War Together?" *Vremya novostei*, May 4, 2006.

[73] Dmitri Polikanov, "Japan As an Important Alternative Power," *Nezavisimaya gazeta*, November 21, 2005.

[74] Interview on Russian-Indian military technology cooperation with Defense Minister Pranab Mukherjee by Aleksander Lomanov, *Vremya novostei*, November 18, 2005.

[75] Arthur Blinov, "Cold War with a Trade Subtext," *Nezavisimaya gazeta*, April 7, 2006.

Weapons aside, India-Russia mutual trade—at just $3.1 billion in 2004—is anemic. In March 2006 Fradkov visited India to discuss the $2.3 billion in Soviet-era debt still owed by India. India is repaying the debt at a rate of about $100 million per year in goods (such as tea and textiles) that Russian firms do not want to take.[76]

Russia held military exercises in India for the first time ever in October 2005, and Moscow is helping New Delhi build India's presence at the Aini airbase in Tajikistan. India has been training the Tajik airforce under an April 2002 agreement and in 2005 began construction work at the disused airport. In December 2005 the two countries began to discuss plans for basing Indian military aircraft in Tajikistan.[77]

Korea

Putin took office in 2000 with hopes that Russia could play the role of an honest broker in resolving the dispute over North Korea's nuclear program and to that end proposed Six-Party Talks with Pyongyang. After finding that Russia had no special influence over Kim Jong-il, however, Beijing effectively marginalized the Russian role in the negotiations.[78] The diplomatic standoff over North Korea has dashed ambitious plans to build new railways and oil and gas pipelines from Russia to South Korea.[79] Despite some expectations, Putin failed to come away from the November 2005 APEC summit in Pusan with a commitment from South Korea to buy Sakhalin gas, either by building a pipeline across North Korea or through LNG deliveries.[80]

Central Asia

Tending to take Central Asia for granted, Moscow expended scant effort toward improving relations with Russia's Eastern "near neighbors."[81] This

---

[76] *Kommersant*, March 20, 2006.

[77] Vladimir Ivanov, "Moscow Style Triple-Shot," *Nezavisimaya gazeta*, December 7, 2005; "IAF to station MIG 29s in Tajikistan," April 20, 2006, http://www.defenceindia.com/17-apr-2k6/news17.html; and Viktor Myasnikov, "New Delhi Is Elbowing Russia Out," *Nezavisimaya gazeta*, April 25, 2006.

[78] "China-Russia: Underwater Reefs in their Relations," Center for Political Information (Moscow), *Information-Analytical Bulletin*, no. 10, 2005.

[79] Hiroshi Kimura, "Putin's policy towards the Korean Peninsula: Why Has Russia Been Losing Its Influence?" (paper presented to the international conference Comparing Different Approaches to Conflict Prevention and Management: Korean Peninsula and the Taiwan Strait, Uppsala, Sweden, December 16–17, 2005).

[80] Anna Nikolaeva, "No Gas Deal," *Vedomosti*, November 21, 2005.

[81] This is now the preferred formula for referring to the former Soviet states, replacing the imperial-sounding "near abroad."

tendency has begun to change over the past two years, however, as Russia's dealings with the Western members of the Commonwealth of Independent States encountered a multitude of problems: democratic revolutions in Georgia and Ukraine; unsolved conflicts in Moldova, Georgia, and Azerbaijan; and a recalcitrant dictator in Belarus. Russian policy toward Central Asia has focused on three main elements: energy trade, fighting terrorism, and preserving political stability through support for incumbent dictators. Russia's strategic goal is to preserve the status quo; Moscow sees rebuilding hegemonic control over the region as neither feasible nor particularly desirable.

Islamist terrorism has been a serious threat to the regimes in the region. Russia (alongside Iran) played a fairly positive role in negotiating an end to the Tajik civil war in 1997. Following September 11th, Kyrgyzstan and Uzbekistan welcomed the introduction of U.S. military bases, hoping to distance themselves from Moscow. Due to the poor human rights and democracy records of Kyrgyzstan and Uzbekistan, however, the U.S. relationship with both countries soured and each gravitated back into a closer relationship with Moscow. The switch in Uzbekistan's orientation over the past year has been particularly dramatic.

Thanks to Russia's location astride the main export routes for Central Asian oil and gas to Western markets, Moscow can extract rents in the form of transit fees. As the main victim of such policies, Turkmenistan has been forced to sell natural gas to Ukraine through Russian intermediaries at a steep discount. In April 2006 Turkmenistan's president, Saparmurat Niyazov, traveled to China, inking a deal to build a pipeline that will supply 40 billion cubic meters of gas per year.[82]

Russia's most important partner in Central Asia is Kazakhstan. Kazakhstan's trade with Russia hit $10 billion in 2005, and the country currently ships 16 million tons of oil a year across Russia via the Chevron-led Caspian Pipeline Consortium. The official line in Moscow and Astana is that there are "almost no difficult unresolved questions" in relations between the two countries.[83] Meanwhile, Kazakh ties with China are growing apace. Mutual trade reached $6 billion in 2005, and in December of the same year China completed construction of the $700 million, 988-km long Atasu-Alashankou pipeline (with an initial capacity of 10 million tons per year).[84] The oil will come from Kumkol fields in south Kazakhstan, which China gained after the acquisition of the PetroKazakhstan oil company; but with

---

[82] *Kommersant*, April 3, 2006.

[83] Dmitri Yermolaev, "A Snow Leopard in Bear's Clothing," *Rossiiskie vesti*, April 6, 2006; and *Nezavisimaya gazeta*, January 11, 2006.

[84] Andrew Neff, *Oil and Gas Journal* 104, no. 9 (March 6, 2006): 41.

TABLE 5   Russian trade with Central Asia ($million)

	Exports			Imports		
	1998	**2001**	**2004**	**1998**	**2001**	**2004**
Kazakhstan	1,881	2,544	4,648	1,877	1,834	3,457
Iran	489	894	1,892	28	34	111
Uzbekistan	485	364	767	521	580	612
Kyrgyzstan	131	83	265	129	61	150
Turkmenistan	94	139	242	43	39	43
Tajikistan	77	69	183	59	129	76
Central Asia total	3,157	4,093	7,997	2,657	2,677	4,449

SOURCE: IMF *Direction of Trade Statistics*, 2005.

the Kumkol fields producing less oil than needed Kazakhstan is looking to Russia for oil to fill the pipe in the interim. In 2003 the Western consortium operating the super-giant Kashagan oilfield on the Caspian blocked the bid to acquire a stake made by the Chinese state-owned company Sinopec.

Russia joined China in a common cause of sorts with regard to Iran's program to acquire nuclear weapons. Russia's abstention during the September 24, 2005 meeting of the International Atomic Energy Agency made it possible for the agency to refer Iran to the UN Security Council, though Russia and China consistently have opposed the threat of UN sanctions. An October 2005 visit to Moscow by U.S. Secretary of State Condoleezza Rice failed to dislodge Russia and China from this position. Foreign Minister Sergei Lavrov explained that "sanctions against Iran are not going to solve the problem of its nuclear program."[85] As an alternative, Moscow floated the idea of a joint venture in Russia that will enrich uranium for Iran's power plants. In February 2005 Russia signed a nuclear fuel supply agreement for the Bushehr nuclear plant that Russia is building for Iran, a project that is close to completion. Under the deal Iran must return to Russia spent nuclear fuel from the reactor.

Regional Cooperation

Putin has been a frequent visitor to Asia and an enthusiastic participant in multilateral bodies such as the Asia Pacific Economic Cooperation (APEC) forum. The most important vehicle for promoting Russia-China

---

[85] *Nezavisimaya gazeta*, February 16, 2006.

cooperation is the Shanghai Cooperation Organization (SCO).[86] Created in 2001, the SCO grew out of meetings that led to a border agreement in 1996 between the "Shanghai Five" (Russia, China, Kazakhstan, Kyrgyzstan, and Tajikistan).[87] Although Russia's presumed preference would have been exclusive leadership of security efforts in the former Soviet Union, Russia seems reconciled to cooperating with China via the SCO.

One of the main goals of the SCO is to fight terrorism and separatism. Along these lines China is particularly interested in suppressing the Uighur separatist movement in Xinjiang.[88] The SCO has created a Regional Anti-Terrorism Structure headquartered in Tashkent. The agreement allows members of organizations that are banned in one SCO country to be arrested in any other SCO country and extradited back to face charges. For example nineteen Hizb-ut-Tahrir activists were extradited from Russia to Uzbekistan.[89]

Commentator Aleksandr Gabuev wrote in May 2006 that "the last twelve months have probably been the most productive period in the development of the SCO. This activization peaked at the SCO summit in Astana on July 5, 2005, where the heads of state issued a resolution all but demanding withdrawal of U.S. military bases from Central Asia."[90] In response to Western criticism over the handling of the Andijan uprising in May 2005, Uzbekistan ordered the United States to quit the Karshi-Khanabad airbase in July. Kyrgyzstan managed to persuade the United States to increase the rent paid for the Manas airbase by hinting that it would otherwise follow the Uzbek example.

The first SCO joint exercise—which involved a scenario of a hijacked airliner—took place in Kazakhstan and China in 2003.[91] August 2005 saw large-scale military exercises between Russia and China for the first time in history. The "Peace Mission" program, which was not part of the SCO framework, involved 70 ships and 10,000 Chinese and 1,800 Russian troops.

---

[86] Huasheng Zhao, "China's Interest in Central Asia and the Future of the Shanghai Cooperation Organization," Center for Strategic and International Studies, August 16, 2005; and Konstantin Lantratov, "Transforming the Six into a Bloc," *Kommersant*, April 27, 2006.

[87] Chzhao Khuashen, "China, Central Asia and the Shanghai Cooperation Organization," Carnegie Center, Moscow, Working Paper, no. 5, June 2005.

[88] Uzbekistan joined in 2001; Mongolia, Iran, India, and Pakistan have observer status.

[89] Mikhail Vinogradov, "Fighters Wwith Terrorism Agree to Cooperate," *Izvestiya*, April 4, 2006.

[90] Aleksander Gabuyev, "The Wall of Shanghai," *Kommersant*, May 16, 2006.

[91] Golts, "Trade Partner, Military Ally."

They practiced amphibious landings on Shandong peninsula, a hypothetical peacekeeping intervention in an ethnic conflict.[92]

Domestic Political Debates

No strong "Asia lobby" is to be discerned in Russia's foreign policymaking. The most easily identified influence group would be the arms exporters that depend on sales to China and India. More broadly argued is that the *siloviki*—the security clan in the presidential entourage—can strengthen their domestic political position by pursuing closer ties with China rather than with the West.[93] Such arguments, however, are quite speculative.

In trade and investment, the key players are the large state-owned corporations (such as Gazprom, Transneft, and Russian Railways) and private companies (such as Lukoil). These companies currently are locked into the European market and are still recuperating from the bitter political struggles surrounding the dismemberment of Yukos and Gazprom's absorption of Sibneft. These key players are, however, actively seeking to establish a global presence and in due course will become more engaged with Asian partners.

Lively debate and deep division exist amongst geopolitical thinkers in Russia over whether closer ties with China serve Russia's long-term national interests. Beijing clearly was a major beneficiary of the Soviet power collapse, as was the United States. Some Russian thinkers want Moscow to continue the policy of the 1990s—that is, to effectively bandwagon with the U.S. superpower. Others encourage Russia to move in the direction of balancing against the United States by allying with China.

Sinophiles range from the right to the left of the political spectrum.[94] Thus the liberal former Yabloko deputy Vyacheslav Igrunov writes that "the West depicts China as a horrible communist monster that jeopardizes democracy. As a corollary, the West urges Russia to sell oil to Japan and not to China."[95] In response to the Council on Foreign Relations report "Russia's Wrong Direction," Konstantin Simonov and Vitalii Ivanov argue that the United States will try to block the VSTO pipeline. They point out

---

[92] The fifth anniversary SCO summit took place in Shanghai on June 15, 2006. To Washington's chagrin, Iranian President Mahmoud Ahmadinejad attended the summit as an observer and broached the idea of Russian-Iranian cooperation to stabilize international prices of natural gas.

[93] Konstantin Simonov, "Property as Key to Success," *Vedomosti*, July 14, 2005.

[94] Alexander Anisimov, "Teeth of the Dragon," *Zavtra*, March 21, 2006.

[95] Vyacheslav Igrunov, "What Is Happening in the Triangle Formed by Moscow, New Delhi and Beijing?" *Izvestiya*, November 1, 2005.

that "China is considered the United States' main opponent in the medium term. How could Uncle Sam beat the dragon? That is very simple—by depriving it of fuel."[96]

These voices are echoed by those of other strategists who see China as a greater threat in the long term than the United States. These strategists cite China's growing economic power, massive population (including a surplus of young males), and sustained military build-up as evidence of this threat.[97] These writers also play into Russian racist stereotypes about the "yellow peril."[98] Adding to distrust of China is the uncomfortable fact that Russia's far eastern territories were expropriated from the Chinese empire in the 18th and 19th centuries.[99] Though Chinese officials never mention the question of these territorial claims to Russia, their silence on the issue does not reassure the Russians. United Russia Duma deputy Nikolai Bezborodov pointedly noted that in the Trans-Baikal area China has 109 divisions, while Russian has but a single division.[100] Sometimes liberals are the ones who play up the China threat in order to justify closer cooperation with Washington.[101] A reporter asked Nikolai Bordyuzha, the Secretary General of the CIS Collective Security Treaty Organization (CSTO), "Do you think that China is our strategic ally or a potential opponent?" Bordyuzha replied: "Nothing in this world lasts forever."[102] Similarly, Vladimir Portyakov argues that blueprints for the creation of a Russia-India-China axis "will continue to gather dust" unless a major crisis transforms these existing relationships.[103]

As for the Russian public, most seem to identify more with Europe than with Asia but few see China as a serious threat. According to a November 2005 VTsIOM poll, 58% think Russia is closer to Europe in culture and way of life; Russia was seen as closer to the East by only 13% and to the United States by only 7%. The United States was seen as a threat by 30% of respondents, followed by China (17%), and Japan a distant third

---

[96] Vitalii Ivanov and Konstantin Simonov, "Russia's Right Path."

[97] Andrei Milovzorov, "China Versus the Rest of the World," http://www.utro.ru, August 17, 2005.

[98] For example, B. Fedortsev quotes a 19th century traveler, Aleksandr Maksimov, on China's "phenomenal evil, hidden behind a smile." See B. Fedortsev, "Russia and the China Syndrome," *EKO*, no. 10 (2005): 134–9.

[99] "China-Russia: Underwater Reefs in their Relations," *Information-Analytical Bulletin*, no. 10 (Moscow: Center for Political Information, 2005).

[100] Vladimir Mukhin, "United Russia Starts Fighting for the Military Vote," *Nezavisimaya gazeta*, December 15, 2005.

[101] Vasilii Mikheev, "The Chinese Riddle," *Pro et Contra* 9, no. 3 (November 2005).

[102] Stepan Sidorchuk, "People Remember the CSTO when a Threat Arises," *Rossiiskie vesti*, no. 3 (January 2006); and Sergei Permyakov, "NATO Reluctant to Cooperate with CSTO," *Voenno-promyshlennyi kurier*, no. 2 (January 18, 2006).

[103] Portyakov, "Russia, China and India in the World Economy."

(6%).[104] According to a November 2004 VTsIOM poll, 40% of respondents regarded relations with China as normal and 34% saw relations as friendly, but only 4% saw China as an enemy. In the event of a conflict between the United States and China, 36% would support China and 21% the United States.[105] Similarly, a U.S.-sponsored international poll found that Russian respondents had a favorable attitude toward China's economic system (67% favorable to 12% unfavorable) and political system (56% favorable to 14% unfavorable).[106]

In the 1990s there was much talk in the West about Russian foreign policy being driven by regional leaders. For example, there was a perceived rift between the federal authorities favoring ties with Beijing and regional leaders in the RFE favoring ties with the United States, Japan, and Korea. Such views led to the hope that outside countries and corporations could deal directly with the regions in the RFE, and thereby bypass Moscow; these speculations proved, however, to be largely wishful thinking. Putin's centralizing reforms, the creation of the federal districts, the reform of the Federation Council, and the taming of the State Duma all have gone a long way toward restoring federal control over the regions. Still, the leaders of mineral-rich regions in Siberia—such as Yakutiya and Krasnoyarsk—are powerful political and economic actors whose views Moscow must take into account.[107]

Conclusion

Economic and strategic trends over the past few years are pushing Russia toward deeper integration with the countries of Asia. This change raises political and even psychological challenges for the Russians, who still see Russia as a European power. Russia's experience with Europe over the past decade, however, has been that an increase in trade does not necessarily bring an end to all political tension and disagreement. Rather than counting on economic integration with either the West or the East to guarantee Russian national security, Russia is using economic ties to boost the Russian economy while maneuvering between the various sides.

---

[104] "Russia Between East and West," VTsIOM press release 361, December 2005, http://www.vciom.ru; and Petr Grinev, "Russians See America as the Enemy," December 22, 2005, http://www.utro-ru.

[105] Dmitri Polikanov and Valeri Fedorov, "Public Opinion and Russian Foreign Policy," *Politiya*, no. 1 (2005): 22-40.

[106] Stephen J. Weber, "How Russians and Americans View Each Other, Themselves, China and Iran," Carnegie Endowment for International Peace, May 31, 2006.

[107] Elizabeth Wishnick, "One Asia Policy or Two? Moscow and the Russian Far East Debate," *NBR Analysis* 13, no. 1 (March 2002).

Even as Russia moves toward closer integration—by pushing ahead with building oil and gas pipelines to bring Siberian resources to China and Japan—many economic and political barriers remain to be overcome. With Russian political and economic institutions still in the process of transition, shifts in the balance of power between rival factions could delay if not derail ambitious energy export projects. The major focus of this uncertainty is finding a replacement for Putin, who will step down in 2008. The leadership succession may open up divisions within the ruling elite between the "statist" lobby of security officials and the heads of state corporations. For the past six years the powerful presence of Putin has kept these rival actors in check as well as subordinated regional leaders to the wishes of Moscow. The post-2008 period could conceivably see a return to the political fragmentation of the 1990s, a development that would complicate the prospects for multi-year, multi-billion dollar investment projects. Nonetheless, with oil and gas flowing from Sakhalin and work having begun on an oil export pipeline from Siberia, Russia will become a growing presence in the East Asian energy market over the next several years.

Some Western observers have sounded an alarm that Russia is turning its back on the West and seeking to project power over neighboring former Soviet states. They see increased Russian energy exports to Asia and strategic cooperation with China as further evidence for this trend. The new emphasis on trade and investment in Russian foreign policy, however, should signal that Russia will be a more cooperative and predictable partner. In expanding ties with Asia, Russia need not be severing relations with the United States and Europe. Given that Russia is currently dependent on Europe for three-quarters of its current trade, the EU will remain Russia's principal trade partner for the foreseeable future. Recognizing that the United States is the dominant world power, Russia sees that maintaining good relations with Washington is in Russia's national interests.

STRATEGIC ASIA 2006–07

REGIONAL STUDIES

EXECUTIVE SUMMARY

This chapter examines whether the economic structures, socio-political conditions, resources, and trade patterns of Central Asia are likely to generate significant regional or international conflict in the coming decade.

MAIN ARGUMENT:

- The energy, mineral, and human resources of the five post-Soviet Central Asian states have spurred economic and political strategies that protect these states from outside intervention and that tend to keep the region from major upsets.

- Being too weak to assure their own security, Kyrgyzstan, Tajikistan, and Turkmenistan must pursue conciliatory foreign policies. By contrast, the presence of exportable staples of oil, natural gas, coal, gold, or cotton has allowed Uzbekistan and Kazakhstan to adopt more assertive policies vis-à-vis their regional neighbors.

- Russia's predominant influence in the region is unlikely to be challenged forcefully by any outside power. While instability within each of these authoritarian regimes could result in violence, outside powers besides Russia are unlikely to step in to restore order.

POLICY IMPLICATIONS:

- The U.S. need not fear that any other power may "lock up" Central Asian energy resources. Increased supplies to China or Russia will help to moderate world prices somewhat.

- To limit the flow of narcotics, arms, human trafficking, and would-be terrorists across Central Asia, cooperation with China and Russia is a promising possibility for the U.S., one that will require openness about the limited intentions of the U.S. and both imagination and coordination with the Central Asian governments themselves.

- While possibilities for the U.S. to obtain mutually beneficial security agreements with individual states in the region do exist, none of these states is likely to become a long-term, reliable ally of NATO, of the U.S., or of any other great power.

Trade, Energy, and Security in the Central Asian Arena

Dina R. Spechler and *Martin C. Spechler*

Despite their remote location and underdeveloped economies, the five post-Soviet republics of Central Asia—Kazakhstan, Turkmenistan, Kyrgyzstan, Uzbekistan, and Tajikistan—have attracted the attention of the United States, Russia, China, and other Eurasian states. First, all five states have unexploited energy resources at a time when most kinds of fuels have become much more expensive. Second, the concern of the People's Republic of China (PRC), a rising economic and military power, about separatism amongst the country's Muslim-Turkic populations has drawn the PRC into the Central Asian arena. Russia and the United States also have a strong interest in containing Islamic extremism on the edge of Central Asia—not to mention reducing trafficking of narcotics, arms, and human beings.[1] Even though all three governments endorse such cooperative goals, these great powers—and some adversaries—suspect one another of trying to gain advantages. A portion of the elites in Russia, China, and even the United States still think in terms of great power rivalry. The "great game" is, however, an outdated metaphor for the behavior of the major powers in this portion of the world.

Dina R. Spechler (PhD, Harvard University) is Associate Professor, Political Science, Indiana University, Bloomington, specializing in the study of Russian and U.S. foreign policy. She can be reached at <spechler@indiana.edu>.

Martin C. Spechler (PhD, Harvard University) is Professor of Economics, Indiana University-Purdue University Indianapolis and faculty affiliate of the Inner Asian and Uralic National Resource Center, Indiana University. He can be reached at <mspechle@iupui.edu>.

The authors wish to thank Pearl Kim and Avi Spechler for research assistance.

[1] An estimated one-third of Afghan drug exports go through Central Asia. Despite increased seizures, much heroin shows up in Russia, Berlin, and New York City. On the way, thousands of Central Asians are corrupted, addicted, and often infected with HIV/AIDS. See "In Afghanistan, Heroin Trade Soars Despite U.S. Aid," *The Wall Street Journal*, January 18, 2006, A1.

All the newly independent Central Asian states are "super-presidential" authoritarian regimes with unclear procedures for succession to the present leadership.[2] Any future instability would be a threat to the energy supplies and security cooperation outside powers wish to have in the Central Asian arena. Were one of these Muslim-majority states to fail and fall into disorde ;, *jihadist* forces might exploit the situation, using the unstable states as a bas(from which to threaten states outside the area, as occurred in Afghanistan prior to September 11, 2001. In the meantime, however, individual Central Asian states have gained enough experience and capability to exploit great power rivalries for purposes of preserving their own freedom of action and advancing their own material development. These increasingly self-confident Central Asian states conduct autonomous policies and successfully extract material benefits from surrounding states by taking advantage of both the competition for energy rights and the common interest in controlling illicit cross-border trafficking through the area.

This chapter seeks to answer three main questions. The first is whether the growing role of outside great powers in developing energy resources in Central Asia will increase the probability of violent conflict among states in the region or, alternatively, will the development of new sources and transportation networks for oil and gas reduce great power tensions. Second is whether economic situations, trade patterns, and natural resources of the Central Asian states will cause conflict among those states or between those states and outsiders. The final question is to what extent political instability in the Central Asian states is likely, and—if such an outcome does occur— to what extent such an occurrence can be expected to result in forcible intervention by outside powers.

The main findings of the chapter are as follows. Concerning the first question, although outsiders will compete for access to natural gas, their quest for oil and gas supplies and for pipelines is unlikely to cause military conflict. The United States has an interest in increasing supplies of Central Asian energy at market prices to the world market, whoever the consumer may be. More secure energy supplies to Russia, China, or other Eurasian powers will reduce the probability of violent conflict and great power tensions, which are more likely to become manifest in other arenas. At the same time, cooperation in Central Asia by the great powers can help both to limit the spread of Islamist extremism and to reduce illicit flows of substances, arms, and people. In answering the second question, this chapter argues that all-out conflict among the Central Asian states is unlikely, but that water issues between upstream and downstream states are the most

---

[2] A "super-presidential" regime is one in which most executive, legislative, and judicial power is concentrated in the hands of the head of state.

likely cause of limited use of force. Outside powers are unlikely to intervene in such clashes. The third and final argument is that political instability is a real possibility in all of the Central Asian states but is not likely to trigger military involvement by outsiders.

The chapter is organized as follows. The first section discusses the economic, political, and strategic environment of the five Central Asian countries and describes their external strategy of *export globalism* by which staples are exported abroad by state-run agencies in exchange for selected capital goods and consumer goods. A second section surveys the energy resource endowments of the states of the region and the outlets through which these resources are and may be exported. A third section examines the directions of trade among these states and between these states and outsiders. A fourth section analyzes the implications of these economic, political, and strategic factors for those outside powers who have both conflicting and cooperative interests in the region; the possibilities for conflict within Central Asia itself; and the likelihood of external intervention. The chapter concludes with implications for U.S. policy in the region.

Economic Background, Socio-Political Conditions, and Strategy

Central Asia is no longer a single, unified region of five ex-Soviet republics but a set of increasingly disparate states with different growth strategies, results, and political orientations (see **Figure 1**). Though all are low-income, the countries of the region can be divided into three classes: the petro-dependent (Kazakhstan and Turkmenistan), the "other-dependent" (Tajikistan and Kyrgyzstan), and the independent (Uzbekistan). The relative strengths and weaknesses of the five states in material and military resources, along with their differing opportunities and leadership styles, condition the foreign policies and security strategies of each.

Kazakhstan

The larger and more important of the two petro-reliant states in Central Asia is Kazakhstan. New wealth and a geographic position adjoining Russia and China make this enormous country an object of keen interest to the great powers. Thanks to increasing revenues from oil leases and exports at high world prices since 2000, Kazakhstan has registered GDP growth rates of almost 10% for the last five years. Additionally, foreign exchange receipts have strengthened the convertible *tenge* and helped reduce domestic

FIGURE 1   Central Asia

inflation. Despite some contractual difficulties, Western oil companies have helped Kazakhstan build facilities for exploitation of deposits along the north Caspian Sea. Kazakhstan has enormous coal reserves—perhaps 4% of the global total—about a third of which are directly exported to Russian thermal power plants. In hopes of increasing production the government is seeking to overcome mine problems (with outside help) and to resolve transportation bottlenecks.[3]

Privatization has proceeded farther in Kazakhstan than in any other Central Asian country, with two-thirds of the economy already in the private sector by 2003.[4] Despite official welcomes, investments in sectors other than banking and energy suffer from an unstable and sometimes corrupt system of law enforcement. Government expenditures constitute about one -quarter of GDP, but programs to reduce poverty have reportedly faltered badly. Despite some early promise of domestic liberalization, the regime of recently re-elected President Nursultan Nazarbayev has become increasingly authoritarian and intolerant of opposition in the press. Consequently, Kazakhstan has joined some neighboring states in turning to the indulgent Russians, who have lately promised $1 billion in

---

[3] American Access Industries Incorporated has interests in the country, as do the Russians. The Kazakhstanis would like to develop electricity exports to Russia, probably in cooperation with that country's Unified Energy Systems combine.

[4] European Bank for Reconstruction and Development (EBRD), http://www.ebrd.com/.

investment. Furthermore, Kazakhstan has consistently sought preferential trade agreements with neighboring states, both Slavic and Central Asian, although so far with little success.

Though growing investments by Russia might imply increasing influence, Kazakhstan's wealth and prosperity have enabled pursuit of a "multi-vectoral" foreign policy that actively cultivates beneficial relations with all major outside powers. Kazakhstan's military cooperation with the United States in Iraq and with NATO has continued at a modest level. Energy deals with China have matured, and informal Sino-Kazakhstani "shuttle trade" is unimpeded.

Turkmenistan

This large but sparsely populated country of 5 million people has the eleventh largest reserves of natural gas in the world. Exports of gas (and some cotton) account for half of GDP. Since these exports now command world prices, instead of those dictated by Moscow, Turkmenistan's exit from the USSR resulted in a considerable improvement in its terms of trade. Nevertheless, subsequent to independence Turkmenistan lost more than half its previous peak output to trade disruptions, and recent growth represents only a partial recovery.

Turkmenistan's natural riches have facilitated arbitrary rule, together with corruption, low taxes, and an overwhelming state sector. The country is dominated by President-for-Life Saparmurat Niyazov, a former Communist functionary whose cult of personality exceeds even that of Joseph Stalin in the late 1940s. He styles himself *Turkmenbashi* (leader of all the Turkmen). Under Niyazov's super-presidential rule, careless and opaque management have been responsible for budgetary deficits, continued double-digit inflation, and necessitating an inconvertible currency, with a black market rate for the manat several times the official one.

Turkmenistan's energy resources have made possible a foreign policy of neutrality and isolationism, albeit with renewed privileges for Russian gas concerns. Cumulative foreign direct investment was only $1.6 billion by 2005, mostly from small-scale oil deals. More so than elsewhere in the region, investors need *proteksia* (protection) to get projects approved and contracts honored. Russia did supply some replacement munitions in the 1990s; the United States has provided some training and equipment as well.[5]

---

[5] Arms Sales Monitoring Project, Database of U.S. Small Arms Shipments, http://www.fas.org/asmp/profiles/smallarmship_db.htm.

Kyrgyzstan

One of the two Central Asian states dependent on outsiders, Kyrgyzstan is a small country of five million people that is deeply divided by both physical and human geography. The capital region around Bishkek is cut off from the populous and poorer south by mountains that are impassable during the long winters. During the Soviet period, this frontier republic was a major producer of military goods for the Red Army. With political independence, Kyrgyzstan lost this market as well as most of the market for hay balers and processed Cuban sugar in the Commonwealth of Independent States (CIS, the successor states to the USSR). Among the Central Asian countries, the Kyrgyz experienced one of the sharpest initial declines in GDP—a roughly 45% decline at the nadir in 1995–96 was accompanied by triple-digit inflation, even though consumption at the time was somewhat shielded by foreign aid. Since that time, recovery has proceeded with only a brief pause, though the 1989 level has not yet been recovered. The country also experienced a large increase in economic inequality among the populace and a decline in local public services (despite high tax rates), resulting in a dramatic rise in the poverty rate that has only abated recently. An estimated 320,000 Kyrgyz work outside the country. Their $95 million in net remittances currently supports some one-fifth of the population.[6] Recent growth has allowed Kyrgyzstan to reduce the external debt burden from its peak. Nevertheless, the government has been forced to devote three-quarters of meager privatization receipts to debt repayment. Debt at the end of 2005 was down to $1.44 billion, nearly half to the World Bank, with Moscow writing off half of Kyrgyzstan's obligations to Russia.

Precious metals and minerals provide almost half of the country's exports. Kyrgyzstan's one notable success in attracting outside private investment is the Kumtor mine, which accounts for more than one-sixth of the country's total output and 40% of industrial output. Now recovered from an accidental cyanide spill near Lake Issyk-Kyl, the mine is nearing depletion. New mines have yet to open. Net foreign direct investment (FDI) is now negative as Kumtor and other mines remit profits. Capital investments have not been sufficient to keep the non-gold capital stock intact. Increasing exports of electricity, which must be transmitted by fixed lines, would make Kyrgyzstan even more dependent on neighbors, which the country already

---

[6] "Kyrgyz Republic: Statistical Appendix," International Monetary Fund, *IMF Country Report*, no. 05/31, February 2005, Table 16.

relies on for oil and gas imports.[7] Unless other industries can be developed in this remote land, the modest per capita income and growth rate of 6% in 2003–05 might not be sustained.

Immediately after independence Kyrgyzstan pursued a policy of neo-liberal reform at the behest of international donors, on whom the country now depends for support. In 1992 half of Kyrgyzstan's 17% budget deficit was covered by international assistance, a pattern that has persisted. With outside help, the state can still devote more than 5% of its income to education, a figure that is quite remarkable for a low-income country. The Kyrgyz Republic was first in the region to have a freely convertible currency (1995), to join the World Trade Organization (1998), and to pursue voucher privatization—all with paltry result. Despite a number of Western-style laws, enforcement of contracts has been unreliable and misappropriations are still widespread. Tariffs are modest, so foreign products enter freely.

Amidst charges of corruption and following a disputed election and widespread demonstrations, President Askar Akaev was replaced as president by Kurmakbek Bakiev. Kyrgyzstan's early liberalization has now been partially reversed. As of mid-2006, the new government of Bakiev and Prime Minister Felix Kulov has not established complete authority. The clans of the Ferghana Valley bitterly complain of neglect and are vulnerable to blockade by Uzbekistan. In February Kulov admitted that 22 "major criminal groups" are active in his country.[8] Militias loyal to local strongmen are ready for action.[9] Thus the situation in Kyrgyzstan is far from stable. Were the criminal gangs (said to control some of the coal industry in the northeast) to gain control of the hydroelectric dams nearby, the Kyrgyz might have to call on foreign forces to restore hydroelectric order and ensure essential deliveries of water.

Despite the many infrastructural projects funded by the Asian Development Bank (ADB), the European Bank for Reconstruction and Development (EBRD), and the World Bank, disappointment with the amounts and results of Western assistance has led Kyrgyzstan to court Russian (and Kazakhstani) investment in agro-processing and other sectors as well as for security assistance. Russia has promised to invest between $2.5 and $3 billion in Kyrgyzstan, mainly in the construction of the Kambar-Ata 1 and 2 hydroelectric power stations on the Naryn River with the

[7] While future export of hydropower is promising for Tajikistan and Kyrgyzstan, both states have in recent years reduced their sales to Uzbekistan and Kazakhstan, both of which have increased their domestic thermal generation. See Clinton R. Shiells and Sarosh Sattar, eds., *The Low-Income Countries of the Commonwealth of Independent States* (Washington, D.C.: IMF, 2004), 286.

[8] Radio Free Europe/Radio Liberty (RFE/RL) Newsline, February 2, 2006.

[9] Rafis Abazov, "The Parliamentary Election in Kyrgyzstan and the 'Tulip Revolutions,'" February and March 2005," (unpublished manuscript, undated).

possibility of building an aluminum smelter using the electricity produced as well.[10] To match the NATO airbase at Ganci (Manas) near the capital, the Russians opened a small airbase at Kant. On a recent trip to Bishkek, G. Vladimir Mikhailov, commander of Russian air forces, announced plans to triple aircraft numbers at Kant and raise its servicemen complement to five hundred. Not surprisingly, given Russian interest, Kyrgyzstan raised the requested lease payments for the NATO airbase.[11] Kyrgyzstan's poverty has brought about a multi-vectoral policy of seeking out the most resources available from any interested party.

Tajikistan

Another poor, mountainous, and dependent country, Tajikistan suffered a disastrous civil war soon after independence. During this same time the country lost more than half its output, and, lacking opportunities in the cities, many Tajiks returned to their villages. According to President Imomali Rakhmonov, 300,000 Tajiks working abroad annually remit $310 million, an amount sufficient to finance the country's trade deficit.[12] Agriculture suffers from avaricious regional officials; industry remains unreformed. Privatization of large enterprises has been very slow, and some of these enterprises' assets have been stolen.[13] Up until this year, the private sector's share had been one of the smallest in the region.[14]

Much as Tajikistan would like more foreign investment—laws on profits, ownership, and foreign exchange accounts are purposefully quite liberal— the unstable and opaque legal regime, as well as the country's remoteness, hinders that development. Although the Soviet Union had planned two large dams, construction has begun on only one, Sangtuda-1, financed by $500 million from Russia's Unified Energy Systems (UES). This project is supposed to begin generating electricity by 2007 and eventually allow export of electricity to Afghanistan or north via Kyrgyzstan and Kazakhstan

---

[10] RFE/RL Newsline, April 27, 2006.

[11] RFE/RL Newsline, February 24, 2006, quoting sources close to President Bakiev. There are 950 U.S. and 75 Danish personnel in Tajikistan. See Christopher Langton, ed., *The Military Balance, 2005–06* (London: The International Institute for Strategic Studies, 2005), 242.

[12] BBC Monitoring Service, "Tajik Labour Migrants' Annual Remittances Amount to 500m Dollars— President," June 16, 2005 (citing Asia-Plus News Agency, Dushanbe); and "Republic of Tajikistan: Selected Issues and Statistical Appendix," International Monetary Fund, *IMF Country Report*, no. 05/131, April 2005, Table A-26.

[13] Shiells and Sattar, *The Low-Income Countries*, 84, 220.

[14] The private sector's share was about 40% in 2000, according to the World Bank, *Low-Income Countries*, 239. During the last year more than 8,000 small- and medium-sized enterprises were privatized, a change that brought the private sector's share to 50%. See European Bank for Reconstruction and Development, *Transition Report 2005* (London: EBRD, 2005), 4.

to the Russian grid. Such an increase in energy production would, however, divert water from the Amu Darya during the summer, affecting cotton fields downstream in neighboring Uzbekistan and likely increasing tensions with that country. Rusal, the Russian aluminum combine, will also help modernize a major smelter and construct a new plant for Tajikistan's crucial state-controlled aluminum industry, the sector which provides the country's staple export.[15] Aside from these promised investments, however, Russia has been able to provide little as development support. Energy-rich Iran has also offered help to the eastern Iranian-speaking Tajiks on some infrastructure projects, as has the Asian Development Bank.

The government under President Rakhmonov remains weak and barely able to restrain the narco-trafficking which originates in Afghanistan. Islamic guerrilla fighters, such as the Islamic Movement of Uzbekistan, have several times penetrated into Tajikistan on their way to attack neighboring Uzbekistan; Tajikistan has retaliated in force. Russian troops, using local volunteers, remain in Tajikistan, but Rakhmonov—adopting a multi-vectoral policy like Kyrgystan's—has also invited some Chinese, Indian, and U.S. military aid.

Uzbekistan

The most populous (26 million) and powerful of the Central Asian states is Uzbekistan, whose capital Tashkent was the main Soviet outpost in the region. With Uzbekistan having experienced negative effects of Soviet dominance—an imposed cotton monoculture and the disaster of the Aral Sea—President Islam Karimov made an early decision to pursue a development model independent of outside aid. To preserve political stability, the new Uzbekistani regime replaced the country's significant Soviet-era subventions by both switching Uzbek cotton exports (still some 40% of export revenues) from CIS to Western markets at much improved prices and by investing in energy and food self-sufficiency. Through heavy taxing of staple exports of cotton, natural gas, and gold, the state retained Uzbekistan's revenue base, avoiding the transitional losses faced by Kyrgyzstan and Tajikistan. Though having suffered from unstable prices for cotton and gold, Uzbekistan nonetheless requires no assistance from foreign experts in order to continue exploiting these resources. Of all the states of the former Soviet Union (FSU), Uzbekistan experienced the shallowest recession in output—only 17.5%—and not only has recorded steady real growth of 4% or more each year since 1996 but also became the first CIS

---

[15] EBRD, *Transition Report 2005*, 186.

state to exceed its pre-independence level of output.[16] The country has done this with almost no outside private support, though the ADB and World Bank have financed infrastructure projects.

As in Russia and Kazakhstan, the recent boom in commodity prices has made internal reform less pressing. Small businesses have multiplied, as they have everywhere else in the region.

In late 2003 a strong austerity program allowed Uzbekistan to restore the country's convertible *soum* currency for trade purposes. Even so, the country remains protectionist, except for machinery and some foodstuffs. Like the other Central Asian states, Uzbekistan has officially welcomed foreign investors from the developed capitalist states. Uzbekistan has been notably reserved, however, about outsider involvement in the country's energy sector. Moreover, bureaucratism, non-transparency, and persistent controls on currency withdrawals all hinder private foreign investment, aside from investment in the mining and hotel sectors. In the absence of significant investment from abroad, Uzbekistan has used state-guaranteed bank loans to invest heavily in the country's textile, chemical, and tourist businesses. Uzbekistan's self-sufficiency in food and energy and booming export surpluses since 2003 have enabled the government to rely entirely on the country's own military for defense. Moreover, Uzbekistan's ethnic homogeneity has allowed the regime to cultivate a distinct Uzbek nationalism.

Uzbekistan spends a relatively high share of national income on education and public health. Child mortality and access to improved water are among the best in the region, despite a per capita income (at purchasing power parity in 2005) of approximately $1,900.

The much-criticized regime of President Karimov keeps a tight control over domestic opposition; thousands of Muslims have been jailed, allegedly for revolutionary activity. Absent popular support, neither Islamist radicals nor irredentist Tajiks have the power to unseat the powerful 67-year-old President, who has had his term extended for a second time.[17] No successor is apparent. Uzbekistanis are famously discreet about their loyalties and fatalistic about politics, so that prediction whether there will be a popular uprising are difficult to make. Such an outcome, however, seems unlikely.

---

[16] For the most detailed surveys of all the Central Asian economies, see Gur Ofer and Richard Pomfret, eds., *The Economic Prospects of the CIS. Sources of Long Term Growth* (Cheltenham, U.K., and Northampton, MA: Edward Elgar, 2004).

[17] Potential Tajik opposition is sometimes overrated. Tajiks officially constitute only 4% of Uzbekistan's population and are usually bilingual, if not intermarried. Some Tajiks elsewhere regard Samarkand and Bukharo as rightfully Tajik cities. Tajikistan obviously has no power (nor apparent interest) in pressing this claim, however, according to the authors' informants.

The state has switched Uzbekistan's primary foreign orientation several times since 1991, though always reserving the freedom to maneuver. Following September 11, 2001, Uzbekistan was quick to offer the United States not only rhetorical support but also an airbase just north of the Afghanistan border. Since 2005, though, Russia has been Uzbekistan's primary patron, though no Russian forces have been allowed into the country; meanwhile, German NATO airmen remain as part of Uzbekistan's continued contribution since 2001 to Operation Enduring Freedom. Quietly accepting a small amount of aid and seeking investment from all sides, Uzbekistan has been able to preserve strategic independence.[18] In practice, if not in rhetoric, the country has been reluctant to participate in regional schemes for trade, joint projects, and the regulation of international water resources. With a strengthened foreign reserve, current account, and budgetary position as well as a docile and isolated population, Uzbekistan can weather outside criticism and pressure for the time being.

Energy Resources and Outlets

Central Asia has significant proven reserves of oil (1–2% of the world total, perhaps more with further exploration) and 3.8% of proven gas reserves. These totals are approximately the same as those of the North Sea; however, Central Asia's output will probably never reach that of Norway and the United Kingdom owing to logistical, technical, financial, and political problems. Rather, by 2010 Caspian oil production (which includes production in Azerbaijan) might optimistically total 60% of the North Sea's current contribution to global oil consumption. Predicted gas production in 2010 might reach 210 billion cubic meters (bcm) per year, about 2–3% of world consumption. Though modest, these energy supplies have regional importance and offer alternative sources should other regions falter.[19] Nearly all of the oil supply growth in the CIS will come from Central Asia.[20]

---

[18] There are about 250,000 ethnic Koreans in Uzbekistan, and South Korea has made significant investments in the country. Korea has announced plans to loan Uzbekistan $30 million for an information technology and education project, and the Korea Resources Corporation has indicated plans to mine uranium, iron, and gold in the country, according to *The Korea Herald,* quoted in RFE/RL Newsline, March 30, 2006. Clearly the Karimov regime still has friends to the east as well as to the north.

[19] James P. Dorian, "Central Asia: A Major Emerging Energy Player in the 21st Century," *Energy Policy* 34, no. 5 (March 2006): 544-55.

[20] International Energy Agency, *World Energy Outlook 2005* (London: IEA, 2005).

Oil

With some of the Caspian's biggest fields on and offshore, Kazakhstan's proved reserves of petroleum has been estimated at between 9 and 29 billion barrels.[21] As of 2003–04 production was about 1 to 1.2 million barrels per day (MMbbl/d) of which only 200 thousand barrels per day (Mbbl/d) was consumed domestically. By 2015 the Kazakhstanis expect to expand output to 3.5 MMbbl/d. Though mediocre in quality, remote in location, and expensive,[22] Kazakhstani oil represents a valuable diversification of supply and has attracted more than $25 billion in foreign investment, of which the state has squirreled away $3.7 billion in a reserve fund.[23] Since refining capacity is still insufficient for domestic uses, Kazakhstan exports crude petroleum. Turkmenistan has some existing oil production capacity, with proven reserves estimated at 273 million barrels, and is producing about 200 Mbbl/d, with little yet available to export.[24] Uzbekistan has working oilfields, but with significant domestic refining and consumption (80% of the country's 152 Mbbl/d production), exports are small and localized. Tajikistan and Kyrgyzstan are oil importers, filling their very modest needs with supplies from surrounding countries.

Several neighboring countries have recently offered to develop the oil deposits thought to lie below the territory of Central Asia. In 2005 Lukoil agreed to partner with the Kazakhstani national oil company to develop a North Caucasus oil and gas field, even though the tax rates will be high. In 2006 Gazprom has vowed to invest "hundreds of millions" to explore Kyrgyzstan for oil. China is the second most active investor behind Russia. China has been a net oil importer since 1993, and its 8–10% growth rates since then make secure oil supply a priority objective.[25] China fears that in an armed conflict, the country's marine shipping lanes from the Middle

---

[21] U.S. Department of Energy, July 2005, http://www.eia.doe.gov. The latter figure is the official Kazakhstani estimate. The latest CIA estimate is 26 billion barrels (bbl), as of January 1, 2004. Kazakhstan's oil, however, has high sulfur content. Ultra-modern techniques both for estimating reserves in deep water and for recovering more of the liquid in oil-bearing rock formations have increased estimates of reserves. Note: multiply bbl/d by 50 to calculate million tons per year.

[22] Foreign oil companies have had recurrent difficulties with the Nazarbaev regime over the terms of their participation. Production-sharing agreements must now yield the national oil company half ownership. A new oil tax is progressive—higher when prices are up—so the government now is to receive 85% instead of 65% of oil income.

[23] RFE/RL Newsline, October 21, 2004.

[24] Based on a mission to Ashgabat in 2005, the International Energy Agency cites estimates much higher—up to 11 bbl—in the Turkmen section of the Caspian alone. See William Tompson, "Caspian Oil in a Global Context" (paper presented at the Europe-Central Asia Forum, Krynica, Poland, December 14–16, 2005), 4. Information from the secretive Turkmenistani regime is always difficult to verify.

[25] China is also taking steps to reduce the growth of oil consumption. According to the International Energy Agency, in 2006 Chinese oil demand will grow only 5.5% because of both higher prices and use of hydropower domestically.

East through the Strait of Hormuz would be blocked.[26] Piracy and terrorism are also threats in the Strait of Malacca, through which half of all oil bound for China passes. China, therefore, has bought rights to several Kazakhstani fields and made preliminary agreements for oil (and gas) development in Turkmenistan. In addition, China has made loans to Turkmenistan to rehabilitate wells there. During Karimov's fourth trip to China, the Chinese National Petroleum Company (CNPC) signed a $600 million agreement with Uzbekistan on energy cooperation on May 26, 2005.[27]

Korea National Oil Corporation (KNOC) has signed a protocol with KazMunaiGas to develop up to 650 million barrels of oil in Caspian fields as well as 200 million barrels at Tengiz. Uzbekneftegas signed a memo with the KNOC and Korea Gas (KOGAS) to explore and possibly develop two oil (as well as two gas) fields in Uzbekistan. India's state-run gas company Gas Authority of India Limited (GAIL) has agreed to build facilities in Uzbekistan to produce some 100 thousand tons of liquefied petroleum gas at a cost of $50–60 million each.[28]

Pipelines

Pipelines to the world market give Kazakhstan and Azerbaijan greater choice of customers and pricing power, not to mention political protection from larger neighbors. Owing to the U.S.-sponsored construction of Baku-Tbilisi-Ceyhan pipeline (BTC, which extends from Baku in Azerbaijan through Tbilisi, Georgia, to the Turkish Mediterranean port of Ceyhan) oil from Kazakhstan can now flow either to Russia through existing pipelines or to Turkey and the West by barge. An underwater pipeline across the Caspian Sea may provide an additional alternative to the route through Russia.[29] As intended, pipelines to the world market give Kazakhstan and

---

[26] According to Pang Xiongqi, a professor at the University of Petroleum in Beijing, who also predicts a peak in Chinese oil production by 2012. See note 4 in James Schlesinger, "Thinking Seriously: About Energy and Oil's Future," *The National Interest* 82 (Winter 2005): 21.

[27] Karimov supposedly hopes for $1.5 billion in additional Chinese investment. RFE/RL, June 27, 2006.

[28] RFE/RL Newsline, May 22, 2006, quoting *Asia Times Online*.

[29] Avoiding more direct routes through Iran or Russia and completed in 2005 at cost of $4 billion, the privately owned BTC pipeline has a capacity of 50 million tons per year. Lukoil withdrew from its minority participation in BTC early in the project. According to a Russian specialist, BTC would need to operate at 70% of capacity in order to reach profitability; Azerbaijan now exports only 5 million tons per year, thus Kazakhstani and Turkmen oil, maybe even Russian, would be needed commercially. Much of the oil would certainly go to the growing Turkish economy. Gennady Starchenkov, "Caspian Oil in the Regional Economic and World Political Contexts," *Central Asia and the Caucasus* 36, no. 6 (2005): 11. Kazakhstan is reportedly ready to commit 25 million tons annually to the BTC. RFE/RL Newsline, May 22, 2006. Deliveries are now also routed via Orenburg and Samara to central Russia by the Caspian Pipeline Consortium—which is slated to double its throughput by 2009—or via Novorossiysk and the Black Sea, then by supertanker through the dangerously congested Turkish Straits.

Azerbaijan more choice of customers and pricing power, not to mention political protection from larger neighbors.

A recently opened pipeline link to the Kazakh-Chinese border will deliver 10 million tons annually to the PRC. This link will be extended to Shanghai by Chinese and foreign oil companies, including Shell, BP, Exxon-Mobil, and Gazprom. Diversification of Kazakhstan's oil customers is thus an accomplished fact. So long as the competition for oil contracts is conducted on a typical commercial basis without government intervention, the existence of multiple export routes should not be a cause for conflict. Conflict may arise, however, if governments provide non-commercial incentives—either positive or negative—inducing Astana to favor one supply route over another. This situation could occur either if the Kazakhstanis have difficulty meeting their contracts or if supplies from other sources are disrupted during an extended period. Although conflict between the governments of consumer countries and the government of Kazakhstan could also arise over transit fees, consumer demand for Kazakhstani petroleum will limit the pressure outsiders might otherwise bring to bear on the supplier.

Natural Gas

Central Asia's natural gas situation differs from that of oil because of the location and size of natural gas deposits, the current need for pipelines, and the much larger ownership role of Russia.[30] Turkmenistan is Central Asia's biggest player with proven reserves of 3 trillion cubic meters, and production of 54.6 billion cubic meters (bcm), of which 38.6 bcm were exported in 2004—mostly to Russia through Soviet-era pipelines crossing Kazakhstan.[31] Though having comparable proven reserves—nearly 2 trillion bcm, one of the twenty greatest in the world—Kazakhstan has had limited production. In 2004 the country produced only 18.5 bcm, of which about 80% was used domestically, leaving only 4.1 bcm for export. Kazakhstan's gas pipelines are mostly in the west and south of the country. Gas exports from Kazakhstan to Russia use the Central Asia-Center pipeline, which also carries gas from both Turkmenistan and Uzbekistan.[32] The eventual

---

[30] According to some U.S. observers, Gazprom has succeeded in establishing Russian predominance in Central Asia by buying up most of gas fields. "Gazprom, Russia's Emerging Powerhouse," Stratfor, December 19, 2004, http://www.stratfor.com (Reports). Gazprom's supposed property rights are hardly secure, as we shall see later in this chapter.

[31] Central Intelligence Agency, *The World Factbook,* https://www.cia.gov/cia/publications/factbook/geos/tx.html (estimate of January 1, 2004).

[32] The Central Asia-Center pipeline has a present capacity of 40 bcm per year, not enough for all prospective users, so the pipeline is to be expanded to 70 bcm per year in the future. See RFE/RL Central Asia Report, May 25, 2006.

customers for most of this gas, as well as for gas of Russian origin, are in Europe. Preferring to diversify available transit routes and perhaps to join the Asian gas grid, the Kazakhstanis are repairing a gas pipeline through Kyrgyzstan.[33]

Uzbekistan has smaller proven reserves—only 1.86 trillion cubic meters as of 2005—but is an established producer with registered output of 55.8 bcm. Of this total 6.5 bcm is exported, mostly to neighboring states, creating an important lever as well as irritant to these states' mutual relations. Kyrgyzstan imports the entire amount of natural gas consumed by the country—1.5 bcm.[34] Tajikistan likewise imports essentially all of the country's natural gas, similar in amount and resulting in cost and political vulnerability for the country.

Natural gas deals have even greater potential for generating conflict than those for oil. Unless, and until, the liquefied form becomes easier and cheaper to produce, gas can be shipped only to a limited number of fixed pipeline terminals. Oil, by contrast, can be transported by tanker to many maritime destinations at minimal cost disadvantage. Thus unlike oil trade at world prices, a natural gas pipeline sets up a bilateral monopoly situation for ongoing negotiation between the source and the end user. Sellers can threaten to cut off supply or to raise prices, either of which inflicts considerable harm on consumers; purchasers can likewise refuse to buy or to pay the price demanded, effectively blocking export of the gas. The Russian gas monopoly Gazprom has been actively signing deals with a number of Central Asian countries to explore for gas to supplement Russia's limited domestic supplies.[35] As part owner, Gazprom presumably, would have some pricing power with respect to these new Central Asian suppliers. Russia will buy 9 bcm from Uzbekistan in 2006 (up from 8 bcm in 2005) at a price of $60 per 1000 cubic meters.[36]

---

[33] RFE/RL Newsline, April 25, 2005. Kazakhstani interest in a gas pipeline under the Caspian Sea to Turkey has faced opposition from the Russians, who may block attempts to build such a line.

[34] Uzbekistan signed an agreement in July 2005 to supply Kyrgyzstan natural gas at $42 per thousand cm—but only after arrears have been paid. A combination of concessionary prices and a willingness to cut off deliveries to Kyrgyzstan gives Uzbekistan the upper hand in relations between the two countries.

[35] Vladimir Milov, "How Sustainable is Russia's Future as an Energy Superpower?" (speech delivered at the Carnegie Endowment in Washington, March 16, 2006), http://www.carnegieendowment.org/events/index.cfm?fa=eventDetail&id=860&&prog=zru. Milov stated that Gazprom will have declines in production beginning in 2008 and will need 100 bcm of gas from Central Asia by 2010, mostly from Turkmenistan.

[36] On a recent visit to Bishkek, Aleksei Miller, CEO of Gazprom, signed a memo calling for "hundreds of millions of dollars" to be invested in a joint venture in the Kyrgyz energy sector. He also promised $6 million to develop four gas fields in Tajikistan with partial Russian ownership. See "Russia-Uzbekistan," Platt's Oilgram News 84, issue 14 (January 23, 2006): 6. Note that LUKOIL JSC is also involved.

Creating an especially sensitive, though sadly comical, situation, President Niyazov has promised considerably more gas deliveries than Turkmenistan can possibly deliver. Turkmenistan's maximum export potential for natural gas is around 100–120 bcm per year.[37] Total production in 2005 was only 63 bcm, of which 45 bcm was exported. Russia's Gazprom is supposed to get all of Turkmenistan's gas exports and more, according to long-term contracts.[38] Moreover, Ukraine's Naftohas Ukrayini has agreed to make payments of $88 million to Turkmenistan for gas as credit against Ukraine debts from 2003–05 of about double that figure. What is more, Niyazov has agreed that China will buy 30 bcms of gas annually for thirty years, beginning in 2009, with the first shipments to come through Uzbekistan and Kazakhstan to Xinjiang and beyond in 2008, though there is no pipeline as yet for such shipments.[39] In addition, Turkmenistan signed an agreement on April 12, 2006, to sell to Iran 8 bcm in 2006 at a price of $65 per thousand cubic meters. Iran expects to purchase 14 bcm from Turkmenistan in 2007.[40] Turkmenistan is also exploring the feasibility of constructing a gas pipeline to supply growing needs in Pakistan and India with gas from Kazakhstan and Uzbekistan.[41] This line would presumably traverse Afghanistan. Furthermore, the Turkmenbashi recently met with the Turkish and U.S. ambassadors to discuss alternative pipeline routes— possibly trans-Caspian, if environmental and political problems can be resolved. All these efforts can, according to Stephen Blank, be interpreted as an attempt to break the "Russian-dominated gas cartel spanning all of Central Asia," the creation of which "has been a major priority of the Putin regime since 2002."[42]

---

[37] Nadejda M. Victor, a Stanford University research fellow, predicts Turkmen gas production may actually decline. By Victor's assertion, the industry is "barely functional" because long-term investors have been scared away by Niyazov's capricious policies. Niyazov recently told his cabinet that the country should be able to produce 10 million tons of oil and 80 bcm of gas in 2006—a substantial increase over the official figures for 2005. RFE/RL Newsline, April 25, 2006.

[38] Turkmenistan has contracted to sell some 68bcm to Russia in 2007, as well as 34 bcm to Ukraine. The price is $65 per 1000 cm from all comers starting later in 2006. Over the last couple of years, Niyazov has demanded ever higher prices from the Russians with little open resistance from them, Economist Intelligence Unit, http://www.eiu.org.

[39] RFE/RL Newsline, April 11, 2006. The extraordinary figure of 50 bcm is mentioned for 2010.

[40] RFE/RL Newsline, April 13, 2006. There is a gas pipeline from the Nebit Deg field to Iran that opened in 1997.

[41] Neil Ford, "Kazakhstan Looks beyond Russia to Market Its Gas to East and Southern Asia," International Gas Report, issue 541 (January 2006): 15.

[42] Stephen Blank, "Turkmenistan Strikes Back: The Energy Wars," Central Asia-Caucasus Analyst, February 22, 2006.

Trade Directions

Oil, gas, gold, and cotton are the main staple commodities that the Central Asian countries are selling at world market prices, with electricity generation a possible new export for Kyrgyzstan, Tajikistan, and Kazakhstan. Though relatively small, each of the Central Asian countries generates merchandise exports that are sizable relative to GDP: 64% for Uzbekistan, 75% for Kyrgyzstan, 81% for Kazakhstan, 111% for Tajikistan, and an estimated 117% for Turkmenistan. These countries' staple exportables are almost entirely under government control, where the state expropriates the surplus over cost for fiscal purposes as well as for purchasing imports of capital goods (machinery) and selected consumer goods. This pattern of export globalism—defined earlier as a strategy by which staples are exported abroad by state-run agencies in exchange for selected capital goods and consumer goods—contrasts with other trading systems: the neo-colonialism of the Soviet past, preferential regional blocs, or multilateralism (which would require a much more decentralized foreign trade sector and membership in the World Trade Organization).[43]

In accord with export globalism, exports and imports of the Central Asian countries to a considerable extent have been directed away from Russia, though the immediate destinations of oil, gold, and cotton do not indicate the eventual customer (see **Figure 2** and **Figure 3**). To take an extreme example, 13.8% of the exports of Kazakhstan go to tiny Bermuda. Additionally, the percentages can vary several points from year to year. Russian-Kyrgyz trade has recently jumped and may reach $1 billion soon, owing to recovery in both countries. Total Central Asian trade with China, the European Union (EU), and the United States has grown faster than that with CIS states outside of Central Asia, particularly Russia and Ukraine. Having risen gradually, Central Asian trade with China, now considerable, would be even higher if shuttle commerce by itinerant traders were included.

There is, of course, trade among the Central Asian countries based in part on the short distances between some of the main border cities.[44] Kazakhstan imports Uzbekistani cement and other construction materials because the high weight-to-value ratio of such products make transportation quite expensive. Diesel oil and gas are smuggled into Kazakhstan from Uzbekistan; flour, in the reverse direction. Owing to

---

[43] As mentioned above, only the Kyrgyz Republic has been accepted as a member of the World Trade Organization, though Kazakhstan may be allowed to join soon.

[44] For instance, Shymkent in Kazakhstan is closer to Tashkent in Uzbekistan than to either Almaty or Astana.

FIGURE 2   Destination of Central Asian country exports (2004)

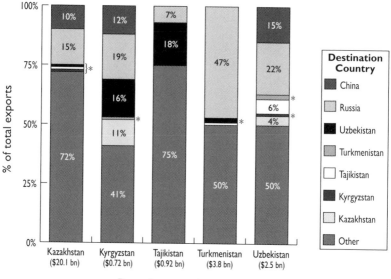

Exporting countries

SOURCE: Central Intelligence Agency, *World Factbook*, 2005; and International Monetary Fund, *Direction of Trade Statistics*, December 2005.

NOTE: Percentages are rounded to nearest whole point; percentages less than 1% are not shown. Figures for Kyrgyzstan's exports to Kazakhstan, Russia, and China are those given by CIA, which were significantly different from IMF and considered by the authors to be more reliable. Figure for Turkmenistan's exports to Russia are for the Ukraine, probably energy exports by pipeline in the direction of Russia.

* *Kazakhstan*: 1% each to Kyrgyzstan, Tajikistan, and Uzbekistan; *Kyrgyzstan*: 1% to Turkmenistan; *Turkmenistan*: 1% to Tajikistan and 2% to Uzbekistan; *Uzbekistan*: 1% to Kyrgyzstan and 2% to Turkmenistan.

Kazakhstan's enormous extent and Soviet-era regional integration, the country still imports electricity and gas in the south. Uzbekistan has agreed to continue supplying nearby south Kazakhstan with natural gas at a below-market price of $55 per thousand cubic meters. Trade turnover between Kazakhstan and Uzbekistan in 2005 was $500 million—a 16% increase over 2004, resulting from accelerated growth in both countries and the warmer relations between these erstwhile rivals for hegemony.

Some analysts have doubted the potential for intra-regional trade on the grounds that the countries are not complementary in their trade. Such an analysis ignores active trade in food as well as in the different forms of energy noted above. Both Tajikistan and Kyrgyzstan are exporters of electricity and importers of oil and gas. Tajikistan barters hydropower for

FIGURE 3   Origin of Central Asian country imports (2004)

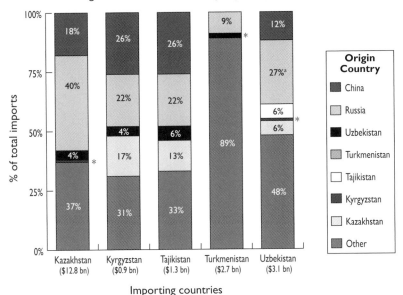

SOURCE: CIA, *World Factbook*, 2005; and IMF, *Direction of Trade Statistics*, December 2005.

NOTE: Percentages are rounded to nearest whole point; percentages less than 1% are not shown. Figures for Uzbekistan's imports from Tajikistan, Kazakhstan, and Russia are those given by CIA, which were significantly different from IMF and considered by the authors to be more reliable. Russian figure includes 4.5% from Ukraine.

* *Kazakhstan*: 1% from Kyrgyzstan; *Turkmenistan*: 2% from Uzbekistan; *Uzbekistan*: 1% from Kyrgyzstan.

gas from Uzbekistan. Uzbekistan also sends north the country's excellent fruits and vegetables, while importing grains from Kazakhstan. Even more important for the future, the countries of the region have unexploited comparative advantages which might come from economies of scale, product differentiation, and labor cost differentials—if free trade or preferential trade agreements were implemented in the region.

An important element of trade not at all registered in official figures is fresh riverine water. As shown in **Figure 4**, the great rivers of this arid and semi-arid region rise in the mountain glaciers of Tajikistan and Kyrgyzstan. The Amu Darya then flows past Afghanistan to Uzbekistan and Turkmenistan before dribbling into the much-reduced southern part of the Aral Sea, an inland lake. The Syr Darya passes through Kazakhstan and Uzbekistan before flowing westward into the northern part of the Aral Sea. Seasonal regulation of the Syr Darya is essential to the irrigated agriculture in both Uzbekistan and Kazakhstan in order to prevent excessive early release of water causing flooding in their valleys across the borders, and insufficient release in the summer killing the field crops. The Interstate Commission for Water Coordination, a water resource consortium established in 1992 to replace the often-violated Soviet-era arrangements, remains ineffective. Consequently, Kyrgyzstan, located up river, is engaged in a chronic dispute with Kazakhstan and Uzbekistan, which are reluctant to compensate Kyrgystan for regulating Syr Darya water. Kyrgyzstan prefers to use the water from the Naryn River tributary trapped by the Toktogul reservoir For hydroelectric power. Kyrgyzstan is delivering 1 billion kilowatt hours of hydroelectric power to Russia at present and would like to build two new up-river facilities that would generate electricity in winter while still allowing collection of water for irrigation. This clever project would, however, be very expensive. Meanwhile, Kyrgyzstan has demanded that the downstream countries help pay both for the $15–$27 million per year in maintenance on the Toktogul reservoir and for the water and power generated. The Kazakhstanis, who generally have workable relations with their smaller neighbor, agreed to pay a modest amount.

China is building an Irtysh-Karamai canal to divert 5–15% of water from the Irtysh River to Lake Ulungur for cotton and grain production in Xinjiang. This diversion will not only impact both Kazakhstan and Russia, which rely on this river, too, but also threaten Kazakhstan's Lake Balkhash.[45]

Far more likely to spark open conflict is the plan of Turkmenistan's dictator to build an artificial lake to irrigate cotton in the eastern region of his country. Were this to come about before Niyazov's passing, the flow of the Amu Darya would be further compromised on its way to Uzbekistan and the Aral Sea.

Interests of Major Outside Powers

Russia

Russia's primary interest in Central Asia is preventing an influx of Islamist radicals, such as those fighting for separation in Chechnya and other militants operating in the rest of the north Caucasus. To the extent that Central Asian states cannot manage their own frontiers and populations so as to avoid negative spillovers into the Russian Federation, the former

---

[45] Justin Odom and Erica Johnson, "The State of Physical Infrastructure in Central Asia: Developments in Transport, Water, Energy, and Telecommunications," National Bureau of Asian Research, *NBR Analysis* 15, no. 5 (December 2005): 108.

FIGURE 4   Great rivers of Central Asia

colonial master will feel compelled to act. Though spillovers such as the armed attack on Beslan are the most threatening, Moscow is watching for ideological contagion in the Turkic and Muslim areas of the Russian Federation. President Putin has emphasized stability as his main objective in Central Asia: "We don't need another Afghanistan in Central Asia, and we will act very carefully there…We need evolution that would lead to consolidation of [democratic] values…but that would prevent outbursts such as the one we witnessed in Andijon."[46]

Moreover, as discussed above, Central Asia is an important source of natural gas, oil, and some other natural resources used or sold by Russia. Projections by the U.S. Energy Information Administration show Russian oil production leveling off from 2007 through 2024; all growth of CIS output will therefore come from Central Asia. Self-sufficient in natural gas, Russia resells gas purchased from Central Asian states in Western Europe at more than twice the price originally paid to Kazakhstan or Turkmenistan. Central Asia's resources are of special importance to companies with close ties to the Kremlin. With the substantial profits from high energy prices, Russian nationalists and security figures (*siloviki*) think they have the means to attempt to reconstitute the Soviet empire, albeit informally, and to head off conceivable Chinese threats to Russia's long-time position in

---

[46] RFE/RL Newsline, February 14, 2006.

Central Asia.[47] Foreign Minister Sergei Lavrov's acknowledged means for accomplishing these objectives is the Collective Security Treaty Organization (CSTO), which excludes China; however, Russian efforts to transform this multilateral organization into an operational force have been in vain.[48] The likelihood is low that the Central Asian states will allow Russian armed intervention to block highly profitable Chinese energy investments which dilute the power of Gazprom.

Nervous about the U.S. military presence in Central Asia since 2001, Russian military and security personnel have emphasized that the U.S. presence is supposed to be strictly temporary, lasting only for the duration of the Afghanistan campaign.

While representing the dominant viewpoints in the foreign policy establishment today, these nationalist and great power security motivations have not gone unchallenged in Russian foreign policy debates. Those liberals and realists who give priority to economic and democratic development in Russia are much more guarded about the importance of Central Asia, aside from basic protection from Islamic radicals. For example, a highly placed official recently wrote:

> The transformation of the [Central Asian] region into a new field of confrontation is not in Russia's interest…Moscow must pursue a reasonable and clear-cut foreign policy and require that Washington make its military actions transparent and predictable. Considering the two countries' common struggle against terror, Washington [should coordinate] its plans with Russia in advance…Russian businesses would benefit from their joint participation with U.S. companies in the development and implementation of large economic projects…Integration measures must also include the targeted financing of nongovernmental institutions of civil society, advocating the real development of democracy in the region and the [observance] of human rights.[49]

---

[47] According to Swedish analyst Lena Jonson, Russia's strategic interest in the 1990s was first "to integrate Central Asian states in the CIS sphere and make them into close allies of Russia and, second, to deny external powers strategic access to Central Asia." See Lena Jonson, "Russia and Central Asia," in *Central Asian Security: The New International Context*, eds. Roy Allison and Lena Jonson (Washington, D.C.: Brookings Institution Press, 2001), 97–101. During 2001–02, though, the Russian "realist" attitude, influential at the time, encouraged cooperation with the United States in Central Asia; afterwards, Russian policy reverted to "great power rivalry." Dina R. Spechler, "Explaining Changes in Russian Foreign Policy," (unpublished manuscript, March 2006).

[48] Kimberly Marten, "Central Asia: Military Modernization and the Great Game," in *Strategic Asia 2005–06: Military Modernization in an Era of Uncertainty*, eds. Ashley J. Tellis and Michael Wills (Seattle: National Bureau of Asian Research, 2005), 219.

[49] Stanislav Chernyavsky, "Central Asia in an Era of Change," *Russia in Global Affairs* 4, no. 1 (January-March 2006): 105–06, http://eng.globalaffairs.ru/docs/2006_english1.pdf. Chernyavsky is Deputy Director of the First Directorate for CIS Countries of the Foreign Ministry of Russia.

Though some Russian military experts could contemplate cooperation with the United States—even to the extent of having shared bases and missions—the Russian army has so far resisted such cooperation.[50]

The present Russian government clearly has a different idea of what democracy entails than does the Bush administration and will take opportunities to trump any card the United States may play. Nonetheless, some Russians are open to joint efforts to stabilize and develop Central Asia, provided that Moscow is afforded an appropriate say and share in any arrangement. To enlist Russia's assistance, the United States would need to be more consultative about the implementation of its limited goals in Central Asia.

China

Central Asia has long been an object of China's imperial interest, though effective control mostly eluded the Chinese.[51] In the opinion of one experienced observer, "Today, China does not want to see a volatile situation in Central Asia, for a stable wider Asia-Pacific is vital for carrying out its economic modernization goals."[52] Even though oil from Kazakhstan would supply no more than 5% of China's consumption needs, China would be more assured owning reserves in a neighboring country rather than owning reserves in Sudan.[53] Beijing also hopes to import electricity from Kyrgyzstan and Tajikistan, a resource that can be important in developing Xinjiang, China's western border region. In exchange for the energy and electricity it

---

[50] Pavel Zolotarev, "The New Bases of the U.S. are Tied to the Regions of Instability" *Nezavisimoye voennoye obozrenie*, August 20, 2004, as quoted in Stephen J. Blank, "After Two Wars: Reflections on the American Strategic Revolution in Central Asia," Strategic Studies Institute, U.S. Army War College, July 2005, 45. Blank bases his view on conversations during 2004 with U.S. military personnel who have tried to arrange such cooperation.

[51] Owen Lattimore, *Inner Asian Frontiers of China* (Boston: Beacon Press, 1940), 171. One of the earliest Western experts on the area, Lattimore estimated that the Chinese emperors controlled parts of Central Asia for "only" 425 of the last 2000 years. The Qing (Manchu) dynasty's power in the area was weakening during the last half of the nineteenth century, though from 1884 Xinjiang province was officially part of China. Between 1933 and 1946 Soviet influence in East Turkestan alternated with Chinese influence, but in 1949 the Xinjiang-Uighur Autonomous Region was proclaimed part of the Communist People's Republic of China. China came to an agreement with Russia, Kazakhstan, Kyrgyzstan, and Tajikistan in 1996–97 over troop reductions in their common border area; more recently these countries agreed to border demarcations.

[52] Russell Ong, "China's Security Interests in Central Asia," *Central Asian Survey* 24, no. 4 (December, 2005): 427.

[53] The figure is based on planned capacity of the Kazakhstan-China pipeline of 400 thousand b/d and likely future consumption. Fu Chengyu, chairman of the China National Offshore Oil Corporation, has been quoted thus: "Technology I can get. Money I have. But if you don't have reserves and production, nobody can help you." See "Global or National?" *Economist*, April 30, 2005, 14 (survey section).

requires, China does sell considerable quantities of cheap consumer goods to Central Asian customers through shuttle traders.

The main point of sensitivity for the PRC is Xinjiang, where some of the indigenous Muslim Uighurs are resentful of Han settlement and domination of the region, even to the point of supporting violent secessionist movements. A small quantity of arms has been smuggled in from Iran, Afghanistan, and even Russia for various Uighur insurgent and guerrilla groups within the region. The Chinese authorities have lost no opportunity to link the Uighur separatists to Al-Qaeda, though such a tie is hardly apparent. The Chinese fear that the granting of concessions or even the appearance of weakness in this vast northwest province would also embolden Tibetan or even Taiwanese separatists. The oppressed Uighurs are presently too weak to cause major trouble.[54] Nonetheless, Chinese efforts in Central Asia can be seen as a means of containing the United States, as well as Islamist threats.

Many Uighurs, ethnic cousins of the Kazakhs and Uzbeks, live over the border in neighboring Central Asian states where there are fewer restraints than in Xinjiang on organizing against sinicization of their homeland. Hence China has had a long-standing policy of conciliating the Central Asian regimes as a means of influencing these regimes to control Uighur irredentists and radicals. China exchanges intelligence about fundamentalists and radicals, seeks their arrest and extradition, and exercises strict control of borders shared with Central Asian states. In 2000–01 China gave Kyrgyzstani and Uzbekistani border guards sniper rifles, flak jackets, night vision goggles, and other equipment worth $1.3 million and funded construction of bunkers on the Kyrgyzstan border. In 2002 Chinese military aid to Kazakhstan amounted to $3 million; in the same year China conducted a first-ever military exercise with Kyrgyzstan. A 2003 joint exercise did not mix the troops but did practice freeing hostages. Notable as well is the rapid growth of trade and exchange of diplomats and increased people flow between China and Central Asia. Concerned that regional conflicts, if allowed to escalate, could spark Uighur unrest, China has a strong interest in peaceful resolution of such conflicts. Thus not only was Beijing content to see the CIS (with Russia in the lead) settle the 1992–97 civil war in Tajikistan but also provided some intelligence to U.S. forces fighting the Taliban in Afghanistan.

Although most Chinese dealings with Central Asian states have been bilateral up until now, Chinese leaders have recently favored adding a multilateral dimension. Most notably, Beijing has promoted the Shanghai

---

[54] Authors' own estimation of the situation based on visits to the area.

Cooperation Organization (SCO) as a high-profile diplomatic effort to counter "U.S. and Russian influence in the region."[55] Though a founding member in 1996, Russia tends to see the SCO as Chinese vehicle; after all, despite joint protests about "big power [i.e., U.S.] monopoly aspirations," the China-Russia relationship has long had underlying tensions. Beijing reportedly made "discreet but clear expressions of interest" in gaining the Karshi-Khanabad air base once the U.S. forces left, a move that Moscow tried to preempt.[56] With their multi-vectoral policies, the Central Asian states welcome infrastructural investments and military training from Russia and China but do not always share the urgency of opposing U.S. "hegemonic" aspirations.

The United States

U.S. interests in the Central Asian region are threefold: access to low-cost energy, democratization and defense of human rights, and halting the flow of drugs, arms, and forced labor from those countries.[57] These objectives are clearly hard to combine, especially in the key country of Uzbekistan, a useful ally in U.S. and NATO peacemaking efforts in Afghanistan from 2001 to 2005.

Under the 2002 Strategic Partnership and Cooperation Agreement with Uzbekistan, U.S. assistance for democratization doubled, including U.S. funding a clinic for human rights law. When somewhat later, independent opposition parties in Uzbekistan were able to hold national meetings but not to register to contest parliamentary elections, the U.S. secretary of state recommend cutting aid to Uzbekistan. The U.S. Department of Defense,

---

[55] Ong, "China's Security Interests," 435. Most observers emphasize that this organization was formed more to counter U.S. influence. The SCO now includes all the Central Asian countries except Turkmenistan, as well as observers from south Asia.

[56] Vladimir Mukhin, *"Poslednaia nabrosok na iuge"* [The Latest Draft on the South], *Nezavisimaia gazeta*, August 8, 2005, quoted by Stephen Blank, "China, Kazakh Energy, and Russia: An Unlikely Ménage à Trois," *China and Eurasia Forum Quarterly* (November 2005): note 31.

[57] According to Matthew Bryza, now Deputy Assistant Secretary of State for European and Eurasian Affairs, speaking from notes at the Conference of the Central Eurasian Studies Society, Harvard University, October, 2004. One might add the following interests: maintaining forward bases for the war on terror, preventing proliferation of nuclear materials, and defending commercial opportunities for U.S. firms hoping to profit from their technology, expertise, and experience. With the predominant ownership of Eurasian oil reserves by the national oil companies (NOC) of the countries in the region, U.S. oil service companies such as Halliburton and Schlumberger have the most acute interest of all U.S. firms in Central Asian energy. "Big Oil" has been confined to the most difficult projects, such as Sakhalin gas. U.S. agricultural implement makers, along with tobacco, soft-drink, and candy makers, have also shown lively willingness to deal with Kazakhstan and Uzbekistan.

however, quickly stepped in to restore some money for priority projects such as non-proliferation of nuclear materials.[58]

With the forced departure of U.S. troops from Uzbekistan's Karshi-Khanabad air base, leaving a base in Kyrgyzstan only, the tone of U.S. officials has grown more pessimistic. At hearings of the Senate Intelligence Committee in early 2006, National Intelligence Director John Negroponte generalized:

> Central Asia remains plagued by political stagnation and repression, rampant corruption, widespread poverty and widening socioeconomic inequalities that nurture nascent radical sentiment and terrorism…in the worst, but not implausible case, central authority in one or more of these states could evaporate as rival clans or regions vie for power, opening the door to an expansion of terrorist and criminal activity on the model of failed states like Somalia…[59]

In its recently released *Quadrennial Defense Review* the Department of Defense gave little attention to Central Asia but did say that "the energy resources of the region offer both an opportunity for economic development, as well as a danger that outside powers may seek to gain influence over these resources."[60] The logic of great power rivalry clearly is just as evident at times in the thinking of U.S. officials as it is behind the opinions of security analysts in Beijing and Moscow. Indeed, the United States is competing with Russia and China to supply military aid to the Kazakhstani government. With new oil money at the country's disposal, Kazakhstan's new military doctrine will include a professional army with rapid-deployment capabilities, new equipment, and "international cooperation both with NATO and Central Asian states."[61]

Other States

As energy importers, European nations (as well as several other large states) clearly are concerned about having both cheaper oil and reliable

---

[58] The United States, in cooperation with the government of Uzbekistan, has recently succeeded in removing significant amounts of weapons-grade uranium from a nuclear facility in Tashkent.

[59] John D. Negroponte, "Annual Threat Assessment of the Director of National Intelligence," statement to the Senate Select Committee on Intelligence , February 2, 2006.

[60] U.S. Department of Defense, *Quadrennial Defense Review Report* (Washington, D.C., 2006), 28.

[61] Col. General Mukhtar Altunbaev, as quoted by Interfax and listed on RFE/RL Newsline, April 4, 2006. Competition to help the Central Asians also can have a downside. According to Oliker and Shlapak: "If the states of Central Asia continue to attempt to play off interested parties against one another, they are less likely to get the assistance they require to eventually manage their own problems. Effective assistance will require coordination and conditionality from a broad range of donors…they need this assistance [from Russia, the U.S. and others] to be coordinated, coherent, and consistent." See Olga Oliker and David A. Shlapak, *U.S. Interests in Central Asia* (Santa Monica: RAND, 2005), 35.

supplies of natural gas at reasonable prices. With demand for energy expected to rise steeply throughout Europe in the next decade and a half, the most accessible new reserves will be located in the Caspian basin or the Middle East. Having provided technical and humanitarian aid pursuant to the partnership and cooperation agreements (PCA) signed in 1999, the EU will continue to do so according to its strategy for Central Asia for 2002–06. As the region's chief policy body, the EU has long been involved in Central Asia for the purpose of protecting these interests. Though natural that Europeans would encourage regional cooperation in Central Asia as a means of promoting economic development given their own successes in regional integration, so far the EU has been able to accomplish little in this regard. Like the United States, Europe is quite interested in democracy and human rights; thus, when Uzbekistan refused an independent investigation into the deaths of hundreds after the May 2005 Andijon massacre, the European Commission sanctioned Uzbekistan by canceling the PCA, denying visas to top officials, and declaring an arms embargo.

For many years Japan was a low-profile participant in efforts to develop Central Asia. As a major importer of oil, mostly from the Persian Gulf, Japan (in competition with China) is seeking energy supplies from Russia for the routing of pipelines in the Siberian Far East. Tokyo thus has an interest in seeing the resources of Central Asia reach world markets, thereby reducing the price to all consumers. Since 1995, Tokyo has not only provided aid but also granted the Central Asian countries preferential status in economic cooperation, most likely to ensure Japan's access to the region's markets. Perhaps in response to increasing tension with China, Japan—more eager for regional friends—has been strengthening overtures to Central Asia. Minister of Foreign Affairs Yoriko Kawaguchi in an August 2004 meeting with the Central Asian foreign ministers in Kazakhstan developed a "Central Asia+Japan" initiative. This new organization was formed to deal with terrorism, drug addiction, mine clearing, public health, environment, water, foreign trade, and transportation. A follow-up at the deputy level meeting was held in Tashkent in March, 2005.[62]

For the same reasons—energy and wariness of China—India has recently been much more active in Central Asia both diplomatically and commercially. With an accelerated growth rate and rising self-confidence, India has made overtures to the Central Asians as a way to avoid geopolitical encirclement by China and China's sometime ally Pakistan.

In sum, Russia's keenest interests in Central Asia are primarily in terms of valuable sources of energy to resell through Russian pipelines, protection

---

[62] Atabek Rizayev, "First meeting of 'Central Asia+Japan' held in Tashkent," *Central Asia-Caucasus Analyst*, May 4, 2005.

from Islamist agitation or terrorism, and markets for Russian manufactured goods and spare labor supplies. Other motivations include Central Asia's kindred Russophone populations and Russia's persistent aspiration for empire or at least for a sphere of influence. Nonetheless, Chinese, American, European, Japanese, and Indian interests are not in acute conflict with Russian objectives. In the interest of the former, promoting democracy is simply neither urgent enough nor sufficiently practical in the political culture of the five Central Asian states. As long as reasonably priced energy emerges from Central Asia and terrorists do not, neither China nor the United States has much reason to oppose a Russian sphere of influence. After all, the Russians are unlikely to oppose normal commercial relations between Central Asians and Chinese traders, who also operate in Russia. Nor will Moscow object to the involvement of U.S. or European oil-service firms, from whose unique expertise Russia, too, stands to benefit. Neither Japan nor India has reason or means to intervene forcefully in the region. If Russia was drawn into an internal problem in Central Asia, no other power would have a strong motive to resist Russia's policing, as none had reason to do so in Tajikistan's civil war.

Possible Conflicts within Central Asia

The most serious conflicts within Central Asia, as indicated above, are between either of the two major powers—Kazakhstan and Uzbekistan—and the three weaker ones. Such conflicts involve water and the interests of ethnic kinsmen rather than territorial claims. In the early 1990s Uzbekistan sent troops into Kyrgyzstan to defend Uzbeks in that country involved in a land dispute with their Kyrgyz neighbors. Complaints of discrimination against Uzbeks living across the Kyrgyz border in Osh and Jalalabad are an ongoing issue. Uzbek citizens also encounter difficulties crossing the irregular Soviet-era border to tiny Uzbek enclaves within Kyrgyzstan. Transit fees, contract fulfillment, and border violations are lesser subjects of contention. In 2005 Uzbekistan annulled a gas contract with Kyrgyzstan for alleged non-payment, a recurrent problem with Tajikistan as well. None of these conflicts, which have led to brief interventions by Uzbekistan on several occasions, will likely lead to major violence, however. This is due to the countries' stark asymmetry in military strength, a consequence of the considerable differences in resource endowment and population size. Notably pacific Kyrgyzstanis spend only a trifle on defense. Kyrgyzstan's Ferghana Valley territory is thus at the mercy of Uzbekistan in any conflict. Uzbekistan spends around 2% of the country's GDP on the military and can field 55,000 soldiers; Kazakhstan spends about the same amount—

$200 million at last count—on a military of similar size and is rapidly modernizing military equipment.

Even smaller and weaker and with troops poorly situated to defend the border from Uzbekistani incursions or to deal with would-be infiltrators, Tajikistan is unable to challenge the sometimes outrageous fees and transit charges imposed on Tajiks trying to pass with their property and goods to the north through Uzbekistan. Non-payment of gas bills by either of the weaker states has been resolved in the past by a temporary shut-off of supplies.

Politically fragile and hindered by antiquated equipment, Turkmenistan managed to spend only a reported 1% of the country's much smaller GDP in 2004. Were the Turkmenbashi's Golden Century Lake project to become operational, the principal site of dispute between Uzbekistan and Turkmenistan would be the border, which is remote from the Turkmen capital and populated by resentful Uzbeks. The Turkmenistanis clearly would have little chance against Karimov's much bigger forces.

The approximate parity in the military power of Kazakhstan and Uzbekistan leaves open the possibility of a Kazakhstan-Uzbekistan war. The two countries' presidents are notorious personal rivals for preeminence in the region. Uzbekistan jealously guards the country's borders; Uzbekistani border guards have been known to kill Kazakhstani citizens carrying contraband into Uzbekistan. Aside from these incidents, however, few conflicts of vital interests exist to divide the two biggest countries in the region; on the contrary, actual and potential trade between Kazakhstan and Uzbekistan is significant.[63] Additionally, Tashkent has dropped accusations against Astana for supposedly sheltering terrorist groups in the south. Given their economic interdependence, the presence of ethnic Kazakhs in Uzbek territory and vice versa, and the lack of burning issues, a Kazakh-Uzbek war is highly improbable. Conflicts in the past have been among regional elites, not between national states, and have not involved disputes over infrastructure or resources.[64]

---

[63] Kazakhstan and Uzbekistan exchange different forms of energy, as noted above. Bilateral trade was $426 million in 2004 and rose to $516 million in 2005. Furthermore, the two countries have acted in a conciliatory and restrained fashion on the several occasions when water or refugee issues have arisen. Having dealt with flooding on the Syr Darya, the two now have cooperated at the local level by splitting the Aral Sea and restoring useful wetlands along the Syr Darya. Their common border, set by Moscow long ago, has been delimited over 2,300 km. Kazakhstan has returned illegal Uzbekistani immigrants who turn up in the cotton fields or construction sites of south Kazakhstan.

[64] Odum and Johnson, "The State of Physical Infrastructure in Central Asia," citing John Schoeberlein, "Bones of Contention: Conflicts over Resources," in *Searing for Peace in Central and South Asia*, Monique Mekenkamp, Paul van Tongeren, and Hans van de Veen, eds. (Boulder, CO: Lynne Rienner, 2002), 85–93.

Important to consider are possible consequences of domestic instability in any of these states having both an authoritarian regime and many poor people who have not had a share in whatever riches the countries' staple exports have provided. There is much loose talk about instability in Central Asia, particularly in Uzbekistan.[65] Journalists and human rights advocates have repeatedly written that the economy in Uzbekistan is faltering, despite statistics to the contrary.[66] Though true that many Uzbekistanis complain about economic policy, the main complaint evidently is against the corrupt government officials.[67] Many observers believe that Karimov has overstayed his welcome and has little support either in the military or the upper levels of the bureaucracy, particularly after his bungling of the Andijon affair and more recent high-handed actions. Yet despite potential instability generated by poverty and inequality or by the instigation of religious extremists, little evidence exists of disorder stemming from such factors. The governments in these countries have generally found any disorder that does occur easy to contain. The events in Andijon were sparked by outrage over misconduct of officials who had imprisoned popular Islamic business people, whose supporters then arranged a jail break—not by economic distress.[68] Most of Uzbekistan's destitution is in the remote countryside, where coercion by local authorities is also a problem. Isolated regions such as Karakalpakstan in Uzbekistan—like Naryn in Kyrgyzstan or Panjakent in Tajikistan—could provide fertile ground for Islamist agitators and unrest but are far from the centers of population and government in rather large countries in which poor communications hinder organization. In Uzbekistani cities, which are economically much better off, occasional outbreaks of rioting over either bazaar regulations or non-payment of wages have been quickly quelled, often with tactical concessions. These cities are doing well enough that their privileged citizens are less inclined toward violent revolution. Large surpluses earned from Uzbekistan's trade in gold and cotton make reform less necessary, as mentioned earlier.

---

[65] None of the twenty most critical "failed states" in the latest rating compiled by the Fund for Peace and the Carnegie Endowment for International Peace are in Central Asia. Uzbekistan and Kyrgyzstan are rated "in danger," however, while Tajikistan and Turkmenistan are "borderline," like Russia. See "The Failed States Index," *Foreign Policy*, no. 154 (May–June 2006): 52.

[66] Annual growth in Uzbekistan is projected by the IMF at over 6%. New gold-mining, textile, and cotton-processing facilities will provide additional employment.

[67] Results of the AsiaBarometer survey of late 2005 showed some 72% of Uzbekistatnis are dissatisfied with economic policy, about the same as for Kyrgyzstan and Tajikistan; 44.5% said they have little or no trust in the central or local governments, often regarded as corrupt, and still less in the police, who take bribes. Of those surveyed, 77% are very concerned about terrorism and 61% about war, yet at the same time have little interest in political participation. See Timur Dadabaev, "Public Confidence, Trust and Participation in Post-Soviet Central Asia," *Central Asia–Caucasus Analyst,* May 31, 2006.

[68] According to author's interviews with well-placed sources.

The same is true for Kasakhstan's trade in oil. Petro-dependent Kazakhstan grapples, however, with high unemployment, struggling agriculture, and blatant inequality. Although Kazakhstan's president Nazarbaev is somewhat more popular than the Uzbekistan's president, Nazarbaev relies for survival on repression of oppositional parties and politicians. The "colored revolutions" in Georgia, Ukraine, and Kyrgyzstan are cited by some observers as possible precedents for Kazakhstan; however all three of these revolutions broke out after contested elections, which so far have not been an issue in the rest of Central Asia. As long as the current rulers remain in power, there is little reason to expect this to change.

The most likely cause of instability in Central Asia would be a succession struggle. None of the strong presidents have a designated vice president or heir, probably for fear of a coup. At the point one of these aging autocrats is incapable of continuing, however, an open fight for power will not necessarily ensue. Many authoritarian and communist regimes have settled the succession within the existing ruling elite with little apparent fuss. In China for example, Jiang Zemin resigned and was replaced by Hu Jintao in 2003. In both Uzbekistan and Kazakhstan the ruling elite have too much at stake to allow a chaotic situation upon the death of the current leader; even if such a situation were to develop, the major powers might not find a strong reason intervene. These powers largely restrained themselves in Kyrgyzstan's recent revolution, and wisely so. As for Turkmenistan, neither Russia nor anyone else will care to intervene as long as the gas continues to flow; any prospective Turkmenistani successor regime will take care to ensure that this critical source of revenue is secure and functioning.

Irregular, porous, and ill guarded, the borders in the Ferghana Valley allow extremists like the Islamic Movement of Uzbekistan (IMU) to move easily into Uzbekistan, their principal target. Karimov's regime is vigilant about Islamic activity and takes no chances with any possible political dissent; nor do Tajikistan and Kyrgyzstan willingly tolerate Islamist radicals. That Hizb-ut-Tahrir is illegal in all three countries is understandable since the goal of this supposedly non-violent organization is to replace the governments with an Islamic caliphate. All the Central Asian states have credibly indicated their willingness to cooperate in opposing both transnational terrorism and narcotics smuggling.

The major outside powers have a strong interest in stability because, were one of these countries to break down in anarchy (even to the extent of Kyrgyzstan's present somewhat chaotic situation), there would be real danger of Islamic radicalism; of the flow of narcotics, refugees, and arms; and of the outbreak of disease. In the early 1990s Russia (and Uzbekistan) did intervene in Tajikistan's civil war, a conflict which neither spread nor involved any forces of other countries. Were a civil war to break out in Kyrgyzstan, Uzbekistan, or Kazakhstan between regionally defined clans, the first impulse of the outside powers would be to refrain from intervention unless an unfriendly regime were to take power—an unlikely scenario given that the urban elites in these countries are predominantly secular, nationalistic, and cognizant of their weakness relative to their bigger neighbors. As argued above, the multi-vectoral policies of all these states stem from objective circumstances, not arbitrary choice.

Conclusions for U.S. Policy

The United States has engaged in a long-term struggle against "terrorism" in which the main enemy is radical Islamist (jihadi) groups, such as Al-Qaeda, and the states which support them. If active defense against this security threat is the primary U.S. vital interest, then Central Asia has a role to play. The United States can try to cooperate with Russia, China, and all the Central Asian governments in suppressing groups like Hizb-ut-Tahrir and the IMU—but at the same time would do well to remain alert to possible negative consequences of such cooperation. Aware of U.S. concern over the spread of Islamic extremism, the authoritarian regimes of the region may exaggerate the Islamist threat in order both to attract military and other assistance and to excuse their lack of restraint in dealing with alleged subversives.[69]

Were an Islamist group to overthrow a friendly regime, such as Pakistan or Afghanistan, the United States might consider armed intervention. To supply a mission in remote areas of Eurasia, bases or base-like forward deployment would be important.[70] Caution is warranted for the United States (and Russia), according to Oliker and Shlapak, because successor regimes in the region may be hostile to the interests of major outside powers. As with military aid, moreover, a U.S. presence may allow these regimes to be even more repressive.[71] U.S. experience in Uzbekistan appears to suggest that it may not be possible for the U.S. to protest brutal actions by Central Asian rulers and at the same time enjoy access to military facilities

---

[69] Marten, "Central Asia: Military Modernization," 235.

[70] A recent RAND study by Oliker and Shlapak likewise recommends minimal forward bases on a "foothold basis" after current operations in Afghanistan wind down.

[71] See Oliker and Shlapak, *U.S. Interests in Central Asia*. Oliker and Shlapak maintain that this was true of the U.S. presence in Uzbekistan (based on the RAND researchers' unspecified interviews in May, 2003).

in their countries.[72] Nonetheless, such bases could be of great importance in the future, for example in dealing with a threat of a nuclear exchange between India and Pakistan.

The present U.S. administration has put great emphasis on promoting liberal democracy and freedom around the world. This goal is supported in general by majority American public opinion, but the United States has limited ability to promote democracy and human rights in Central Asia, especially when a country in the region supplies energy and troops to the West. Given the relative unimportance for U.S. policy of Central Asia compared to other regions, Washington would be prudent to exercise patience and emphasize low-level capacity building and training for the future, while avoiding political involvement. Based the authors' experience and observations, many well-placed officials in these countries do see the need for economic reform, judicial and media independence, and decentralization of authority—if not (publicly) noting the need for a change of leadership at the top.

The United States certainly needs lower prices for energy, and with inelastic demand for the liquid oil products necessary for vehicles, small increases in supply can have a major effect in reducing crude oil prices worldwide since this fungible commodity is traded on world markets at closely related prices. Accordingly, the United States should welcome the efforts of Russian, Chinese, and Japanese companies to build pipelines at their own expense for bringing Central Asian and Russian oil to both the markets of both their own countries and the world. Little realistic possibility exists that any of these states can corner the market or close off Western supplies for more than a few days. Once more easily and cheaply available in liquid form, natural gas too will become a fungible, worldwide commodity. Meanwhile, pipelines to China or Turkey from Central Asia will increase supply and reinforce Central Asian's independence and bargaining power. The Central Asians themselves can be depended upon to prevent Russia from bottling up energy sources, an outcome some U.S. observers have feared.

---

[72] A wide assumption is that U.S. government criticism in the wake of the massacre at Andijon was one reason why U.S. forces were expelled from the Karshi-Khanabad base in Uzbekistan. In interviews conducted with Uzbek officials in the summer of 2005, however, these officials cited the uncertain legal status of U.S. troops, inadequate compensation for the facilities, and the U.S. demand for rapid renovation of the runway as reasons for requesting the troops leave. As Oliker and Shlapak write: "Uzbek officials indicated that events at Andijan were not the cause of the eviction notice. Neither, they said, was U.S. pressure on neighboring Kyrgyzstan to release refugees…In fact, the Uzbek note indicated a desire for continued cooperation in areas of shared interest." See Oliker and Shlapak, *U.S. Interests in Central Asia*. We believe the last sentence of the RAND report; USAID continues to operate there.

U.S. allies in Europe will, of course, have to pay for the gas they obtain from pipelines originating in Central Asia. Gazprom's unreliability as a provider of gas from the region may have been exaggerated recently; moreover the Europeans have alternative sources, as well as some liquefied gas and nuclear energy on which to rely. Pipeline politics so far has neither been a casus belli nor even a cause for threats of the use of force. If wishing to take a leadership role in the world management of energy, including the supplies coming from Central Asia, the United States would be advised to remain in talks with Russian, Chinese, Japanese, Indian, and European leaders, who share many of the same concerns.

In conclusion, this chapter implies a more stable status quo than appearances might suggest. The major powers have cooperative interests in expanding energy exports and limiting illicit drugs and arms from Central Asia; trade will also benefit the five countries of the area, which are deriving material benefits from their "multi-vectoral" policies. For many reasons, this region is a natural Russian sphere of influence; the United States and China have no compelling reason to challenge that primacy. Outside intervention is not likely to be required to address either conflicts or instability within the region, barring a threat to energy exports. Not only is the capacity to influence the course of politics in these authoritarian states limited, but all the major powers have more important concerns elsewhere.

Executive Summary

This chapter addresses economic relations in South Asia, particularly India's economic interactions with its neighbors and security implications for the region.

MAIN ARGUMENT:
- Political conflict, poor physical connectivity, trade barriers, a lack of trade complementarity, and impediments to cross-border investment are primary factors in South Asia's weak economic integration.

- While having some impact, the new regional trade agreement (SAFTA) will not fundamentally create powerful new interest groups in the immediate future, especially in the critical India-Pakistan case, as long as the military remains the preeminent actor in Pakistan. Trade between India and Pakistan is too insignificant to be a mitigating factor in any India-Pakistan conflict.

- Investments in physical networks encompassing water and energy offer greater security payoffs in South Asia than trade. These networks range from oil and gas pipelines to electricity grids and river water schemes. However, the projects are likely to be realized only if they involve several countries and multilateral financing and guarantees.

POLICY IMPLICATIONS:
- Positive security externalities are more likely to arise if economic interactions are either part of cross-border networks of production or the result of large fixed network investments in goods and services where substitution is very difficult.

- Increasing intra-industry and cross-border trade in services are essential to economic growth and economic integration in South Asia. Two specific areas of potential cooperation are energy (pipelines and power grids) and river basin resource sharing and management; U.S. support for such cross-border projects could be quite helpful.

- While the Indo-U.S. nuclear deal potentially offers India an important mechanism to address its burgeoning energy needs, its failure to materialize would sharply increase India's incentives to secure access to Iran's sizeable gas supplies.

The Limits of Integration in Improving South Asian Security

Devesh Kapur and *Kavita Iyengar*

This chapter addresses the characteristics of and trends in economic relations in South Asia, focusing particularly on India's economic interactions with Pakistan and China as well as the security implications for the region. Although the region has bucked the global trend of regional trade integration, significant differences are emerging as India's trade relations with Sri Lanka and China are booming while those with Pakistan remain moribund. In addressing the trade-security nexus in the region the paper makes four key points.

First, substantial trade integration between India and Pakistan is unlikely in the foreseeable future. The primary barriers are domestic politics in both countries and, in particular, the role of the Pakistani army as the preeminent actor in Pakistan. The sort of normalization that accompanies significant economic interactions would pose severe challenges for the *raison d'etre* of the military's dominance in that country. Furthermore, trade between the two countries will continue to be hostage to periodic bouts of terrorist attacks in India. In the foreseeable future the Pakistani military will be both unable and unwilling to completely stamp out the *jihadi* groups, and governance weaknesses will continue to make India susceptible to such attacks, which will continue to disrupt relations with Pakistan. Business (and trade) can handle risk more easily than uncertainty, and terrorist attacks sharply increase the strategic uncertainty facing cross-border traders. If the

Devesh Kapur holds the Madan Lal Sobti Professorship for the Study of Contemporary India and is Director, Center for Advanced Study of India, University of Pennsylvania. He can be reached at <dkapur@sas.upenn.edu>.

Kavita S. Iyengar is Senior Consultant, Regional Cooperation, at the Asian Development Bank's India Resident Mission. She can be reached at <kiyengar@adb.org>.

logic of business is hostage to chronic uncertainty, business is unlikely to thrive.

Second, the paper is more sanguine about growing trade relations between China and India notwithstanding the fact that the two countries will continue to be strategic competitors. With their rapid growth the two countries have much to gain from each other's markets. Additionally, China and India do not have the sort of domestic compulsions that are a critical hindrance in India's relations with Pakistan. Much of the China-India trade will not, however, be driven by cross-border investments; this trade therefore is unlikely to create the sort of deeper integration usually arising from such investments. China will continue to keep India off-balance through its support for Pakistan (and other countries in the region that have contentious relations with India), while at the same time seeking economic gains through closer trade links with India. India is likely to redouble efforts to seek closer relations in China's near-abroad, especially with Japan and Myanmar (Burma).

Third, the chapter argues that physical networks encompassing water and energy offer greater possibilities of security payoffs in South Asia than does trade. These networks range from oil and gas pipelines to electricity grids and river water schemes. Given low levels of trust and the large capital expenses, however, the projects are likely to be realized only if they involve several countries as well as multilateral financing and guarantees.

Finally the paper cautions against drawing any simple conclusion from growing trade volumes to positive security externalities. In contrast to other time periods, global trade is much more competitive; this change implies that if security issues cause a disruption in supplies than substitution possibilities are much easier and therefore less expensive. This is especially true of products traded among developing countries since these rarely include hi-tech items where markets may be more oligopolistic (and therefore have higher costs of disruption). Moreover, a major share of non-commodity trade is driven by intra-industry trade arising from cross-border investments and regional production networks. Investments and production networks are critical and their absence in the region will limit the positive security spillover effects of trade.

The structure of this chapter is as follows. The first section overviews recent economic and trade developments in the region and then examines the key characteristics of the region's trade. The next section analyzes the institutional arrangements that undergrid cross-border trade. The chapter subsequently examines a broader gamut of economic relations extending beyond trade to cross-border investments and physical networks—especially in energy and river basins. The final part of the paper discusses the security implications of the differing patterns of cross-border economic relations in the region and draws implications for U.S. policy.

Macroeconomic and International Trade Trends in South Asia

Over the past quarter-century South Asia has experienced the second fastest growth in the world (after East Asia). Annual average growth in South Asia has been 5.6% compared to 7.7% in East Asia (see **Table 1**).[1]

As to be expected given India's dominance, the region's growth has been driven by India, although Bangladesh has also done well and Pakistan somewhat less so (see **Table 2**). A comparison of gross domestic product (GDP) and population growth is instructive. From 1990 to 2003 average population growth rates for Bangladesh, India, Pakistan, and China were 1.96%, 1.95%, 2.88%, and 1% respectively. Per capita growth rate differences are amplified by the much higher population growth rates of Pakistan on the one hand and much lower rates of China on the other, with Bangladesh and India in the middle.

With the exception of India and to a lesser extent Bangladesh, the recent economic performance of South Asian countries has been relatively weak, especially when compared to East Asia. Bangladesh has been an unsung success story in the last few decades, given its bleak prospects when the country became independent. Yet with the exception of garment exports (which are threatened by the demise of the Multifibre Arrangement or MFA), Bangladesh has had little success in developing other modern sectors, leaving few viable drivers of future growth. In the 1980s the country best poised in the region to emulate the newly industrialized countries of East Asian was Sri Lanka. Although Sri Lanka has not done badly, the civil war has severely curtailed those ambitions. While Nepal's prospects were earlier smothered by foreign aid, more recently political conflict within the democracy movement, the monarchy, and a crippling Maoist movement have all had ruinous consequences. The recent political settlement, however, offers some hope that the worst may be behind. After a dismal decade in the 1990s, the Pakistan economy has shown surprising buoyancy since 2002. The degree to which national resources are preempted by the military, the weakness of Pakistan's human capital, and the importance of the military's self-interest as the driver of policymaking all, however, present daunting challenges to Pakistan's medium term prospects.

---

[1] By comparison world GDP growth over this period was 2.9%.

TABLE 1   GDP growth, 1980–2004 (annual average)

Region	1980–84	1985–89	1990–94	1995–99	2000–04
East Asia and Pacific	7.20	7.80	9.40	6.80	7.2
Europe and Central Asia	n/a	n/a	–5.20	2.00	5.2
Latin America and Caribbean	1.40	2.20	3.60	2.40	2.2
Middle East and North Africa	3.80	1.20	4.60	3.40	4.4
South Asia	5.40	6.00	5.00	5.80	5.6
Sub-Saharan Africa	1.60	2.40	0.60	3.60	3.4
World	2.40	4.00	2.40	3.00	2.8

SOURCE: The World Bank, *An East Asian Renaissance: Ideas for Economic Growth* (Washington D.C.: World Bank, 2006).

TABLE 2   GDP growth trends in Bangladesh, India, Pakistan, and China (period average)

	1990–95	1995–2000	2000–05
Bangladesh	4.6	5.2	5.5
India	5.2	6.2	6.4
Pakistan	4.9	4.2	4.9
China	10.5	8.6	9.2

SOURCE: The World Bank, *World Development Indicators*, 2005 (Washington, D.C.: World Bank, 2005).

The Indian economy grew at about 3% per annum between 1950 and 1980. Since 1980, the Indian economy has grown steadily at about 6 % per annum making it one of the fastest growing economies of the world. In per capita terms, growth has quadrupled (from about 1% to nearly 4% per annum). Long a closed economy, India has witnessed a rapid growth of trade since beginning to liberalize its economy in 1991. Additionally, India's exports and imports have grown at more than twice the rate of GDP, exceeding $100 billion in fiscal year (FY) 2005–06 (though India's exports are still barely 15% of China's). Having built up record reserves and few external liabilities, India is much less prone to external shocks compared to the past. Until the 1980s, Pakistan's export performance had been superior to India's. Since then, however, Pakistan's export performance has faltered, reflecting the country's modest overall economic performance.

Growth in the region has been accompanied by structural transformation. Although agriculture accounted for more than half of GDP at the time of independence a half-century ago, the share has fallen to between one-fifth and one-quarter in all countries except Bangladesh and Bhutan (see **Table 3**). In sharp contrast to China and other East Asian countries, however, South Asia has seen services rather than industry emerge as the dominant sector. Recently Kochhar and others have highlighted India's "exceptionalism"—the dominance of services in a relative low-income economy.[2] Yet the share of services in Bangladesh, Pakistan, and Sri Lanka is as high as in India. Although the underlying causes may vary, the economic structure of South Asian countries (and not just India) has an exceptionally high share of services given the relatively low level of income.

The positive economic developments in the region mask some disquieting trends. Unlike China where the most populous provinces have been growing the fastest, India's densely populated northern belt has grown much more slowly than the less-populated south and west. Public investments in both human and physical capital in these regions have been short-changed by profligate government consumption spending. Stagnation in agricultural growth, coupled with the slow growth of labor-intensive manufacturing, has limited employment opportunities for the burgeoning young labor force. Additionally, resource constraints—particularly in energy and water—loom large and will pose increasingly serious economic and security challenges for the region.

The greater importance of trade has increased the region's integration with world markets. The trade-to-GDP ratio of all the countries in the region has significantly increased, with India witnessing the largest change (see **Table 4**). Nonetheless India continues to have the lowest trade-to-GDP ratio in the region, partly due to the country's large domestic market.

The Direction of Trade

Although South Asian exports continue to depend heavily upon developed country markets, over the past decade a rising trend in the share of exports heading to East Asian and Chinese markets has been observable (see **Table 5**). India's merchandise trade has been shifting toward Asia and away from Europe since the early 1990s. In the case of services exports (especially information technology or IT), however, industrialized countries

[2] Kalpana Kochhar, Utsav Kumar, Raghuram Rajan, Arvind Subramanian, and Ioannis Tokatlidis, "India's Pattern of Development: What Happened, What Follows?" IMF Working Paper, no. 06/22, January 2006.

TABLE 3 Sectoral composition of production in South Asia and China, 2003 (% GDP)

	Agriculture	Industry	Services
South Asia	23	26	51
Bangladesh	22	26	52
Bhutan	33	40	27
India	22	27	51
Nepal	41	22	37
Pakistan	23	24	53
Sri Lanka	19	26	55
China	15	52	33

SOURCE: The World Bank, *World Development Indicators*, 2005.

TABLE 4 Trade in South Asia and China (% GDP)

	1980–89	2003
South Asia	18.5	33.5
Bangladesh	19.2	34.3
India	14.1	30.5
Nepal	31.8	45.4
Pakistan	34.5	40.8
Sri Lanka	68.2	78.1
China	21.5	66.1

SOURCE: The World Bank, *World Development Indicators*, 2005.

account for 90% of the exports and the United States alone accounts for nearly two-thirds.

The Composition of Trade

The share of food and raw material in merchandise exports has been declining for all countries of South Asia while the share of manufactures (the largest category) has steadily increased (see **Table 6**). Manufactures are the dominant import category for all countries in the region, however, followed by fuels (except for Bangladesh where food imports are the second-largest imports). This data ignores a growing category of exports, namely commercial services such as IT. The value of exports of commercial services (including IT, communications, financial, transport, and travel services) has more than quadrupled for all of South Asia since 1990. Information and

TABLE 5 Direction of merchandise trade of select Asian countries, 1990–2004 (% of total)

		Asia		Europe		North America		Middle East		Rest of the world	
		1990	2004	1990	2004	1990	2004	1990	2004	1990	2004
Merchandise exports	Bangladesh	14.8	7.0	41.8	51.0	32.3	26.5	4.9	1.3	6.1	14.2
	India	21.0	32.4	47.2	24.8	16.3	20.7	7.1	13.5	8.3	8.7
	Nepal	14.7	53.7	60.0	18.8	24.1	24.1	0.1	0.1	1.2	3.4
	Pakistan	30.6	22.4	41.0	29.9	14.3	23.8	8.7	17.8	5.5	6.2
	Sri Lanka	14.8	14.3	30.9	36.9	28.8	33.4	17.7	8.1	7.7	7.3
	China	68.3	43.3	14.8	20.5	10.2	26.1	2.3	3.0	4.5	7.2
Merchandise imports	Bangladesh	47.7	59.6	22.0	10.6	8.4	3.1	5.1	8.2	16.8	18.5
	India	17.4	27.8	41.3	28.6	12.9	7.9	18.3	5.9	10.1	29.7
	Nepal	69.4	67.7	20.1	6.3	2.9	2.5	0.0	18.5	7.6	5.0
	Pakistan	31.6	35.1	29.3	22.1	14.2	11.8	19.1	26.6	5.8	4.4
	Sri Lanka	47.5	55.3	18.0	23.0	9.0	2.8	11.5	9.0	14.0	9.9
	China	48.5	46.7	26.2	16.0	16.0	9.6	0.9	3.6	8.4	24.1

SOURCE: Asian Development Bank, *Key Indicators*, available at http://www.adb.org/Statistics/ki.asp.

TABLE 6   Structure of merchandise trade of South Asia and China, 2003
(% of total)

		South Asia	Bangladesh	India	Nepal	Pakistan	Sri Lanka	China
Merchandise exports	Food	11.3	7.7	11.3	9.9	10.4	15.1	4.4
	Agric. raw materials	1.4	2.1	1.3	0.5	1.6	2.4	0.6
	Fuels	4.9	0.6	5.8	0.0	2.4	0.1	2.5
	Ores and metals	3.2	0.0	4.1	0.2	0.3	0.5	1.6
	Manu-factures	78.3	89.5	76.5	66.7	85.1	40.5	90.6
Merchandise imports	Food	7.9	19.8	5.8	12.6	10.3	9.8	3.6
	Agric. raw materials	4.1	7.3	3.3	3.8	6.0	1.1	3.8
	Fuels	27.8	7.7	31.5	16.3	22.0	–	7.0
	Ores and metals	3.9	2.3	4.3	3.0	2.7	0.8	5.3
	Manu-factures	55.8	62.8	54.3	49.1	58.6	43.0	80.0

SOURCE: Computed from the World Bank, *World Development Indicators*, 2005. Data for Nepal is for 2000; data for Sri Lanka is average for 1990–99.

communication technology outsourcing and related services from India, which exceeded $23 billion in FY2006, constitute the major driving force.

Inter-regional and Intra-regional Trade in South Asia

Despite several favorable conditions for a successful preferential trading arrangement in South Asia—the geographic proximity of countries, high pre-tariff rates and protection measures, and high level of informal trade between countries—South Asia is currently one of the most weakly integrated regions in the world.[3] Intra-regional trade in South Asia is only 2% of GDP, compared with 37% in NAFTA, 63% in the European Union, and 38% in ASEAN. In 2003 exports of Bangladesh, India, Pakistan, and Sri Lanka to South Asian countries constituted 1.6%, 4.6%, 0.4%, and 3.6% respectively of each country's total exports. The share of exports within

---

[3] Sanjib Pohit and Nisha Taneja, "India's Informal Trade with Bangladesh and Nepal: A Qualitative Assessment," Indian Council for Research on Economic Relations (ICRIER), July 2000.

the bloc was 5.2% in 1980 and dropped to 3.2% in 1990. Though having gradually climbed since then (to 5.6% in 2003) intra-regional trade in South Asia is barely above that of a quarter-century ago (see **Table 7**).

Unsurprisingly, chronic political tensions in the region are the principal reason for the low level of economic integration.[4] Many analysts remain pessimistic about the chances for significant changes in the political climate that would allow for greater economic integration.[5] This is especially the case in the relations between India and Pakistan (and to a lesser extent Bangladesh). In the case of Bhutan, Nepal, Sri Lanka, and (more recently) Myanmar, however, the prospects are much more favorable.

Several additional factors contribute to weak integration in the region. First, physical connectivity—cross-border road and rail links—is quite limited.[6] Second, there is lack of trade complementarity, similarity in comparative advantage, and a limited export basket due to relatively inefficient production structures in neighboring countries.[7] Third, tariff and non-tariff barriers (NTB) continue to be high; even compared to the import substituting liberalization period of other regions of the world, South Asia still has the highest levels of tariff.[8] Even as tariff declined in the 1990s, NTBs increased.[9] Additional "behind the border" constraints—such as connectivity across contiguous countries, documentation requirements, clearance procedures, and border conditions, approaches, and facilities—all effectively thwart intra-regional trade flows.[10] Fourth and finally, as a result

---

[4] Indra Nath Mukherji, "Towards a Free Trade Area in South Asia: Charting a Feasible Course for Trade Liberalization with Reference to India's Role," Research and Information Systems for Non-aligned and Other Developing Countries, Discussion Paper, December 2004.

[5] Jayatilake S. Bandara and Wusheng Yu, "How Desirable is the South Asian Free Trade Area? A Quantitative Assessment," NJF Seminar, no. 325, Helsinki, 2001; and Elizabeth Krueger, Rossan Pinto, Valerie Thomas, and Tristan To, "Impacts of the South Asia Free Trade Agreement," Policy Analysis Workshop, Public Affairs 869, University of Wisconsin-Madison, 2004.

[6] Praful Patel, "Building Highways and Skyways Will Make for an Integrated South Asia," Development Dialogue, *The World Bank in India*, January 2006.

[7] M. Agarwala and P. Pandey, "Prospects of Trade Expansion in the SAARC Region," *The Developing Economies* 30, no. 1 (1992); R.H.S Samaratunga, "Essays in Trade Policy and Economic Integration with Special Reference to South Asia" (thesis, La Trobe University, Melbourne, 1999); and A.R. Kemal, Musleh-ud Din, Kalbe Abbas, and Usman Qadir, "A Plan to Strengthen Regional Trade Cooperation in South Asia," in *Trade Finance and Investment in South Asia*, ed. T. N. Srinivasan (New Delhi: Social Science Press, 2002).

[8] Jayanta Roy, "South Asian Regional Trade Agreements: Perspectives, Issues and Options" (paper presented at the International Trade Roundtable: The WTO at 10 Years: The Regional Challenge to Multilateralism, Brussels, 2005).

[9] The most common NTBs are sanitary and phytosanitary measures (SPS) and technical barriers to trade (TBT), followed by quotas, anti-dumping measures, license requirements, and countervailing measures.

[10] B. Bhattacharya and Somasri Mukhopadhyay, "Non-Tariff Measures on South Asia's Exports: An Assessment," South Asian Association for Regional Cooperation (SAARC) Chamber of Commerce and Industry, December 2002.

TABLE 7   SAARC intra-regional trade

	Merchandise exports within bloc ($millions)	% of total bloc exports
1980	664	5.2
1990	863	3.2
2000	2,593	4.1
2003	4,773	5.6

SOURCE: The World Bank, *World Development Indicators*, 2005.

NOTE: SAARC is the South Asian Association for Regional Cooperation.

of high barriers to cross-border investment, a key driver of international trade in recent years—intra-industry trade—is completely absent in the region. Investment linkages within South Asia are even weaker than trade linkages. While India has bilateral promotion and protection agreements (BIPA) with 46 countries (with a further 11 in the process of ratification) the only one in South Asia is with Sri Lanka.[11] In the case of China, New Delhi and Beijing have inked an Agreement on the Avoidance of Double Taxation (DTA) and are negotiating a BIPA.

A major reason for increased intra-industry trade is the growth of cross-country production sharing arrangements, often among affiliates of the same firm. This type of arrangement accounts for approximately 35% of world trade in manufactured goods.[12] In South Asia the proportion of intra-industry trade in total trade has been very low for most products. This low level is reflected in the average bilateral Grubel-Lloyd indices of intra-industry trade.[13] Intra-industry trade was only 1%, 0.08%, and 0.01% of Bangladesh's bilateral trade with India, Pakistan, and Sri Lanka respectively, while intra-industry trade between India and Nepal was 14% of their total bilateral trade (see **Table 8**). Intra-industry trade with Pakistan and Sri Lanka was only 8.3% and 1.7% respectively of India's bilateral trade with these countries, while that between Nepal and Pakistan is practically zero. While about 40% of Nepal's trade with Sri Lanka is of the intra-industry variety, overall trade between the two countries is quite small.

---

[11] The principal elements of BIPAs include national treatment for foreign investment, MFN treatment for foreign investment and investors, free repatriation, recourse to domestic dispute resolution, and international arbitration.

[12] Alexander Yeats, "Just How Big Is Global Production Sharing?" World Bank, World Bank Policy Research Paper, WP 1871, January 31, 1998.

[13] The index has a lower bound of zero and an upper bound of one, with larger values reflecting a greater degree of intra-industry trade. See A. R. Kemal, M. K. Abbas, and U. Qadir, "A Plan to Strengthen Regional Trade and Co-operation in South Asia" in T.N. Srinivasan ed., *Trade Finance and Investment in South Asia* (New Delhi: Social Science Press, 2002).

TABLE 8   Average bilateral Grubel-Lloyd indices of intra-industry trade in
South Asia

	Bangladesh	India	Nepal	Pakistan	Sri Lanka
Bangladesh	–	0.010	0.000	0.008	0.001
India	–	–	0.140	0.083	0.017
Nepal	–	–	–	0.000	0.393
Pakistan	–	–	–	–	0.068
Sri Lanka	–	–	–	–	–

SOURCE: Kemal, Din, Abbas, and Qadir, "A Plan to Strengthen Regional Trade
Cooperation."

Thus economic integration in the region continues to be very limited by
virtually any measure. The next section looks at institutional arrangements
that may explain why this is the case.

Institutional Arrangements Underpinning Economic Integration

Many observers have emphasized that, even in the absence of major
political measures, economic integration would bring significant benefits
to the people of the region quite apart from possible political and security
payoffs.[14] Until India began to open its economy in 1991, India's illiberal
trade policies were a major obstacle to greater economic linkages with the
country's neighbors. Even after 1991, India had a "big brother attitude"
toward smaller neighbors that proved unhelpful in building an economic
community in the region. Though India's trade and foreign polices have
undergone significant changes in recent years, the neighbors have been
less forthcoming, as evidenced by the checkered history of the South
Asia Preferential Trading Area (SAPTA). The institutional framework for
regional cooperation was first laid with the establishment of the South
Asia Association for Regional Cooperation (SAARC) in 1985. Economic
cooperation became part of the association's agenda only in 1993, however,
with an agreement to form SAPTA. Since that time three rounds of
preferential tariff reductions have been implemented: SAPTA1 and SAPTA2
covered a mere 226 and 1,800 items respectively. SAPTA3, concluded in
1998, covered 2,700 items, but following the India-Pakistan Kargil war in

---

[14] For the Kashmir region in particular see, Ambassador Teresita Schaffer, *Kashmir—The Economics
of Peace Building* (Washington, D.C.: CSIS, 2005).

1999, SAPTA4 was halted. The twelfth SAARC summit in 2004 at Islamabad agreed to initiate the South Asia Free Trade Area (SAFTA), which came into effect in mid-2006.

A major impediment for SAFTA has been the view among some influential elites in Pakistan that "given India's strong interest in SAFTA, Pakistan could leverage its entry by getting concessions from New Delhi on Kashmir."[15] As a result trade between the two countries languished at a few hundred million dollars, with a surplus in India's favor (unofficial trade, mainly through Dubai and Singapore, has been several times larger). While India gave MFN status to Pakistan, the latter has refused to reciprocate despite its obligations under the World Trade Organization (WTO).[16] This exclusion has mattered little to India given both the very limited India-Pakistani trade and the absence of any trade-specific leverage enjoyed by Pakistan.

There has been a modest upturn in bilateral trade, driven by changes in the domestic and external environments of the two countries. After a long period of stagnation, official bilateral trade in 2004–05 doubled from the year before to $835 million (with Pakistan's exports at $288 million and its imports from India at $547 million) and is expected to exceed $1 billion in 2006. In 2004 as relations between the two countries recovered from their nadir, Pakistan scrapped import duties on thirteen commodities from India that were scarce in local markets (especially food related items) and expanded the positive list by 773 items (to a total of 1,059 items). Pakistan has stepped up imports from India, particularly bulk items with high transport costs for which demand is relatively price inelastic (therefore shortages can sharply drive up domestic prices). These imports include food items such as tea, meat, and sugar as well as such bulk items as cement.[17] In the aftermath of the avian flu outbreak in Pakistan in early 2006, a sharp fall in poultry consumption and commensurate rise in beef prices lead to an increase in imports from India.[18] The fact is that many common-use items in short supply in either country are available in the other country and

---

[15] Shahid Javed Burki, "Safta Needs a Patron," *Dawn*, February 21, 2006.

[16] According to WTO rules, all member states must provide each other with MFN status. A failure to comply can lead to a complaint being lodged by a state that has not been given the status by another member.

[17] Last year Pakistan imported nearly 9.5 million kg of Indian tea (constituting 7% of its total tea imports). The bulk of Pakistan's tea imports (nearly four-fifths) are imported from Kenya.

[18] Importers were booking fifteen to twenty containers per month, each loaded with 27.5 tons of meat. Pakistani traders import Indian red meat at 75 rupees per kg; another 30 rupees is added to the cost by the time the meat reaches a middleman and an additional 25 rupees at the butcher's shop. See "Import of Red Meat from India Increases," *Dawn*, March 24, 2006, http://www.dawn.com/2006/03/24/top5.htm.

(conditional on the infrastructure for trade being in place) can be quickly transported and could therefore ease short-term price spikes.

The principal reasons underlying this upturn in trade include the following: the easing of tensions between the two countries, the launch of SAFTA, the opening of rail and road links, and—in particular for politically sensitive basic consumer commodities in Pakistan—price hikes. Although first proposed in 1995, SAFTA did not get off the ground for reasons mentioned earlier. Then from the late 1990s—and in sharp contrast to India's earlier reactive stance on international trade issues—a new activism on economic diplomacy became an important feature of India's foreign relations. This new approach focused especially on trade agreements mainly with other developing countries. In essence, India merely joined the FTA bandwagon that many Asian countries have joined since 1999. China set the cat among the pigeons by offering to negotiate an FTA with ASEAN, even pledging to liberalize key sectors ahead of schedule. Fearing the potential discriminatory effects, other countries such as Japan and India were forced to counter. As a result nearly 60 such agreements are either in effect or under negotiation in the region.

The weakness of regional integration has led South Asian countries to diversify outside the region, although Bhutan and Nepal continue to be strongly dependent on India for their trade. Smaller countries have sought to augment their bargaining power with India by reaching out to China.[19] India in turn has been seeking to break out of the region's limitations by consciously pursuing a "look east" policy—an economic and strategic orientation toward Southeast Asia. To circumvent Pakistan's foot dragging on SAFTA, India catalyzed the creation of another regional trade agreement (RTA)—the Bay of Bengal Initiative for Multi-Sectoral Technical and Economic Cooperation (BIMSTEC) comprising all countries of SAARC (with the exception of Pakistan and the Maldives but including Myanmar and Thailand). India also established bilateral free trade areas with Nepal and Sri Lanka, a limited free trade agreement with Thailand (in 2003), and a number of preferential trade agreements (tariff concession schemes) with Afghanistan, Chile, and Mercosur (the Latin American trade grouping comprised of Argentina, Brazil, Paraguay, Uruguay, and Venezuela). The Comprehensive Economic Cooperation Agreement (CECA) with Singapore in 2005 was perhaps India's first "comprehensive" FTA. This is likely to become a model, with a Comprehensive Economic Partnership Agreement with Sri Lanka to follow. India currently is in the process of negotiating trade

---

[19] Anand Kumar, "Making a Beeline for SAARC," South Asia Analysis Group, Paper no. 1770, April 17, 2006. Bangladesh and Nepal blocked Afghanistan's entry into SAARC until China was granted observer status.

agreements with ASEAN, the Gulf Cooperation Council states, Mauritius, South Korea, and the Southern African Customs Union. Two other regional groupings with which India is looking to diversify its trade relationships are the India-Brazil-South Africa triangle (as a potential trilateral FTA) and the Ganga-Mekong Cooperation program (established in 2000). The latter (comprising Cambodia, India, Laos, Myanmar, Thailand, and Vietnam) currently deals primarily in four areas of mutual cooperation—tourism, culture, human resources development, and transportation linkages—but again with the intention of laying the foundation for future cooperation in trade and investment.[20]

Faced with the prospect that SAFTA might be Pakistan's only chance to be part of a significant RTA, Pakistan agreed to ratify SAFTA, which came into effect in 2006. If followed through, SAFTA will sharply reduce tariffs and trade-related barriers in the region. The developing members of SAFTA (Pakistan, India, and Sri Lanka) will slash their customs duties to 0–5% within seven years after the pact comes into effect, while the least developed members (Bangladesh, Bhutan, Nepal, and the Maldives) will do the same in ten years. The Indian and Pakistani governments, meanwhile, have agreed to take steps for protecting the subcontinental identity of Basmati rice and to file jointly for geographical indication under the WTO. Nonetheless, since SAFTA covers only goods (not services and investments and subject to the list of "sensitive items"), this agreement will inevitably limit the possibilities of increased intra-regional trade. Since trade and production structures of the trading partners lack strong complementarities, intra-industry trade can play a pivotal role in promoting regional integration in South Asia and dynamic scale economies. Also, given that services are more than half of GDP in the region's economies, the absence of services agreements is bound to further limit cross-border economic integration. Additionally, the degree to which trade increases are irreversible will depend on far greater physical and commercial connectivity and investments include the opening of bus routes, shipping, train services, the establishment of bank branches, business links between Pakistani and Indian insurance companies, agreements on mutual investments and the capital market, and agreements both on standards and conformance and on sanitary and phytosanitary issues.

For the present there is no indication that Pakistan will drop its refusal to allow Indian portfolio investment or participation in the privatization program or will even officially allow distribution of Indian films (which have been banned in Pakistan since 1965). Pakistan's refusal to allow transit

---

[20] For an official list of India's current engagement with RTAs see Government of India Ministry of Commerce and Industry, Department of Commerce, "India's Current Engagement RTAs," http://commerce.nic.in/india_rta_main.htm.

access for trade to Afghanistan through Pakistani territory has led India to try bypassing Pakistan by building the Zaranj-Delaram road connecting the Iranian port of Chabahar with Afghanistan's Garland highway and onwards to Uzbekistan and Tajikistan. This construction in turn has invited attacks on Indian personnel working on the project, leading to the deployment of Indian security personnel in proximity of restive areas near the Pakistan border and further rankling Pakistani sensitivities.[21]

According to one recent analysis, economic cooperation between India and Pakistan requires either prior security cooperation or, as a substitute, de facto deterrence.[22] Explicit nuclearization (coupled with missile delivery systems) has assured Pakistan's security in a way that should reduce the country's sensitivity to India's relative gains in the military sphere. Furthermore, the Kargil fiasco in 1999 has demonstrated to Pakistan the limits of using the shield of nuclear capability to launch a military offensive designed to force India to compromise on Kashmir. In other words, Pakistan is more secure from an Indian military threat but at the same time less able to threaten conventional force as a means to resolve the Kashmir dispute. In the past, Pakistan had feared that economic cooperation with India might give the latter greater economic gains that would translate both into Indian military gains and ever-widening gaps in military capabilities. Now, however, Pakistan's relative gains in the security sphere should reduce Pakistani sensitivity to relative gains by India in the economic sphere, making Islamabad more amenable to economic cooperation with New Delhi.

The argument is compelling but omits a critical variable: the interests of key domestic actors. In the case of Pakistan the preeminent domestic actor is the army. The sort of normalization that accompanies significant economic interactions would pose severe challenges for the *raison d'être* of military dominance in that country. Furthermore, trade between the two countries will continue to be hostage to periodic bouts of terrorist attacks in India as evidenced by the bomb blasts in Mumbai in July 2006. In the aftermath, trade delegations canceled trips as well as trade fairs. Fond hopes aside, terrorist attacks in India will unfortunately continue to be a periodic feature of the Indian landscape. In the foreseeable future the Pakistani military will be both unable and unwilling to stamp out the jihadi groups completely— not just as a leverage to prod India on Kashmir but also because Islamic

---

[21] There is some speculation that the Pakistani intelligence is behind the changing nature of the Taliban's demands, from localized demands (such as securing the release of comrades) to explicitly broad demands (in particular asking Indians to quit the country).

[22] E. Sridharan, "Improving Indo-Pakistan Relations: International Relations Theory, Nuclear Deterrence and Possibilities for Economic Cooperation," *Contemporary South Asia* 14, no. 3 (2005): 321–39.

parties (some of which are linked to these jihadi groups) are an important ally in its quest to stay in power in Pakistan. India's governance weaknesses will continue to make the country susceptible to such attacks; lacking the capacity to address domestic weaknesses to minimize such attacks, India will have little option but to put a brake on relations with Pakistan. By and large business can deal with risk by pricing it and acting accordingly. Business finds dealing with uncertainty to be much harder, however, a fact that will continue to bedevil relations between the two countries in the foreseeable future.

This equilibrium could change if a civilian government were in power in Pakistan (though the Pakistani military has been known to call the shots even when out of power). Since politicians need business allies for their financial support, business could emerge as an important domestic interest group favoring closer trade links with India if trade offers significant financial gains. In contrast, with autonomous sources of patronage, the army does not need trade to secure its own financial and corporate interests.

Security relations between Bangladesh and India have deteriorated in recent years, with India claiming that Bangladesh has become both a haven for a number of insurgent groups fighting Indian rule in the remote northeast and a transit to Pakistan for Islamic terrorists. The large numbers of illegal Bangladeshi migrants are changing the ethnic and religious character of India's eastern border areas. The Indian reaction—to build a 4,000 km (2,500 mile) fence on the India-Bangladesh border—has been deemed as yet another unfriendly act by Bangladesh. Not surprisingly, these strains have put a damper on trade and investment flows. Although enjoying a considerable bilateral trade surplus (of about $1.5 billion in 2005), India has not agreed to Bangladesh's demands for duty-free access to Indian markets given Bangladesh's refusal to allow India transit access to the country's northeast. A more positive reaction to stem the flow of migrants has been offered by India's finance minister, P. Chidambaram, who has argued that another way of tackling the migration problem would be to aid Bangladesh's economy: "What is the point in calling ourselves a regional economic power if we can't help our neighbors?"[23] It remains to be seen how substantial will be the effects of the ratification of SAFTA in increasing trade between the two countries. There are few Indian investments in Bangladesh. Recently India's Tata group, one of the country's most respected business houses, proposed a $3 billion investment in Bangladesh, the largest single foreign investment proposal ever made

---

[23] Quoted in "A Problem Shared," *Economist*, March 23, 2006.

in that country.[24] This proposal too has faltered, a victim of Bangladesh's domestic politics.

The changing dynamics of Indian-Sri Lankan relations offers the clearest case in the region of the positive security externalities from increasing trade relations. During the 1980s ties between the two countries were at their nadir in the aftermath of India's botched attempt to insert itself in Sri Lanka's civil war. Colombo was also wary of closer economic links between the two countries because Sri Lanka had a more liberal trade regime and feared being swamped by imports from India's much stronger and diversified economy. To overcome these fears and build Sri Lankan confidence, India made asymmetrical concessions in the Indo-Sri Lanka Free Trade Agreement of 1998. The resulting trade growth (with Sri Lanka's exports to India growing more rapidly than imports) has further alleviated apprehensions. The two countries are negotiating a Comprehensive Economic Partnership Agreement that, unlike SAFTA, includes services as well as cross-border investment. Meanwhile, there is increasing Indian investment in Sri Lanka.[25]

India-China Economic Relations

Economic integration and interdependence in Asia has been growing, underpinned by investment, production, and trade networks on the one hand and on the other a shared interest in preventing and managing future crises, whether the roots might be economic, natural, or political. At the same time, however, the rivalry among Asia's leading powers—in particular between China on one side and Japan and India on the other—is a reminder that the intensity of shared interests cannot be taken for granted.

There is little doubt that a qualitative transformation in Sino-Indian relations took place in the period between Indian prime minister Rajiv Gandhi's 1988 breakthrough trip to China and Chinese premier Wen Jiabao's 2005 visit that included the signing of a "strategic and cooperative partnership." China has moved from a pure "containment" strategy to a mixed strategy that also includes cooperation and cooptation. This shift has been driven by China's wary relationships with Japan and the United States, by growing strategic closeness between India and the United States, and by India's surging economy. As noted below, unlike the 1950s this relationship has a stronger pragmatic and economic content.

---

[24] The investments included a 2.4 million-ton steel plant, a one million-ton urea fertilizer plant, a 500 megawatt coal-fired power plant and a 1,000 MW gas-fired power plant. The offer included a 10 % equity stake for the Bangladesh government in all projects as well as plans to tap the capital market in Bangladesh.

[25] For instance the principal oil company in Sri Lanka is largely Indian-owned.

Indian analysts believe that an India containment strategy continues to be influential among a section of military and strategic experts in China. Although economic, political, and military support to Pakistan continues to be a lynchpin of this strategy, close relations with the military junta in Myanmar and building relations with Bangladesh, Nepal, and Sri Lanka have emerged as important elements as well. Already the largest supplier of weaponry to Bangladesh, China has emerged as that country's largest source of imports as well. Beijing has leveraged these links in order to gain inclusion in the region's regional groupings, hoping to offset India's growing dominance. Thus China was granted observer status at the SAARC November 2005 summit in Dhaka as a result of efforts by Nepal, Pakistan, and Bangladesh and despite Indian reluctance. Nepal even threatened to veto Afghanistan's entry into SAARC, which India supported, unless China was granted observer status, in part because China had been supplying small arms to the embattled King against India's wishes.

China concurrently has managed to exclude India from the emerging East Asian Community (EAC) by encouraging Malaysia's fears that the region would be divided into two blocs; one bloc being the core or primary states with China as the leader inside the ASEAN+3 grouping (including China, South Korea, and Japan) and the other being the secondary states of India, Australia, and New Zealand that together with the EAC are part of the East Asian Summit (EAS).[26] Additionally, at the global level, China's blocking of Japan's bid for a Security Council seat ensured that India's claims were shut out as well.

In contrast, at the bilateral level political and commercial relations have been on an upswing. Trade between India and China stood at $2.4 million in 1977. After similar low levels through the 1980s, trade between the countries picked up in the 1990s. India-China bilateral trade has grown from $339 million in 1990 to $13.6 billion in 2004 and $18 billion in 2005, with India enjoying a trade surplus. If, as expected, bilateral trade crosses the $20 billion mark in 2007, China will overtake the United States as India's largest trading partner. In an effort to enhance bilateral trade to $50 billion by 2010, the India-China Joint Economic Group meeting in March 2006 decided to set up six task forces related to the WTO, harmonization of standards, rules of origin, NTBs, agriculture, and reconciliation of trade. Apart from deciding to put in place a CEO forum to facilitate business relationships, India and China have also agreed to examine the possibility

---

[26] India, Australia, and New Zealand have been limited to being dialogue partners on regional issues such as terrorism and avian flu.

of inking a regional trade agreement along with an investment protection agreement.[27]

Although China is becoming an important source of India's imports and destination for its exports, India's position in total Chinese trade is still barely above 1%. In terms of product composition, India's exports to China are dominated by primary and semi-finished steel, iron ore, low-value minerals, and plastics and linoleum products, while China's exports to India are dominated by electronic goods and medicinal and pharmaceutical products. In all cases the elasticities of substitution from suppliers from other countries are fairly large, implying that trade disruptions will carry little costs to China and somewhat additional, but not large, costs for India. Physical connectivity between the two countries, a major barrier to trade and virtually absent until a few years ago, is growing.[28] China's recognition of Sikkim as a part of India has paved the way for the opening of the Nathu La pass in Sikkim, which potentially could provide much quicker access to the sea from Tibet. This is the third crossing between the two countries to have opened since the border closure following the 1962 war. Under the Bangladesh, China, India, and Myanmar initiative (BCIM, also known as the Kunming initiative), efforts are in place to link the contiguous areas of the four countries, providing a shorter access to the coast and to China's western provinces (especially Yunnan). India, however, continues to harbor fears of potentially destabilizing effects both on security and on domestic industry; as a result, New Delhi has allowed only "border trade." Thus while China has extensively upgraded infrastructure at the border crossings in anticipation of greater trade, the transport infrastructure on the Indian side is in poor condition. Despite considerable interest by China, India has not been enthusiastic about, for example, reviving the old Stilwell road connecting India's northeast to Yunnan, even though greater economic exchanges across the land border with China are likely to be beneficial both to China's impoverished western provinces and Yunnan and to India's eastern provinces and restive northeast.

Despite growing outward foreign direct investment by both China and India, the two invest very little in each other.[29] As with India's other neighbors, investment linkages between India and China are very weak. Total Chinese investments in India amount to about $150 million whereas

---

[27] For details, see "Report of the India-China Joint Study Group on Comprehensive Trade and Economic Cooperation," Ministry of External Affairs, Government of India, November 2005.

[28] There are now direct flights between Bejing and Delhi as well as (beginning in December 2005) direct telecom connection between China and India (hitherto calls were routed through Europe and the United States). The agreement—between India's Reliance Infocomm and China Telecom, the country's main fixed-line carrier—decreased phone tariffs by more than 50%.

[29] Outward FDI by China was $6.9 billion in 2005 and by India, $6 billion.

Indian investments in China are close to $100 million. Security concerns have limited Chinese investments in India. In the telecom sector the Indian government has put on hold expansion plans of the two largest Chinese telecom equipment makers—Zhongxing Telecom Co. (ZTE) and Huawei Technologies (the latter of which has a major software development center in Bangalore)—as well as proposed investments in Indian ports by Hutchinson.[30] At the time of this writing, the reformist Marxist government of West Bengal was wooing Chinese investment in that state, a development offering greater possibilities. China, in contrast, has been more forthcoming, calling upon Indian companies to pick up equity in China's state-owned enterprises through the Beijing Equity Exchange (BEE) and successfully wooing major Indian software companies to set up shop in China.[31]

Physical Networks, Connectivity, and Economic Interlinkages

The level of bilateral trade among India, Pakistan, and China is too limited to create the sorts of domestic constituencies that would significantly reshape security relations between these countries. Even if trade were to grow substantially, trade disruption will not impose onerous costs on any of these countries and hence will not be a major factor as they contemplate their security stance. Might economic linkages that are network based and establish physical "facts on ground"—cross-border production networks based on mutual investments, energy networks (whether oil and gas pipelines or power grids), and river basin sharing—have a greater impact on security? To analyze this argument, this section considers two examples— energy and river basin waters.

Guaranteeing Energy Security

Both China and India have stepped up their efforts to secure energy supplies that are critical to sustaining their rapid economic growth. Estimates are that if India's economy grows at 7–8% over the next quarter-century, the country's primary energy demand will increase three to four times. Currently India is the world's sixth largest consumer of energy, importing over 70% of the country's crude oil needs. The Indian public

---

[30] Monica Gupta, "Chinese Investments Face Security Hurdles," *Business Standard*, June 19, 2006. Huawei's connections to the Chinese military (to which it is a leading IT provider) have raised security concerns in India.

[31] K.G. Narendranath, "Beijing Wants India Inc to Pick Up Stake in Chinese PSUs," *Financial Express*, April 20, 2006, http://www.financialexpress.com/fe_full_story.php?content_id=124362.

sector Oil and Natural Gas Company (ONGC) has invested $3.5 billion in overseas exploration since 2000. In the foreseeable future, India has little option but to import increasing amounts of oil and gas to meet the country's energy needs.

In addition to the sharp growth in bilateral trade between China and India, the most visible manifestation of the mixed strategy of cooperation and competition has been in the energy sector. China has repeatedly got the better of India in the competition for global energy resources, whether in Myanmar, Kazakhstan, Angola, Ecuador, or Nigeria. China National Petroleum Corporation (CNPC) bested India's ONGC in a battle for control of PetroKazakhstan as well as for Nations Energy, a Canada-based company with oil fields in Central Asia. While China may yet pay the penalty of the "winner's curse" for such aggressive bidding, the reality is that China is better prepared for future energy uncertainties than is India. India's efforts have been stymied both by traditional governmental lethargy and by an absence of coherent foreign, trade, and energy policies and geo-strategic goals.

Having failed to best China, India is relying on cooperation with China as a "strategic partner" in their mutual hunt for energy, proving once again that—at least in India's case—hope may well triumph over experience. Since joint bids would diffuse opposition, China's partnership strategy with India is at least partly designed to make China's international energy deals more palatable to the international community. Additionally, it makes sense for the two countries to cooperate, even tacitly, to improve their bargaining position since competition between the two has simply bid up oil and gas asset prices. The oil and gas giants from the two countries—Indian Oil Corporation (IOC) and China Petroleum and Chemical Corporation (Sinopec), both of which are public sector dominated—have been discussing floating a special-purpose vehicle to participate in the Singapore Platt window for Oman and Dubai crude oil to challenge the so-called "Asian premium" the two are paying to buy from global suppliers. The two companies are also beginning joint bids for overseas oil and gas fields. In 2005 CNPC and ONGC reached agreement to buy a stake in Syria's largest oil producer (the first time groups from each country have secured upstream resources in the Middle East) and in 2006 they teamed up to buy a 50% stake in Omimex de Colombia.

To obtain gas for its energy requirements, India is simultaneously pursing three options: development of domestic resources, pursuit of long-term liquefied natural gas (LNG) contracts, and participation in transnational gas pipeline projects. India has had some success in the first option with gas discoveries, particularly those in the Krishna-Godavari basin. As for the second option, India has entered into separate LNG contracts with Qatar and Iran for supply of five million tons per annum over 25 years. While supplies from Qatar have been flowing in since 2004 those from Iran are scheduled to commence from 2009. With sanctions affecting Iran's ability to avail of critical LNG technologies, however, it is unclear if this will indeed occur.

The last option, the creation of a regional gas grid, has the most significant implications—if any manage to get off the ground. Of the three current proposals, all are fraught with political and security-related problems.

The IPI pipeline. Though the Iran-Pakistan-India pipeline was first conceived in 1989, little progress was made until tensions and deep mistrust between India and Pakistan ebbed. In early 2005 Iran agreed to separate agreements with the two countries: a straightforward purchase of Iranian gas at the Indian border (90 million standard cubic meters [scm] per day), and a separate agreement with Pakistan covering the supply of gas to that country (60 million scm per day) as well as payments for transit rights of the gas pipeline to India. With strong opposition from the United States, India will face difficulty securing the large financing for the project (estimated at $7 billion); other significant issues—technical, commercial, and legal—remain as well, especially those related to gas price and project structure. This situation could change if U.S.-Iran relations improve or perhaps if the Indo-U.S. nuclear deal comes unstuck. The latter would reduce India's incentives to toe the U.S. line since Indian energy security will be put under double jeopardy, with India having neither access to sizeable gas supplies nor to nuclear energy. U.S. pressure on India to drop this project may simply allow China to emerge as a key player. In early 2006, China proposed that regardless of whether New Delhi builds a pipeline from Iran to India via Pakistan, the Chinese would be willing to pay for and construct the pipeline from Pakistan into western China, thus providing a critical alternative source of funding and construction for both Iran and Pakistan if India withdraws from the project.

The TAPI natural gas pipeline. The Turkmenistan-Afghanistan-Pakistan-India pipeline project was first envisaged in the mid-1990s as the Turkmenistan-Afghanistan-Pakistan gas pipeline (TAP) but could not make headway on account of the civil war in Afghanistan. Interest in the project revived after the installation of the Karzai Government, with the Asian Development Bank (ADB) as the lead development manager and consultant. With India formally joining the project in May 2006, the proposed pipeline would extend from the Turkmenistan border to Multan, Pakistan, with a 640 km extension to India. Lower costs (estimates are that TAPI would cost about $5 billion), the availability of multilateral financing, and the absence of fears of sanctions by the United States all portend greater success. The project has considerable geopolitical significance in that, for the first time, South Asia would have access to gas from Central Asia. There is the possibility that once the pipeline is operational pipelines from other Central Asian republics could also link up with this pipeline to meet the increasing demands of South Asia.

As an alternative to the TAPI project, the United States has proposed a large electricity transmission project (a 500 kilovolt line) from Central Asia across Afghanistan to Pakistan and India. Under the plan, a regional power grid stretching from Almaty to New Delhi would be fed by oil and gas from Kazakhstan and Turkmenistan and by hydropower from Tajikistan and Kyrgyzstan—a grid that would drive regional economic development and integration. For the United States "the opening of Afghanistan has transformed it from an obstacle separating Central from South Asia into a 'bridge' connecting the two."[32] The project promises closer economic ties between Central and South Asia on the one hand and among South Asian antagonists (Afghanistan, India, and Pakistan) on the other. While the project is closely aligned with U.S. objectives in the region, Turkmenistan appears more inclined to favoring pipelines to Russia and China.

The Myanmar-Bangladesh-India pipeline. Originally, India had sought to tap into the substantial natural gas reserves of Bangladesh being developed by Unocal. Nationalist pressures in Bangladesh nixed this option. Subsequently when rebuilding its relations with Myanmar after a long hiatus, India attempted to build a pipeline through Bangladesh (the shortest and hence least expensive route) to transport gas from an offshore project off the Rakhine Coast of Myanmar (a project in which India's ONGC and GAIL have equity stakes). This pipeline would have not only benefited the power-starved northeastern states of India (Bengal in particular) but also provide much-needed revenues to the Bangladeshi government. Progress was stalled, however, by Myanmar's misgivings towards Bangladesh and Dhaka's demands on New Delhi for trade concessions as a precondition for participating in the project, leading Myanmar to enter into an agreement with China.

Despite Myanmar being in favor of a pipeline running entirely through Indian territory India continued to put hope over realism, believing that the benefits to Bangladesh and the reduced costs of a pipeline through Bangladesh would boost relations between the two countries. Only in early 2006 did India begin a serious effort to examine the feasibility of a Myanmar–

---

[32] Richard A. Boucher, Assistant Secretary of State for South and Central Asian Affairs, statement before the House International Relations Committee Subcommittee on the Middle East and Central Asia, Washington, D.C., April 26, 2006.

India pipeline via the northeastern states; such a project would purposefully bypass Bangladesh so as not to allow Dhaka to hold the project to ransom.[33] In March 2006 following a visit to Myanmar by India's President APJ Abdul Kalam (the first Indian president to visit the country), Myanmar and India agreed to a long-term plan to supply natural gas to India, underlying India's efforts to foster closer economic ties with that country.[34]

River Basin Sharing

The most manifest interdependencies within South Asia concern the sharing of river waters. Though a source of chronic tension, these natural interdependencies also hold potential for substantially greater cooperation. The most cited example has been the Indus Water Treaty between India and Pakistan that has withstood the vicissitudes of the relations between the two countries since its 1960 signing.

When India and Pakistan became independent in 1947, the political boundary between the two countries cut across the Indus basin. The lower riparian state—Pakistan—found that the headworks of the country's principal irrigation canals were in Indian territory (one at Madhopur on the Ravi River and one at Ferozepur on the Sutlej River). An institutionalized mechanism for sharing the waters of the Indus basin was put into place through the Indus Water Treaty in 1960. The agreement gave India exclusive rights over three eastern rivers—Sutlej, Beas, and Ravi—leaving Chenab, Jhelum, and Indus to Pakistan while allowing India limited use of the latter, provided there was no obstruction to the flow of waters into Pakistan.

The treaty worked well for years. Despite decades of strained relations between India and Pakistan, the cost/benefit ratio helped the Indus water treaty withstand all pressures.[35] Since the 1980s, however, there have been

---

[33] The proposed Myanmar-India pipeline will be routed through the Indian states of Mizoram, Assam, Bengal, and Bihar where it will join the proposed Jagdishpur-Haldia pipeline. The line will also have the provision to transport gas from developing gas fields from India's landlocked northeastern states of Tripura and Assam.

[34] Jill McGivering, "India Signs Burma Gas Agreement," *BBC News*, March 9 2006, http://news.bbc.co.uk/go/pr/fr/-/1/hi/world/south_asia/4791078.stm. India has offered to buy natural gas from Myanmar's offshore Shwe fields (where Indian companies have a 30% stake and Korean companies the rest) on "a take-or-pay" basis in an effort to offer a better deal than the Chinese. India is also considering implementing the proposal for the Tamanthi hydro-electric project on the Chindwin river in Myanmar, barely 40 km from the Nagaland border, that can provide 1200 MW for Nagaland and Manipur. See Chietigj Bajpaee, "India Recovers Lost Ground in the International Energy Game," *Power and Interest News Report* (PINR), March 16, 2005; and Richa Mishra, "Myanmar Gas: India Works Out Route Bypassing Bangladesh," *Hindu Business Line*, May 7, 2006.

[35] There is some reason to believe that fears of Indian control of the headwaters of the Indus in Kashmir have played an important role in strategic thinking in Pakistan. If so, it is not clear why India has not attempted to use that control to pressure Pakistan, particularly at the height of the insurgency in the 1990s.

a growing number of unresolved disputes. Given Pakistan's lower riparian status, virtually all disputes understandably have entailed Pakistani objections to Indian projects—the Wullar Barrage/Tulbul navigation project on the Jhelum, the Swalakote hydroelectric project and Dul Hasti hydroelectric project on the Chenab, and the Kishanganga hydroelectric project on the Kishanganga in Jammu and Kashmir. The most vexing disagreement to emerge involves India's Baglihar Hydropower Project (BHP) on the river Chenab in the Doda district in Jammu and Kashmir. Conceived in 1992, the Rs 40 billion (about US$1 billion) project is scheduled to be completed in 2007 and is designed to generate 450 megawatts (MW) in phase I and 900 MW in phase II.

Pakistan has objected to several features of the project, contending that they violate the Indus Water Treaty. India disagreed and Pakistan approached the World Bank (which had brokered the treaty) to appoint a neutral expert to resolve the differences. The Permanent Indus Commission (PIC) set up by the two countries under the Indus Water Treaty had been meeting regularly to sort out any differences but for the first time failed to resolve the issue, leading Pakistan to invoke the provision to approach the World Bank.[36]

China controls the upper part of the Brahmaputra River (called Meghna in Bangladesh and Sang Po in Tibet) as well as the Indus. Press reports have indicated that China was preparing a scheme to divert waters from Tibet to the parched Yellow River in the country's west and was putting up a barrage on the Parichu River in Tibet (which when it enters India is known as the Sutlej) and on the Sang Po. There have also been flash floods in the Indian state of Himachal Pradesh that have resulted from landslides in the upper reaches in Tibet. All of these issues have raised security concerns in India (the lower riparian state) and—although Dhaka has chosen to ignore them—have also become part of India's dialogue with Bangladesh.

South Asia faces a looming water crisis. The problems stemming from increased demand and poor water usage in South Asia will be compounded by changing river-flow patterns resulting from increased glacier melting in the Himalayas and possibly from changes in the South Asian monsoon. The lack of trust and comprehensive agreements is compounded by the fact that China, India, and Pakistan are not signatories to the Convention on the Non-Navigational Uses of International Water Courses (adopted at the General Assembly in 1997) and consequently are not obligated to inform each other when they build new dams. Nonetheless, as Ben Crowe and

---

[36] The World Bank has appointed an expert (as a guarantor to the treaty, the bank will not directly participate in any discussion or exchange on the subject), and the arbitration clause has come into operation for the first time in the 45-year history of the treaty.

Nirvikar Singh argue, innovations such as an explicit economic evaluation of water development alternatives (power generation, flood mitigation, and availability for agriculture or human consumption) would allow for a more transparent assessment of international exchange.[37] Moving some of the issues from inter-state bilateral diplomacy to multilateral regional fora would expand the scope for exchanges and bargaining. In addition, bringing in private economic actors would create new interests and trading arrangements. Such arrangements involving the trading of water rights across borders are likely to have substantial effects in binding the region together—more so than merchandise trade. Plenty of international substitutes exist for the latter but virtually none for the former.

Conclusion: Security Implications for the Region and for the United States

Conventional theories of the links between trade and security shed little light on how India's relations with its neighbors, especially Pakistan and China, are likely to evolve. Indeed most studies that purport to show the link between trade and security do a poor job in specifying the causal direction as well as the effects of changes in the composition and forces driving global trade. The fact that Japan's largest trading partner is China, that Japan hosts the second largest number of overseas students from China, and that Japan is also the second largest investor in China, does not negate the reality that relations between the two countries are less than warm. One could argue that strong economic bonds have curbed the possibility of bilateral tensions from spiraling out of control. Such an argument implies, however, that in the absence of these economic links, relations would indeed have spiraled out of control.

As the *Economist* has noted in the case of Bangladesh and India, "Geography, like history, should bind the two together. Such has been the climate of mutual suspicion that it has instead kept them apart."[38] Not only is the level of trade in the region too small, but even if such economic ties were to grow substantially, bilateral trade will remain a modest fraction of overall trade—too small to matter especially given the high degree of substitutability of products available in highly competitive global trade markets. Trade disruption will not impose onerous costs on any of these countries and hence will not be a significant factor as they contemplate their

---

[37] Ben Crowe and Nirvikar Singh, "Floods and International Relations in South Asia: An Assessment of Multi-Track Diplomacy," (unpublished manuscript, University of California, Santa Cruz, 2004).

[38] "A Problem Shared," *Economist*, March 23, 2006.

security stance. Other economic linkages that are network based—cross-border production networks based on cross-border investments, energy networks (whether oil and gas pipelines or power grids), and river basin sharing—offer much greater "lock-in" effects where any disruption will impose substantial costs on all parties.

India's contrasting fortunes in using economic linkages to improve security ties with Bangladesh on the one hand and with Myanmar and Sri Lanka on the other point both to the possibilities and limitations of a strategy of using economic linkages to tame security challenges when confronted with the imperatives of domestic politics and geography. In the case of Bangladesh, economic links have languished and security tensions have grown, while India's relations with Myanmar and Sri Lanka have improved considerably in recent years. As a result of both the sharp political polarization in Bangladesh and the existing historical baggage, relations with India have become hostage to the country's domestic politics. Geography has amplified the mistrust in two distinct ways: first, migration from Bangladesh into geographically contiguous areas of India's northeast is significantly reshaping the demography of a part of India that is already prone to ethnic strife and separatist movements. If even modest projections of global warming come to pass, rising sea levels will pose enormous challenges to Bangladesh and in turn are bound to exacerbate migratory and demographic pressures on India. Secondly, given that Bangladesh's downstream riparian status has made the sharing of river waters a ticklish political issue between the two countries, looming water shortages will exacerbate such tensions and pose substantially greater political challenges.

India has only belatedly pursued opportunities in Myanmar as part of its "look east" policy. For much of the 1990s India's support both for multi-party democracy in Myanmar and for the release of opposition leader Aung San Suu Kyi left little room for striking deals with the military regime. Isolating Myanmar proved costly and India gained little in return. The shift in India's stance was the result of several factors: a growing realization of the significant inroads the Chinese were making in India's restive eastern border, a desire to tap into the region's energy resources, gaining access to the markets of Southeast Asia, and securing Myanmar's help in cracking down on insurgency in the northeast. Wary of becoming overdependent on China and wanting to hedge its bets, Myanmar's military regime responded with alacrity once India shifted its posture. India has emerged as one of Myanmar's largest export markets and Myanmar now views itself as the "land bridge" linking India with Southeast Asia.

The turnaround in India's relations with Sri Lanka and Myanmar offers a window into the Indian policies most likely to elicit greater cooperation in the region. Given the country's regional dominance and historical baggage, India would benefit from placing a greater onus on the so-called Gujral doctrine, which called for disproportionate reciprocity by the dominant power (India) towards its smaller neighbors.[39] Such an approach is most feasible in the realm of economic interactions and might mitigate the deep distrust in the region. These may still not yield any fruits given the crucial role of domestic politics in Bangladesh and Pakistan—yet in their absence failure is certain.

The China-India dynamic reflects the ambivalences in the security-trade nexus. On the one hand relations between the two countries are the best they have been in the last half-century. Though not resolved, border issues have been contained. Meanwhile India's trade with China has grown exponentially, positioning China to emerge as India's largest trading partner by the end of this decade. At the same time, however, both countries are quietly developing security assets to counter each other. As China continues to provide strong military and financial support to Pakistan, India's mixed strategy—balancing against China by developing closer security ties with the United States as well as bandwagoning with China in developing closer economic ties—is one that other countries in the region (notably Australia and Japan) are also cultivating.

This mix of competition, cooperation, and confrontation will continue. Increased levels of trade alone will not be sufficient to ensure against unbridled competition spilling over into confrontation. Positive security externalities are more likely to arise if economic interactions are part of cross-border networks of production or the result of large fixed network investments in areas where substitution is very difficult. The areas where the possibilities are most likely are in supply chain-linked investments in production, oil and gas pipelines, power grids, water, and transport. The United States can play a vital role in supporting these investments, especially through private and multilateral financing. The scope for a positive U.S. role is most apparent in supporting cross-border energy investments: dams in Nepal, gas investments and pipelines connecting Bangladesh and India, and gas and energy grids connecting India with Pakistan, Afghanistan, and Central Asia. In light of ongoing negotiations on the Indo-U.S. nuclear deal, it should be noted that a key goal of this deal is to address India's burgeoning energy needs. If, for whatever reason, the deal fails to materialize there is little doubt that India's incentives to secure access to Iran's sizeable gas supplies would sharply increase, a scenario the United States must keep in mind while negotiating the details of the nuclear deal.

---

[39] I.K. Gujral was India's foreign minister (1989–1990) and prime minister (1997–98).

The United States also can play an important role in the provision of trade infrastructure. A major impediment to regional trade is the lack of facilitative infrastructure. Given NAFTA and burgeoning U.S. trade with Canada and Mexico, the United States has considerable experience in the procedures and institutional and physical infrastructure (such as facilities, documentation requirements, and clearance procedures) required to reduce congestion times, ensure transparency, and minimize security fears. This experience, combined with multilateral financing, could considerably enhance trade within the new SAFTA institutional arrangements.

EXECUTIVE SUMMARY

This chapter examines the evolving geo-economic environment in Southeast Asia, particularly the rise and high visibility of the PRC, and the implications for U.S. economic, political, and security interests in the ASEAN region.

MAIN ARGUMENT:

Despite the growth in influence of the PRC in the region, Japan, the EU, and the U.S. are still major economic partners of ASEAN and the U.S. is the grouping's most important security partner. ASEAN is constructing a hub and spoke system of multiple ASEAN+1 connections in which both Washington and Beijing are important in a regional distribution of power that can promote the interests of China, the U.S., and ASEAN.

POLICY IMPLICATIONS:

- The building of the ASEAN-U.S. Enhanced Partnership will act as a balance to China. To be successful, the partnership will require moving beyond economic relations in the building of functional links to promote greater multilateral political interdependencies in the region.

- The Enhanced Partnership's economic strategy of building a regional network of free trade agreements will require the reauthorization of the U.S. president's fast track trade authority in 2007.

- The key bilateral relationship for the U.S. in ASEAN is with Indonesia. Continued U.S. support of the Yudhoyono government's efforts at reform and development will provide further substance to what the U.S. now defines as its "strategic partnership" with Indonesia. A strong Indonesia has the potential once again to lead ASEAN.

- The economic and security platforms supporting U.S. strategic interests in Southeast Asia are stable. The political platform needs shoring up with respect both to formal U.S. association with ASEAN's Treaty of Amity and Cooperation (TAC) and to U.S. differences with ASEAN over issues of democratization and human rights in Myanmar (Burma).

Strategic Dimensions of Economic Interdependence in Southeast Asia

Donald E. Weatherbee

The leitmotif of contemporary analyses of the international relations and political economy of East and Southeast Asia has become the "rise of China." Some observers see China's heightened economic role—particularly as expressed by China's relatively sudden prominence as a major trade partner of the ASEAN states—as playing a key part in a perceived decline of U.S. influence in Southeast Asia. Many also see China's emerging regional posture as challenging a fundamental basis of U.S. strategic policy in the region since 1950. The U.S. security role in Southeast Asia has been crucial to peace, stability, and the maintenance of the regional balance of power, with the United States being the predominant extra-regional great-power.

Now, China's place in what had for decades been an essentially unchallenged U.S.-centered strategic ordering of Southeast Asia poses the question as to whether U.S. dominance is a necessary condition for the promotion of U.S. national interests in the region. Alternatively, will U.S. adaptations and adjustments to an emerging balance of power or, in the worst case jeremiads, Chinese predominance, be sufficient to safeguard the U.S. stake in Southeast Asia's future? If either China or the United States decides that its national interests require the exclusion or containment of the other, then tension, conflict, and insecurity will mark future regional relations.

The regional security interest of the Southeast Asian states themselves is thus to avoid that kind of outcome by helping to promote a strategic environment that is non-threatening to either China or the United States.

Donald E. Weatherbee (PhD, Johns Hopkins School of Advanced International Studies) is the Donald S. Russell Distinguished Professor Emeritus at the University of South Carolina. He specializes in politics and international relations in Southeast Asia. He can be reached at <donald.e.weatherbee@verizon. net>.

For the ASEAN states, their bilateral relations with extra-regional powers are increasingly linked to their group relations in ASEAN+1 formats or other multilateral frameworks such as the security oriented ASEAN Regional Forum (ARF). ASEAN as a regional policy platform is becoming even more important to its members as they begin to move toward a more integrated regional organizational format. Both China and the United States recognize the importance of ASEAN to its members and have placed their bilateral relations in Southeast Asia in the contextual setting of developing ASEAN regionalism. Within this setting, ASEAN states hope that growing region-wide interdependencies involving both China and the United States will mediate their regional relationship through a joint interest in the maintenance of a stable strategic environment. The economic dimensions of the interdependencies are expressed through a proliferation of market-driven bilateral free trade agreements and region-wide ASEAN+1 trading and functional cooperation agreements, all of which also have a political foundation in extending the scope of multilateral activities.

The China "dazzle" has tended to eclipse the fact that ASEAN's economic ties to the United States, Japan, and the European Union (EU) in sum far outweigh those of China. Furthermore, China's new "partnership" links in Southeast Asia are not unique. Even as ASEAN becomes closer to China, it is forging stronger ties with all important trading partners. Contradicting the view that a China-centric, geo-economic unit is emerging in Southeast Asia, ASEAN appears to be taking an omnidirectional strategy, hedging and balancing its links to any single extra-regional power. The United States understands that its future role in Southeast Asia will depend on U.S. policy capabilities across the full range of international transactions. This is apparent in Washington's new initiative, the ASEAN-U.S. Enhanced Partnership, which—if promoted and supported—has the potential to ensure that the United States will remain, if not the extra-regional predominant actor in Southeast Asia, at least a significant actor that can defend its interests in the emerging new distribution of power.

This chapter first examines China's role in the evolving structure of ASEAN's intra-regional East Asian economic interdependencies, outlining the web of bilateral ASEAN+1 trade agreements and "strategic partnerships" that ASEAN has negotiated or is negotiating. The next section then examines the comparable U.S. economic presence in the region with particular attention to the building of an ASEAN-U.S. Enhanced Partnership. The following section addresses the strategic implications of the economic dynamics as underpinned by the U.S. security presence. The chapter concludes by examining the implications for future ASEAN-U.S. relations in an ASEAN-centered system of multiple "+1s" and the political requisites of a truly enhanced ASEAN-U.S. relationship.

ASEAN, China, and East Asian Integration

Some analysts have argued that "American interests are in trouble throughout the Asia-Pacific region."[1] This claim derives in part from a perception of a new pattern of international transactions centered on China: "the predominant trend in the region is the creation of an extensive web of mutual interdependencies among state and non-state actors, with China increasingly at the center of the web."[2] This China-centric web is perhaps most clearly visible in Southeast Asia where an overarching network of multilateral ASEAN-China functional agreements and strategic partnership now complement China's burgeoning bilateral ties with the ASEAN states.[3] Historical reference to traditional Chinese statecraft in the dependent lands to the South—the "Nanyang"—has already been introduced as factor in explaining contemporary is informing contemporary Chinese policy[4] Concerns have been expressed that China's strategic ambitions seem to be focusing on establishing a preeminent sphere of influence designed ultimately to bind Southeast Asia to China.[5] Viewing China's role in Southeast Asia from the antipodes, veteran Australian analyst Milton Osborne describes China as the "paramount regional power."[6]

Singapore's Tommy Koh, perhaps Southeast Asia's most influential diplomatic luminary, has opined that the United States "is losing the competition for influence in Southeast Asia. The winner, at least for the time being, is the People's Republic of China."[7] Two retired U.S. ambassadors with

---

[1] Bernard K. Gordon, "Asia's New Trade Pattern: Implications for Indonesia, the US and Beyond" (paper presented at a USINDO Open Forum, February 28, 2006).

[2] David Shambaugh, ed., *Power Shift: China and Asia's New Dynamic* (Berkeley: University of California Press, 2006), 23.

[3] Kuik Cheng-Chwee, "Multilateralism in China's ASEAN Policy: Its Evolution, Characteristics, and Aspirations," *Contemporary Southeast Asia* 27, no. 1 (April 2005): 102–22.

[4] Martin Stuart-Fox, "Southeast Asia and China: The Role of History and Culture in Shaping Future Relations," *Contemporary Southeast Asia* 26, no. 1 (April 2004): 116–39.

[5] Marvin C. Ott, "China's Strategic Reach into Southeast Asia," (written presentation to the United States–China Economic and Security Review Commission, July, 22 2005), http://www.uscc.gov/2005hearings/written_testimonies/05_ 07_21_22wrts/ott_marvin.

[6] Milton Osborne, "A Changing Dynamic in the Region: China is Starting to Flex its Muscles down South," *The Australian*, April 7, 2006. Osborne took pains, however, to distinguish paramountcy from hegemony in that China was "tolerant" of ASEAN's other external relations—including those with the United States.

[7] Tommy Koh, "America's Role in Asia: What Does Southeast Asia Want from Washington?" *PacNet* 53, December 21, 2004.

extensive Southeast Asia experience have noted that, although the United States still has a significant but receding presence in the area, U.S. policies are "spasmodic," lack coherence, and "are not commensurate with its interests."[8] Another commentator has charged Washington with being "comparatively inattentive and inert" in the contest for the future of Southeast Asia.[9] The U.S. strategic concentration in Asia has mainly been on immediate issues, such as the growing military capabilities of China, counterterrorism, the proliferation of WMD (especially the nuclear problem in North Korea), and the Taiwan problem. When giving attention to longer-term interests, the United States has often only done so from a zero-sum perspective in which the United States and China are rivals, with any gain for China viewed as diminishing the position of the United States.[10] In this zero-sum atmosphere, the United States appears to be falling behind.[11]

This U.S. fixation on Sino-U.S. competition in Southeast Asia neglects the fact that the competition is mediated by ASEAN and its member states. ASEAN gives the Southeast Asian states more strategic levers to use in maneuvering between the great powers.[12] Enhanced autonomy may in fact be allowing the ASEAN states to devise their own strategies for moving between the great powers as opposed to "bandwagoning" or becoming simply dependent end points on a new hub and spoke system.[13] ASEAN's latitude for movement has been enlarged through engagement, balancing, and hedging, thus keeping open more than one option for ASEAN states.[14]

China's Economic Position in ASEAN

China's rate of market growth in the region exceeds that of ASEAN's other major trading partners (see **Tables 1–3**). The relatively recent blossoming of ASEAN-China trade can be linked to the staged implementation of an

---

[8] Morton Abramowitz and Stephen Bosworth, "Rethinking Southeast Asia," The Century Foundation, April 21, 2005, http://www.tcf.org/list.asp?Type=NC&pubid=955.

[9] Ott, "China's Strategic Reach."

[10] Bruce Vaughn, *China-Southeast Asia Relations: Trends, Issues, and Implications for the United States* (Washington, D.C.: Congressional Research Service, February 8, 2005), 26.

[11] "New Glue or New Gloss? Southeast Asian Regionalism and US Policy," Stanley Foundation, *Policy Bulletin*, http://www.stanleyfoundation.org/reports/SEAc04pb.pdf.

[12] Shannon Tow, "Southeast Asia in the Sino-U.S. Strategic Balance," *Contemporary Southeast Asia* 26, no. 3 (December 2004): 434–59.

[13] Gaye Christopherson, "The Role of East Asia in Sino-U.S. Relations," *Asian Survey* 42, no. 3 (May/June 2002): 370.

[14] Denny Roy, "Southeast Asia and China: Balancing or Bandwagoning?" *Contemporary Southeast Asia* 27, no. 2 (August 2005): 305–22; Joseph Chinyong Liow, "Balancing, Bandwagoning, or Hedging? Strategic and Security patterns in Malaysia's Relations with China, 1981–2003," in *China and Southeast Asia: Global Changes and Regional Challenges*, eds. Ho Khai Leong and Samuel C. Y. Ku, (Singapore: Institute of Southeast Asian Studies, 2005), 281–306.

ASEAN-China Free Trade Agreement. An "early harvest" group of items for tariff reduction was specified in the 2002 ASEAN-China Comprehensive Economic Co-operation Framework Agreement.[15] A 2004 ASEAN-China Agreement on Trade in Goods between ASEAN and the PRC identified "normal" and "sensitive" tracks for liberalization of trade to be achieved both for the ASEAN-6 by 2010 and for the CLMV group (the newer members of ASEAN: Cambodia, Laos, Myanmar [Burma], and Vietnam) by 2015. In negotiating the ASEAN-China FTA, which went into effect in 2005, the ASEAN strategy was to include the products that would generate the quickest benefits for ASEAN. ASEAN-China agreements on services and investment liberalization are still being negotiated.

From 2000 to 2004, the growth rate of ASEAN's exports to China was far greater than that of ASEAN's exports to the United States (see **Table 1**). The growth rate in 2004 for ASEAN exports to China was 43%, whereas the growth rate for exports to the United States—after being flat for three years—was 22%. Over the full half-decade, ASEAN exports to China increased by 175%. The post-2001 growth in ASEAN's trade with China is associated in part with its 2001 accession to the WTO. The negative and low growth of ASEAN exports to the United States reflects a trade diversion from ASEAN origin to Chinese origin in the U.S. market for labor-intensive goods. Spurring ASEAN to become more competitive and move up the technology ladder is one of the goals of the ASEAN Free Trade Area (AFTA). **Table 2** shows ASEAN imports on an annual basis from 2000 to 2004. In 2004, the ASEAN surplus with the United States was more than $20 billion and ASEAN's deficit with China was a little more than $5 billion. **Table 3** shows the total two-way trade for ASEAN and its major partners. The U.S. share of ASEAN's total trade in 2004 of 13.2% is 3% less than what it was in 2000, while China's share increased from 4.3% to 8.3%. The trend line for China bent sharply upwards in 2005 as the FTA's "early harvest" boosted ASEAN-China trade to $130 billion, an almost 60% increase over 2004.[16] The U.S. 2005 year-end figure was $148.5 billion, only a 9% gain over 2004 but still 14% more than China's 2005 two-way trade.[17] In 2005,

[15] All references in this chapter to ASEAN documents and agreements are available at http://www.aseansec.org.

[16] Comparable ASEAN statistics for 2005 to those used in tables 1–3 will not be available until the publication of the *ASEAN Statistical Yearbook 2006*. The 2005 China trade figure is that given by the PRC Ministry of Commerce 2005 Export–Import data for ASEAN. The figure is higher than the $120 billion Sino-ASEAN trade reported in the *China Daily* (January 9, 2006).

[17] The U.S. figures are from the Department of Commerce's trade statistics. U.S. figures are not directly comparable to ASEAN figures since there is approximately a 14% difference once customs, insurance, and freight (CIF) are added to the value of U.S. imports of ASEAN goods. Even though trade figures may not be the same, the magnitudes, percentages of change, and trends revealed are accurate.

T A B L E 1   ASEAN exports 2000–04 ($million)

Country	2000	2001	2002	2003	2004
U.S.	73,769.0	62,741.0	61,557.0	61,439.7	75,175.8
EU-15	62,905.0	56,690.2	54,386.3	57,003.8	69,412.3
Japan	50,559.0	48,250.0	44,503.4	50,345.9	63,760.9
China	14,178.9	14,516.0	19,547.0	27,044.2	38,647.0
Total	410,140.6	370,355.7	383,854.1	431,033.4	525,635.8

S O U R C E :   *ASEAN Statistical Yearbook*, 2005, Table V.7, 71.

T A B L E 2   ASEAN imports 2002–04 ($million)

Country	2000	2001	2002	2003	2004
Japan	65,630.8	53,258.5	53,083.7	58,077.8	72,497.6
U.S.	48,448.0	45,618.8	43,397.4	49,924.5	54,583.8
EU-15	39,093.2	39,681.5	40,041.8	42,815.8	51,803.7
China	18,137.0	17,399.2	23,212.2	28,272.2	43,210.5
Total	345,856.7	317,128.6	328,112.6	359,890.0	459,944.0

S O U R C E :   *ASEAN Statistical Yearbook*, 2005, Table V.8, 73.

T A B L E 3   ASEAN two-way trade 2000–04 ($million)

Country	2000	2001	2002	2003	2004
U.S.	122,217.0	108,360.3	104,954.4	119,517.5	129,759.6
Japan	116,229.8	101,505.5	97,587.1	108,423.7	136,258.5
EU-15	101,997.2	96,371.7	94,428.1	99,819.6	121,216.0
China	32,159.9	21,915.2	42,759.0	55,316.4	81,857.5
Total	755,997.3	687,484.3	711,966.3	790,923.4	985,580.4

S O U R C E :   Original data from *ASEAN Statistical Yearbook*, 2005, Table V7 and Table V8, combined.

Chinese exports to ASEAN ($55 billion) for the first time exceeded the U.S. exports ($49.6 billion). The U.S. trade deficit with ASEAN was $40 billion, while China's deficit was $20 billion. China's trade with ASEAN will likely exceed that of the United States by 2007 or even as early as 2006.

The aggregate data presented by ASEAN, while reflecting ASEAN regional trade orientations, does not reflect the differing importance in ASEAN trade of the individual members. More than 90% of ASEAN trade is carried out by the ASEAN-5 core members, with Singapore, Malaysia, and Thailand leading the group. These countries have the greatest strategic economic value to both China and the United States. Having economically broken out of the CLMV group, Vietnam presents economic opportunities for both China and the United States. Other strategic considerations enter into play as well. The impetus for China's economic relations with Myanmar (Burma) and Laos lies in the borderland proximity of these countries to China. The U.S. sanctions regime against Myanmar (Burma) is made possible by strategic indifference. Furthermore, unlike the United States, China does not prioritize economic interests in a framework that includes human rights, environmental concerns, labor rights, and other items that are not directly trade related.

The composition of ASEAN-China trade is changing. While China's search for primary products continues, there is a growing volume of intra-industry trade between ASEAN and China given that regional production networks and supply chains by Asian multinational corporations (MNC) promote real integration (as opposed to government-to-government deals with greater political than economic meaning). Some caveats are necessary, however. There is no guarantee that the present surge in ASEAN-China trade will continue. The current situation is fueled by China's unprecedented growth in productive capacity and income; whether the boom can continue at the same rate is a matter of debate. With the lowest fruits of the FTA having been picked, Southeast Asian resistance to the flood of cheaper Chinese fruits, vegetables, textiles, and other consumer goods is already building in vulnerable sectors. In addition, China's own economy may face a slowdown as a result of mounting internal economic, political, and social tensions. Some have raised dire predictions that ASEAN economies will become mere appendages of the Chinese economy in a kind of neo-traditional suzerain-vassal relationship. Such warnings do not seem to take into account ASEAN's hedging strategy in East Asia that forges tighter links with South Korea, Japan, and beyond—including the United States.

Merchandise trade is only one part of the economic web of goods, services, and finance that has integrated ASEAN into the global economy. China does not loom large in these broader dimensions of ASEAN's international economic relations. The productive capabilities and infrastructure supporting the market economies of Southeast Asia require access both to capital from international financial institutions (IFI) in the forms of grants and loans and to bilateral foreign direct investment (FDI). Among the IFIs with strong regional presence in Southeast Asia, the United States, Japan, and other developed liberal democracies have a commanding presence. The same is true of country-specific or situational donor consortiums, such as the consortium groups for Indonesia, Cambodia, and East Timor or the donor groups for post-conflict reconstruction and development in Aceh and Mindanao. Disaster and humanitarian relief assistance also have an economic impact on Southeast Asia, with the response of such groups to the December 2004 tsunami being the most recent dramatic example. There are no multilateral frameworks into which China can be fitted comfortably as a donor. The United States, acting through the U.S. Agency for International Development, is the largest source of bilateral official development assistance in the ASEAN region, followed by Japan. Chinese "assistance" takes the form of concessional loans and credits that are linked to Chinese companies, often with strategic purposes.

FDI has played the most critical role in the industrial development that has propelled ASEAN GDP growth rates (which have now recovered from the financial crash of 1997–98). As the single largest source of FDI to the ASEAN region, the United States in 2004 provided nearly a quarter of all new FDI in ASEAN (see **Table 4**). The United States, the EU-15, and Japan are the source of 60% of ASEAN FDI. The aggregate figures do not reflect the direction of investment. In 2004, four ASEAN countries received 92.4% of all FDI, with Singapore alone winning 62%. In value, the numbers were: Singapore, $16 billion; Malaysia, $4.6 billion; Vietnam, $1.6 billion; and Thailand, $1.4 billion.[18] For the first time, Vietnam outperformed Thailand in competition for FDI.

China is not an important FDI source for ASEAN but is rather a global competitor. One of ASEAN's major concerns is that China is appropriating FDI that might otherwise come to ASEAN. Over the last half-decade, FDI flows to ASEAN have increased, yet such flows to China have grown much faster. Up to 70% of new FDI in East Asia (excluding Japan) is going to China and only 20% to ASEAN.[19] This disparity is due in part to the comparative advantage China holds with regard to cheap labor and in part to the attractiveness of the Chinese market. The diversion of FDI to China is one reason ASEAN is moving from AFTA to an ASEAN Economic Community, making the region—with a potential market of nearly 600 million people—more attractive to FDI. While moving up the technological and services ladder and with GDP growing at high rates, ASEAN certainly is not going to adopt investment and financial policies with China that would exclude the United States or its other major partners.

---

[18] ASEAN Secretariat, *ASEAN Statistical Yearbook*, 2005, (report prepared by the ASEAN Secretariat, Jakarta, November 2005), 139. Note that the total ASEAN FDI in Table VI.1 ($25.6 billion) is higher than the total in Table VI.2 ($21.8 billion) because the former also includes Singapore's reinvested earnings.

[19] Figures as given by Ambassador Chan Heng Chee in "China and ASEAN: A Growing Relationship" (presentation to the Asia Society Texas Annual Ambassadors Forum and Corporate Conference, Houston, Feburary 3, 2006), http://aoo.mfa.gov.sg/pr/read_content.asp?view, 124416.

TABLE 4   FDI in ASEAN by 10 leading sources, 2004 ($million)

Country	FDI	% share
EU 15	5,420.5	24.8
United States	5,051.9	23.7
Japan	2,538.2	11.6
Intra-ASEAN	2,432.7	11.2
Taiwan	1,188.6	5.4
Other EU	937.2	4.3
South Korea	896.5	4.1
Australia	392.5	1.8
Hong Kong	344.9	1.7
China	225.9	1.0
Canada	92.1	0.4
Rest of World	2,217.4	10.4
Total	21,803.8	100.0

SOURCE: *ASEAN Statistical Yearbook*, 2005, Table VI.2, 143.

ASEAN's East Asian Response

As suggested above, the new ASEAN-China economic connections are best viewed within the broader pattern of trade liberalization and expansion in the Asian region. In a strikingly frank assessment, a senior ASEAN economic official stated that because "ASEAN does not wish to be in a tributary relationship with China, its most sensible strategy is to move closer to the other dialogue partners, even as it moves closer to China."[20] This is the essence of hedging. A framework for Comprehensive Economic Partnership forged between ASEAN and Japan in 2003 has led to negotiations between the two for an Economic Partnership Agreement (EPA) that is essentially an FTA expanded to include services and investment facilitation provisions. The goal is to have the EPA in place by 2007. The third round of negotiations began in April 2006, with an FTA to be fully phased in by 2012. Japan has also pressed for bilateral EPAs in the ASEAN region. The Japan-Singapore EPA went into force in 2002; a Japan-Malaysia EPA was inked in 2005. Japan's EPA with Thailand, scheduled to have been signed in April 2006, was delayed by the collapse of Prime Minister Thaksin Shinawatra's

[20] Lee Yoong Yoong, "FTAs with Dialogue Partners: Compatible with ASEAN Integration?" *ASEANONE*, January 2005, 6.

government and awaits a new Thai government to be formed after October 2006 elections. The EPA between Japan and the Philippines is on track for a 2006 signing. Japan held a fourth round of EPA negotiations with Indonesia in April 2006, and Indonesia has indicated it wishes to hasten the process. Vietnam and Japan have begun a feasibility study looking toward an FTA, which, if launched, would be Vietnam's first such agreement. The competition in Southeast Asia between China and Japan is in some respects nearly as fraught with economic consequences for ASEAN as is the Sino-U.S. relationship.

ASEAN is also working with its other dialogue and trading partners in Asia both on bilateral frameworks of trade liberalization and on FTAs. The Republic of Korea and ASEAN signed a 2004 joint declaration on partnership and a subsequent ASEAN-ROK Framework Agreement for an FTA was reached in May 2006. This was an ASEAN minus 1 document since Thailand refused to sign due to South Korea's reluctance to liberalize rice imports. An ASEAN-ROK agreement on services and investment is hoped to be concluded by the end of 2006. Australia and New Zealand are also pressing for an FTA with ASEAN that builds on the existing Australia-New Zealand Closer Economic Relations Trade Agreement (CER).[21] The principles governing negotiations for an FTA between Australia and New Zealand were established in 2004. With six rounds of negotiations having already taken place by April 2006, the FTA should hopefully be concluded by 2007.[22]

Significantly, India—which has the economic potential to rival China in the future—has embarked on a bilateral FTA negotiation with ASEAN. Although India's framework agreement with ASEAN was set forth in 2003, at the 2005 ASEAN-India summit the ASEAN side noted that the negotiations for an FTA had not moved forward as "expeditiously" as hoped. Due to difficulties over rules of origin and ASEAN's agricultural exports to India, the proposed implementation of the FTA was postponed from January 2006 to January 2007. When Indian restrictions (that would have reduced the trade covered to less than the required 80%) threatened further delays, direct intervention by the Indian prime minister Manmohan Singh forced India's negotiators to give way. Prime Minister Singh's action showed how important the FTA was to India's goal of positioning itself as a potential fourth major extra-regional actor in Southeast Asia. Even

---

[21] In ASEAN's external economic relationships, Australia and New Zealand are paired as a single economic unit because of the Closer Economic Relationship (CER) agreement governing trade and investment between them.

[22] The course of the negotiations can be tracked round by round at the Australian Department of Foreign Affairs and Trade website, http//www.dfat.gov.au/trade/fta/ASEAN.

with the Indian prime minister's push, the 2007 date is in doubt since the negotiation was suspended by ASEAN in July 2006, frustrated by India's continued reluctance to reduce even further its "sensitive list." India, in response, dispatched a special envoy to ASEAN in an effort to revive the talks. ASEAN in August cautiously agreed to a resumption of talks but with a demand for Indian concessions.

ASEAN hopes to put its standing with its other East Asian Partners on the same footing as it has with China in more than just trade relations. In the ASEAN+3 grouping (China, Japan, South Korea), the ASEAN-China Strategic Partnership for Peace and Prosperity is matched by the ASEAN-Japan Strategic Partnership and the ASEAN-ROK Joint Declaration on Comprehensive Cooperation Partnership. The partnership concept has been extended in an ASEAN-India Partnership for Peace, Progress, and Shared Prosperity as well as an ASEAN-Russia Partnership for Peace and Security, and Prosperity and Development in the Asia-Pacific Region. These declaratory statements calling for good and cooperative relations have little real strategic significance. As the ASEAN-China agreement states, the "Strategic Partnership is nonaligned, non-military, and non-exclusive, and does not prevent the participants from developing their all-directional ties of friendship and cooperation with others." The value of such partnerships to ASEAN is in the explicit guarantee to peaceful bilateral relations, which gives further normative substance to the multilateral guarantee ASEAN's partners—with the exception of the United States—have made in acceding to the Treaty of Amity and Cooperation in Southeast Asia (TAC).

In a competitive thrust at China, the Japanese minister of trade proposed in April 2006 that talks begin in 2008 on an East Asian FTA that would incorporate ASEAN, Japan, South Korea, China, Australia, New Zealand, and India. This was not a new idea; the notion of an East Asian FTA as a building block for an East Asian Community had been subject to ASEAN+3 studies and statements since first mooted in 1998. The Japanese *démarche* fell into the same black hole as other specific suggestions to give institutional substance to rhetorical expressions of "East Asian-ness" (defined by the December 2005 East Asia Summit to include India, Australia, New Zealand, and, in the future, Russia as well as possibly the United States). U.S. apprehension that the deepening economic interdependencies in the ASEAN+3 regional grouping will lead to substantive institution-building that excludes the United States does not take into full account the economic, political, cultural, and historical differences and tensions among putative members that militate against such integration. Trade alone will not bind them.[23]

U.S. Initiatives

Southeast Asian countries had criticized the Bush administration for focusing U.S. policy toward the region so narrowly on the war on terrorism that Washington was neglecting other important interest areas. Even though administration officials had always taken pains to address the breadth of U.S. political, security, strategic, economic, and cultural interests in the area, the rhetoric was not always accompanied by deeds that could functionally link those interests to regional interests. It has taken China's new economic prominence to refocus the United States on Southeast Asia as an interest area in its own right, not just a theater of the war on terrorism.

U.S. trade relations with the six significant ASEAN economies—the ASEAN core five members plus Vietnam— are, with the exception of the Philippines, healthy and growing (see **Table 5**). Only in the past four years, however, have U.S. bilateral economic relations with the ASEAN states been explicitly viewed by American policy makers in a regional context. Since 2002, the United States has moved toward a regionalized trade agenda to complement the existing political and security agenda. In that year, Bush announced a new Enterprise for ASEAN Initiative (EAI) that provided a roadmap for measures to move from bilateral trade and investment framework agreements (TIFA) to FTAs.[24] A TIFA is consultative; an FTA is binding, with dispute resolution mechanisms available. The United States has TIFAs with the Philippines (1989), Indonesia (1996), Brunei (2002), Thailand (2002), and Malaysia (2004). Negotiations for a TIFA with Cambodia began after Cambodia became a WTO member in 2004. In addition, the exports of the Philippines, Thailand, Cambodia, and Indonesia to the United States are all boosted through their inclusion in the U.S. Generalized System of Preferences (GSP).[25] The trading status of the ASEAN countries and the United States is outlined in **Table 6**. The objective of the EAI is to transform the TIFAs into a network of bilateral FTAs. Though operationally bilateral, the EAI projected for the first time a regionalist dimension to U.S. trade and investment. A major study of EAI

---

[23] This is the argument in Edward J. Lincoln, *East Asian Economic Regionalism* (Washington, D.C.: Brookings Institution Press, 2004).

[24] Office of the Press Secretary, "Enterprise for ASEAN Initiative (EAI)," October 16, 2002, http://www.state.gov./p/eap/rls/14700.htm.

[25] The GSP is administered by the USTR. It provides preferentially reduced tariffs or duty-free import in the United States for more than 4,600 products from 144 developing countries.

TABLE 5   U.S.-Southeast Asia two-way trade, 2001–05 ($million)

Country	2001	2002	2003	2004	2005
Malaysia	31,726	34,357	36,357	39,191	44,153
Singapore	32,598	31,013	31,705	34,905	35,823
Thailand	20,723	19,658	21,021	23,939	27,125
Philippines	19,994	18,225	18,052	16,215	16,140
Indonesia	12,603	12,523	12,040	13,480	15,051
Vietnam	1,513	2,915	5,879	6,439	7,822

SOURCE: U.S. Department of Commerce, *Trade Statistics Express*.

TABLE 6   U.S.-ASEAN free trade efforts

Country	FTA	TIFA	WTO	GSP
Brunei		✓	✓	Not Eligible
Burma			✓	Not Eligible
Cambodia		Negotiating	✓	✓
Indonesia		✓	✓	✓
Laos			Negotiating	Not Eligible
Malaysia	Negotiating	✓	✓	Not Eligible
Philippines		✓	✓	✓
Singapore	✓	✓	✓	Not Eligible
Thailand	Negotiating	✓	✓	✓
Vietnam			Negotiating	✓
ASEAN		Negotiating		

SOURCE: Office of the United States Trade Representative, May 2006.

and the FTA negotiations has concluded that the EAI is a defensive strategy for ASEAN, a pro-active commercial policy for the United States, and a strategic imperative for both.[26] Furthermore, the U.S. approach to TIFAs and FTAs is "WTO plus," that is, both more liberal than WTO standards require in trade and investment rules and includes areas of negotiation that are not directly trade related (such as labor and environmental concerns). The U.S. position is also "TRIPS plus," going beyond the minimum standards of the 1986 WTO Agreement on Trade Related Aspects of Intellectual Property Rights (TRIPS).

---

[26] Seiji F. Naya and Michael Plummer, *The Economics of the Enterprise for ASEAN Initiative* (Singapore: Institute of Southeast Asian Studies, 2005).

From the announcement of the EAI, discussion between the United States and its ASEAN partners was underway to explore an intensification of ASEAN-U.S. cooperative activities in a comprehensive and action-oriented program. One immediate goal of ASEAN was to negotiate a regional TIFA with the United States. The two sides have stated that they are mutually resolved to strengthen relations, including developing a strategic partnership covering a broad range of issues of mutual interest.[27] This commitment was a major thrust of the Joint Vision Statement for an ASEAN-U.S. Enhanced Partnership announced at a quasi-summit meeting of Bush and seven of his ASEAN counterparts during the November 2005 APEC meeting.[28] At that meeting, the United States and ASEAN agreed to launch an Enhanced Partnership "that is comprehensive, action-oriented and forward-looking, and comprising political and security cooperation, economic cooperation and social and development cooperation."

An ASEAN-U.S. Plan of Action has been developed to implement the Enhanced Partnership. According to the United States, the Enhanced Partnership and its Plan of Action will be the "cornerstone" for growing U.S. engagement in the region, as the United States is "moving toward a new, deeper phase in our relations with ASEAN."[29] On July 27, 2006, at the annual ASEAN Ministerial Meeting, a five-year Framework Document for the Plan of Action was ceremonially signed by Secretary of State Condoleezza Rice and her ten ASEAN counterparts. On the trade agenda, the EAI was again endorsed and it was agreed to work towards concluding an ASEAN-U.S. regional TIFA. This was signed in August at the ASEAN Economic Ministers Meeting (AEM) attended by USTR Susan Schwab. The real challenge, however, will be to go from a regional TIFA to an FTA. On the U.S. side the momentum relies on congressional reauthorization of presidential fast-track authority that currently expires in July 2007. The Framework Document also provides for broader cooperation in political, security, and socio-economic development areas of U.S.-ASEAN relations and enhanced communications between relevant government agencies.

[27] ASEAN Press Release, "Joint Press Statement of the 18th U.S.-ASEAN Dialogue," Washington D.C., June 28, 2005, http://www.aseansec.org.

[28] "Joint Vision Statement for an ASEAN-U.S. Enhanced Partnership," accessed at http://www.state.gov/p/eap/ris/ot/57078.htm.

[29] Deputy Assistant Secretary of State for East Asian and Pacific Affairs Eric G. John, "The U.S. and Indonesia: Toward a Strategic Partnership," (policy speech delivered to the United States–Indonesia Society, December 20, 2005).

Economic Relations with ASEAN-5

The first FTA that the United States entered into with an Asian country was with Singapore. The U.S.-Singapore agreement, signed in May 2003, went into force on January 1, 2004. The FTA has been described by the U.S. Trade Representative as a leading-edge agreement that will be a foundation for the United States to pursue other FTAs in Southeast Asia under the EAI.[30] This "WTO plus" document expands market access in goods, services, investment, government procurement, and intellectual property. Considered groundbreaking in the protection of labor rights and the environment, the agreement is more comprehensive than other FTAs signed or proposed by ASEAN or its members with regional partners, including China. In the agreement's first year of operation, there was a 10% boost in two-way trade between the United States and Singapore that was sustained in 2005. Singapore has aggressively sought FTA links around the world. That Singapore was the first ASEAN country to pen such an agreement with the United States signifies U.S. recognition that the city-state not only is the single most important economic partner of the United States in Southeast Asia but also is the region's most important commercial, financial, and IT center.

Thailand has sought to emulate Singapore by seeking to increase market access through bilateral FTAs. Unlike Singapore, the Thai FTA strategy has been characterized as being "unserious" and "trade-light," with the proposed WTO plus Thailand-United States FTA being the "sole exception."[31] On October 19, 2003, President Bush announced the intention to negotiate a Thai-U.S. FTA under the EAI.[32] This followed the desire expressed by Bush and Prime Minister Thaksin at a June 2003 White House meeting to expand the robust economic ties between the two countries.[33] Thailand is the third largest trading partner of the United States in Southeast Asia and in 2004 was the 20th largest goods trading partner of the United States in the world.[34] Bilateral trade grew 13% between 2004 and 2005. Prime Minister Thaksin underlined the importance of the FTA to Thailand, emphasizing

[30] Documentation for the U.S-Singapore FTA is available at http://www.ustr.gov (Trade Agreements).

[31] This FTA is "WTO plus." Razeen Sally, "Thailand's New FTAs and Its Trade Policies Post-Asian Crisis: An Assessment," National Research Council of Thailand, December 20, 2005, http://www.bilaterals.org/article.php3?id_article=3310&var_recherce=Razeen+Sally.

[32] Office of the Press Secretary, "Statement on U.S.–Thailand FTA negotiations," October 19, 2003, http://www.whitehouse.gov/news/releases/2003/10/2001019-1.html.

[33] Office of the Press Secretary, "Joint Statement Between the United States of America and the Kingdom of Thailand," June 10, 2003, http://www.whitehouse.gov/news/releases/2003/06/2003961-1.html.

[34] Office of the United States Trade Representative, "Facts on the U.S.–Thailand Free Trade Agreement Negotiations," *Trade Facts*, July 11, 2005, http://www.ustr.gov.

that the alternative was to lose out as other countries pursue their own deals.[35] This view was echoed at the end of the sixth round of negotiations in January 2006 by the USTR negotiator, who warned that "without such an FTA, Thailand's exporters will lose the competitive advantage they would gain against some of their fiercest competitors in the region."[36] Those competitors include Malaysia and a surging Vietnam. The negotiations are on hold pending the resolution of the Thai political crisis and formation of a new government.

The United States launched FTA negotiations with Malaysia in March 2006. Malaysia is the United States' largest trading partner in Southeast Asia and its 10th largest trading partner worldwide.[37] The United States is Malaysia's largest market. U.S.-Malaysia trade has increased by 28% over the half-decade from 2001 to 2005 and, after the TIFA, by 11.3% between 2004 and 2005 alone. The United States is also Malaysia's largest provider of FDI. In 2005, such investment was nearly $1.4 billion, a more than 40% increase over 2004 and in 2005 the equivalent to nearly 30% of Malaysia's FDI.[38] Malaysia is undertaking the FTA negotiations fully aware that the model agreement for the United States is the U.S.-Singapore FTA and is keeping abreast of the status of U.S.-Thai FTA bargaining.

At the close of the first round of negotiation in June 2006, both the United States and Malaysia were reasonably confident that a deal could be struck by the end of the year. Malaysia's trade minister Rafidah Aziz has said that she sees absolutely no opposition from the Malaysian side and no contradiction between forging bilateral FTAs while simultaneously engaging in multilateral framework negotiations. Citing the different levels of economic development within ASEAN, Rafidah pointed out that Malaysia's market access goals may not be the same as those of other ASEAN members.[39] Her argument implicitly underscores not only the impact of economic tiering on ASEAN's regional framework agreements and FTA negotiations but also the gulf between "WTO plus" and the basic rules of the WTO as the negotiating goal.

---

[35] As quoted in Tony Alllison, "Thailand, US inch ahead on trade accord," *Asia Times*, January 14, 2006.

[36] Office of the United States Trade Representative, "Statement of Barbara Weisel Assistant U.S. Trade Representative Regarding the 6th Round of the US–Thailand FTA Negotiations," January 13, 2006, http://www.ustr.gov/Document_Library/Press_Releases/2006/January/Section_Index.html.

[37] Press Release, Office of the United States Trade Representative, "United States, Malaysia Announce Intention to Negotiate Free Trade Agreement," March 8, 2006, http://www.ustr.gov./Document_Library/Press_Releases/2006/March/Section_Index.html.

[38] "Foreign Investment at Four-Year High," *BizNews Databank*, February 2, 2006, http://english.biznewsdb.com.

[39] "Rafidah: ASEAN Vision for Economic Integration Shouldn't Block Individual FTA Talks," *The Star*, April 4, 2006.

Leaving aside the special case of Myanmar (Burma), the Philippines is the only ASEAN country with which U.S. trade has not increased over the half-decade from 2000 to 2004. In 2005, Sino-Philippine trade (valued at $17.5 billion) for the first time exceeded U.S.-Philippine trade. Sino-Philippine trade in 2005 was valued at $13.3, nearly a 32% increase over 2004. Philippine exports to China more than doubled imports.[40] For U.S.-Philippine trade, the 2005 figures represented the latest in a series of annual declines (see **Table 5**). This trend can be explained only in part by the fact that the Philippines is less competitive than other ASEAN countries or by issues related to the liberalization of the country's trade and investment regimes.

The government of President Gloria Macapagal-Arroyo has responded in kind to China's special efforts to court the Philippines. In his 2005 state visit to the Philippines, Chinese president Hu Jintao set a $30 billion Sino-Philippine trade target for 2010. The Philippines appears to have adopted a hedging strategy.[41] In a 2003 speech to Philippine ambassadors, Arroyo stated that China, along with Japan and the United States, has "a determining influence in the security situation and the economic evolution of East Asia."[42] For China, an initial payoff has been Philippine acquiescence to a joint development scheme for potential oil and gas reserves in South China Sea jurisdictions claimed by the Philippines. China also seeks to balance the military re-engagement of the United States and the Philippines. Arroyo's 2004 visit to China was upgraded from "official" to "state" following both withdrawal of the Philippine contingent from Iraq and Philippine preparations to sign a spate of functional bilateral agreements.

Indonesia, with half of ASEAN's population and major resources, looms large both for the United States and for ASEAN's future development. Since the election of President Susilo Bambang Yudhoyono in September 2004, the Indonesian government's economic focus has been on reforms and incentives to improve the country's performance in the international economy. Given the importance of foreign relations in this area of governance, Yudhoyono in three meetings with Bush has expressed the significance of the U.S.-Indonesia relationship.[43] The United States has

---

[40] The data on Sino-Philippine trade is available at http://www.Philembassy-China.org.

[41] Philippines analyst Renato Cruz De Castro outlined the Philippine hedging strategy in a February 2006 presentation at the conference "China in Asia: Chinese Influence, Asian Strategies, and U.S. Policy Responses" sponsored by the National Defense University and the American Enterprise Institute. *The Executive Summary* is available at http://www.ndu.edu/inss (Regional Security Studies).

[42] As quoted in "Arroyo Meets Hu in China for Talks," *The Straits Times*, September 2, 2004.

[43] Office of the Press Secretary, "Joint Statement Between the United States of America and the Republic of Indonesia," May 25, 2005, http://www.whithouse.gov/news/releases/2005/20050525-11.html.

framed the relationship as a developing strategic partnership "concentrating not on what we can't do together, but on what we can."[44] U.S. assistance to Indonesia in fiscal year (FY) 2006 will exceed $500 million. Secretary of State Rice calls the bilateral relationship a "democratic partnership" in which free trade will help support Yudhoyono's "pro-growth, pro-jobs, pro-poor" mission.[45]

The burgeoning relations hold promise for lifting the U.S. economic presence out of the relative doldrums brought on by the financial crisis of 1997–98 and the fall of former president Suharto. China-Indonesia trade in 2004 was $13.5 billion, evenly matching U.S.-Indonesia trade. During Hu Jintao's 2005 state visit to Indonesia, the two countries announced a goal of $20 billion in two-way trade by 2007. Indonesian trade minister Mari Pangestu called for an increase in Sino-Indonesian trade of $30 billion by 2010. The shortfall in the growth of Indonesian exports to the United States is in part due to U.S. importers turning to Vietnamese products. Indonesian officials openly acknowledge that their rival for the U.S. market is Vietnam, not China.[46] The United States has particularly welcomed the new Indonesian government's decision to press forward with a trade agenda that builds on the 1996 bilateral TIFA. In June 2005, the U.S-Indonesia TIFA Council met for the first time in five years. Subsequent meetings led to a decision to accelerate TIFA consultations, intensifying the process of moving toward a future FTA. The Indonesian government is already studying the costs and benefits of an FTA.

To expand trade Indonesia must attract FDI for new or unused productive capacity. A continuing pattern of disinvestment, amounting in 2005 to more than $3 billion, has posed a serious problem for Indonesia.[47] Indonesia has been praised by the United States for efforts under Yudhoyono to tackle corruption, regulative disincentives, the complexities of decentralization, and legal uncertainty, as well as issues related to tax, custom, and labor reform and other internal obstacles to expanded trade and investment. Indonesia's seriousness of purpose was exemplified by Yudhoyono's decisive intervention in March 2006 to cut through the political, bureaucratic, and corruption logjam that had thwarted Exxon Mobil's development of Central Java's Cepu oil field. The United States is prepared as well to assist in strengthening Indonesia's investment climate.

---

[44] John, "The U.S. and Indonesia."

[45] Transcript of remarks by Secretary of State Condoleezza Rice at the Indonesia World Affairs Council, March 15, 2006, http://www.state.gov/secretary/m/2006/63160.htm.

[46] Remarks by Indonesian Minister of Trade Mari Elke Pangestu, U.S.-Indonesia Chamber of Commerce lunch, New York, March 5, 2005.

[47] World Bank, "Indonesia Key Indicators," *East Asia Update*, March 2006.

Implementation of all the Yudhoyono government reform policies will take time; as the policies unfold under the liberalized bilateral economic relationship envisioned in Jakarta and Washington, however, the economic role of the United States in Indonesian development can only be enhanced.

The CLMV Countries

Of ASEAN's "second tier" economies, Vietnam will be the first to be promoted to the first rank. Vietnam's GDP growth rate is one of the highest in the world, averaging 7.4% per annum in the last half-decade. Socialist Vietnam has been a "little China" in terms of having undergone dramatic economic and financial transformation. Merrill Lynch strategists view Vietnam as Asia's economic frontier, whose growth in the next decade will be far more exciting than any other country in ASEAN.[48] Vietnam's largest single trading partner is China. Two-way trade between Vietnam and China in 2005 was valued at $8.2 billion, an increase of 21% over 2004.[49] U.S.-Vietnam bilateral trade in 2005 was only $400 million less than China-Vietnam trade (see **Table 5**). The official China-Vietnam trade figures do not include "informal" cross-border trade. Most striking is the more than 400% increase in value of Vietnam's trade with the United States since the December 2001 enactment of the Vietnam-U.S. bilateral trade agreement. Vietnam's WTO accession negotiations, which began over a decade ago, are approaching a successful conclusion. The goal is for Vietnam to have WTO membership by the time the country hosts the November 2006 Asia Pacific Economic Cooperation (APEC) forum that will be attended by President Bush and will again include a mini-summit of ASEAN leaders. Successful conclusion of WTO accession negotiations and a favorable vote by the U.S. Congress on Permanent Normal Trade Relations (PNTR) would likely bring even greater opportunities for expanding U.S.-Vietnam trade.[50] PNTR status for Vietnam, which is the only ASEAN nation that does not enjoy this status, is not a certainty. If Vietnam remains a "country of particular concern" (CPC) on the religious freedom list, Congress may be reluctant to give up its annual vote on normal trade relations with Vietnam by granting PNTR status. Congress designated Vietnam a CPC in 2004 but withheld sanctions.

---

[48] Merrill Lynch Asia Pacific Strategy Group, "Buy Vietnam—The Emerging Frontier of ASEAN," *Asian Insights*, February 2, 2006.

[49] Figures as cited by *People's Daily* online, February 8, 2006.

[50] Vietnam has been accorded normal trade relations (NTR) status on an annual basis since 1998. This requires an executive waiver of the Jackson-Vanik amendment, a congressional debate, and a congressional vote. Though permanent normal trade relations (PNTR) is not a requirement of WTO membership, without it the United States would have to permit Vietnam to withhold from the U.S. commitments generalized to other WTO member states. Nor, as the case of Myanmar (Burma) shows, does PNTR status give immunity from trade sanctions.

The United States recognizes that progress has been made in Vietnam and the CPC label could possibly be removed in 2006. Once Vietnam is in the WTO and has PNTR status with the United States, a TIFA further boosting the economic ties between the two countries would be the next step.

Although still impeded by the bureaucratic and political obstacles of the socialist state system, Vietnam's rapid growth also reflects the ongoing opening of the country's economic and financial sectors to global capitalism. As noted above, Vietnam has emerged as the third most attractive target for FDI in ASEAN, trailing only Singapore and Malaysia. The United States has become an important source of investment in Vietnam's growth. From 1998 to the end of 2005, U.S. businesses directly invested $730 million. The cumulative combination of U.S. business investment with investment from U.S. third-country subsidiaries makes the United States the largest foreign investor in Vietnam.[51] In March 2006 the giant computer firm Intel announced a $300 million investment in Vietnam to package and test microchips. This announcement gave substance to the 2005 promise of Bush and the Vietnamese prime minister, Phan Van Khai, that the two countries would work together to promote favorable conditions for increased U.S. investment in Vietnam.[52]

The CLM countries present a different picture. Due both to lack of economic incentive in Cambodia and Laos and to the political situation in Myanmar (Burma), very little American trade and investment goes to the former two countries and virtually none to the latter. China has strategic and political incentives for close economic relations with the CLMV group because of the security implications of contiguity and the benefits these countries offer as economic hinterlands for South China. The border regions in both Myanmar (Burma) and Laos are becoming informal trans-China markets and areas of ethnic-Chinese settlement. China's interests in the development of the Mekong basin can be seen in its Laos and Cambodia policies. Japan, also interested in Mekong development, has hastened bilateral talks with Cambodia and Laos on development assistance. An additional interest for China in Cambodia is gaining access to the deepwater port at Sihanoukville. In 2006, China's premier Wen Jiabao pledged $600 million in loans and grants for Cambodian infrastructure and hydropower

---

[51] Deputy Assistant Secretary of State for East Asia and the Pacific Eric John, testimony before the U.S. Congressional subcommittees on Asia and the Pacific, Global Human Rights, and International Operations, House International Relations Committee, March 25, 2006, http://www.usinfo.state.gov/eap/ris/ m/.63826.htm.

[52] Office of the Press Secretary, "Joint Statement of the United States of America and the Socialist Republic of Vietnam," June 21, 2005, http://www.whitehouse.gov/news.releases/2995/06/20050621-2.html.

projects tied to Chinese state companies.[53] The annual foreign assistance donors' consortium pledge to Cambodia for 2006 was $601 million, with the largest single pledge being $164 million from the United States.

U.S. sanctions toward Myanmar (Burma) and strong U.S. encouragement for the democratic and quasi-democratic states of ASEAN to pressure the intransigent junta have further isolated Myanmar (Burma) internationally. ASEAN is in disarray on policy toward the Myanmar (Burma) regime, with senior foreign policy officials in Malaysia, Indonesia, the Philippines, and Thailand unable to conceal their frustration with the Burmese generals over their nose-thumbing at ASEAN colleagues. In the judgment of the Malaysian foreign minister, Myanmar (Burma) is holding ASEAN hostage and bringing the organization into disrepute.[54] On the other hand, neither Washington nor ASEAN is going to allow the junta's intransigence on democratization, human rights, and the issue of freedom for Aung San Suu Kyi to paralyze ASEAN-U.S. relations. Secretary Rice's deliberate absence from the 2005 ASEAN ministerial made two points: the first was that business could not proceed as usual if Myanmar (Burma) were to chair ASEAN, and the second was that ASEAN must reassess its priorities. Despite some internal ASEAN foot dragging by Vietnam, Laos, and Cambodia, the ASEAN-6 seem prepared—even if in an "ASEAN minus" formula—to regularize an ASEAN-U.S. summit outside of an official ASEAN meeting on the sidelines of APEC, to which neither Myanmar (Burma), Laos, nor Cambodia would belong. The United States, in turn, is willing to accept a working engagement with Myanmar (Burma) as an ASEAN member at lower bureaucratic levels. Myanmar (Burma) is represented in the ASEAN-U.S. Dialogue. It can be noted that at the Kuala Lumpur July 2006 signing of the Framework Document for the ASEAN-U.S. Enhanced Partnership, Secretary Rice shook hands with all of the ASEAN foreign ministers including the Burmese.

Sanctioned by the United States and the European Union, estranged from ASEAN, and snubbed as a pariah state by democrats around the world, the Burmese junta—dug into its Pyinmana redoubt—increasingly depends on China for political and economic support. The China-Myanmar (Burma) entente does not seem to have given Myanmar (Burma) much leverage in its relations with either the United States or ASEAN. Any diplomatic leverage the junta might enjoy is in the China-India competition over Myanmar's (Burma's) natural resources, particularly over Myanmar's (Burma's) offshore gas fields. Burmese prime minister Soe Win's visit to China in February

---

[53] "China Boosts Cambodian Relations with $600m Pledge," *FT.Com*, April 9, 2006.

[54] "Myanmar Holding ASEAN Hostage: KL," *Straits Times Interactive*, April 18, 2006.

2006 was followed by Indian president Abdul Kalam's visit to Myanmar (Burma) in March. ASEAN in a sense has thrown up its hands, calling on China and India to persuade Myanmar (Burma) to reform. Following the April 2006 ASEAN foreign ministers meeting, the organization's secretary-general said that India and China had both stronger economic leverage on Myanmar (Burma) and the leverage of common borders.[55] China's intimate relations with the Burmese junta could present problems for Beijing should there emerge a future "ASEAN minus Myanmar (Burma)" regional setting of an institutionalized ASEAN with a new legal charter and non-consensus based decision-making procedures.

The Strategic Environment of Interdependence

In discussing the direct economic effect of bilateral and multilateral FTAs in Southeast Asia, important is to note that these agreements are acts of political will and have political effects. Thus more than a statement of commercial policy, U.S. trade policy toward Southeast Asia (first in the framework of the EAI and now embodied in the Enhanced Partnership) is also a strategically significant expression of the U.S. commitment to remain a major regional actor. The economic data clearly refutes alarmist claims that China is economically pushing the United States out of Southeast Asia. In aggregate dollar terms, the economic position of the United States in the region is stronger than ever before. Across all economic transactions— trade, investment, development assistance—the United States is still Southeast Asia's largest partner. Even as China has risen, the United States has advanced as well. In the ASEAN-U.S. relationship, the important bilateral links are healthy by almost any measure. Certainly, the relative share held by the United States in the ASEAN economy has declined. This trend is not as alarming as it may seem given that, as trade figures show, ASEAN economic transactions are expanding across the board and the U.S. "slice of this pie" is actually expanding in absolute, although not relative, terms. The U.S. strategy in the EAI is focused on long-range rather short-term gains. Negotiations to turn TIFAs into FTAs will be lengthy and not necessarily always successful. The existence of the goal and especially the intermediate steps and agreements undertaken in pursuit of the goal will, however, help move the ASEAN-U.S. relationship to even higher levels of trade and investment liberalization and interdependence.

The ASEAN-U.S. Enhanced Partnership builds on economic interdependencies, but the ASEAN region views this partnership as a

---

reaffirmation of the U.S. intention to maintain a major presence in the region and be a contributor to regional stability. In that sense, the partnership is a kind of confidence building measure. Opening the May 2006 ASEAN-U.S. Dialogue, the Thai chair welcomed the Enhanced Partnership as further promoting a vibrant ASEAN-U.S. relationship that was a "solid foundation in maintaining peace, security, and prosperity in the overall regional architecture."[56] In insuring the U.S. regional role and commitment to the promotion of economic growth and development, the partnership broadens the legitimacy of the U.S. security role in defense cooperation.

The strategic environment in which ASEAN and its +1 partners can best achieve their goals (as expressed in their comprehensive partnerships and trade agreements) is a peaceful and politically stable Southeast Asia that is open to all. ASEAN views positively China's transformation over the last decade from a looming territorial and ideological threat to a cooperative and collaborative economic, political, and security partner.[57] China's peaceful disposition in the "modern global grid" is welcomed.[58] Moreover the 2002 ASEAN-China Declaration on the Conduct of Parties in the South China Sea, and subsequent steps to implement it, dampened, if not fully extinguished, a potential disruptive flash point. In 2005, Vietnam, China, and the Philippines agreed to conduct a joint survey of the disputed area's oil potential. This survey was a landmark confidence building measure and was described as "model-setting" by the Philippine foreign minister.[59] This cooperative effort also reduced the possibility of a face-off between the United States and China. The two countries have similar interests in maintaining the security of sea lanes through Southeast Asia and the critical straits choke points. Both Beijing and Washington have committed their support to ASEAN in a variety of multilateral non-traditional security areas: counter-narcotics, counter-piracy, and counter-trafficking in persons. The United States and China have been proactive with ASEAN on other transnational issues, such as combating the spread of pandemic disease (including HIV/AIDS, SARS, and avian influenza).

From ASEAN's vantage, both China and the United States are playing positive roles. The ASEAN states have tried to translate great-power concerns over competing interests in Southeast Asia—the potential "negatives" in

[56] "Joint Press Statement of the 19th ASEAN-U.S. Dialogue," Bangkok, May 23, 2006.

[57] Alice Ba, "China and ASEAN: Renavigating Relations for a 21st Century," *Asian Survey* 43, no. 4 (September/October 2003): 622–47.

[58] Kishore Mahbubani, "Understanding China," *Foreign Affairs* 84, no. 5 (September/October 2005): 59.

[59] "China, Philippines, Vietnam sign South China Sea agreement," ABC Radio Australia, March 14, 2005.

the relationship—into "positives" for the defense and advancement of their own strategic interests with the great powers. In an atmosphere of interest convergence, the outcome—at least in some critical policy areas—can be win-win-win, although some actors will win more than others.

This understanding has not stopped key ASEAN states from hedging and balancing against a future that might not be as bright as the welter of pacts and partnerships promise. There still exist concerns regarding China's ultimate non-economic objectives in the region. The power-projection capabilities China's navy is acquiring can be used both vis-à-vis Taiwan as well as in safeguarding sea lines of communication to protect energy imports. For ASEAN's core-5 at least, the constancy of the U.S. security presence underpins the Enhanced Partnership. China's heightened importance on the economic and political horizons of the Southeast Asian states has had no perceptible negative impact on the long-standing U.S. security role in the region. Though the U.S. war in Iraq is generally unpopular in Southeast Asia, not only have defense ties not been curtailed but the impetus of congruent U.S. and Southeast Asian counter-terrorism interests has in fact strengthened and deepened U.S. defense links with its ASEAN friends and allies. The commonality of Chinese, ASEAN, and U.S. views of the terrorist threat has been expressed in bilateral terms, ASEAN formulations, and the multilateral deliberations of the ASEAN Regional Forum (ARF). Unlike China, the United States has numerous capabilities (military operational, facility use, training, and interoperability) in Southeast Asia that give it a unique extra-regional strategic access.

The U.S. commitment to regional security is expressed in a robust program of bilateral and multilateral exercises and exchanges between U.S. forces in the Pacific Command and friendly and allied Southeast Asian forces. The U.S. International Military Education and Training (IMET) program has graduated tens of thousands of Southeast Asian students (see **Table 7**), including President Yudhoyono. The United States is also the major extra-regional defense supplier to the key ASEAN countries (**Table 8**). The United States has formal defense alliance relationships with the Philippines and Thailand, both now officially designated Major Non-NATO Allies. In the Philippines, on the basis of the Mutual Defense Agreement and under the shelter of the Visiting Forces Agreement, the United States maintains what a former U.S. ambassador to the Philippines described as a "semi-continuous" presence in the country.[60] In November 2005, a bilateral "strategic dialogue" took place in Bangkok between senior Thai and U.S. security officials, renewing a process that began in 1993. Although the

[60] Ambassador Francis Ricciardone as quoted in Herbert Docena, "When Uncle Sam Comes Marching In," *Asia Times*, January 3, 2006.

TABLE 7   ASEAN IMET students

Country	FY 2000	FY 2001	FY 2002	FY 2003	FY 2004	FY 1990–2004
Indonesia			30	41	32	8,275
Malaysia	26	66	48	47	93	2,939
Philippines	90	124	145	185	176	25,085
Singapore						271
Thailand	94	152	179	140	43	23,637
Total	210	342	402	413	344	60,207

SOURCE: U.S. Department of Defense Security Assistance Agency, *Fact Book 2004*, 119.

NOTE: This excludes IMET participants from pre-1975 Vietnam, Laos, and Cambodia.

TABLE 8   ASEAN-U.S. foreign military sales agreements, FY 2000–04 ($thousand)

Country	FY 2000	FY 2001	FY 2002	FY 2003	FY 2004	Totals
Brunei	353					353
Cambodia	463	325	424			1,212
Laos		82				82
Malaysia	5,071	3,014	22,821	9,396	19,714	60,016
Philippines	13,628	7,012	14,189	43,748	51,626	130,203
Singapore	103,512	653,271	146,755	155,520	141,510	1,200,568
Thailand	173,569	56,881	84,116	78,434	30,250	423,250
Total	342,596	720,585	268,305	287,098	43,100	1,861,684

SOURCE: U.S. Department of Defense Security Assistance Agency, *Fact Book 2004*, 2.

United States and Singapore have never had a formal alliance, Singapore's political and military relationship as a Major Security Cooperation Partner makes the city-state the closest U.S. ally in Southeast Asia.[61] In July 2005, Singapore and the United States signed a Strategic Framework Agreement providing for even closer cooperation in defense and security.[62] Even Vietnam—motivated by concerns about China—has strengthened U.S. defense ties, including for the first time sending participants to IMET in

---

[61] Anthony L. Smith, "Singapore and the United States 2004–2005: Steadfast Friends," *Special Assessment: The Asia-Pacific and the United States 2004–2005* (Honolulu: Asia-Pacific Center for Security Studies, February 2005).

[62] Office of the Press Secretary, "Joint Statement between President Bush and Prime Minister Lee of Singapore," July 12, 2005, http://www.whitehouose.gov/news/releases/2005/07/20050712.html.

2006. Only Laos among the former battlefields of Indochina has resisted a vitalization of military-to-military links to the United States.

A major hole in the pattern of U.S. security relations in Southeast Asia was the disruption in defense and security ties with Indonesia—an interruption imposed by restrictions placed by the U.S. Congress that date back to 1992 and were strengthened in 1998. The United States views Indonesia's position in Southeast Asia as strategically unique—given that Indonesia contains nearly half of Southeast Asia's population, has the largest Muslim population in the world, is located on critical Asian sea lane choke points, is a key ally in the war on terrorism, and is a remerging leader of ASEAN. At the May 2005 meeting between Bush and Yudhoyono, the two agreed that "normal military relations would be in the interest of both parties."[63] The political stumbling blocks had been overcome by the Yudhoyono government's democratic spirit, commitment to reform, and cooperation on both human rights and counter-terrorism issues. In fact, the first steps toward normalization had been taken by the time the two presidents met. In February 2005, the United States determined that Indonesia could resume full participation in the IMET program and restored foreign military sales (FMS) for non-lethal items in May. In November 2005, continuing the process of reengagement with Indonesia, Secretary of State Rice waived all remaining legislative restrictions on U.S. military assistance to Indonesia, allowing foreign military financing (FMF) and defense exports.[64] In March 2006, the State Department posted formal notice permitting the sale of lethal military equipment to Indonesia on a case-by-case basis.[65]

With the removal of restrictions, the Commander of the U.S. Pacific Command has called for a "rapid, concerted infusion" of military assistance to Indonesia.[66] The foreign operations budget request for FY 2007 calls for major increases in military assistance for Indonesia.[67] Perhaps the most telling sign for the new U.S.-Indonesia defense relationship is the return to grace of the Indonesian Army's Special Forces (KOPASSUS), which

---

[63] Office of the Press Secretary, "Joint Statement between the United States of America and the Republic of Indonesia," May 25, 2005, http://www.whitehouse.gov/news/releases/2005/05/20050525-11.htm.

[64] U.S. Department of State Office of the Spokesman, "Indonesia–Military Assistance," January 4, 2006, http://www.state.gov?r/pa/prs/2006/58686.htm.

[65] Federal Register 71, no. 60 (March 13, 2006): 15797.

[66] Admiral William J. Fallon, "Statement to the U.S. Senate Armed Services Committee on Pacific Command Posture," March 7, 2006, http://www.armed-services.senate.gov/statement.2006/March/Fallon%2003-07-06.pdf.

[67] U.S. Department of State, Congressional Budget Justification, Foreign Operations, Fiscal Year 2007, http://www.state.gov/documents/organization/60643.pdf.

was held responsible for some of the military's most egregious human rights outrages. For the first time in eight years, KOPASSUS was invited to participate in the 2006 annual PACOM-sponsored Pacific Area Special Operations Conference (PASOC) in Hawaii.

From a military point of view, the restoration of normal relations allows the United States to again contribute to Indonesia's military modernization and capacity building, aid that will better allow Indonesia to support common strategic interests in counter-terrorism and maritime security. These changes will also enhance Indonesia's ability to work with Singapore, Malaysia, and Thailand in their joint security presence in the Strait of Malacca. With access to U.S. assistance and equipment reopened, the Indonesian military's capacity for interoperability with other U.S. friends and allies in the ASEAN region will be increased. The reintegration of Indonesia into the PACOM–centered security nexus in Southeast Asia also is expected to give further incentives to the Indonesian military for reform and professionalization. As important as normalization is for the military, the greatest strategic significance is the new political quality that normalization lends to the bilateral relationship. While visiting Jakarta in March 2006, Secretary Rice underlined the importance of "the growing strategic partnership and strategic relationship of the United States and Indonesia."[68] Although the bilateral security dialogue (both Track I and Track II) between Jakarta and Washington was never broken, the dialogue had no real functional programmatic underpinnings to give credibility to a U.S.-Indonesia security partnership—a partnership that Indonesia insists must be symmetrical. Given Indonesia's critical role in ASEAN, the U.S.-Indonesia "strategic partnership" is a necessary key ingredient to the ASEAN-U.S. Enhanced Partnership.

Together the reformist Indonesian government and the normalization of the U.S.-Indonesian defense relationship bolster ASEAN's collective capability both to hedge and balance in pursuit of interests with the United States and China and to do so without threatening the interests of either of these great powers. The message from Washington to Southeast Asia is that while intent upon broadening and deepening U.S. ties to ASEAN—perhaps even to balance China in some respects—the United States is not trying to contain China in Southeast Asia. Visiting Asia in March 2006, Secretary Rice took pains to emphasize the obligations and responsibilities of the United States and its friends to create conditions for China to be a positive force

[68] U.S. Department of State, "Transcript of Press Conference with Indonesia's Foreign Minister Noer Hasan Wirajuda," http://www.state.gov/secretary/rm/2006/63087.htm.

in the region.[69] ASEAN depends on a stable strategic Sino-U.S. relationship for the maintenance of Southeast Asia's political autonomy and economic well-being. The potential for Sino-U.S. conflict to pose real problems for ASEAN does not come from a clash of interests in Southeast Asia but rather from confrontation between Beijing and Washington in Northeast Asia, particularly Taiwan, and the possible spillover into Southeast Asia.

Conclusion: An ASEAN-centered System and U.S. Policy

The economic and political data presented above does not support the thesis that the Southeast Asian states are integrating their economies into a web with China at the hub. ASEAN is at the hub of its own global network with spokes of differing sizes running to the United States, the EU, Japan, China, and India. The multiple ASEAN+1s are deepening ASEAN's global interdependencies. The real economic dynamic within any ASEAN+1 is not ASEAN as a unitary actor but rather ASEAN as a network of the individual state's bilateral trade and investment relations. ASEAN's strategy not only seeks to carry out geopolitical goals (such as hedging and balancing) but also has an economic component, seeking to maximize its member's global market access to support GDP growth and economic development. In the years ahead, however, if ASEAN (with or without Myanmar [Burma]) achieves its stated intentions, the organization will move to a new format of rules-based greater institutionalization, legal personality, and a stronger international bargaining position. The elements of a draft charter are slated to be ready for the ASEAN leaders at their December 2006 summit. Looking toward a more coherent ASEAN, U.S. Senate Foreign Relations Committee chair Richard Lugar already has introduced a bill to appoint a U.S. ambassador to ASEAN.[70] Lugar's initiative, though perhaps premature, nevertheless suggests that the ASEAN+1 multilateral format will become increasingly significant for the United States in the next five years.

President Bush has conspicuously adopted multilateralism as an important complement to its bilateral ties in his administration's approach to Southeast Asia—a strategy China has adopted for more than a decade.[71] The same strategy has been adopted by China's other competitors in the

---

[69] As quoted in Jane Perlez, "As Rice visits Asia a China subtext looms," *New York Times*, March 13, 2006.

[70] The bill, co-sponsored by Senators Biden, Kerry, and Obama, http://Lugar.senate.gov/pressapp/record.cfm?id=255076.

[71] Kuik, "Multilateralism and China's ASEAN policy."

region. The United States is just now catching up. Implementation of the ASEAN-U.S. Enhanced Partnership presumes a strategic environment in which a prospering economic relationship and commitment of a continuing U.S. security presence in the region will be accompanied by a more intensive political relationship. An institutionalization of regular ASEAN-U.S. summits would place the United States at a level already enjoyed by China, Japan, Korea, Russia, India, and Australia.

As ASEAN begins the process of reinventing itself, maintaining the momentum in the "ASEANization" of U.S. policy will be important. Three issues in particular will require attention. One threat to stability in the ASEAN-U.S. relationship is growing protectionist sentiment in the United States. A legislative backlash by Congress against what many members claim are unfair Chinese trade practices could spill over and harm the EAI strategy and the ASEAN-U.S. Enhanced Partnership. A new Congress in 2007 will have to reauthorize the president's trade authority.

Second, the evolution of the reinvigorated U.S.-Indonesia relationship will not likely be totally smooth. Indonesia is re-emerging as Southeast Asia's policy leader. Revitalized Indonesia is a prime mover in the effort to restructure ASEAN. From Jakarta's point of view, Indonesia is expected to take the leadership in ASEAN since "the future of [ASEAN's] 500 million people depends on Indonesia."[72] Looking at Yudhoyono's Indonesia, a former editor of the *Far Eastern Economic Review* stated that "it is time for the country to revive its role in regional and world affairs."[73] The importance of Indonesia in defining the future overall strategic environment for U.S. policy in Southeast Asia is sometimes obscured by greater attention to immediate issues. Because of Jakarta's past human rights record, Congressional voices still are raised against normalization of military relations with Indonesia. The Yudhoyono government has been criticized for not taking stronger action against radical Islam. There has been discord at official levels about the conduct of the war on terror. Indonesia's sensitivity about its territorial integrity is touched off by U.S. voices favoring independence for Indonesia's Papua provinces. The United States would benefit by making every effort to prevent these issues (and others that will arise) from negatively impacting U.S.-Indonesian cooperation and, by extension, the U.S. partnership with ASEAN.

Finally, a firmer political foundation will be needed for the U.S. partnership with ASEAN to prosper fully in an enhancement of functional economic, political, and security links. This will be especially true if, over the

---

[72] Opinion and Editorial "Leading ASEAN," *The Jakarta Post*, August 12, 2004.

[73] Michael Vatikiotis, "Susilo, Regional Affairs, and Lessons from Suharto," *The Jakarta Post*, November 3, 2004.

next half-decade or so, ASEAN succeeds in reshaping itself institutionally. Before U.S. relations with ASEAN can be on an equal political footing with the other important ASEAN+1 partners, the United States will have to find a way to formally associate itself with the Treaty of Amity and Cooperation in Southeast Asia (TAC). This treaty is essentially a regional nonaggression treaty and commitment to the pacific settlement of disputes, with Australia, China, India, Japan, Mongolia, New Zealand, Pakistan, Papua New Guinea, the Republic of Korea, and the Russian Federation all being signatories. The ASEAN goal in extending the TAC to other countries with interests in Southeast Asia (the next being France and East Timor) was to have these countries commit to the normative framework which theoretically governed regional international relations. The ASEAN states repeatedly have asked the United States to accede, always to be refused.

Allies of the United States in the Pacific region acceded to the TAC without modification of their security treaty relations and obligations with the United States, as the ASEAN-Australian understanding makes clear.[74] The TAC's dispute resolution mechanism (which has never been used) has no compulsory jurisdiction. In the "vision statement" for the Enhanced Partnership, President Bush did acknowledge that the TAC

> acts as a code of conduct governing inter-state relations in the region for the promotion of peace and stability, and its role as a unifying concept for ASEAN and respect the spirit and principles of the TAC, in line with the commitment of ASEAN and the United States to enhance their partnership.[75]

To "acknowledge" is not to commit. The question is, if there are no real strategic or political objections, why does the United States continue to hold back? The answer appears to lie in U.S. constitutional processes and concern that the Senate might fail to ratify, thus worsening the U.S. TAC problem with ASEAN. Other ways exist for a U.S. president to make international commitments that are more binding then simply "acknowledgment." Remaining to be explored is the question of what level of U.S. obligation to abide by TAC would both be satisfactory to ASEAN and win the United States an invitation to the East Asian Summit. As it is, the economic and security platforms supporting U.S. strategic interests in Southeast Asia are firm; resolution of the TAC problem would give the political platform a much needed shoring up.

---

[74] The Australian understandings are stated in the government's submission of the TAC to Parliament in August 2006, http://woparad.parl.net/house/committee/usct/9august2005/treaties/tac_text.pdf.

[75] "Joint Vision Statement," paragraph 3.

STRATEGIC ASIA 2006–07

SPECIAL STUDIES

EXECUTIVE SUMMARY

This chapter examines whether political reform is necessary in China in order for the country to sustain economic growth into the future.

MAIN ARGUMENT:
Though the Chinese government so far has managed the rising tensions between economic modernization, on the one hand, and the many institutional flaws of authoritarian rule (e.g., lack of political accountability, weak rule of law, bureaucratic ossification, and endemic corruption), on the other, China will not likely continue this course of rapid growth without undertaking the necessary political reforms to make the Chinese political system more responsive and respectful of property and individual rights.

POLICY IMPLICATIONS:
- Western policymakers need to re-examine their assumptions about the sustainability of China's authoritarian developmental model.

- The U.S. government would benefit, in particular, from rebalancing and shifting U.S. policy toward China from the current focus on security issues to a new focus on non-traditional threats such as corruption, environmental degradation, and public-health disasters.

- A re-energized human rights approach to China by the West could emphasize domestic political change in China as the measurement of China's performance as a responsible global power.

- Given that China's political system is unfriendly to competitive markets, Western businesses have the same interests as Western governments in promoting democratic change in China. Western businesses would benefit from building a united front in their dealings with China.

China: Can Economic Growth Continue without Political Reform?

Minxin Pei

Though having become a great power, China faces a highly uncertain future. This uncertainty has now become one of the decisive factors influencing the policy of the West toward China. In the minds of key Western decisionmakers and strategic thinkers loom two questions: whether China will democratize and whether China can continue its rapid economic ascendance without democratic reforms. The strategic uncertainties facing these policymakers are illustrated by the matrix of potential outcomes based on the interplay between the two crucial variables: democratization and economic growth in China (**Table 1**). The most desirable outcome is Scenario I, which sees a China that has successfully democratized its political system, developed its economy, and become a strong partner of the West and Asian allies of the West. Each of the three other outcomes would create a different set of difficulties. Notably, sustained growth under authoritarian rule (Scenario II) would allow China to acquire military capabilities and economic influence with which to challenge and compete against the West. Yet an authoritarian China that falters economically (Scenario IV) is also likely both to experience political strife at home and to behave unpredictably abroad. If economic growth were to stagnate despite the democratization of the Chinese political system (Scenario III), China likely would pose a lesser traditional security threat but, due to its economic weakness, would generate many non-traditional threats, such as illegal immigration, environmental degradation, and epidemics. (These non-traditional threats are equally likely under Scenario IV.)

Minxin Pei is a senior associate and the director of the China Program at the Carnegie Endowment for International Peace. His latest book is *China's Trapped Transition: The Limits of Developmental Autocracy* (Harvard University Press, 2006). He can be reached at <mpei@carnegieendowment.org>.

TABLE 1   Democracy and economic growth: four scenarios for China

	Democratic reform	Authoritarian rule
Sustained growth	Liberal Dream: A strong partner for the West (*Scenario I*)	Authoritarian Nightmare: A formidable competitor (*Scenario II*)
Faltering growth	Democratic Disappointment: A weak, peaceful power (*Scenario III*)	Frail Giant: A stagnant and insecure regime (*Scenario IV*)

The primary objective of this chapter is to address the question of whether China will continue to maintain rapid economic growth without undertaking democratic reforms. Although the most haunting specter for most Western strategic thinkers is Scenario II, this chapter argues that the country's economic rise is unlikely to continue if China fails to purse the long-delayed political reforms. That the Chinese Communist Party (CCP) has consistently resisted democratic reforms in the last three decades while delivering impressive economic growth does not necessarily indicate that the party will be able to successfully do so in the future. On the contrary, the CCP's ability to delay introducing regime-changing political reforms has contributed to the accumulation of massive governance deficits and systemic risks; to the extent that these deficits and risks have real and substantial economic costs, China's economic prospects will suffer. In other words, without democratic reform the most likely outcome for China is Scenario IV—a faltering authoritarian giant beset by internal woes. Unfortunately, Western policymakers seem to be unprepared for this outcome.

This chapter first briefly reviews the history of rapid economic growth in post-Mao China, analyzes the main factors behind such growth, and then explains why massive socioeconomic modernization has not led to a democratic breakthrough in China. This is followed by a description of the economic and social consequences of lagging democratization. The next section explores the various mechanisms through which the absence of political reform would likely become a drag on China's economic performance in the next ten to fifteen years. The conclusion presents an analysis both of the prospects for political reform and of the policy implications of China's uncertain future.

The Chinese Economic Miracle

China's rapid economic growth—averaging about 9% a year since the late 1970s—has defied projections of not only pessimists skeptical of the capacity of China's authoritarian regime to deliver long-term superior economic performance but also of optimists confident of the democratizing effects of sustained economic development. In less than three decades China has increased per capita income 1,000%, more than doubled the urbanization rate, and transformed itself from a negligible participant in the world economy to the third-largest global trading power. This process of fast-paced economic modernization and liberalization also has produced millions of professional workers and private entrepreneurs who have become a vital source of social dynamism and—potentially—political change. Indeed, judging by any measurement of economic development, the Chinese experience during the reform era has been nothing but a resounding success.

Such an assessment may fit well the theory of the developmental state derived from the historical experience of rapid industrialization in East Asia (Japan, South Korea, Taiwan, and Singapore).[1] In particular, the earlier literature on the developmental state implicitly credits authoritarian rule with the capacity to overcome the collective action problem of providing leadership in late-developing societies and to mobilize the financial and administrative resources in achieving rapid growth; to this extent the Chinese case provides yet another empirical confirmation, albeit on a gigantic scale. To advocates of the theory of the developmental state, the Chinese experience is thus hardly surprising. The linkage between democratic reform and superior economic growth performance is (if such a link exists at all) most likely to be negative: democratic reform may be not only unnecessary but also positively harmful for sustaining economic growth.[2]

Yet, the theory of the developmental state may be useful only in explaining *ex post facto* how some states managed to achieve rapid growth while others did not. The implicit linkage between authoritarianism and superior growth is tenuous because of the selection bias problem. A review of empirical evidence shows no systematic relationship between regime type and growth performance.[3] At the same time, the theory of the developmental state must contend with the powerful insights of the institutionalist school

[1] Stephan Haggard, *Pathways from the Periphery* (Ithaca, NY: Cornell University Press, 1991); Thomas Gold, *State and Society in the Taiwan Miracle* (Armonk, NY: M. E. Sharpe, 1997); Robert Wade, *Governing the Market: Theory and the Role of Government in East Asian Industrialization* (Princeton, NJ: Princeton University Press, 1990); and Chalmers Johnson, *MITI and the Japanese Miracle: The Growth of Industrial Policy, 1925-1975* (Stanford, CA: Stanford University Press, 1983).

[2] Robert Wade, *Governing the Market: Theory and the Role of Government in East Asian Industrialization* (Princeton, NJ: Princeton University Press, 1990).

[3] Adam Przeworski et al., *Democracy and Development: Political Institutions and Well-being in the World, 1950-1990* (New York: Cambridge University Press, 2000).

of economic development.[4] According to the institutionalist school, superior long-run economic growth can only be sustained by political and legal institutions that protect property rights and restrain the predatory appetite of the state.[5] To the extent that an authoritarian regime, unconstrained by the rule of law and political competition, is more likely to be a predator than a nurturer, an autocracy will be unlikely to maintain strong economic performance—unless it implements political reforms that would build and strengthen the institutions of the rule of law and expand political participation.[6] From this perspective, pessimists are theoretically justified in questioning the durability of China's "authoritarian developmental state." Empirically, the spectacular collapse of Suharto's regime in Indonesia in 1998 also validates the view that, without political reform, even one of the most successful authoritarian developmental states could degenerate into a predatory one, with catastrophic consequences.[7]

For the moment, however, China's economic miracle appears to have clearly defied both orthodox theory and doomsayers. The economic locomotive is real and seems unstoppable. Unadjusted for quality (which will complicate matters a great deal since the social costs of environmental degradation, rising income inequality, and corruption would be included to offset the rise in income), the rate of growth China has achieved since 1978 is among the highest for a major economy. Between 1978 and 2003, China recorded an annual growth rate of 9.4%.[8] A quarter-century of high growth has completely transformed the Chinese economy. The aggregate size of the Chinese economy in 2003 (adjusted for inflation) was more than eight times larger than in 1978.[9] Structurally, the share of the modern sectors (manufacturing and service) rose from 72% to 85%, with manufacturing

---

[4] Douglass North, *Institutions, Institutional Change, and Economic Performance* (New York: Cambridge University Press, 1990); and Thrainn Eggertsson, *Economic Behavior and Institutions* (New York: Cambridge University Press, 1990).

[5] Margaret Levi, *Of Rule and Revenue* (Berkeley: University of California Press, 1989); and North, *Institutions, Institutional Change, and Economic Performance.*

[6] In the institutionalist literature, the connection between strong protection of property rights provided by the rule of law and superior long-run economic performance is undisputed but the effects of democracy on growth remain unproven. In the contemporary world, however, the rule of law and democratization are politically interdependent. Authoritarian rulers are unlikely to subject themselves to the rule of law without the pressures of democratization. Therefore, political reform must include both legal and democratic reforms.

[7] In East Asia, the two most successful developmental autocracies—Taiwan and South Korea—avoided such a catastrophe mainly because their ruling elites allowed political contestation to increase gradually. There were competitive elections and strong civic forces that helped check the state's predatory instincts. In Singapore, the rule of law and clean elections also acted as a self-enforcing mechanism against abuse of power by the ruling People's Action Party.

[8] *Statistical Yearbook of China 2004* (Beijing: China Statistical Publishing Co., 2005), 25.

[9] Ibid., 56.

accounting for 52% of the economy.[10] The material well-being for Chinese citizens has improved dramatically, as reflected in the increase of per capita income from $150 in 1978 to roughly $1,700 in 2005. The improvement of the standard of living can be seen clearly in the data in **Table 2** as well. Obviously, rapid growth has significantly reduced poverty. According to the World Bank, about 402 million people were lifted out of abject poverty (defined as living on $1 a day) from 1981 to 2002, with the total population of the impoverished falling from 490 to 88 million in this period.[11]

TABLE 2   Rising standards of living in China, selected indicators (1978–2000)

Selected indicators of standard of living	1978	1983	1990	1992	2000
Passenger cars (per 1,000 people)	–	–	1.43	–	6.74
Air transport, passengers carried (million)	1.54	–	–	–	61.89
Malnutrition prevalence, weight for age (% of children under 5)	–	–	–	17.40	10.00
Immunization, DPT (% of children ages 12–23 months)	–	58.00	–	–	89.00
Television sets (per 1,000 people)	2.62	–	–	–	304.16
Literacy rate, adult total (% of people ages 15 and above)	64.10	–	–	–	90.90

SOURCE: The World Bank, *World Development Indicators*, various years.

For the world economy, the most important aspect of China's economic modernization is the explosive growth of its foreign trade. The extensive linkages with the world economy have made China a critical component of the global supply chain. The participation of tens of millions of rural laborers in the export-oriented manufacturing sector has strengthened China's comparative advantage and contributed to low inflation around the world. China's enormous gains from international trade have given Beijing an unprecedented level of influence in the economic integration in East Asia (as seen from its leadership's role in helping establish free-trade zones in the region). With China's foreign currency reserves approaching $1 trillion in 2006, China has become a pivotal player in international finance because its exchange rate and reserve policies can move both interest and exchange rates around the world.

---

[10] *Statistical Yearbook of China 2004*, 54.

[11] The World Bank, "Shanghai Poverty Conference: Case Study Summary," http://info.worldbank. org/etools/docs/reducingpoverty/case/33/summary/China-8-7PovertyReduction%20Summary. pdf.

Many factors have contributed to China's rapid economic gains in the reform era. Compared with the more developed state-socialist economies in the former Soviet bloc, the pre-reform Chinese economy had more favorable structural and institutional conditions, such as a less extensive welfare state and less bureaucratic centralization.[12] These pre-conditions allowed China to avoid major economic disruptions since non-state firms could emerge and eventually replace state-owned firms as the main engine of growth and employment generation.[13] One scholar aptly named this strategy "growing out of the plan."[14] Additionally, China, by fortune of geography, is located in a "good neighborhood"—the fastest-growing region in the world economy. With proximity to the so-called "dragon economies" in general, and access to the business networks of ethnic-Chinese in East Asia in particular, China could not only benefit from the inflows of foreign direct investment from these economies, but also tap into the enormous pool of intangible wealth of entrepreneurial knowledge and connections accumulated by the Chinese diaspora. Indeed, China could not likely have built its competitive export-oriented industrial base without the contributions of direct investment and knowledge from the businesses in Hong Kong and Taiwan.[15]

To what extent should the Chinese government be given the credit for this economic miracle? In answering this question, one must disaggregate the effects of policy and strategy from those of authoritarian rule. The majority of mainstream economists, for example, firmly believe that China's gradualist reform strategy was responsible both for the massive expansion of output during the reform era and for the minimization of transition costs.[16] In addition, the decision to launch economic reform first in the countryside ensured success in the early, and most difficult, stage of economic transition and later generated powerful momentum for extending the reform into urban areas.[17] The policy of decentralization also appears to have offered enormous incentives for local elites to promote economic

---

[12] Yingyi Qian and Chenggang Xu, "Why China's Economic Reforms Differ: The M-form Hierarchy and Entry/Expansion of the Non-state Sector," *Economics of Transition* 1, no. 2 (1993): 135–70.

[13] Jeffrey Sachs and Wing Thye Woo, "Structural Factors in the Economic Reforms of China, Eastern Europe, and the Former Soviet Union," *Economic Policy* 18 (1994): 102–45.

[14] Barry Naughton, *Growing Out of the Plan: Chinese Economic Reform, 1978–1993* (New York: Cambridge University Press, 1995).

[15] Hongying Wang, *Weak State, Strong Networks* (New York: Oxford University Press, 2002).

[16] Lawrence Lau, Yingyi Qian, and Gerard Roland, "Reform without Losers: An Interpretation of China's Dual-Track Approach to Transition," *Journal of Political Economy* 108, no. 1 (2000): 120–43; and Gerard Roland, *Transition and Economics: Politics, Markets, and Firms* (Cambridge: MIT Press, 2000).

[17] Jean Oi, *Rural China Takes Off: Institutional Foundations of Economic Reform* (Berkeley: University of California Press 1999).

growth.[18] Conservative macroeconomic management, despite several episodes of high inflation, is another much-praised policy adopted by the Chinese government in maintaining a stable pro-growth environment.[19] Lastly, by embracing globalization and aggressively courting foreign direct investment, China has managed to maximize its comparative advantage and significantly expand its foreign trade.[20]

Much more problematic is the assessment of the extent to which China's authoritarian rule has contributed to the delivery of rapid growth for nearly three decades. Conceivably, one can make three arguments for the case that authoritarian rule has provided the political guarantee for superior economic performance in China since the late 1970s. First, compared to a democratic regime in a comparable developing country, China's authoritarian political system is more capable of mobilizing the resources for rapid development. Unconstrained by opposition parties, civil society groups, courts, and the press, an authoritarian regime has greater discretion and capacity to increase investment and build the physical infrastructure needed for economic take-off. This can be seen in China's very high investment rates and ability to develop its critical infrastructure with impressive speed, which stands in contrast to the low investment rates and slow infrastructural development in India. Second, China's authoritarian rule has suppressed labor costs and helped maintain the country's comparative advantage in the international economy. In particular, by prohibiting independent labor unions, China has made itself an attractive destiny for foreign direct investment in labor-intensive manufacturing. Third, as the disastrous experience of the former Soviet Union shows, adopting democratic reforms before economic reform bears fruit can unleash dangerous centrifugal forces and cause an anti-regime revolution. The subsequent political chaos and social unrest will cause an economic collapse with devastating consequences. The Chinese government, in particular, is fond of crediting the breathtaking economic take-off in the 1990s to the political stability that prevailed after the bloody suppression of the pro-democracy movement in June 1989.

Of these three arguments, the most serious and plausible is the second one. Authoritarian rule is most likely an ally of international capital in search of cheap labor. The enormous advantage of cheap labor has definitely been the most important factor in the explosive growth of China's labor-intensive export sector. The linkage between authoritarian rule and resource

---

[18] Susan Shirk, *The Political Logic of Economic Reform in China* (Berkeley: University of California Press, 1993); and Yasheng Huang, *Investment and Inflation Control in China: The Political Economy of Central-Local Relations during the Reform Era* (New York: Cambridge University Press, 1996).

[19] The World Bank, *China, 2020* (Washington, D.C.: The World Bank, 1997).

[20] Shang-jin Wei, ed., *The Globalization of the Chinese Economy* (London: Edward Elgar, 2002).

mobilization capacity may appear obvious and intuitive. Yet—given the ease with which authoritarian regimes can mobilize resources and the enormous discretion with which such regimes use them—waste and corruption is likely to be endemic under authoritarian rule, resulting in inefficient use of resources. One telltale example of systemic waste in China is the huge stockpile of non-performing loans in the financial system (about $700 billion in 2005), despite rapid growth (normally, banks thrive in fast-growing economies, but not in China).[21] The so-called Chinese model compares well only with Russia but not with many of the East European countries, which achieved the democratic breakthrough and successfully adopted radical economic reforms. Today, these countries rank higher in governance indicators, have much lower level of corruption, and enjoy greater economic freedom than China.[22] Of course, if we factor in the personal welfare loss from living under authoritarian rule (lack of political choices, fear of the secret police, and denied access to information) then gains in the material standards of living must be discounted, and China's achievement would lose a great deal of luster.

Regardless of the degree to which authoritarian rule contributes to or undermines China's growth performance, the most important question is whether Chinese economic growth will continue to surge ahead at high speed *without* political reform. For the next decade, many of the economic fundamentals remain positive and China's strong growth momentum will most likely continue. The most important favorable economic factors include:

High savings rate. The national savings rate (combining household, corporate, and government savings) will remain well above 30% for at least a decade, providing the funds needed to sustain high rates of investment, the most powerful and proven engine of growth. Some optimists even claim that, based on the experience of East Asia's newly industrialized countries (NIC), high savings rates, not the health of political and economic institutions, determine long-run growth performance.[23] The connection between high savings and high growth is, however, not a certain one. Aside from the issue of whether savings are efficiently invested in China, changing demographics, especially the rapid growth of an elderly population in the mid-2010s, is likely to reduce savings rate. High savings in China are

[21] *The Financial Times*, May 3, 2006, 1.

[22] See the World Bank Institute, "Governance Indicators," http://www.worldbank.org/wbi/governance/data.html; Transparency International, *Corruption Perception Index*, http://www.transparency.org/; and the Fraser Institute, "Economic Freedom in the World," http://www.fraserinstitute.ca/economicfreedom/index.asp?snav=ef.

[23] Jonathan Anderson, "How to Think about China," (UBS Securities, 2005).

maintained, at present, by households' uncertainty about their pensions, healthcare, and educational expenditures. Ironically, successful reforms that would increase confidence in the government's ability to pay for these social services in the future could reduce public uncertainty, increase consumption, and reduce savings. The net result is not necessarily slower growth but a different—and perhaps more healthy—type of growth that is driven by consumption, not investment.

Migration of rural labor. The massive migration of rural labor that is of marginal productivity to the modern sectors in urban areas has been a principal contributor to the increase in productivity and economic growth in the reform period. In the past quarter-century, an estimated 150 million rural migrants have been absorbed into the manufacturing, construction, and service sectors in China. In the next two decades, more than 200 million rural residents are expected to move to more productive employment in the cities.[24] The participation of this huge labor pool in the modern sectors will not only maintain China's low-wage cost advantage but also generate its own growth momentum.

Growing and dynamic private sector. Despite the Chinese government's discrimination against the private sector, private Chinese firms have become the main engine of economic growth and employment generation. As indigenous private Chinese firms continue to gain market share, talent, and financial clout, they will provide a key source of momentum for the Chinese economy.[25]

Spreading growth clusters. As a continental economy, China will gain additional advantage from the spread of growth clusters from the more prosperous coastal areas to the agrarian hinterland. To date, growth has concentrated mostly along the east coast. Although this concentration has greatly exacerbated regional economic disparities, the migration of growth clusters, driven by manufacturing companies' search for cheaper locations to relocate, will provide a powerful stimulus to economic growth in the agrarian provinces located in the central part of the country.

Globalization. By embracing globalization, China has maximized its comparative advantage of abundant low-cost labor.[26] The outsourcing of manufacturing activities to China by firms with higher labor costs has been a main driver of export growth and improvement in quality for products

---

[24] *The 2005 China Development Report* says that the "cumulative number" of rural migrants to the cities will be "well over 200 million" over the next approximately fifteen years, http://www.undp.org.cn/downloads/nhdr2005/NHDR2005_complete.pdf, 102.

[25] See OECD, *Economic Survey: China* (Paris: OECD, 2005).

[26] See Peter Nolan, *Transforming China: Globalization, Transition, and Development* (New York: Cambridge University Press, 2004).

made in China. Although China's explosive growth in exports has met with
increasing protectionism in its main markets (the United States and Europe),
China's extensive ties with the global economy will allow China to tap into
the huge pool of foreign technology, management know-how, and—to a
decreasing extent—capital in maintaining its growth momentum.[27]

Political Reform: A Critical Assessment

If China's success in achieving three decades of high growth has
confounded skeptics, the dearth of evidence that the three decades of
unprecedented economic modernization have made the Chinese political
system more democratic has equally challenged the theoretical validity
of the school of "democratic evolution," which asserts that economic
development has liberalizing effects on authoritarian political systems. Of
course, it would be false to claim that Chinese politics has not changed.
Compared to the era of mass terror under the rule of the late leader Mao
Zedong, Chinese society today is much more free, diverse, and autonomous.
Despite an overall poor human rights record and a history of repression,
Chinese politics has also become much less brutal and more constrained
by rules and norms.[28] The Chinese Communist Party (CCP) even has
undertaken limited administrative and institutional reforms, including
strengthening the legislative branch, building a modern legal system, and
even experimenting with grassroots democracy in villages.[29] Nevertheless,
judging by the most basic criteria of democratization (such as the
emergence of an organized opposition, autonomous civil society, and civil
liberties) the Chinese political system remains unmistakably authoritarian,
not democratic.

More disturbingly, the Chinese experience, especially since the 1990s,
seems to have stood on its head the liberal modernization theory predicting
democratization as a result of economic development. The reality in China
is the reverse: while China's economic take-off was barely beginning,
Beijing was more tolerant of experiments with democratic reforms, but as
the country has grown richer, China's political system has failed to grow

[27] See Nicholas Lardy, *Integrating China into the Global Economy* (Washington, D.C.: Brookings
Institution Press, 2001).

[28] Andrew Nathan, "Authoritarian Resilience," *Journal of Democracy* 14, no. 1 (2003): 6–17.

[29] Randall Peerenboom, *China's Long March Toward Rule of Law* (New York: Cambridge University
Press, 2002); and Murray Scot Tanner, *The Politics of Lawmaking in Post-Mao China: Institutions,
Processes, and Democratic Prospects* (New York: Oxford University Press, 1999).

more democratic.[30] In some respects, the Chinese political system today has become even less democratic than in the 1980s. For example, the Communist Party has discontinued the experiment with so-called inner-party democracy, which allowed limited competitive elections within the Central Committee. The discussion of political reform has similarly been banned in public discourse; in contrast, the top leadership seriously explored various options of political reform in the late 1980s.[31]

The reverse relationship between economic development and democratic change in China can be seen more clearly in the limits of the three most important institutional reforms endorsed and implemented by the Chinese Communist Party since the late 1970s: strengthening the legislative branch, building a modern legal system, and instituting semi-competitive elections in villages.

Strengthening the Legislative Branch

China's efforts to strengthen the role of the legislative branch—mainly the National People's Congress (NPC) and, to a lesser extent, local people's congresses (LPC)—in decisionmaking is generally considered one of the most important steps of political institutionalization.[32] If successful, this reform measure would introduce institutional pluralism into an authoritarian political system. While the importance of strengthening the legislative branch is widely recognized, research on the actual achievement of this reform has yielded different assessments. Kevin O'Brien's study of the NPC in the 1980s finds no evidence that this key legislative institution became more competitive or responsive. Instead, the reform merely strengthened the CCP's hold on the legislative branch.[33] Murray Scot Tanner's research, however, offers a more upbeat assessment of China's legislative reforms. Tanner argues that these reforms have considerably reduced the control of the CCP in policymaking by enhancing the political standing of the NPC and making the NPC an influential player in China's decisionmaking process. This does not mean that the legislative process in China has been democratized. The NPC is merely another bureaucratic player in a

---

[30] In the 1980s, senior leaders, including Deng Xiaoping and Peng Zeng, pushed for legal reforms, village elections, and the strengthening of the National People's Congress. Deng himself called for democratic reform in the mid-1980s as a means of overcoming bureaucratic resistance to economic reform. Regarding Peng's role in reforming the NPC, see Michael Dowdle, "The Constitutional Development and Operations of the National People's Congress," *Columbia Journal of Asian Law*, 11 (1997): 1–123.

[31] Wu Guoguang, *Political Reform Under Zhao Ziyang* (Taipei: Yuanjing Publishing Co., 1997).

[32] Tanner, *The Politics of Lawmaking in Post-Mao China*.

[33] Kevin O'Brien, *Reform Without Liberalization* (New York: Cambridge University Press, 1990).

decidedly authoritarian policymaking process.[34] Evidence shows that the NPC is, at best, a secondary bureaucratic player that routinely endorses the bills drafted by the executive branch. For example, the Standing Committee of the NPC rejected the bills proposed by the government only three times in 28 years.[35] Official figures also indicate that individual legislators play an insignificant role in law-making. For example, from 1983 to 1995 more than five thousand bills were proposed by delegates, but only 933 (18%) of them were referred to committees. There was no record that any of the proposed bills ever became law.[36]

In practical terms, the most visible progress in China's legislative reform is the hundreds of laws and resolutions issued by the NPC since the late 1970s. These laws have provided the legal framework for China's economic reform (about a third of all the laws passed since 1978 are classified as "economic laws" that govern commercial activities), as well as codified administrative rules and procedures (about half of the new laws are considered administrative laws). Compared with the Maoist era—during which Mao's personal edicts and the CCP's documents served as the supreme laws of the land—the new laws passed by the NPC were certainly a huge improvement, especially since they adopted many Western legal concepts. Yet Stanley Lubman, an authority on Chinese law, finds shortcomings in the laws and rules passed by the NPC. He believes that the language of these laws often is too vague and is intentionally designed to maximize the flexibility and discretion of the government rather than to constrain the power of the state.[37]

Legal Reform

The rule of law is the institutional foundation for sustainable long-run growth. As such, China's effort since 1976 to build a modern legal system is key to the success of Chinese economic reform.[38] Though the Chinese government likes to showcase its achievements in legal reform, any impact on protecting property and individual rights or on constraining the power of the ruling party and the state has been mixed. China has undeniably passed

---

[34] Tanner, *The Politics of Lawmaking in Post-Mao China*.

[35] These bills were the law on residents' committees in 1989, the highway law in 1999, and the draft law on the bankruptcy of state-owned enterprises in 1987.

[36] *Shidai zhuren* [Master of the Times], 7 (1999): 23.

[37] Stanley Lubman, "Bird in a Cage: Chinese Law Reform after Twenty Years," *Northwestern Journal of International Law and Business*, 20 (2000): 383–423.

[38] For two excellent studies of China's legal reform, see Pitman Potter, ed., *Domestic Law Reforms in Post-Mao China* (Armonk: M. E. Sharpe, 1994); and Stanley Lubman, ed., *China's Legal Reforms* (Oxford: Oxford University Press, 1996).

several hundred laws, made huge investments in raising the professional qualifications of its judges and lawyers, and improved judicial procedures, but the Chinese legal system—operating as it does under the strict controls imposed by the CCP—lacks the independence necessary to function as the guarantor of the rule of law.[39] Several key indicators suggest that legal reform began to lose momentum in the late 1990s. The growth of civil and administrative litigation has registered a net decline in recent years. The total number of civil and commercial cases fell from more than 5 million in 1999 to about 4.4 million in 2002 (a 12% decline over three years). The decrease in the number of administrative litigation cases (lawsuits filed against the government) was especially notable. The number of such lawsuits fell in 2002 to about 80,000, back to the level of 1996 (when court data indicated that plaintiffs could win or gain favorable settlements in two out of five cases).[40] Falling litigation may indicate the erosion of the public's confidence in the impartiality of the Chinese courts. One measurement is the rapid fall of plaintiffs' "win rate" in lawsuits filed against the government. In 1996, plaintiffs suing the government could expect to gain favorable court rulings and settlements in 41% of the cases. This rate fell, however, to 32% in 1999 and it plunged to 20.6% by 2002.[41] If anything, the courts have become less willing to rule against the government or to force it to settle with plaintiffs.

China's legal reform has lost momentum for one main reason: despite nearly three decades of institutional experiments, the Chinese legal system has not freed itself from the political dominance of the ruling CCP and, consequently, is deprived of the institutional independence and authority needed to perform its functions effectively. The CCP's political dominance can be seen throughout the organizational structure and routine operations of the courts. The CCP has a special political and legal committee (*zhengfa weiyuanhui*) headed by a senior party official who oversees the courts and law enforcement. The committee often determines the outcomes of major court cases. Candidates for the presidents and vice presidents of courts are nominated by the CCP. Local governments also have substantial control over the courts because the presidents and vice presidents of local courts are appointed by the local governments, which also control the budgets and personnel appointments of the courts. If the CCP's dominance has deeply politicized the judicial system, the significant influence of local governments

---

[39] Peerenboom gives a relatively upbeat assessment of China's legal reform in his book: Randall Peerenboom, *China's Long March toward Rule of Law* (New York: Cambridge University Press, 2002).

[40] *Law Yearbook of China, 2003*, (Beijing: *Zhongguo tongji chubanshe*, 2004), 149.

[41] Calculated from data supplied by *Zhongguo falü nianjian* [Law Yearbook of China], various years (Beijing: *Zhongfuo falü nianjian chubanshe*).

over the courts has fragmented the authority of the judiciary and greatly limited its effectiveness. Of note is that these two institutional flaws of the Chinese legal system are well-known, yet none of the legal reform measures implemented to date address these two defining features of the Chinese judiciary.

In retrospect, one should not be surprised by this outcome. The CCP's desire to maintain political monopoly is fundamentally incompatible with the nature of the rule of law. The party's primary objective for legal reform is to make the legal system more effective in serving the CCP's overall strategy of maintaining power through economic reform; therefore, legal reform will not be allowed to undermine party authority.

Village Elections

Of all the limited political reform initiatives, instituting village elections has been heralded as the most promising step toward genuine democratization (despite the fact that the elected villager are, legally, only civic groups empowered with self-government). Promoters of village elections, both in and outside China, argue that village elections make local governments more accountable, help protect the individual rights of villagers, improve local governance, and empower the peasantry.[42] Yet, seventeen years after village elections, significant controversy remains as to whether village elections have delivered their promises or substantively democratized politics at the grassroots level. Researchers have found that village elections have failed to empower the peasantry and to end the dominance of the CCP's cells in the villages. For example, local CCP bosses continued to control key levers of power, especially village finance and personnel appointments.[43]

To be sure, important progress has been made in advancing village-level democratization. This progress has resulted from both the political entrepreneurship of reformers within the government and the political pressure and innovation of villagers. For example, the draft law on village elections passed in 1988 had few useful provisions on how elections should be held. After rural voters experimented with and on their own adopted many important procedural innovations, the government eventually

---

[42] Kevin O'Brien and Lianjiang Li, "Accommodating Democracy in a One-Party State: Introducing Village Elections in China," *The China Quarterly*, 162 (2000): 465–89; Robert Pastor and Qingshan Tan, "The Meaning of China's Village Elections," *The China Quarterly*, 162 (2000): 490–512; and Allen Choate, "Local Governance in China: An Assessment of Villagers Committees," (Working Paper no. 1, The Asia Foundation, 1997).

[43] Oi and Rozelle, "Elections and Power: The Locus of Decision Making in Chinese Villages," *The China Quarterly*, 162 (2000): 513–39; and Björn Alpermann, "The Post-Election Administration of Chinese Villages," *The China Journal*, 46 (2001): 45–67.

revised many of these innovations into the law in 1998. Another important measure of progress in this regard is that—nearly two decades after the experiment was launched—village elections have become an established political institution in China, with most provinces having held more than three rounds of such elections by 2000. A survey conducted in 2002 shows that 83% of the villagers polled reported elections in their villages in 2002, compared with 76% in 1993, with voter turnout rising from 63% in 1993 to 69% in the 2002 poll.[44]

That village elections are now regularly held throughout China does not mean that these contests are genuinely competitive. In fact, many studies show a very mixed picture. If the baseline for measuring progress is whether multiple candidates compete in these elections, much improvement has been made. The percentage of villages having multi-candidate elections rose from 53 in 1993 to 70 in 2002. Yet this measurement does not fully reflect the competitiveness of village elections, since the local authorities can manipulate the nomination process to ensure that their choices get on the ballots. As a result, only 43% of the villages used the free primary method of nomination and 35% of villages adopted nomination procedures that violate the legal provisions on village elections. If the electoral provisions in the Organic Law on Village Committees are strictly applied, only 31% of the villages in China are in compliance.[45]

Since most village elections are manipulated by local officials, these elections have little effect on local governance.[46] Worse still, unelected local authorities and CCP party organizations also routinely usurp the power of financial control of villager committees and illegally dismiss elected village committee members. In one jurisdiction in Hubei province, 187 of the 329 village committee chairmen elected in September 1999 were illegally removed by township governments before their terms expired. Replacements were not elected but appointed—illegally—by local authorities. Similar incidents were reported in many other parts of China.[47] The most serious failure of village elections is that they have failed to counter the power of the CCP in rural China. Although having allowed village elections, the CCP is unwilling to cede power at the grassroots level. Consequently, elected villager committees are constantly engaged in a power struggle (mostly over the village's budgets and personnel decisions) with the village

---

[44] Tianjian Shi, "Election Reform in China" (unpublished manuscript, Department of Political Science, Duke University, 2004).

[45] Ibid.

[46] John James Kennedy, "The Face of 'Grassroots Democracy' in Rural China," *Asian Survey* 42, no. 3 (2002): 456–82.

[47] *Nanfang Zhoumo* [Southern Weekend], September 12, 2002.

CCP branches. In a study of 500 villages in Hunan, the elected villager committees were totally powerless in 40% of the villages surveyed because the CCP cells monopolized key decisionmaking power.[48] Another survey of 2,600 rural residents in 1999 found that local government officials and party organizations were perceived as more powerful than the newly elected villager committees.[49]

The results of China's political reform since the late 1970s have been disappointing but not unexpected. Except for the small group of liberals who lost power in the late 1980s, the CCP leadership has been dominated by political conservatives who steadfastly have resisted substantive political reforms that would have undermined the party's political supremacy. Since leadership choices determine the timing of democratic transition, the extremely limited progress toward a more democratic political system in China is predicted by the regime transition theory.[50] If the leadership had any incentive to open up the political system in the 1980s because of the strategic necessity of generating the needed momentum for economic reform, such incentives completely vanished in the 1990s when the economy began to take-off explosively. Instead of producing the desired democratizing effects, rapid economic transformation has enabled the CCP to strengthen hold on power.

Autocracy and Development: Why Politics Matter

Given the breathtaking economic growth China has attained under authoritarian rule during the reform era, the very question of whether the lack of political reform has been a drag on economic performance may seem odd, if not ludicrous. The record of nearly three decades of high growth is in itself testimony to many that China does not need democratizing reform to improve economic performance. If anything, this record proves the superiority of the authoritarian developmental state.

Economic growth is not, however, the only measure of the progress of a society. A political regime that is credited with achieving rapid economic growth can, nevertheless, conceivably perform poorly on many indicators of governance or have paid enormous social costs for high rates of growth. More important, the quality of growth must also be taken into account when

---

[48] *Zhongguo gaige (nongcunban)* [China Reform, rural edition], 2 (2003): 15.

[49] David Zweig, "Democratic Values, Political Structures, and Alternative Politics in Greater China," *Peaceworks*, no. 44, July 2002, 45.

[50] Guillermo O'Donnell and Philippe Schmitter, *Transitions from Authoritarian Rule: Tentative Conclusions about Uncertain Democracies* (Baltimore: Johns Hopkins University Press, 1986).

evaluating any country's economic performance.[51] Obviously, a society that has achieved high rates of growth at the expense of massive environmental decay, rising inequality, rampant corruption, and underinvestment in public goods cannot be judged to have delivered superior performance. When this yardstick—quality-adjusted growth—is applied, China's record begins to lose luster.[52] Although establishing rigorous relationships between a certain regime type and quality-adjusted growth performance may be methodologically difficult, it is possible, at least in the Chinese case, to trace many societal ills to the strategies and policies adopted by the CCP to maximize its chances of political survival. This section explores, mostly at the theoretical level, why and how autocracy impedes sustainable economic growth.

A post-communist authoritarian developmental state, such as the post-Mao Chinese state, is constrained by the overriding objective of delivering and maintaining rapid economic growth on the one hand (because economic performance is critical to political survival) and by the inherent institutional flaws of autocracy that undermine efficiency, distort incentives, and exacerbate the principal-agent problem on the other. Economic growth may provide the authoritarian developmental state the fiscal and technocratic resources to offset the effects of the pathologies of an authoritarian regime.[53] It is doubtful, however, that an authoritarian developmental state can grow out of these flaws without undertaking the necessary political reforms that will remove these underlying growth-limiting institutional obstacles.

Constituency Maintenance, Inequity, and Inefficiency

Contrary to conventional wisdom, an authoritarian developmental state is not immune to capture by interest groups. The differences between state capture under autocracy and state capture under democracy lie mainly in the rules under which politically powerful interest groups influence the policies of the state and the degree of transparency of the political process in which state capture takes place.[54] Maintaining the support of key political constituencies is a particularly tough challenge for post-communist

---

[51] High-quality growth is that which is achieved with relatively less environmental degradation, socioeconomic inequality, neglect of basic needs, and corruption.

[52] The quality of economic growth can be measured by social costs (inequality and corruption) and environmental costs. High growth accompanied by high social and environmental costs is low quality growth. See Minxin Pei, "The Dark Side of China's Rise," *Foreign Policy* (March/April 2006): 32–40.

[53] The rise of technocracy in China is viewed by most scholars as a positive development. See Cheng Li, *China's Leaders* (New York: Rowman and Littlefield, 2001).

[54] Joel Hellman and Daniel Kaufmann, "Confronting the Challenge of State Capture in Transition Economies: Oligarchy and Economic Reform," *Finance and Development* 38, no. 3 (2001): 31–42.

autocracies. Lacking charismatic leadership and ideological appeal, a post-communist authoritarian regime has few instruments to motivate its supporters and retain their loyalty—other than to provide them with costly economic privileges and patronage. The imperative of regime survival thus necessitates policies favoring the key constituencies of the authoritarian developmental state, such as the security apparatus, the state bureaucracy, the ruling party's core membership, and selected social elites. These policies, designed to secure the support of the elite, have serious effects on both social equity and economic efficiency.

In an elitist authoritarian regime, public policies unavoidably favor the politically powerful and discriminate against the weak.[55] Unless motivated by enlightened self-interest for its long-term survival (rarely seen among authoritarian regimes), an elitist autocracy faces insurmountable obstacles to taking effective measures (such as fiscal redistribution or human capital investment targeting the underprivileged groups) to mitigate the effects of their policies on social injustice. In elitist autocracies in which the state controls valuable economic resources (such as land, credit, and under-priced state-owned assets) and access to commercial opportunities (permission to enter restricted markets or establish new businesses), politically privileged groups can readily turn their access to power into easy acquisition of private wealth, a practice commonly known as crony-capitalism.[56] Needless to say, the redistribution of assets under crony-capitalism further entrenches the underlying socioeconomic structures that produce inequality and injustice. Based on available data from China, pro-elite policies are among the contributing factors for rising inequality in the last three decades. Estimates from various sources suggest that the Gini coefficient of income has increased from 0.28 to around 0.45 during this period.[57]

Economically, pro-elite policies could harm growth because rising public frustrations with social injustice breed political instability.[58] Politically, pro-elite policies tend to perpetuate a vicious cycle: the more dependent an authoritarian regime is on elitist constituencies, the more privileges the regime tends to provide to these favored groups to maintain

---

[55] The CCP under Jiang Zemin became an elitist regime. See Cheng Li, "One Party, Two Systems: Bipartisanship in the Making?" paper presented at the Carnegie Endowment for International Peace, November 2, 2005.

[56] For a discussion on crony-capitalism see David Kang, *Crony Capitalism: Corruption and Development in South Korea and the Philippines* (New York: Cambridge University Press, 2002).

[57] One study by the Ministry of Finance in 2003 shows that the Gini index was 0.28 in 1991 and 0.458 in 2000. See Lian Yuming ed., *China by the Numbers* (Beijing: Zhongguo shidai jingji chubanshe 2004), 354. Also see OECD, "China in the Global Economy; Income Disparities in China: An OECD Perspective," (Paris: OECD, 2004).

[58] Alberto Alesina and Roberto Perotti "Income Distribution, Political Instability, and Investment." *European Economic Review* 40, no. 6 (1996).

their support, and the more fearful of democratization the ruling elites grow because liberalizing politics would threaten not only their political power but also their deeply entrenched economic privileges. As a result, elitist authoritarian regimes typically apply more repression, not pro-poor redistributive policies, to deal with rising social discontent.

Policies favoring a small group of elites that constitute the core supporters of an authoritarian regime also harm economic efficiency for two reasons. First, the state must devote enormous fiscal resources to provide the material privileges expected by these elites. For example, in China, administrative expenditures accounted for 19% of the total government spending in 2003, exceeding the combined government spending on education, health, and scientific research.[59] Second, the authoritarian regime must also protect the economic interests of these elites both by preserving their rent-seeking opportunities and by supplying them with various subsidies to maintain the viability of their businesses. In the Chinese case, evidence of this tendency can be seen in both the size of the political patronage of the CCP and the financial performance of the state-owned enterprises (SOE). According to official data, the CCP appoints 81% of the managers of SOEs and 56% of all enterprise managers. In 2003, 5.3 million CCP officials—about 8% of the CCP's total membership and 16% of its urban members—held executive positions in SOEs.[60] The flawed property rights and political patronage result in enormous waste and inefficiency, as reflected in the miserable financial performance of SOEs. For example, the median rate of return on assets was a only 1.5% for SOEs in 2003. As a group, more than 35% of SOEs lose money and one in six has negative equity.[61]

Incentive Structure and Social Deficits

Without question, the incentive structure of any political system motivates its ruling elites and determines their responsiveness to public needs. In a democratic system in which the ruling elites are periodically held to account for their performance by the electoral system, these elites have the incentive to respond to the needs of the voters or the interest groups that can influence electoral outcomes. In an authoritarian system, on the other hand, the ruling elites are held accountable by their superiors in a bureaucratic hierarchy. As a result, authoritarian ruling elites are conditioned to respond not to public needs but to the top policy priorities

---

[59] *Statistical Yearbook of China 2004*, 293.

[60] *China News*, http://www.chinanews.com.cn, October 20, 2003 and June 3, 2004; and *Dangzheng ganbu wenzhai* [Digest for Party and Government Officials] 6 (2002): 48.

[61] See OECD, *Economic Survey: China* (Paris: OECD 2005), 40.

valued by their bureaucratic superiors, who determine their job security and political careers. In pre-reform communist systems, as in Castro's Cuba and Maoist China, the regimes' preferences for providing public goods (health and education in particular) over ensuring economic growth can result in higher levels of human development attainment relative to income.[62] Once the top priorities of the regime change from favoring social investment to emphasizing rapid economic growth, however, the ruling elites at all levels of the system rationally alter their behavior and concentrate their efforts on tasks that will meet the growth targets expected of them by their superiors. In the Chinese case, such a shift of priorities has resulted in an excessive increase in investments in fixed assets (needed both for growth and for establishing a tangible record of managerial competence of the local elites), but at the expense of a significant reduction in social investments.

The extent of the massive shift can be seen from data on government expenditures. In the 1990s—the decade following the Tiananmen crackdown in 1989 and the collapse of communist regimes in the former Soviet bloc—maintaining high rates of growth was the centerpiece of the CCP's survival strategy. In this decade of China's awe-inspiring economic take-off, however, the state's social investments plunged. Under the pretext of "marketization," the government systematically reduced its role even in areas (such as public health and primary education) where market forces simply did not exist. The government's spending on education fell nearly twenty percentage points as a share of total education spending in the 1990s. Social policy became highly regressive as well. For instance, China's rural residents, the country's most disadvantaged and poorest group, have to pay out of their meager income 78% of all the education funding (the central government provides only 1% of the funding for rural education).[63] Investment in public health has also suffered. In the 1980s, the Chinese government funded 36% of all health-care costs. By 2000, however, the share of government spending in total health-care expenditures had fallen to less than 15%. As in the case of education, China's health-care policy is regressive to the extreme, providing the ruling elites with high-quality medical services for free and forcing the poorest to pay for their own health-care needs. In terms of financial equity, a report by the World Health Organization rates China's health-care system higher than only two countries—Brazil and Myanmar.[64] A majority of the population are denied access to the health-care system for financial reasons. The Chinese Ministry of Health disclosed in late 2005 that two-thirds of the

---

[62] This can be seen in the ranking of human development for China, Vietnam, and Cuba in the United Nations Development Program's *Human Development Report*.

[63] Lian, *China by the Numbers*, 385–86.

[64] The World Health Organization, *World Health Report*, 2000.

population do not have any type of health insurance and that about half of the people who become ill do not seek professional medical attention or treatment.[65] Education and public health are not the only areas in which the shift in regime priorities has led to sustained underinvestment and neglect. Potentially far more dangerous is the massive environmental degradation that has ensued as the elites have pursued high economic growth at all cost.[66]

Since the Chinese leadership headed by Hu Jintao came to power in early 2003, the issue of China's social deficits has become a highly contentious topic. Sensing potential political gains from this debate, the new leadership has announced a series of measures to reduce rural taxation and increase spending on health care, education, and infrastructure in the countryside. Judging, however, by the relatively small amounts of new spending on social investment, this step, although welcome, will make only a small difference in reducing the accumulated social deficits.[67]

Most notable is that in the raging debate on social deficits in China the most sensitive political topic—how to reform the political incentive structure so that the local elites would behave more responsively to public needs—is studiously avoided. The modest spending increases are accompanied neither by administrative reforms to streamline a bloated and parasitic rural bureaucracy nor by new measures to empower rural residents politically so that they can hold local elites accountable for inadequate delivery of social services. The omission of these political reforms makes reorientation of the priorities of local governments more difficult, thereby ensuring the continuing accumulation of social deficits. Blaming local elites—the proverbial scapegoats—for their failure to make the necessary social investments would, however, be unfair because they are merely responding at the local level to the incentive structure embedded in China's developmental autocracy. In other words, as long as the ruling elites in Beijing deem continued high economic growth more important to regime survival than increased social investments—and continue to evaluate local elites accordingly—local officials will behave rationally by focusing on growth despite ballooning social deficits.

---

[65] *China News*, January 6, 2006 and Dec. 22, 2005, http://www.chinanews.com.cn; and *China Newsweek*, August 22, 2005, 24. For the latest review of China's health-care system, see the World Health Organization, *A Health Situation Assessment of the People's Republic of China*, http://www. wpro.who.int/NR/rdonlyres/0267DCE8-07AB-437A-8B01-03D474D922CD/0/hsa_en.pdf.

[66] See Elizabeth Economy, *The River Runs Black: The Environmental Challenge to China's Future* (Ithaca: Cornell University Press, 2003); and Vaclav Smil, *China's Past, China's Future* (London: RoutledgeCurzon, 2003).

[67] The new leadership announced a 13% increase, or $5.6 billion, for rural spending in 2006. See Edward Cody, "China Plans to Boost Spending in Rural Areas," *The Washington Post*, March 5, 2006, A19.

Information Asymmetry, Monitoring of Agents, and Corruption

The apparent strength of an authoritarian developmental state is its capacity to mobilize the resources (mainly fiscal revenue) needed to increase investment in the economic sectors targeted by the government as engines of growth. The literature on the developmental state focuses on the state's capacity to overcome the collective action problem and market failure as the key to generating above-trend growth in late-developers. Unfortunately, the theory of the developmental state overlooks or assumes away another issue—the principal-agent problem. Like all large organizations, an autocratic developmental state relies on individual bureaucratic agents to implement its policies. Given the inherent problems of information asymmetry, an authoritarian state has great difficulty in monitoring and policing its own agents. Theoretically, authoritarian regimes should have greater problems of information asymmetry and difficulties in policing their agents because of the absence of a free press, opposition parties, and a strong civil society. In practical terms, an authoritarian developmental state with a serious problem of information asymmetry and a weak capacity to monitor and police its agents unavoidably will lose the ability to control the corruption by the same agents.[68] In other words, corruption by the insiders of the regime is the Achilles' heel of an authoritarian developmental state.

Post-Mao China is no exception to this rule. As a key part of reforms, China decentralized the control rights of the state's property (land, factories, and natural resources) and transferred significant administrative power to the lower echelons of the government. Such decentralization was meant to encourage local elites to take greater initiatives and increase economic efficiency. Whereas decentralization may have improved the incentive structure for local elites, it was not, however, accompanied by institutional reforms that would have increased the state's capacity to monitor and police these agents as well. To make matters worse, the failure to introduce democratic reforms in general and the suppression of the freedom of the press and civil society in particular have allowed newly empowered local elites to form rent-seeking collusive alliances among themselves (the most egregious manifestation of which is the local mafia states). Authoritarian developmental states are, therefore, always at risk of degenerating into authoritarian predatory states.[69]

---

[68] For studies on how the Chinese government evaluates its officials, see Barry Naughton and Dali Yang, eds., *Holding China Together: Diversity and National Integration in the Post-Deng Era* (New York: Cambridge University Press, 2004); and Susan Whiting, *Power and Wealth in Rural China* (New York: Cambridge University Press, 2000).

[69] For a discussion on state degeneration, see Minxin Pei, *China's Trapped Transition: The Limits of Developmental Autocracy* (Cambridge: Harvard University Press, 2006).

Academic studies indicate that such a degenerative process is quite advanced in China.[70] Official data and countless anecdotes in the Chinese press also provide several disturbing clues to the extent of official corruption. First, the amount of wealth looted by corrupt officials has increased dramatically, as indicated by the "large-sum cases" prosecuted by the court, which doubled in number from 1992 to 2002. Second, corruption is reaching the higher levels of the ruling elites. For example, the number of officials at the county-level and above prosecuted each year by the government rose from 1,386 in 1992 to 2,925 in 2002.[71] Third, collusive corruption involving a group of officials now has become widespread. Select regional data suggests that these cases account for 30–60% of all corruption cases.[72] In an authoritarian developmental state, collusive corruption is inevitable, being the optimal survival strategy for local elites who face no democratic constraints from below and know how to use the advantage of information asymmetry to deceive their superiors. In such an environment, denunciation by other local elites poses the most dangerous threat. The optimal strategy for eliminating this threat is to cooperate—indeed collude—with these elites.

The more that an authoritarian regime must depend on the same agents, whose corruption is endangering the long-term survival of the regime, to maintain the regime's security and power, the more the autocracy is ill-positioned to fight corruption; a serious anti-corruption drive will likely turn many of the regime's most loyal agents into its fierce foes and put the survival of the regime at great risk. This enforcement dilemma is clearly reflected in the Chinese government's half-hearted approach to combating corruption: as shown by official data, most corrupt officials face no serious punishment.

On average, each year in the 1990s 140,000 Communist Party officials and members were caught in corruption scandals, but 82% received no punishment and only 5.6% were criminally prosecuted. Despite the new leadership's vow to eradicate corruption, in 2004, of the 170,850 CCP

---

[70] Yan Sun, *Corruption and Market in Contemporary China* (Ithaca: Cornell University Press, 2004); Xiaobo Lu, "From Rank-Seeking to Rent-Seeking: Changing Administrative Ethos and Corruption in Reform China," *Crime, Law and Social Change* 32, no. 4 (1999): 347–70; and Xiaobo Lu, "Booty Socialism, Bureau-preneurs, and the State in Transition: Organizational Corruption in China," *Comparative Politics* 32, no. 3 (2000): 273–94.

[71] *Zhongguo falü nianjian*, various years.

[72] http://www.jcrb.com.cn, Feb. 27, 2002; *China News*, Feb. 25, 2002, http://www.chinanews.com.cn; and http://www.jcrb.com, Nov. 5, 2002.

members whom government investigators found to have engaged in wrong-doing, only 4,915 were prosecuted.[73]

Conclusion: Risk Factors for Future Growth

As discussed in the preceding section, certain growth-inhibiting characteristics are embedded in an authoritarian developmental state. Economic growth will be difficult to sustain unless these intrinsic characteristics of authoritarianism are removed or their ill effects mitigated through political reform. Undertaking political reform—especially democratizing reform—would, however, at the same time endanger the survival of the authoritarian regime itself, though such reform may improve the prospects of long-run economic growth. Understandably, few authoritarian regimes willingly reform themselves out of existence unless the alternative is imminent demise. Based on this perspective, the current Chinese leadership's uncompromising stance *against* political reform is completely rational, and the CCP will unlikely initiate political reform without first experiencing a powerful political or economic shock.

Yet the institutional flaws of autocracy materially affect economic performance and social stability. Maintaining the status quo for another ten to fifteen years in China will most likely result in faltering growth due to persistent economic inefficiency, rising systemic risks, and accelerated political decay.

Persistent Economic Inefficiency

To the extent that the CCP must maintain a huge political patronage as its base of support, systemic economic waste and inefficiency will be a significant drag on economic performance. The most obvious symptoms of such waste and inefficiency will be chronic financial hemorrhaging in SOEs, massive overcapacity, and misguided investment projects built more to burnish the record of local elites than to generate real economic returns. At the aggregate level, China's banking system, through which the CCP allocates investment capital, will bear the brunt of systemic inefficiency.[74] The system will continue to use cheap or free credit to sustain politically favored sectors and firms, while at the same time discriminating against the private

---

[73] *Zhongguo jian jianchabao* [China Prosecutors' Gazette], September 25, 1997, 1–4; and *China News*, Jan. 21, 2005, http://www.chinanews.com.cn.

[74] *Putting China's Capital to Work: The Value of Financial System Reform*, McKinsey Global Institute, May 2006, http://www.mckinsey.com/mgi/publications/china_capital/index.asp; Richard Podpiera, "Progress in China's Banking Sector Reform: Has Bank Behavior Changed?" *IMF Working Paper* 06/71 (Washington, D.C.: International Monetary Fund, 2006).

sector. Given the logic of political patronage and crony-capitalism, the state will keep protecting its monopolies in the most important economic sectors (such as finance, energy, natural resources, transportation, and telecom services). The allocation of factor inputs, most importantly land, will be determined not by market forces but by government fiat. The consequences of these systemic inefficiencies will be low returns on invested capital and an extremely fragile financial system saddled with impaired assets. Inefficiencies caused by flawed political institutions may not immediately drag down growth as long as China has strong economic fundamentals, especially high savings and investment rates. At the moment, China boasts a domestic savings rate above 40% of GDP and attracts $50 billion of foreign direct investment per year. This pool of capital allows China to maintain an investment rate in excess of 40% of GDP and to generate robust growth even in an inefficient economic system. China, however, will unlikely be able to maintain such a high savings rate forever. Demographic changes around 2015 will increase both the population of retirees and the dependency ratio, inevitably causing the savings rate to fall. The fragility of the financial system will also prompt domestic investors to transfer wealth abroad, especially at a point when China's capital control becomes even more porous or is removed.

Rising Systemic Risks

A fast-growing economy that is simultaneously experiencing a rapid increase in inequality, massive environmental degradation, and social deficits will unavoidably accumulate systemic risks. At the current rate of increase, socioeconomic inequality in China could soon reach the level commonly associated with Latin American countries such as Mexico. High inequality may slow down economic growth both by limiting the growth of domestic consumption (since the poor will lack the purchasing power) and by increasing instability and lawlessness (as inequality exacerbates social frustrations and even legitimizes criminal behavior directed at the wealthy). Fearful of political instability and social disorder, investors would lose confidence and move their capital elsewhere. Environmental degradation poses a much greater risk. Estimates put the cost of environmental damage in China at roughly 8% of GDP.[75] With severely polluted major rivers, depleted underground aquifers, and inefficient use of water, China is experiencing enormous water-related environmental strains. The economic costs of water shortage, already severe, will likely exact a high price on growth performance, especially in the northern plains of China.

---

[75] The World Bank, *China 2020* (Washington, D.C.: The World Bank, 1997), 77.

Environmental degradation could spark political turmoil and social conflict as well, as its victims blame the state for inaction or even complicity and use desperate means to protect their livelihoods. The likelihood of an ecological disaster—such as a large-scale toxic spill polluting a major waterway, massive floods, or prolonged drought—increases dramatically in this high-risk environment. Even if such nightmarish scenarios fail to materialize, repairing the environmental damage that already has occurred will require tens of billions of dollars in spending, forcing the government to divert capital away from fixed investment and slow down economic growth. The additional health-care costs resulting from the effects of pollution will also be considerable.

The Chinese government's neglect of education and public health could endanger future growth prospects as well. This neglect obviously will result in a population that is not as well-educated, healthy, or productive. More important, underinvestment in education and public health tend to hurt the most disadvantaged and vulnerable segments of the population, thus directly contributing to inequality (with all its attendant ill consequences). The risks of a major public health disaster, such as an uncontrollable epidemic, will increase significantly. As demonstrated by China's faltering fight against the spread of AIDS and stumble in responding to the 2003 SARS epidemic, future public health shocks (for example, an avian flu pandemic) are likely and could be devastating in terms both of human lives and of economic costs.

Accelerated Political Decay

The ability of the CCP to overcome its manifold challenges depends to a critical degree on whether the party can effectively stop and reverse the political decay that, based on the symptoms and scope of corruption, appears to be well-advanced. The record of autocratic regimes in combating corruption, however, inspires little confidence. Because of several factors— dysfunctional mechanisms of political accountability, the suppression of both freedom of press and civil liberties, and the rule by man rather than by law—a monopolistic ruling party is extremely unlikely to be able to restrain the predatory behavior of its agents without introducing reforms that would empower civil society or strengthen the rule of law. If such is the case in China, the process of political decay will only accelerate in the decade to come.

Accelerated political decay inevitably will sap China's economic vigor. Corruption will weaken China's most vital economic organs, especially financial services (including banking) and infrastructure, which are critical to future growth. Shady deals in the privatization of state-owned assets and in real estate development will deprive the state of much-needed revenues while enriching well-connected individuals. Pervasive crony-capitalistic practices will protect the vested interests of rent-seekers, thus limiting market competition and perpetuating inefficiency. Political decay also will undermine the Chinese state's capacity to cope with environmental degradation and public health crises because a corrupt officialdom habitually conceals information, covers up mistakes, and takes slow and inadequate actions against these threats to public welfare.

Ironically, the greatest victim of accelerated political decay would be the CCP itself, as the ruling party. The spread of collusive corruption within the party will fragment the CCP's authority and allow local elites to usurp party power. Once entrenched, networks formed by collusive officials would grow resistant to purges and anti-corruption campaigns launched by the central government. As its agents' own parochial interests diverge from the corporate interests of the CCP, the ruling party also will face increasing difficulty in implementing policies, having neither the means to motivate party agents nor the coercive instruments to force compliance. To the extent that corruption worsens socioeconomic inequality and de-legitimizes the ruling elites, political decay will further alienate the Chinese people from the CCP and further fuel social frustrations. Enfeebled from within and unloved by its own people, the CCP would be precariously positioned to weather the political and economic shocks made more likely by the process of accelerated political decay itself.

We may thus rule out the scenario of "Liberal Dream" (a strong democratic China transformed through peaceful evolution) and that of "Authoritarian Nightmare" (an economically and militarily powerful China ruled by a thoroughly unreconstructed autocracy). Given the pathologies embedded in a post-communist authoritarian regime, the most likely scenario for China would be either a frail autocratic giant or a weak new democracy. Yet the current policies of the West are based either on the "Liberal Dream" scenario (which justifies engagement) or on the "Authoritarian Nightmare" scenario (which calls for covert containment or, euphemistically, "strategic hedging"). Little serious thought or intellectual exercise appears to have been devoted to scenarios of a weak China, either democratic or authoritarian. Has China's past economic performance been so dazzling that those in the West have grown complacent and dismissive of China's underlying institutional flaws and frailties? If so, such complacency is irresponsible because these flaws—now more than just obvious—will inevitably derail China's rise.

For the global economy in general, and China's chief trading partners in particular, an economically faltering China would have serious practical consequences. Many of the rosy long-term scenarios of the growth in demand within China would not materialize. The price of commodities would likely fall as well. The much-feared oil shortage, based almost entirely on China's unquenchable thirst, would unlikely come true. In geopolitical terms, the critical bilateral relationships now cultivated by China with African, Latin American, and Asian countries likely would undergo gradual erosion; an economically stagnant China would not be able to underwrite these relationships with economic benefits (such as direct investments, aid, and imports), thus disappointing the countries in these regions that may have counted on China as an economic counterweight to the West. China would see its geopolitical influence quickly plummet in these regions. In Asia, China might find itself experiencing the same setback dealt to Japan after the bursting of the bubble economy in the 1990s. Beijing's capacity to wield economic power to gain influence in Asia would likely be undercut severely. Should India's economic rise continue at its current rapid pace, Asia's regional leadership role would migrate from Beijing to New Delhi.

Similarly, the business community in the West would experience a rude awakening as a result of such a scenario. Having bet heavily on China both as a source of demand for their products and as an offshore manufacturing center, these companies could find that strategies pursued on this basis fail to deliver the promised economic rewards. Subsequent re-thinking of the China market by these companies could lead to a dramatic curtailment of direct investment in, and sourcing from, China—a step that, while surely further exacerbating China's economic woes, nonetheless would fully reflect the habitual fickleness of foreign capital. China's relations with the West would likely deteriorate, not merely as a result of Beijing's declining economic importance but also because disappointed Western businesses would be much less willing to defend China's interests in their local capitals. Depending on the specific scenarios under which China's economic decline were to unfold, Beijing quite conceivable might accuse Western businesses and investors (especially hedge funds) of conspiring against the Chinese economy and causing the decline, a strategy that would help focus the attention of the Chinese public elsewhere but could further alienate Western businessmen and their politicians.

China's economic faltering would be a mixed blessing for the United States. The security threat envisioned by the Pentagon's planners would disappear, with China's military modernization grinding to a halt due to a lack of resources. Washington would no longer fear China's expanding influence in Latin America, the Middle East, Southeast Asia, and Africa.

The United States, however, would suffer economically. Because of the close economic interdependence between China and the United States, any significant economic decline in China would diminish U.S. access to markets, cheap credit, and profitable investments. More important would be that China's weakness would stimulate new non-traditional security threats that would emerge—potentially including risks of proliferation of weapons of mass destruction, massive environmental degradation, public health disasters, drug trafficking, illegal migration, money laundering, and counterfeiting. In many respects, the United States would have more difficulty addressing these threats since all originate within China and are protected by Chinese borders. Unless Washington finds a strong partner in the Chinese government, the United States would have few effective tools to contain these threats directly.

Since the West's economic and security interests would suffer significantly should China's economy falter as a result of the country's political stagnation, the strategic interests of the West would be best served by a rethinking of the current approach to China and an adjustment to the strategy of focusing on economic engagement as the principal instrument of integrating China into the global community. The current approach, though having yielded rich dividends in the last three decades, also has shown its limits, especially in helping transform the Chinese political system. A new approach, emphasizing China's domestic political reform as a benchmark of its integration with the West, would better serve Western interests. Western governments and businesses would do well to work as partners, not adversaries, to better protect long-term interests in China; rather than hoping for modernization-induced political change, the new course would aggressively promote democracy, human rights, and the rule of law.

EXECUTIVE SUMMARY

This chapter examines how economic interdependence has shaped the emergence of new great powers, as well as the responses of existing powers to their rise, and explores how these historical patterns might apply to 21st century Asia, particularly to relations among the U.S., China, and India.

MAIN ARGUMENT:

- In the last 500 years, no new great power has managed to evade substantial warfare around the time of its entry into elite status.

- Economic interdependence is hardly a "silver bullet" guaranteed to pacify interstate conflicts. Though it may constrain conflict escalation processes, interdependence also generates serious economic frictions that can easily offset or overwhelm its conflict-suppressing effects.

POLICY IMPLICATIONS:

- China's compliance with trade commitments needs to be monitored and enforced; little is to be gained, however, by bilateralizing economic frictions. In particular, U.S. legislation aimed at China-specific trade and exchange rate regulation and executive branch punitive actions directed at China are best avoided. If Chinese leaders lower their estimates of the future benefits of trade and cross investment, then economic interdependence will be less likely to constrain their political and military behavior.

- While the U.S.-Indian rapprochement is a welcome development, tighter integration of India into the U.S. strategic network, bolstering India's strategic capabilities, and overt attempts to use India as a strategic counterweight to help contain China carry the risk of triggering unwanted Chinese countermeasures.

- If the U.S. should fail to innovate on a virtually continuous basis in the 21st century the country will be faced with ongoing losses of market shares and employment to hard-charging, low-cost challengers, such as China and India, as they converge on the industries associated with the last cluster of technological innovations.

Will Economic Interdependence Encourage China's and India's Peaceful Ascent?

David P. Rapkin and William R. Thompson

How have incumbent great powers responded to emerging challengers seeking to break into, or move up, the great power ranks? How might these responses have been shaped by considerations of economic interdependence? There likely are a number of approaches to answering these questions. Lacking a well-documented theory of great power ascent conditioned by economic interdependence, however, one approach is to examine systematically earlier episodes of great power transitions. The point of such an exercise is to extract generalizable information about elite upward mobility in interdependent circumstances. A major operative assumption is that previous behavior could have some applicability both to the contemporary world and to the immediate future despite obvious contextual changes in degrees of interdependence and lethality over the past several centuries.[1] This chapter thus aims to uncover historical patterns in the responses to challenges among interdependent actors and to explore how these patterns might apply to 21st century interactions with Asia, where we find an incumbent system leader (or global power), one great power, and another seeking great power status (the United States, China, and India, respectively). What historical lessons, with special emphasis on

David P. Rapkin is Associate Professor, University of Nebraska, where he has served as department chair and graduate chair. He has also been a visiting professor at Tsukuba University in Japan during 1988–90 and 1996–98. He can be reached at <drapkin2@unl.edu>.

William R. Thompson is Rogers Professor of Political Science at Indiana University, Bloomington and has served as president of the International Studies Association (2005–06). His most recent books are *Puzzles of the Democratic Peace* (with Karen Rasler, 2005) and *Globalization and Global History* (co-edited with Barry Gills, 2006). He can be reached at <wthompso@indiana.edu>.

[1] Economic interdependence and lethality, generally, have increased over the past five hundred years, but both substantial interdependence and lethality already were in evidence around 1500.

this volume's economic interdependence theme, might point toward ways to reduce (or increase) the probability that future transition processes involving these three states will be as violent as many (though not all) such transitions have been in the past?

To address these questions, the balance of the chapter is divided int) six sections. The first section provides historical evidence substantiating the violent character of great power ascensions. The next section focuses on economic interdependence: should interdependence matter to the question of whether ascensions are violent? The empirical evidence on the claim that economic interdependence is a powerful constraint on conflict escalation, however, is less supportive than one might expect. Nor is economic interdependence best viewed as a single process; it actually is better construed as encompassing a number of different processes, some of which may constrain conflict while others exacerbate tensions. The question then is: what is the net effect likely to be? The third section delineates four important sources of economic friction that have served as obstacles to the emergence of great powers insofar as these four factors appear to have offset any pacifying effects of economic interdependence in prior great power transitions. The fourth section assesses the relevance of these obstacles to foreseeable 21st century transitions involving the United States, China, and India. The next-to-last section focuses on two 21st century departures from the regularities observed in previous periods of transition: the dissymmetry of U.S.-China economic interdependence and U.S. moves to facilitate India's emergence as a great power. A consideration of the policy implications for the United States concludes the essay.

Violent Conflict and the Emergence of Great Powers

The history of status mobility at the apex of the international system is characterized quite demonstrably by considerable violence. Upwardly mobile states invariably have had to fight their way into the elite subset of powers referred to as great or major powers. States that ascend to the status of lead economy in the world system also have had to fight to maintain that status. The consistency of the record does not necessarily imply that contemporary or future states will have to fight because their predecessors have done so in the past. The record does suggest, however, that there is ample reason to anticipate conflict being associated with the emergence of new powers.

There are fairly easy ways to check this generalization. One approach involves looking at the roster of states designated as great powers over the past five hundred years. Jack S. Levy provides the following list of great powers at his chosen 1495 starting date: France, England/Great Britain, Spain, Austria, and the Ottoman Empire.[2] The Netherlands joined in 1609, Sweden in 1617, Russia in 1721, Prussia/Germany in 1740, Italy in 1861, the United States in 1898, Japan in 1905, and China in 1949.[3] While it is easy to quarrel about the validity of some entries and the absence of a few others, this list is highly representative of the powers that international relations specialists consider to be the political-military elite of the past half-millennium. The list is amended here only slightly for immediate purposes by treating the 1870–71 transformation of Prussia into Germany as a new great power.

This list will be used as a guideline in asking what happened when new great powers emerged. **Table 1** summarizes the conflicts that occurred within twenty-five years both before and after the year a new great power entered the elite list.[4]

Nine new great power entries are listed in **Table 1**. The table shows that no newly emerged great power managed to evade participation in extensive warfare. No single reason explains this rather unambiguous outcome, yet neither is each great power's story entirely unique. Instead, three factors seem most prominent. The most overarching factor is that great powers have operated like Mafioso hit men. To gain status, they have had to first "make their bones"—in organized crime parlance, kill someone. Among great powers, making one's bones means defeating another state in combat. The target state need not be a great power but this certainly helps. If the opponent is a very strong power, victory is not absolutely necessary. Merely demonstrating that a state can hold its own against major power competition may suffice—as in the case of seventeenth century Netherlands' long struggle with Spain or twentieth century China's clashes with the United States and the Soviet Union. Otherwise, the victory should be a very clear-cut demonstration of the new elite's military power capabilities (as in the cases of Sweden, Russia, Prussia/Germany, the United States, and Japan). Only Italy never really satisfied this criterion and, as a consequence, that country's status as a great power was always considered suspect.[5]

---

[2] Jack S. Levy, *War in the Modern Great Power System, 1495–1975* (Lexington: University Press of Kentucky, 1983), 48. Austria dropped out of the great power ranks in 1918, the Ottoman Empire in 1699, and Spain in 1808.

[3] According to Levy, the Netherlands left the great power system in 1713, Sweden in 1721, Italy in 1943, and Japan in 1945.

[4] Given the assumption that states listed as great powers in 1495 entered the great power list at some point prior to 1495, these states have been excluded from this examination of new entries.

[5] See, for example, R.J.B. Bosworth, *Italy, the Least of the Great Powers: Italian Foreign Policy before the First World War* (Cambridge: Cambridge University Press, 2005).

TABLE 1   Warfare and entry into the great power ranks

Great power	Entry date	Warfare within 25 years before and after entry into great power ranks
The Netherlands	1609	• Dutch revolt from late 1560s • English intervention in 1585 • Spanish intervention in France, 1589 • Dutch war with Spain renewed in 1621 ending a truce begun in 1609
Sweden	1617	• War with Russia, 1570–95 • Polish invasion, 1592–98 • War with Poland over Livonia, 1600–11 • War with Russia, 1613–17 • War with Poland, 1617–29 • "Bloodless war" with Poland, 1634–53 • Swedish intervention in Thirty Years' War, 1630–48
Russia	1721	• Russo-Turkish war, 1695–1700 • Great Northern War, 1700–21 • War with Persia, 1722–23 • War of the Polish Succession, 1733–38 • Austro-Russian-Turkish war, 1736–39 • War with Sweden, 1741–43
Prussia	1740	• War of Austrian Succession, 1740–48 • Seven Years' War, 1756–63
Italy	1861	• Italian War of Independence, 1848–49 • Crimean War, 1854–56 • War with Austria, 1859 • Italo-Roman war, 1860 • Italo-Sicilian war, 1860 • Seven Weeks' War with Austria, 1866
United States	1898	• War with Spain, 1898 • Boxer Rebellion, 1900 • World War I, 1917–18
Japan	1905	• Intervention in Korea, 1882–85 • Sino-Japanese War, 1894–95 • Boxer Rebellion, 1900 • Russo-Japanese war, 1904–05 • World War I, 1914–18 • Intervention in China, 1927–29
China	1949	• Japanese intervention, 1927–29 • Japanese expansion in China, 1931–45 • Korean War, 1950–53 • War with India, 1962

SOURCE: War data is taken from Jack S. Levy, *War in the Modern Great Power System, 1495–1975* (Lexington: University Press of Kentucky, 1983): 88–91.

A second factor is that most great powers emerged in fairly tough neighborhoods. To emerge in the eastern Baltic or central Europe meant that an ascending state would probably have to fight its immediate neighbors over territory and trade. In some cases, decisionmakers felt compelled to fight in order to gain control over adjacent or nearby pieces of territory—either by taking the territory from neighbors or by preventing the neighbors from taking the territories. Sweden fought to acquire Pomerania, Prussia battled to seize Silesia, and Japan desired to gain dominion over Korea. In other cases, independence had to be wrested away from overlords (e.g., by the Netherlands and Italy). To emerge as a great power is rather difficult if one's state remains a subordinate part of an imperial order.

The third factor is related to states that emerge not only as a great power but also as the predominant great power in their home region. Russia did this in the Baltic in the early eighteenth century. So, too, did the United States in the late nineteenth century. When this type of regional power transition occurs, there has been a tendency to resort to coercion as a way to accelerate the reorganization of the region. Evicting Spain from Cuba, preventing Russian inroads into Northeastern Asia, or punishing India over alleged border transgressions are the types of behaviors toward which newly ascendant regional hegemons are inclined. A successful demonstration of force helps to underscore their asserted position in the regional pecking order.[6]

Nothing about the history of entry into the great power ranks implies that states have no choice but to fight for any of the above reasons. Yet the historical record gives considerable reason to think some increased level of conflict is quite likely because the circumstances of elite emergence have encouraged it. In the modern era (i.e., the last five hundred years) no new great power has managed to evade substantial warfare around the time of its entry into elite status.

Yet there is also an economic dimension to emergence and ascent that must be taken into account. Some new great powers are just that: one new member among several members of an elite club. Some leap immediately to regional predominance. Still others are viewed as challengers for the

---

[6] This process is similar to the tendency for ancient rulers to demonstrate their coercive prowess early in their rule as a demonstration effect, thereby avoiding the need thereafter to rely constantly on force.

lead economy position in the world system.[7] Implicit in the concept of a lead economy is some likelihood that one state is recognized as the most innovative center of economic production and exchange. The United States has occupied this position since at least the mid-twentieth century. In the nineteenth century, Britain held the lead economy position. Before Britain, the United Provinces of the Netherlands enjoyed this status in the seventeenth century. Before the Dutch, the Portuguese briefly claimed this role by finding a way around Africa and into the Indian Ocean, thereby breaking the Venetian-Mamluk lock on east-west Eurasian trade.[8]

The added complexity of a second arena of action focused on economic competition, technological and industrial leadership, and long-distance commercial supremacy suggests an additional test. Are challengers for the lead economy position any more likely to escape the heightened conflict associated with emergence into the great power club? The quick historical summary presented in **Table 2** suggests that extensive warfare has been the norm, though with at least some exceptions.

The Portuguese took more than three generations to work their way around the African continent once they had begun their initial and largely unsuccessful efforts to expand into Morocco in 1415. Once in the Indian Ocean, the better-armed Portuguese were able to establish a maritime protection racket, requiring that those shipping to the west of India pay to participate in trade. For a few decades the Portuguese were also able to monopolize the delivery of spices to European markets; in the fifteenth century a Venetian-Egyptian Mamluk combination had controlled this monopoly but the Portuguese movement into the Indian Ocean circumvented the earlier pattern of control. To hold onto their new-found market control, the Portuguese had to fight Gujerati, Mamluk, and Ottoman opposition; but by contrast the Venetian resistance avoided any direct physical confrontation with the Portuguese.[9] That the Italian state

---

[7] Assumed here is a distinction between regional and global politics. At the regional level, actors have tended to focus on local territorial expansion, with regional hegemony the ultimate prize. At the global level, a few actors have focused on long-distance and inter-regional commerce. Predominance in trade and, later, industrial production are the primary goals. This distinction has gradually emerged over the past millennium. One of the implications is the existence of regional elite states and global elite states, some of which have dual status (e.g., the contemporary United States holds the regional position in North America and the lead position at the global level) but others that have had either one role or the other (e.g., Austria, the Ottoman Empire, Sweden, Italy, and, to date, China).

[8] Another assumption made here is that east-west trade initially between parts of Asia and western Europe has been characterized by an increasing level of economic interdependence throughout the past five hundred years.

[9] See, for instance, George Modelski, "Enduring Rivalry in the Democratic Lineage: The Venice-Portugal Case," in *Great Power Rivalries*, ed. William R. Thompson (Columbia: University of South Carolina Press, 1999), 153–71.

TABLE 2   Global lead economies and challenges

Century	Lead economy	Principal challenger(s)	Outcome
Late 15th to Early 16th	Venice	Portugal	Only indirect conflict between Venice and Portugal
Late 16th to Mid 17th	Portugal/Spain	The Netherlands	Extensive warfare (Dutch Revolt, 1560s; Thirty Years War, 1648)
Mid 17th to Early 18th	The Netherlands	France, England	Extensive warfare with England/Britain aligning ultimately with the Netherlands (1652–55, 1665–67, 1672–78, 1688–97, 1700–13)
Mid 18th to Early 19th	Britain	France	Extensive warfare (1741–48, 1755–63, 1778–83, 1793–1815)
Late 19th to Early 20th	Britain	Germany, United States	Extensive warfare (World War I, 1914; World War II, 1945)
Mid to late 20th	United States	Soviet Union	Cold War (1945–1989)
Mid 21st	*United States?*	*China?*	*?*

system was under siege thanks to French and Spanish interventions over succession rights may have had something to do with Venetian restraint.

The Dutch independence movement ensured there would be Dutch-Spanish fighting in the sixteenth century. With the Spanish absorption of Portugal and its empire in 1581, the partially merged Iberian entity became a broader target. This was all the more true after the Dutch decision in the 1590s to circumvent the ports on the Iberian peninsula and to establish networks of their own in Asia and the Americas.[10] There ensued Dutch-Portuguese combat in Brazil, Africa, and the southern tier of Asia, with the Dutch attempting to displace both the Portuguese trading regime in the Indian Ocean and its enclaves along the Afro-Eurasian coastline. By the time the Dutch had established independence, the conflict had escalated to a struggle to become the lead economy of the global system—a struggle eventually won by the Dutch within the context of some eighty years of intermittent conflict ranging throughout the world.

---

[10] The Dutch decision was a reaction to the belated Spanish decision to close Iberian ports to Dutch shipping long after the Dutch Revolt had begun. The choice faced by the Dutch was whether to accept being closed out of Asian and Mediterranean markets to which they had earlier had access via Spanish ports or to go around the Spanish ports and develop Dutch routes beyond Europe.

In the second half of the seventeenth century the Dutch came under attack from both the English and the French. Decisionmakers in both challenger states had concluded that the Dutch controlled too much of Europe's trade volume, making it incumbent upon them to take away from the Dutch as much of the trade as they possibly could. While the English and Dutch fought three wars in the 1650s to 70s, France had ambitions that went beyond merely grabbing some portion of Dutch trade: the French wanted to supplant the Netherlands as the lead economy.[11] To accomplish this meant subordinating the Dutch to French supremacy in Europe and beyond. Warfare had begun by 1672 and continued intermittently to 1713. Along the way, the Dutch *stadtholder* was able to re-align English foreign policy by essentially seizing the English throne by force and committing England to the anti-French coalition. Ironically, however, the Dutch were bankrupted by the 1688–1713 combat and forced to cede their lead economic position to Britain.

While the Dutch were eclipsed by the conflicts with the French, France's bid to translate the country's massive size within the European region into global predominance was not extinguished in 1713. Warfare with Britain resumed in the 1740s, the 1750s to 60s, and the 1770s to 80s, finally peaking in the 1793–1815 French Revolutionary and Napoleonic Wars. The ultimate outcome was the failure of the French challenge and the loss of French imperial territory in Canada, the Caribbean, and India. Victory for the British was marred only by the loss of their thirteen American colonies.

Britain's Industrial Revolution in the late eighteenth century altered the terrain of global economic competition by substituting an emphasis on industrial production for the previous focus on control of commercial markets. Innovating new waves of technology henceforth became the primary criterion for economic leadership. Britain led the first two waves centered on textiles, iron, and steam/railroads but faltered as the focus shifted to chemicals, steel, and electricity. Germany and the United States were better prepared to assume the lead in these key sectors and thus to challenge the British lead economy position. But which one posed the greatest threat to Britain's position? In the long run, the U.S. potential was considerable and might have led to British efforts to thwart U.S. economic ascendance. Instead, British decisionmakers took the position that the U.S. rise was nearly inevitable and the German threat more immediate and

---

[11] On Dutch foreign policy problems of this era, see Jack S. Levy, "Economic Competition, Domestic Politics, and Systemic Change," in *Great Power Rivalries*, ed. William R. Thompson (Columbia: University of South Carolina Press, 1999), 172–200; and Jack S. Levy and Salvatore Ali, "From Commercial Conflict to Strategic Rivalry to War: The Evolution of the Anglo-Dutch Rivalry, 1609–52," in *The Dynamics of Enduring Rivalries*, ed. Paul F. Diehl (Urbana: University of Illinois Press, 1999), 29–63.

closer to home—in terms of both European and Middle Eastern markets and Germany's North Sea location.[12]

As a consequence, the British negotiated themselves out of three ongoing rivalries (with the United States, France, and Russia), struck a deal with the Japanese, and retrenched their naval forces in European waters in order to better concentrate on the German threat. The two world wars thus were fought in part to resolve the German economic challenge to Britain's position. World War I was inconclusive, although it was clear in the war's immediate aftermath that the incumbent system leader, Britain, was unlikely to recover fully from the costs of that war. World War II was decisive in that the British were exhausted, the Germans were defeated resoundingly, and the United States was clearly both on top of the global system and in charge of the introduction of new technology to the world economy.

The one wrinkle for the United States in this global economic predominance was the withdrawal of the Communist world from full participation in the world economy and the reluctance of the Soviet Union as leader of the Communist subsystem to acknowledge or accept the U.S. global lead. Some 45 years of cold war competition ensued, ending without direct major power violence with the collapse of the Soviet Union in the late 1980s.[13] The Soviets, overextended in the Third World and unable to meet the technological requirements necessary at the highest levels of economic competition, acknowledged defeat (at least indirectly) and altered their grand strategy. In the process of attempting to reform their approach to competing in world politics, the Soviets lost control of Eastern Europe, the Caucuses, and Central Asia. Their vaunted military prowess was revealed to be far less formidable than often feared. The Russian ability to participate, let alone compete, as a great power in world politics was called into question and still has not been fully resolved.

So, while the United States appears to retain the lead in the introduction and diffusion of information technology, the real test will come with subsequent waves of technology later in the 21st century.[14] How many innovative challengers will emerge? If multiple challengers do emerge, will the United States designate one as the principal threat, then concede or ally

---

[12] Incumbent system leaders, other things being equal, tend to focus on more direct threats, as opposed to more abstract threats. See William R. Thompson, "The Evolution of Political-Commercial Challenges in the Active Zone," *Review of International Political Economy* 4, no. 2 (September 1997): 285–317.

[13] That Soviet pilots flew North Korean planes in the Korean War appears to have been the sole exception. A series of limited proxy wars in developing countries might also be considered as a kind of indirect, surrogate U.S.-Soviet military competition.

[14] See, for example, William R. Thompson, "Systemic Leadership, Evolutionary Processes, and International Relations Theory: The Unipolarity Question." *International Studies Review* 8, no.1 (2006): 1–22.

with the others in an attempt to thwart at least one challenger? Or might the United States revitalize itself once again and widen the U.S. technological lead? Can China harness the country's huge domestic market to attain technological preeminence? What about Europe's efforts under European Union auspices to consolidate European capabilities in one regional-sized competitor? Where might India fit into this picture? India also has a large domestic market and some fledgling information technology capability but even more acute poverty and underdevelopment to overcome than China.

Important to keep in mind, however, is that these are not questions that can be answered in the near term. These questions refer to processes that currently are underway but are still highly open-ended and may require several decades or more to reach fruition. All of the potential challengers currently visible on the horizon could undergo various types of disintegration in the next several decades, thereby undermining the intensity of the challenge they might pose. The rapid pace of Chinese development could founder due to resource shortages or political dissent (see Minxin Pei's chapter in this volume). The European Union (EU) could become quite prosperous and yet lack leadership in advanced technology and production. India may generate population faster than it can transform the nation's still largely agrarian economy.

Though difficult to forecast precisely who may challenge and when, the anticipation that some level of heightened conflict is likely to be associated with a period of structural transition is not without reason. The past five hundred years of great and global power competition is more than suggestive. As established earlier, the emergence of new powers is a process characterized by substantial stresses and strains which have proven difficult for the powers involved to manage without resorting to large-scale violence. The payoffs linked to mobility in the world system, especially at or toward the very top of the stratification hierarchy, are apt to be seen as very high. As can safely be concluded from the data in Tables 1 and 2, willingness to engage in warfare appears to be especially strong.

Does Economic Interdependence Suppress International Conflict?

This brief survey of the evidence of violence in the emergence of historical great powers seems to provide a strong basis for skepticism about the conflict-suppressing effects of economic interdependence; safe to say at the least is that little violence seems to have been suppressed in the past. Quite different expectations, however, flow from the central premise of economic interdependence arguments: increased levels of interdependence, while bringing definite benefits, also raise the costs of severing or otherwise disrupting the economic relationship. Conflict between trading partners, therefore, should be less likely than between pairs of states that do not trade. More dynamically, partners that are increasing their trading activity should become more concerned with avoiding increasingly costly disruptions—again, in comparison to states that are not increasing their trading activity.

This expectation that economic interdependence serves to dampen conflict ultimately stems from the calculus of national leaders seeking to maximize their state's benefits and minimize its costs. Interdependent relationships are assumed to increase benefits, while also raising the costs of ending the relationship. As Thomas Moore and Dixia Yang point out, an assortment of state and non-state actors, all of which encourage deepening economic interdependence, influences the cost-benefit calculations of China (and other countries) through a variety of channels: person-to-person contacts, multilateral economic institutions, transfer of economic ideas and norms, inter-governmental pressure, multinational corporations, transnational manufacturing networks, and global markets.[15]

Yet even allowing that such conflict-suppressing interdependence effects obtain, there is little basis to expect that these effects will be the sole consequence of increased trade and other forms of economic interaction.[16] Historical processes in general, and interdependence processes in particular, are apt to have mixed effects. There is indeed ample historical evidence suggesting that the restraining effects can be offset or overwhelmed by other, contrary effects. For example, increases in trade are also likely to bring increased trade frictions of different sorts. The economic interdependence argument does not tell us how strong the effect should be or whether it is likely to be stronger or weaker than other putative effects that pull in the opposite direction.

How then can we know when and under what circumstances interdependence effects are likely to constrain—or alternatively, give way to—conflictual tendencies? One persuasive answer is provided by Dale Copeland, who argues that it is not the level of interdependence per se but rather decisionmaker expectations about future interdependence benefits that influence whether peace or conflict prevails. If interdependence

---

[15] Thomas G. Moore and Dixia Yang, "Empowered and Restrained: Chinese Foreign Policy in the Age of Economic Interdependence," in *The Making of Chinese Foreign and Security Policy in the Era of Reform*, ed. David M Lampton (Stanford, CA: Stanford University Press, 2001), 193–98.

[16] Space constraints do not permit more detailed consideration of the different effects likely to result from different forms of economic interaction, for example, trade and direct foreign investment. For a thorough explication of this distinction, see Stephen G. Brooks, *Producing Security: Multinational Corporations, Globalization, and the Changing Calculus of Conflict* (Princeton, NJ: Princeton University Press, 2005).

benefits are projected into the future, then conflict is less likely; but if such benefits are expected to be cut off or sharply diminished, then the conflict-suppressing effects of interdependence are weakened.[17] What is left unspecified, however, are the circumstances that influence the expectations of decisionmakers.

It should not be surprising that the empirical evidence on economic interdependence operating as a constraint on political-military conflict is quite mixed—especially absent systematic data concerning decisionmaker's expectations of the future economic benefits of interdependence. For every analysis finding a negative relationship (the greater the economic interdependence between two states, the less the likelihood of conflict escalation between them), there is another study finding a positive relationship or the absence of any significant relationship.[18] Thus not yet known is whether interdependence in any given context will constrain or aggravate conflict escalation. One reason for these mixed findings is that the relative strength of interdependence constraints appears to be fairly weak. A number of other realpolitik-type variables—for instance, ongoing territorial disputes, rivalry, relative capability, distance—have a much stronger impact on conflict escalation. Only regime type—whether one or both of the states in a dyadic pair is democratic—has less impact than economic interdependence.[19] The first cautionary note, therefore, is that economic interdependence is hardly a "silver bullet" guaranteed to pacify interstate conflicts, especially compared to the more robust relationships involving grievance issues and military power. Though probably true that economic interdependence may constrain conflict escalation processes, that the effects

---

[17] Dale Copeland, "Economic Interdependence and War: A Theory of Trade Expectations," *International Security* 20, no. 4 (Spring 1996): 5-41; and Dale Copeland, "Economic Interdependence and the Future of U.S.-Chinese Relations," in *International Relations Theory and the Asia-Pacific*, ed. G. John Ikenberry and Michael Mastanduno (NY: Columbia University Press, 2003), 323–52. The former examines the cases of Germany prior to the two world wars; the latter looks both at Japan prior to WWI and at contemporary China. See also Rex Li, "Security Challenge of an Ascendant China: Great Power Emergence and International Stability," in *Chinese Foreign Policy: Pragmatism and Strategic Behavior* ed. Suisheng Zhao (New York: M.E. Sharpe, 2004), 39, for another application of Copeland's framework that finds that, "For the moment, China's expectations of future trade with both its Asian neighbors and Western nations are by and large positive."

[18] This negative finding is based on a review of 34 empirical analyses reported in Karen Rasler and William R. Thompson, "Assessing Inducements and Suppressors of Interstate Conflict Escalation" (paper presented at the annual meeting of the International Studies Association, San Diego, California, March 22–25, 2006). One strongly contrasting view on the role of economic interdependence is Bruce Russett and John R. Oneal, *Triangulating Peace: Democracy, Interdependence and International Organizations* (New York: Norton, 2001).

[19] These findings are reported in Rasler and Thompson, "Assessing Inducements and Suppressors of Interstate Conflict Escalation." They are based on a quantitative analysis of militarized interstate disputes for the post-World War II period utilizing databases that allow analysts to avoid the extensive missing data problems that characterized empirical analyses involving gross domestic product information prior to the last three to four years.

will necessarily be all that strong or consistent is far from clear. Other factors that appear to be more important to conflict escalation can either mitigate, trump, or accentuate any possible effects of interdependence. These findings do not mean that the effects of economic interdependence are substantively nil, but only that a variety of other variables appear to count more when the time comes to engage in, or desist from, conflict escalation.

What features of great power competition might help to account for these ambivalent results? This chapter suggests that the history of the past five centuries indicates that states seeking to expand their industrial and commercial activities in the world economy, especially latecomers trying to catch up with an established system leader, have recurrently encountered at least four major types of obstacles that can diminish the constraining effects of economic interdependence: (1) the perception that the prevailing status quo is relatively closed to newly ascending powers, (2) the process of catching up to early leaders encourages the adoption of strategies that are likely to be perceived as unfair, (3) the process of catching up usually involves ascending actors converging on production and trade of the same goods as the targets of their catch-up efforts, and (4) similar economic activities demand similar and possibly scarce energy sources.

Implicit in each of these problem areas is that increased economic interaction and interdependence might also be accompanied by increased conflict among the most important economic actors. Any of these four problems might alone be sufficient to override the interdependence constraints expected to prevent costly disruptions of commerce. The four combined, or even smaller combinations of two or three problems, could certainly overwhelm the more pacific effects of increased interdependence.

How prominent have these four sources of trouble been in the great power conflicts of the modern era? More specifically, are these problem areas especially apt to be manifest in situations involving latecomers seeking a position at or near the apex of the world economy? There are two historical "laboratories" within which to uncover recognizable patterns that bear on the challenges posed by emerging powers: (1) the historical experience of the European *region* and (2) the waves of competition over *global* elite status that followed and were often joined to the intra-European struggles. Historically, then, a number of trials are available for examination. The question is: what patterns characterized these trials? And, to what extent are the patterns found in the 16th through the 20th centuries likely to have relevance for the 21st century emergence of China and India as great powers?

Obstacles to Great Power Emergence

Markets are Already Staked Out

Latecomers confront a world economy in which markets and imperial territories are already staked out. States that develop control of trade routes, markets, and leading industrial sectors get "there" first. These states create strategically located bases, enclaves, raw material sources, and consumer market shares.[20] Later developers, who need access to the same trade routes and markets, will desire bases and enclaves in more or less the same locations. As a consequence, latecomers perceive the need to fight their way in because the states that have preceded them are unlikely to surrender their positions and market shares peacefully.[21]

Many of the commercial commodities valued in early modern Europe were cultivated in few places. Silver came primarily from Spanish mines in South America after the 1550s. Spices came primarily from a few of the islands in the Indonesian archipelago. Sugar was produced in Brazil after earlier sites lying closer to the Mediterranean proved less productive; sugar production subsequently migrated increasingly to selected Caribbean islands.[22] Tobacco was grown on the eastern seaboard of North America, tea came from China, and so on. The point is that traders in pursuit of these products were apt to bump into one another. Whoever controlled access to the most valued commodities could set prices to some extent and determine who gained access to the commodities. The temptation to take the sources of production away from the initial possessors must have been strong.

As a consequence, the French and British fought in part over who could gain access to Spain's Latin American colonies. The Dutch and Portuguese fought over the control of Brazilian sugar production. The Dutch, English, and Portuguese fought over who could have access to the Spice Islands. The perception that the system was relatively closed to newcomers was not always unrealistic, but perceptions of closure could also be exaggerated. Entering the Indian Ocean, the Portuguese assumed that local markets would be closed to them because Muslim traders were thought to have total control over the distribution of traded commodities. Though exaggerated,

---

[20] On the overlap in basing choices over the last half-millennium, see Robert Harkavy, "Long Cycle Theory and the Hegemonic Powers' Basing Networks," *Political Geography* 18, no. 8 (November 1999): 941–972.

[21] The dissatisfaction of latecomers is a point featured prominently in power-transition arguments. See A.F.K. Organski, *World Politics* (New York: Random House, 1958); and A. F. K. Organski and Jacek Kugler, *The War Ledger* (Chicago, Il.: University of Chicago Press, 1981).

[22] The Dutch had attempted to seize Brazil from the Portuguese; once that project had failed, the Dutch were important agents in shifting sugar production to Caribbean islands controlled by England.

this assumption nonetheless encouraged the Portuguese to enter Indian trading ports prepared to do battle and thus to initiate a self-fulfilling prophecy.[23]

Similarly, the wish of France and England was not simply to compete with Dutch commerce in the seventeenth century. Rather, their assumption was that European trade was a fixed volume. Whatever France and England could acquire would have to come at the expense of what the Dutch already controlled. British and French colonies or enclaves in North America, the Caribbean, and India might have coexisted but the British and French tended ultimately to function on mutually exclusive principles. Neither North America nor India was large enough for both British and French agents to compete and coexist; one or the other had to be ousted. In the Caribbean, islands initially changed hands with some frequency; but gradually France and England developed an increased reluctance to surrender island territory gained in eighteenth century warfare.

Bending the Rules with Strategic Trade Policies

As Alexander Gerschenkron emphasized, latecomers have tended to develop more centralized strategies—government intervention and protection, subsidies, industrial policies—to improve their chances of breaking into the elite ranks.[24] States that are more oriented to the status quo are likely to perceive the actions of new competitors as unfair (e.g., dumping, predatory trade policies, manipulation of exchange rates) and thus overreact to the new competitors' efforts to catch up by enacting punitive policies.[25]

Industrialization did not diminish the mercantilist tendency to view great power conflict in zero-sum terms but instead is more likely to have hardened this view. The early lead of the British in industrialization prompted Napoleon's attempt to close European markets to British exports in order to provide French industry some time to become more competitive. Later in the nineteenth century, both Germany and the United States also became highly protectionist, recognizing the need to insulate their economies from the competitive advantages of British producers. The

---

[23] The Portuguese were in essence extending by assumption and practice the centuries-long Christian-Muslim struggle in the Mediterranean to the Indian Ocean.

[24] The Gerschenkron effect refers to the argument that late developers must overcome more obstacles to growth than early developers and, therefore, are more likely to rely on authoritarian governments, central planning, and banking-business partnerships in attempts to catch up with the growth leaders. See Alexander Gerschenkron, *Economic Backwardness in Historical Perspective* (Cambridge, MA: Belknap Press, 1962).

[25] See Paul Kennedy, *The Rise of the Anglo-German Antagonism, 1860–1914* (London: George Allen and Unwin, 1980), 291–305.

Soviets went even further in attempts to insulate their industries from world capitalism and the competition it would have brought. In an industrialized world, challengers are the ones who are most likely to protect their domestic industries from external competition; apparent to the challengers is their own inability to compete initially with the front runner(s) without some leveling of the playing field via protectionist policies. If newcomers enter the field on the front runner's rules, the odds are biased against winning or even holding one's own.

Catching up, therefore, encourages ascending actors to bend the rules.[26] They dump products at unprofitably low prices and tell lies both about competitors and about the quality and safety of their own products. Even if the states catching up do not engage much in these predatory practices, they are apt to be accused of doing so. How else to explain their unexpected success against the established industrial powers? Challengers may enact border measures that strategically discriminate against the lead economy's products or make other, less transparent attempts to increase market shares by denying the lead economy's comparative advantages. Such actions have often engendered responses in kind, sometimes leading to conflict spirals of retaliation and counter-retaliation.[27]

Convergence on the Same Sectors and Industries

Economic development tends to result in competitors converging on the same technologies, sectors, and industries—rather than the complementarity thought to follow from specialization based on comparative advantage and a deepening division of labor. At the technological high end (and depending on the time period) all advanced economies tend to produce steel, automobiles, or computers. These economies also tend to require external markets to accommodate their scale of production. Similar products and finite markets predict to surplus capacity and, ultimately, to intensified competition that is often construed in zero-sum terms. These effects are exacerbated in the case of industries that are—or at least are thought to be—critical to national security.[28] Concepts such as comparative advantage, specialization, and division of labor apply for most situations.

---

[26] Note that "the rules" tend to be set by the early developers and are not necessarily accepted by later developers. Free trade, for instance, is most appealing to an economy that can out-produce all other economies.

[27] In general, see John A.C. Conybeare, *Trade Wars: The Theory and Practice of International Commercial Policy* (New York: Columbia University Press, 1987). For more specific examples relating to late nineteenth century business competition, see Kennedy, *Anglo-German Antagonism,* 41–58, 291–305.

[28] These elements are emphasized in Gautam Sen, *The Military Origins of Industrialized and International Trade Rivalry* (London: Pinter, 1983).

These concepts apply less well, however, to the elite ranks attempting to operate on the technological frontier.

The problem is made even worse by the tendency for new technologies to appear in clusters. Textiles and iron were followed by steam engines and railroads. Chemicals, steel, and electricity came next, followed by automobiles. More recently, aerospace and electronics, followed by information technology, have all played their respective roles as strategic industries which represented high value added, best practices, skilled employment, and relatively high profits and wages as well as being critically important to military capabilities.

Modern clusters of technologies are seemingly difficult to skip; that is, those playing catch-up industrialization do not leap-frog from textiles to electronics without also mastering steel and automobiles in-between. To be competitive with the world's lead economy, it is therefore necessary for the challenger to gain competitiveness in the same industries in which the leader excels or has excelled. If the leader stumbles and commits prematurely to an eventually uncompetitive path (as did Britain, in steel) or if the leader becomes overly complacent and allows competitors to improve on prevailing practices (as did the United States, in automobiles), challengers may be able to surpass leaders; but even if unable to become the new leader, challengers are forced by the nature of modern economic development to compete in the same industrial sectors more or less at the same time. Intra-industry trade can ameliorate but not eliminate this problem.[29] This complication operates between leaders and challengers but applies as well among challengers: in a situation involving multiple challengers, all are likely to be trying to produce similar types of widgets at roughly the same time.

As trading complementarities are lost in the process, so too are some of the potential constraints of economic interdependence. Economies of scale encourage the production of more than is likely to be consumed by home markets, resulting in tendencies toward chronic surplus production. Competitors may become even more cutthroat in their efforts to outsell each other in third-country markets, leading back in some cases to the type of predatory practices associated with catch-up development strategies.

National defense concerns are an additional element encouraging similarities in industrial structure. Perceived security imperatives suggest that industrial development must be encouraged at all costs: certain industries are essential to being able to operate at the military technology

---

[29] For an argument that increasingly globalized production by multinational corporations substantially reduces major power conflict, see Brooks, *Producing Security.* Interestingly, though, Brooks explicitly excludes developing countries from this generalization.

frontier. Nuclear physics capabilities are critical in an era of both missiles with nuclear warheads and submarines with nuclear reactors for propulsion. Information technology is vital in an era emphasizing closer coordination and control of multiple military weapons, forces, and theaters. Both nuclear physics and information technology are important to launching satellites and space missions. Biochemistry cannot be ignored as long as chemical and biological weapons are developed, even if their use remains improbable. Even more purely commercial industries, like automobile production, are strategically linked to tank and truck production. Again, the point is that the nature of interstate competition tends to lead elite economic actors to specialize in the same production areas at roughly the same time. Less interdependence and more competition can be anticipated as a result.

Competition for Access to Energy

The question of competition for energy supplies is a special case of the "markets are already staked out" category discussed earlier, but the strategic importance of energy (to industrial production, distribution, and military power projection) warrants separate consideration. If elite economies tend to have similar industrial structures and production orientations, also probable is that these economies will all need reliable and relatively inexpensive access to energy resources.[30] To the extent that supplies of these energy sources are scarce (or worse yet, diminishing), or that growing demand for these sources is outpacing supply, conflict over access to the same energy resources needed to operate advanced economies becomes more likely.

In the age of maritime commerce, such competition might seem to have been fairly inconsequential. After all, building sailing ships that exploited readily available wind systems would not seem to have been an insurmountable task. Yet even in this context supply problems arose. Sailing ships had to be built from tall timber. Much of Europe was deforested, thereby placing a premium on Baltic and North American forests as prizes to be controlled, if possible. Wind may be widely distributed, but the most efficient sailing routes were more delimited. Control of the primary trade routes gave one's own national shipping a global edge.

Industrialization has of course made this problem even more acute. In an age of steam propulsion, coal supplies were critical. Access to petroleum becomes indispensable if the primary source of propulsion (on land, in the air, or under the sea) is the internal combustion engine. It was therefore

---

[30] Resources are emphasized in Stephen G. Bunker and Paul S. Ciccantell, *Globalization and the Race for Resources* (Baltimore: Johns Hopkins University Press, 2005).

not surprising that prior to World War II the United States went to great lengths, in competition with Britain, to develop control of as many major oil fields as possible.[31] Concerns about access to coal and petroleum helped determine Japan's acquisitive strategies toward Manchuria and Southeast Asia.[32] Additionally, problems in acquiring sufficient access to petroleum contributed to Germany's defeat in World War II.[33]

Coal, natural gas, and petroleum are characterized by uneven geographical distributions. Some actors have large amounts of natural coal, oil and gas, or both, while others are highly dependent on external supplies. Most contemporary great powers are especially dependent on petroleum supplies controlled by non-great powers. Courting these oil producers and competing to arrange secure access to energy sources becomes a preoccupation of ascending and incumbent powers alike.

21st Century Relevance

Will these characteristic problems recur in the 21st century? Might economic interdependence suppress or counteract the urge to fall back on coercive resolution of the issues at stake? How might the emergence and ascent of China and India be affected? The authors do not mean to imply that the contemporary examples presented in this chapter amount to evidence that historical patterns are being repeated. These patterns do suggest, however, that certain features of great power emergence and transition appear to be at least latent in the early 21st century.

By this point in time, the seizure of resource-rich territories, trade routes, or strategic locations staked out either by great power rivals or by indigenous peoples is no longer regarded as legitimate state practice. While prevailing norms now (more or less) effectively prohibit overt forms of state conquest and direct control, the nationalistic urge to exert as much control as possible over raw materials, bases, or territory deemed essential to national welfare, security, or both still persists. This urge, however, now

---

[31] On the U.S. effort to acquire secure access to oil prior to World War II, see Ed Shaffer, *The United States and the Control of World Oil* (New York: St. Martin's Press, 1983); and William R. Thompson, "Global War and the Foundations of U.S. Systemic Leadership," in *War and Power: Defining the American State*, ed. James Fuller and Lawrence Sondhaus (London: Routledge, forthcoming).

[32] See, for instance, Jonathan Marshall, *To Have and Have Not: Southeast Asian Raw Materials and the Origins of the Pacific War* (Berkeley: University of California Press, 1995); and David P. Rapkin, "The Emergence and Intensification of the US-Japan Rivalry in the Early Twentieth Century," in *Great Power Rivalries*, ed. William R. Thompson (Columbia: University of South Carolina Press, 1999), 337–370.

[33] Support for this observation is found in, among other places, Richard Overy, *Why the Allies Won* (New York: Norton, 1995), 228–234.

takes less overt and direct forms which are more congenial to those states that possess the desired resources or locations.

The experience of explosive economic growth in recent decades has strained China's ability to secure enough raw materials for the country's burgeoning industries. Indeed, so rapid have been the increases in China's demand for various raw materials that the country has had difficulty finding adequate supplies. World markets for various basic commodities—from copper, zinc, aluminum, iron, and scrap steel to oil and natural gas—have been booming in consequence of China's, and to a much lesser extent India's, contributions to world demand.[34] By and large, China and India have increased their reliance on markets to meet their needs; but both countries (and particularly China) seem to harbor a residual distrust of market mechanisms and an unwillingness to rely exclusively on such mechanisms when other options, such as long-term contracts with raw material suppliers, are available. In China's case, this "obsession for possession" has become global in scope, involving long-term commitments—often at above-market prices—with suppliers not just in Southeast Asia but also in Africa, the Middle East, Latin America, Russia and Australia. David Hale has opined that, "…like previous Great Powers, Beijing will develop a foreign policy and military strategy to protect its access to raw materials."[35]

U.S. response has been critical. For instance, in the March 2006 National Security Strategy (approved by President Bush), the U.S. government complains that China's leaders are "expanding trade, but acting as if they can somehow 'lock up' energy supplies around the world or seek to direct markets rather than opening them up, as if they can follow a mercantilism borrowed from a discredited era."[36] Most objectionable from the perspective of the Bush administration are China's arrangements with and support for states that the United States views as foreign policy problems (e.g., Iran, Sudan, Venezuela, and Myanmar) owing mainly to their human rights or proliferation policies, as well as to their overt anti-U.S. stance. To date, China's efforts to secure access to raw materials have not precipitated direct confrontation with the United States; but as 1.3 billion citizens/consumers in China, combined with a like number in India as well as others in Southeast Asia and elsewhere become more affluent and consume increasing amounts

---

[34] Consider some illustrative examples of recent growth in China's resource consumption between 1990 and 2003: China's iron ore imports increased from 14 to 148 million tons, aluminum from 1 to 5.6 million tons, refined copper from 20,000 tons to 1.2 million tons, platinum from 20,000 ounces to 1.6 million ounces, and nickel from zero to 61,500 tons as reported in David Hale, "China's Growing Appetites," *National Interest*, no. 76 (Summer 2004), 138.

[35] Hale, "China's Growing Appetites, 141.

[36] Cited in David E. Sanger, "China's Rising Need for Oil Is High on U.S. Agenda," *New York Times*, April 18, 2006.

of housing, appliances, automobiles, and other resource-intensive products, great power competition to "lock up" supplies of scarce raw materials is likely to intensify. The resulting frictions may or may not lead to overt confrontation but can reasonably be expected to pull in the opposite direction from whatever conflict-dampening effects follow from increased economic interdependence.

The perceived imperative of securing sources of raw materials and their transport, joined with traditional geostrategic concerns, have led both China and India to begin to adopt the strategy used by past and present great powers of establishing networks of naval facilities in the Indian Ocean. China is heavily involved in establishing a port facility at Gwadar in Pakistan as part of its "string of pearls" maritime basing strategy, which also encompasses facilities in Bangladesh, Myanmar, Thailand, Cambodia, and the South China Sea. As noted by one U.S. defense contractor, "China is building strategic relationships along the sea lanes from the Middle East to the South China Sea in ways that suggest defensive and offensive positioning to protect China's energy interests, but also to serve broad security objectives."[37] India, for its part, has opened a new naval base of its own at Karwar, aims to build a port at Dawei in Myanmar, is planning to set up a monitoring station in Madagascar, and has been increasing its coordination with the U.S. Navy.

Complaints about unfair commercial practices, trade and investment protectionism, and state support for targeted industries—all characteristic of the Gerschenkronian catch-up industrialization model—were most fully articulated in the U.S. critique of Japan in the 1980s and early 1990s. This critique and accompanying trade frictions subsided by the mid-1990s, however, by which time Japan's protracted stagnation attenuated the country's image as a formidable economic threat. Similar issues surfaced in connection with the policies of the World Bank and the International Monetary Fund toward Asia's "developmental states," particularly during the Asian financial crisis of 1997–98.

More recently, in the context of China's large and growing bilateral current account surplus with the United States, similar complaints with Chinese economic policies have emerged in the United States, particularly in the Congress, though these complaints have not yet been translated into punitive policies. Important to note is that the basis for U.S. dissatisfaction with Chinese policies is narrower than in the earlier Japanese case because China, with some significant exceptions, has been more open to imports and much more open to direct foreign investment than was Japan. Hence,

[37] From a report by Booz Allen Hamilton, "Energy Futures in Asia," cited in Sudha Ramachandran, "China's Pearl in Pakistan's Waters," *Asia Times*, March 4, 2005.

U.S. complaints have focused on lax protection of intellectual property rights, state subsidization of Chinese industries, and—most prominently— allegations that China is a "currency manipulator," i.e., that China routinely intervenes in currency markets in order to maintain a significantly undervalued Chinese yuan. In turn, the undervalued "peg" in relation to the U.S. dollar is alleged to contribute to the bilateral imbalance as (artificially) cheaper Chinese goods flood U.S. markets and (artificially) more expensive U.S. goods have a harder time penetrating Chinese markets.[38]

According to Lawrence Lindsey, former chief economic adviser to President George W. Bush, the critique of Chinese exchange rate policies is rooted in deeper ideological considerations centering on "...whether markets or government policies will be the fundamental drivers of global trade." More specifically, Lindsey posits that "...under an exchange rate fixed by Chinese authorities and not the market, it is the Chinese government that implicitly decides who in America benefits from our trade relationship: consumers or producers, borrowers or lenders. American sensibilities hold that this is a matter best left to the market."[39] Whether these trade frictions rise to the point where they out weigh the constraints posed by the complexities of U.S.-Chinese interdependence is of course a question that draws much speculation and analysis.

Similar strains have not surfaced in the U.S.-India economic relationship, largely because trade between the two is much smaller. While there is some popular concern over the outsourcing of jobs to India, especially high-end, skilled jobs in the information sector, most Americans seem to realize that these interdependence costs result from decisions by U.S. firms rather than from the actions of the Indian state or Indian firms. Likewise, India's trade with China, while growing rapidly, is not of sufficient scale to generate much by way of trade frictions. Moreover, India—with a legacy of an extensive state role in economic development and with market-oriented reforms that lag behind those of China—is unlikely any time soon to share U.S. objections to the role of the Chinese government in China's trade and exchange-rate policies. Instead, owing to the two countries' experiences with Western intrusion and domination, they are more likely to be aligned in defense of traditional conceptions of state sovereignty vis-à-vis external pressures to change economic policies in a liberalizing direction.

The process by which states, both first-comers and latecomers, converge on the same limited set of industries has in recent decades accelerated.

---

[38] For the conventional economic view that the bilateral imbalance is a consequence of low U.S. and high Chinese savings rates and thus is not amenable to solution by changes in exchange rates, see Ronald I. McKinnon, "Currency Manipulator?" *Wall Street Journal*, April 20, 2006.

[39] Lawrence B. Lindsey, "Yuan Compromise?" *Wall Street Journal*, April 6, 2006.

Product cycles have shortened dramatically, partly due to the ability of highly mobile multinational firms to exploit information technologies to control far-flung production networks. Perhaps more important has been the effectiveness of developing countries, especially China and India, in enhancing the engineering and scientific skills of their workforces; in attracting world-class technology firms, including their research-and-development activities; and in developing indigenous technology firms. The confluence of these developments has enabled China and India to move quickly up the "value chain" and to begin challenging more developed countries not just in "low end" manufacturing and services but also increasingly in industries that the latter had regarded as their preserve, at least in the near-to-medium term.

China's comparative advantages have been in manufacturing, including computer hardware, while India has found some large niches in services and software, with the effect that both have caused costly adjustments in the United States, Japan, and elsewhere. As for interdependence between China and India, their respective hardware-software specializations have so far limited competitive frictions, but this complementarity is likely to diminish as China seeks competitiveness in software and India aims to strengthen its manufacturing capabilities. Srinivasan, for example, anticipates that "China could surpass India as a software power in a decade."[40] Others in the industry estimate that "given three to five years they will close the gap."[41] India is not expected to catch up with China in manufacturing within such a short timeframe, but its skilled, low-wage labor force and large markets are expected to draw increasing foreign and domestic investment in manufacturing activities, especially if wages in China continue to rise.[42]

Space technology, owing to its dual (commercial and military) salience, is likely to engage the United States, China, and India in competition at the high end of the technological ladder, thus reflecting the 21st century logic of convergence described above. Posen describes how space capabilities— specifically reconnaissance, navigation, and communications satellites— contribute to American "command of the commons" (also encompassing sea and air power), noting that Secretary of Defense Donald Rumsfeld has emphasized the importance of the military exploitation of space and has set

[40] T.N. Srinivasan, "Economic Reforms and Global Integration," in *The India-China Relationship: What the United States Needs to Know*, ed. Francine R. Frankel and Harry Harding (New York: Columbia University Press, 2004), 240.

[41] Vineet Toshniwai, an executive with the Indian software firm, Infosys, as quoted in Pallavi Aiyar, "China-India IT Cooperation: One 'Pagoda' Short," *Asia Times*, March 23, 2006.

[42] See Anand Giridharadas, "In India, 'Next Great' Industrial Story," *International Herald Tribune*, April 17, 2006.

the military the mission of "space control."[43] China, which "hasn't missed an opportunity to use its success in space to showcase China's rising power," views the prospect of American dominance of space as a serious threat.[44] Viewing space prowess as integral to any bid for great power status, New Delhi too is intent on developing India's space capabilities, "the crown jewel of [the country's] technological achievements in the post-Independence period".[45] Accordingly, following the successful May, 2005 launch of India's eleventh remote-sensing satellite, Prime Minister Manmohan Singh declared to the Indian parliament that the launch "reaffirms the emergence of India as a major space power."[46]

Though having various space-based weapons under development, the United States has so far refrained (as have other space-faring countries) from actually deploying space weapons. Various satellite technologies do, however, have dual (i.e., commercial and military) applications that are strategically important without crossing the weapons-in-space threshold. The ability to launch navigation satellites, for instance, is linked directly to the launch, guidance, and accuracy of ballistic missiles; therein lie American concerns with China's participation in Europe's Galileo global positioning project. Ballistic missile defense, which would jeopardize the integrity of China's nuclear deterrent, relies upon reconnaissance satellites. In addition, U.S. ability to project conventional force around the globe depends on all three types of satellites. Deployment of space-based weaponry would up the strategic ante even higher.[47] In sum, space technology exemplifies one dual-use industrial sector that great powers have converged on and competed over, a sector in which strategic considerations usually trump the pacifying effects of economic interdependence.

If the availability of energy resources becomes (or is expected to become) problematic—due either to scarce supplies or to increased demand because emerging economies are expanding their energy consumption—competition among major powers for control over or access to energy supplies is likely to escalate in intensity and political significance. Both scarcer supply and mounting demand characterize contemporary energy

---

[43] Barry Posen, "Command of the Commons: The Military Foundation of U.S. Hegemony," *International Security* 28, no. 1 (Summer 2003), 5–46.

[44] Antoaneta Bezlova, "Beijing: We Have Lift Off," *Asia Times*, October 14, 2005.

[45] Ashley Tellis, "India as a New Global Power: An Action Agenda for the United States," Carnegie Endowment for International Peace, 2005, 34. See pages. 34–8 for the ambitious agenda Tellis presents for enhanced U.S.-India cooperation on space.

[46] Quoted in Siddharth Srivastava, "India Races into Space," *Asia Times*, May 20, 2005.

[47] For a cautionary view of the likely effects of U.S. weaponization of space, see Michael Krepon, "Lost in Space: the Misguided Drive Toward Antisatellite Weapons," *Foreign Affairs* 80, no. 3 (May/June 2001): 2–8.

markets, especially oil. Many industry analysts estimate that a global "Hubbert's peak"—the point at which half the world's oil reserves have been extracted and after which remaining supplies become more expensive and less price competitive compared with alternative energy sources—is already upon us.[48] While there are optimists who question the dire supply-side implications of Hubbert's peak advocates, there can be no quarrel with the demand side facts: U.S. demand, about 25–30% of world consumption, continues unabated. The oil demand of China and India, while low on a per capita basis, has each increased significantly.[49] China is now the world's second largest consumer, India the fourth largest, and other Asian countries—notably Japan, Korea, and to a lesser extent Southeast Asian countries—are also large-scale oil importers.[50] All countries depend on the same sources of oil supply, most of which are located in the volatile Middle East where the world's largest reserves (about two-thirds of the world total) are found.

These circumstances seem certain to lead to sharp geopolitical competition for secure access to oil and other energy sources. China's strategic vulnerabilities with respect to oil are exacerbated by the fact that the U.S. Navy controls the sea lines of communication through which Asia's energy imports flow, and thus would be able to choke off China's supplies in the event of military conflict in the Taiwan Strait or elsewhere.[51] As mentioned above, China's efforts to ameliorate this vulnerability have resulted in long-term arrangements with various regimes, notably Iran, Sudan, Burma, and Venezuela, that are at cross purposes with the United States on various strategic and human rights issues and have engendered U.S. complaints of mercantilist attempts to "lock up" supplies of energy. As gas prices increase and U.S. consumer discontent grows, U.S.-China competition for oil could very likely intensify. China and India face what James Clad terms a "common predicament" in so far as both have very

[48] Kenneth S. Deffeyes, *Beyond Oil: the View from Hubbert's Peak* (NY: Hill and Wang, 2005).

[49] The optimist position is based on the premises that new oil fields will be discovered and that new extraction technology will be developed that will reduce the price of pumping oil from places that are difficult to extract cheaply. The argument relates less to the world's oil supply and more to what can be extracted at what price.

[50] For more detailed data on China's and India's energy consumption patterns, as well as those of other Asian countries, see Mikkal E. Herberg, "Asia's Energy Insecurity: Cooperation or Conflict," in *Strategic Asia 2004–05: Confronting Terrorism in the Pursuit of Power*, ed. Ashley J. Tellis and Michael Wills (Seattle: National Bureau of Asian Research, 2004), 339–78.

[51] Thus, in addition to trying to diversify the kinds of energy resources it uses (more natural gas and coal so as to lessen oil dependence) and the sources of such energy (i.e., sourcing from Africa, Latin America, and Central Asia, as well as the Persian Gulf), China is also moving to diversify the modes of transportation by which its energy supplies are delivered: overland pipelines from Central Asia and Russia are partly intended to reduce China's vulnerability to potential supply disruption caused by the U.S. Navy.

limited domestic sources of supply, both are highly dependent on the same sources of energy imports, and both are in transition from direct state control of energy decisions to a more market-oriented approach.[52] Thus there are also opportunities for the two to generate "common responses," which is not quite the equivalent of cooperative responses. There have been some explicit cooperative responses, such as the January, 2006 agreement "to cooperate down the entire hydrocarbon value chain,"[53] but whether this cooperation will endure is unclear. Moreover, not everyone views this cooperation in altogether positive terms: "India, sharing a ravenous thirst for oil, has joined China in an increasingly naked grab at oil and natural gas fields that has the world's two most populous nations bidding up energy prices and racing against each other and global energy companies."[54]

We agree with Mikkal Herberg's judgment that across Asia, "…to this point the evidence suggests that cooperation is falling behind competition in the search for energy security in the region." It is of course preferable that China and India, as well as all other Asian states and the United States, continue to try to temper energy competition with whatever cooperation is feasible, though we harbor some doubts that cooperative arrangements will remain intact should a direct conflict of interests arise over oil or other geostrategic issues.

Contemporary Departures from Historical-Structural Expectations?

There are two features of the contemporary global political economy that might limit the generalizability of historical-structural patterns. One is what we term the "dissymmetry" of U.S.-China interdependence: the comparatively wealthier United States provides a relatively open market for China's rapidly growing manufactured exports, while the much poorer China translates its sizeable bilateral trade surplus with the United States into international reserves that, in turn, are used to supply unprecedented flows of capital to finance continued U.S. consumption of Chinese products (see Stephen Cohen's chapter in this volume). In interdependence terms,

---

[52] James Clad, "Convergent Chinese and Indian Perspectives on the Global Order," in *The India-China Relationship: What the United States Needs to Know*, ed. Francine R. Frankel and Harry Harding (New York: Columbia University Press, 2004), 271–76. We are inclined to think that Clad overestimates the extent to which China and India have shifted to market-oriented approaches to their energy problems.

[53] Mani Shankar Aiyar, India's petroleum and natural gas minister, as quoted in Sarutha Rai, "China and India: Bidding Partners, At Least on Paper," *International Herald Tribune*, January 20, 2006.

[54] Keith Bradsher, "2 Big Appetites Take Seats at the Oil Table," *New York Times*, February 18, 2005.

the relationship between the two may be symmetrical or balanced, in the sense that both may be comparably vulnerable to costly disruptions; the relationship is dissymmetric, however, in so far as both parties have very different kinds of stakes at play. This situation is quite different from more ordinary, garden-variety forms of interdependence in which two countries increase their trade or investment with each other.[55]

Closure of U.S. markets would seriously crimp China's export-led development strategy, while cessation of China's purchases of U.S. treasury bonds would trigger a chain of consequences: the reduction in inexpensive imports would combine with dollar depreciation to increase inflationary pressures, and increases in interest rates would likely be accompanied by a slowdown in the U.S. economy as well as greater difficulty in financing budget and current account deficits. In addition, the costs to U.S. firms doing business in China would be substantial. A depreciated dollar would devalue China's stock of U.S. Treasury dollar-denominated holdings (expected to reach one trillion dollars by the end of the year) and diminish Beijing's ability to manage the value of the yuan by means of intervention in currency markets. Moreover, in view of the size and pivotal positions of the U.S. and Chinese economies, the repercussions of an economic meltdown on such a scale would surely reverberate across the Asian region and, in all likelihood, across the global economy as well. For many observers, the centrality of such arrangements (in what is arguably the world's most important bilateral economic relationship) cannot be sustained indefinitely. What remains to be determined, from this perspective, is whether a "soft landing" can be engineered or if a much harsher adjustment, or "hard landing," is unavoidable.

Little wonder, then, that former U.S. treasury secretary, Lawrence Summers, describes the U.S.-Chinese economic relationship as a "balance of financial terror," while others adjust the cold war acronym to "mutually assured *economic* destruction."[56] These hyperbolic formulations reflect the assessment that the costs of disrupting the economic relationship would be quite substantial. We argue that because dissymmetric interdependence rests on a kind of complementarity, such interdependence allows these higher economic stakes to cumulate. Were the United States to acknowledge

---

[55] We tentatively suggest that dissymmetric interdependence may make it more difficult to resolve economic disputes because negotiations are over dissimilar "goods" that are hard to directly compare (i.e., apples and oranges). In contrast, in negotiations over like goods (such as market openings, tariff reductions, increased exports or imports, national treatment, and customs or phytosanitary standards), it is easier to quantify the value of concessions and to "split the difference" in order to reach agreement.

[56] Quoted in Frederick Kempe, "U.S., China Stage an Economic Balancing Act," *Wall Street Journal*, March 28, 2006.

balance of payments constraints, take steps to increase its savings rate, and rein in its twin deficits and were China both to encourage domestic consumption rather than savings and to reduce the size of its international reserves, neither China's stake in access to U.S. markets nor the U.S. stake in continued inward capital flows would have reached such proportions.

It is improbable that decisionmakers on either side would enact the economic policies that would bring about the kind of meltdown described above, at least not on economic grounds alone. Yet what if other, perhaps strategic, stakes are factored into the cost-benefit calculations of the two sides? Would U.S.-China economic interdependence be sufficient to dissuade U.S. or Chinese decisionmakers from resorting to force in the event of a confrontation in the Taiwan Strait? While providing a definitive answer to this question is not possible, we do think that dissymmetric interdependence has increased the vulnerability of both countries and thereby raised the disincentives for either country's disruption of their economic relationship.

Generalizing about the emergence of new great powers would be much simpler if the historical patterns we have examined, insofar as they are structural in nature, yielded identical implications for both China and India. Such simplicity is elusive, however, as given not only variation in the number of simultaneous challengers but also variation in the responses of existing powers to the newcomers challenging them and the international order they have constructed. As mentioned earlier, incumbent system leaders facing multiple challengers have in the past chosen to focus their resistance, which has often taken the form of seeking to contain the challenger thought to be most threatening to the status quo. For example, Britain designated late nineteenth century Germany as the challenger most in need of containment, while at the same time enlisting the United States, also a rival, to help thwart the German challenge. In other words, some emergent challengers face containment and perhaps even confrontation, while others find their interests accommodated as they are in effect invited into the ranks of the great powers.

Has a similar pattern begun to emerge? Is the United States (or at least certain elements inside and outside of the U.S. government) in the process of defining China as the challenger posing the greatest potential threat and thus warranting containment—while at the same time enlisting (or coopting) India to that (and other) cause(s)? Along these lines, there have been considerable references to the United States and India as "natural allies." This formulation is usually predicated on three factors: both countries are large, multiethnic democracies; India, though lagging behind China in terms of liberalizing reforms, has a well-established, independent judiciary which enforces property rights and contracts and thus will prove in the longer-run to be a more valuable economic partner; and both the United States and India share an interest in preventing the emergence of China as a regional hegemon. In this context, India is often construed as a significant counterweight to rising Chinese power. Moreover, the Bush administration has declared that the United States intends to "help India become a major power in the 21st century." In addition, as Rumsfeld has made clear, the United States already differentiates its responses to the two: "We anticipate that the relationship with India will continue to be strengthened. With respect to China, it's not completely clear which way they are going."[57]

Still unclear, however, is whether the U.S. Congress is going to endorse the nuclear energy package that the Bush and Singh administrations have forged as a centerpiece of their "strategic partnership" or whether it will be willing to accept the corollary damage to the already weakened Treaty on the Non-Proliferation of Nuclear Weapons (NPT). These conditions will be necessary to cement the current U.S.-India rapprochement. Also uncertain is whether India, in view of its not-so-distant history as a leader of the Non-Aligned Movement and with vocal domestic opposition, will be willing to accept the costs to autonomy entailed in being co-opted (as some see it) by the United States. India's relations with Iran and the status of bilateral natural gas and pipeline deals will likely prove an early test of India's readiness to bend its interests to accommodate those of the United States. India may choose a more independent path.[58]

From another standpoint, Tellis observes that "two power transitions—not one—appear to be occurring concurrently in Asia today." One is the much-discussed U.S.-China power transition; the other is between China and India, both of which are "emerging powers that, growing at historically rapid rates, having fought wars previously, and abutting one another along the Asian landmass, remain natural competitors."[59] We think this "dual transition" approach is the most useful way to think about the political economy of Asia in the 21st century, though as the conceptualization makes

---

[57] Quoted in Anand Giridharadas, "India Portrays Itself as a New Type of Superpower," *International Herald Tribune*, July 21, 2005.

[58] A recent example of an independent Indian position, at least rhetorically, that the U.S. is unlikely to find congenial involves Prime Minister Singh questioning the patterns of trade and capital flows described in the preceding section: "Given the potential for investment demand in the region, we must find ways of making better use of our savings. How can we make sure that the savings and surpluses generated in our region can find investment avenues within our region?" Quoted in Anand Giridharadas, "Singh Urges Less Money for Financing U.S. Debt," *International Herald Tribune*, May 5, 2006. It is difficult to interpret this statement as other than a call for regional coordination and self-reliance and a shift away from Asian financing of American consumption.

[59] Ashley Tellis, "China and India in Asia," in *The India-China Relationship: What the United States Needs to Know*, ed. Francine R. Frankel and Harry Harding (New York: Columbia University Press, 2004), 172.

clear, regional dynamics will become much more complex as the century unfolds. For now, to the extent that the quite different U.S. reactions to the emergence of these two Asian states is perceived by China's leaders to facilitate India's emergence at the expense of China's and to more deeply integrate India into the U.S. strategic network, we expect that the two countries' trajectories, roles, and degrees of satisfaction with the status quo will likely diverge.

Conclusion: Policy Implications for the United States

This chapter has presented historical findings that depict the process of great power emergence as being both fraught with mercantilist competition and prone to large-scale violence, patterns that can offset or overwhelm the conflict-dampening effects of economic interdependence. Yet we resist the tendency to reify these patterns into immutable laws of the global political economy that are destined to recur in the interactions of the United States, China, and India in the balance of this century. Nor do we think that the presence of these patterns implies that cooperative (bilateral and multilateral) solutions are bound to be fruitless. Rather, we view the explication of historical patterns as opportunities for social, or more aptly strategic, learning that can lessen the probability that the deadly dynamics of great power interactions characteristic of prior centuries will be repeated. Accordingly, we focus on four implications for United States policy.

First, the United States would benefit from monitoring and enforcing China's compliance with its trade commitments, but there is little to be gained by bilateralizing economic frictions. If things go awry economically—for example, worsening bilateral imbalances, a collapse of the U.S. dollar, or a bursting of the housing market bubble—then avoiding the temptation to scapegoat China would be prudent. In particular, China-specific trade and exchange rate legislation and punitive executive branch actions are best avoided. Such measures encourage Americans and Chinese alike to think of these problems in zero-sum terms. If Chinese leaders lower their estimates of the future benefits of trade and cross investment, then economic interdependence will be less likely to constrain China's political and military behavior.

Second, since secure access to energy and other raw materials looms as a likely near- to medium-term point of contention, cooperative arrangements need to be forged to cope with what will be thorny, difficult-to-solve problems in the best of circumstances. We doubt seriously that national elites in any of the major resource-importing countries believe that markets, which in the energy case do not operate as economic textbooks suggest, will sort these matters out to their satisfaction.

Third, while the U.S.-Indian rapprochement is a welcome development, tighter integration of India into the U.S. strategic network, bolstering of India's strategic capabilities, and overt attempts to use India as a strategic counterweight to help contain China carry the risk of triggering unwanted Chinese countermeasures—e.g., strengthening Pakistan's nuclear and missile capabilities or augmenting China's own modest nuclear forces. Hence, the United States and India should tread carefully, building on their compatibilities and shared interests while avoiding unnecessarily provocative steps that worsen China's security dilemmas, lest China take steps to worsen theirs.

Finally, the clearest implication to emerge from historical-structural approaches is that sustained scientific and technological innovation and the resulting capacity to generate transformative technologies and leading sectors is an essential way to protect national interests amidst the turbulence associated with great power emergence and transition. As evidenced by the information technology–spurred revitalization of the United States in the 1990s, the flexibility and innovation of the U.S. economy translates into the ability to maintain the U.S. position as the world's lead economy. Failure to innovate on a virtually continuous basis in the 21st century will mean that the United States will be faced with ongoing losses of both market shares and employment to hard-charging, low-cost challengers, such as China and India, as they converge on the industries associated with the last cluster of technological innovations.

EXECUTIVE SUMMARY

This chapter examines the potential impacts of an avian flu pandemic in the Asia-Pacific, in particular the effects on regional economic integration, effectiveness of regional responses, and implications for the United States.

MAIN ARGUMENT:
East and Southeast Asia will be the center of the pandemic influenza that most public health authorities predict will likely sweep the global community in the near future. Such an outbreak will transform the region's relationship both among its increasingly integrated member economies and with the world at large. Though local and national public health structures are being urgently reinforced, the regional structures that are currently in place will likely prove inadequate to coordinate transnational activities in the event of a pandemic.

POLICY IMPLICATIONS:

- The ongoing process of economic integration within the region is at risk in a pandemic scenario.

- If a pandemic occurs within Asia's human population, regional cooperative forums on public health issues might be ineffective as many agreements are as of yet little more than declarations of intent and most are grossly underfunded.

- International collaboration to strengthen public health defenses and contain the pandemic threat is active but may not prove adequate.

- The United States has a major role to play, and how that role is played over the next decade will impact Washington's relationships in and with the region.

- Consensus and cooperation with strong accountability are cornerstones of successful technical collaboration.

When the Flu Comes: Political and Economic Risks of Pandemic Disease in Asia

Ann Marie Kimball

Ecologically, demographically, and epidemiologically the Asia-Pacific is "ground zero" for epidemics of new human pathogens, both imported and "home grown." The region is characterized by the collocation of dense communities of humans and animals (especially birds), a situation which creates opportunities for the emergence of new human pathogens. In addition, the World Bank has recently ranked the region as the world's "most open" for international trade, giving the Asia-Pacific ongoing exposure to agents arising elsewhere which make their way via travelers or commodities in global trade.[1] The security of the Asia-Pacific region is increasingly hinging on the ability of countries to maintain the security of human populations against emergent diseases. Recurrent emergent epidemics and human pandemics in the Asia-Pacific are thus an important optic with which to examine trends in a variety of other aspects of regional change. Though the previous decade witnessed numerous new human pathogens, SARS in particular served as an important "wake up call" for this need for regional change.[2]

Ann Marie Kimball (MD, MPH, University of Washington) is Professor of Epidemiology and Health Services at the University of Washington School of Public Health and Community Medicine and Director of the APEC Emerging Infections Network. She can be reached at <akimball@u.washington.edu>.

[1] The World Bank, "East Asia Update," March 2006, http://www.worldbank.org.

[2] HIV/AIDS is an example of an infection that, having entered Asia through trade and travel, now creates a "background" condition of vulnerability to other infections in the immunocompromise it causes. The incursion of HIV/AIDS into the region and the coincident aging of the populations in many countries (such as China and Japan) are creating new vulnerabilities. Human "host defenses" (i.e., the ability of the body to "fight off" infections) decline both in people infected with the HIV virus and in people as they age; Asia has increasing populations of both types of individuals. The challenge of new disease emergence will only grow over coming years.

This chapter will begin with a brief overview of the how the repeated emergence and extension of outbreaks of new infectious agents in the Asia-Pacific has transformed the regional on many levels. A second section presents a series of case studies of disease in the Asia-Pacific and examines their economic (including trade) effects. A third section then gauges the current risk of H5N1 avian influenza (or "bird flu") breaking out in the region. As a means of analyzing the potential of regional organizations to cope with such outbreaks, a fourth section contrasts the experience of the European Union (EU) and the Asia-Pacific in responding to highly pathogenic avian influenza. The chapter concludes with an analysis of the likely impact of a major pandemic outbreak in East Asia and draws implications for the United States.

Epidemics: Transformative Events

During the past decade numerous new human agents have "emerged" from the Asia-Pacific, and other emergent human agents have arrived in the region via travel and trade. These emergences have severely tested the public-health safety nets in the region. Public safety systems—water, sanitation, disease surveillance, laboratory capacity, epidemic investigation and containment, and health care systems—have all been tested and often found in need of urgent repair. First, neurologic illness (such as bovine spongiform encephalopathy, also known as BSE or "mad cow" disease) and immunocompromise and enteric disease (such as HIV/AIDS and E. Coli 0157:H7, respectively) arrive through trade and travel. Second, the region also has a propensity for spawning its own new agents. Most new human pathogens "jump" from other vertebrate species, and—for reasons which are not clear—the ecology of the Asia-Pacific favors this phenomenon.[3] This ecological reality poses challenges to the health and public health systems of the region, both national and international.

In each case of epidemic disease, ripple effects have occurred across such diverse elements of society as legal regimens, trade, and travel. Though contemporary attention is focused on the potential for pandemic flu and the incursion of H5N1 into an ever-increasing geographical range of bird populations, this is only the most recent of new pathogens to affect the region. Previous events include the introduction and spread in the 1980s

---

[3] Seventy percent of new agents of human infection arise from the jumping of pathogens from other vertebrates into humans. This has been true for such agents as tuberculosis and influenza. The mechanism by which pathogens successfully move from one species to another is not known, nor are the factors that might create opportunity for species jumping well delineated.

of HIV/AIDS through travel and contaminated product.[4] Additionally, the prion agent of BSE and new variant Creutzfeldt-Jacob disease (nvCJD in humans) from Europe has reached the region both in contaminated surgical product and in animal feeds.[5] E. Coli 0157:H7, imported into Japan in radish seeds, has caused a major outbreak in the past.[6] The region has also spawned new agents, however, including the Nipah virus, Enterovirus 71, SARS coronavirus, and most recently H5N1 avian influenza.

Why is this region at such high risk? The dense populations of human, birds, pigs, and other animals at or near burgeoning population centers create the spatial proximity for species jumping.[7] Intensification of agriculture, uneven sanitary infrastructure, and changes in production and food handling also likely play a role.

What each of these outbreak events brings to the societies they infect is profound. When relatively unknown to science and medicine, a new pathogen is more deeply frightening to both policymakers and the general population. There are no well-known effective treatments for individuals. Efforts to limit the spread of infection are hampered by the unknown nature of how the infection is spread. Is the new illness spread person-to-person? Transferred by air or by droplet? Spread fecal-orally? Carried in food, water, or other items consumed by humans?

Finally there are generally imperfect protections available against infection. Antiviral drugs for example may or may not be useful against a newly evolved viral infection such as avian influenza. Vaccines are rarely available and must be developed. Personal protective measures—such as hand washing, masks, and gloves—are often employed but have been poorly studied for their efficacy.

From the perspective of government, measures to contain infections include both domestic control within borders and consideration of transnational transmission threats. If the infection is occurring in an economy open to trade or tourism, governments may react with measures

---

[4] Ann Marie Kimball, Yuzo Arima, and Jill R. Hodges, "Stealth Infections and Global Trade: Farther, Faster, Quieter," *Globalization and Health* 1 (May 2005).

[5] Kozo Mizoguchi, "Japan Will Destroy 45 Cows Suspected of Having Mad Cow Disease," Associated Press, February 9, 2006. Prion (short for proteinaceous infectious particle) agents are unique because they are made only of proteins and are characterized by their hardy nature that is resistant to most techniques of sterilization. Prion agents cause progressive and fatal neurodegenerative disorders in both humans and animals.

[6] H. Michino et al., "Massive Outbreak of Escherichia Coli 0157:H7 Infection in School Children in Sakai City, Japan Associated with Consumption of White Radish Sprouts," *American Journal of Epidemiology* 150, no. 8 (October 15, 1999): 787–96.

[7] Asian palates prefer fresh poultry. Thus with the ongoing urbanization of population in Asia, intensive poultry enterprises are located as close as possible to the urban markets in order to facilitate freshness and reduce transportation costs.

to interrupt the traffic of people or goods to limit risk. Ideally, costs of all measures are weighed against the benefits of success and the risks of failure to combat epidemic disease. The ability to actually quantify costs and benefits is, however, not possible for new emergent infections. Timely information from other affected countries is slow and usually not available when decisions need to be taken. For the Asia-Pacific, with its heavy reliance on regional and international trade and "just in time" commerce, epidemics pose a grave threat.

A History of Regional Emergent and Imported Infections

Case studies allow a closer understanding of the broad-ranging impact of infectious disease outbreaks in the region at the local, national, and international levels. This section reviews a number of case studies, the lessons from which are summarized in **Table 1** below. By highlighting the dynamics of epidemic disease in the region, these cases help us understand the alarm that the pandemic influenza is currently causing. While many different "measures" of impact have been put forward, no single measure— be it loss of life, illness rates, economic loss, or geographic range—serves to untangle the complexity of how these events affect the societies in which they occur.

The Migration of Disease in Southeast Asia: The Nipah Virus

In late 1998 an illness broke out among livestock workers in Malaysia. The health authorities initially suspected Japanese encephalitis, a serious illness that is found in the region. Vaccination for this disease was not effective in protecting against the illness, however, and scientists soon realized that this disease was novel. Of 265 people infected and clinically ill, 105 died.[8] Some scientists felt that the emergence of the new Nipah virus was the product of an ecological chain of events that was occurring in the archipelago nations of Indonesia and Malaysia. Over the past two decades pulpwood and industrial implantation has caused extensive deforestation, reducing the natural habitat of the large fruit bat. In 1997 slash-and-burn clearing in Indonesia resulted in a significant haze of particulate pollutants that ranged over the neighboring countries of Malaysia and Singapore, darkening the skies. There is evidence that the loss of habitat and reduction

---

[8] World Health Organization, "Nipah Virus," http://www.who.int/mediacentre/factsheets/fs262/en/.

TABLE 1   Lessons learned from selected disease outbreaks

Case study	Disease	Lessons learned
Malaysia, Singapore	Nipah virus	• New disease • Widespread dislocation of industry • Transnational spread through trade
Malaysia, Taiwan	Enterovirus 71	• Poor scientific communication due to WHO structure (exclusion of Taiwan) • Increased tension in foreign relations
Japan, U.S.	E. Coli 0157:H7, BSE	• Tension in international relations • Importation of disease in trade
Vietnam	Influenza	• Increased food price • Increased international assistance
Hong Kong	Avian influenza	• "Rapid Response" • Importance of transparency • Importance of control measures
PRC	SARS	• Lack of transparency • Weak science • Transnational spread

of flowering fruit trees from both deforestation and the unseasonable haze drove the bats to forage in cultivated fruit orchards where they became collocated with large piggeries. The nipah outbreak occurred when the virus jumped from bats to pigs and then infected humans. Note that more than 90% of the human cases occurred in piggery workers.[9]

The outbreak illustrates again the close trading relationships and economic ties among countries in the region. Eleven abbatoir workers in Singapore became ill from contact with imported pigs, with one succumbing to the disease.[10] Malaysia is a predominantly Muslim society and many of the piggery workers were non-Muslim migrant laborers. Many workers were deported because of the outbreak, and half of the piggeries were shut down. Thus the outbreak of a new agent caused divisions within the affected society, the expulsion of a particular high risk group, and transmission to a trading partner. The intraregional transmission of the Nipah virus in pigs is typical of microbial traffic during outbreaks in the region.

---

[9] K. B. Chua, B. H. Chua, and C. W. Wang, "Anthropogenic Deforestation, El Nino and the Emergence of Nipah Virus in Malaysia" *Malys J Pathol* 1 (June 24, 2002): 15.

[10] N.I. Paton et al., "Outbreak of Nipah-Virus Infection among Abattoir Workers in Singapore" *Lancet* 354, no. 9186 (October 9, 1999): 1253–56.

The Slow Flow of Science in a Fractured Region: Enterovirus 71

Enterovirus 71 is a relatively unknown viral infection which causes human hand, foot, and mouth disease (HFMD)—an eruption of blister-like rash on the hands and feet and in the mouths of children. In 1997 a particularly severe cluster of illness occurred in Sarawak, Malaysia, resulting in a number of deaths. The identity of the agent was not known for some time. The following year, Taiwan experienced a major outbreak of a similar clinical illness across the entire island, an outbreak that lasted months. Of these cases, 405 were serious enough to require hospitalization and 78 children died.[11] Taiwan managed both to identify the virus as Enterovirus 71 and to complete a description of its genome.[12] Not a member of the United Nations, Taiwan is excluded from the World Health Organization (WHO). During the outbreak the ongoing investigation and results were broadcast through the APEC Emerging Infections Network and thus reached Taiwan. While this "workaround" is useful, the exclusion of Taiwan from the WHO has been very problematic for prevention and control efforts, not only for these outbreaks of Enterovirus in the late 1990s but for the ensuing SARS crisis of 2003.

The International Politics of Disease: U.S.-Japan Relations

E. Coli 0157 H7. In 1993 a large outbreak of E. Coli 0157 H7, an enteric pathogen, occurred in five western states of the United States. Appearing due to the consolidation of feedlots, slaughtering, and meat processing, the relatively unknown pathogen was transmitted in undercooked hamburger. In 1996 a large outbreak—10,000 cases—of the disease occurred among school children and factory workers in Sakai, Japan.[13] After extensive investigation, health experts traced the outbreak to hydroponically sprouted radish seeds. The Japanese imported white radish seeds from two sources: Oregon state in the United States and New Zealand. Molecular studies suggested that the source was the Oregon sprouts, and Japan ceased importation of the sprouts from the United States. This outbreak brought to light difficulties in assuring public health in Japan when two Ministries (in this case, the Ministry of Health and the Ministry of Education) were involved. The Japanese subsequently carried out a major revision of their 150-year-old public health laws to create a more powerful mandate for public health in

---

[11] J. Mackenzi et al., "Emerging Viral Diseases of Southeast Asia and the Western Pacific," *Emerging Infections* 7, no. 3 (2001).

[12] Health experts established in 2006 that the two outbreaks of Enterovirus 71 involved different strains of the virus and thus one economy did not pass contagion to another.

[13] Michimo et al., "Massive Outbreak of Escherichia Coli 0157:H7 Infection."

that country. The outbreak further highlighted the ability of such incidents to create tensions between trading economies. The trade in radish seeds was halted by Japan, but the U.S. Food and Drug Administration (FDA) did not accept much of the Japanese evidence and thus resisted taking any action against the producers.

HIV/AIDS. A second case of disease affecting U.S.-Japan relations has been HIV/AIDS, which arrived in Asia in the 1980s. Though travel was probably most important in introducing the infection to Thailand, contaminated Factor VIII (a biological product used to treat hemophilia) was indisputably an important source of introduction into Japan.[14] Despite knowledge of the risk, the four U.S. pharmaceutical houses producing Factor VIII were not asked by the FDA to recall their product. When a safer product (i.e., "heat treated" factor) became available the Japanese elected to require additional clinical trials of the new product rather than allowing it to be licensed as a substitute for the unsafe product. This decision, which was taken in part to prevent permanent U.S. domination of the Japanese market for blood factor, created delay which cost lives.[15] Litigation continues in the courts over both the contaminated products and the failure to substitute safer alternative products in Japan.

Mad cow disease. The above two examples created tension between the United States and Japan. Probably no issue is as contentious, however, as the current impasse in the trade of beef related to mad cow disease. After a three-year embargo in response to BSE, the Japanese tentatively opened their market to U.S. beef, only to close it after the first shipment arrived with neural tissues such as brain and spinal cord included—against an express agreement between the two countries. Policies on screening herds for BSE differ between the two countries, and the ongoing beef embargo costs U.S. producers $1.9 billion annually. In the meanwhile, Canada documented another case of mad cow disease in its herds in July 2006, though importation of beef from Canada to Japan had already resumed in December 2005. Producers in both Canada and Japan have undergone on-site inspection by Japanese regulators as a prerequisite for Canada to regain access to the Japanese market. The United States feels that the reinstatement of import bans of beef by Japan is thus an overreaction, and U.S. Embassy officials in Tokyo have voiced their frustration.

---

[14] Ann Marie Kimball, Yuzo Arima, and Jill R. Hodges, "Stealth Infections: Farther, Faster, Quieter" *Globalization and Health* 1 (2005).

[15] Public Works and Government Services, Health Canada, *Commission of Inquiry on the Blood System in Canada,* report prepared by the Krever Commission Report, (Ottawa, Ontario, Canada: Health Canada, 1997).

Government Response to Epidemics: SARS in Hong Kong

There is likely no better illustration of the ability of transnational disease transmission to foster major change in "non health" affairs than severe acute respiratory distress syndrome (SARS). In February of 2003 the Global Public Health Information Network (GPHIN) noted an unusual report of pneumonia from the People's Republic of China (PRC).[16] Reports of an atypical pneumonia appearing in Guangzhou were not confirmed by the Chinese authorities. Information continued to reach the international community, however, on hundreds of cases of a type of pneumonia that was not responsive to treatment. Government scientists announced the culprit was chlamydia, a well-known pathogen. Reports surfaced of anxious citizens mobbing pharmacies. When transnational transmission occurred in March of 2003 and was traced to a Chinese individual ill with the new disease in Hong Kong, the WHO began an intense and unprecedented international effort to orchestrate disease investigation and control. At the time the first SARS cases appeared in China, the PRC considered the unauthorized reporting of disease to be a violation of national security. In 2002 for example, a Fulbright scholar had been detained and imprisoned for publishing HIV/AIDS reports on the Internet.[17]

During the crisis, the WHO took four very important steps. First, by choosing a non-regional-specific name for the unknown disease, the organization avoided the risk of stigmatizing Asia and more specifically China (note that influenza has been commonly named "The Hong Kong flu" for the origin of its first appearance).

Second, the WHO elected to define risky areas for travel through travel advisories that were based not only on reports from the country involved (which were decided in part on how control within that country's borders was proceeding) but also on the reports of cases in other countries which were traced to the country of origin. Thus although the mayor of Toronto was adamant that Toronto should be removed from the travel advisory list because there was no risk in that city, cases transmitted in Toronto which

---

[16] Designed and built by the government of Canada in the 1990s, GPHIN is an electronic "webcrawler" that visits key websites in multiple languages on a continuous basis to pick up phrases suggestive of new outbreaks. Rumors picked up by GPHIN are then processed in Toronto and sent to Geneva where the team contacts their in-country counterparts to confirm, deny, or elaborate on the GPHIN information. Within the WHO's Global Outbreak Alert and Response (GOARN) group, GPHIN has become a central source of disease reporting. For more information on GPHIN, see http://www.phac-aspc.gc.ca/media/nr-rp/2004/2004_gphin-rmispbk_e.html.

[17] Dr. Yanhai Wan, a 2002 Fulbright New Century scholar, was detained for interrogation for posting reports of the HIV/AIDS epidemic in China—an act believed by authorities to be in violation of the State Secrets law. Wan was released September 20, 2002 after about five weeks of questioning.

were reported both in the Philippines and to the WHO kept Toronto on the list.[18]

Third, the WHO employed electronic communications and created a consortium of research laboratories in a collective effort to describe the agent of the disease. Brokered by the WHO, the eleven laboratories—including some in Asia—worked collaboratively with daily postings of new findings on a secure site so each laboratory could proceed as rapidly as possible to discover the identity of the pathogen. This resulted in the complete genetic mapping of the new coronavirus in one month.[19]

Finally, rather than simply maintaining all operations at the headquarters in Geneva, the WHO began to use its regional office—the Western Pacific Regional Office (WPRO) in Manila—as an important coordination center. This decision allowed both for the timely fielding of teams into affected areas and for the speedier provision of information.

SARS had enormous impact on travel and somewhat of a lesser effect on trade. The impact on travel was already beginning prior to the issuance of WHO advisories, but these advisories probably exacerbated the loss of travel dollars in affected economies. At the same time the greater information base provided to the public by the WHO in their advisories may have spared non-affected areas from such losses. The Asian Development Bank has estimated the cost of SARS at $59 billion for East and Southeast Asian economies, with a GDP growth decline of 0.6%.[20]

One area which was not well addressed during the SARS crisis was the need for cross-country communication between the ministries of commerce, finance, tourism, and health. Within APEC the Emerging Infections Network, which links commerce and health, was thrust into serving this communications function. This lack of international communication between various ministries remains an area of concern in many countries.[21]

Following the SARS outbreak major changes in transparency occurred throughout the governments of the region. The PRC revised the legal basis for disease reporting and welcomed extensive international technical assistance in designing and upgrading laboratories and information systems, including Internet-based systems. Though there continues to be operational issues, the collaboration between the PRC and the WHO has

---

[18] *CBC News*, "Toronto Mayor Rails against WHO Warning," April 24, 2003, http://www.cbc.ca/news/.

[19] Debora MacKenzie, "Genetic Sequence of SARS Virus Revealed," *NewScientist*, April 14, 2003, http://www.newscientist.com.

[20] Asian Development Bank, "Assessing the Impact and Cost of SARS in Developing Asia," Asian Development Bank Outlook 2003 Update, 75–92.

[21] Nedra Pautler and Ann Marie Kimball, "Lessons of SARS: The APEC EINet Experience," APEC Special Report, May 6, 2003, http:www.apec.org.

become much more constructive. Acutely aware of the loss of confidence that SARS provoked among its Asian neighbors, the PRC has taken a number of positive steps in regaining this confidence. One such step has been hosting both the World Bank's pledging meeting on avian influenza in 2005 and the APEC Emerging Infections Symposium in 2006.

Domestic and Economic Repercussions of Epidemics: Vietnam

Vietnam provides an illustrative case in the epic of highly pathogenic avian influenza in Southeast Asia. Vietnam was among the countries hit by the SARS pandemic in 2003. Sixty-two cases of SARS occurred, resulting in six deaths.[22] One year later, in October of 2004, three outbreaks of highly pathogenic avian influenza occurred in Tien Giang, Long An, and Soc Trang. By the close of 2004, estimates hold that 45 million poultry either were culled or died.[23]

In Vietnam, as in much of the rest of Southeast Asia, poultry is largely kept in backyard flocks, with 95% of flocks containing less than 50 birds.[24] Approximately half of all households in Vietnam (rural or urban) keep chickens, and in rural areas the ratio jumps to seven of ten households. Given the $1 farm-gate price of a bird, the overall loss from the Vietnamese economy was about $45 million—or 0.1 % GDP—in 2004. Egg production slid by more than 1 billion units between 2003 and 2004. Consumers substituted pork and other meats for poultry and eggs and thus paid a higher price for food, which led to an increase in inflation from 3% to 9.5% in mid-2004.[25]

In terms of the human toll, 23 cases and 16 deaths had occurred in the country by the end of 2004. Human cases occurred in 13 provinces, and avian cases occurred in 57 provinces. Vietnam has taken stringent methods to control avian influenza outbreaks. A team of WHO technical advisers was mobilized to assist the government's investigation and control of the human disease. In seeking to control the four waves of avian influenza Vietnam has experienced, Hanoi has welcomed assistance from the WHO, Food and Agriculture Organization (FAO), and World Organization for

---

[22] This experience has been well described in the clinical and epidemiologic literature. See Hoang Thu Vu et al., "Clinical Description of a Completed Outbreak of SARS in Vietnam, February-May 2003," *Emerging Infectious Diseases* 10, no. 2 (February 2004).

[23] Viet Tuan Dihn, Martin Rama, and Vivek Suri, "The Costs of Avian Influenza in Vietnam," Policy Note, October 11, 2005, http://www.worldbank.org.

[24] Food and Agriculture Organization of the United Nations, "The Hen Which Lays the Golden Eggs—Or Why Backyard Poultry Are So Popular," FAO Publication, 2006.

[25] The World Bank, "Vietnam at a Glance", September 9, 2005, http://devdata.worldbank.org/AAG/vnm_saag.pdf.

Animal Health (OIE). Along with technical assistance has come badly needed financial support from a variety of sources including the U.S. government, World Bank, and others. Extensive public education about the risks associated with sick poultry, the signs of the disease in both birds and humans, and the urgency of reporting has been carried out. Compensation for culling moved from 10% to 50% of farm-gate price by June of 2005. In contrast to neighboring Thailand, Vietnam has embarked on an ambitious poultry vaccination scheme with plans to vaccinate up to 60 million birds. Vietnam has already imported 120 million doses of H5N1 vaccine from Harbin, China and plans to import an additional 260 million doses.

The Vietnamese have received unprecedented amounts of foreign assistance, which have been accompanied by foreign visitors and have enhanced foreign collaboration. The Canadians have launched one initiative in the region to strengthen public health.[26] Vietnam has begun to take a leadership role within the APEC Health Task Force and hosted an APEC health ministers' summit in Da Nang in May of 2006. Long absent from the high-speed communications networks in the region, Vietnam is participating with foreign partners to bring research and education networks to the country.[27] Enhanced Internet access will assure timely information for disease control.

Thus in a low income country, the impact of this new scourge has been to raise the price of food, decrease the production of poultry, and open the society to more transnational assistance. Political consequences to Vietnam are seen in the country's determination to use assistance to reinforce its public health infrastructure and to collaborate in the leadership of economic fora such as APEC. This last point is remarkable in a society which had long been seen as a former Soviet client state with a socialized economy.

---

[26] In September 2005 Canada announced a five-year, $15-million project to strengthen the capacity of public health systems in both Southeast Asia and China to detect and respond effectively to emerging infectious diseases. See J. Mackenzi et al., "Emerging Viral Diseases of Southeast Asia and the Western Pacific." The Canada-Asia Regional Emerging Infectious Diseases (CAREID) project will focus on assisting the region by improving surveillance and outbreak investigation and response, strengthening lab systems, increasing preparedness, and improving effective communications and public education. The project is the result of meetings and consultations with international partners as well as a mission by CAREID to the region to assess their capacity needs to combat emerging infectious diseases.

[27] The European Union and others are bringing the TIEN2 network into the Mekong Basin region in June, 2006. See "Joint Media Release," Delegation of the European Commission to Vietnam, http://www.delvnm.cec.eu.int/en/whatsnew/news240.tom. Additional information on the TEIN2 networking effort is available at http://www.TEIN2.net.

The Current Risk of Flu: Avian Influenza

Given the background of emergent diseases in the above case studies, we can now outline the risk of the current pandemic flu threat, setting up for the next section's assessment of the competency in the region to address this threat. Highly pathogenic avian influenza (HPAI) has been the bane of the commercial poultry industry since modern techniques for raising fowl were introduced. Influenza in poultry flocks, which strikes suddenly in closely crowded industrial settings, has a very short duration and high lethality. Outbreaks have occurred in Europe and North America, but the ongoing outbreaks of HPAI in the Asia-Pacific have been unusual in that they have been widespread geographically, have been recurrent over a period of three years and have included an increasing toll of sporadic human cases with a high mortality rate.

There are a number of strains of viruses which cause HPAI. The most recent and destructive to date is H5N1. The importance of these outbreaks of avian flu in the human community is twofold: (1) widespread loss of a food resource given the destruction of flocks through disease or culling and (2) a continuing source of potential human pandemic influenza. Human influenza pandemics are believed to arise when viruses jump species to humans from their natural reservoir in the pig or the bird populations. Given that the major historical influenza pandemics of 1918, 1957, and 1968 preceded the technology for actually tracking genetic change in viruses, some of what is posited below is thus hypothetical. The 1918 virion has, however, just been detailed using modern techniques, and this new science demonstrates the alarming possibility that just one or two mutations are sufficient to allow an avian virus to gain the ability to transmit efficiently from human to human.[28] Prior both to this work and the 1997 cluster of bird flu that appeared in humans in Hong Kong (described above), scientists had believed that an intermediate animal (such as the pig) had to be infected with and then transmit an avian virus to humans in order for efficient human-to-human infection to take place.[29] Swine infection has also been documented with the H5 subtype, and this is a second potential "reservoir" for the sparking of a global pandemic.[30] Recent reports from Indonesia (which has recorded the greatest number of human bird flu cases and a mortality rate of over 60%) are rekindling pandemic concern. An extended

---

[28] Jeffrey K. Taubenberger et al., "Initial Genetic Characterization of the 1918 'Spanish' Influenza Virus," *Science* 275, no. 5307 (March 21, 1997): 1793–96.

[29] Chan PK. "Outbreak of Avian Influenza A (H5N1) Virus Infection in Hong Kong in 1997" *Clinical Infectious Disease* 34, no. 2 (March 21, 2002): S58–64.

[30] David B. Lewis, "Avian Flu to Human Influenza," *Annual Review of Medicine* 57(2006): 139–54.

family in northern Sumatra suffered eight cases of bird flu with six deaths. While exposures from poultry have occurred, authorities are struggling to rule out human-to-human transmission. In Indonesia, the spread of the virus among swine has also caused concern about a potential additional reservoir for human infection.[31]

Human influenza is well known.[32] Every year influenza circulates around the globe in both the temperate and the southern regions. In each hemisphere the circulation coincides with colder times of the year. Outbreaks routinely cause increased deaths, especially among the elderly and chronically ill. The belief is that in the tropics the various flu viruses circulate irregularly, with different viruses circulating at the same time, and circulation occurring throughout the calendar year. Occasionally, flu becomes much more deadly. In 1918 the great pandemic of influenza killed an estimated 50 million people.[33]

A signal event of human-to-human spread of the virus in an efficient manner would alert the world to the inception of a global pandemic. When avian influenza first emerged in humans in Hong Kong (1997) the territory mounted a vigorous response. Eighteen human cases with six deaths occurred, and exposure to live poultry was implicated. Hong Kong authorities were prompt in alerting the WHO. Extensive international assistance from the WHO coupled with very strong political and technical measures imposed by the government succeeded in preventing further spread. Following the initial small cluster of human cases, the Hong Kong government slaughtered over one million birds. "Live markets" for meat— very popular in the territory—were closed, reorganized to prevent co-mingling of different species of birds, disinfected, and finally re-opened. At that time the Hong Kong authorities began requiring that all birds imported be vaccinated.[34]

---

[31] D. Cryanoski, "Bird Flu Spreads among Java's Pigs," *Nature* 435, (May 26, 2005): 390–91.

[32] The scientific puzzle of what "flu" really is and why it becomes so deadly from time to time has, however, been the object of consistent research. Influenza is actually caused by a family of viruses which are, like the coronavirus and the HIV virus, built of RNA. RNA viruses are much more likely to "make mistakes" or mutate when replicating. RNA viruses have just one strand of genetic material whereas the more stable double helix of DNA has two. But in the world of viral life, mistakes can mean flexibility for survival of the species. So these viruses are constantly changing their characteristics, becoming more or less virulent (serious in the clinical illness they cause) and more or less infectious to humans.

[33] Jeffrey K. Taunenberger and David M. Morens, "1918 Influenza: The Mother of All Pandemics" *Emerging Infectious Disease* 12, no. 1 (January 2006): 15–22.

[34] Interestingly, Hong Kong has been spared from the recent HPAI outbreaks and has no reported human cases of avian influenza.

Since the first cases were reported from South Korea three years ago, the Asian avian epidemic has been recurring in flocks throughout Asia.[35] The illness in birds has ominously been accompanied by an increasing number of sporadic human infections. The particular influenza virus involved, H5N1, was first identified in 1996 in geese in southern China.[36] In fact the "agricultural revolution" of poultry in Asia has been remarkably rapid, with exports from East Asia of poultry products increasing 25 fold between 1990 and 2000 (See **Figure 1**).

The incursion of the H5N1 virus into flocks of birds has extended into Europe and Africa through two possible routes: wild bird migration and illicit traffic of infected poultry. Of great concern to policymakers is the ongoing tally of sporadic human cases of severe influenza due to the same virus. To date ten countries have reported to the WHO a total of 196 cases of human bird flu with 110 deaths. Indonesia has recently surpassed Vietnam in reporting the largest proportion of cases and deaths. To date 93 cases and 42 deaths have occurred in Vietnam, where clusters of cases possibly related to human-to-human transmission have also occurred. A mere four countries (Vietnam, Indonesia, Thailand, and China) have reported more than 80% of the cases and deaths over the past three years. This link between the disease in birds and human illness has created alarm with authorities at the national and international levels of public health. Countries and organizations have launched major efforts to prepare for an eventual pandemic of human influenza if and when the virus is able to jump more consistently between species. Though at its core a public health issue, pandemic preparedness is an activity that also extends across all sectors.

There is no doubt that the consequences of highly pathogenic bird flu in Asia have been devastating for the poultry industry in the affected areas. Widespread culling of infected flocks and quarantines to limit traffic to and from geographically proximate farms have crippled the production and trade of poultry. Both the sheer loss in numbers of birds over the three-year period in affected countries and the number and nature of trade restrictions put into place against affected countries demonstrate the severity of the situation.

---

[35] "Avian Influenza—South Korea: Suspected," *PROMED* archive no. 20031212.3047, December 12, 2003.

[36] Interestingly, recent reports hold that these same geese (Bar-headed geese) have been the subject of a recent breeding program in China. This breeding effort, begun in 2003, is directed toward domestication and repopulation of this species. See PROMED "Avian Influenza: China, Laos" 114, abstracted from news, *Nature* 441 (May 18, 2006): 263.

FIGURE 1   Poultry exports from East Asian countries (1961–2002)

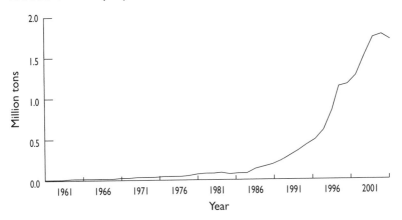

SOURCE: Data for this table sourced from Food and Agriculture Organization of the United Nations (FAOSTAT), 2003, http://faostat.fao.org.

Enhanced Regional Cooperation?

Health authorities have long been concerned about the "biosecurity" of the region, but only did the incursion of HIV/AIDS help elevate that concern to the level of regional political and economic fora. In 1994 the International AIDS Conference was convened in Japan, marking the first global conference on AIDS to be convened in Asia. Coincident with the conference were initial business-outreach efforts in an effort to ally the goals of enterprises with those of public health and safety in the combating of epidemic threat. Initiated as the USAID-funded Asia Pacific Alliance Against AIDS, these efforts eventually led to the creation of the Global Business Coalition on HIV/AIDS by the World Health Organization. This group has worked to bring AIDS to the attention of the Davos Summit participants. The global focus on a single epidemic trumped, however, the concerns of the Asia-Pacific relating to the general risk of disease emergence. The Asia-Pacific Economic Cooperation (APEC) forum recognized the broader area of concern in both the 2000 and the 2002 Leaders' Declaration.[37]

The SARS epidemic galvanized both these groups and the countries in the region to begin intensive preparedness activities designed to contain and prevent epidemic threats. The increasing economic integration of the region brings at least three major assets to this effort: (1) intensive investment in

---

[37] Citation of Leaders' Declarations from the 2000 and 2002 APEC summits, http://www.apec.org (Leaders' Declarations); "Facing Globalization the APEC Way: Report to the APEC Economic Leaders, 2000," Apec Business Advisory Council, October 2000; and APEC Economic Leaders Declaration, Los Cabos, Mexico, October 27, 2002.

transnational science and research collaboration, (2) a common interest in preventing the heavy human and economic cost that trade and travel disruption causes, and (3) an increasingly robust electronic communications architecture within and across borders in the region. These three drivers have come to serve not public health but rather economic development. Each contributes to public health aims, however, especially in terms of disease preparedness. Pandemic preparedness for influenza, which is only the more recent version of SARS preparedness, typifies the aligning of these interests for the common defense.

Following the SARS epidemic of 2003 and 2004 many countries maintained heightened vigilance. Singapore General Hospital, for example, did not relax its SARS precautions for nearly a year following the last case of SARS. Epidemiologists did not know if SARS would recur in 2005. Preparations for such a recurrence were undertaken not only nationally using health assets but also transnationally through policy dialogue APEC convened its first health ministerial and commissioned an ad hoc SARS taskforce. With the assistance of the WHO and other international partners the PRC instituted new information and surveillance systems. New infectious disease hospitals were built with explicit design features for isolation and quarantine near Shanghai and other population centers.

The threat of a human pandemic of bird flu in 2003 further advanced the dialogue and activities of preparedness. The concern has now effectively joined the sectors of commerce and health in local, national, and transnational responses. Governments have played an important role in the process, as have formal international organizations such as the WHO, OIE, FAO, and others. In addition, the combined efforts of healthcare systems and business are leading to unprecedented levels of cooperation and is advancing preparedness and response capabilities.

Avian Influenza: A Tale of Two Regions

Pandemics follow trade and travel routes in people, animals, and goods; at the same time, however, the value of crossborder traffic and trade is such that the threats of pandemic disease are seen as "common" by communities that are more closely integrated. This appreciation of the common threat increases the possibility of collective, cooperative response as opposed to fragmented single-nation efforts. The importance of such a response can be appreciated if the experience of the Asia-Pacific is contrasted with that of the EU in combating HPAI.

The European Union case. The EU is a treaty-based regional organization that works under treaty law; the Asia-Pacific is a much more diverse collection of nations which has increasingly developed pragmatic cooperation on trade and health. Similarly transnational cooperation on health issues is more formalized in the EU than in the Asia-Pacific. Perhaps in consequence, the response in the world of commerce to avian influenza in Asia is in stark contrast to that of the EU in 2003.

When outbreaks of H7N7 virus occurred in the Netherlands, Belgium, and Germany, the EU successfully (1) contained the outbreak among poultry through a vigorous early response, (2) played down fears of a consequent human outbreak despite the occurrence of human cases of disease, and (3) used "regionalization" effectively as a means of maintaining poultry trade despite the presence of the disease in poultry. This has not been the experience with the highly pathogenic avian influenza in Asia. Specifically, the measures taken by the EU to control the outbreak were vigorous and included:

- standstills on the transportation of live poultry, hatching, and slurry

- destruction of affected and proximate flocks to prevent disease spread

- significant surveillance and monitoring measures within a wide radius of outbreak locations

- strict sanitation measures regarding table eggs and poultry intended for slaughter

- movement restrictions and protective measures for people working on poultry farms and handling poultry

- bans on poultry exports from the "protected zones" to outside countries and the use of specific labeling measures for domestic sales[38]

The European avian influenza episode was also characterized by scrupulous "regionalization" of trade sanctions against any and all infected EU member economies, a step that encouraged trading partners to limit imports only from the afflicted areas of the given country. Although the Netherlands is a tiny country, its EU trading partners were careful to allow the Hague authorities to demarcate "infected" versus "disease free" areas for bird flu, allowing trade in poultry to continue at a reduced rate throughout much of the crisis. Clearly a high degree of transparency and trust among trading partners is required for this strategy to work.

---

[38] European Commission, "Avian Influenza (AI) in the Netherlands, Belgium, and Germany—Chronology of Main Events and List of Decisions Adopted by the Commission," http://ec.europa.eu/food/fs/ah_pcad/ah_pcad_77_en.pdf.

Regional organizations in the Asian theater. In contrast to the highly integrated European model discussed above, the more diverse regional organization of the Asia-Pacific did not succeed in stemming the spread of HPAI among fowl over the past three years. There are a variety of reasons for this failure. First, disease detection and reporting in the region has historically been problematic. The EU enjoys integrated and transparent disease-specific surveillance systems. The Asia-Pacific does not have such an asset. A second reason is that trade—especially over land routes—is less manageable by governments. Borders in many areas are porous and illicit trade in poultry products has stumped efforts to put into place the strict measures that are necessary to control HPAI. Yet another reason is that poultry is central to the diet and income of many poor families in the region who simply cannot afford to destroy flocks and therefore are reluctant to report disease.[39] Finally, the regional cooperation mechanisms that are currently in place lack the foundation of treaty law (as is the case with the EU states). A foundation in treaty law would enhance the perception of permanence and therein invite more serious investment in systems such as transparent collaborative systems.

While the primary purpose of most regional cooperation programs is economic in nature, Asian states have used these cooperative venues to promote regional health programs and complement national pandemic plans. Since 2000, the APEC Leaders' Declaration has emphasized the need to combat emerging infections. In 1996 APEC's Industrial Science and Technology Workgroup funded the first regional cooperative health project, the Emerging Infections Network. Following the SARS outbreak, APEC convened its first meeting of health ministers and launched a new health task force on cooperative efforts to combat avian influenza. Both the lack of financial support and the difficulty in coordinating across numerous working groups have hampered APEC's response to date.

The SARS epidemic convinced Asian political leaders of the importance of regional cooperation on public health goods. In mid-December 2005, sixteen Asian leaders signed the East Asian Summit Declaration on Avian Influenza Prevention, Control and Response at the first ever East Asian Summit. Regional cooperation and coordination at the cabinet-level was enhanced with the establishment of an ASEAN HPAI task force in October

---

[39] The Indonesian experience is particularly instructive here. In many poor countries farmers are understandably reluctant to report sick birds and even more reluctant to sacrifice their flocks through extensive culling. Though there is no unified expert opinion on vaccination as an option, vaccination of flocks is in use in Vietnam, China, and to a limited extent Indonesia. See "Avian influenza A(H5N1), update 18: FAO/OIE/WHO Technical Consultation on the Control of Avian Influenza, Situation (human) in Thailand and Viet Nam Feb 05 2004," *PROMED* archive no. 20040205.0421, February 5, 2004. Consultation held February 3–4. Report dated February 2, 2004.

2004. Health ministers from the ASEAN+3 countries met in late November 2004 to discuss the avian flu. The ASEAN Health Group on Communicable Diseases monitors human health aspects through the ASEAN+3 Emerging Infectious Disease program while an ASEAN Animal Health Trust Fund has also been established. The Ayeyawady-Chao Phraya-Mekong Economic Cooperation Strategy (ACMECS) is one of the newer regional groupings, but at the second summit meeting in November 2005 the five members adopted the Declaration on Partnership in Combating Avian Influenza and Other Infectious Diseases. Closer cooperation on monitoring and surveillance, sharing of information and best practices, and developing rapid response teams, as well as the possibility of establishing a regional stockpile of drugs were also discussed.[40]

If a pandemic occurs within the human population in Asia, these regional cooperative forums on public health might be ineffective as many agreements are as yet little more than declarations of intent and most are grossly underfunded. Experience has shown that pandemics place extreme economic and political stress on relationships among regional economies. Despite discussion there has been no consensus on protocols in the area of stockpiling for sharing resources, much less "drills" on how such agreements would actually be operationalized. During the SARS epidemic—which killed fewer than a thousand people worldwide—most activities that required face-to-face interaction, such as entertainment, retail shopping, and travel activities—were severely curtailed. Economies such as Hong Kong that rely on tourism to promote employment and earn foreign exchange earnings were severely affected. An H5N1 human pandemic can be expected to result in greater impact on overall economic activity. Movement of poultry between China and Vietnam has already been curtailed. China and Thailand alone account for 15% of global poultry shipments, but their products have been banned in Japan, their biggest export market. A human influenza pandemic in Asia would likely lead to a further tightening of trade restrictions.

An Asian influenza pandemic would likely impinge on the movement of labor within countries; restriction of travel between the interior and coastal regions of China would have a deleterious effect on China's economic growth rates, not to mention the likely impact on employment generation. Concurrently, economic activity would be severely curtailed by the restriction of labor movement between countries—such as between the Philippines, the Middle East, and Thailand (which receives over a million laborers from its neighboring countries). Migrant laborers frequently have neither legal status in the host country nor access to public health facilities.

---

[40] Songrit PhonNgern, "Laos Today: Laos and ACMECD Partners to Increase Cooperation on Bird Flu," *Laos Today*, December 7, 2006, http://www.voanews.com/lao/2006-07-12-voa1.cfm.

A large scale pandemic likely will lead to more stringent border controls, possibly complemented by deportation of labor, as well as to acute suffering among migrants.[41]

International Organizations

Increasing clout. International global organizations are increasing their influence and clout in Asia. This development may be in part due to the lack of strong regional structures as described above, the increasing perceptions of the region as a global threat given the repeated emergence of infections with pandemic potential, or to a combination of these two factors.[42] This "new activism" of international organizations in the region can be seen in the enactment of travel advisories during SARS, the passage of the new International Health Regulations, and other actions discussed as follows. In the wake of the SARS outbreak the World Health Assembly passed the new International Health Regulations. These regulations had been revised over the previous seven years, with extensive consultation of national and regional authorities. The new regulations formalized a number of innovative elements:

- increased diversity of information sources on potential outbreaks;

- a decision tree for the declaration of public health emergencies;

- a positive obligation for all countries to establish capacity to control disease within their borders, and an exhortation to donor countries to assist poorer member countries in achieving this; and

- criteria on which travel advisories will be declared. The regulations, which are to be phased in over the next two to three years, clearly will bolster the efforts of regional entities to cope with pandemic threats in Asia.

The loosely integrated APEC or ASEAN can not, however, provide the kind of strong, central coordination that was crucial in orchestrating the response within the European Union to infection in the Netherlands. World Health Organization presence in the region is also fragmented between the WPRO in Manila and the Southeast Asia Regional Office (SEARO)

---

[41] C. C. Tchoyoson et al., "Nipah Virus Encephalitis: Serial MR Study of an Emerging Disease," *Radiology*, 222, no. 1 (2002): 219–26. As noted in the Malaysian scenario, piggery workers were deported during the Nipah crisis. Stigmatization and exclusion of immigrants is an unfortunate but common occurrence during epidemics.

[42] Of note is that influenza pandemics historically often were named for their origin, as for example the Spanish flu (1918), the Asian flu (1957) and the Hong Kong flu (1968), which also "fixed" Asia as a source of health threats in the minds of many in the West.

in New Delhi. A great deal of authority rests with WHO headquarters in Geneva, an arrangement that was problematic during SARS. Though since that time some progress toward empowering the regional offices has taken place, collaboration between the two Asia offices is less than perfect. The continent is arbitrarily divided with North Korea as a SEARO member state and South Korea as a WPRO state. As mentioned earlier, UN recognition of China leaves Taiwan excluded entirely from the WHO.

Limitations of cross-border cooperation. In light of the lessons learned through the case studies, whether the international response to influenza will be adequate is not clear. In particular, supply and stockpiling antiviral and vaccines are contentious topics among nations. Countries with relatively poor economies, such as Indonesia, do not have the capacity to stockpile antiviral as do wealthier countries, such as Singapore. Experience has shown, however, that with transborder traffic flu quickly spreads to all economies if not controlled effectively at the primary site of transmission. Thailand has publicly offered 35,000 doses of Tamiflu to the first economy to report human-to-human transmission. Such regional "sharing" of medications or vaccine has not been extensively discussed, however, and thus will not likely happen.

Attempts to strengthen regional data sharing for surveillance have been equally mixed. Although influenza laboratory surveillance has been strengthened, notably in China, the Mekong Basin nations have worked for nearly a decade to share disease surveillance information and had mixed success. Political divisions in the diverse region of the Asia-Pacific translate to perpetually weak regional structures, which bode ill for effective transnational collaboration in times of pandemic emergency.

Conclusion

The Lowy Institute recently has published a study on the macroeconomic consequences of pandemic influenza. The findings are based on a global equilibrium (G-cubed) model developed for the Asia-Pacific situation.[43] The projected impacts, even from a mild scenario, are very large echoing the relatively large impacts seen in the case study descriptions here. How different regions are affected and how regions eventually emerge from a

---

[43] Warwick McKibben projects a global loss of $330 billion with a mild scenario of pandemic influenza. A massive scenario would incur about $4.4 trillion in losses. See Warwick J. McKibben and Alexandra A. Sidorenko, "Global Macroeconomic Consequences of Pandemic Influenza," Lowy Institute for International Politics, February 2006, http://www.lowyinstitute.org/Publication. asp?pid=345.

potential pandemic such as avian influenza will also depend on a number of long-term factors, outlined below.

Impact on labor availability. Absenteeism and mortality will increase in the short term. In the longer term, the impact of an avian influenza pandemic will depend on mortality and diminution of human labor skills. The overall impact on labor will depend on a long list of variables including unemployment and underemployment levels, the ability to switch to more capital-intensive means of production, and the impact on the relative price of labor. Given that human capital shortages are real and acute for most developing countries, however, an avian influenza pandemic—is a threat to economic prosperity because of the impact on labor competitiveness.

Impact on the structure of the family. The family is the basic unit of production in most of the Asian agrarian-based economies. The family is also the primary source of insurance and transmitter of culture and knowledge across generations. The HIV/AIDS epidemic has shown that humans have great capacity to adapt and ensure survival, even in a very high-prevalence environment. The avian influenza pandemic is different, however, in that infection is rapid, allowing little time or scope for families to devise survival strategies.

Impact on savings and investment. The pandemic will have an impact on long-term saving and investment. Savings—which have traditionally been very high in Asia—may be reduced as a consequence of reduced output and increased health expenditures. There may be less incentive to save and invest, depending on how expectations concerning future economic prosperity are formulated. Regions strongly affected by a pandemic may also become less attractive to external investors.

Personal medical care systems. Some countries, such as Singapore and Thailand, have world-class personal medical care systems and thriving medical tourism industries.[44] SARS demonstrated the vulnerability of these economic engines to infectious disease. Hospitals not only were the major source of infection where infection control was weak but were swamped with the ill and forced to cancel all elective admissions for weeks during the outbreak. Such will be even more the case with an influenza pandemic. The WHO has recommended the use of tamiflu prophylaxis for medical personnel if and when the pandemic spark ignites. Stocks of this antiviral are in short supply and their deployment likely will be contentious within countries as well as internationally, as discussed above.

Relationships between countries. The trust and confidence that countries have in each other will be affected both by what happens during the

[44] "Medical tourism" here is used in the WTO, GATS sense, i.e., international health seeking by persons willing to cross borders for medical care in pursuit of quality or price reduction.

pandemic and by the situation in the new steady state once the pandemic has run its course. The most important factor likely to test relationships during a pandemic is how well regional agreements and commitments to cooperation stand up to the actual pandemic. One issue in particular will be rapid and adequate access to regional stockpiles of drugs. The burden that specific countries or groups of countries are expected to shoulder in limiting the further spread of the pandemic—whether in terms of cost or diversion of resources from other pressing social and health issues—will also test relationships as will preemptive bans and controls on movement of people and goods from HPAI-affected regions. Post-pandemic relations between different regions will be determined by both the extent of damage suffered and the resilience of individual countries. All states will suffer from some form of economic and political disruption, but states that were already poor may find their status greatly reduced in comparison to states that are better able to insulate themselves from HPAI. The poorer states' resulting sense of insecurity could contribute to a reduction in regional cooperative arrangements or to the rise of aggressive unilateral actions.

Regardless of how Asia emerges from an avian influenza pandemic, the steady roll of emergent infections in the region is a guarantee that this will not be the last challenge from new infectious disease the region must face. Within the region, transnational systems of cooperation and working relationships among public health authorities are being strengthened at all levels—universities, governments, and civil society, including business. The marked uptick in investment in science and technology is also contributing to this cooperation.[45] Traditional trade forums such as ASEAN and APEC have begun to define their role in public safety in relation to that of the WHO. The World Bank "pledging" conference held in Beijing brought together a number of intersecting partners but did not include the trade community. In May 2006 ABAC—the business group supporting APEC— convened a workshop in Hong Kong to insure business continuity; the WHO is not represented, although the Health Task Force of APEC is. Ideally these two major sectors—health care and trade—would be synchronized in a flexible and effective strategy for pandemic response, however, that vision has not crystallized as regional preparedness efforts proceed.

---

[45] Richard P. Suttmeier, "Science and Technology: A New World in the Making?" in *Strategic Asia, 2004–05: Confronting Terrorism in the Pursuit of Power*, ed. Ashley J. Tellis and Michael Wills (Seattle: The National Bureau of Asian Research, 2004), 456–86.

Implications for the United States

The implications for the United States in terms of public safety, political leadership, and economic well-being are profound. The United States has been an active provider of technical assistance and financing for preparedness, though some aspects of this outreach have been less successful than others. Given the rapid economic integration of the region, U.S. national interest will be best served by positioning the United States as a reliable partner in this effort.

In 2003 President George Bush elaborated a bilateral bio-security agreement with Singapore that centered on assuring security from infectious disease.[46] The agreement established the Regional Emerging Disease Intervention Center (REDI) in Singapore to be supported by the two governments. The center initially was a surprise to the WHO, although a visit by the Director General was hastily arranged after the announcement. The Center provided the United States with an opportunity to demonstrate U.S. sincerity in regional collaboration against pandemic threats; however, two years later the burden of supporting the center fell primarily to the Singaporean government.[47]

The central hurdle for the United States most likely will be demonstrating that U.S. actions in public health are collaborative and not simply directed toward thwarting potential bioterror attacks against the American people. Pandemic preparedness offers an opportunity for the United States to do this. Compared to Australia, Canada, and other donor nations, the United States has been less nimble in actually expending funds successfully in recipient countries. The amount slated to be spent under the Center for Disease Control's Global Disease Detection initiative and other such initiatives is substantial, however, and recently released "Requests for Agreements" from the Center for Disease Control invite foreign governments to request U.S. assistance for pandemic preparedness in substantial amounts.[48]

As demonstrated above, the impact of a pandemic or other emergent disease threat in the Asia-Pacific is profound and crosses many sectors both within the affected countries and transnationally. Thus for the United States the stakes in "getting it right" are high, given that many U.S. major financial partners and trading partners reside across the Pacific. Beyond the scope of

---

[46] The Whitehouse, Press Release, "Health Security Initiative: Presidential Action," October 21, 2003, http://www.whitehouse.gov/news/releases/2003/10/20031021-5.html.

[47] Some disgruntled wags referred to the center located in the Biopolis complex of Singapore as the "not ready" center. The center has subsequently seen much more generous and sincere support from the United States as the pandemic flu threat has sharpened, thus quieting some of the criticism.

[48] See "Surveillance and Response to Avian and Pandemic Influenza," Funding Opportunity Number CDC-RFA-C106-607, http://www.cdc.gov/od/pgo/funding/CI06-607.htm.

this chapter but of note is that U.S. Pacific Command (PACOM) has taken a leadership role in preparing the region's militaries for cooperative response and planning. This activity will undoubtedly prove of central value in the event of a pandemic.[49]

In particular, governments with strategic vision will increasingly focus on recognizing and enabling direct collaboration between the various sectors—the commercial and industrial sector, the trade and transportation sectors, the medical care industry, and the traditionally "public" public health sector. Far from benign neglect, this is a stance of active involvement in which governments assist in the evolution of equitable, sustainable systems that provide public goods—such as population safety from infectious diseases. By becoming an integral element of how business is done in the region, through corporate citizenship or public private partnerships, the establishment of population biosecurity will be more timely and in scale with the needs of the region.[50]

---

[49] Andrew S. Erickson, "Combating a Collective Threat: Protecting U.S. Forces and the Asia-Pacific from Pandemic Threat," and James R. Campbell, "Military Preparation and Response to Pandemic Influenza Outbreak in the Asia-Pacific Region," in *An Avian Flu Pandemic, What Would It Mean and What Can We Do?* NBR Pacific Health Summit briefing book, June 2006.

[50] Melinda Moore, "Influenza Surveillance in the Asia-Pacific Region: A New Role for Business," and Andrina Lever and Roberto Romulo, "Business, AI and APEC: Putting Rubber to Road—A Response Plan for Every Business," in *An Avian Flu Pandemic, What Would It Mean and What Can We Do?* (Emerging Infections/Pandemics Workgroup publication for the Pacific Health Summit, Seattle, June 20–22, 2006).

STRATEGIC ASIA 2006–07

INDICATORS

TABLE OF CONTENTS

Strategic Asia
by the Numbers

The following twenty pages contain tables and figures drawn from NBR's Strategic Asia on-line database and its sources. This appendix consists of 23 tables covering: economic growth, trade and foreign investment, population size and growth; politics and international relations; energy consumption and oil supplies; and armed forces, defense expenditures, conventional military capabilities, and weapons of mass destruction. The data sets presented here summarize the critical trends in the region as well as changes underway in the balance of power in Asia.

The Strategic Asia database contains additional data for all 37 countries in Strategic Asia. Hosted on the program's website (http://strategicasia. nbr.org), the database is a repository for authoritative data for every year since 1990, and is continually updated. The 70 indicators are arranged in 10 broad thematic areas: economy, finance, trade and investment, government spending, population, energy and environment, communications and transportation, armed forces, weapons of mass destruction, and politics and international relations. The Strategic Asia database was developed with .NET, Microsoft's XML-based platform, which allows users to dynamically link to all or part of the Strategic Asia Program's data set and facilitates easy data sharing. The database also includes additional links that allow users to seamlessly access related on-line resources.

The information for *Strategic Asia by the Numbers* was compiled by Strategic Asia research assistants Peter Mattis and Evan Morrisey and Next Generation research fellow Tim Cook.

Economies

Driven by continued rapid growth in China, economic recovery in Japan, and strong growth in India, plus robust inflows of foreign investment, average GDP growth across Asia of 7% is well ahead of the global average of 4.7%. Consumer demand is increasing as incomes rise across Asia, further supporting economic growth in many states.

- China surpassed the United Kingdom and France to become the world's fourth largest economy in 2005 and remains the second largest in purchasing power parity terms.

- Japan's economy is recovering from its decade-long stagnation, prompting the first interest rate rise—from a base rate of zero—in almost six years.

- Despite recent corruption scandals, the South Korean economy is improving as the service sector strengthens along with increasing consumer demand.

- Bolstered by high oil prices, growing domestic demand, and investment, Russia has become the world's twelfth largest economy.

TABLE 1   Gross domestic product

	GDP ($bn constant 2000)				Rank	
	1990	1995	2000	2004	1990	2004
United States	7,055.0	7,972.8	9,764.8	10,763.9	1	1
Japan	4,130.4	4,456.2	4,746.1	4,932.9	2	2
China	444.6	792.8	1,198.5	1,715.0	4	3
Canada	535.6	583.0	714.4	789.4	3	4
South Korea	283.6	413.0	511.7	613.1	6	5
India	268.0	345.4	457.4	581.2	8	6
Australia	273.2	320.5	387.5	444.1	7	7
Taiwan	–	–	321.3	344.9	–	8
Russia	385.9	239.7	259.7	328.8	5	9
Indonesia	109.2	159.4	165.0	197.2	9	10
Hong Kong	106.2	139.4	165.4	188.9	10	11
Thailand	79.4	120.0	122.7	150.1	11	12
Malaysia	45.5	71.5	90.3	106.8	13	13
Singapore	43.9	67.5	91.5	102.5	14	14
Philippines	56.2	62.6	75.9	88.5	12	15

SOURCE: The World Bank, *World Development Indicators*, 2006; (data for Taiwan) Central Bank of China, 2005.
NOTE: These values show GDP converted from domestic currencies using 2000 exchange rates. Figures for Taiwan are calculated using the average exchange rate for 2000. Dash indicates that no data is available.

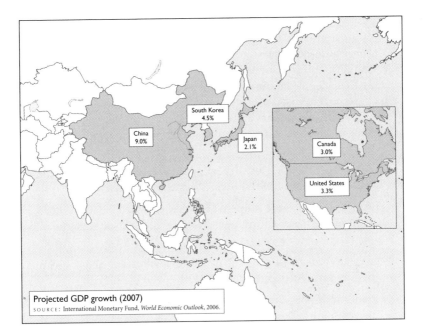

Projected GDP growth (2007)
SOURCE: International Monetary Fund, *World Economic Outlook*, 2006.

TABLE 2   GDP growth and inflation rate

	GDP growth (%)			Inflation rate (%)		
	1990–99	2000–04	2005	1990–99	2000–04	2005
United States	2.6	3.0	3.5	3.0	2.5	3.2
Japan	1.5	1.3	2.7	1.3	-0.5	–0.3
China	9.3	8.4	9.9	7.4	0.8	1.8
Canada	2.1	3.0	2.9	2.1	2.4	2.2
South Korea	6.2	5.7	3.9	5.6	3.0	2.8
India	4.8	5.7	7.6	10.0	5.0	4.2
Australia	3.4	3.9	2.5	2.6	2.1	2.7
Taiwan	5.8	3.4	3.8	3.2	0.6	2.3
Russia	–6.6	5.7	6.4	34.8	15.9	12.7
Hong Kong	3.5	4.6	7.3	6.8	0.4	0.9
Indonesia	3.6	4.1	5.6	19.3	9.1	10.5
Thailand	5.1	4.7	4.5	5.1	1.8	4.5
Malaysia	6.6	5.0	5.3	10.5	1.5	3.0
Singapore	6.9	3.8	6.4	2.0	1.0	0.4
Philippines	2.7	4.2	5.1	9.2	4.5	7.6

SOURCE: Central Intelligence Agency, *The World Factbook*, various editions.

Trade

Trade is a cornerstone of economic growth in Asia, particularly in the emerging economies of East and Southeast Asia. With global trade policy in disarray after the suspension of the Doha Round, many states are focusing their efforts on the pursuit of bilateral and multilateral free trade agreements. While regional trade appears healthy, higher energy prices and protectionist sentiments in advanced Asian economies could slow cooperation.

- China's global trade surplus reached a new high of $102 billion in 2005, triple that of 2004. Beijing's yuan revaluation and other minor trade concessions have failed to alleviate U.S. concerns.

- Russia's global trade surplus exceeded that of China's in 2005 at $120 billion—a result of high global oil and gas prices. Japan also maintained a wide surplus.

- ASEAN is increasingly seeking bilateral trade agreements with its trading partners (e.g. India, South Korea, and the EU).

- Poor transportation and port infrastructure, combined with burdensome customs regulations, challenge trade in South Asia.

TABLE 3   Trade flow

	Trade flow ($bn constant 2000)				Rank	
	1990	1995	2000	2004	1990	2004
United States	1,159.6	1,627.3	2,572.1	2,582.1	1	1
China	129.9	283.9	530.2	1,186.9	6	2
Japan	649.4	763.5	957.6	1,028.6	2	3
Hong Kong	197.3	380.7	475.3	651.7	5	4
Canada	296.3	414.3	617.4	604.2	4	5
South Korea	118.0	235.4	401.6	585.0	7	6
Russia	305.9	157.0	176.8	289.5	3	7
Malaysia	67.0	150.0	206.7	248.9	10	8
India	39.8	83.8	130.5	222.4	13	9
Australia	88.1	127.7	178.0	203.9	8	10
Thailand	68.3	131.9	153.3	197.5	9	11
Indonesia	66.2	118.8	117.9	143.3	11	12
Philippines	42.8	67.9	82.7	101.2	12	13
Vietnam	4.1	14.1	35.1	65.4	15	14
New Zealand	21.6	29.2	36.6	43.1	14	15

SOURCE: The World Bank, *World Development Indicators*, 2006.
NOTE: Data for United States, Japan, Canada, Australia, and New Zealand is for 2003 rather than 2004. No data is available for Singapore or Taiwan.

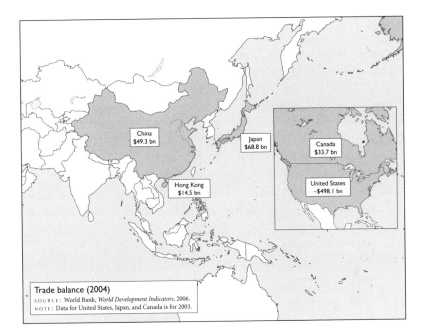

Trade balance (2004)
SOURCE: World Bank, *World Development Indicators*, 2006.
NOTE: Data for United States, Japan, and Canada is for 2003.

TABLE 4   Exports and export partners

	Exports ($bn) 2005	Export destinations (top three partners in 2005 with percentage share of total exports)
United States	927.5	Canada (23%), Mexico (13%), Japan (6%)
China	752.2	U.S. (21%), Hong Kong (16%), Japan (11%)
Japan	550.5	U.S. (23%), China (13%), South Korea (8%)
Hong Kong	286.3	China (45%), U.S. (16%), Japan (5%)
Canada	364.8	U.S. (84%), Japan (2%), UK (2%)
South Korea	288.2	China (25%), U.S. (15%), Japan (8%)

SOURCE: Central Intelligence Agency, *The World Factbook*, 2006.

TABLE 5   Import and import partners

	Imports ($bn) 2005	Import origins (top three partners in 2005 with percentage share of total imports)
United States	1,727.0	Canada (15%), China (15%), Mexico (10%)
China	631.8	Japan (17%), South Korea (12%), Taiwan (11%)
Japan	451.1	China (21%), U.S. (13%), Saudi Arabia (6%)
Hong Kong	291.6	China (45%), Japan (11%), Taiwan (7%)
Canada	317.7	U.S. (58%), China (7%), Mexico (4%)
South Korea	256.0	Japan (19%), China (14%), U.S. (11%)

SOURCE: Central Intelligence Agency, *The World Factbook*, 2006.

Trade Dependency

Most Asian states are highly dependent on trade, particularly many of the smaller Southeast and East Asia states. Asia accounts for 21% of world exports, and intra-regional trade comprises 40% of Asia's exports. While export-driven expansion has greatly contributed to these states' economic development, their high dependency on trade suggests structural vulnerabilities, including susceptibility to global financial shocks.

- Trade was equivalent to 65% of GDP in China and 57% in Russia, higher than in India, Japan, and the United States.

- China's merchandise exports growth continued to expand by nearly 30% in 2005, but import growth was nearly halved at 17.6%.

- Though high in Northeast and Southeast Asia, intra-regional trade and investment are significantly lower in South Asia, where lack of complementarities in trade and cool political relations remain stumbling blocks to regional integration.

- Although low in volume, oil exports are causing Central Asia's trade to accelerate faster than that of other subregions.

TABLE 6   Trade intensity

	Trade as a share of GDP (%)				Rank	
	1990	1995	2000	2004	1990	2004
Hong Kong	255.9	294.7	287.4	376.2	1	1
Malaysia	147.0	192.1	228.9	221.1	3	2
Mongolia	76.9	97.2	128.0	162.3	7	3
Macao	164.2	119.9	152.7	161.8	2	4
Cambodia	18.9	77.7	111.6	140.5	13	5
Vietnam	81.3	74.7	112.5	140.0	5	6
Thailand	75.8	90.4	124.9	136.4	8	7
Papua New Guinea	89.6	105.6	134.8	126.0	4	8
Turkmenistan	–	170.4	179.7	123.5	–	9
Tajikistan	63.0	131.7	170.6	110.6	10	10
Philippines	60.8	80.5	108.9	102.4	11	11
Kazakhstan	–	82.5	105.4	101.1	–	12
Kyrgyzstan	78.8	71.8	89.4	95.4	6	13
South Korea	57.0	58.7	78.5	83.8	12	14
Sri Lanka	67.2	81.6	88.6	81.9	9	15

SOURCE: The World Bank, *World Development Indicators*, 2006.
NOTE: Data for Macao is for 2002 rather than 2004. No data is available for Singapore or Taiwan. Dash indicates that no data is available.

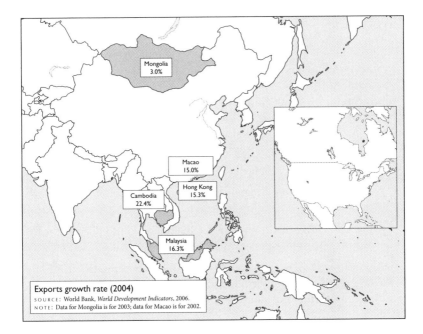

Exports growth rate (2004)

Mongolia 3.0%
Macao 15.0%
Hong Kong 15.3%
Cambodia 22.4%
Malaysia 16.3%

SOURCE: World Bank, *World Development Indicators*, 2006.
NOTE: Data for Mongolia is for 2003; data for Macao is for 2002.

TABLE 7   Trade with Asia and the United States

	Share of trade with Asia (%)			Share of trade with the United States (%)		
	1990	2000	2004	1990	2000	2004
Hong Kong	53.1	66.5	72.1	16.1	14.8	11.0
Malaysia	46.0	59.9	61.6	16.9	18.8	37.1
Mongolia	26.0	72.5	68.7	0.9	13.8	10.7
Macao	45.0	49.0	56.6	21.5	27.7	24.0
Cambodia	70.8	53.9	59.0	–	30.3	24.6
Vietnam	34.6	70.5	63.8	0.0	3.6	11.0
Thailand	32.6	54.5	58.1	15.7	16.8	21.3
Papua New Guinea	30.9	31.6	26.9	5.9	1.5	1.7
Turkmenistan	–	38.5	12.5	–	1.8	6.1
Tajikistan	–	56.4	29.9	–	2.0	5.2
Philippines	31.9	51.5	61.3	26.6	24.5	33.8
Kazakhstan	–	42.3	48.4	–	3.3	2.4
Kyrgyzstan	–	56.8	62.7	–	5.4	2.5
South Korea	22.4	46.5	51.7	27.0	20.2	15.1
Sri Lanka	30.0	42.9	45.7	15.4	20.1	15.3

SOURCE: International Monetary Fund, *Direction of Trade Statistics*, various editions.
NOTE: Data after 1990 includes trade with Russia and Central Asia. Dash indicates that no data is available.

Investment

Investment is a crucial component of economic growth in Asia. While investment in China is higher than in any other state in the region, Russia, India, and Australia are also attracting increasing amounts of foreign investment. Japan, South Korea, and China are leading sources of FDI in developing Asia, particularly in Southeast Asia.

- Asia is attracting nearly 25% of global FDI. Inflows are highest in China, Russia, and Asia's newly industrialized economies—Hong Kong, South Korea, Singapore, and Taiwan.

- In Southeast Asia, Thailand, Vietnam, Indonesia, and Malaysia have relaxed foreign ownership controls to attract greater inward FDI.

- Inward FDI growth in Russia is rapid, totaling $14.1 billion in the first half of 2006—almost equal to the $14.6 billion total gain in 2005.

- India received record-level FDI in 2004, concentrated in IT and other skill-intensive sectors. Indian outward FDI, particularly in IT, manufacturing, and natural resources, is also rising.

TABLE 8   Flow of foreign direct investment

	FDI inflow ($bn)				Rank	
	1990	1995	2000	2004	1990	2004
United States	48.5	57.8	321.3	106.8	1	1
China	3.5	35.8	38.4	54.9	5	2
Australia	8.1	12.0	13.6	42.9	2	3
Hong Kong	–	–	61.9	34.0	–	4
Singapore	5.6	11.6	16.5	16.0	4	5
Russia	–	2.1	2.7	15.4	–	6
South Korea	0.8	1.8	9.3	9.2	10	7
Japan	1.8	0.0	8.2	7.8	8	8
Canada	7.6	9.3	66.1	6.3	3	9
India	–	2.1	3.6	5.3	–	10
Malaysia	2.3	4.2	3.8	4.6	7	11
Kazakhstan	–	1.0	1.3	4.1	–	12
New Zealand	1.7	3.7	4.0	2.5	9	13
Vietnam	–	–	1.3	1.6	–	14
Thailand	2.4	2.1	3.4	1.4	6	15

SOURCE: International Monetary Fund, *International Financial Statistics*, 2006.
NOTE: Data for India in 2004 is from United Nations Conference on Trade and Development, *World Investment Report*, 2005. Dash indicates that no data is available.

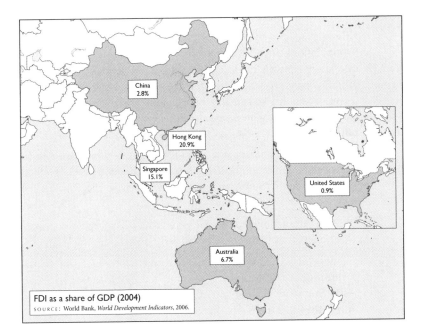

FDI as a share of GDP (2004)
SOURCE: World Bank, *World Development Indicators*, 2006.

TABLE 9 Origins of FDI

	Origins of FDI (leading countries of origin for inward investment in 2004)
United States	UK, Netherlands, Japan
China	Hong Kong, Virgin Islands, Japan
Australia	U.S., UK, Japan
Hong Kong	Germany, Singapore, U.S.
Singapore	EU, U.S., Japan
Russia	UK, Luxembourg, Netherlands
South Korea	U.S., EU, Japan
Japan	U.S., Netherlands, France
Canada	U.S., EU, Japan
India	Mauritius, U.S., UK
Malaysia	Germany, Singapore, U.S.
Kazakhstan	U.S., UK, Netherlands
New Zealand	Australia, U.S., Netherlands
Vietnam	U.S., UK, Netherlands
Thailand	Japan, Germany, U.S.

SOURCE: U.S. Department of Commerce, *Country Commercial Guides*, 2005 and 2006; and *Economist Intelligence Unit*, 2006.

NOTE: Since data for FDI by country is not reported in a consistent form and varies across sources, this table shows only the main countries of origin for FDI and omits the values and percentage share.

Population

Large populations are a source of both strength and weakness in Asia and, despite falling growth rates in Northeast Asia, they will continue to expand overall. Larger populations, combined with rising incomes, will increase competition for resources and consumer demand in line with growth, but could be a drag on economic development in China and Japan as aging populations challenge social safety nets and shrink workforces.

- Russia will face a demographic crisis if the country does not reverse the current population decline. Government initiatives such as amnesty for illegal immigrants are being tested in the Russian Far East, where population decline is most acute.

- South Asia populations are growing the fastest of all regions in Asia and are concentrated mostly in urban areas and the coastal plains.

- Dense populations, as well as close proximity of human and animal populations, have led to a rise in the emergence of infectious diseases in Asia. Indonesia has so far experienced the highest number of fatalities attributed to avian influenza.

TABLE 10   Population

	Population (million)				Rank	
	1990	1995	2000	2004	1990	2004
China	1,135.2	1,204.9	1,262.6	1,296.2	1	1
India	849.5	932.2	1,015.9	1,079.7	2	2
United States	249.6	266.3	282.2	293.7	3	3
Indonesia	178.2	192.8	206.3	217.6	4	4
Pakistan	108.0	122.4	138.1	152.1	7	5
Russia	148.3	148.1	146.3	143.8	5	6
Bangladesh	104.0	116.5	128.9	139.2	8	7
Japan	123.5	125.4	126.9	127.8	6	8
Vietnam	66.2	73.0	78.5	82.2	9	9
Philippines	61.1	68.4	75.8	81.6	10	10
Thailand	54.6	58.3	61.4	63.7	11	11
Myanmar (Burma)	40.8	44.5	47.7	50.0	13	12
South Korea	42.9	45.1	47.0	48.1	12	13
Canada	27.8	29.4	30.8	32.0	14	14
Nepal	19.1	21.7	24.4	26.6	15	15

SOURCE: The World Bank, *World Development Indicators*, 2006.

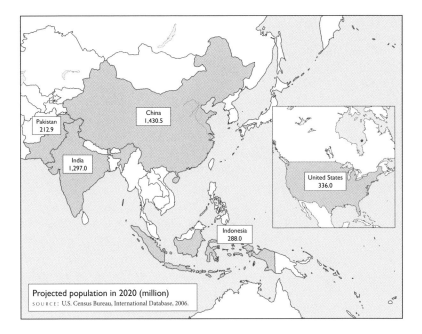

Projected population in 2020 (million)
SOURCE: U.S. Census Bureau, International Database, 2006.

TABLE 11   Population growth and life expectancy

	Population growth (annual %)			Life expectancy at birth (yrs)		
	1990	2000	2004	1990	2000	2004
China	1.5	0.7	0.6	69	70	71
India	2.0	1.7	1.4	59	63	63
United States	1.1	1.1	1.0	75	77	77
Indonesia	1.8	1.3	1.3	62	66	67
Pakistan	2.5	2.4	2.4	59	63	65
Russia	0.4	−0.0	−0.5	69	65	65
Bangladesh	2.3	2.0	1.9	55	62	63
Japan	0.3	0.2	0.1	79	81	82
Vietnam	2.2	1.3	1.0	65	69	70
Philippines	2.3	2.0	1.8	66	70	71
Thailand	1.4	1.0	0.9	68	69	71
Myanmar (Burma)	1.8	1.3	1.1	56	59	61
South Korea	1.1	0.8	0.5	71	76	77
Canada	1.5	0.9	1.1	77	79	80
Nepal	2.4	2.3	2.0	55	61	62

SOURCE: The World Bank, *World Development Indicators*, 2006.

Politics and International Relations

Transition is the watchword for Asian politics as many important states, including China, India, Japan, and South Korea, either will be facing or have recently experienced leadership changes. U.S. diplomacy has focused intently on improving relations with Asia to garner support for dealing with North Korea and the Iranian nuclear crisis.

- Relations between Tokyo and Seoul have worsened both over responses to North Korea's July 2006 missile tests and over historical grievances, placing Washington in a difficult position with two key alliance partners in Northeast Asia.

- India is becoming a more assertive global power, while popular discontent has made domestic politics in Pakistan unstable. Relations between the two states are increasingly delicate after the Mumbai bombings in July 2006.

- U.S.-Russian relations are deteriorating due to U.S. pressure both for democratic reforms in Russia and for better protection of intellectual property, as well as over failure to agree on Russia's WTO accession.

TABLE 12 Political leadership

	Political leadership	Date assumed office	Next election
Australia	Prime Minister John Winston Howard	March 1996	2008
Canada	Prime Minister Stephen Harper	February 2006	2011
China	President Hu Jintao	March 2003	N.A.
India	Prime Minister Manmohan Singh	May 2004	2009
Indonesia	President Susilo Bambang Yudhoyono	October 2004	2009
Japan	Prime Minister Junichiro Koizumi	April 2001	2007
Kazakhstan	President Nursultan A. Nazarbayev	December 1991	2012
Malaysia	Prime Minister Abdullah bin Ahmad Badawi	October 2003	2009
Pakistan	President Pervez Musharraf	June 2001	2007
Philippines	President Gloria Macapagal-Arroyo	January 2001	2010
Russia	President Vladimir Vladimirovich Putin	May 2000	2008
South Korea	President Roh Moo-hyun	February 2003	2007
Taiwan	President Chen Shui-bian	May 2000	2008
Thailand	Prime Minister Thaksin Shinawatra	February 2001	2006
United States	President George W. Bush	January 2001	2008

SOURCE: Central Intelligence Agency, *The World Factbook*, 2006.
NOTE: Japan's prime minister will step down in September 2006. Thailand is holding new elections in October 2006. Table shows next election year in which the given leader may lose or retain his position. In some countries, elections may be called before these years.

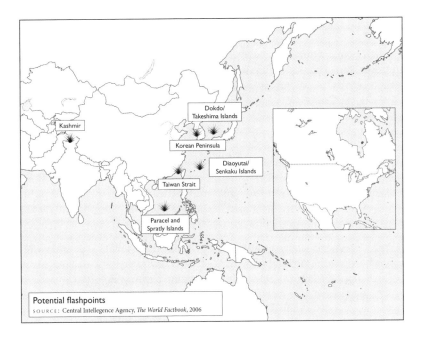

Potential flashpoints
SOURCE: Central Intellegence Agency, *The World Factbook*, 2006

TABLE 13 Political rights, corruption, and globalization rankings

	Political rights score		Corruption score		Globalization index	
	2000	2005	2000	2005	2001	2005
Australia	1	1	8.3	8.8	23	13
Canada	1	1	9.2	8.4	10	6
China	7	7	3.1	3.2	47	54
India	2	2	2.8	2.9	48	61
Indonesia	3	2	1.7	2.2	38	60
Japan	1	1	6.4	7.3	29	28
Kazakhstan	6	6	3.0	2.6	–	–
Malaysia	5	4	4.8	5.1	20	19
Pakistan	6	6	–	2.1	–	50
Philippines	2	3	2.8	2.5	33	32
Russia	5	6	2.1	2.4	44	52
South Korea	2	1	4.0	5.0	31	30
Taiwan	1	1	5.5	5.9	–	36
Thailand	2	3	3.2	3.8	30	46
United States	1	1	7.8	7.6	12	4

SOURCE: Freedom House, *Freedom in the World*, 2001 and 2005; Transparency International, *Corruption Perception Score*, 2001 and 2005; and AT Kearney/Foreign Policy, *Globalization Index*, 2001 and 2006.
NOTE: Political rights = ability of the people to participate freely in the political process (1 = most free/7 = least free). Corruption = degree to which public official corruption is perceived to exist (1 = most corrupt/10 = most open). The globalization index tracks changes in economic integration, technological connectivity, personal contact, and political engagement (rank of 62 countries, 1 = most globalized). Dash indicates that no data is available.

Energy

Economic growth is accelerating energy demand throughout Asia and net exporters, such as Malaysia, Russia, Central Asia, and Australia, stand to gain. Coal—an abundant resource in countries such as China, India and Australia—remains an important fuel, especially in the face of rising oil and gas prices.

- China and India drive much of the expanding global energy demand and could surpass the United States as the world's leading oil consumers within 30 years.

- China began exploratory oil drilling near disputed territory with Japan in August 2005, while South Korea and Japan continue to dispute ownership of the Dokdo/Takeshima islands.

- Kazakhstan and China recently completed a pipeline that carries oil between the two states as well as from Russia to China. Kazakhstan is planning to double oil production within the next decade.

- Renewed interest in nuclear power could open up new markets for Russia, South Korea, and China to export equipment and expertise.

TABLE 14   Energy consumption

	Energy consumption (quadrillion Btu)				Rank	
	1990	1995	2000	2004	1990	2004
United States	84.6	91.2	98.9	100.4	1	1
China	27.0	35.2	38.8	59.6	2	2
Russia	–	27.9	27.5	30.1	–	3
Japan	18.4	20.7	22.4	22.6	3	4
India	8.0	11.5	13.6	15.4	5	5
Canada	11.1	12.2	13.0	13.6	4	6
South Korea	3.8	6.5	7.9	9.0	6	7
Australia	3.7	4.1	4.8	5.3	7	8
Indonesia	2.2	3.3	4.1	4.7	8	9
Taiwan	2.0	2.9	3.8	4.4	9	10
Thailand	1.3	2.2	2.6	3.4	10	11
Malaysia	1.0	1.5	1.9	2.5	12	12
Uzbekistan	–	1.8	1.9	2.3	–	13
Kazakhstan	–	1.9	1.9	2.2	–	14
Pakistan	1.2	1.6	1.9	2.0	11	15

SOURCE: U.S. Department of Energy, *Energy Information Administration*, 2006.
NOTE: Table shows energy consumption of petroleum, natural gas, coal, hydroelectric, nuclear, geothermal, solar, wind, and wood and waste power. Dash indicates that no data is available.

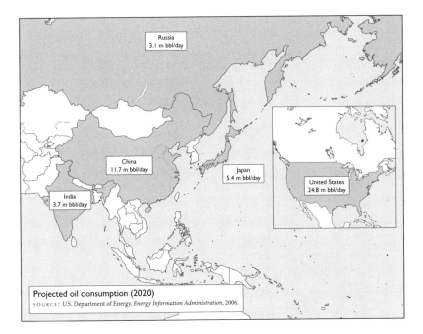

Projected oil consumption (2020)
SOURCE: U.S. Department of Energy, *Energy Information Administration*, 2006.

TABLE 15   Oil supplies and reserves, 2004

	Oil supply (M bbl/d)*			Proven oil reserves (bn barrels; main fields)
	Product.	Consum.	Imports	
United States	8.7	20.6	12.6	21.9 (Gulf of Mexico, Alaska)
China	3.6	6.4	2.9	18.3 (Daqing, Shengli)
Russia	9.3	2.8	–6.6	60.0 (Samotlor, Romashkin)
Japan	0.1	5.4	5.3	< 0.1
India	0.8	2.5	1.7	5.4 (Mumbai, Upper Assam)
Canada	3.1	2.3	–0.8	178.9 (Alberta, British Columbia)
South Korea	< 0.1	2.2	0.7	–
Australia	0.6	0.9	0.4	3.5 (Bass Strait, Carnarvon Basin)
Indonesia	1.0	1.2	0.2	4.7 (Duri, Minas)
Taiwan	< 0.1	1.0	0.9	< 0.1
Thailand	0.3	0.9	0.6	0.6 (Gulf of Thailand)
Malaysia	0.9	0.5	–0.3	3.0 (Peninsular Malaysia)
Uzbekistan	0.1	0.2	< 0.1	0.6 (Kokdumalask, Shurtan)
Kazakhstan	1.2	0.2	–0.9	9.0–36.9 (Tengiz, Karachaganak)
Pakistan	0.1	0.3	0.3	0.3 (Potwar Plateau, Sindh prov.)

SOURCE: U.S. Department of Energy, *Energy Information Administration*, 2006.
NOTE: Estimates for Kazakhstan's proven oil reserves vary. Dash indicates that no data is available.
* Thousand barrels per day.

Defense Spending

Regional defense expenditures continue to grow as Asian states undergo military modernization. Increased budget outlays reflect corresponding economic growth rather than signaling a regional arms race. Asia remains relatively stable through a combination of regional balancing, cooperation, and the U.S. security presence.

• Between 2001 and 2006, the United States has increased defense spending by 48%, largely directing this spending toward research and development, equipment replacement, and deployments in Iraq and Afghanistan.

• The United States and countries in Asia are calling for increased transparency in China's defense expenditures, which officially increased 14.7% to roughly $35 billion. Analysts place the figure as high as three times that amount.

• Japan has the world's sixth largest defense budget. Although agreeing to pay three-fifths of the estimated $10 billion to relocate U.S. troops to Guam, Japan is resuming a trend of defense expenditure cuts.

TABLE 16   Total defense expenditure

	Expenditure ($bn)				Rank	
	1990	1995	2000	2004	1990	2004
United States	293.0	267.9	300.5	465.0	1	1
China	11.3	33.0	42.0	62.5	3	2
Russia	–	82.0	60.0	61.9	–	3
Japan	28.7	50.2	45.6	45.1	2	4
India	10.1	10.0	14.7	19.6	6	5
South Korea	10.6	14.2	12.8	16.3	4	6
Australia	7.3	8.4	7.1	14.3	8	7
Canada	10.3	9.1	8.1	11.4	5	8
Indonesia	1.6	4.4	1.5	7.6	11	9
Taiwan	8.7	13.1	17.6	7.5	7	10
Myanmar (Burma)	0.9	1.9	2.1	6.2	12	11
North Korea	–	5.2	2.1	5.5	–	12
Singapore	1.7	4.0	4.8	5.0	10	13
Pakistan	2.9	3.6	3.7	3.3	9	14
Vietnam	–	0.9	1.0	3.2	–	15

SOURCE: International Institute of Strategic Studies, *The Military Balance*, various editions.
NOTE: Estimates for China and North Korea vary widely. Dash indicates that no data is available.

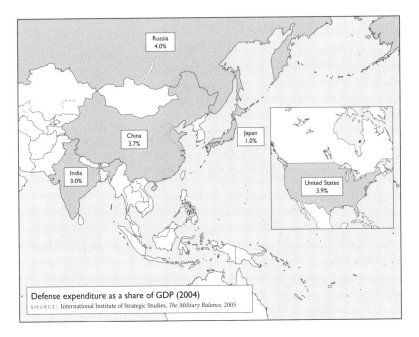

Defense expenditure as a share of GDP (2004)
SOURCE: International Institute of Strategic Studies, *The Military Balance*, 2005

TABLE 17   Defense expenditure as share of GDP and CGE

	Defense expenditure as a share of GDP (%)			Defense expenditure as a share of CGE (%)		
	1990–94	1995–99	2000–04	1990–94	1995–99	2000–04
United States	4.9	3.4	3.4	20.6	16.3	17.3
China	4.9	5.6	3.9	31.3	25.3	19.4
Russia	7.7	6.0	4.5	29.7	24.0	18.4
Japan	1.0	1.0	1.0	7.8	7.0	–
India	2.8	3.1	2.9	15.9	15.1	14.4
South Korea	3.7	3.2	2.7	13.4	17.7	13.9
Australia	2.4	2.2	2.2	9.5	8.6	7.2
Canada	1.9	1.3	1.2	7.1	6.2	6.3
Indonesia	1.5	1.7	2.1	15.8	11.0	7.8
Taiwan	5.0	4.9	2.7	31.8	27.7	–
Myanmar (Burma)	4.2	6.9	5.8	71.7	122.3	–
North Korea	25.5	14.7	19.9	28.5	–	–
Singapore	4.9	5.3	5.0	28.4	32.5	29.3
Pakistan	7.3	6.2	4.1	33.7	28.1	25.3
Vietnam	9.6	3.8	7.2	11.1	11.5	–

SOURCE: The World Bank, *World Development Indicators*, 2006; and International Institute of Strategic Studies, *The Military Balance*, various editions; U.S. Department of State, *World Military Expenditures and Arms Transfers*, 2003.
NOTE: Data for some countries over certain periods is partial. Dash indicates that no data is available.

Conventional Military Capabilities

Asia is a growing market for military equipment as many states replace or upgrade outdated hardware. Although much of the region is wary of China's rise and increasing military strength, this has not yet triggered significant balancing behavior. Nevertheless, many states pursue modest hedging strategies to ensure security and freedom of action.

- China's equipment upgrades are in line with improvements made in recent years. In 2005–06 China accepted shipments of new destroyers, submarines, and combat aircraft from Russia.

- U.S.-Southeast Asia military relations continue to expand as more countries participate in annual Cobra Gold and CARAT exercises. The United States recently restored IMET training and aid to Indonesia.

- Russia continues to reform and modernize its military, notably through reforms in elite and specialist units.

- Military modernization is proceeding slowly in Southeast and Central Asia due to budget constraints and is largely aimed at bolstering their abilities to manage low-intensity internal conflicts.

TABLE 18   Manpower

	Armed forces (thousand)				Rank	
	1990	1995	2000	2005	1990	2005
China	3,030	2,930	2,470	2,255	2	1
United States	2,118	1,547	1,366	1,474	3	2
India	1,262	1,145	1,303	1,325	4	3
North Korea	1,111	1,128	1,082	1,106	5	4
Russia	3,988	1,520	1,004	1,037	1	5
South Korea	750	633	683	688	7	6
Pakistan	550	587	612	619	8	7
Vietnam	1,052	572	484	484	6	8
Myanmar (Burma)	230	286	344	428	13	9
Thailand	283	259	301	307	10	10
Indonesia	283	275	297	302	10	11
Taiwan	370	376	370	290	9	12
Japan	249	240	237	240	12	13
Bangladesh	103	116	137	126	14	14
Sri Lanka	65	125	–	111	15	15

SOURCE: International Institute of Strategic Studies, *The Military Balance*, various editions.
NOTE: Active duty and military personnel only. Data value for Russia in 1990 includes all territories of the Soviet Union. Dash indicates that no data is available.

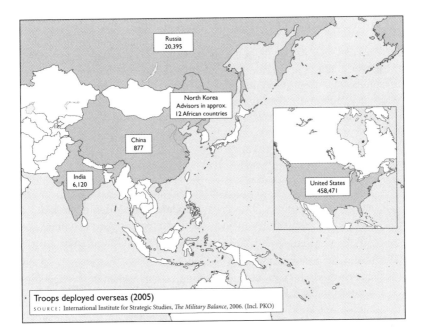

Troops deployed overseas (2005)
SOURCE: International Institute for Strategic Studies, *The Military Balance*, 2006. (Incl. PKO)

TABLE 19 Conventional warfare capabilities, 2005

	Tanks, artillery, APCs/LAVs	Combat aircraft	Principal surface combatants	Submarines
China	29,780	2,643	63	70
United States	29,050	5,421	118	96
India	17,660	886	54	19
North Korea	24,460	590	9	88
Russia	62,895	2,118	66	69
South Korea	15,944	556	43	20
Pakistan	8,018	340	7	11
Vietnam	6,355	221	11	2
Burma	968	125	4	0
Thailand	4,343	205	18	0
Indonesia	1,766	142	29	2
Taiwan	4,596	511	32	4
Japan	3,690	400	53	16
Bangladesh	590	83	5	0
Sri Lanka	1,217	21	0	0

SOURCE: International Institute of Strategic Studies, *The Military Balance*, 2005.

Weapons of Mass Destruction

Asia is home to the highest concentration of nuclear weapons states in the world and is the region that presents the greatest number of threats to established non-proliferation regimes. Efforts by the United States and others in the region to bolster non-proliferation initiatives, through both active interdiction and diplomacy, have yielded few positive results to date.

- North Korea tested seven missiles in July. Although considered a failure, the tests cast further doubt on prospects for success in the stalled Six-Party Talks.

- Advocates of the U.S.-India nuclear deal maintain that the agreement will regulate India's nuclear development and could provide a partnership that hedges against China's influence; critics contend the deal will further erode the NPT and non-proliferation regimes.

- India and Pakistan tested ballistic missiles in May and July of 2006 in efforts to enhance their expanding missile capabilities. Each side notified the other prior to the tests in accordance with established confidence-building protocols.

TABLE 20   Nuclear weapons

	Nuclear weapons possession				Warheads
	1990	1995	2000	2005	2005
Russia	✓	✓	✓	✓	~ 16,000
United States	✓	✓	✓	✓	~ 10,300
China	✓	✓	✓	✓	410
India	✓	✓	✓	✓	70–110
Pakistan	–	–	✓	✓	50–110
North Korea	?	?	?	prob.	~ 5–10

SOURCE: Carnegie Endowment for International Peace, Monterey Institute for International Studies.
NOTE: Table shows confirmed (✓), probable (prob.), and unknown (?) possession of nuclear weapons. Dash indicates that no data is available.

TABLE 21   Intercontinental ballistic missiles

	Number of ICBMs			
	1990	1995	2000	2005
Russia	1,398	930	776	570
United States	1,000	580	550	550
China	8	17+	20+	40+
India	–	–	–	–
Pakistan	–	–	–	–
North Korea	–	–	–	?

SOURCE: International Institute of Strategic Studies, *The Military Balance*, various editions.
NOTE: Question mark (?) indicates unknown possession of ICBMs. Dash indicates that no data is available.

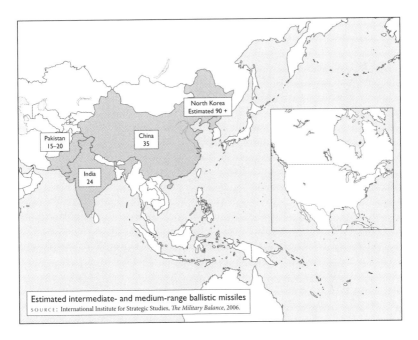

Estimated intermediate- and medium-range ballistic missiles
S O U R C E : International Institute for Strategic Studies, *The Military Balance*, 2006.

TABLE 22   Non-proliferation treaties

	NPT	Additional Protocol	CTBT	CWC	BTWC
Russia	Ratified	Signatory	Ratified	Ratified	Ratified
United States	Ratified	Signatory	Signatory	Ratified	Ratified
China	Ratified	Ratified	Signatory	Ratified	Ratified
India	–	–	–	Ratified	Ratified
Pakistan	–	–	–	Ratified	Ratified
North Korea	Withdrew	–	–	–	Acceded

S O U R C E : Nuclear Threat Initiative, Monterey Institute of International Studies.
N O T E : NPT = Non-proliferation Treaty, CTBT = Comprehensive Test Ban Treaty, CWC = Chemical Weapons Convention, BTWC = Biological and Toxic Weapons Convention, Additional Protocol = IAEA Additional Protocol. Dash indicates non-participation.

TABLE 23   WMD export control regimes

	Nuclear Suppliers Group	Australia Group	Wassenaar Arrangement	Zangger Committee	MTCR
Russia	Member	–	Member	Member	Member
United States	Member	Member	Member	Member	Member
China	Member	–	–	Member	–
India	–	–	–	–	–
Pakistan	–	–	–	–	–
North Korea	–	–	–	–	–

S O U R C E : Nuclear Threat Initiative, Monterey Institute of International Studies.
N O T E : MTCR = Missile Technology Control Regime. Dash indicates non-participation.

Index

About the Authors

Michael R. Chambers (PhD, Columbia University) is Associate Professor of Political Science at Indiana State University. He has taught at St. Olaf College and was a visiting scholar at the John K. Fairbank Center for East Asian Research at Harvard University from 2003 to 2004. Since December 2004 he has served as an editor of the journal *Asian Security*. Dr. Chambers has published on China's relations with its East Asian neighbors and on China's alliance behavior, including articles in *Current History*, the *Journal of East Asian Studies*, and the *Journal of Contemporary China*. He is also the editor of *South Asia in 2020: Future Strategic Balances and Alliances* (2002). He was a member of the "Contending Perspectives: Southeast Asian and American Views of a Rising China" project sponsored by NBR and Singapore's IDSS.

Stephen D. Cohen is Professor, School of International Service, American University, Washington, D.C., and Director of the International Economic Relations Field. His research and teaching interests center on foreign trade policy, international finance, and foreign direct investment. Among his books are *International Monetary Reform, 1964–69: The Political Dimension*; *The Making of U.S. International Economic Policy*; *Cowboys and Samurai: Why the U.S. Is Losing the Battle with the Japanese and Why It Matters*; and *An Ocean Apart: Explaining Three Decades of U.S.-Japanese Trade Frictions*. He is the principal author of *Fundamentals of U.S. Foreign Trade Policy: Economics, Politics, Laws, and Issues*. His new book, tentatively titled *Foreign Direct Investment and Multinational Corporations: Avoiding Simplicity, Embracing Complexity*, will be published later this year.

Richard J. Ellings (PhD, University of Washington) is President and Co-founder of The National Bureau of Asian Research (NBR). He is also Affiliate Professor of International Studies at the Henry M. Jackson School of International Studies, University of Washington. Prior to serving with NBR, from 1986–89, he was Assistant Director and on the faculty of the Jackson School, where he received the Distinguished Teaching Award. He served as Legislative Assistant in the United States Senate, office of Senator Slade Gorton, in 1984 and 1985. Dr. Ellings is the author of *Embargoes and World Power: Lessons from American Foreign Policy* (1985); co-author of *Private Property and National Security* (1991); co-editor (with Aaron Friedberg) of *Fragility and Crisis* (2003), *Asian Aftershocks* (2002), and *Power and Purpose* (2001); co-editor of *Korea's Future and the Great Powers* (2001, with Nicholas Eberstadt) and *Southeast Asian Security in the New Millennium* (1996, with Sheldon Simon); and the founding editor of the *NBR Analysis* publication series. He established the Strategic Asia Program and AccessAsia, the national clearinghouse that tracks specialists and their research on Asia.

Kavita Iyengar (PhD, Clark University) is currently a consultant with the Asian Development Bank, New Delhi, where she is working on regional cooperation issues for South Asia. Prior to this she was Commissioning Editor with Oxford University Press in India responsible for the economics, business and ecology areas. In her previous assignments, Dr. Iyengar has worked on trade and environment issues with the Energy Research Institute in India and in the United States with Industrial Economics, Inc. An undergraduate from Delhi University, Dr. Iyengar received her Master's degree in Economics from Jawaharlal Nehru University in New Delhi.

David C. Kang (PhD, UC Berkeley) is Associate Professor of Government and Adjunct Associate Professor and Research Director at the Center for International Business at the Tuck School of Business at Dartmouth College. He has been a visiting professor at Stanford University and Yale University. Dr. Kang is finishing a book about East Asia's response to China's rise. He is the author of *Crony Capitalism: Corruption and Development in South Korea and the Philippines* (2002), and co-author (with Victor Cha) of *Nuclear North Korea: A Debate on Engagement Strategies* (2003). Dr. Kang has published numerous scholarly articles as well as opinion pieces in the *New York Times*, the *Financial Times*, the *Washington Post*, the *Los Angeles Times*, and numerous Korean and Chinese newspapers. Dr. Kang is a member of the editorial boards of *Political Science Quarterly*, *Asia Policy*, *IRI Review*, *Business and Politics*, and the *Journal of International Business Education*.

Devesh Kapur (PhD, Princeton University) holds the Madan Lal Sobti Professorship for the Study of Contemporary India and is Director, Center for Advanced Study of India, University of Pennsylvania. He is a senior associate of the Global Economic Governance Programme at the University of Oxford and Non-Resident Fellow at the Center for Global Development, Washington, D.C. His research examines local-global linkages in political and economic change in developing countries (particularly India), focusing on the role of domestic and international institutions (especially the Bretton Woods Institutions) and international migration. He is the co-author (with John Lewis and Richard Webb) of *The World Bank: Its First Half Century*, co-author (with John McHale) of *Give Us Your Best and Brightest: The Global Hunt for Talent and Its Impact on the Developing World*, and co-editor (with Pratap Mehta) of *Public Institutions in India: Performance and Design*. He is currently working on a book manuscript *Democracy, Death and Diamonds: The Impact of Migration From India On India* for Princeton University Press. He received the Joseph R. Levenson Teaching Prize awarded to the best junior faculty, Harvard College, in 2005.

Ann Marie Kimball (MD, MPH, University of Washington) is Professor of Epidemiology and Health Services at the University of Washington School of Public Health and Community Medicine and Director of the APEC Emerging Infections Network. Dr. Kimball is an adjunct professor in Medicine with the School of Medicine and is an attending physician on staff at Harborview Medical Center. Her research interests are in emerging infections and global epidemic prevention, surveillance, investigation and control of infectious diseases. In 2000 she was named as a New Century Scholar for Fulbright, and in 2004 she received a Guggenheim Foundation scholar award for her work. She has worked extensively in the areas of trade policy and disease control, telecommunications, disease surveillance, and alert systems. Her latest book is *Risky Trade: Infectious Diseases in an Era of Global Trade*. Formerly Dr. Kimball served as Regional Advisor for HIV/AIDS with the Pan American Health Organization (WHO). She has also served as Director of the Washington State HIV/AIDS/STD Program and as Chair of the National Alliance of State and Territorial AIDS Directors in the United States.

Michael Mastanduno (PhD, Princeton University) is Nelson A. Rockefeller Professor of Government and Associate Dean for the Social Sciences at Dartmouth College. Dr. Mastanduno joined the Dartmouth faculty in 1987. His areas of research and teaching specialization include international relations, U.S. foreign policy, and the politics of the global economy. He is the author or editor of numerous books including *Economic Containment* (1992), *Unipolar Politics* (1999), *International Relations Theory and the Asia Pacific* (2003), and *U.S. Hegemony and International Organizations* (2003). His recent articles on Asia appear in *International Relations of the Asia-Pacific* and *Australian Journal of International Affairs*. Dr. Mastanduno has been a guest faculty member at the Graduate School of Economics and International Relations at Milan, at the Geneva Center for Security

Policy, and at the University of Tokyo as an Abe Fellow. He has been awarded fellowships from the Brookings Institution, the Council of Foreign Relations, the East-West Center, and the Salzburg Seminar. He served during a sabbatical from Dartmouth as a special assistant for Japan in the Office of the U.S. Trade Representative. He is a member of the Council of Foreign Relations and Phi Beta Kappa.

Minxin Pei (PhD, Harvard University) is Senior Associate and Director of the China Program at the Carnegie Endowment for International Peace in Washington, D.C. Prior to this, he taught politics at Princeton University from 1992 to 1998. His main interest is U.S.-China relations, the development of democratic political systems, and Chinese politics. Dr. Pei is the author of *From Reform to Revolution: The Demise of Communism in China and the Soviet Union* (Harvard University Press, 1994) and *China's Trapped Transition: The Limits of Developmental Autocracy* (Harvard University Press, 2006). His research has been published in *Foreign Policy, Foreign Affairs, The National Interest, Modern China, China Quarterly, Journal of Democracy*, and many edited books. His op-eds have appeared in the *Financial Times, New York Times, Washington Post, Christian Science Monitor*, and other major newspapers.

David P. Rapkin is Associate Professor, University of Nebraska, where he has served as department chair and graduate chair. He has also been a visiting professor at Tsukuba University in Japan during 1988–90 and 1996–98. His major research and teaching interests are in global political economy with an emphasis on East Asia. His recent articles have appeared in *New Political Economy, World Development*, and *The World Economy*.

Peter Rutland (PhD, University of York) has been a Professor of Government at Wesleyan University in Connecticut since 1989. From 1995 to 1997 he was Assistant Director of the Open Media Research Institute in Prague. From 1997 to 1998 he chaired the Olin Security Studies Seminar at the Davis Center, Harvard University, and from 1999 to 2000 he was executive director of the Caspian Studies Program at the Kennedy School of Government, Harvard. He has taught as a Fulbright professor in St. Petersburg (2000) and at Sophia University in Tokyo (2003–04). He is the author of *The Myth of the Plan* (1986) and *The Politics of Economic Stagnation in the Soviet Union* (1992) as well as editor of *Business and the State in Contemporary Russia* (2000). Recent articles include "The Reform of the Electricity Sector," in *The Dynamics of Russian Politics II* (edited by Peter Reddaway and Robert Orttung, 2005).

Dina Rome Spechler (PhD, Harvard University) is Associate Professor, Political Science, Indiana University Bloomington, specializing in the study of Russian and U.S. foreign policy. She is the author of *Permitted Dissent in the USSR and Domestic Influences on Soviet Foreign Policy* and co-author (with Martin C. Spechler) of "Conflict and Cooperation in Central Asia after 9/11," in *Eurasia in Balance*, (ed. Ariel Cohen, 2005). Her current research deals with major changes in the foreign policies of the United States, Russia, and Israel.

Martin C. Spechler (PhD, Harvard University) is Professor of Economics, Indiana University-Purdue University Indianapolis and faculty affiliate of the Inner Asian and Uralic National Resource Center, Indiana University. He is the author of *Perspectives in Economic Thought* and many articles on Central Asia. He is also the book review editor of *Comparative Economic Studies*. Martin Spechler is currently completing a book on the political economy of Central Asia.

Ashley J. Tellis (PhD, University of Chicago) is Senior Associate at the Carnegie Endowment for International Peace, specializing in international security, defense, and Asian strategic issues. He was recently on assignment to the U.S. Department of State as Senior Advisor to the Undersecretary of State for Political Affairs, during which time he was intimately involved in negotiating the civil nuclear agreement with India. He is Research Director of the Strategic Asia Program at NBR and co-editor of *Strategic Asia 2005–06: Military Modernization in an Era of Uncertainty* and *Strategic Asia 2004–05: Confronting Terrorism in the Pursuit of Power*. Previously he was commissioned into the Foreign Service and served as Senior Advisor to the Ambassador at the U.S. embassy in New Delhi. He also served on the National Security Council staff as Special Assistant to the President and Senior Director for Strategic Planning and Southwest Asia. Prior to his government service, Dr. Tellis was Senior Policy Analyst at the RAND Corporation and Professor of Policy Analysis at the RAND Graduate School. He is the author of *India's Emerging Nuclear Posture* (2001) and co-author (with Michael D. Swaine) of *Interpreting China's Grand Strategy: Past, Present, and Future* (2000). His academic publications have also appeared in many edited volumes and journals.

William R. Thompson is Rogers Professor of Political Science at Indiana University, Bloomington and served as president of the International Studies Association (2005–06). His books include *The Comparative Analysis of Politics* (with Monte Palmer, 1978), *Contending Approaches to World System Analysis* (1983), *Rhythms in Politics and Economics* (with Paul Johnson,

1985), *Seapower in Global Politics, 1494–1993* (with George Modelski, 1988), *On Global War: Historical-Structural Approaches to World Politics* (1988), *War and State Making: The Shaping of the Global Powers* (with Karen Rasler, 1990), *The Great Powers and Global Struggle, 1490–1990* (with Karen Rasler, 1994), *Leading Sectors and World Politics: Coevolution in Global Economics and Politics* (with George Modelski, 1996), *Great Power Rivalrie.* (1999), *The Emergence of the Global Political Economy* (2000), *Evolutionary Interpretations of World Politics* (2001), and *Growth, Trade, and Systemic Leadership* (with Rafael Reuveny, 2004). His most recent books are *Puzzles of the Democratic Peace* (with Karen Rasler, 2005) and *Globalization and Global History* (co-edited with Barry Gills, 2006).

Donald E. Weatherbee (PhD, Johns Hopkins School of Advanced International Studies) is the Donald S. Russell Distinguished Professor Emeritus at the University of South Carolina. Specializing in politics and international relations in Southeast Asia, he received his BA from Bates College and MA and PhD from the Johns Hopkins School of Advanced International Studies. He has held teaching and research appointments at universities and research centers in Indonesia, Singapore, Malaysia, Thailand, the United Kingdom, Germany, and the Netherlands as well as at the U.S. Army War College. He was awarded the U.S. Army's Distinguished Civilian Service medal for his work on the post-Vietnam War strategic profile of Southeast Asia. His most recent major publication is the book *International Relations in Southeast Asia: The Struggle for Autonomy* (2005).

Michael Wills is Director of the Strategic Asia Program at The National Bureau of Asian Research. He is co-editor of *Strategic Asia 2005–06: Military Modernization in an Era of Uncertainty* and *Strategic Asia 2004–05: Confronting Terrorism in the Pursuit of Power*. He was a contributing editor to *Strategic Asia 2003–04: Fragility and Crisis* and *Strategic Asia 2002–03: Asian Aftershocks*, and has served as technical editor on numerous books and articles, including *Religion and Conflict in Southeast Asia: Disrupting Violence* (forthcoming), *Strategic Asia 2001–02: Power and Purpose*, and *The Many Faces of Asian Security*. Before joining NBR, Mr. Wills worked at the Cambodia Development Resource Institute in Phnom Penh, and prior to that with the international political and security risk management firm Control Risks Group in London. He holds a BA (Honors) in Chinese Studies from the University of Oxford.

About Strategic Asia

The **Strategic Asia Program** at The National Bureau of Asian Research (NBR) is a major ongoing research initiative that draws together top Asia studies specialists and international relations experts to assess the changing strategic environment in the Asia-Pacific. The Strategic Asia Program transcends traditional estimates of military balance by incorporating economic, political, and demographic data and by focusing on the strategies and perceptions that drive policy in the region. The program's integrated set of products and activities includes:

- an annual edited volume written by leading specialists,

- an executive summary tailored for public and private sector decisionmakers and strategic planners,

- an on-line database that tracks key strategic indicators,

- briefings and presentations for government, business, and academe that are designed to foster in-depth discussions revolving around major, relevant public issues.

Special briefings are held for key committees of Congress and the executive branch, and other government agencies as well as for the intelligence community. The principal audiences for the program's research findings are the U.S. policymaking and research communities, the media, the business community, and academe.

The Strategic Asia Program's on-line database contains an unprecedented selection of strategic indicators—economic, financial, military, technological, energy, political, and demographic—for all of the countries in the Asia-Pacific region. The database, together with previous volumes and executive summaries, are hosted on the Strategic Asia website at http://strategicasia.nbr.org.

Previous Strategic Asia Volumes

Over the past six years this series has addressed how Asia is increasingly functioning as a zone of strategic interaction—one riddled with fault lines and contending with an uncertain balance of power. The first volume, *Strategic Asia 2001–02: Power and Purpose*, established a baseline assessment for understanding the strategies and interactions of the major states within the region—notably China, India, Japan, Russia, and South Korea. The second volume, *Strategic Asia 2002–03: Asian Aftershocks*, drew upon this baseline to analyze the changes in these states' grand strategies and relationships in the aftermath of the September 11, 2001 terrorist attacks. *Strategic Asia 2003–04: Fragility and Crisis* examined the fragile balance of power in Asia, drawing out the key domestic political and economic trends in Asian states supporting or undermining this tenuous equilibrium. Building upon established themes, *Strategic Asia 2004–05: Confronting Terrorism in the Pursuit of Power* explored the effect of the U.S.-led war on terrorism on the political, economic, social, and strategic transformations underway in Asia. *Strategic Asia 2005–06: Military Modernization in an Era of Uncertainty* appraised the progress of Asian military modernization programs and developed a touchstone to evaluate future military changes to the balance of power.

Research and Management Team

The Strategic Asia research team consists of leading international relations and security specialists from universities and research institutions across the United States. A new research team is selected each year. The research team for 2006 is led by Ashley J. Tellis (Carnegie Endowment for International Peace). General John Shalikashvili (former Chairman of the Joint Chiefs of Staff), Aaron Friedberg (Princeton University, and Strategic Asia's founding research director), and Richard Ellings (The National Bureau of Asian Research, and Strategic Asia's founding program director) serve as senior advisors. Advising the program is the executive committee, composed of Herbert Ellison (University of Washington), Donald Emmerson (Stanford University), Francine Frankel (University of Pennsylvania), Mark Hamilton (University of Alaska), Kenneth Pyle (University of Washington), Richard Samuels (Massachusetts Institute of Technology), Robert Scalapino (University of California-Berkeley), Enders Wimbush (Hudson Institute), and William Wohlforth (Dartmouth College).

The Strategic Asia Program depends on a diverse funding base of foundations, government, and corporations, supplemented by income from publication sales. Support for the program in 2006 comes from the GE

Foundation, Lynde and Harry Bradley Foundation, and National Nuclear Security Administration at the U.S. Department of Energy.

Attribution

Readers of Strategic Asia reports and visitors to the Strategic Asia website may use data, charts, graphs, and quotes from these sources without requesting permission from The National Bureau of Asian Research on the condition that they cite NBR *and* the appropriate primary source in any published work. No report, chapter, separate study, extensive text, or any other substantial part of the Strategic Asia Program's products may be reproduced without the written permission of The National Bureau of Asian Research. To request permission, please write to:

The NBR Editor
The National Bureau of Asian Research
4518 University Way NE, Suite 300
Seattle, WA 98105
nbr@nbr.org.

The National Bureau of Asian Research

The National Bureau of Asian Research is a nonprofit, nonpartisan research institution dedicated to informing and strengthening policy in the Asia-Pacific. NBR conducts advanced independent research on strategic, political, economic, globalization, health, and energy issues affecting U.S. relations with Asia. Drawing upon an extensive network of the world's leading specialists and leveraging the latest technology, NBR bridges the academic, business, and policy arenas. The institution disseminates its research through briefings, publications, conferences, Congressional testimony, and email forums, and by collaborating with leading institutions worldwide. NBR also provides exceptional internship opportunities to graduate and undergraduate students for the purpose of attracting and training the next generation of Asia specialists.